The Neville Chamberlain
Diary Letters

'The Smiling Chancellor': Budget Day 1934

The Neville Chamberlain
Diary Letters

VOLUME THREE

The Heir Apparent, 1928–33

edited by

ROBERT SELF

ASHGATE

Published by
Ashgate Publishing Limited
Gower House
Croft Road
Aldershot
Hants GU11 3HR
England

Ashgate Publishing Company
131 Main Street
Burlington, VT 05401-5600 USA

Ashgate website: http://www.ashgate.com

ISBN 1 84014 693 1

British Library Cataloguing in Publication Data
Chamberlain, Neville, 1869–1940
    The Neville Chamberlain diary letters
    Vol. 3: The heir apparent, 1928–33 edited by Robert Self
    1. Chamberlain, Neville, 1869–1940 2. Chamberlain, Neville,
    1869–1940 – Correspondence 3. Politicians – Great Britain – Biography 4. Great
    Britain – Politics and government – 1901–1936
    I. Title II. Self, Robert C., 1953–
    941'.083'092

Library of Congress Cataloging-in-Publication Data
Chamberlain, Neville, 1869–1940.
    [Correspondence. Selections]
    The Neville Chamberlain diary letters / edited by Robert Self.
        p. cm. Includes bibliographical references. (v. 3 : alk. paper)
    Contents: v. 3. The heir apparent, 1928–33
        1. Chamberlain, Neville, 1869–1940–Correspondence. 2. Great Britain–
    Politics and government–20th century. 3. Prime ministers–Great Britain–
    Correspondence. I. Self, Robert C., 1953– II. Title.

    DA585.C5 Z48 2000
    941.083'092–dc21   00–026601

This volume is printed on acid free paper.

Typeset by Manton Typesetters, Louth, Lincolnshire, UK.
Printed and bound in Great Britain by TJ International Ltd, Padstow, Cornwall.

Contents

Acknowledgements

A large number of debts are incurred during the preparation of a study of this sort. First and most obvious, I owe an immense debt of gratitude to the generosity of the University of Birmingham for granting its kind permission to reproduce so extensively the letters of Neville Chamberlain to his sisters and to quote from other Chamberlain family correspondence in their care. Thanks are due to Miss Christine Penney and the Special Collection staff of the Heslop Room at Birmingham University Library who cheerfully provided so much valuable assistance during this research and to Mr Jim Davies of the Photographic Department of Birmingham University Library for copying material from Chamberlain's Papers. By the same token, the editor is indebted to the owners, custodians and archivists of the other collections of private papers and diaries used in the preparation of the text. For access and permission to quote from material in privately owned collections I am grateful to Viscount Addison, the Earl of Derby, John Grigg, Captain J. Headlam, Vice-Admiral Sir Ian Hogg, the Syndics of Cambridge University Library, the Warden and Fellows of New College Oxford, the Marquess of Salisbury, Mrs A. Stacey and the Trustees of the Bridgeman family archive, Mrs R.M. Stafford, the Clerk of Records of the House of Lords acting on behalf of the Beaverbrook Foundation Trust, the Masters and Fellows of Churchill College, Cambridge and the Conservative Party. I have also consulted archive collections held by a number of other libraries and institutions, namely Birmingham Central Library, Department of Western Manuscripts of the Bodleian Library, British Library, British Library of Political and Economic Science, Durham Record Office, House of Lords Record Office, Liverpool City Central Library, National Archives of Scotland, National Library of Scotland, Public Record Office, Rhodes House Library, Oxford and Sheffield University Library. My thanks are due to the keepers, librarians and curators of these institutions and their staff. Every effort has been made to trace the copyright holders of unpublished documents from which quotations have been made. To anyone whose copyright I have unwittingly infringed I offer my sincere apologies. A good deal of the research upon which this book is based was made possible by an award from the Arts & Humanities Research Board under the Research Leave Scheme which permitted me to devote an entire academic year to the preparation of these volumes in 1999–2000.

Debts of a more personal kind also exist. I am particularly deeply indebted to Mr James Lloyd, Neville Chamberlain's grandson, for his kindness, assistance and patience in answering many questions about his family and to Dr Stuart Ball for all the practical and scholarly assistance he has so freely given during the course of this project. By the same token, Professors John Ramsden, Iwan Morgan, Peter Mandler and Brian Harrison all provided valuable advice or assistance on various aspects of this work. Alec McAulay of Ashgate Publishing provided unstinting enthusiasm and support at the commencement of this project and without his great vision and encouragement it may never have come to fruition. At the other end of the publishing process, Ruth Peters has consistently proved a patient and very helpful source of guidance, good judgement and support throughout. Thanks are also due to Helen Dalton, Dan Herbert, Christine Smart and their colleagues at the London Guildhall University Library who have been unfailing in their assistance during the research for these volumes and to Louisa Hoff who provided invaluable information on Chamberlain's art and music interests. Finally, there is the vast debt of gratitude I owe to Katie – for all she has contributed to this project and for just being there.

Editor's Note

Although the general approach to the task of editing these letters is thoroughly discussed in the introduction to the first volume, the reader should note that where sentences and paragraphs have been removed these have all been marked by the use of suspension dots. In every other respect the letters themselves have been reproduced in their original form. Although Neville Chamberlain's punctuation and use of capital letters is erratic and inconsistent and his spelling of surnames is idiosyncratic, his abbreviations and original spellings have been retained throughout. Editorial insertions have been made in some places for the sake of clarity, but these are always denoted by a square bracket. Only the style of dating has been standardised in the interests of consistency. Chamberlain almost always closed his letters with 'Your affecte. brother, Neville Chamberlain'. These words have been omitted to avoid needless repetition.

Volume Two: Errata

Page 296 footnote 31 should read:
Wilfred William Ashley (1867–1939). Conservative MP for Blackpool 1906–18, Fylde 1918–22 and New Forest 1922–32. Chairman, Anti-Socialist Union. Unionist Whip 1911–12; Parliamentary Secretary, Ministry of Transport 1922–23; Under-Secretary, War Office 1923–24; Minister of Transport 1924–29. Created Baron Mount Temple 1932.

Page 418 footnote 48 should read:
John William Davis (1873–1955). American lawyer and politician. Member, US House of Representatives 1911–13; US Solicitor-General 1913–18; US Ambassador to London 1918–21 and adviser to President Wilson and US delegation to Paris Peace Conference 1919; Democratic Presidential candidate 1924.

List of Abbreviations

ADC	Aide-de-Camp
AG	Attorney-General
AJB	A.J. Balfour
AMC	Association of Municipal Corporations
BBC	British Broadcasting Corporation
BDP	Birmingham Daily Post
BL	Andrew Bonar Law
BMA	British Medical Association
BSA	Birmingham Small Arms Company
B/T	Board of Trade
BUA	Birmingham Conservative & Unionist Association
Bart	Baronet
CC	County Council
CCA	County Council Association
CCC	Conservative Cabinet Committee
CCO	Conservative Central Office
C/E	Chancellor of Exchequer
C-in-C	Commander-in-Chief
CMB	Central Midwives Board
CO	Colonial Office
CRD	Conservative Research Department
DC	District Council
DH	Daily Herald
DM	Daily Mail
DO	Dominion Office
DT	Daily Telegraph
EAC	Economic Advisory Council
EMC	Elliott's Metal Company
FBI	Federation of British Industry
FE	F.E. Smith, Lord Birkenhead
FO	Foreign Office
FS	Foreign Secretary
GC	Guardians Committee
GG	Governor-General
GHK	George Hamilton Kenrick

GM	Germain Martin
GOC	General Officer Commanding
IDAC	Import Duties Advisory Committee
ILP	Independant Labour Party
JC	Joseph Chamberlain
JHT	J.H. Thomas
JLG	J.L. Garvin
KCB	Knight Commander of the Order of the Bath
KG	Knight of the Order of the Garter
LA	Local Authority
LCC	London County Council
LGB	Local Government Board
LMS	London Midlands & Scottish Railway
LSA	Leo Amery
LlG	David Lloyd George
M & CW	Mother & Child Welfare
MD	Mental Deficiency [Bill]
MFGB	Miners' Federation of Great Britain
MH	Ministry of Health
MOH	Medical Officer of Health
MP	Morning Post
MU	Midland Union (of Conservative & Unionist Associations)
NFU	National Farmers Union
NUA	National Unionist Association
NUCUA	National Union of Conservative & Unionist Associations
NUR	National Union of Railwaymen
OD	Outdoor relief, Poor Law
PAC	Public Assistance Committee
PL	Poor Law
PLP	Parliamentary Labour Party
PMG	Post-Master General
PO	Post Office
PPS	Parliamentary Private Secretary
PR	Proportional Representation
PS	Private Secretary
RAMC	Royal Army Medical Corps
RC	Royal Commission
RDC	Rural District Council
RHS	Royal Horticultural Society
RM	Ramsay MacDonald
Refm	Referendum [on food taxes]
SB	Stanley Baldwin
TM	Their Majesties

TU	Trades Union
TUC	Trades Union Congress
UAB	Unemployment Assistance Board
UDC	Urban District Council
WI	Women's Institute
WO	War Office
YMCA	Young Men's Christian Association

Other Personal Nicknames

All Highest	Lord Curzon
Bal	Earl of Crawford (and Balcarres)
Beaver	Lord Beaverbrook
Bobby	Bolton Eyres-Monsell
Bosky	Arthur Griffith-Boscawen
David	J.C.C. Davidson
Jix/Jicks	William Joynson-Hicks
Leo	Leo Amery
Linky	Lord Hugh Cecil
Max	Lord Beaverbrook
Our Herb	Herbert Samuel
Philip	Philip Cunliffe-Lister
Sam	Samuel Hoare
The Goat	David Lloyd George
Top	Viscount Wolmer
Uncle Arthur	Arthur Henderson
Van	Robert Vansittart
Wee Frees	Independent (Asquithian) Liberal Party
Worthy	Laming Worthington-Evans

1

Introduction
Neville Chamberlain, 1928–33:
The Heir Apparent

I

The Local Government Act of 1929 represented a fitting culmination of Neville Chamberlain's reforming record at the Ministry of Health and he presciently anticipated that it would 'prove to have been my magnum opus when my obituary notice is written'.[1] Although in many respects its sheer scope gave it the appearance of a consolidation Act, the measure combined three central themes of Chamberlain's long-term thinking about local government in Britain. Firstly, its long-awaited reform of the Poor Law completed his comprehensive review of local government services and provision. Under the Act, Chamberlain sought finally to 'break up the Poor Law' by subsuming it within a unified system of provision for all citizens under the direct democratic control of local councils. Secondly, the Act involved the fundamental restructuring of a system of local government finance largely untouched since the establishment of the county councils in 1888 and which required radical attention even without the parallel reform of the Poor Law because of its lack of coordination and the distorting effect it had upon the distribution of central government support. Worse still, its inequitable financial burdens fell most heavily upon those depressed areas and heavy industries least able to afford it, leaving manufacturers clamouring for relief from a growing burden of local taxation which represented a major cause of their own lack of competitiveness.[2] The final aspect of continuity concerned the enlargement of local government units which Chamberlain had favoured since advocating the Birmingham Extension Bill in 1910.[3] As Minister of Health, he became convinced of the benefits of poor relief and public health services administered by larger units able to spread the financial burden more evenly to ensure that richer areas assisted poorer ones. The Poor Law Unions which replaced the parish as the geographical unit for relief in 1834 were thus in their turn replaced by the county and country boroughs, while scheduled roads were also transferred from district to county councils.

---

[1] N. Chamberlain to Ida Chamberlain, 17 November 1929.

[2] Bryan Keith-Lucas, *The History of Local Government in England* (London, 1970), pp. 231–32. 'Memo on the Chancellor's scheme', n.d. (December 1927), NC7/9/16.

[3] N. Chamberlain to Hilda, 1 August 1920, Robert Self (ed.), *The Neville Chamberlain Diary Letters, Volume I, The Making of a Politician, 1915–20* (Aldershot, 2000), pp. 44–45, 382.

Despite the importance of his legislative triumph in 1929, Chamberlain's path was a difficult one.[4] Since he had first raised the prospect of Poor Law reform in 1925, Chamberlain's cautious plan of advance had become ensnared in Churchill's far more grandiose design for the wholesale restructuring of local government finance. From the outset, the differences in style and habits of mind between the two men were as painfully obvious as those in their policy objectives. Both men thus recognised the need for the personal and departmental support of the other but were contemptuous of their rival's methods and policy priorities. Churchill lamented Chamberlain's lack of vision in adhering so rigidly to his own more limited scheme, but recognised that he could not carry his own plans without the support of the Cabinet's expert on local government and the minister most directly responsible for it.[5] Conversely, Chamberlain recognised the desirability of derating and Treasury block grants for health services and necessitous areas in order to relate central government's financial support to local need rather than current level of expenditure, but he was far more sceptical about the practicality of Churchill's broader scheme.[6] Moreover, his orderly, fastidious mind and faith in careful preparation were equally outraged by Churchill's febrile flights of imagination and regular brainstorms.[7] 'There is too deep a difference between our natures for me to feel at home with him or to regard him with affection', Chamberlain confessed to Lord Irwin after the battle was over. 'He is a brilliant wayward child who compels admiration but who wears out his guardians with the constant strain he puts upon them'.[8] Yet for all that, he also recognised that he needed Churchill's support in order to remove Cabinet faintheartedness about so controversial a reform and to provide the necessary additional finance to overcome local authority resistance to the plan.

After a year of erratic development with regular changes of mind and direction, the outlines of Churchill's derating scheme were finally complete in mid-December 1927.[9] Chamberlain's initial response was to promise to consider the plan carefully, but he noted that 'it is only fair to say that in its present form I see

---

[4] For a good account of these negotiations see David Dilks, *Neville Chamberlain: Volume I, Pioneering and Reform 1869–1929* (Cambridge, 1984), pp. 534–77.

[5] Churchill to N. Chamberlain, 13 March 1928, NC7/9/22.

[6] N. Chamberlain to Baldwin, 24 December 1927, Baldwin MSS 5 (Cambridge University Library).

[7] Neville Chamberlain Diary, 16 June 1927; N. Chamberlain to Hilda, 24 July, 30 October and 12 November 1927, Robert Self (ed.), *The Neville Chamberlain Diary Letters, Volume II, The Reform Years 1921–27* (Aldershot, 2000), pp. 417, 427, 428; N. Chamberlain to Lord Irwin, Christmas Day 1927 and 12 August 1928, Eur.c. 152/17/227A and 152/18/114A (Oriental and India Offices Collections, British Library).

[8] N. Chamberlain to Irwin 12 August 1928, Irwin MSS Eur.c. 152/18/114A.

[9] Churchill to Baldwin, 17 December 1927, Baldwin MSS 5; Churchill to N. Chamberlain, 17 December 1927, NC7/9/14.

grave difficulties departmental or administrative, financial and political'.[10] Reinforced by the knowledge that Churchill had 'some vy knobbly criticisms' both from the industrialists he had consulted and his own Treasury officials,[11] and convinced that Churchill 'doesn't want another Gallipoli', Chamberlain then set about drafting a critique which would mobilise the language of cautious support and constructive criticism while demolishing any prospect of the plan being ready for the 1928 Budget or being tied to his own scheme for Poor Law reform.[12] Thus, at a practical level, Chamberlain pointed to the need for 'careful and perhaps prolonged negotiations' with the many vested interests, the probable underestimate of the cost of rate relief and the likely criticism that the imposition of necessary further taxation would injure national credit and prove electorally unpopular. He was even more alarmed by the adverse implications for local government. By removing any direct financial interest in local authority expenditure, derating would reduce still further the supply of practical men of business coming forward as candidates with the result that local government would become dominated by 'those representatives of "Labour" who regard office as a means of advancing Socialist theories and benefiting their own particular supporters at the expense of the community'.[13] He also objected that derating would so drastically reduce the income of many local authorities that they would have no resources from which to meet the cost of new services other than by demanding progressively larger block grants with the result that 'the finance of the scheme would be still further swelled'. While posing as a sympathiser with the bold concept, therefore, Chamberlain concluded that 'the subject is so complicated that prolonged examination would be necessary and I am doubtful whether it could be completed in time for legislation next year'.[14]

Chamberlain briefly appeared to have won this first round. Confronted by the weight of his arguments for caution, Baldwin agreed they should devote the next year to working out the details and promised to tackle Churchill about its postponement.[15] Yet the victory was short-lived. By 2 January Churchill had substantially amended the scheme and then he bombarded Baldwin with a powerful counter-barrage arguing that with partial remission he was 'defacing the classical purity of the conception for the sake of an easier passage!', but that 'it is this year or never'.[16] Moreover, when the Chancellor outlined his revised

---

[10] N. Chamberlain to Churchill, 20 December 1927, NC7/9/18.

[11] Churchill to N. Chamberlain, 21 December 1927, NC7/10/8.

[12] N. Chamberlain Diary, 22 December 1927; N. Chamberlain to Irwin, Christmas Day, 1927.

[13] N. Chamberlain to Irwin, 12 August 1928.

[14] See draft 'Memo on the Chancellor's Scheme', n.d., NC7/9/16 and N. Chamberlain to Baldwin, 24 December 1927, Baldwin MSS 5. N. Chamberlain to Cunliffe-Lister, 27 December 1927, Swinton MSS 174/2/1/5 (Churchill College, Cambridge).

[15] Baldwin to N. Chamberlain, 27 December 1927, NC7/11/20/c.

[16] Churchill to Baldwin, 4 and 7 January 1928, Baldwin MSS 5 and Martin Gilbert, *Winston S. Churchill, Volume V, 1922–1939* (London, 1976), p. 264.

proposals to Cabinet on 20 January, even by Chamberlain's own account, they received 'very favourable consideration'.[17] In the Policy Committee established to consider them further, the battle was largely fought over two key issues related to the timing of implementation and the more important question of whether local or central government should receive the product of the fixed national rate to be levied on largely derated properties. Although Chamberlain had reluctantly accepted the proposal of a fixed rate, at their meeting on 27 February he argued strongly for its proceeds to go to the local authorities rather than the Exchequer, and he was supported by most of the committee on 5 March.[18] Without notice to the others, however, Churchill then issued a paper repeating his objections in such forceful terms that Chamberlain went to the next Policy Committee 'in a high state of indignation and hit back as hard as [he] could', concluding with a blank threat to refuse to undertake negotiations on such lines.[19]

Churchill responded to this outburst with a combination of coaxing and veiled threats. His acknowledgement that Chamberlain was 'the master' and that he could 'make no progress in the face of yr opposition' was thus accompanied by the warning that as Chancellor his 'only remedy if I find the task too hard or too wearisome will be to withdraw the scheme', but that 'Without it there cd be no Poor Law reform in this Parliament'.[20] This threat provoked another strong reply from Chamberlain next day in which he declared coldly that 'if we are to work together there must be give and take on both sides', but that hitherto 'I have done all the giving, but very little weight has been attached to my views if they have differed from yours'.[21] This uncharacteristically angry letter, blazing with pent-up wrath and righteous indignation, had a chastening effect upon Churchill who was 'almost elaborately forthcoming and friendly' at their meeting next day at which Chamberlain again 'seized the opportunity to do some plain talking'. The result, he believed, was that he had left Churchill 'with a clearer understanding of my difficulties and perhaps of my character'.[22]

Although David Dilks denies the allegation that Chamberlain was 'sulkily negative' in his conduct of these negotiations,[23] there is some evidence to suggest more than a hint of the 'not invented here' syndrome in his attitude. 'The plan is a gamble', he confessed revealingly to his sisters in mid-March, 'I am trying at least to reduce the risks *but I cannot be as enthusiastic about it as about my own*

---

[17] N. Chamberlain to Hilda, 22 January 1928. CAB 2(28)1, 20 January 1928, CAB 23/57.

[18] CP 105(28), Policy Committee: Second Report, 29 March 1928, CAB 24/194. CPC 3rd and 4th Conclusions, CAB 27/364.

[19] N. Chamberlain to Hilda, 18 March 1928.

[20] Churchill to N. Chamberlain, 13 March 1928, NC7/9/22.

[21] N. Chamberlain to Churchill, 14 March 1928, NC7/9/23.

[22] N. Chamberlain to Hilda, 18 March 1928.

[23] Dilks, *Neville Chamberlain*, p. 547.

scheme which it supersedes.[24] In private, Chamberlain conceded that his real problem was that he 'never found the ground on which [he] could take a definite stand, except that of the retention of the flat rate'.[25] In an effort to extend the ground on which to make a stand, he consequently reopened the battle over the scope of the scheme. Six days after their meeting to clear the air, the Policy Committee thus witnessed another clash over the derating of railways, canals, harbours and docks which Chamberlain opposed as an additional burden on the Exchequer for what he correctly believed to be a barely 'camouflaged subsidy' which could be more effectively dealt with directly.[26] This conflict rumbled on in the Policy Committee until 26 March when, in the absence of officials, the committee agreed to exclude railways and docks.[27]

Two days after this momentary success, Chamberlain finally unburdened himself of his frustrations to Baldwin in such a way as to increase significantly his leverage in Cabinet. Declaring that he 'had an unhappy week facing up to resignation', he professed himself 'determined to withdraw rather than assent to a scheme which [he] believed to be dangerous to the future of local government'. After Baldwin assured him that the Cabinet would not allow him to resign, Chamberlain explained what in effect were his terms, involving the exclusion of railways and the retention of the fixed rate by the local authorities. At this juncture Baldwin appeared to accept the force of Chamberlain's argument on the grounds that the Cabinet needed to be united to proceed with the plan;[28] a priority which subsequently proved equally persuasive to the Cabinet as a whole after three full meetings devoted to the issue on 2–3 April. Accordingly, Chamberlain's views prevailed over the exclusion of railways and the need for some form of partial rather than total remission for productive industry, although the proportion to be paid was postponed to enable the relevant ministers to consider the question.[29] After another heated meeting of the Policy Committee, the two main adversaries compromised on a three-quarter remission. As Chamberlain later recorded, it was 'a very notable victory & I feel like a man who has been standing a siege for many months & at length has finally succeeded in beating off the enemy!'[30]

'The Plan has at last been settled', Chamberlain noted prematurely on 4 April.[31] Although Churchill attempted to reopen the railway exemption issue three days later, this time the opposition of Cunliffe-Lister and senior Treasury officials

---

[24] N. Chamberlain to Hilda, 18 March 1928. Emphasis added.

[25] Neville Chamberlain Diary, 21 March 1928.

[26] Neville Chamberlain Diary, 18 April 1928; N. Chamberlain to Hilda, 29 April 1928; N. Chamberlain to Irwin, 12 August 1928.

[27] CPC 7th Conclusions, 26 March 1928, CAB 27/364.

[28] Neville Chamberlain Diary, 28 March 1928.

[29] Neville Chamberlain Diary, 4 August 1928. CAB 19(28)4, 3 April 1928, CAB 23/57.

[30] Neville Chamberlain Diary, 4 April 1928.

[31] Ibid.

persuaded him to abandon the plan. Within days, however, Baldwin had also come round to the view that the railway question should be reconsidered. On 18 April a 'very worried' Baldwin explained to Chamberlain the Central Office fear that these modifications had now robbed the scheme of much of its original appeal. Moreover, despite Baldwin's apparent acceptance of Chamberlain's reasoned case for the amendments he 'maintained his troubled look'. When they met again over dinner that evening, Baldwin revealed that he had endured intense pressure to return to the original scheme from Cunliffe-Lister, Walter Guinness and Churchill, the last-mentioned clearly so much overwrought that he 'marched about the room shouting and shaking his fist and had launched out a tremendous tirade against [Chamberlain]' for his constant cold water and jealousy. Although Chamberlain dismissed Churchill's tantrums as 'too childish & contemptible ... to be upset over', Baldwin then crucially revealed his own doubts over the exclusion of railways and asked him to reconsider.[32]

By the following morning Chamberlain had already decided to surrender to Baldwin's appeal 'on account of [his] personal affection for him & because ... he had a real flair for the way things would appear to the man in the street'.[33] After another long talk with Baldwin 'to liberate [his] soul' about the many frustrations endured in his dealings with Churchill, Chamberlain agreed that at the next Cabinet he would restate his case before making it clear that he would not obstruct Cabinet agreement – a remarkably magnanimous gesture given Baldwin's own earlier admission that Chamberlain still commanded a majority in Cabinet, but one which reflected his responsiveness to Baldwin's personal appeal in circumstances in which no major personal or departmental issues were perceived to be at stake.[34] He also derived some consolation from the belief that his Cabinet position had been strengthened by a gesture which made it correspondingly less easy for Baldwin to evade his commitment to Poor Law reform.[35]

Events soon fulfilled Chamberlain's gloomy prediction that he had 'a horrible session' ahead in which 'Winston will do all the prancing and I shall do all the drudgery'.[36] The derating scheme figured prominently in Churchill's 3½ hour Budget speech delivered on 24 April to an admiring Parliament.[37] Conversely, Chamberlain was left to steer the complex Rating and Valuation (Apportionment) Bill through Parliament in order to pave the way for the full measure in the next session. Yet although the Bill appeared to Chamberlain 'the most difficult and

---

[32] Neville Chamberlain Diary, 18 April 1928.

[33] Neville Chamberlain Diary, 18 and 19 April 1928.

[34] N. Chamberlain to Ida, 21 April and to Hilda, 29 April 1928; Neville Chamberlain Diary, 19 April 1928.

[35] Neville Chamberlain Diary, 20 April 1928; CAB 23(28)4, 20 April 1928, CAB 23/57.

[36] N. Chamberlain to Hilda, 15 April 1928.

[37] Baldwin to the King, 26 April 1928, Baldwin MSS, 63/243.

vulnerable I have ever introduced', it proved to be 'child's play',[38] partly due to his care in drafting and ministerial mastery of its complicated provisions, but more to the 'incredible feebleness, laziness & incompetence of both oppositions'.[39] At the same time Chamberlain was busily engaged in drafting the Local Government Bill and then going through every clause and contingency to remove all possible objections and to construct a watertight defence against the remainder. After four months negotiating with the various local authority bodies and the Poor Law Guardians, the Bill of 115 clauses and twelve schedules covering 127 closely printed pages was introduced to Parliament on 13 November. As the *Annual Register* noted, by any standard it was 'a stupendous measure', with many of its clauses as long as an ordinary Act of Parliament.[40]

On 26 November Chamberlain moved the Second Reading of the Local Government Bill in a masterly two and a half hour speech to which (even by his own meticulous standards of preparation) he had devoted 'an immense amount of trouble'.[41] Declaring the measure among the greatest to come before Parliament for many years, he set his plan for the comprehensive reform of the entire structure of local government within the context of its historic development since the Poor Law Amendment Act of 1834 and the Acts of 1888 and 1894. Explaining the trends of population, shifting patterns of industry and the development of new services which had occurred to render that machinery obsolete and outmoded, he summed up the deficiencies of the existing structure under the five headings which had changed little since his provisional programme of legislation in November 1924.[42] This 'masterly piece of exposition and argument' earned him 'unstinting praise from all sides of the House'.[43] According to one observer, the speech was 'listened to in almost complete silence and the closest attention'. Moreover, its appeal to the collective sentiment of the Commons was increased by the fact that it contained 'more human touches and humour than is customary with Neville's speeches';[44] personal embellishments about local government as it appeared to the people of Birmingham, introduced at his wife's instigation 'to put in something human lest the speech shd appear to be devoted too exclusively to the coldly mechanical efficiency of administration'. When he sat down, he did so to vigorous and enthusiastic cheering from all parts of the House for longer than Worthington-

---

[38] N. Chamberlain to Irwin, 12 August 1928.

[39] Neville Chamberlain Diary, 30 July 1928; N. Chamberlain to Hilda, 8 July 1928.

[40] M. Epstein (ed.), *The Annual Register 1928* (London, 1929), p. 108.

[41] Neville Chamberlain Diary, 1 December 1928; N. Chamberlain to Sir Gilbert Barling, 4 December 1928, Letters Additional 4.

[42] CP 499(24), 'Provisional Programme of Legislation', 19 November 1924, CAB 24/168. See also CP 386(26), 'Poor Law Reform', 18 November 1926, CAB 24/182.

[43] *Annual Register 1928*, pp. 109–10. See also Baldwin to the King, 27 November 1928, Baldwin MSS 63.

[44] Winterton Diary, 26 November 1928, Earl Winterton, *Orders of the Day* (London, 1953), p. 153.

Evans recalled in his eighteen years in the Commons. Certainly Chamberlain confessed himself to be well satisfied with the speech and gratified by its results – particularly the fact that his lucid exposition enabled MPs to recognise, for perhaps the first time, that this represented 'a great help towards a happy result at the Gen. Election'.[45] After an easy passage through Parliament the Bill received Royal Assent on 27 March 1929.

At the heart of the Local Government Act (and its Scottish counterpart) was the formal separation of the highly problematic and demoralising dual responsibility of the Poor Law for both the able-bodied unemployed and the non-able-bodied who were confined largely to the institutions. Henceforth, the former were to be administered by newly established Public Assistance Committees appointed by local authorities and funded jointly from the rates and the Exchequer. In contrast, the Poor Law Unions, Boards of Guardians and Scottish parochial boards were abolished and the care of the non-able-bodied poor was transferred to the county and county borough councils while the powers, duties, assets and institutions of the 625 Poor Law Unions were assigned to existing specialist council committees in order to improve the quality of provision. Under this arrangement, workhouse infirmaries were assigned to council health committees where they were intended to develop into general and municipal hospitals without their previous stigma of destitution and pauperism, while responsibility for the education of Poor Law children was transferred from the workhouse to local education committees. In this manner, the major local authorities were finally empowered to 'break up the Poor Law', to end the wasteful duplication of services which had so appalled reformers since the Poor Law Commission in 1909 and to unify provision for the destitute and able-bodied unemployed on the same terms as the rest of the community. On this basis, the measure was hailed by reformers of all persuasions as 'a sentence of death' on the century-old Boards of Guardians, the concept of 'less eligibility' and the other principles of 1834.[46]

The actual impact of the Local Government Act is difficult to assess fairly given the almost immediate onset of the Great Depression which inhibited local authorities from grasping the full opportunities offered by the measure, and then the onset of the Second World War which effectively uprooted the entire structure. Nevertheless, while some contend that in the longer term 'both the structural and the financial reforms were improvements of great importance',[47] many modern commentators follow the Webbs in lamenting that although the administrative structures and titles changed, the old Poor Law remained largely untouched in its fundamentals with regard to the notion of relief and the stigma

---

[45] Neville Chamberlain Diary, 1 December 1928 and 24 February 1929. See also Lord Onslow to N. Chamberlain, 18 February 1929, NC7/11/22/22.

[46] Sidney and Beatrice Webb, *English Poor Law History: Part II, The Last Hundred Years* (London, 1929), pp. 985, 1019.

[47] John Ramsden, *The Age of Balfour and Baldwin* (London, 1978), p. 290.

of pauperism.[48] As Bentley Gilbert contends, 'beyond the disappearance of the guardians themselves, the expansion of hospital facilities by some, by no means all, local authorities, turned out to be almost the only notable change in the durable apparatus of local welfare functions'. As a result, the following decade witnessed a continuation of the previous 'rudderless drifting towards specialised institutions'.[49] All of this fell considerably short of Chamberlain's optimistic vision of a national hospital service with local government leading the way towards greater coordination in health provision and the translation of general workhouse institutions into public hospitals.[50] For the poor receiving indoor relief the picture was very similar. Although the 1929 Act was intended to improve treatment in specialist institutions, economic slump ensured that 'all the Act could do was to reshuffle existing resources rather than encourage innovation'. As a historian of the workhouse notes, 'Chamberlain had laid the foundations of a more specialised system of residential institutions, but a corresponding social investment was not made until the more prosperous 1950s'.[51] At a practical level, the physical legacy of the Poor Law persisted for still longer in the continued use of old workhouse buildings, while the extremely hierarchical administrative structures and authoritarian attitudes acquired in Poor Law years too often persisted into the newly created PACs and NHS.[52]

In the shorter term, Chamberlain's view of the vote-winning potential of derating and local government reform was somewhat ambivalent. After the annual party conference at Yarmouth in September 1928, at which he enjoyed 'the success of [his] life', his mood was distinctly optimistic.[53] At other times, however, he more soberly reflected that the measure was 'too technical and too involved ever to make much appeal to the man in the street' and he reconciled himself to the belief that it would be 'remembered to our credit hereafter'.[54] The latter judgement came far closer to the truth. Since the defeat of the General Strike in 1926, the government had increasingly demonstrated symptoms of a debilitating *malaise d'ennui* which carried them listlessly into the 1929 general election. By the end of 1928 Lord Robert Cecil reported: 'the fourth year decay of a Government's policy ... is in full swing',[55] and without the electoral fillip of

---

[48] Webb, *English Poor Law*, pp. 986–87; Keith-Lucas, *The History of Local Government*, p. 231; Bentley B. Gilbert, *British Social Policy, 1914–1939* (London, 1976), pp. 229, 232; M.A. Crowther, *The Workhouse System, 1834–1929* (London, 1981), p. 109.

[49] Gilbert, *British Social Policy*, pp. 203–4, 232–33; Pat Thane, *The Foundations of the Welfare State* (London, 1982), p. 176.

[50] N. Chamberlain in *The Times*, 11 April 1929.

[51] Crowther, *The Workhouse System*, pp. 110, 153.

[52] Ibid., pp. 112, 154–55; Thane, *Foundations*, p. 176.

[53] N. Chamberlain to Ida, 28 September 1928; Neville Chamberlain Diary, 1 November 1928. See also Neville Chamberlain Diary, 1 December 1928 and 24 February 1929.

[54] N. Chamberlain to Ida, 4 November 1928. Also N. Chamberlain to Irwin, 12 August 1928.

[55] Lord Robert Cecil to Irwin, 30 August 1928, Cecil MSS 51084/63 (British Library).

Cabinet reconstruction or any radical commitment to tariffs, the Conservatives fell back upon a sound but unexciting record of domestic legislation and an uninspiring employment policy firmly rooted in Treasury orthodoxy and derating. Yet despite these problems, like most other observers, Chamberlain never really doubted their ability to return from the election with an overall working majority. In Birmingham, he anticipated that the Conservatives would lose Yardley but hold all eleven other seats in the city.[56] In the event, although Chamberlain enjoyed a far less rowdy election in the safety of Edgbaston than at Ladywood in 1924, within the city as a whole the election was a near disaster for the Conservatives. Since 1886 the Unionists had never lost more than one seat in Birmingham. In 1929 Labour were in confident mood and took no fewer than six of its twelve seats including that of a Cabinet Minister in Erdington, while in West Birmingham Austen Chamberlain only just scraped in by forty-three votes in a seat held continuously by a Chamberlain for almost half a century. In reality, the Labour advance in the city was based on flimsy foundations, but it was still a tremendous blow to Chamberlain and the Conservatives. Among the fallen was Geoffrey Lloyd who, despite vast exertions to cultivate Chamberlain's former constituency, was defeated in Ladywood by eleven votes.[57]

Initial explanations for defeat tended to vary in emphasis but the 'natural swing of the pendulum' was believed to have been aggravated by specific discontents. Certainly Chamberlain was convinced that the key factor had been 'the ceaseless propaganda that has been going on for years among the working classes to the effect that things would never be right for them till a "Labour" Govt came in. Every grievance has been exploited to point this moral ... there is no conversion to Socialism. It is merely the present discontents showing themselves in a desire for change'.[58] Yet as he was also aware, even his own achievements as a social reformer had contributed to their defeat because his pensions and housing policies probably won no new votes but alienated those who did not benefit from such measures.[59] At a more general level, no one contributed more in tangible policy terms to the government's disquieting reputation for 'socialistic tendencies' than Chamberlain had at the Ministry of Health.[60] Yet despite this direct responsibility for the unpopularity of certain aspects of policy, throughout the 1924–29 government Chamberlain had progressively strengthened his position as Baldwin's principal lieutenant and as

---

[56] N. Chamberlain to Hilda, 25 May 1929.

[57] Chief Agent's Report to the Birmingham Unionist Association Management Committee, 21 September and 12 October 1928, Steel-Maitland MSS GD 193/209/223–24, 230 (National Archives of Scotland).

[58] Neville Chamberlain Diary, 8 June 1929.

[59] N. Chamberlain to Ida, 2 June 1929. Also Bridgeman Diary, July 1929 (Shropshire Record Office, SRO 4629); G. Lane-Fox to Irwin, 26 September 1927, Irwin MSS Eur.c. 152/17/256d.

[60] Lord Younger to Davidson, 27 December 1926, Baldwin MSS 53/31–33.

a future leader of the party – particularly after Baldwin removed Douglas Hogg from the running by forcing upon him the Lord Chancellorship in March 1928 at a time when he was considered the more likely successor.[61] In the immediate aftermath of defeat in June 1929, however, his transition from heir apparent to the leadership was generally assumed to be a long way off, not least because Chamberlain was 'too loyal to S.B. to attempt to dislodge him'.[62] During the next two years, however, a ferocious period of internecine warfare shook Baldwin's leadership to its foundations and brought Chamberlain almost to the point of succession.

II

Depression, distaste for politics and gloomy forebodings about the future are natural emotional responses to electoral defeat among those so rudely deprived of office, status and worthwhile occupation. Chamberlain was no exception. Indeed, for a man who could more genuinely claim than most of his colleagues that his 'pleasure is in administration rather than in politics', the transition to the Opposition benches was a painful and traumatic experience. Within days of the election, Chamberlain predicted that Labour would spend two years establishing their credibility in office, then introduce a popular budget as a prelude to a general election designed to usher in a full term of majority government and the socialist millennium. He was thus soon dismally contemplating the prospect of seven years in Opposition, by which time he would be sixty-seven, with his powers in decline and with a new generation of leaders emerging to obstruct any future claim he may have to office. 'It is hard to bear & it will take time to recover spirits', he confessed to his sisters, consoling himself with the thought that 'there is no certainty in politics and that is why one does not go out in despair. The most unexpected things may happen and we may return to office sooner than seems possible now'.[63]

In political terms the prospects were equally cheerless. As in 1924, Chamberlain believed that electoral disillusion with the reality of Labour government was a necessary but prolonged prophylactic against continued Labour growth and future ascendancy.[64] Yet a united and combative Opposition with strong leadership and a clear constructive vision was an essential corollary of such a strategy and

---

[61] Baldwin to Irwin, 15 September 1927, Irwin MSS Eur.c. 152/17/253–54 and Keith Middlemas (ed.), *Thomas Jones: Whitehall Diary*, 2 vols (London, 1969), I, pp. 105–6.

[62] Jones Diary, 19 June 1929, *Whitehall Diary*, II, p. 189.

[63] N. Chamberlain to Ida, 2 June 1929. Also N. Chamberlain to Mary Carnegie, 1 June 1929, NC1/20/1/147 and Neville Chamberlain Diary, 8 June 1929.

[64] N. Chamberlain to Hilda, 9 June 1929; N. Chamberlain to Baldwin, 2 June 1929, Baldwin MSS 36/211.

in the immediate aftermath of defeat he privately lamented that Baldwin lacked the necessary qualities for such conditions;[65] apprehensions substantiated within months by widespread criticism of Baldwin's inertia and lack of leadership even among his most sympathetic supporters.[66] Moreover, these failures were particularly alarming because factious intra-party disputes over tariffs and the food tax incubus had boiled to the surface almost immediately the Conservatives left office, provoked by speeches from Amery and Chamberlain in early July and the simultaneous launch of Lord Beaverbrook's Crusade for 'Empire Free Trade' with its direct assault upon the 'outworn fallacy of the "Dear Loaf"'.[67]

Mounting party disenchantment with Baldwin's leadership placed Chamberlain in an invidious personal position. Although he continued to hope that Baldwin's lethargy was a 'passing phase', Chamberlain confessed in October 1929 that it 'is all very depressing and particularly embarrassing for me because everyone I meet tells me of S.B.'s failings and many suggest that I should do better in his place. Heaven knows I dont want the job. It is a thankless one at any time & never more so than now when the party is all to pieces'. Moreover, as Baldwin was his friend as well as his leader, Chamberlain was determined that he would 'not on any account play L.G. to his Asquith'. On the other hand, he was tormented by the fear that Baldwin's temperamental distaste for Opposition may prompt him to retire, leaving him to contest the succession with Churchill; an eventuality which prompted the confession that 'I dont know which I should dislike most!'[68]

Reluctant to assume the leadership himself but adamantly opposed to Churchill's succession, Chamberlain thus became even more firmly committed to the maintenance of Baldwin's position. In late October, he warned Baldwin of the poor state of party morale and urged him to 'do violence to his instincts, give a lead and attack the enemy'. He also attempted to persuade him that tariffs were 'the only thing which could pull [our] people together and that an advance there was the thing to work for'. This logic implied the need to achieve an accommodation with Beaverbrook, despite the fact that Chamberlain believed Empire Free Trade was so 'woolly' that it would not only be 'riddled with criticisms' if adopted as party policy but also likely to jeopardise his own plans to 'make tariffs ... only part of a larger Imperial trade policy'.[69] Yet encouraged by Harold Macmillan into believing that 'with a "few kind words" he might be

[65] Neville Chamberlain Diary, 8 June and 26 July 1929.

[66] N. Chamberlain to Ida, 22 October 1929; N. Chamberlain to his wife, 22 and 26 October 1929, NC1/26/416, 418.

[67] Lord Beaverbrook, 'Who is for the Empire?' and 'The New Project of Empire', *Sunday Express*, 30 June and 7 July 1929. For Conservative free trade apprehensions at this apparently concerted protectionist démarche see Churchill to Lord Linlithgow, 10 July 1929, Hopetoun MSS 1002 (National Register of Archives, Scotland).

[68] N. Chamberlain to Hilda, 13 and 26 October 1929.

[69] N. Chamberlain to his wife, 25 October 1929, NC1/26/417.

won over', Chamberlain and Hoare met Beaverbrook on 4 November. Although discouraged by Beaverbrook's equivocation, 'strong personal hostility to SB' and intransigence over the full food tax policy, on the following morning Beaverbrook informed Hoare that after Chamberlain's forthcoming East African tour if they went to him 'meaning business he would be prepared to do a deal ... and ... his personal feelings about S.B. wd not stand in the way as he cared much more about Empire Free Trade than he did about his vendetta'.[70] On this basis, the accommodation was consummated at a personal meeting between Baldwin and Beaverbrook and a few sympathetic words in the leader's Albert Hall speech on 21 November. Chamberlain also rejoiced at Baldwin's speech on the grounds that it represented the first step on the road to the abandonment of past pledges on tariffs and the adoption of the 'free hand' he had desired since entering Opposition. At this juncture he believed Baldwin was 'quite sound on the merits, but wavers backwards and forwards on the expediency according to the last person who talked to him'.[71] As a result, Chamberlain and Hoare carefully worked in concert to sustain the protectionist pressure on Baldwin. 'He is like a top', Chamberlain told his sisters, 'You must keep whipping him or he falls over!'[72]

The rapprochement which Chamberlain had negotiated with Beaverbrook before his departure proved as short-lived as it was superficial. Urged on by Lord Rothermere's demands for a more aggressive strategy to contest by-elections with an organisation similar to his own Anti-Waste League a decade earlier, Beaverbrook dispensed with official Conservative support and launched the United Empire Party on 18 February to carry the fight to the constituencies. Having done so, he then almost immediately abandoned Rothermere after becoming 'really frightened at the utter lack of statesmanship and knowledge of politics' displayed by his fellow press baron.[73] At a private meeting on 3 March, Baldwin then agreed to a referendum on food taxes after the next general election as the price of reunion with the erratic Beaverbrook. On the following day Baldwin announced the referendum as official policy in a speech at the Hotel Cecil. When Chamberlain arrived home from Africa four days later he thus found a manifestly changed situation. Now restored physically and mentally, within days he had taken up the reins of his new domain at the Conservative Research Department, persuaded Baldwin to establish a 'Committee of Business' as 'a sort of inner Shadow Cabinet' and renewed his cordial relations with an evidently discontented Beaverbrook.[74] During a long talk on 11 March, Beaverbrook gave vent to his renewed suspicions of the sincerity of Central

---

[70] Neville Chamberlain Diary, 4 and 5 November 1929.

[71] Neville Chamberlain Diary, 8 December 1929.

[72] N. Chamberlain to Hilda, 24 November 1929.

[73] H.A. Gwynne to Baldwin, 21 February 1930, Gwynne MSS 15 (Bodleian Library, Oxford).

[74] N. Chamberlain to Ida, 22 March 1930.

Office and Davidson, the Party Chairman, and announced that he hoped the referendum would soon be dropped; an opinion Chamberlain begged him to suppress for fear of alarming fiscally less-advanced opinion in Parliament and the constituencies. By the end of this meeting Beaverbrook expressed his probably sincere gratitude for 'the first good conversation he had had' and one based on a growing sense of mutual respect.[75]

Despite Chamberlain's reassuring effect, the volatile Beaverbrook soon rebelled again. Provoked by the publication of an aggressively free trade letter from Lord Salisbury in *The Times* which left him 'very restless and angry',[76] at an unpleasant meeting with Davidson and Chamberlain on 25 March Beaverbrook announced his intention to revive his Empire Crusade. After this meeting, Davidson's attitude towards Beaverbrook hardened dramatically. 'Not at all happy about the situation' and scandalised by the hectoring threats and demands, Davidson noted prophetically that Beaverbrook 'wants everything and will give nothing. He will take every opportunity which is given by the luke-warm or clumsy advocacy … of Empire Free Trade as a reason why he should be critical of our sincerity, and at the same time find some excuse for not giving any support whatever to our campaign in the country'. Moreover, as it would be 'intolerable' for Beaverbrook to 'call the tune and write the slogans', Davidson urged Chamberlain to ascertain the limits of his support for the forthcoming Conservative 'Home and Empire' campaign and for candidates fighting on the Hotel Cecil policy.[77] If, as Davidson subsequently claimed, the referendum was merely a device 'to lead [Beaverbrook] on a bit' and detach him from the hated and implacable Rothermere,[78] the limits of his indulgence were reached by the end of March and the ensuing conflict over the Nottingham by-election and the Home and Empire campaign were manifestations of this resolve. Conversely, the direct consequence of these tensions was to drive Beaverbrook back into the arms of Rothermere as a prelude to renewed hostilities against the Conservative Party – and in particular against Davidson, in the belief that his 'destruction would be a deadly blow to Baldwin' just as Acland-Hood's had been to Balfour.[79]

Yet whatever Beaverbrook would have liked to believe, he only represented an indirect danger to Davidson by illuminating his shortcomings. The principal

---

[75] 'Notes re Empire Free Trade', hereafter called Elibank Diary, 10 and 11 March 1930, Elibank MSS GD 32/25/69 fols 29–30 (National Archives of Scotland). Also Neville Chamberlain Diary, 12 March 1930 and Hannon Diary, 11 March 1930, Hannon MSS (House of Lords Records Office, Hist. Coll. 189).

[76] Elibank Diary, 25 March 1930, fol. 43.

[77] Davidson to Chamberlain, 26 March 1930, Davidson MSS 190 (House of Lords Records Office, Hist. Coll. 187).

[78] Draft memoir, R.R. James, *Memoirs of a Conservative: J.C.C. Davidson's Memoirs and Papers, 1910–37* (London, 1969), p. 322.

[79] Beaverbrook to Rothermere, 3 July 1929, Beaverbrook MSS C/284 (House of Lords Records Office, Hist. Coll. 184).

threat to his continued influence came from Chamberlain. By March 1930 Chamberlain had resolved to remove Davidson from the party chairmanship because he was 'a fool and a danger in his post': a view he communicated to Beaverbrook.[80] After consultation with his half-brother and Cunliffe-Lister, Chamberlain thus suggested to Davidson on 3 April that 'he had better go before he was fired out'.[81] Davidson's position then became untenable during May when Robert Topping, the Principal Agent, produced a calculated memorandum of concern about the 'extremely disturbing' deterioration of party morale since the dismal failure of the Home and Empire campaign. If another electoral disaster was to be avoided, Topping warned, the party needed a lasting accommodation with Beaverbrook.[82] As Davidson was manifestly incapable of repairing the breach, Topping's memorandum was of considerable importance in undermining his intra-party position. Chamberlain had initially intended that Geoffrey Ellis should succeed Davidson as he was already familiar with Central Office and his 'ideas about the C.O. and politics generally accord[ed] very closely with [his] own'. Discreetly trying to avoid the appearance of a plot, Chamberlain thus began to canvass support for Ellis during April and at one point even hoped to induce Davidson to propose Ellis himself.[83] In the event, however, the suspicion that the prevarication of Baldwin and Davidson over the succession was intended to leave Topping in effective control of Central Office induced Chamberlain to abandon the Ellis candidature and to assume the chairmanship himself on 23 June.[84]

Chamberlain was only too well aware of the sacrifices which the chairmanship entailed, having previously rejected any idea of accepting such 'a soulless job' in 1921 and 1924.[85] Yet despite his palpable lack of enthusiasm, the decision offered a variety of advantages for the party and even for Chamberlain himself. Firstly, he rightly believed that Beaverbrook respected his intentions and sincerity and 'at the Central Office I may have perhaps a better chance of convincing him where the true interests of his policy lie'.[86] Secondly, although a second-best solution for Chamberlain, it had the merit of averting a greater evil, namely the prospect that Baldwin's retirement might force him reluctantly to become leader to prevent Churchill from doing so.[87] Thirdly, from Baldwin's perspective, it

---

[80] Elibank Diary, 29 March 1930, fol. 43; N. Chamberlain to Ida, 6 April 1930.

[81] N. Chamberlain to his wife, 4 April 1930, NC1/26/422. Also Davidson to Chamberlain, 3 April 1930, Davidson MSS.

[82] Topping memorandum to Davidson, 2 May 1930, Davidson MSS 190.

[83] N. Chamberlain to Ida, 6 April and to Hilda, 12 April 1930.

[84] N. Chamberlain to Hilda, 25 May and 21 June 1930. Also Neville Chamberlain Diary, 22 June 1930; Hoare to Irwin, 31 May 1930, Irwin MSS Eur.c. 152/19/71.

[85] N. Chamberlain to Ida, 21 August 1921 and to Hilda, 18 May 1924. Self (ed.), *Neville Chamberlain Diary Letters*, II, pp. 78 and 223.

[86] N. Chamberlain to Lord Derby, 27 June 1930, Derby MSS (Liverpool Central Library).

[87] For these fears see N. Chamberlain to Hilda, 10 May and 8 June and to Ida 17 May 1930.

effectively neutralised the party's most likely alternative leader by inextricably associating Chamberlain's reputation and future with Baldwin's own; a risk of which Chamberlain, his wife and half-brother were all keenly aware. Finally, in the short term, Chamberlain's appointment served to infuse the leadership with a new sense of purpose and direction in challenging its critics.[88] Thus, as a direct result of Chamberlain's initiative, at the Caxton Hall meeting on 24 June Baldwin launched an abrasive attack upon the Press Lords and their pretensions to dictate policy to the Conservative Party. While the 'Old Gang' could congratulate themselves upon a largely organisationally contrived victory, however, it had not removed the fundamental problem. To this end, Baldwin again authorised Chamberlain to approach Beaverbrook.

From the outset Chamberlain had sought permanent reconciliation with Beaverbrook because he could 'be equally a very valuable friend and a very formidable enemy'.[89] Although increasingly frustrated by Beaverbrook's continual charges of bad faith, his vanity, recklessness and complete lack of constancy of purpose, Chamberlain's growing regard for Beaverbrook was fully reciprocated.[90] On this basis, Chamberlain implicitly subscribed to Davidson's belief that if only 'he would make a real friend of someone who is not in the dregs of politics … we could change the whole of his outlook' – particularly if the party could 'devise some policy which would make a spiritual semi-sentimental appeal'.[91] Within a fortnight of the Caxton Hall meeting, Chamberlain thus invited Beaverbrook to meet 'to settle whether we are to be at peace or war'.[92] On 18 July at a private dinner at Eaton Square, Chamberlain, Cunliffe-Lister and Hoare 'profoundly impressed and depressed' Beaverbrook with warnings that Labour's rumoured plans for import boards, quotas and bulk purchase from the empire would sabotage Empire Free Trade. Chamberlain then played his 'trump card and … brought … home to Max the absolute folly of quarrelling with [the] Party and the necessity of finding some way of destroying the Labour Party before they destroyed his policy'. On this basis, Beaverbrook agreed to cease his attacks and rival candidatures in return for official toleration towards Conservative candidates sympathetic to his policy. Although Baldwin appeared 'half disappointed' by the possibility of agreement, Chamberlain believed that they would be 'in clover' if it materialised and Topping rejoiced at 'the first gleam of light after many months of gloom'.[93]

---

[88] N. Chamberlain to Hilda, 21 June 1930.

[89] N. Chamberlain to Ida, 22 March 1930.

[90] Ibid. See also Beaverbrook to Hoare, 18 May 1930, Beaverbrook MSS C/307 and his remarks in Davidson memoranda dated 12 and 14 March 1930, Davidson MSS.

[91] Davidson to N. Chamberlain, 15 April 1930, Davidson MSS 190.

[92] N. Chamberlain to Ida, 12 July 1930 and to Beaverbrook, 11 July 1930, Beaverbrook MSS C/60; Neville Chamberlain Diary, 19 July 1930.

[93] Neville Chamberlain Diary, 19 and 20 July 1930.

Conservative satisfaction was short-lived. Less than a week after their meeting, another split occurred over Beaverbrook's decision to support Rothermere and the UEP against the Conservatives at the Bromley by-election: a rift widened by the resumption of attacks in the *Daily Express* and Chamberlain's discovery that Beaverbrook had not only 'been playing a double game ... all through' the Bromley negotiations, but that he had told a group of MPs he was only cooperating 'to keep Neville sweet'.[94] In language very similar to that employed towards Hitler after the betrayal of his hopes about Munich, Chamberlain recorded that 'I had given my trust and it had been abused and I was bitterly humiliated and outraged'. This he considered to be 'one of [Beaverbrook's] biggest blunders. He has destroyed my confidence in him', he told his sisters bitterly, 'and when that has happened I won't readily give it up again vide Lloyd George'.[95] In practice, this fiasco over Bromley was symptomatic of Beaverbrook's fundamental inability to choose between Rothermere and the Conservative Party as the best means to achieve his desired end in circumstances in which the antipathy between the two rendered the alternative alliances mutually exclusive. It also brutally exposed his chronic political unreliability. Thus, within days of the breach with Chamberlain, Beaverbrook had quarrelled with Rothermere and withdrawn from further participation in the by-election. Yet Chamberlain was now in an altogether less forgiving mood. Moreover, believing Beaverbrook to be 'in very low spirits and anxious for an excuse for reconciliation', Chamberlain's decision to 'let him stew in his own juice' reflected the conviction that unless Beaverbrook was forced finally to choose between his two allies, lasting accommodation would always be impossible.[96]

At the same time Chamberlain took an equally robust stance towards the problem of party discontent with the failure of Baldwin's leadership and lack of progress towards his own more aggressive tariff policy. Despite warnings that '[a]ny policy which Baldwin launches as leader is doomed as a damp squib because he has lost the confidence of the Party and will never regain it',[97] by early October Chamberlain concluded that only by committing Baldwin to the latter could intra-party criticism of the former be dispelled. With this in mind, he had already prepared the ground for Baldwin's public conversion to the new policy by launching his own 'unauthorised programme' in a speech at Crystal Palace on 20 September calling for drastic economy (especially on unemployment insurance), an emergency tariff, a wheat – and possibly meat – quota and the abandonment of the referendum to permit a free hand on other imports to

---

[94] Neville Chamberlain Diary, 29 and 30 July 1930.

[95] N. Chamberlain to Hilda, 4 August 1930. Also N. Chamberlain to his wife, 4 August 1930, NC1/26/434.

[96] N. Chamberlain to Hilda, 21 September 1930.

[97] Sir Henry Page Croft to Chamberlain, 4 October 1930, Croft MSS 1/7/6; Neville Chamberlain Diary, 11 October 1930.

improve imperial economic relations. Yet although he had been pleasantly surprised by Baldwin's determined lead in accepting the new tariff programme at the Business Conference on 7 October, there is evidence to suggest that later that evening Chamberlain consulted his half-brother and Hoare about calling a frontbench meeting in Baldwin's absence to discuss leadership and ultimately to change it in his favour. By the following day, however, he abandoned the plan because 'if any move is made, it should really come from the House of Commons – the body which makes, and can presumably unmake, leaders'. Instead he drafted an exchange of letters with Baldwin articulating the new policy 'in such a way as to tide us over the immediate difficulties, and to give an opportunity to those who are still loyal, to renew their allegiance'.[98]

In the event, the Canadian Premier's offer at the Imperial Conference of a reciprocal preference arrangement provided a 'Heaven-sent opportunity' of attaching Baldwin to the 'unauthorised programme'[99] and Chamberlain immediately issued a statement over Baldwin's name declaring that '[w]hatever the Socialist Government may do the Conservative Party accept[ed] the principle put forward with such weight and unanimity'.[100] In the long term, Chamberlain's statement represented a personal triumph and a crucial reorientation of Conservative tariff policy. The referendum had been buried and Chamberlain's 'unauthorised programme' had become official party policy ultimately to bear fruit in 1931–32. In the short term, Chamberlain's initiative also radically transformed leadership perceptions of the threat posed by Beaverbrook and the forthcoming party meeting. Although still harbouring grave doubts about Baldwin's ability to remain as leader indefinitely, Chamberlain's second public letter to himself from Baldwin the following week reaffirming their commitment to the 'unauthorised programme' was designed merely to 'save S.B.'s bacon long enough to enable him to go later without a triumph for R[othermere] and B[eaverbrook]'. In the interim he was content to 'await events'.[101] Should Baldwin recover his position then no harm would be done: if he did not, then the parliamentary party could disown him without directly implicating Chamberlain in his downfall.

During October Baldwin emerged briefly from the morose apathy into which news of his unpopularity had thrown him, to demonstrate a new vigour and determination. Baldwin's short speech to the party meeting of nearly 600 peers, MPs and candidates at the Caxton Hall on 30 October unveiled the new policy and obtained its endorsement with only one dissident – Beaverbrook. Baldwin then withdrew to allow the attack on the leadership to be defeated by 462 to 116.

---

[98] For oblique references to the plot see Neville Chamberlain to Austen Chamberlain, 8 and 10 October 1930 and reply, Austen Chamberlain MSS (Birmingham University Library), AC39/2/39–40 and AC58/75. See also Neville Chamberlain Diary, 11 October 1930.

[99] N. Chamberlain to A. Chamberlain, 10 October 1930, AC58/75.

[100] *The Times*, 10 October 1930; Neville Chamberlain Diary, 11 October 1930.

[101] N. Chamberlain to Ida, 11 October 1930.

In such a highly-charged atmosphere, the news that a Crusader candidate had defeated the official Conservative to win South Paddington by 914 votes was recognised on both sides to be 'a Pyrrhic victory'.[102] Thus, when Chamberlain met Beaverbrook a week later, he was surprised to find 'a New Max' with all his assurance gone and 'at times almost humble in manner'.[103] This was fortunate for Chamberlain, for although he had adopted 'the stiffest possible attitude' towards the wayward Press Lord, fears of an early election and a serious shortage of funds and candidates due to continued uncertainty about Beaverbrook made an accommodation imperative.[104] In the belief that 'he really does mean, this time, to come in' Chamberlain arranged a public exchange of letters between Beaverbrook and Baldwin on 21 November as the basis for full cooperation.[105] Again, however, the promise of accommodation proved illusory and the resumption of the Press and by-election offensive in December finally disabused Chamberlain of his last illusions about Beaverbrook. 'He is as unstable as water, without patience, balance or self-control', Chamberlain lamented. 'He can never wait, and his restless vanity impels and compels him always to keep himself in the limelight'.[106]

Although Chamberlain successfully undermined the UEP campaign at the East Islington by-election, the crisis of confidence in Baldwin's leadership reached a climax in February 1931. Inundated with letters from all over the country informing him 'that people have lost all trust in his ability or will to carry anything', Chamberlain finally concluded that his succession was the 'natural outcome'.[107] His problem, however, was that while he was the only person able to bring about Baldwin's retirement, he could not act without the appearance of self-seeking disloyalty. Fortunately, this potentially compromising dilemma was resolved by the decisive intervention of Robert Topping, General Director at Central Office. Topping probably consciously set out to be the *deus ex machina* in Chamberlain's strategy and he had certainly given him advance warning about his intentions.[108] In a brutally uncompromising memorandum in late February 1931 Topping reported that support for Baldwin's leadership had declined so dramatically since October that even his most loyal supporters now shared the widespread feeling that 'in the interests of the Party … the Leader should reconsider his position'. While conceding that Churchill's Indian policy was more popular with the party than Baldwin's, Topping expressed the view

---

[102] Neville Chamberlain Diary, 6 November 1930; Beaverbrook to Croft, 4 November 1930, Croft MSS 1/4/14.

[103] Neville Chamberlain Diary, 6 November 1930; N. Chamberlain to Ida, 8 November 1930.

[104] See George Bowyer, 'Memo on Candidates', 1 December 1930, Baldwin MSS 48/187–92.

[105] N. Chamberlain to Bridgeman, 18 November 1930, NC8/10/16d.

[106] N. Chamberlain to Hilda, 14 December 1930; Neville Chamberlain Diary, 1 February 1931.

[107] Neville Chamberlain Diary, 23 February 1931. Also N. Chamberlain to Hilda, 14 February 1931.

[108] Neville Chamberlain Diary, 23 February 1931.

that they 'would prefer ... that if a new Leader is to be chosen, he should be elected on broad policy and not on any one single issue'. In short, by claiming to speak for the bulk of party sentiment, Topping had provided Chamberlain with a weapon to unseat Baldwin, to exclude Churchill from the succession and put himself forward as the only alternative and natural leader. Moreover, he precipitated the crisis in such a way as to leave Chamberlain uncompromised by allegations of self-interest.

Chamberlain's consultation with senior colleagues ended in a unanimous decision to inform Baldwin of Topping's report, although Hailsham had prevailed in delaying its disclosure until after Baldwin's Newton Abbott speech on 6 March; a proposal Chamberlain accepted against his own better judgement because he 'did not relish the prospect of hearing ... that [he] had shown indecent haste in pushing SB off the throne'. In the event, the news that Moore-Brabazon had withdrawn his candidature for the forthcoming St George's by-election rather than defend Baldwin's leadership provided the pretext for the immediate presentation of Topping's memorandum to Baldwin. Having read it, Baldwin summoned Chamberlain to announce that he had decided to resign without consulting his colleagues and offered to help him to obtain the leadership to prevent Churchill doing so.[109] Later that evening, however, the leadership was effectively snatched from Chamberlain's grasp by Lord Bridgeman who convinced Baldwin that resignation 'would be a base surrender and desertion in the face of the enemy' and that he should 'challenge the right of the press millionaires to dictate procedure to the Party' by contesting the St George's by-election himself. Even if defeated, Bridgeman argued, Baldwin could then retire 'with honour and dignity as the champion of a cause which 99 per cent of the people knew in their hearts was right'.[110] Baldwin found it rather less easy to convince Chamberlain who appeared 'very cold' when the subject was broached next morning and pointed to the difficulties which Baldwin's defeat would create for his successor; a far from disinterested calculation which prompted the curt reply, 'I don't give a damn about my successor, Neville'.[111]

Baldwin's new determination did not significantly modify Chamberlain's perception of the situation or its likely outcome. In the belief that Baldwin could not remain leader much longer, on 5 March Chamberlain and Hailsham agreed privately that they were prepared to serve under each other as a 'partnership', but never under Churchill. Baldwin's reaction to these arrangements was predictably brusque and a few days later he gave it to be understood that he was

---

[109] Neville Chamberlain Diary, 1 March 1931.

[110] Neville Chamberlain Diary, 3 March 1931; Bridgeman Diary, 1 March 1931, Political Notes II, fols 229–33; N. Chamberlain to Ida, 7 March 1931. Also Davidson to Irwin, 6 March 1931, Irwin MSS Eur.c. 152/19/254.

[111] Neville Chamberlain Diary, 3 March 1931; Keith Middlemas and John Barnes, *Baldwin: A Biography* (London, 1969), p. 590.

'very angry with "some of his colleagues", particularly Hailsham who had he believed been plotting against him'. Although Chamberlain was not among 'the chief sinners', Baldwin was known to be 'sore against [him] for not having supported him more stoutly' – an accusation Chamberlain understandably found 'difficult to stomach without resentment'.[112] In this atmosphere of mutual suspicion and resentment within the leadership, the final crisis was precipitated by Chamberlain's half-brother. Austen Chamberlain had always opposed his brother's decision to accept the party chairmanship, and by March 1931 he believed that this was severely jeopardising his chances of the succession.[113] Having figured prominently in the confidential discussions between Neville, Amery and Hoare designed to engineer Baldwin's resignation during the first week in March, at the Business Committee on 11 March Austen bluntly enquired when Baldwin was going to relieve his brother at Central Office, as his debating talents were desperately required on the front bench.[114] Although he had not warned his half-brother in advance, perhaps because of his previous veto of a similar scheme due to the closeness of the family relationship, to all present it was 'pretty plain what [Austen] had in mind' and 'even SB could hardly miss the underlying implication that it was to free Neville for the successorship'.[115] By this stage, however, even Chamberlain inclined to the view that Austen was correct in his view and in an icy conversation with Baldwin two days later he explained his desire to resign as Chairman, only to be astonished and wounded to hear absolutely no word of surprise, regret or appreciation.[116] After this, he curtly completed the explanatory letter to accompany his formal resignation, denying foreknowledge of his half-brother's plans, explaining his own 'singularly painful and embarrassing position' when confronted by the Topping memorandum and objecting that it was 'intensely disagreeable' to feel his motives were regarded as self-interested.[117]

Chamberlain's anger and frustration at Baldwin's behaviour was intensified by the activities of the Press Lords whose impudent intervention in the St George's by-election represented both the climax of their campaign against Baldwin and the end of Chamberlain's hopes of replacing him before he was ready to go. As Chamberlain lamented, 'it is in accord with the irony of politics that just as I was about to take the step which must have resulted in the speedy retirement of SB Max comes in with a move which must cause him to dig his

---

[112] Neville Chamberlain Diary, 11 March 1931.

[113] A. Chamberlain to Hilda, 7 March 1931, AC5/1/533, Robert Self (ed.), *The Austen Chamberlain Diary Letters* (Cambridge, 1995), pp. 365–66.

[114] A. Chamberlain to Ida, 13 March 1931, AC5/1/534, Self (ed.), *Austen Chamberlain*, pp. 366–67.

[115] Neville Chamberlain Diary, 11 March 1931; Amery Diary, 7 and 11 March 1931.

[116] Neville Chamberlain Diary, 14 March 1931.

[117] N. Chamberlain to Baldwin, 13 March 1931, Baldwin MSS 166/58–60.

toes in and will rally to him many who wish for a change'.[118] During an often scurrilous and abusive campaign, Baldwin and Duff Cooper easily subordinated questions of policy to the moral right of the party to choose its own leader without dictation from an 'insolent and irresponsible plutocracy'.[119] After Cooper's comfortable victory, all that remained was to resolve outstanding difficulties. Although Baldwin soon let it be known that he was 'anxious to avoid a rift' with Chamberlain, there were further angry scenes and their breach was not formally resolved until 24 March, after a 'frank not to say brutal talk' had enabled them to part 'shaking hands with the clouds removed'.[120] On the same day, Chamberlain reluctantly reopened negotiations with Beaverbrook and an agreed exchange of letters was published on 31 March after Chamberlain thwarted a last-ditch effort to give the appearance that the Conservatives had changed their policy to accommodate Beaverbrook.[121] In retrospect, the Empire Crusade had been a farcical episode. The tariff policies which Chamberlain introduced less than a year after the St George's by-election borrowed nothing in their conception from Beaverbrook or Empire Free Trade. Upon going into Opposition in 1929 a party committee had been established to make proposals on 'the general industrial policy which the Party should adopt'.[122] Here, and in Chamberlain's Conservative Research Department, the tariff policy had been in gestation since early 1930. When Cunliffe-Lister's committee produced its hundred-page report in June 1931 after eighteen months of intensive deliberation, the Conservatives were armed with an all-embracing protectionist policy and 'a definite, practical working plan, which can be put into operation without delay'.[123] All that remained was to find an opportunity to put these plans into effect.

III

In the immediate aftermath of defeat in 1929, Chamberlain had anticipated seven years in Opposition. Eighteen months later he was doubtful whether the Labour government could survive much longer and talked more in terms of months rather than years.[124] To accelerate the process of government collapse, since November 1930 Chamberlain had been planning to destroy it from within by encouraging the development of an independent 'Liberal-Unionist' group of

---

[118] Neville Chamberlain Diary, 1 March 1931.

[119] Baldwin to Col. Butchart, *Morning Post*, 8 March 1931.

[120] Neville Chamberlain Diary, 21 and 25 March 1931.

[121] Neville Chamberlain Diary, 28 and 31 March 1931.

[122] Cunliffe-Lister to Steel-Maitland, 17 July 1929, Steel-Maitland MSS GD193/120/3(2).

[123] N. Chamberlain to Cunliffe-Lister, 16 July 1931 and to Lady Cunliffe-Lister, 6 February 1932, Swinton MSS 174/2/4.

[124] N. Chamberlain to Hilda, 3 January and 14 February 1931; Lord Selborne to his wife, 23 April 1931, reporting Chamberlain's view, Selborne MSS 106/117 (Bodleian Library, Oxford).

MPs prepared to join with the Conservatives to oust Labour in return for suitable guarantees about their own position.[125] As the Liberals moved closer to Labour during 1931, Chamberlain even encouraged secret negotiations with Lloyd George during July in order to obtain his support to defeat the government in return for some limited measure of electoral reform.[126] In the event, the arrival of the European financial crisis in London during the same month rendered such combinations unnecessary for both sides in the negotiations.[127]

Chamberlain was the principal architect of the Conservative Party's evolving response towards the crisis. In practice, Baldwin clearly did envisage an ideal outcome from the crisis. In July and August he had consistently declared that he would assist the government with economies but never join another coalition.[128] He also believed that 'in the long view it is all to the good that the govt have to look after their own chickens as they come home to roost, and get a lot of the dirt cleared before we come in'.[129] Yet, in reality, he abdicated any influence he might have had early in the negotiations by appearing 'not … to have a strong view one way or the other' and by leaving London.[130] After only six hours in London for crisis meetings on 13 August, Baldwin intimated to Chamberlain his desire to return to his holiday in France. Chamberlain's failure to remonstrate betrayed a deeper relief.[131] Free from interference and surveillance, Chamberlain conducted negotiations as he desired. Certainly his clarity of mind and grasp of detail ensured he was almost alone in knowing precisely what he wanted from the situation. As such, his thoughts, actions and motives are central to the principal remaining controversy surrounding the events of 1931, relating to the allegation that this was 'a "Conservative ramp"' and that Chamberlain 'displayed unique qualities of leadership and foresight' in deliberately exploiting the financial crisis to pursue 'a strategy that ensured the downfall of Labour and prepared the way for a National Government under Conservative control'.[132]

In recent years this view of a Conservative conspiracy has been subjected to vigorous scholarly rebuttal, principally on the grounds that the formation of the

---

[125] Neville Chamberlain Diary, 21 November 1931; N. Chamberlain to Grigg, 20 February 1931 and Grigg to Baldwin, 27 February 1931, Altrincham MSS (Bodleian Library, Oxford). Also N. Chamberlain to Hilda, 1 March 1931.

[126] N. Chamberlain to Hilda, 4 July 1931; Neville Chamberlain Diary, 6 July 1931.

[127] Neville Chamberlain Diary, 24 July 1931.

[128] Amery Diary, 31 July 1931; Baldwin at Hull, 17 July 1931, Middlemas and Barnes, *Baldwin*, pp. 613, 617, 620, 621.

[129] Baldwin to N. Chamberlain, 15 August 1931, NC7/11/24/1.

[130] 'The First National Government', n.d. Templewood MSS VII/1 (Cambridge University Library).

[131] N. Chamberlain to Hilda, 16 August 1931.

[132] J.D. Fair, 'The Conservative Basis for the Formation of the National Government of 1931', *Journal of British Studies* 19 (1980), pp. 143, 164. For earlier suspicions of 'a subcutaneous Conservative plan', see L.C.B. Seaman, *Post-Victorian Britain 1902–51* (London, 1966), p. 233; Gilbert, *British Social Policy*, pp. 174–76.

National Government was 'neither sought nor desired' by the Conservatives, but rather something into which they were 'stampeded' by the panic atmosphere of August 1931 and then accepted out of national duty and an ardent desire for economy. As a result, the allegation that 'any Conservatives were principally concerned ... with cunning notions of wrecking the Labour party' is dismissed as 'patently absurd'.[133] As one recent study notes, 'Despite playing a prominent role in the negotiations which led up to the establishment of the National Government, [Chamberlain] neither foresaw the manner of the crisis's outcome nor tried to direct the discussion against the trend of events'.[134] Yet although this counter-view has now undoubtedly become the established orthodoxy, the problem with rebuttals based on a close examination of the events of August 1931 is that they often obscure the partisan dimension underlying Chamberlain's longer-term strategy. In this context, the creation of a National Government may not have been the outcome that Chamberlain initially anticipated or consistently desired, but in a crucial sense it was the logical outcome of the strategy he had pursued throughout the preceding year. As such, in a very important sense, he was the principal arbiter of the Labour government's fortunes and the outcome of the crisis.

In Opposition, the Conservatives had consistently condemned the government's allegedly irresponsible finance and demanded economy, particularly in relation to borrowing for the Unemployment Insurance Fund. Indeed, soon after the 1929 election Chamberlain had predicted that unemployment insurance 'would be the "Achilles heel" of the Labour Government',[135] and by February 1931 he was confidently predicting that 'the Govt cannot maintain themselves in office for many more months' because their 'policy of spending will have its effect in the money market and public opinion will make itself felt in condemnation'.[136] On this basis, Chamberlain had countered Baldwin's vehement objections to the widely rumoured idea of a National Government in July with a remarkably prescient assessment of the crisis as it eventually developed: 'What I foresaw the possibility of was a panic in the City[,] a hundred million deficit in the Budget, a flight from the £ & industry going smash; such a position that it could only be met by such drastic steps as Germany & Austria were taking. It was then that R.M[acDonald] would come to him because he would not be able

---

[133] David Wrench, '"Cashing in": The Parties and the National Government, August 1931–September 1932', *Journal of British Studies* 23 (1984), pp. 135–53; Stuart Ball, 'The Conservative Party and the Formation of the National Government, August 1931', *Historical Journal* 29 (1986), pp. 159–82 and *Baldwin and the Conservative Party: the Crisis of 1929–31* (New Haven and London, 1988), pp. 151–97; Andrew Thorpe, *Britain in the 1930s: The Deceptive Decade* (Oxford, 1992), p. 10.

[134] Graham Stewart, *Burying Caesar: Churchill, Chamberlain and the Battle for the Tory Party* (London, 1999), p. 112.

[135] Harold Macmillan, *Winds of Change, 1914–1939* (London, 1966), p. 260.

[136] N. Chamberlain to Hilda, 14 February 1931. Also N. Chamberlain to Ida, 25 July 1931.

to count on his own people to support him'. At this juncture, Chamberlain loathed the idea of National Government, but he was sufficiently realistic to recognise that in panic circumstances such a demand 'might be very hard to refuse'.[137]

It is undeniable that Chamberlain passionately and sincerely believed that it was crucial to balance the budget and reduce public expenditure – particularly with regard to unemployment insurance. In order to achieve these goals, he was prepared to sacrifice much in the national interest. It is also clear that the Conservatives stood every chance of winning the next election with an overall majority even without the devastating effects of a political crisis and schism within Labour ranks. But the truth of these propositions should not obscure the equally fundamental fact that Chamberlain clearly perceived an opportunity to achieve a massive and enduring partisan advantage in pursuit of these national goals and that he actively manipulated the crisis discussions in order to bring this about. In this context, Chamberlain's calculations and strategy as the crisis unfolded during August 1931 were guided by two central assumptions. Firstly, he was rightly convinced that '[f]rom the party point of view the chance of getting "economy" out of the way before a General Election and of destroying the enemy's most dangerous weapon by identifying the present Government with "economy" is so important that it would be worth much to obtain it'.[138] This was particularly so as since the New Year his optimism about the imminent fall of the Labour government had been accompanied by the grim realisation that they had 'left us a damnosa hereditas and I dont look forward to any share I may have in clearing up the mess'.[139] Secondly, if successful in this immediate objective, Chamberlain anticipated either 'a new alignment of parties' or 'an appeal to the country in conditions offering the utmost advantage, seeing that we could no longer be saddled with the unpopularity of economy, but could concentrate on tariffs and Imp[erial] Preference as the restorers of prosperity'.[140]

In the event, the publication of the May Report on National Expenditure on 31 July, with its gloomy prediction of a £120 million budget deficit and proposals for drastic retrenchment of £97 million (including £66.5 million from unemployment insurance), provided Chamberlain with the weapon he needed to saddle the Labour government with all the opprobrium of passing such drastic measures while undermining its electoral support and Cabinet unity. In late July Chamberlain had made it clear to Bank of England officials that the Conservatives would 'back up the Chancellor if he will squarely face the issues ... *even if his*

---

[137] Neville Chamberlain Diary, 24 July 1931. Also N. Chamberlain to Hilda, 18 July 1931.

[138] N. Chamberlain to H.A. Gwynne, 13 August 1931, Gwynne MSS 17.

[139] N. Chamberlain to Hilda, 3 January 1931. Also N. Chamberlain to Elibank, 7 January 1931, Elibank MSS GD32/25/75.

[140] N. Chamberlain to Hilda, 16 August 1931.

own side should go against him.[141] He then left London when the Commons went into recess and remained in Scotland on his fishing holiday convinced that 'one can best leave things to go on simmering for the present'.[142] In this respect, Chamberlain was fortunate that the Bank of England's efforts to exert pressure on the Cabinet to reduce expenditure coincided with his own objectives, and he had been 'agreeably surprised to note the extent to which the Bankers had succeeded in frightening Ramsay' by their first crisis meeting on 13 August.[143]

Chamberlain 'had done some pretty hard thinking' before this first meeting with MacDonald and Snowden on 13 August.[144] At this juncture he knew precisely what he wanted in both financial and political terms but lacked the means to bring it about. As he complained to the editor of the *Morning Post*, when his City editor 'speaks of our "insisting" on this or that I am not sure that he realises our limitations'. As the Conservatives were not being asked to join the government, 'our only "sanction" may be to withdraw support from proposals which both on National and Party grounds we may very anxiously desire to see forwarded'.[145] In the event, this latter scenario precisely outlined the turn of events. On the same day, with the French and American loans almost exhausted, Bank of England soundings in New York confirmed that there was no prospect of any further credits unless the Labour government could obtain the support of the other parties for their economy programme. Chamberlain now had the fulcrum upon which the leverage supplied by the May Committee could be exerted. From this moment, MacDonald effectively became the prisoner of the Opposition parties.[146] All that remained was for Chamberlain to offer terms for Opposition support which the Cabinet could not accept and remain either united or electorally credible.

By sticking rigidly and single-mindedly to the argument 'that retrenchment was the vital thing', and particularly by making a 10 per cent cut in unemployment insurance the acid test of the Labour Cabinet's economic responsibility and willingness to 'squarely face the issues', Chamberlain sought to detach those ministers committed to responsible government and balanced budgets from the rest of the Cabinet committed primarily to the defence of sectional class interests and party unity.[147] As he rightly predicted to his wife on 21 August, 'one of two

---

[141] E.R. Peacock to F.S. Oliver, 1 August 1931, Philip Williamson, 'A "Bankers' Ramp"?: Financiers and the Political Crisis of August 1931', *English Historical Review* 94 (1984), p. 788. Emphasis added.

[142] N. Chamberlain to Ida, 9 August 1931.

[143] Geoffrey Lloyd to Cunliffe-Lister, 14 August 1931, Swinton MSS 174/2/1/27.

[144] N. Chamberlain to Cunliffe-Lister, 15 August 1931, Swinton MSS 174/2/1/12.

[145] N. Chamberlain to Gwynne, 13 August 1931, Gwynne MSS 17.

[146] N. Chamberlain to A. Chamberlain, 14 August 1931, AC39/3/26; to Cunliffe-Lister, 15 August 1931, Swinton MSS 174/2/1/11–12; and to his wife, 23 August 1931, NC1/26/44767.

[147] Neville Chamberlain Diary, 22 August 1931; N. Chamberlain to his wife, 23 August 1931, NC1/26/447.

things may happen. Either R.M. may surrender to his malcontents & put forward inadequate proposals in which case I am told he will lose Snowden and the flight from the £ will set in, or he will part with Henderson & others and open negotiations for a National Govt'.[148] To increase this pressure, Chamberlain adamantly refused to be diverted from the central question of economies and their composition by other potential distractions such as tariffs, despite the evident frustration of more short-sighted protectionist followers.[149] He equally prudently refused to be drawn by MacDonald's efforts on 21 August to put an exact figure on the level of economies the Conservatives would accept, for fear of being drawn into a bargaining process which would end in a lower figure than he thought acceptable either on national grounds or on grounds of achieving his partisan expectations. At the same time, however, he consistently emphasised that unless the Opposition parties' terms were met they would turn the government out immediately, but that it was 'the P.M.'s bounden duty to avoid [the] crash' and that they 'were ready to give him any support in our power for that purpose either with his present or in a reconstructed Govt'.[150] Given the clarity of Chamberlain's objectives and the undeviating determination with which he pursued them, it was little wonder that when colleagues reassembled in London on 21 August they agreed that 'Neville is handling the situation admirably'. As Cunliffe-Lister recorded after the briefing, 'everything turns on whether the Government will cut the dole – without that you can't get the necessary economies, and … the other economies hang on it. Nor can you justify taxation. A tariff is no alternative. First and foremost you must have drastic economy. That alone will save the situation. Whatever happens there will be a political crisis'.[151]

In this context, the principal flaw in the 'Conservative ramp' thesis lies not in the assertion that Chamberlain manipulated the crisis to achieve conveniently overlapping national and party goals, but rather in the claim that this crucially involved an outcome defined in terms of a Conservative-dominated National Government. In reality, the successful pursuit of Chamberlain's objectives did not necessarily imply a National Government and historians too often overstate and pre-date the moment at which the idea of a National Government began to germinate in Chamberlain's mind as a convenient outcome to the crisis.[152] Chamberlain's initial intention had been to force the Labour government to shoulder all of the opprobrium for economies while giving them all necessary external support to achieve this goal but avoiding any sort of coalition. Rumours of MacDonald's desire for a National Government in early July had thus been dismissed because

---

[148] N. Chamberlain to his wife, 21 August 1931, NC1/26/446.

[149] Neville Chamberlain Diary, 22 August 1931.

[150] Ibid.

[151] Cunliffe-Lister to his wife, n.d. Friday (21 August 1931), Swinton MSS 313/1/5.

[152] Middlemas and Barnes, *Baldwin*, p. 621. See also Roy Jenkins, *The Chancellors* (London, 1998), p. 342 saying he was convinced of the need for a National Government by the end of July.

the leadership disliked the idea and the party 'would not stand it for a moment'.[153] By the end of the month, however, the crisis had deepened sufficiently for a meeting of the two Chamberlains, Hailsham, Hoare and Cunliffe-Lister to agree that coalition could still be averted, but 'might be unavoidable' and that, if so, such an arrangement would only be acceptable if accompanied by a commitment to tariffs.[154] When the final crisis erupted on 23 August after the Labour Cabinet could not agree to the level of economies demanded by Chamberlain and the other Opposition leaders, Chamberlain and Hoare had 'already come to the conclusion that a National Government was inevitable'.[155] Confronted by the prospect of MacDonald's resignation and a minority Conservative ministry, Chamberlain thus urged upon Baldwin the need 'first to try and get Ramsay Snowden & one or two other members of the Govt in even if they brought no one with them'. Moreover, later that day, when MacDonald declined to accept the idea on the grounds that he would be 'a ridiculous figure unable to command support and would bring odium on us as well as himself', Chamberlain swiftly retorted that his adhesion would substantially strengthen any National combination because of the support he commanded in the country and (more important) its beneficial effects on foreign confidence. Shifting from flattery to cajolery, he also warned of the criticism likely to follow if MacDonald refused to join such a government when he supported its policy.[156]

The outcome of the political crisis of August 1931 thus represented a major personal triumph for Chamberlain. The formation of a National Government was never one of his primary goals, but when it emerged as the option most likely to deliver his central objectives, its adoption did not necessitate a fundamental reappraisal of broader strategy. The Labour Cabinet split down the middle over the crucial question of whether to accept the demanded cut in unemployment insurance; MacDonald was persuaded to remain as Prime Minister in an all-party combination committed to execute necessary but unpopular economies;[157] and by the terms of the Buckingham Palace concordat the government was committed to deal only with the financial emergency before a dissolution and a party election which could only be held in circumstances of the utmost advantage to the Conservatives. At the same time, Chamberlain's will had prevailed over Baldwin's deeply ingrained antipathy towards the idea of joining another coalition.[158] Little wonder that, when looking back on the outcome

---

[153] Neville Chamberlain Diary, 6 July 1931.

[154] N. Chamberlain to Hilda, 2 August 1931; A. Chamberlain to Ida, 2 August 1931, AC5/1/550, Self (ed.), *Austen Chamberlain*, pp. 374–75; Cunliffe-Lister to his wife, 'Friday' (30 July 1931), Swinton MSS 270/3/22.

[155] 'The Second Labour Government', Templewood MSS VI/2.

[156] Neville Chamberlain Diary, 23 August 1931.

[157] Ibid.

[158] Middlemas and Barnes, *Baldwin*, pp. 621, 626, 629. Viscount Templewood, *Nine Troubled Years* (London, 1954), p. 18; James, *Memoirs of a Conservative*, pp. 365, 368.

of the crisis, Chamberlain felt that he had committed no tactical errors with which to reproach himself.[159] As Chamberlain's principal lieutenant throughout the crisis, Sir Samuel Hoare was in a better position to judge than most when he later told Chamberlain that he was 'certain that if you had not at the very outset of the negotiations adopted not only the right line but also the right tone the country might have been plunged into an irrevocable catastrophe. It is such crises that really test a man's judgement'.[160] Throughout the crisis Chamberlain had repeatedly remarked that 'the mercy of God was vouchsafed in three ways, Lloyd George was in bed: Winston was in Biarritz and S.B. was at Aix'.[161] Yet as Hoare noted, 'The greatest of all [good luck] ... was the series of events that left you in full control of a situation that particularly demanded your qualities of quick decision and consistent action'.[162] Certainly looking back in amazement in the aftermath of their election landslide two months later, Conservative Central Office (CCO) believed 'that but for [Chamberlain] the Conservative Party would not be where it is to-day'.[163] Against this background, there would appear to be a fairly strong case for reviewing the current orthodoxy about the role of Chamberlain and his motives during the political crisis of 1931.

IV

Economy dominated the National Government's labours during its first month but these measures were themselves overtaken by further disasters. Newly obtained credits were almost exhausted when the Home Fleet at Invergordon, incensed by unannounced cuts in pay, staged its famous 'mutiny'. The consequent loss of confidence in sterling and the outflow of gold from London largely negated the Cabinet's frenetic exertions of the past month. On 21 September, after a 'terrible week' in which 'the atmosphere ha[d] been as depressing as it [was] possible to imagine', a Bill suspending the gold standard was hastily passed.[164] Yet even before the defence of sterling had failed, it was apparent that 'the task of setting our house in order will not be fulfilled unless measures are taken to redress the unfavourable balance of trade'.[165] Expectations nurtured by free traders after the Buckingham Palace agreement (that they could fight as separate parties preaching their own nostrums when sterling had been saved) were also destroyed. Of gold, the bankers told MacDonald that such a course

---

[159] N. Chamberlain to Hoare, 24 August 1931, Templewood MSS VII/1.
[160] Hoare to N. Chamberlain, n.d. (?24–25 August 1931), NC7/11/24/13.
[161] A. Chamberlain to his wife, 28 August 1931, AC6/1/806.
[162] Hoare to N. Chamberlain, n.d., NC7/11/24/13.
[163] Marjorie Maxse to N. Chamberlain, 28 October 1931, NC7/11/24/22.
[164] N. Chamberlain to Ida, 19 September 1931.
[165] Neville Chamberlain Diary, 19 September 1931.

would disastrously undermine foreign confidence unless fought on an agreed programme to restore the trade balance.[166] The need for agreement upon measures to correct the balance of trade thus became inextricably associated with Conservative clamour for an election and the implementation of tariff reform at a time when the party's leadership recognised that 'pressure from the Conservative rank and file for an election is so overwhelming that the members of the Cabinet "would be left high and dry" if it does not come off'.[167]

Yet rather than rank and file aspiration redirecting Chamberlain's intentions, it permitted the realisation of his long-term strategy. By mid-September he was already saying that 'Nothing but a protective tariff of the kind ... worked out in the last six months, would ... be effective and ... therefore ... any attempt to buy Liberal support by compromising on this all-important matter would [not] be in the interests either of the Party or the Country'. As such, 'the Liberal Party will have to face up to the fiscal decision ... The decision will split it from top to bottom, and ... will end it, the two sections going off in opposite directions; and bring us back nearly to the two party system'.[168] Nevertheless, although his own 'idiotic party' wanted to fight on party lines, Chamberlain was convinced that 'the only way to secure the sort of majority which would give the world confidence is to go as a National Government, perhaps even as a National Party carrying MacDonald and his colleagues with us together with as many Liberals as [they] could get'.[169] In order to achieve these goals Chamberlain was resolved to make 'the Prime Minister ... face up to [the tariff], to decide by a majority to adopt it, to accept Samuel's resignation and after filling his place ... go to the country as a National Government on a programme of the full tariff and a free hand to save the country'.[170]

After an inconclusive Cabinet meeting on 28 September which left the Conservatives 'very depressed by the Prime Minister's attitude', Chamberlain was determined to see MacDonald in the hope of 'influencing him to a firmer stand'.[171] That evening he drafted the election statement already agreed by the Conservative Business Committee calling for a free hand 'to control imports, whether by prohibition, tariffs or other measures'.[172] By the following morning the Prime Minister had learned of his expulsion from the Labour Party and he appeared 'very low and depressed', but he read the draft attentively and seemed 'very pleased with it saying he agreed to every word but was doubtful whether

---

[166] Hankey Diary, 20 September 1931, Hankey MSS 1/7 fol. 28 (Churchill College, Cambridge).

[167] Hankey Diary, 25 September 1931, Hankey MSS 1/7 fol. 30 reporting Hoare.

[168] N. Chamberlain to Sir Edward Grigg, 16 September 1931, Altrincham MSS. Also Neville Chamberlain Diary, 19 September 1931.

[169] N. Chamberlain to Ida, 19 September 1931.

[170] Neville Chamberlain Diary, 19 and 24 September 1931.

[171] Neville Chamberlain Diary, 29 September 1931.

[172] A copy can be found in Samuel MSS A81/20, 21b (House of Lords Records Office, Hist. Coll. 128).

the Libs wd. accept it'. In fact, MacDonald's apprehension outlined Chamberlain's precise intention.[173] Determined that Samuel and his free trade Liberals 'shall swallow the whole programme or go out',[174] Chamberlain's strategy when drafting the statement was to demand the restriction of imports without reference to the specific method in the hope that if MacDonald 'accepted it and then H.S[amuel] objected he might get annoyed and perhaps be ready to go on without him'.[175]

Despite unsuccessful efforts to press the issue to a breach at Cabinet between 29 September and 2 October,[176] the conflict was postponed until 5 October. At a crucial meeting with MacDonald shortly before the Cabinet met on this date, Chamberlain and Baldwin had insisted upon the inclusion of the contentious commitment to control imports and supported it with a threat to resign if MacDonald refused.[177] Moreover, 'in the last stage of exasperation and almost in despair', Chamberlain had already resolved that if MacDonald could not find a solution he would force the issue to a crisis himself.[178] The Cabinet meeting fully justified his expectations. MacDonald's initial attempts at evasion provoked considerable Conservative consternation and, according to MacDonald, prompted Chamberlain to scribble a note to Thomas threatening resignation.[179] Recognising that it was 'useless and impossible',[180] MacDonald then abruptly announced that an election was inevitable and only the platform remained to be agreed. Sensing a rupture, Baldwin's valedictory speech was cut short, however, when Samuel suddenly produced a typed statement accepting that the Prime Minister should issue his own statement, agreed by the party leaders, with a separate appeal by each party.[181] The crisis was over. 'I was never so surprised in my life', Sankey recalled in his diary, 'in less than 90 seconds we decided to stick together when it appeared hopeless'.[182] On the following morning MacDonald obtained a dissolution.

Although Chamberlain had secured a qualified Tory victory, the general election fully vindicated his strategy. Fighting on a uniquely advantageous battleground, the Conservatives carried all before them. Yet as all recognised, the future tenor

---

[173] Neville Chamberlain Diary, 29 September and 1 October 1931.

[174] N. Chamberlain to Hilda, 26 September 1931.

[175] N. Chamberlain to Ida, 4 October 1931.

[176] Neville Chamberlain Diary, 29 September and 2 October 1931. See also Hankey's 'Notes on events during the week ended Saturday 3 October 1931', Magnum Opus MSS (31)7, CAB 63/44 (Public Record Office).

[177] Neville Chamberlain Diary, 5 October 1931.

[178] A. Chamberlain to his wife, 5 October 1931, AC6/1/324 and to Hilda, 3 October 1931, AC5/1/556, Self (ed.), *Austen Chamberlain*, pp. 386–88.

[179] MacDonald Diary, 5 October 1931, MacDonald MSS 30/69/1753 fol. 402 (Public Record Office). Neither Chamberlain nor Hankey refer to this in their diaries although Amery records Cunliffe-Lister saying 'S.B. and Neville intimated resignation'.

[180] Ibid.

[181] Neville Chamberlain Diary, 5 October 1931.

[182] Sankey Diary, 5 October 1931, Sankey MSS c.285 fol. 81 (Bodleian Library, Oxford).

of the government would be determined by the political and fiscal complexion of the Chancellor of the Exchequer. Before the election some Conservatives had feared that MacDonald might attempt to demonstrate his independence by putting a Samuelite or one of his own supporters at the Exchequer with Baldwin's acquiescence.[183] After the election, however, the Conservatives were in both the mood and position to veto any such a proposal.[184] Moreover, this time, Chamberlain experienced none of the personal reluctance or administrative distaste for the idea of the Treasury that had inhibited him both in 1923[185] and during talk of Cabinet reconstruction in 1928–29.[186] Determined to ensure that the Treasury and Board of Trade were not both held by tariff reformers,[187] MacDonald had initially hoped to persuade Baldwin that Chamberlain should remain at the Ministry of Health so 'that someone with leanings on the whole to the other side should take the Exchequer, as Cunliffe-Lister is so good at the Board of Trade'.[188] By 5 November, however, MacDonald was forced to concede and Chamberlain became Chancellor while Walter Runciman, feared by the Conservatives as an inveterate free trader, accepted the Board of Trade.

Despite the necessary concession to free trade sensibilities, Chamberlain remained 'very optimistic',[189] for although there were 'some suspicious elements in [the Cabinet] ... they will not really have much chance of obstructing, even if they ... wish to do so'.[190] Moreover, despite Runciman's reputation as a difficult colleague, Chamberlain was sanguine because he 'like[d] Runciman personally and I fancy he likes me so that at least we ought to start fair'.[191] This optimism about Runciman was not misplaced. Although a lifelong Liberal free trader, during the August crisis Runciman's interpretation of the priorities of Gladstonian orthodoxy lent greater emphasis to retrenchment than to free trade on the grounds that 'during this present emergency we may have to take many emergency steps as we did in time of war'.[192] By September 1931, therefore, while unconvinced about food taxes and still proudly proclaiming himself 'the most bigoted Free

---

[183] N. Chamberlain to Hilda, 10 October 1931; A. Chamberlain to Ida, 11 October 1931, AC5/1/560, Self (ed.), *Austen Chamberlain*, p. 390; Amery Diary, 18 October 1931.

[184] Bridgeman to Baldwin, 2 November 1931, Baldwin MSS 45/194–95; Beaverbrook to N. Chamberlain, 4 November 1931, Beaverbrook MSS C/80; A. Chamberlain to his wife, 30 October 1931, AC6/1/850.

[185] See Self (ed.), *Neville Chamberlain Diary Letters*, II, pp. 12, 163–64, 177–78.

[186] Neville Chamberlain Diary, 11 March 1929.

[187] MacDonald Diary, 1 November 1931, fol. 403. Hankey Diary, 30 October 1931, fol. 40.

[188] MacDonald to Baldwin, 3 November 1931, Baldwin MSS 45/199.

[189] Amery Diary, 31 October 1931.

[190] N. Chamberlain to Elibank, 10 November 1931, Elibank MSS GD32/25/75.

[191] N. Chamberlain to Hilda, 7 November 1931. For a contrary view of the 'nervous tension' between them see Victor Cazalet Diary, 7 June 1932, Robert Rhodes James, *Victor Cazalet: A Portrait* (London, 1976), p. 144.

[192] Runciman to Lord Forres, 6 October 1931, Runciman MSS 245 (Newcastle University Library).

Trader in the House',[193] Runciman had come as far as any Simonite on industrial protectionism and the need to address the adverse balance of trade. On this basis, harmony rather than dissension characterised the relationship between Chamberlain and Runciman during the remainder of 1931 as they erected an emergency tariff wall against foreign dumping.[194]

It suggests much about the divergent aspirations within the National Government that while MacDonald regarded the onset of 1932 with 'many forebodings',[195] Chamberlain eagerly heralded it as 'the year of opportunity':

> Although 1931 was a year of unhappiness, and then a wonderful exhibition of determination and courage on the part of the Nation, 1932 will be the year of opportunity, and, if we do not make good use of it, we shall deserve the condemnation which posterity will certainly mete out to us. In my present office I feel I have perhaps a greater share of the responsibility for the use that is to be made of our wonderful majority than anyone else ... Frankly, although the burden is heavy, I rejoice at it. To be given the chance of directing such great forces where I am convinced they should be applied, is such a privilege as one had no right to hope for; and I intend to make the most of it.[196]

Above all, Chamberlain expected to use his position to impart substance to the incorporeal vision of a scientific tariff and imperial preference invoked by his father some thirty years before. As he rightly forecast, 1932 would be a 'very momentous year ... the turning point or perhaps ... rather ... the critical point in my political career'.[197]

As in the previous September, Chamberlain regarded MacDonald as 'the key to the situation' in his advance towards a general tariff. Believing his views on tariffs were still largely uncrystallised, Chamberlain considered that the Prime Minister would accept any reasonable solution if it did not involve 'embarrassing political complications' – albeit that he was acutely sensitive to MacDonald's anxiety at being portrayed by critics as 'a mere figurehead, obliged to accept holus-bolus any policy which might be imposed upon him by his Tory colleagues'.[198] While Chamberlain, rather erroneously, believed that MacDonald liked him personally and showed much deference to his opinions,[199] he was a Conservative and thus

---

[193] *Parliamentary Debates: House of Commons Debates*, 5th ser. (hereafter *H.C. Debs.* 5s.), 256, col. 331, 10 September 1931; Runciman to E.J. Beavis, 5 November 1931, Runciman MSS 221.

[194] See Robert Self, *Tories and Tariffs: The Conservative Party and the Politics of Tariff Reform 1922–1932* (New York and London, 1986), pp. 666–72.

[195] MacDonald to Lady Londonderry, n.d., David Marquand, *Ramsay MacDonald* (London, 1977), p. 690.

[196] Chamberlain to Sir Francis Humphrys, 8 January 1932, NC7/11/24/15.

[197] N. Chamberlain to Hilda, 3 January 1932.

[198] 'Notes on Proceedings in Cabinet and elsewhere on the formulation of Government Policy on the Balance of Trade, concluded 30 January 1932' (hereafter Chamberlain memo). NC8/18/1, para. 5.

[199] See MacDonald Diary, 21 and 31 July 1930 and 20 September 1931, fols 331, 399.

disqualified from insulating the Prime Minister from such allegations. Protectionist advance, therefore, depended upon Chamberlain's ability to win the support of a 'sufficiently influential non-Tory section of the Cabinet' to relieve MacDonald's anxiety and to ensure that he 'remained fairly comfortable'. In particular, if Runciman's assent could be secured for the proposals emanating from the Balance of Trade Committee, Chamberlain felt he 'could have no greater certainty of winning … the support of the Prime Minister'.[200] Although Runciman had displayed an unexpected flexibility over the emergency tariffs in November–December 1931, in a number of private conversations during December Chamberlain found him intractable over tariffs on fundamentals like meat, wheat and steel. Nevertheless, despite Chamberlain's overestimate of the progress made in these talks,[201] Runciman still played a pivotal role in designing the Import Duties Bill and in securing Snowden's promise not to oppose these proposals in the Balance of Trade Committee.[202] To this extent at least, Chamberlain was successful in creating an understanding which left MacDonald 'very glad' that they were 'getting together and hammering out agreements on some of the big subjects' before them.[203]

The Committee on the Balance of Trade, established in early December to advise upon remedies, was crucial to Chamberlain's strategy of legitimating protectionist aspirations in such a way as to reassure MacDonald of a 'National' consensus. Having skilfully outmanoeuvred MacDonald over the Committee's composition and organisation, Chamberlain intended 'to bring on the battle at an early stage' so the 'fight will come in Committee' which, as Chairman, he would dominate.[204] His manipulation of the Committee's proceedings was characteristically adroit. After a discursive first session, debate was almost entirely confined to memoranda prepared by Chamberlain and Runciman, thereby compelling the free traders to argue their case within the parameters defined by protectionist initiative. Moreover, by the penultimate session, all the Committee's members except Thomas (who 'could be relied upon to support') and Samuel had been persuaded to accept Chamberlain's proposals for a flat rate tariff with selective surtaxes to be imposed by an independent Import Duties Advisory Committee.[205] At this meeting, however, Chamberlain's strategy virtually collapsed when Snowden suddenly launched into an 'old time Free Trade disquisition' against a general tariff[206] and then adamantly refused to listen to pleas from Runciman and Chamberlain designed to change

---

[200] Chamberlain memo, para. 5.

[201] For his more equivocal account of these talks see Runciman to MacDonald, 21 December 1931, Runciman MSS 245.

[202] Chamberlain memo, para. 7.

[203] MacDonald to Runciman, 26 December 1931, Runciman MSS 245.

[204] Chamberlain memo, paras 2–4; N. Chamberlain to Ida, 12 December 1931.

[205] BT(31), 4th Conclusions, 13 January 1932, CAB 27/467; Chamberlain memo, paras 7, 8, 11.

[206] N. Chamberlain to Hilda, 17 January 1932.

his mind.[207] In order to reconcile the committee's divergent opinions, at their final meeting on 18 January Samuel and Snowden were permitted to submit separate memoranda of dissent.

Although Chamberlain had initially hoped to carry the whole committee with him, once the split occurred he found it relatively easy to portray the majority as moderate pragmatic realists and the dissenters as inflexible doctrinaire free traders. The magnitude of his success in isolating the free traders became fully apparent during two Cabinet meetings on 21 January to discuss the reports. When the Cabinet reassembled next day, therefore, Samuel's offer 'to sit down again and try to find some other way of agreement'[208] was vetoed by Chamberlain, who merely reassured MacDonald about their continued confidence in him and the continuation of the 'National' element in the government after the Samuelite departure.[209] Yet at this point, 'when there seemed nothing to do except say "goodbye"',[210] Hailsham proposed an 'agreement to differ', suspending collective responsibility to permit the dissentients to 'go "as they pleased" on the tariff question': a suggestion which met with immediate approval although Chamberlain was manifestly 'not enthusiastic about their remaining'.[211] In this context, the supreme irony was that Chamberlain, who had been trying to engineer the Samuelite resignation since October 1931, had initially proposed this expedient to MacDonald on the previous afternoon in order to retain Snowden in the Lords without apparently having ever considered the possibility of its application to Liberal ministers in the Commons.[212] Despite the retention of the Samuelites, however, even Chamberlain professed himself 'well satisfied'. Not only had he prevailed on the tariff, but the public formalisation of free trade dissent served to insulate his position against the intra-party criticism that he had 'sold the pass' by being insufficiently assertive in imposing tariffs on the rest of the Cabinet.[213]

Introducing the Import Duties Bill on 4 February, Chamberlain carried the House with emotion and a sense of historical fulfilment on 'the great day of [his] life'.[214] Although Chamberlain confessed that he would have preferred to have kept his feelings to himself for fear of losing control of his voice, he relented when he 'realised that this would have been misunderstood when everyone else was full of the historic completeness of it all'.[215] Thus, in a moving 'personal note' he concluded with a tribute to his father's frustrated

---

[207] Chamberlain memo, para. 11; Chamberlain to Snowden, 15 January and reply 16 January 1932, NC7/11/25/41–42.

[208] Chamberlain memo, para. 16.

[209] Neville Chamberlain Diary, 22 January 1932; N. Chamberlain to Ida, 23 January 1932.

[210] Chamberlain memo, para. 17.

[211] Sankey Diary, 22 January 1932, Sankey MSS c. 286 fol. 8.

[212] Neville Chamberlain Diary, 22 January 1932; N. Chamberlain to Ida, 23 January 1932.

[213] Ibid. Also N. Chamberlain to Elibank, 5 February 1932, Elibank MSS GD32/25/30.

[214] N. Chamberlain to Ida, 6 February 1932.

[215] N. Chamberlain to Mary Carnegie, 6 February 1932, NC/20/1/156.

exertions in the belief that 'he would have found consolation for the bitterness of his disappointment if he could have foreseen that these proposals, which are the direct and legitimate descendants of his own conception, would be laid before the House of Commons ... in the presence of one and by the lips of the other of the two immediate successors to his name and blood'.[216] Thereafter, in spite of public hostility to the Bill from the ministerial free traders, it enjoyed a remarkably smooth legislative passage and by the end of February had passed into law. Only the empire now remained to be integrated into British tariff arrangements to complete the Chamberlainite edifice.

In this context, the decision to reconvene the deadlocked 1930 Imperial Economic Conference at Ottawa during the summer of 1932 was a fortuitous bonus for Conservative protectionists and imperial visionaries already flushed with domestic success. Although the established pattern of imperial economic relations during the preceding decade had become one of 'Dominion importunity, and British intransigence',[217] the Import Duties Act promised to end this deadlock by furnishing the British with a bargaining position from which to negotiate reciprocal arrangements and it soon became apparent that they intended to make full use of their opportunity. Yet from the outset, the Ottawa Preparatory Committee witnessed a conflict of perspectives about imperial economic relations which soon turned into a personal confrontation between Chamberlain and J.H. Thomas, the Dominion Secretary. Thomas continued to adhere to the established orthodoxy that preference should retain the traditional form of unilateral non-discriminatory concessions within the empire rather than bilateral agreements which might produce 'political and economic dangers of the very gravest character'. Although he intended to press for the maximum concession at Ottawa, therefore, the maintenance of imperial unity would remain his first priority. In contrast to Thomas's calculated altruism, Chamberlain preferred to place his faith in bilateral bargaining in the belief that 'the policy of the generous gesture' had failed to produce any striking results in the past and that in the prevailing economic climate Dominion politicians would find negotiated agreements with a specific *quid pro quo* easier to defend to their own electorate.[218] Moreover, believing the point to be fundamental, this conflict was eventually resolved in Chamberlain's favour by early December.[219] Two weeks later he achieved an equally crucial victory over MacDonald's prevarication when the Cabinet agreed to two schedules of food products upon which they would grant complete or partial preference in return for adequate concessions from the Dominions.[220]

---

[216] *H.C. Debs.* 5s., 261, col. 296, 4 February 1932.

[217] Ian M. Drummond, *Imperial Economic Policy, 1917–1939: Studies in Expansion and Protection* (London, 1974), p. 171.

[218] OC(31), 1st meeting, 16 November 1931, CAB 27/473.

[219] CAB 84(31)2, 2 December 1931, CAB 23/69.

[220] CAB 92(31)5, 16 December 1931.

Yet although he had succeeded in forcing the Cabinet to 'face realities' over food bargaining at Ottawa in December,[221] Chamberlain recognised that the future shape of imperial economic relations depended upon negotiations at Ottawa and upon Thomas's leadership of the British delegation. As a result, having begun by seeking to circumscribe his freedom to manoeuvre, from the end of January it appears that Chamberlain decided that he, and not Thomas, should play the leading role at Ottawa. Chamberlain was not alone in these concerns. Although Thomas had a well-established reputation as a committed tariff reformer and a zealous imperialist,[222] his retention of the Dominion Office after 1931 engendered considerable misgivings among Dominion leaders and particularly for R.B. Bennett, the mercurial Canadian Premier, who warned Conservative ministers in November 1931 that 'the Canadians [were] extremely anxious that JHT should not visit the Dominions where ... he would degrade the whole Dominion conception of a British statesman'.[223] Yet the full extent of the danger involved in Thomas's leadership at Ottawa only became apparent in February 1932. In drafting the Import Duties Bill, Chamberlain had intended to grant a 33⅓ per cent preference to the empire, retaining the remainder for bargaining at Ottawa. Having been 'begged' by Thomas to offer no preference as 'he wanted all he could get to bargain with', Chamberlain acquiesced, assuming Thomas 'knew his business well enough to be sure that no mischief would be done' and because 'it seemed rather difficult ... as Chancellor to urge a project involving a loss of revenue against a Minister responsible for the Department which [would] benefit'.[224] Four days later, however, Chamberlain learned from Howard Ferguson, the Canadian High Commissioner and an intimate of Bennett's, not only that Thomas was wrong in making this proposal, but that he had been warned of hostile Canadian reactions three weeks earlier. Although Chamberlain then revised the Bill accordingly to give the Dominions free entry until 15 November 1932, after this it was perhaps scarcely surprising either that he had 'cold shivers to think how near we were to a colossal blunder' or that he feared Thomas would destroy all hope of success at Ottawa.[225] Apprehensions of this kind, combined with suspicions that Thomas wished to exclude him from Ottawa,

---

[221] N. Chamberlain to Hilda, 6 December 1931.

[222] Lionel Curtis to Nancy Astor, 30 January 1924, Astor MSS 1416/1/4/34 (Reading University Library); Dalton Diary, 21 February 1924, Dalton MSS 4 (British Library of Political and Economic Science); J.L. Garvin to Thomas, 1 June 1930, Thomas MSS U1625/c45 (Centre for Kentish Studies, Maidstone); Hewins Diary, 1 May 1924 (University of Sheffield Library).

[223] N. Chamberlain to Ida, 29 November 1931.

[224] N. Chamberlain to Ida, 6 February 1932.

[225] Ibid. Drummond, *Imperial Economic Policy*, p. 183, incorrectly states that the preferences were 'considerable sacrifices from an economy-minded Chancellor' offered against Chamberlain's wishes but 'questions of negotiating strategy won out, defeating the Chancellor in his search for revenue'. In fact, Chamberlain clearly subordinated revenue to negotiating strategy and his strategy triumphed over Thomas's negotiating strategy.

thus induced him to persuade Baldwin that he should formally lead the delegation himself, thereby enabling Chamberlain to control negotiations while Baldwin performed the purely ceremonial functions of leader.[226]

Although Baldwin was gratified by Chamberlain's proposal, both men were sensitive to the danger that such a suggestion would arouse suspicions of a Conservative conspiracy. Two days later, however, Thomas solved the problem by engaging in a drunken quarrel with Ferguson at a large public dinner during which only Austen Chamberlain's intervention to 'knock … their heads together' averted a diplomatic disaster.[227] After this incident Chamberlain persuaded Baldwin to write to MacDonald proposing the plan and he did so himself.[228] Again, Chamberlain was successful. Thomas's ruffled dignity was appeased with the promise that he should be second in order of precedence and in return he agreed to Chamberlain's inclusion to 'complete [his] father's work'. Yet as Chamberlain later observed with justifiable cynicism, 'I fear that [Thomas] will find that his precedence doesn't really depend on his place in a list'.[229]

As one chronicler has observed, the delegates departing for Ottawa on 13 July hoped to 'save the Empire by their energy and save the world by their example'.[230] Before departing Chamberlain confessed to being 'very anxious' about the conference because so much was expected that 'disappointment was inevitable',[231] particularly as he realised that even if they obtained all they asked from the Dominions, the extra trade and employment generated during the next year would be far from substantial.[232] Having never really shared the more sentimental imperial vision of his half-brother and Amery, for Chamberlain the opportunities of Ottawa were essentially pragmatic and commercial: 'its real importance', he told his sisters, 'lies in starting the Empire on the new path of mutual preference and provided it does that any initial failures are of minor importance … [because] the future possibilities of Empire trade … must be infinitely greater than anything we can hope for from the foreigner'.[233] Yet while recognising that the Dominions were 'likely to be very exacting, and … claim what will be very difficult for us to give while withholding much of what we should like to have', even Chamberlain sustained his optimism about the possibilities of success almost until the very end.[234]

---

[226] N. Chamberlain to Hilda, 27 February 1932.

[227] A. Chamberlain to Hilda, 5 March 1932, AC5/1/577, Self (ed.), *Austen Chamberlain*, p. 408.

[228] N. Chamberlain to Ida, 5 March 1932; Baldwin to MacDonald, 5 March 1932 and Chamberlain to MacDonald, 6 March 1932. MacDonald MSS 30/69/2/12 II.

[229] N. Chamberlain to Hilda, 12 March 1932.

[230] W.K. Hancock, *Survey of British Commonwealth Affairs, Volume II, Problems of Economic Policy, 1918–1939* (London, 1940), p. 217.

[231] N. Chamberlain to Mary Carnegie, 13 July 1932, NC1/20/1/159.

[232] N. Chamberlain to his wife, 24 July 1932, NC1/26/469.

[233] N. Chamberlain to Hilda, 11 June 1932.

[234] N. Chamberlain to Mary Carnegie, 13 July 1932, NC1/20/1/159.

At Ottawa the work of the conference was interminable and exhausting and the bulk of the labour and strain fell directly upon Chamberlain.[235] In the thirty-one days between the first preliminary session on 20 July and the final session on 20 August, the British delegation attended 112 meetings, were circulated with 169 documents and endured constant briefings from official advisers and unofficial lobbyists. Yet in spite of their physical and mental exhaustion, the British delegation remained united throughout and Chamberlain considered it a 'pleasure to work with such a team … in which there are no difficulties and no jealousies'. Even Thomas greatly enhanced his reputation, moving up 'several notches in [Chamberlain's] opinion', as scorn gave way to respect for his 'great discretion and great loyalty'.[236] Only Chamberlain's exhaustion under the burden of assumed leadership, with the recurrence of trouble in his right eye and the gout which had plagued him at the Lausanne conference, gave cause for serious concern. It was indicative of the delegation's harmony in their efforts to reach agreement with the Dominions that they should have remained united for so long while conceding so much.

The attitude of Bennett, the Canadian Prime Minister, was conducive to British unity while shaking their faith in imperial sentiment to its foundations. Bennett's attitude towards Britain and imperial economic unity had hardened substantially since 1930 and his niggardly list of proposed concessions only increased British suspicion.[237] Bennett had little more faith in British intentions, and his efforts to coerce them into surrendering more than they intended made a deplorable impression upon all concerned. To the British, Bennett had 'the manners of a Chicago policeman and the temperament of a Hollywood film actor'.[238] Negotiation showed him to be a 'sharper and a crook'[239] and on departure one of the industrial advisers insulted him to his face.[240] With Chamberlain, who initially believed he inspired Bennett's confidence, he 'behaved … like a pig'.[241] Despite his realism before leaving England, therefore, it was apparent to all observers that Chamberlain found this kind of negotiation a 'sad disillusionment'.[242] When a *News Chronicle* correspondent declared that Bennett was as 'passionate as a spoilt child, as slippery as an eel, as

---

[235] N. Chamberlain to Ida, 21 August 1932; Cunliffe-Lister to his wife, 27 July and 19 August 1932, quoted in Alan Earl, 'The Political Life of Viscount Swinton, 1918–1938', MA thesis, Manchester, 1960, pp. 244, 248.

[236] N. Chamberlain to his wife, 10 August 1932, NC1/26/473.

[237] For Bennett's attitude see R.N. Kottman, *Reciprocity and the North Atlantic Triangle, 1932–1938* (Ithaca, 1968), pp. 27, 34–35; O(UK) 30th and 32nd Conclusions, 4 August 1932, CAB 32/101.

[238] N. Chamberlain to Hilda, 11 August 1932.

[239] Ottawa Diary, 17 August 1932; O(UK) 60th Conclusions, 17 August 1932, CAB 32/102.

[240] N. Chamberlain to Ida, 21 August 1932.

[241] N. Chamberlain to his wife, 16 August 1932, NC1/26/474.

[242] Cunliffe-Lister to his wife, 19 August 1932, quoted in Earl, 'Viscount Swinton', p. 248.

stubborn as a mule, and as hysterical as a woman who ha[d] lost her lover', Chamberlain added warmly that he also 'lied like a trooper and … alternately blustered, bullied, sobbed, prevaricated, delayed and obstructed to the very last moment'.[243]

Yet, for Chamberlain, personal injury only highlighted a more profound political frustration. 'He [had] looked forward to the prospect of the culmination of his work with sympathetic and willing partners; and Bennett had treated him like a trickster'.[244] In particular, his 'real disappointment' lay in his failure to secure agreement on the general resolutions he had drafted on the outward voyage for acceptance when the conference opened.[245] Instead, the conference had adopted a series of innocuous declarations on their final day, which all recognised to be nothing but pious platitudes without binding force or enduring significance. Rebuffed, Chamberlain could only console himself with the thought that 'the time was not ripe' for such resolutions, but that the conference had 'been in time to stop the rot' within the fabric of the empire itself and time would heal the rest.[246] In the event, after the formulation of seven major trade agreements in thirty-one days, exhausted ministers felt justified in commending themselves upon their 'wonderful achievement';[247] self-congratulation less perhaps at the terms of the agreements than at their existence at all. As Chamberlain informed the Cabinet after his return to London, he had been forcefully impressed by 'how thin the bonds of Empire had worn, and the growth of nationalism in the Dominions. He did not think that the bonds could have survived but for this Conference, which had strengthened the sense of belonging to a great Commonwealth and the advantages to be derived therefrom'.[248]

If the bonds of empire were allegedly strengthened by Ottawa, those binding the Cabinet were certainly not. MacDonald had always recognised that the likely resignation of the Cabinet free traders over Ottawa would mean that nothing stood between him and the Tory domination he had so long feared.[249] Yet as Chamberlain assured him, the Cabinet 'looked to him not [as] the leader of the Tory Party but as the symbol of [their] faith that until prosperity returned country must come before party'. He was equally sincere in the view that Samuel was 'emphatically not a man to go tiger hunting with & with his disappearance & that of his satellite "Archie" [Sinclair] we should be far more homogeneous and we should … move towards the fused party under a National

---

[243] N. Chamberlain to Ida, 21 August 1932. Also Ottawa Diary, 15 and 17 August 1932.

[244] Cunliffe-Lister to his wife, 19 August 1932.

[245] CAB 46(32)1, 27 August 1932, CAB 23/72.

[246] Ottawa Diary, 20 August 1932.

[247] N. Chamberlain to Ida, 21 August 1932.

[248] CAB 46(32)1, 27 August 1932.

[249] MacDonald to Thomas, 7 September 1932, Thomas MSS U1625/c105.

name which I regard as certain to come'.[250] Chamberlain thus wooed the Liberal Nationals[251] while simultaneously making himself 'as disagreeable as possible' with Samuel and Sinclair over their failure to cut police pay in the hope they might resign as a means of extricating themselves from an increasingly embarrassing position.[252] In the event, although MacDonald postponed the crisis, at Cabinet on 28 September Chamberlain adamantly excluded any prospect of further compromise and the free traders finally departed to provide him belatedly with yet another crucial victory.[253]

V

Alongside his tariff triumph, during 1932 Chamberlain also laid the foundations of the monetary policy which prevailed throughout the rest of the decade. Having been forced off the gold standard in September 1931, monetary expansion through a 'cheap money' policy became a feasible option and interest rates fell sharply from a crisis peak of 6 per cent in September 1931 to 5 per cent on 18 February before continuing in a series of cuts through the spring of 1932 to a thirty-five-year low of 2 per cent by 30 June where it remained (except for a brief period in August–September 1939) until November 1951. In retrospect, at least, Chamberlain came to regard tariffs and cheap money as the two key strands of his policy for domestic economic recovery and by 1934 the Governor of the Bank of England was complaining that the Chancellor was already quite satisfied that these policies had solved the country's economic problem.[254] Two years later in his Budget statement, Chamberlain thus specifically attributed the remarkable economic recovery since his first Budget in 1932 to these 'two main pillars' of his policy.[255]

Considerable controversy surrounds the precise impact of 'cheap money' in contributing to recovery. For example, some economic historians argue strongly that the cheap money policy of the 1930s was the fulfilment of Treasury's plans since the mid-1920s to aid recovery by stimulating investment, enterprise and profits.[256] As such, cheap money is credited with a significant role in laying the permissive foundations for the general recovery of trade and prosperity and in

---

[250] N. Chamberlain to Hilda, 30 August and 18 September 1932. For his private hope that 'we may presently develop into a National Party and get rid of the odious title of Conservative which has kept so many from joining us in the past', see N. Chamberlain to Hilda, 24 October 1931.

[251] Hore-Belisha to Runciman, 8 September 1932, Runciman MSS 254.

[252] N. Chamberlain to Hilda, 18 September 1932.

[253] CAB 47(32)1, 28 September 1932, CAB 32/72.

[254] Sir Henry Clay, *Lord Norman* (London, 1957), p. 442.

[255] B.E.V. Sabine, *British Budgets in Peace and War, 1932–1945* (London, 1970), p. 80.

[256] Susan Howson, *Domestic Monetary Management in Britain, 1919–38* (Cambridge, 1975), pp. 68, 90–95, 106–7; G.C. Peden, 'The "Treasury View" on Public Works and Employment in the Inter-War Period', *Economic History Review* 2nd ser., 37 (1984), pp. 177–78.

either stimulating the 'housing boom' of the 1930s or at least sustaining it once prices began to rise.[257] Conversely, others are more sceptical about the effect of cheap money as a stimulus to the housing boom, and portray it less as a conscious recovery policy than as initially an offshoot of foreign exchange policy designed to keep the value of sterling down during 1932 in the face of an influx of foreign capital into London. In the short term, it also enabled the Treasury to satisfy its more traditional preoccupation with easing the interest burden on the national debt and only in the longer term was it regarded as a means to assist with recovery from depression.[258]

In practice, the objectives behind cheap money developed as policy-makers became increasingly aware of its possibilities. Nevertheless, even during the first half of Chamberlain's Chancellorship their 'main object' was 'to get trade going with as much vigour as adverse world conditions permit'. To this end, Treasury officials argued in October 1932 that it was 'highly desirable' that 'the present low rate of interest should gradually permeate the economic structure and quicken industrial enterprise', particularly in house construction.[259] Although recent analysis suggests that these aspirations did not achieve their desired goal in the simple causal manner anticipated by the Chancellor, the fact remains that whatever the outcome of the policy, the objective reflected a conscious response to slump and a positive recovery policy. As such, it is a partial refutation of the claim that the National Government had no active policy to address the depression except to wait upon the natural processes of recovery. Certainly the independent Committee on Economic Information in October 1933, backed by the Chancellor and President of the Board of Trade, believed that cheap money had played a key role in recovery.[260] On the other hand, insofar as these monetary priorities imposed a constraint upon the range of policy instruments and options open to the Chancellor by compelling a trade-off with a more expansionist fiscal and budgetary policy, it meant that Chamberlain appeared to be inactive, complacent and helpless in the face of mass unemployment and demands for 'imaginative finance'.[261]

One immediate benefit of this shift to cheap money was that it made possible the conversion of the 5 per cent War Loan 1929/47 to a lower rate of interest

---

[257] Ibid., Also Keith Feiling, *The Life of Neville Chamberlain* (London, 1946), p. 283; Jenkins, *The Chancellors*, p. 351; N.H. Dimsdale, 'British Monetary Policy and the Exchange Rate, 1920–1938', *Oxford Economic Papers*, supplement 33 (1981), pp. 338–40.

[258] Donald Winch, *Economics and Policy: A Historical Study* (Fontana edn, 1969), p. 213; Edward Nevin, *The Mechanism of Cheap Money: A Study of British Monetary Policy, 1931–1939* (Cardiff, 1955), pp. 92, 273–74 and ch. 8; Derek Aldcroft, *The British Economy: Volume I, The Years of Turmoil, 1920–1951* (Brighton, 1986), pp. 85, 90–95.

[259] Sir Frederick Phillips to Hopkins and Chancellor of Exchequer, 19 October 1932, T175/70.

[260] CAB 61(33)10, 8 November 1933, CAB 23/77.

[261] Howson, *Domestic Monetary Management*, p. 92; Aldcroft, *British Economy*, p. 114. For Chamberlain's recognition of this trade-off and problem see *H.C. Debs.* 5s., 277, col. 61, 25 April 1933.

following the precedent set by Goschen's conversion operation in 1888. This was certainly not a new policy objective. Debt conversion had been under discussion since 1927, but by the time that Chamberlain became Chancellor Britain's departure from the gold standard had permitted lower interest rates and the necessary legal powers to achieve debt conversion had been obtained in the September 1931 Finance Bill.[262] Having bided his time until conditions were favourable, Chamberlain returned secretly from the Lausanne conference on 30 June to inform the Cabinet that later that evening he would announce the conversion of the entire 5 per cent War Loan to a 3½ per cent basis.[263] Explaining his reasons for prompt action to a delighted House of Commons, Chamberlain highlighted the benefits in terms of balancing the budget at a lower level by reducing the interest charges on some 27 per cent of the total National Debt at a saving of £30 million in a full year. By removing this great mass of high interest-bearing debt which had been 'hanging like a cloud over the capital market' and preventing a fall in general interest rates, he also hoped the measure would assist industry to obtain capital at a lower cost and thus stimulate investment and recovery. The strongest argument, however, related to 'the spirit in the country. After a long period of depression we have recovered our freedom in monetary matters'. Having balanced the Budget, Chamberlain was thus 'convinced that the country is in the mood for great enterprises, and is both able and determined to carry them through to a successful conclusion'.[264]

The conversion operation represented a major triumph for Chamberlain. Although still wearing his gout boot, he appeared 'in excellent spirits and his voice was particularly strong'.[265] His hopes that the country would respond generously to a patriotic appeal were more than fulfilled.[266] Of the £2,084,994,086 in 5 per cent War Loan 1929/47 outstanding on 31 March 1932, no less than £1,920,804,243 was converted to 3½ per cent War Loan 1952, some 92 per cent of the total. A variety of market factors explain the success of the operation, but this positive response was easily interpreted by supporters as a vindication of the Chancellor's emphasis upon the crucial importance of restoring confidence in the government's financial policy through balanced budgets and a managed currency.[267] For a government apparently 'flagging' in public esteem, the 'widest enthusiasm' for this 'sterling act of Courage' was also believed to have restored some of its popularity.[268]

---

[262] Howson, *Domestic Monetary Management*, pp. 71–74, 76, 88.

[263] CAB 41(32)3, 30 June 1932, CAB 23/72.

[264] *H.C. Debs.* 5s., 268, cols 2121–26, 30 June 1932.

[265] A. Chamberlain to Hilda, 2 July 1932, AC5/1/588, Self (ed.), *Austen Chamberlain*, p. 414.

[266] N. Chamberlain to Beaverbrook, 30 June 1932, Beaverbrook MSS C/80.

[267] Ibid. Also CAB 50(32)2, 11 October 1932, CAB 23/72.

[268] Hore-Belisha to Runciman, 1 July 1932, Runciman MSS 260. Also Beaverbrook to Chamberlain, 2 July 1932, Beaverbrook MSS C/80.

In parallel with the adoption of 'cheap money', Chamberlain's Treasury also moved towards a managed currency to still further insulate business confidence from external speculative pressures. Although the suspension of the gold standard in September 1931 had been regarded by politicians, Treasury officials and the Bank of England as a 'very great disaster',[269] apocalyptic forebodings about a dramatic fall in the exchange rate and rapid domestic inflation did not materialise. Although the value of sterling fell sharply from its $4.86 parity on the gold standard to $3.40 on 25 September and then $3.23 in early December before a revival of confidence produced a period of stability at around $3.40, this fall was not accompanied by financial panic or hyperinflation. On the contrary, the authorities soon recognised that there were distinct advantages to be derived from a lower exchange value in the hope that (together with cheap money) this would assist the Treasury to achieve its primary objectives of raising wholesale prices, reducing the burden of debt and increasing export competitiveness through currency depreciation.[270] 'The City is buzzing with activity, the Govt stocks are booming[,] the foreigners are buying sterling and we are sitting with all our weight on its head lest it should soar up to undesirable heights', Chamberlain noted in late February 1932. Little wonder that Treasury officials felt happier than at any time since 1927 or that the Chancellor should rejoice that 'it is indeed wonderful that the National Government should have so quickly restored confidence when we seemed about to plunge to disaster only a few months ago'.[271]

Having recognised the benefits of a managed currency, the Treasury swiftly took steps to arm itself with the necessary tools for the job. In a 'very secret' memorandum prepared by the Treasury and circulated exclusively to Chamberlain, MacDonald and Reading on 13 October 1931, an 'especially secret' paragraph warned of the very real danger of panic selling of sterling and the need for 'a cushion with which to support the pound'.[272] Out of these concerns grew the impetus to establish an Exchange Equalisation Account (EEA), announced in the Budget in April 1932, with the aim of checking the undue speculative fluctuations in the exchange value of sterling so damaging to domestic investment and output while at the same time helping to maintain 'cheap money' as an aid to economic recovery.[273] Of the two objectives, it was perhaps the domestic goals which increasingly predominated throughout the 1930s.[274]

---

[269] Niemeyer memorandum, 26 September 1931, T 175/56. Also Clay, *Lord Norman*, pp. 399–400; Howson, *Domestic Monetary Management*, pp. 78–79.

[270] Phillips, 'The Present Position of the Pound', 24 February 1932, T 175/57.

[271] N. Chamberlain to Hilda, 27 February and 12 March 1932.

[272] 'Very secret' memo, 3 October 1931, para. 16, NC8/12/1–2.

[273] Susan Howson, *Sterling's Managed Float: the Operation of the Exchange Equalization Account, 1932–39* (Princeton, 1980), pp. 1, 7–8. See also CAB 14(33)2, 6 March 1933, CAB 23/75.

[274] Howson, *Domestic Monetary Management*, pp. 83, 173–79.

Although cheap money and a managed currency provided Chamberlain with solid grounds for optimism about recovery, Treasury policy-makers also recognised the critical need to find an acceptable settlement of the vexed problem of war debts.[275] Moreover, although these negotiations were officially a matter for the Foreign Office, from the outset Chamberlain was determined to ensure that he should be directly consulted before any action was taken[276] and in reality he largely dictated the policy actually pursued. From Chamberlain's perspective, the myopic intransigence, political cynicism and self-interested greed of France and the USA over intergovernmental debts threatened to undermine world economic recovery. 'Any Reparations settlement or adjustment must be accompanied by a corresponding settlement or adjustment of war debts', Chamberlain explained to his sisters in December 1931. 'Hoover knows it but daren't say so. Unless he says so France darent move and so we are all locked in a suicidal embrace which will probably drown the lot of us!'[277] In order to escape from this hopeless impasse, Chamberlain intended to proceed in two quite distinct negotiating phases while at the same time ensuring that the problems of reparations and war debts remained inextricably bound together. He was thus prepared to accept postponement of the planned Lausanne conference on reparations in January 1932 until there was some certainty of a negotiated European agreement on their cancellation, in the belief that this would massively strengthen the force of Anglo-French overtures to the United States requesting that they should 'make their contribution' by cancelling Allied war debts.[278]

The Lausanne Conference convened on 16 June 1932. Within three days Chamberlain was stricken with a severe recurrence of the gout which had flared up immediately after the Budget two months earlier as 'a sign of overwork on the machine'.[279] In April the attack had been so debilitating that Chamberlain was unable to use the usual gout boot and was forced onto crutches, while the condition and its medication had such a depressing effect on his constitution that 'life seem[ed] insupportable at times'.[280] At one stage in late May he seriously considered the possibility that its persistence might force his reluctant retirement from politics altogether.[281] This recurrence at Lausanne was even more unfortunate because MacDonald's chairmanship of the conference, his own ill-health and vagueness about the financial detail ensured that Chamberlain was recognised from the outset as the effective

---

[275] For the background to these issues see Derek Aldcroft, *From Versailles to Wall Street 1919–1929* (London, 1977), ch. 4; Patricia Clavin, *The Failure of Economic Diplomacy: Britain, Germany, France and the United States, 1931–36* (London, 1996).

[276] N. Chamberlain to Hilda, 26 November 1932.

[277] N. Chamberlain to Hilda, 6 December 1931.

[278] N. Chamberlain to Hilda, 11 January 1932.

[279] N. Chamberlain to Hilda, 23 April 1932.

[280] N. Chamberlain to Ida, 30 April 1932.

[281] N. Chamberlain to Ida, 21 May 1932.

leader of the British delegation.[282] Instead, the remorseless hard work of the past months provoked a near complete physical collapse, during which Chamberlain was compelled to take to his bed, and he only re-emerged in a gout boot on 23 June; a deeply frustrated man humiliated at his inability to pull his weight.[283] Ultimately, however, no one doubted that at Lausanne Chamberlain had been 'the chief factor in the consummation' of an agreement which Runciman hailed as 'a triumph of British policy and statesmanship'.[284]

Central to British planning for Lausanne was the hope that at an early stage in the proceedings delegates would pass a resolution declaring that in the interests of world recovery there should be an all-round cancellation of all war debts and reparations.[285] In the event, after a 'very strenuous time' wrestling with the other delegations, the declaration was adopted by the Conference on 17 June – although only after Chamberlain made himself distinctly 'disagreeable' to Herriot.[286] Unfortunately, for a man of Chamberlain's direct and businesslike habits, the defensive posturing of European diplomacy was immensely frustrating and progress initially proved to be painfully slow. After many dashed hopes and reverses, however, by the end of June a British scheme had been accepted involving the total cancellation of all European reparations and war debts subject to a German lump sum payment into a fund for European reconstruction, which satisfied the French need to demonstrate that Germany had not been allowed to escape all further burdens while German opinion could be pacified with the thought that the payment would not be paid directly to France. After a further crisis over the amount of Germany's lump sum payment, agreement was finally reached on 8 July after a relaxed dinner between Herriot and Chamberlain at which they had negotiated late into the night to produce a final settlement sketched out on the latter's napkin. To obtain French agreement, the British also entered into a secret 'Gentleman's Agreement' postponing ratification until a 'satisfactory settlement' had been reached between the European powers and the United States over their own war debts.

The principal problem confronting Chamberlain's two-stage strategy was that the White House and Congress were adamantly opposed to any remission or cancellation of Anglo-French war debts. Nevertheless, although he found their idiocy and cynicism 'simply infuriat[ing]', Chamberlain remained hopeful that 'we shall last out long enough to enable even the Americans to learn a little sense'.[287] As he assured a sceptical French delegation at Lausanne, what the

---

[282] Sir John Simon to N. Chamberlain, 7 January 1932, N7/11/25/37.

[283] N. Chamberlain to Hilda, 26 June 1932.

[284] Runciman to Chamberlain, 10 July 1932, NC7/11/25/33.

[285] CAB 32(32)1, 8 June 1932 and CP 191(32), 'Reparations', by Simon, 31 May 1932, CAB 24/230.

[286] N. Chamberlain to Hilda, 19 June 1932; Simon to Vansittart, 20 June 1932 appended to CAB 37(32), 22 June 1932, CAB 23/72. See also N. Chamberlain's Lausanne Diary, NC2/16/1–2.

[287] N. Chamberlain to Hilda, 15 May 1932; N. Chamberlain to Ida, 5 June 1932.

Hoover Administration said for domestic consumption before the presidential elections in November may not be the same as their policy afterwards. 'The important thing was to say nothing to them now but to come to a settlement ourselves' on the grounds that if it commended itself to world opinion it would be difficult for the United States to resist; an expectation reinforced three days after the Lausanne conference commenced by hints from an American intermediary that if the European powers ensured the issue remained off the American electoral platform it may be possible for Hoover to defer the next war debt payment due on 15 December until a negotiated settlement had been reached.[288]

In accordance with this strategy, on 10 November 1932, within days of Hoover's defeat in the election, the British Ambassador at Washington presented a Note during Secretary of State Stimson's 'Diplomatic Hour' set aside for ambassadorial visits. In many ways, the Note established all of the central themes of the British case on war debts as it would develop over the next two years. While accepting that the one-year Hoover moratorium on intergovernmental debts announced in June 1931 had been a useful first step, the British argued that it had not realised its objective. The Note also pointed to the final settlement of the reparations problem at Lausanne as a major step 'towards the early restoration of world prosperity' and called upon the US government to enter into a corresponding review of European war debts to America. As a final settlement was impossible before the next British payment was due on 15 December, the specific purpose of the Note was to urge suspension of this payment to enable negotiations to take place unencumbered by such a burden in a manner similar to that employed at Lausanne.[289] Stimson's reply to the British Note on 23 November offered little hope of compromise. Reiterating the established American position that reparations were a European issue which did not directly involve the United States, Stimson did acknowledge the sacrifice of the European creditors in cancelling reparations, but he also asserted that they could not disregard the effects of the British proposal on the American taxpayer in the depths of the slump. Indeed, he asserted that the American government and people attached such importance to the maintenance of the original debt agreements that the arguments for a full payment in December 'far outweigh any reasons now apparent for its suspension'.[290] At this juncture, Chamberlain found it 'very hard to control [his] feelings about the Americans' who 'haven't a scrap of moral courage'. Yet he still 'clung obstinately' to the hope that they would suspend the

---

[288] N. Chamberlain to Ida, 20 June 1932. Also Simon to Vansittart, 20 June 1932, appended to CAB 37(32), 22 June 1932.

[289] CP 389 (32), 'British War Debts to America', 10 November 1932, CAB 24/234. Published as Cmd. 4192 (1932).

[290] Cmd. 4203, Note Addressed by the US Government to His Majesty's Government in reply to a Note dated November 10 1932 relating to British War Debts, Washington, 23 November 1932. See also Martin L. Fausold, *The Presidency of Herbert C. Hoover* (Lawrence, Kansas, 1985), pp. 216–17.

December payment even though he recognised he was 'almost alone in this view'.[291]

American intransigence confronted the British with a stark dilemma. As Chamberlain noted with more than a touch of Shakespearean drama for the first (but by no means the last) time in November 1932: 'To pay or not to pay, that is the question'. On the one hand, defaulting on the debt would encourage every other small debtor nation to do the same and gravely undermine confidence in Britain's moral leadership as well as its credit. On the other hand, payment would only serve to vindicate American cynicism and obduracy towards its European debtors to the detriment of world recovery and encourage them to expect further instalments at a time when the nominal balance owed by the British amounted to $4700 million – larger than the original advance of $4300 million after nearly half of that original sum had already been paid. Against this background, Chamberlain concluded initially that 'it really requires more courage to refuse to pay than to pay' and after Stimson's note in late November he was inclined towards non-payment. 'I should not repudiate; I should expressly admit the obligation but at the last moment I should inform the Yanks that my conscience would not allow me to take such a step which I was convinced would upset the world & throw back all chance of recovery for an indefinite period'.[292] Such a stance conformed well with his broader two-stage strategy of first educating the French at Lausanne before going on to do the same with American opinion in the belief that 'the longer they go without payment the more easy will it be for them to accept the prospect that there never will be any payment'.[293] To this end, as he explained to Flandin in mid-November, his strategy was to work for a moratorium of at least three years with 'a lump sum payment of enormously reduced amount, so that the Americans could tell their Congress that they had refused to listen to cancellation; but the amount would, in fact, be so small as to be nearly the same thing'.[294]

The crucial turning point in the development of Chamberlain's thinking occurred on the afternoon of Sunday 27 November, at a meeting with the Governor of the Bank of England. Here Chamberlain was informed that Ogden Mills, the US Treasury Secretary, agreed privately with the British stance and had expounded a secret plan in which Britain should propose to a sympathetic American Administration that it wished to separate payments towards the principal and interest of the war debt. This would enable Britain to avail itself of its right to suspend payments on the former for two years and (although only Congress could remit the interest) Britain should offer to make payment on the interest in

[291] N. Chamberlain to Hilda, 26 November 1932.

[292] Ibid.

[293] N. Chamberlain to Ida, 4 December 1932.

[294] N. Chamberlain to Lord Tyrrell, 17 November 1932 and accompanying 'Notes of Conversations with M. Flandin, November 1932', NC7/11/25/47–48.

the form of bonds maturing over a three-year period to be held by the US government until maturity. From Chamberlain's perspective, there were two obvious objections to the plan. Firstly, American refusal to extend the offer to the French (to whom they were violently hostile) was 'very serious, for it would involve the default of France and the non ratification of Lausanne'. It would also expose Britain to French allegations that it had betrayed its ally and their 'gentleman's agreement' in pursuit of purely selfish national interests. Secondly, the Governor warned that British default would set a dangerous precedent for a creditor nation and prompt Australia, Argentina and Germany (among others) to default on their payments to her.[295] This meeting with Montagu Norman provoked a complete and immediate *volte face* in the Chancellor's position insofar as he now concluded that although default may be unavoidable 'the consequences of non payment were so serious that ... we ought to avoid them as long as there remained even a remote chance of a happy ending'.[296]

Against a background of 'great nervousness' in the City created by American hostility,[297] an informal meeting of ministers was called on 28 November to avoid the public speculation and alarm likely to attend a full session of Cabinet. Outlining Ogden Mills's scheme to his colleagues, Chamberlain enunciated his own new thinking in favour of payment. He thus emphasised the twin dangers of antagonising France, as this would react on the Disarmament Conference 'and the peace of Europe', and the damaging precedent that British default would create among smaller debtor nations and the 'terrific shock' which such an action would administer 'to a very large number of the best of our people who would feel that Englands name had been dragged in the mud and would suffer humiliation accordingly'.[298] On these grounds, Chamberlain informed his colleagues that 'he had at last come to the conclusion that we ought ... to pay' – albeit while simultaneously impressing upon Congress the adverse consequences of a resumption of payments for American recovery and the hope that before the next scheduled payment in June they would have entered into negotiations for a final settlement. After Runciman, Hailsham and Cunliffe-Lister emerged as the only advocates of default, Baldwin then decisively stated his support for Chamberlain's arguments, noting that repudiation was 'an ugly word' and that it 'might bring the world within sight of the end of Capitalism. Our word is unique in the world'.[299]

When the Cabinet reassembled the next evening, the battle lines of the previous day re-emerged more clearly. Having urged the Cabinet to make the full December

---

[295] Meeting of Ministers, 28 November 1932 appended to CAB 63(32), CAB 23/73. Also N. Chamberlain to Ida, 4 December 1932.

[296] N. Chamberlain to Ida, 4 December 1932.

[297] N. Chamberlain to Ida, 19 November 1932.

[298] N. Chamberlain to Ida, 4 December 1932.

[299] Meeting of Ministers, 28 November 1932, appended to CAB 63(32)1, 29 November 1932, CAB 23/73.

payment if the Americans refused a final request to extend the Mills plan to other European debtors, much to Chamberlain's consternation, 'a strong section' led by Cunliffe-Lister and Hailsham (but not now Runciman) were in favour of unilaterally accepting the Mills plan and 'let[ting] the French go hang'. At this juncture, things 'got a bit warm' as Chamberlain was determined to resign rather than accept 'a betrayal of our Ally and a fatal blow to Lausanne'.[300] Chamberlain then read the Cabinet a full summary of the draft Note expounding the complete British case for suspension of the December payment before, at MacDonald's suggestion, it was resolved to delete the final section saying that if Congress refused to do so the payment would be made in full.[301] The fourteen-page British Note was then despatched for submission to the American government along with a request to extend the offer to France. At the same time, the French were to be given a general account of developments in the vague hope of obtaining their consent to British acceptance of the Mills offer.[302]

Although Chamberlain's Note represented a powerful and comprehensive exposition of the British case for debt revision, its appeal to enlightened self-interest and American fairness received 'a bad reception in the United States' where Congress 'closed their eyes to it'. At the same time, informal consultations on the unofficial American offer indicated a much less attractive proposal than that originally communicated by Mills. As these changes rendered the Mills plan unacceptable, the full British payment was made in gold on 10 December as Chamberlain wished.[303] At the same time, having decided that 'the time had come to be a little more outspoken', Chamberlain's accompanying Note stopped short of the threat of repudiation but explained unambiguously that the December payment should not be regarded as a resumption of annual payments, but as an 'exceptional and abnormal' capital advance against final settlement;[304] a form of words designed to educate American public opinion and indicate clearly that there were 'limits to our squeezability'.[305] He followed this on 14 December with the first of several robust speeches outlining British policy which received widespread domestic acclaim.[306]

Despite these disappointments over the December payment, collective wishful thinking in London was sustained by the belief that the incoming President would be far more amenable to British pleas than his predecessor. In late

[300] N. Chamberlain to Ida, 4 December 1932.

[301] CAB 63(32)1, 29 November 1932, CAB 23/73.

[302] Ibid. CP 416(32), 'British War Debt to America', 1 December 1932, CAB 24/235.

[303] CAB 65(31)1, 7 December 1932.

[304] Cmd. 4215, Further Note by His Majesty's Government to the United States Government related to British War Debts, 11 December 1932.

[305] N. Chamberlain to Hilda, 10 December 1932.

[306] Headlam Diary, 14 December 1932, Stuart Ball (ed.), *Parliament and Politics in the Age of Baldwin and MacDonald: The Headlam Diaries, 1923–1935* (London, 1992), p. 254; N. Chamberlain to Ida, 17 December 1932.

August, A.J. Cummings of the *News Chronicle* had a 'very long and important talk' with Governor Roosevelt which he reported confidentially to Runciman at Roosevelt's request. According to Cummings, Roosevelt 'has liberal views and is undoubtedly a real friend to this country'.[307] On the subject of war debts, Roosevelt explained that he was personally in favour of cancellation, but he 'made it equally clear that in the present state of politics and industry in the U.S.A. it would be impossible officially to advocate this course ... "We must ask you all", he said "to acknowledge the debt, but you would find us an extremely indulgent creditor ..."'.[308] These hopes were reinforced at the end of January 1933 when Roosevelt sent an intermediary to meet MacDonald and Chamberlain to discuss war debts. Although of 'an exploratory character', the meeting radiated goodwill and encouraged British expectations of an early settlement. The Cabinet were also reassured by news that the President-Elect was prepared to make a similar offer to the other European debtors and that he was considering a moratorium which (according to MacDonald's account) 'might last so long that the American public could forget what was to be paid'.[309]

On the basis of these indications, Chamberlain was able to reassure the Cabinet that their strategy was apparently bearing fruit:

> It was obvious that American public opinion had a long way to go, as had Mr Roosevelt himself, before their ideas approached to our own. For this a certain amount of time was necessary. So long as we could obtain a moratorium during the conversations it was unnecessary to agitate ourselves about delay. Time must work in our favour, for the facts of the situation would tend to bring the Americans to see the ill effects on the United States of a continuation of payments. Although it was impossible as yet to see our way through the jungle, nevertheless he felt fairly confident in his own mind.

In the belief that any new President was in his strongest position with Congress at the start of his term, the Cabinet responded positively to Roosevelt's eagerness for a private and secret understanding before his inauguration on 4 March. To make this possible, at Chamberlain's suggestion, it was decided to use the British Ambassador in Washington as an intermediary. Sir Ronald Lindsay was thus recalled to London with the effect that Roosevelt immediately invited him to an interview before his departure.[310]

Lindsay's meeting with Roosevelt took place at Warm Springs on 29 January 1933. According to the Ambassador's report to London, Roosevelt 'spoke throughout with remarkable frankness' about his desire for 'a comprehensive

---

[307] A.J. Cummings to Runciman, 9 September 1932, Runciman MSS 259/30–31.

[308] 'Memorandum on conversation with Governor Roosevelt at Albany on 31 August 1932', by A.J. Cummings, Runciman MSS 259/32–38.

[309] CAB 5(33), Appendix: 'Summary of Statements made to the Cabinet ... on British War Debts to the US on Monday, 30 January 1933 at 3pm', CAB 23/75.

[310] Ibid.

programme in which debts and other questions will automatically fall into their proper places', but of his refusal to contemplate piecemeal action because 'only by presenting Congress with the prospect of curing the world as well as the domestic situation can he hope to ensure its support'. To this end, he wished negotiations to begin immediately after his inauguration and 'to be pressed forward with the utmost energy' in order to be completed by 20 April when he planned 'to present to Congress without delay 5 or 6 great and important measures, to force it to confine itself to these, and to use pressure to make it adjourn within 60 days'. To achieve this goal, Roosevelt proposed that the 'British "number 2 man"' should arrive by 6 March to engage in private conversations in the hope that after ten days sufficient progress would have been made to enable the Prime Minister 'to come out in person to finish matters off'. On the substance of the debt issue, however, Roosevelt was less encouraging. Offering essentially a modification of the existing terms, rather than the immediate final settlement envisaged by Britain and France, Roosevelt asserted that the 'really terrible' condition of the country meant that 'if he and Hoover and an archangel from Heaven were all to be united in asking it for more it would not avail'.[311]

Lindsay's account of American opposition to any settlement on terms satisfactory to Britain reaffirmed Chamberlain's primary emphasis upon the need for a moratorium on debt payments until American opinion had progressed sufficiently to recognise its own best interests. To pave the way for such a step, Chamberlain proposed that Lindsay should persuade the President to send a message to Congress declaring that war debts could not be settled until the questions of tariffs, world prices and currency were discussed at the forthcoming World Economic Conference, and that to assist the separate but concurrent talks on war debts a moratorium should be offered until a final settlement was announced. In order 'to sweeten Congress', Chamberlain was even prepared to consider changing the venue of the World Economic Conference from London to Washington to assist 'the education of the Americans' – but only so long as MacDonald retained the chairmanship on which he had 'set his heart'.[312] Confident of eventual success, even when Lindsay reported 'most gloomily' on his conversations with Roosevelt in late February, Chamberlain refused to be despondent.[313] 'The picture could hardly look blacker than it does', he confessed to Lord Lothian, 'but, nevertheless, I am not unhopeful of the future since the facts and time are on our side'.[314] Ironically, what he failed to recognise was that his own robust public utterances about the damaging effects of war debts and the

[311] CP 29(33), Secret decipher of Lindsay telegrams, 30 January 1933, CAB 24/237.
[312] N. Chamberlain to Ida, 12 February 1933. Also N. Chamberlain to Lord Lothian, 17 February 1933, Lothian MSS GD40/17/200/220–21.
[313] N. Chamberlain to Ida, 25 February 1933 and 1 April and to Hilda, 1 April and 29 April 1933.
[314] N. Chamberlain to Lothian, 17 February 1933, Lothian MSS GD40/17/200/220–21.

British terms for settlement made this prospect progressively less likely. Indeed, Chamberlain's speech at Leeds on 24 January had been bitterly resented by American opinion and had greatly inflamed the situation. As Norman Davis, a close adviser and confidant of Roosevelt, urged Lothian to tell MacDonald, 'F[ranklin] R[oosevelt] is taking his political life in his hands' and 'N[eville] C[hamberlain] is making it more and more difficult':[315] a concern about Chamberlain's 'rather crude' observations which the President-Elect expressed himself to the British Ambassador in late January.[316]

In the event, Roosevelt departed little from Hoover's policy on war debts. Although he recognised that full payment was increasingly less likely, Congress had forbidden the President to reduce or cancel the debts and Roosevelt was far too shrewd a player of presidential transactional politics to squander his personal capital and leverage in hopeless and peripheral efforts to alter its stance when he had far more fundamental battles to fight over the New Deal at home.[317] Yet this did not prevent Roosevelt from stringing the British along over the prospects of an eventual settlement while engaging in a variety of confidential communications designed to obtain a more favourable general agreement on issues of importance to the United States. After a tour to America where he 'saw almost everyone of importance except the incoming President',[318] Lord Lothian acted as an unofficial intermediary between the Prime Minister and the veteran American diplomat Colonel House who was now part of Roosevelt's stable of advisers and a direct connection to the new American leadership.[319] Similarly, less than a month after Roosevelt's inauguration, a close presidential adviser met Runciman to emphasise American fears about the British obsession with war debts and to suggest that there were 'other matters of much greater importance' to deal with concerning the reduction of tariffs and disarmament and that only through cooperation on these 'great world problems' would 'the American mind ... be reconciled to any new method of dealing with war debts'.[320]

Despite these efforts to divert British attention into channels more acceptable to American opinion, an apparent ray of hope emerged during MacDonald's visit to Washington in April 1933 when Roosevelt gave a 'very firm pledge' to seek powers to act on war debts before Congress rose.[321] Although by the end of

---

[315] Lothian notes, 'Lamont dinner', n.d. See also W.Y. Elliott to Lothian, 1 February 1933, Lothian MSS GD40/17/199/138–39, 183; Felix Frankfurter to Roosevelt, 28 January 1933, Max Freedman (ed.), *Roosevelt and Frankfurter: Their Correspondence, 1928–1945* (London, 1967), p. 105.

[316] CP 29(33). Secret decipher of Lindsay telegrams, 30 January 1933, CAB 24/237.

[317] James MacGregor Burns, *Roosevelt: The Lion and the Fox* (New York, 1956), p. 249.

[318] Lothian to Chamberlain, Runciman, Baldwin and Simon, 16 February 1933, Lothian MSS GD40/17/200/218.

[319] Sir William Wiseman to Lothian, 23 February 1933; Lothian to Col. House, 13 February 1933, Lothian MSS GD40/17/200/241, 208.

[320] Runciman untitled memorandum, 31 March 1933, Runciman MSS 259/49–54.

[321] CAB 33(33)2, 5 May 1933, CAB 23/76.

May the position still remained 'very obscure',[322] all the available indications encouraged the belief that the President would send a message to Congress requesting a moratorium.[323] In the event, however, these expectations proved to be tantalisingly short-lived. As the President informed Lindsay on 8 June, 'a very serious deterioration had taken place in the Congressional situation and it was absolutely impossible now to send any such messages. In the temper of Congress at this moment such action might provoke them to pass every kind of legislation, mischievous not only to the United States but even to the world in general'. The President thus returned to the initial request for an interim part-payment of $10,000,000 which Roosevelt declared he would accept as a contribution towards the final settlement, although 'he knew perfectly well that that meant nothing at all'.[324]

When the Cabinet considered the American offer on 9 June, Chamberlain's position was significantly less conciliatory than before. Although the December payment had been designed to avoid default, 'that payment had not done us much good, as Congress appeared more obdurate than ever. If we paid 10,000,000 Dollars now there was no reason why we should not be asked to pay the same again next December, and two payments of 10,000,000 Dollars would amount to a big figure in one year'. As it would also threaten Lausanne, by compelling Britain to demand more in repayments from her own debtors, he declared a part-payment in June 'would ... be a mistake, but a token payment as a recognition of the legal position, might be regarded in a different light'. As a result, he proposed to offer 10,000,000 ounces of silver, both to emphasise the token nature of the payment and because it was worth only $5,000,000 – but only on condition that the President gave prior assurances that this would not be regarded as default.[325] As in the previous November, Runciman, Hailsham and Cunliffe-Lister emerged as the principal challengers to Chamberlain's authority arguing strongly that although default and deferment were 'ugly words', with awkward implications for a creditor nation like Britain, 'to make payment at the expense of our equilibrium and of our recuperative strength is still more dangerous. The ugly words we can survive, but the strain on our country's heart and strength may prove to be the beginning of a catastrophe'.[326] Despite this opposition, however, when challenged directly by the Chancellor on whether 'if the worst came to the worst, we should not pay', there was a general consensus that they should.[327]

---

[322] CAB 38(33)1, 31 May 1933.

[323] Telegrams 381–82 from Sir Ronald Lindsay, 8 June 1933 appended to CAB 39(33)2, 9 June 1933, CAB 23/77.

[324] Ibid.

[325] CAB 39(33)2, 9 June 1933.

[326] CP 134(33), 'War Debts' by Runciman, 24 May 1933, CAB 24/241.

[327] CAB 39(33)2, 9 June 1933.

After 'a last and urgent appeal' from the White House for $10,000,000 on the grounds that it would make a far more favourable impression on American opinion than the British counter-offer, the Cabinet accepted Chamberlain's advice and agreed to the American terms.[328] On the following day the announcement to the Commons was 'received with unanimous applause and congratulations'.[329] Britain then made a token payment of $10,000,000 in silver while six other debtors made no payment at all. From Chamberlain's perspective it was 'a great relief to my mind, for we were in a dilemma of the most embarrassing kind, and, up to almost the last moment, I did not know whether we should secure what I wanted'.[330] Having done so, however, he regarded it as the best of all possible outcomes on the grounds that 'it is not a nice thing to default and yet payment again really was not possible'.[331] Equally important, he regarded the arrangement as 'a substantial advance in the education of the American people: God knows they want it'.[332]

Despite Chamberlain's sanguine optimism, within two weeks the collapse of the World Economic Conference after Roosevelt's famous 'bombshell message' on 4 July opposing currency stabilisation removed any prospect of better Anglo-American relations. Already convinced of his 'misfortune to be dealing with a nation of cads',[333] Chamberlain angrily contended that 'there has never been a case of a Conference being so completely smashed by one of the participants'.[334] His only consolations were derived from a malicious delight at a further slump on the New York Stock Exchange which highlighted the dangers of Roosevelt's New Deal[335] and the modestly mitigating effects of a post-conference Dominion declaration on imperial monetary policy as a 'sort of sequel to Ottawa'.[336] Yet, the American retreat into economic nationalism and isolation left the war debt question effectively unresolvable on terms satisfactory to the British. In late September 1933, Sir Frederick Leith-Ross, the government's Chief Economic Adviser, sailed for New York to begin the long-awaited preliminary discussions. A month later, however, Chamberlain reported to the Cabinet that 'the American President was being influenced by the difficulties of his political situation and that in order to escape rebuff, he would have to avoid any controversial settlement'. Advised by Lindsay and Leith-Ross that a permanent settlement was beyond their

---

[328] CAB 41(33)1, 13 June 1933, with telegrams in Appendix I–V, CAB 23/77.

[329] Neville Chamberlain Diary, 14 June 1933. Also Headlam Diary, 14 June 1933, Ball (ed.), *Parliament and Politics*, p. 273.

[330] N. Chamberlain to L.S. Amery, 16 June 1933, NC7/2/62.

[331] N. Chamberlain to Hilda, 10 June 1933.

[332] N. Chamberlain to Amery, 16 June 1933.

[333] N. Chamberlain to Hilda, 4 February 1933.

[334] N. Chamberlain to Ida, 15 July 1933.

[335] N. Chamberlain to Hilda, 23 July 1933.

[336] Ibid.

reach, Chamberlain thus abandoned hope of anything but a temporary three-year settlement to help reduce American expectations.[337]

This time, however, Cabinet opposition to the Chancellor's policy was considerably stiffer from the 'good many [who] would like just to sit back & refuse any payment'.[338] Again, the leading critics 'in full cry for default' were Runciman, Cunliffe-Lister and Hailsham supported by Ormsby-Gore.[339] As the usually opaque Cabinet record ominously noted, 'The general tenor of the discussion revealed some hardening of opinion on the subject of payments'.[340] Yet despite this influential and increasingly determined opposition, Chamberlain remained convinced that it was still 'worth our while to pay something though not too much to avoid being denounced however unjustly as defaulters'.[341] In taking this stand, he commanded the support of not only Baldwin and MacDonald but also most of those less directly involved. A note from Lord Irwin passed across the Cabinet table during the harangue against payment thus bore the simple message, 'Two or three of us who are ignorant & therefore silent, shall trust your judgement better than others; & you may as well know it'.[342] After Roosevelt rejected both the proposed British permanent and temporary settlements in favour of another token payment, Chamberlain thus persuaded the Cabinet to accept this course as the least objectionable option and in the belief that default would wreck all hope of eventual cancellation.[343]

In the event, this further token payment in December 1933 prompted a full-scale row with the United States which culminated in the Johnson Act in June 1934, prohibiting loans to governments defaulting or behind with their payments to the US.[344] The Johnson Act effectively resolved the British dilemma by precluding the use of token payments as a means of avoiding default. Confronted by a choice between defaulting or paying the full outstanding balance to the detriment of its own economic recovery, and in the certain knowledge that it would receive no further repayments from its own debtors, Britain finally suspended all war debt payments. Despite the blow to national pride and the defeat of all Chamberlain's hopes, the action made the achievement of a balanced budget significantly easier by further reducing the burden of debt servicing from over 8 per cent of National Income in 1931 to under 5 per cent by 1935.

---

[337] CAB 58(33)1, 26 October 1933, CAB 23/77.

[338] N. Chamberlain to Ida, 28 October 1933.

[339] Irwin note to Chamberlain, n.d. (28 October 1933), NC7/10. Runciman to Lord Hailsham and reply, 27 September 1933. Also Leith-Ross to Runciman, 27 September 1933, Runciman MSS 259/17–18 and 265/53.

[340] CAB 58(33)1, 26 October 1933.

[341] N. Chamberlain to Ida, 28 October 1933.

[342] Irwin note to Chamberlain, n.d., 28 October 1933.

[343] CAB 59(33)6, 2 November 1933.

[344] Wayne S. Cole, *Roosevelt and the Isolationists, 1932–45* (Lincoln, Nebraska, 1983), ch. 7.

VI

By the end of 1933 the most difficult phase of Chamberlain's Chancellorship was drawing to an end along with the worst of the Great Depression. Since November 1931, Chamberlain had reigned supreme over economic policy and had increasingly established his more general policy dominance within the Cabinet. From the outset he was determined to ensure that there was no repetition of the unwanted Prime Ministerial interference with Treasury business which Snowden had suffered for so long and of which he had warned Chamberlain.[345] As a result, he resolved that 'if he continues to act as though he were Dictator & not P.M. I shall watch for a suitable opportunity & then show my teeth'.[346] By the end of November a suitable pretext presented itself. When Chamberlain learned that MacDonald had resumed his previous habit of discussing economic policy with private meetings of economists, he acted immediately to curtail this interference, speculating with his sisters whether there was 'any velvet glove thick enough to overcome the disagreeable impression of the metallic substance inside'.[347] In the event, MacDonald took the rebuff 'extremely well', but thereafter he proved circumspect in dealing with a Chancellor who he increasingly recognised to be the effective policy leader of the majority party. For his own part, Chamberlain was also keenly aware that he occupied 'a different position in this Cabinet from any other that I have sat in. It seems to me that I carry more weight. I certainly speak more; the P.M. shows much deference to what I say and as S.B. mostly remains silent our people look to me for the lead and I see that they get it'.[348]

Beyond his own department, this new status often gave him the authority and confidence to intervene as he wished. Cabinet colleagues were still more than capable of mounting resistance on crucial collective questions like payment of the American debt or where the primary interests of their own departments were at stake – as demonstrated by the battle over Chamberlain's plans for a radical new Unemployment Bill in 1933–34 and Simon's rejection of his suggestions about disarmament. Yet in reality, Chamberlain often still prevailed even outside the area of his own virtually all-encompassing domain at the Treasury. 'It amuses me to find a new policy for each of my colleagues in turn and though I can't imagine that all my ideas are the best that can be found, most of them seem to be adopted faute de mieux!'[349] Towards the Commons, he appeared to approach his task as Chancellor 'from the standpoint of the plain businessman', addressing the House 'in the tone and manner of a company chairman speaking to a

---

[345] Snowden to N. Chamberlain, 29 December 1931, NC7/11/24/30.
[346] N. Chamberlain to Ida, 15 November 1931.
[347] N. Chamberlain to Ida, 29 November 1931.
[348] N. Chamberlain to Ida, 12 December 1931.
[349] N. Chamberlain to Hilda, 30 October 1932.

meeting of shareholders' to provide them with 'a straightforward, matter-of-fact statement of expenditure and income' without dramatics or imaginative flights.[350] Yet his old acerbity and mastery of details still made him a formidable force, particularly when supported by a Treasury machine which shared his values and policy priorities and was led by men who admired his decisive, hard-working style of leadership. Indeed, in Warren Fisher, the Permanent Secretary at the Treasury, and an official who judged ministers on precisely these qualities, Chamberlain inspired something approaching adoration.[351]

During this period, Chamberlain laid the foundations of an economic strategy upon which he placed his hopes of recovery. Contemporary critics of the National Government were vocal in their condemnation of Chamberlain's policy as something which 'tinkered with the cancer of massive unemployment ... It was all small, haphazard, essentially palliative, and unrelated to any long-term constructive economic policy'.[352] For many later historians, the National Government's failure on unemployment also placed Chamberlain 'closer to the older orthodoxies of *laissez faire*, essentially pursuing a "good housekeeping" policy while waiting for the natural self-righting forces of the free market to bring back prosperity. His keen but narrow business mind made him an appropriate executor of his strategy'.[353] He has thus been portrayed as 'a pure Cobdenite in his reliance on "natural" forces and individual enterprise' and his lack of sympathy with the burgeoning 'middle opinion' of the 1930s as it moved towards planning and more interventionist forms of capitalism.[354] In his response to regional and industrial problems particularly, many economic historians have condemned the government's 'piecemeal and opportunist' policies which amounted not to 'a consistent and coherent ... policy worthy of the name, more a hotch-potch of *ad hoc* measures to meet particular circumstances'.[355]

Although such an indictment appears compelling given the persistence of regional mass unemployment throughout the 1930s, such judgements obscure much of the logic, coherence and bolder vision contained within Chamberlain's plans. Furthermore, although there is a tendency to attribute recovery to a

---

[350] F.W. Pethick-Lawrence, *Fate Has Been Kind* (London, n.d.), p. 190. Gervais Rentoul, *This is My Case: An Autobiography* (London, n.d.), p. 120; D. Walker-Smith, *Neville Chamberlain: Man of Peace* (London, n.d. 1939–40), p. 177.

[351] See N. Chamberlain to Hilda, 5 January 1924; Warren Fisher to N. Chamberlain, 4 June 1924, NC7/11/17/7 and 18 January 1937, NC7/11/30/48.

[352] Robert Boothby, *My Yesterday, Your Tomorrow* (London, 1962), p. 125.

[353] Peter Clarke, *A Question of Leadership: Gladstone to Thatcher* (Penguin edn, London, 1992), p. 119.

[354] A.J.P. Taylor, *English History 1914–1945* (Harmondsworth, 1975), p. 375. Kevin Jeffreys, *The Churchill Coalition and Wartime Politics, 1940–45* (Manchester, 1991), p. 13; Robert Blake, *The Conservative Party from Peel to Thatcher* (Fontana edn, 1985), pp. 237, 245.

[355] Winch, *Economics and Policy*, p. 224; Aldcroft, *The British Economy*, pp. 110–14, 119, 125, 131; M.W. Kirby, *The Decline of British Industrial Power Since 1870* (London, 1981), pp. 67–68.

variety of spontaneous causes and non-policy factors, it is wrong to dismiss entirely the impact of significant shifts in policy introduced during his Chancellorship on the grounds that most 'pointed in the right direction' and that 'in each case a policy-on situation was better for employment than the alternative of no policy change at all'.[356] In 1932 the success of the debt conversion operation had been accompanied by a managed currency protected by the Exchange Equalisation Account. 'Cheap money' helped provide at least the permissive foundations for the housing boom which became one of the most prominent features of the rising economic activity during the 1930s. At the same time, the Import Duties Act had created the 'scientific' tariff structure which Chamberlain had planned for so long and had commended to Parliament as a panacea for virtually all of the nation's industrial and economic ills.[357] Contrary to the standard indictment, therefore, a reasonable case can be made for regarding Chamberlain's Chancellorship as the period in which Britain took its first significant steps towards 'supportive' management of the economy – albeit, admittedly, a managed economy of a distinctly non-Keynesian variety.[358]

With the benefit of hindsight, it is clear that the general tariff was far less successful than policy-makers believed at the time. The Ottawa agreements probably only diverted existing trade into slower-growing imperial channels rather than creating new trade. They may also have had adverse repercussions for imperial trade *vis-à-vis* foreign markets and, as Runciman anticipated, probably created difficulties in negotiating bilateral trade agreements with non-imperial countries.[359] Moreover, as the 'effective rate' of protection given by the tariff was often far lower than the nominal rate, the Import Duties Act often exposed or even disadvantaged some of those industries it was supposed to be protecting.[360] Yet without the benefit of complex econometric analysis, the perceived reality for Chamberlain and his colleagues during the 1930s was that by protecting domestic industry in the home market from foreign competitors 'the tariff proved on balance of significant and essential value in aiding British recovery, not only by giving an initial stimulus to rise from the slough, but in the longer-term also'.[361] Moreover,

---

[356] Aldcroft, *The British Economy*, pp. 134–35.

[357] *H.C. Debs.* 5s., 261, cols 286–88, 4 February 1932.

[358] Samuel H. Beer, *Modern British Politics: A Study of Parties and Pressure Groups* (London, 1965), ch. 10; Alan Booth, 'Britain in the 1930s: a managed economy?', *Economic History Review*, 2nd ser., 40 (1987), pp. 499, 522.

[359] Drummond, *Imperial Economic Policy*, pp. 284–89; Runciman to MacDonald, 2 September 1932, MacDonald MSS 30/69/1/594.

[360] Forrest Capie, 'The British Tariff and Industrial Protection in the 1930s', *Economic History Review*, 31 (1978), pp. 399–409 and *Depression and Protectionism: Britain Between the Wars* (London, 1983), ch. 8. But see J. Foreman-Peck's more positive view of the impact of tariffs on output and employment in *Economic History Review*, 2nd ser., 34 (1981), pp. 132–39.

[361] Sir Herbert Hutchinson, *Tariff Making and Industrial Reconstruction: An Account of the Work of the Import Duties Advisory Committee, 1932–1939* (London, 1965), p. 165.

as with the evaluation of 'cheap money', the fundamental point is that whatever the retrospective effect of tariff policy during the 1930s, the contemporary intent was consciously and explicitly to arm the government with a flexible tool with which to manage the economy and restore industrial prosperity. In this respect, above all, the Import Duties Act represented a victory for the pragmatic protectionists like Chamberlain over the vague but grandiose aspirations of sentimental imperial visionaries like Amery. Ultimately, for Chamberlain, tariff reform was to be sought less as an end in itself than as an instrumental step towards a far broader and more ambitious economic objective. Nowhere was this more apparent than in the perceived relationship between the Import Duties Act and the reorganisation of industry.

Industrial reorganisation and rationalisation had been central to discussion about Safeguarding policy towards iron and steel during the 1924–29 government.[362] Baldwin's electoral pledges and Churchill's free trade obstructionism, however, made rationalisation appear as an alternative rather than an adjunct to tariff protection. Yet after 1931, Chamberlain had the opportunity to make the latter conditional upon the former. As he informed Snowden:

> the coupling with this flat rate tariff of additional powers [to impose selective surtaxes] provides us with such a lever as has never been possessed before by any Government, for inducing or, if you like, forcing industry to set its house in order. I have in mind particularly iron and steel and cotton: and my belief in the advantages of Protection is not so fanatical as to close my eyes to the vital importance of a thorough reorganisation of such industries as these, if they were even to keep their heads above water in the future.

As Chamberlain emphasised consistently in the Balance of Trade Committee and later in Cabinet,[363] the basis of his long-term industrial strategy was to enable the independent Import Duties Advisory Committee to inform ailing and uncompetitive industries that if 'you want help … you must first put your house in order'.[364] To exercise this leverage effectively, he actively sought out a like-minded chairman to employ these powers in a suitably interventionist manner. As a result, it is perhaps not surprising that both contemporary testimony and econometric analysis suggests that despite IDAC's 'independent' status it recommended selective duties in accordance with governmental priorities rather than the objective merits of the case or the level of import penetration.[365] Against this background, it is thus both unjust and unhistorical to argue that the National Government did not have a positive unemployment policy or that

---

[362] Self, *Tories and Tariffs*, ch. VIII.

[363] See, for example, BT(31) 2nd and 4th Conclusions, 8, 13 January 1932, CAB 27/467; CP 25(32), 19 January 1932, Committee on the Balance of Trade: Report, para. 22. Also CAB 5–6(32)1 and CAB 10(32)2, 21 and 29 January 1932, CAB 23/70.

[364] CAB 5(32)1, 21 January 1932.

[365] Hutchinson, *Tariff Making*, pp. 155–56.

'when Neville Chamberlain introduced the Import Duties Bill he was fulfilling the dreams of his father as much as prescribing for the depression'.[366]

While historians have too often understated and ignored Chamberlain's breadth of ambition in tariff and industrial policy, they have generally been far more critical of his budgetary orthodoxy and adherence to the so-called 'Treasury view'. Certainly during Chamberlain's Chancellorship public expenditure as a share of national output did fall between 1931 and 1934 before stabilising and then rising sharply from 1937 as the effect of rearmament became apparent. In this respect, Britain was far more orthodox than almost any other European state in its policy on balanced budgets[367] – albeit that even modern econometric calculations have not yet resolved the question of whether the real effects of Chamberlain's budgetary stance was broadly neutral in its impact (as Broadberry argues)[368] or more deflationary than it appears from conventional budgetary analysis (as Middleton contends on the basis of the constant employment budget).[369]

Yet what is absolutely certain is that policy-makers in the 1930s perceived the achievement of a budgetary balance to be a crucial cornerstone for any broader policy designed to sustain low interest rates and cheap money, while preventing inflation and maintaining confidence in the economy; forces for fiscal conservatism reinforced still further by London's emergence at the centre of a sterling area of states (both within the empire and beyond it) who pegged their exchange rates to the pound and held considerable sterling balances in London.[370] While Keynesian historians have been dismissive of Chamberlain's emphasis on unprovable psychological arguments about the importance of confidence,[371] such scepticism often underestimates the impact of the traumatic perceived lessons of 1931. 'Hot money' had fled catastrophically from London then, and the Treasury had reason to fear that it would do so again if the budget was not balanced and the canons of 'responsible' finance were not respected. Given the circumstances which had brought the National Government to office in the first place, therefore, Chamberlain was determined that there should be nothing in his economic strategy to jeopardise

---

[366] H.W. Richardson, 'The Economic Significance of the Depression in Britain', *Journal of Contemporary History* (1969), pp. 3–19.

[367] Roger Middleton, *Towards the Managed Economy: Keynes, the Treasury and the Fiscal Policy Debate of the 1930s* (London, 1985), pp. 111–12; Jim Tomlinson, *Public Policy and the Economy Since 1900* (Oxford, 1990), pp. 111–12.

[368] S.N. Broadberry, 'Fiscal Policy in Britain during the 1930s', *Economic History Review*, 2nd ser., 37 (1984), pp. 95–102.

[369] R. Middleton, 'The Constant Employment Budget Balance and British Budgetary Policy 1929–39', *Economic History Review*, 2nd ser., 34 (1981), pp. 266–86.

[370] Tomlinson, *Public Policy*, p. 112. I.M. Drummond, *The Floating Pound and the Sterling Area, 1931–39* (Cambridge, 1981), pp. 15, 22, 25–26, 123, 130–32. H.W. Richardson, *Economic Recovery in Britain 1932–39* (London, 1967), pp. 218–19.

[371] Winch, *Economics and Policy*, p. 218.

business or investment confidence through the adoption of destabilising or 'flashy' short-term expedients. When Keynes criticised the 1932 Budget on the grounds that '"Sound" finance may be right psychologically, but economically it is a depressing influence', he did so as an expansionist economist anticipating an employment multiplier effect from government expenditure on public works, but even he conceded privately that there were 'enormous psychological advantages in the appearance of economy' in order to prepare the ground for debt conversion and lower long-term interest rates.[372]

Ultimately, it was the crucial importance of this psychological sense of economic confidence, derived from the appearance of 'sound' finance, for which Chamberlain was prepared to play the long game. 'After such a long period of unsound management, especially in finance, it would be foolish to expect a very rapid recovery' the Chancellor confided to a close friend in January 1932. 'There are serried ranks of apparently insoluble problems in front of us; but given a few years, we shall work through them'.[373] Confronting a gloomy trade and financial position six months later, he consoled himself with the confidence that 'one must take a longer view and there are some more hopeful signs'.[374] One such sign was a report from the Committee on Economic Information that 'Psychologically, there is a greater steadiness and confidence in business and industrial circles in Great Britain than in most other countries'.[375] Yet as Chamberlain also recognised, playing the long game had significant adverse implications for his reputation in the short term. After his 1933 Budget he thus gloomily reflected that 'there will be no praise for the Chancellor till one of my successors is fortunate enough to come in on the upward turn of trade. For myself I must be content to do my duty as I see it and trust to recognition in the future'. At times, Chamberlain found this need for patient stoicism 'a depressing business'. Looking ahead to nothing but 'long struggles against a gradually more & more disgruntled public opinion' he even talked briefly (but unconvincingly) about retirement after the next election.[376]

These values, priorities and expectations were grimly reflected in Chamberlain's budgetary policy during the first half of his Chancellorship. Although encouraged by early signs of apparent recovery in the spring of 1932, his prudent expectations of reduced revenue for the coming year reinforced an already strong instinctive inclination towards fiscal conservatism. Alarmed by press speculation about a reduction in direct and indirect taxation in the forthcoming Budget after an

---

[372] *Evening Standard*, 20 April 1932; Keynes to Macmillan, 6 June 1932, quoted in Robert Skidelsky, *John Maynard Keynes: Volume Two, The Economist as Saviour, 1920–1937* (London, 1992), p. 436.

[373] N. Chamberlain to Sir Francis Humphreys, 8 January 1932, NC7/11/24/15.

[374] N. Chamberlain to Hilda, 11 June 1932.

[375] CP 161(32), 'Economic Advisory Council: Third Report of the Committee on Economic Information: Survey of the Economic Situation', 25 May 1932, para. 14, CAB 24/230.

[376] N. Chamberlain to Hilda, 29 April 1933.

overly optimistic speech by Baldwin at Ilford in March 1932, Chamberlain promptly 'damped them down' three days later in a speech at Birmingham in the belief that 'it is certainly too soon to begin dividing up the skin of the bear'.[377] Response to his first Budget on 19 April 1932 varied considerably. Although the King was gratified to find 'at this very critical time in the history of the world' that he had 'a government of all the Talents and a Chancellor of the Exchequer in whom everyone has the fullest confidence',[378] and Cabinet colleagues communicated their customary congratulations, the Prime Minister was privately far more critical of a Budget speech with 'too many small and wearisome details', a poor ending and little cheering. 'Chancellor not in form and showed his weakness', MacDonald noted in his diary, 'lack of imagination and especially of coordinating vision'.[379] Among his own backbenchers, although by common consent 'a dull and boring' speech, there was also a recognition that 'no one could have made a very successful speech with such a financial situation to unfold'.[380] In contrast, *The Times* characteristically described the Budget as one of 'puritanical severity' for its lack of concessions and unnecessary orthodoxy on debt redemption.[381]

Yet from Chamberlain's own perspective, the 1932 Budget achieved his limited objectives and, despite sustained backbench criticism of the failure to reduce beer duty to assist the brewing industry, he concluded that he had 'got off very cheaply with such an unpopular Budget' and consoled himself with the many 'very gratifying comments showing the wisdom as well as the courage of refusing to make concessions'. He was particularly gratified by those from the City and the Governor of the Bank of England noting that it was 'almost the first honest Budget since the War'.[382] Besides bolstering confidence that there would be none of the irresponsible finance and unbalanced Budgets which had created the 1931 financial crisis, Chamberlain was also motivated by the conviction that Britain still needed to make 'further great economies'. As such, he was 'determined to give the grumblers a run for their money and make them face up to realities'. By being 'very cautious and guarded in [his] language', the intention was thus to create an atmosphere 'in which the disagreeable things become possible'.[383]

Chamberlain's problem was that his hopes of creating a suitable climate of opinion in which 'disagreeable things' became possible actually required

[377] N. Chamberlain to Ida, 5 March and to Hilda, 12 March 1932.

[378] Sir Clive Wigram to N. Chamberlain, 16 April 1932, NC7/11/25/49.

[379] MacDonald Diary, 19 April 1932, fol. 414.

[380] Headlam Diary, 19 and 20 April 1932, Ball (ed.), *Parliament and Politics*, p. 236.

[381] Jenkins, *The Chancellors*, p. 349.

[382] N. Chamberlain to Hilda, 23 April 1932; Montagu Norman to N. Chamberlain, 22 April 1932, NC8/16/4.

[383] N. Chamberlain to Hilda, 15 and 29 May 1932.

enormous forbearance and vision from Parliament and electors. Yet in reality, desperate economic conditions often fostered an ambivalence about dull but 'responsible' policy options which ended in an enthusiasm for more radical solutions. Chamberlain thus found himself assailed both by 'economisers' who advocated far greater budgetary severity and 'unbalancers' who believed that salvation depended on deficit finance to fund large-scale public works. Predictably, the 'economisers' were largely to be found on the government's own benches. Cuthbert Headlam spoke for many mainstream Tories when he lamented after the 1932 Budget that 'the Cabinet has not gone nearly far enough in economies … the truth of the matter is this Government like any ordinary government, funks taking a really strong line'.[384] When Chamberlain warned these critics during the debate on the Finance Bill that 'before embarking on serious changes of national policy … some hard thinking should be done',[385] the Conservative backbench 1922 Committee responded by establishing a subcommittee to achieve 'drastic public economy on a scale not yet contemplated'.[386] In the event, the report of 'The Economy Bunglers' was rudely brushed aside by both the Press and many Conservative backbenchers alarmed by the political implications of such draconian cuts. By this stage, however, the same government backbenchers had already lost their enthusiasm for Chamberlain's consistent message about the need for continued financial stringency. After one such gloomy exposition of government policy during a Labour censure debate in February 1933, even Chamberlain confessed to being 'a little depressed when after all the work I had put in on [the speech] I didn't succeed in carrying the sentiment of the House with me'.[387] Yet despite this conspicuously chilly response, Chamberlain soon recovered his usual equilibrium, confident in the knowledge that he had 'deliberately said unpleasant things because … it was necessary that people should be told the truth'. As he noted characteristically, 'they will presently see that I was right and respect me all the more for saying what others are afraid to say'.[388] Although he was so inspired by the need to tell the truth that he intended to make it a recurrent theme in his speeches thereafter,[389] even within the Cabinet the Chancellor's gloomy emphasis upon the obstacles to recovery was conceded to be 'unfortunate, and really unfair to himself', but a habit which reflected 'a fault more of manner than of argument'.[390]

---

[384] Headlam Diary, 26 April 1932, Ball (ed.), *Parliament and Politics*, pp. 236–37.

[385] *H.C. Debs.* 5s., 266, cols 2267–348, 10 June 1932.

[386] Philip Goodhart, *The 1922: The Story of the 1922 Committee* (London, 1973), pp. 52–62. Stuart Ball, 'The 1922 Committee: The Formative Years, 1922–1945', *Parliamentary History* 9 (1990), pp. 141–45.

[387] N. Chamberlain to Hilda, 18 February 1933. See also Headlam Diary, 16 February 1933, Ball (ed.), *Parliament and Politics*, p. 260; *The Annual Register, 1933* (1934), pp. 9–10, 20.

[388] N. Chamberlain to Hilda, 18 February 1933.

[389] Ibid.; N. Chamberlain to Arthur Chamberlain, 20 February 1933, NC7/11/26/9.

[390] Runciman to J.F. Simpson, 21 March 1933, Runciman MSS 265/26.

Chamberlain's second Budget on 25 April 1933 followed in 'an orderly and unexciting way' in the logical series from 1932 to 1935.[391] Confronted by what he believed to be an unparalleled level of 'barracking' and the demands for 'imaginative finance' and a fiscal stimulus, Chamberlain recognised that he would 'soon be the most unpopular man in the country' but he adamantly refused to yield.[392] There were thus no concessions on expenditure at the bottom of the slump and the Budget was notable only for a reduction in beer duty and the taxation of Co-operative Societies – the latter providing the only flash of controversy and interest during the otherwise 'calm and tranquil' progress of the Finance Bill.[393] Beneath the surface, however, although Chamberlain believed that the Budget had been received 'with general approval though without enthusiasm',[394] critical backbenchers lamented the Chancellor's Budget speech had been 'a cheerless performance and very distinctly depressed the House. Nor did the customary vindication of financial soundness, though acquiesced in by the House, evoke any applause at all. It was a pure Treasury Budget with no glimmering of any constructive solution for the economic problem'.[395]

Of all the aspects of Chamberlain's stewardship of the economy, this failure to deviate from an ostensibly severe balanced budget orthodoxy into the realms of large-scale public works to stimulate recovery has perhaps aroused most condemnation. For these critics, the maintenance of such a policy long after the crisis had passed suggests that the balanced budget had become 'a fetish to be worshipped in its own right regardless of circumstance'.[396] Even at the time, Chamberlain rapidly came under strong pressure to relax his iron grip on public expenditure as soon as the worst of the depression had passed. In November 1932 the Economic Advisory Council's Committee on Economic Information had noted signs of recovery and urged active support for public works to stimulate revival.[397] When nothing happened, they wrote to the Prime Minister with a vigorous plea for a radical change of policy. Conceding that the restoration of confidence in financial policy had been the 'paramount consideration' in 1931, the committee argued that in the past eighteen months the change in economic circumstances had been 'so radical as to amount to a complete transformation'. As a result, 'in accordance with the traditional precepts of trade cycle theory', they urged a substantial public expenditure stimulus 'to enable the forces of recuperation to gain the upper hand' at a time when the Chancellor's stringent

[391] Jenkins, *The Chancellors*, p. 351.

[392] N. Chamberlain to Hilda, 1 April 1933.

[393] Sabine, *British Budgets in Peace and War*, p. 29.

[394] Neville Chamberlain Diary, 8 May 1933.

[395] Amery Diary, 25 April 1933, John Barnes and David Nicholson (eds), *The Empire at Bay: The Leo Amery Diaries, 1929–1945* (London, 1988), p. 292. Headlam Diary, 25 April 1933, p. 267.

[396] Winch, *Economics and Policy*, p. 215.

[397] Committee on Economic Information: Fifth Report, 14 November 1932, CAB 58/30.

budgetary policy was acting as 'a definite adverse influence' upon recovery.[398] A month later, the already critical *Times* published four articles by Keynes also arguing that depressed business expectations required the Chancellor to pump £110 million worth of additional purchasing power into the economy through tax cuts and loan-financed public works to stimulate aggregate demand and assist in domestic and world reflation[399] – a lead which was subsequently endorsed by thirty-seven academic economists and was even taken up by the *Daily Express* and the *Mail*.[400] Shortly before the 1933 Budget even Sir Ralph Hawtrey, the Treasury's only professional economist, was saying that 'it was no use to imagine that anything could be done to set the economic situation right so long as the present people were in control at the Treasury and the Bank of England'.[401]

The compelling potency of these arguments for deficit finance gained considerably from the triumph of Keynesian economics during and after the Second World War. Moreover, in some respects Treasury opposition to public works in the 1930s does appear to have advanced very little since the Edwardian era in the belief that they simply diverted money from normal trade to abnormal relief works, were exceedingly expensive, difficult to organise and short term in their effects.[402] Yet, in fairness, indictments of Chamberlain's Chancellorship in this sphere often fail to understand his policy preferences and prejudices within the context of the fears, uncertainties and theory of his own time.[403] At one level, there can be no doubt that 'by temperament and conviction [Chamberlain] was as wedded to orthodoxy as Snowden'; an adherence to 'a hairshirt philosophy of economic policy' based partly on his view of budgetary policy as a 'quasi-moral issue'. From this perspective, policy-makers confronted a stark choice between the difficult path of fiscal rectitude with its attendant odium and the deceptively easy path along which lesser men might succumb to the temptation to seek popular solutions and peddle half-truths rather than face 'disagreeable' facts.[404] Yet while an excess of puritan zeal and temperament may help to explain the undeviating clarity of Chamberlain's tone, it does not entirely explain a policy preference for the appearance of balanced budgets which stemmed principally from a sincere belief that they would induce the confidence necessary for recovery while unbalanced budgets would retard or jeopardise that process. Moreover,

---

[398] CP 34(33), 'Financial Policy and Trade Activity', 15 February 1933, CAB 24/238.

[399] *The Times*, 13–16 March 1933. Expanded and reprinted as *The Means to Prosperity* (1933).

[400] *The Times*, 10 March 1933; Winch, *Economics and Policy*, p. 217.

[401] Amery Diary, 8 April 1933, Barnes and Nicholson (eds), *The Empire at Bay*, p. 292.

[402] Treasury memorandum, 'The Level of Prices as Effected by Monetary Policy', 29 September 1932, T172/1814.

[403] See Aldcroft, *The British Economy*, pp. 95–114 for a discussion of constraints.

[404] Middleton, *Towards the Managed Economy*, pp. 114–15. For lesser men and disagreeable facts see N. Chamberlain to Hilda, 18 February and 1 April 1933 and to Arthur Chamberlain, 20 February 1933, NC7/11/26/9.

during the 1930s a variety of additional factors substantially reinforced Chamberlain's profound instinctive scepticism about public works and the economics of budgetary expansion.

Firstly, there was the problem of deciding whose alternative theory to embrace. It was a good joke to claim that 'where five economists are gathered together there will be six conflicting opinions and two of them will be held by Keynes!', but its pungency was derived from its underlying grain of truth at a time when his ideas were still evolving.[405] As a senior Treasury official warned the Chancellor in October 1932, 'there is no criterion for determining the proper economists to follow, and whoever one chooses, one is apt to find oneself led into actions which are either repugnant to commonsense or incapable of practical achievement'.[406] From Chamberlain's perspective, both objections applied powerfully to Keynesian nostrums in 1932–33. As John Ramsden shrewdly notes, the adoption of an expansionist policy may have led to financial crisis, 'not because it is wrong, but because it was *believed* to be wrong',[407] at a time when 'the canons of financial rectitude were so deeply engrained within society that any attempt to resort to unusual financial practices would create renewed worries about British financial integrity, the strength of the currency, fear of inflation and the prospects of a flight of capital, which would have brought back "the nightmare of recession"'.[408]

Secondly, the problems of theory became even greater when applied to their practical translation into policy. In retrospect, it is clear that public works on the scale of Lloyd George's 1929 programme would have been far too small to have dealt with the subsequent increase in unemployment. They would also have encountered major balance of payments problems and near insuperable practical and administrative constraints beyond the power and authority of a democratic state to overcome.[409] Furthermore, recent calculations of the likely employment multiplier effect suggests that to deal effectively with 3 million unemployed the government needed to expend anything between £537 million and £752 million – sums which represent an equivalent of at least half of the total budgetary outlay in 1932 and between 14 and 19.3 per cent of GNP.[410] Even excluding the question of where such funds would come from in a bond market where interest rates were at rock bottom, a deficit of this level must have represented a major

---

[405] Thomas Jones to his daughter, 20 October 1931, Thomas Jones, *A Diary with Letters, 1931–1950* (London, 1954), p. 19.

[406] Sir Richard Hopkins to Chancellor of Exchequer, 20 October 1932, T175/70.

[407] Ramsden, *Age of Balfour and Baldwin*, p. 339.

[408] Aldcroft, *The British Economy*, p. 105.

[409] Roger Middleton, 'The Treasury in the 1930s: Political and Administrative Constraints to the Acceptance of the "New" Economics', *Oxford Economic Papers* 34 (1982), pp. 48–77 and 'The Treasury and Public Investment: A Perspective on Inter-War Economic Management', *Public Administration* 61 (1983), pp. 351–70.

[410] Aldcroft, *The British Economy*, pp. 110–12.

threat to confidence given the fact that a projected deficit of £120 million in 1931 had brought the entire financial system to the edge of the abyss.

A third problem was that international lessons proved no more attractive for the Chancellor's view of deficit finance and public works, contrary to the view of many later economic historians. Even if it is accepted that policies abroad, particularly in Sweden and the United States, demonstrate that unorthodox budgetary policies did not automatically lead to financial disaster, the Treasury's observation at the time suggested that they would be more likely to precipitate another crisis of confidence than lead Britain on to the road to recovery.[411] In his 1933 Budget statement, Chamberlain thus devoted four columns of Hansard to his reasons for adamantly rejecting pressure to unbalance the Budget in favour of 'imaginative finance': a case based largely on the fact that badly unbalanced Budgets were 'the rule rather than the exception', but that such states had not enjoyed the benefits the expansionists had claimed but rather deepening depression, falling price levels and 'the fear that things are going to get worse'. In contrast, Chamberlain claimed that Britain had 'stood the test with the greatest measure of success' and was free from such fears largely because it had balanced the Budget and pursued a sound financial policy.[412] In drawing this international comparison, Chamberlain had been accused of 'crude empiricism'.[413] Yet whether fair or not, his profoundly contemptuous view of Roosevelt and the New Deal was echoed by both Cabinet colleagues and by his key Treasury advisers. After war debt discussions with the President, both the British Ambassador and the government's Chief Economic Adviser concluded independently that Roosevelt was completely out of his depth with economic and financial questions.[414] It was scarcely surprising that Chamberlain subscribed to a similar view. In his assessment of the New Deal to Cabinet in October 1933, Chamberlain had thus employed a supremely dismissive analogy which represented 'the Yanks as a barbarous tribe and Roosevelt as a medicine man whose superiority over other medicine men consisted in the astonishing agility with which when one kind of Mumbo Jumbo failed, he produced another'.[415] In 1935, Leith-Ross provided an equally typical response to Lloyd George's call for a British version of the New Deal:

> In the United States ... gambling holds much the same place in national life as cricket does in ours. Nothing, therefore, is more natural than that the American government should indulge in a gamble while a British government has to keep a straight bat and sometimes to stone wall. Such tactics may not appeal to those spectators who have more enthusiasm than knowledge of the pitch, but it is to be

---

[411] For these fears see N. Chamberlain to Hilda, 24 June 1933 and to Ida, 28 October 1933.
[412] *H.C. Debs.* 5s., 277, cols 57–61, 25 April 1933.
[413] Middleton, *Towards the Managed Economy*, p. 115.
[414] See CP 29(33), 10 February 1933 and Appendix to CAB 65(33)1, 29 November 1933.
[415] N. Chamberlain to Ida, 28 October 1933.

hoped that the barracking will not affect the batsmen. For the state of England is not such that they can afford to take great risks.[416]

Although it is tempting to sneer at the sporting metaphors and misplaced superiority, as Chamberlain never tired of saying both in public and in private, it was easy for others without direct responsibility to demand 'imaginative finance', but as Chancellor he had to be 'very sure that the old principles have really failed before we abandon them, and that new experiments are really likely to succeed before we venture to embark upon them'.[417] Convinced that balanced budgets paved the way for cheap money and that this (in conjunction with tariffs) was already producing recovery, the instinct for cautious national self-preservation became almost irresistible.

A fourth constraint upon the Chancellor was that the Treasury were less convinced that the economy had turned the corner to sustained recovery in 1933 than the Committee on Economic Information and his other critics.[418] Moreover, even if Britain was through the worst, the unsettled state of the world economy offered little certainty that it would not be plunged into another crisis as suddenly as in August 1931. Contemplating a decline in revenue during 1932, he thus warned that it was 'most important not to do anything which would give the impression that the bad times are over and we can begin to slack off our efforts'.[419] By sustaining the impression that the budgetary crisis had never subsided, Chamberlain thus found both a justification for the rigour of his orthodoxy and a longer-term opportunity to build national finances into such an unassailable position that a progressive relaxation of the fiscal stance would eventually become possible as the crowning culmination of his Chancellorship.[420] Finally, on top of all these economic factors, during the worst of the slump in 1932 and 1933 Chamberlain was also increasingly mindful of the adverse effects of a reflationary cut in income tax on war debt negotiations, and specifically 'on the mind of the Middle Western Farmer!'[421]

Despite the criticism of those bored with sound finance or actively committed to budgetary expansion, therefore, Chamberlain was resolutely determined to resist pressure from reflationists and the 'pontifical scolding' of *The Times* in favour of an unbalanced Budget.[422] On 17 March 1933, the day after the last of his articles in *The Times*, Keynes spent an hour with Chamberlain during which

[416] G.C. Peden, *British Economic and Social Policy: Lloyd George to Margaret Thatcher* (Oxford, 1985), p. 118.

[417] Speech at Lord Mayor of London's dinner in his honour, 1933. Walker-Smith, *Neville Chamberlain*, pp. 181–82.

[418] Hopkins to the Chancellor, 16 February 1933, T175/93.

[419] N. Chamberlain to MacDonald, 6 September 1932, MacDonald MSS 30/69/2/12 II.

[420] CAB 68(33)5, 6 December 1933, CAB 23/77.

[421] N. Chamberlain to Ida, 25 February 1933.

[422] Ibid. For *The Times* criticism in its leaders see Winch, *Economics and Policy*, p. 217.

he warned that 'the more pessimistic the Chancellor's policy, the more likely it is that pessimistic anticipations will be realised and vice versa. Whatever the Chancellor dreams, will come true'.[423] For his part, Chamberlain found Keynes's ideas 'even worse than [he] had supposed', but he noted shrewdly that 'the trouble is that he is so plausible & confident that people like the ordinary back bencher who have not much knowledge are very likely to be attracted especially when he is backed so strenuously by the Times':[424] a suspicion of future trouble confirmed by Baldwin's own anxiety about the backbench unrest already provoked by support for Keynes's articles.[425] Indeed, even the Chancellor's own half-brother had been briefly attracted by these ideas before the cautious side of his nature made him draw back when it became evident that 'it would be a pure gamble which might well end in disaster'.[426] Chamberlain was equally concerned by the launch of Roosevelt's New Deal, on the grounds that if it succeeded it 'will be embarrassing because people will want to know why I haven't done the same'.[427] From the outset, however, he anticipated that it would fail to produce the desired recovery and the slump on the New York Stock Exchange in July 1933 thus provoked some savage amusement when it 'absolutely silenced the critics who were asking why our Chancellor could not be brave as well as wise like the American President'. As time exposed further dangers of the New Deal, he thus believed 'our people may gradually come to realise that our slower and less sensational methods are more satisfactory in the long run'.[428] While Chamberlain remained Chancellor this policy priority would not change, as Lloyd George found to his cost when he attempted to foist a similar scheme for a New Deal on the National Government in January 1935.[429]

In fairness, notwithstanding his profound personal animus towards Lloyd George and contempt for Roosevelt's economic understanding, Chamberlain's opposition to expansionist adventures should not be taken to imply a dogged adherence to the canons of nineteenth-century financial orthodoxy. On the contrary, the years after 1932 witnessed a number of major departures from orthodoxy at the Treasury. With regard to debt management policy, the Treasury suspended its Sinking Fund provision in 1933 and continued the practice throughout the 1930s. In 1932 a completely new departure was also made with regard to forward budgetary planning when Chamberlain instructed the Treasury to compile an 'Old Moore's Almanack' with detailed estimates of the scope for fiscal relaxation leading up to 1935. From

---

[423] Skidelsky, *John Maynard Keynes*, II, p. 474.

[424] N. Chamberlain to Hilda, 18 March 1933. For the Treasury response to Keynes's articles see items in T175/17.

[425] N. Chamberlain to Ida, 25 March 1933.

[426] A. Chamberlain to Ida, 30 April 1933, AC5/1/615, Self (ed.), *Austen Chamberlain*, p. 438.

[427] N. Chamberlain to Hilda, 24 June 1933.

[428] N. Chamberlain to Hilda, 23 July and to Ida, 28 October 1933.

[429] Nick Smart, *The National Government, 1931–40* (London, 1999), pp. 106–10.

1933 onwards, Chamberlain also actively engaged in 'fiscal window dressing' in order to shroud deficits with the appearance of balanced budgeting without the full deflationary reality. Similarly, recognising that a further tightening of the fiscal stance was impracticable given the prevailing mood of pessimism which threatened recovery, the Treasury had adopted a 'very negative reaction' to the Ray Committee's recommendations on local expenditure which entailed controversial cuts of £35–40 million without any reference to their likely consequences. Thus, as Roger Middleton argues persuasively, the orthodoxy which infuriated many contemporaries (and subsequent historians) provided 'an excellent shield for his less orthodox actions' which were simultaneously radical but 'subtle [and] largely invisible to those outside the Treasury and Cabinet'.[430]

By the same token, Chamberlain's orthodox language, opposition to deliberately unbalanced budgets and confidence in the 'natural' process of recovery should not obscure his support for other forms of direct State intervention and public expenditure to assist the economy. Chamberlain had never been a blinkered enthusiast of the untrammelled sanctity of the free market. On the contrary, throughout his political career he had rejoiced when condemned as 'a rank socialist' by old Tories alarmed by his radical views on State intervention to restrict the market mechanism and curb the freedom of private enterprise.[431] During the 1930s these radical instincts remained active, as he demonstrated by his enthusiasm for the potentialities of IDAC and marketing boards and other restrictionist strategies designed to raise world wholesale prices. Moreover, at precisely the time he opposed deficit finance, Chamberlain had played a pivotal role in forcing through the construction of the uncompleted *Queen Mary* and the merger of the Cunard and White Star Lines in order to create a single powerful British force capable of dominating the North Atlantic trade, not as a disquieting exercise in misplaced 'sentimentality', as Cabinet opponents claimed,[432] but rather because he had always 'been after much larger game'. 'To my mind this is an excellent example of how National financial resources can & should be used to remove an otherwise insuperable obstacle to the effective working of private enterprise'.[433] To do so by unbalancing the Budget and at the risk of national credit and confidence, however, was an entirely different matter.

Despite the persistence of high levels of unemployment in the depressed areas and staple trades, Chamberlain's confidence in the efficacy of his own measures

---

[430] Middleton, *Towards the Managed Economy*, pp. 104, 114, 115, 209.

[431] See N. Chamberlain to Hilda, 2, 15 March 1919 and 12 July 1924, Self (ed.), *Neville Chamberlain Diary Letters*, I, pp. 311–14 and II, p. 237.

[432] Runciman to MacDonald, 12 August 1933, Runciman MSS 265/67. Also CAB 49(33)2 and CAB 69(33)4, 28 July and 13 December 1933.

[433] N. Chamberlain to Ida, 17 December 1933. For his full case for this intervention see N. Chamberlain to Runciman, 27 August 1933, Runciman MSS 265/62 and CAB 69(33)4, 13 December 1933.

soon appeared to be vindicated. As early as May 1932 the Committee on Economic Information reported that without 'the threatening international outlook, there would be … substantial grounds for confidence in the position of Great Britain', given improved competitive power and an almost unique level of domestic stability and financial confidence.[434] Certainly, the period from September 1932 until 1934 witnessed a continuous and accelerating recovery before it slowed somewhat during 1934 and most of 1935. Reporting a rise in wholesale prices, record low levels in short-term interest rates, rising industrial production and the achievement of equilibrium in the balance of payments, in his 1934 Budget the Chancellor declared with a Dickensian flourish that 'we have now finished the story of *Bleak House* and are sitting down this afternoon to enjoy the first chapter of *Great Expectations*'.[435] Confident of recovery, Chamberlain finally felt able to ease the fiscal burden and to restore half of the cuts imposed in 1931. In Chamberlain's mind this was the direct outcome of a preconceived plan, relating both to economic management and the most effective presentation of that policy, which stretched back to the very start of his Chancellorship. As he explained revealingly to the Cabinet in December 1933:

> when he took office he had made it his definite aim, in dealing with national finance, to build up the resources of the nation until they were in an unassailable condition. He had wanted to demonstrate the strengthening of the national resources by progressive remissions in successive Budgets. So far he had been successful in carrying out that policy. It had been almost an essential of that policy that his first Budget should be an unpopular one. His second Budget had been a little better, and he hoped his third would be better still. To complete the policy it was important to avoid an anti-climax in his fourth Budget …[436]

Such claims owed nothing to *ex post facto* rationalisation. In order to achieve this goal, the Chancellor had instructed the Treasury in March 1932 to plan for a reduction of taxation and an increase in expenditure over a three- to four-year period.[437] Having reconciled himself to harsh measures and personal unpopularity in the early years, as the economy recovered Chamberlain's posture as the courageous and incorruptible saviour of the nation's finances only further reinforced his status as the driving force behind the National Government and as a future Prime Minister. From this position, Chamberlain had every reason to believe that it would be but a short step to the Premiership itself.

---

[434] CP 161(32), EAC: Third Report of the Committee on Economic Information: Survey of Economic Situation, 25 May 1932, para. 13, CAB 24/230.

[435] *H.C. Debs.* 5s., 288, col. 903, 17 April 1934.

[436] CAB 68(33)5, 6 December 1933, CAB 23/77. Also MacDonald Diary, 6 December 1933.

[437] Hopkins to the Chancellor, 'Speculative Forecast of 1935 on the Basis of "Old Moore's Almanack"', 21 March 1932, T188/48.

2

1928

'Winston's Plan ... Changes Like a Kaleidoscope': Derating and the Battle for Local Government Reform

22 January 1928
Westbourne
Edgbaston

My dear Hilda,

...

... I think both Annie & I are distinctly better for our holiday; at any rate all my friends remark upon my healthy appearance and she says her nerves are quieted down so the trip appears to have fulfilled its main purpose and has moreover given us some fresh ideas and interests.

I forget if I told you of the negotiations for the purchase of Elliotts ordinary shares by Imperial Chemical Industries. The terms which are advantageous to Elliotts have now been agreed by the Directors & assuming they are endorsed by the shareholders they will go through. They will not make me richer but they will enable me to spread my interests over a wider field as there is a much bigger market in I.C.I. than in Elliotts and I was getting a little anxious at having so large a part of my capital in one concern over which I no longer retained any control. But sentimentally I cannot help regretting a change which destroys the individuality of the old firm and of course alters the prospects for Frank.[1] He might still find employment there but it cannot be the same thing as I had imagined at one time.

Hoskins people appear more hopeful about the future and they have a fair amount of work on hand & in prospect. But prices are very low and the first half of their year which begins on the first of August shows no better results than last. So the prospects of a resumption of dividends are not very hopeful.

The Winstonian scheme [for rating reform] seemed very near death when I went away but it has revived during my absence and a preliminary description has received very favourable consideration from the Cabinet. We shall examine it in Committee and my endeavour must be to tie P.L. on to it if it is not postponed to a later date.

---

[1] Frank Chamberlain (1914–65). See Appendix I: 'The Chamberlain Household and Family'.

Northampton[2] is considered very encouraging not only because we can say with fair plausibility that we should have won it if Hailwood had not intervened but because the Liberal vote dropped below Labour by 5000. I hear that the Liberals are very downhearted and that Rothermere[3] is thinking of dropping Ll.G.![4]

...

18 March 1928
Westbourne

My dear Hilda,

So many weeks have gone by since I last wrote that it is difficult to remember where we were then or how far we have got since in our sporadic and interrupted meetings. But I dont think it is any use going back further than last week.

...

Did you hear that the wretched Orpen[5] failed Annie a second time. A second time we had invited a small & select party to meet him and at the last moment he wrote to say he was ill & could neither lunch nor paint. I have since been told that he gets fits of this kind when he is going to paint a picture: apparently its a form of nerves. He must be a true artist but I wonder whether he will ever paint my portrait. I fixed March because it was the easiest month in which to spare the time, now it has more than half gone and nothing done.

I had a weary day on Tuesday listening to the Labour members steady stream of irrelevant sobstuff mingled with abuse of the Minister of Health. Their gross exaggerations, their dishonesty in slurring over facts that tell against them, and their utter inability to appreciate a reasonable argument do embitter my soul sometimes & if I seem hard and unsympathetic to them it is the reaction brought about by their own attitude. But I suspect that with certain exceptions they dont hate me as much as they are supposed to ...

There have been stormy times this week but they have ended in a lull if not a calm.

------

[2] Northampton by-election, 9 January 1928. A Conservative majority of 971 in 1924 was turned into a Labour majority of 557 through the intervention of E.A. Hailwood as an Independent Conservative who received 1093 votes.

[3] Harold Sidney Harmsworth (1868–1940). Northcliffe's brother. Proprietor, *Daily Mirror* 1914–31; *Daily Mail*, *Evening News* and Associated Newspapers Ltd 1922–40; Secretary for Air 1917–18. Created Baron Rothermere 1914 and Viscount 1919.

[4] David Lloyd George (1863–1945). Liberal MP for Caernarvon Boroughs 1890–1945. President, Board of Trade 1906–8; Chancellor of Exchequer 1908–15; Minister of Munitions 1915–16; Secretary for War 1916; Prime Minister 1916–22. Created Earl Lloyd-George of Dwyfor 1945.

[5] William Orpen (1878–1931). Irish painter. War artist and official painter at Paris Peace Conference. Famous for portraits. Knighted 1918.

Eaton Square ... Thank you for your birthday wishes. My family make such a fuss about it that it cannot be ignored and though I do not think that one can be congratulated on one's near approach to the age of 60 there are many compensations for the loss of youth in family affection and a more philosophical and less agitated mentality. It is a great happiness to me that you & Ida have not been pushed out of my life by my marriage; for that we must largely be grateful to Annie who has a "genius for friendship". We have missed your letters quite uncomfortably since you have been in London.

I was just beginning to tell you of the troubles of the week. I have been urging a certain modification of the "plan". Winston[6] began by thinking it made so small a change that with it he would buy my support dirt cheap. Consultation with the Eminence Grise of the Treasury however caused him to declare that it impugned a fundamental principle. Submitted to the Committee they declared in effect that they didn't quite understand it, but if the M/H wanted it they would support him as he had to do the difficult part of the job. W. was upset at this and asked that a final decision might be postponed to last Monday. I readily agreed but imagine my wrath & indignation at finding he had circulated on *Saturday* a fresh memorandum violently attacking my proposal. I went to the meeting in a high state of indignation and hit back as hard as I could finishing up with the flat statement that if the Committee now went against me I shd tell the Cabinet that I would not undertake negotiations on such lines. This was a bombshell and the Committee hastily adjourned the discussion on that part of the subject. The next day I had a long letter from W. He was concerned, startled, puzzled. Why was I so chilly? Why was he left so lonely in the shafts? Would I come & see him. I couldn't at the moment. Instead I sent a reply which Annie thought "rather strong" though the P.M. says W. was very pleased with it. The next day I went; he was almost elaborately forthcoming and friendly. He had handled the thing badly. He would always see me privately in future before fighting in Committee. He recognised that I must be the final arbiter. On my side I seized the opportunity to do some plain talking. For the first time I almost monopolised the conversation and we parted amicably with a clearer understanding of my difficulties and perhaps of my character. The plan is a gamble; I am trying at least to reduce the risks but I cannot be as enthusiastic about it as about my own scheme which it supersedes.

---

[6] Winston Leonard Spencer Churchill (1874–1965). Conservative MP for Oldham 1900–1904 (as a Liberal 1904–6). Liberal MP for Manchester North-West 1906–8 and Dundee 1908–22. Conservative MP for Epping 1924–45 and Woodford 1945–64. Under-Secretary for Colonies 1905–8; President, Board of Trade 1908–10; Home Secretary 1910–11; First Lord of Admiralty 1911–15 and 1939–40; Chancellor, Duchy of Lancaster 1915; Minister of Munitions 1917–19; Secretary for War and Air 1919–21; Colonial Secretary 1921–22; Chancellor of Exchequer 1924–29; Prime Minister 1940–45 and 1951–55. Minister of Defence 1940–45 and 1951–52. Created KG 1953.

We went to Winchester last week. ... I enjoyed seeing Frank and I had satisfactory talks with his housemaster whom I like very much. It is evident to me that life is very different for Frank from what mine was at school. ...

I had a terrible dinner to attend on Saturday from 7 to 11.15! I thought it would never end. But today has been lovely. The crocuses were blazing at Westbourne under the azaleas, in the grass & over the south border. Apiculata Sancta Godseffire and Oppositifolia are flowering as they never have before and the Cymbidiums are superb. I have been trying to photograph them experimenting with a colour filter, but I made a dreadful lot of mistakes.

This afternoon I went a longish walk with Platten and still wonder at the limberness of my knees after it. I am busy selling out my shares in I.C.I. and reinvesting elsewhere. P's account of what has happened there does not increase my confidence in these huge unwieldly [sic] concerns. It is rather tragic that Elliotts should have been absorbed into the colossus because they had not got a strong enough personnel to stand up on their own.

   ...

24 March 1928
Westbourne

My dear Ida,

   ...

You do seem to have had a heavy week and I dont wonder you were a bit worried over it but I congratulate you on your successful presentation of Estimates. There is nothing like thorough preparation of your subject to get things through especially at the beginning. You build up a reputation in that way so that people come to assume that you know what you are talking about and in the end it saves you trouble because your word is taken and you are not subjected to the questioning which is inevitable where there is no confidence. Rating in particular is so technical that few people will take the trouble to master it and I reckon I have got my R.&V. Bill through so easily simply on my reputation, so that the Labour Party have never found out what the real weakness of our position was and have persistently barked up the wrong tree.

I am glad to hear there are signs of movement in Rural Housing. We have got a debate coming on in the House about it soon and I hope it will show that if it has not yet acquired much momentum it is not a dead letter. I believe in some Scotch counties it has really gone quite well.

The Zinovieff debate went very well. Stanley[7] did not make his points quite as pointedly as he might have done but the revelation of the informant of the D.M.

---

[7] Stanley Baldwin (1867–1947). Conservative MP for Bewdley 1908–37. Joint Financial Secretary

was a bombshell and Douglas Hogg[8] fairly pounded Ramsay[9] to a jelly at the end of the evening. I am sure Ramsay would be glad never to hear the name of Zinovieff again.

On Tuesday we dined at Admiralty House to meet their Majesties. The party went off extremely well and we all enjoyed ourselves right ealong [sic]. The King[10] was in great spirits roaring with laughter & jabbing the first Sea Lord in the ribs with immense gusto. ...

Last night I came down with Sam Hoare[11] who was addressing the Conservative Club & spent the night here and tonight I have been dining with the Birmingham agents. Most of them have been changed lately and we have really got quite a good team now. I spoke to them collectively and afterwards had a private talk with each of them, eleven in all. I was encouraged on the whole. We shall have a tough job to keep some of the seats but I am hopeful of preserving Ladywood and winning Kings Norton provided we dont strike some new trouble in the meantime.

That brings up Winston's plan. It changes like a kaleidoscope so that even now I dont know what form it will take when it comes before the Cabinet on Thursday. But I am *not* looking forward to this week as I shall have to take my decision whether I am going to support the Chancellor oppose him or press for modifications. A great responsibility rests on me for half the Cabinet dont in the least understand the question (including the P.M.) and I believe they really rely on me to give them the lead. At this moment Winston is under the impression that he has squared me but till I see the final form I dont know whether he has or not and I much fear it will not be possible for me to give my convinced & enthusiastic approbation.

---

to Treasury 1917–21; President, Board of Trade 1921–22; Chancellor of Exchequer 1922–23; Prime Minister 1923–24, 1924–29, 1935–37; Lord President of the Council 1931–35. Created KG and Earl Baldwin of Bewdley 1937.

[8] Douglas McGarel Hogg (1872–1950). Conservative MP for St Marylebone 1922–28. Attorney-General 1922–24, 1924–28; Lord Chancellor 1928–29, 1935–38; Secretary for War 1931–35; Lord President 1938; Conservative Leader in the Lords 1931–35. Knighted 1922. Created Baron Hailsham 1928 and Viscount 1929.

[9] James Ramsay MacDonald (1866–1937). Labour MP for Leicester 1906–18, Aberavon 1922–29, Seaham 1929–31; National Labour MP for Seaham 1931–35 and Scottish Universities 1936–37. Labour Party Secretary 1900–1912; Chairman 1912–14 and Leader 1922–31. Prime Minister and Foreign Secretary 1924; Prime Minister 1929–35; Lord President 1935–37.

[10] George Frederick Ernest (1865–1936). Created Prince of Wales 1901; succeeded as King George V 1910.

[11] Samuel John Gurney Hoare (1880–1959). Conservative MP for Chelsea 1910–44. Secretary for Air 1922–24, 1924–29, 1940. Secretary for India 1931–35; Foreign Secretary 1935; First Lord of Admiralty 1936–37; Home Secretary 1937–39; Lord Privy Seal 1939–40. Ambassador in Madrid 1940–44. Conservative Party Treasurer 1930–31. Succeeded as Bart 1915. Created Viscount Templewood 1944.

On Monday I have to take a debate in the House but about Tuesday I shall have to see the P.M. and give him my views.

...

31 March 1928
Westbourne

My dear Hilda,

...

You are right about Douglas Hogg. I regard his promotion as rather a calamity and it was all rushed through in a very unfortunate way. He had always told me that he would want my advice before he decided but on Friday the 23rd the P.M. sent for him & after telling him that F.E.[12] had refused represented that it was inevitable that he should take it. Douglas was taken aback and felt he ought not to refuse when it was put that way and though he didn't think he had quite committed himself he admitted when he came to see me on .... [sic] that he had not been quite definite in saying what he would do. I strongly urged him to delay and said I would ask the P.M. to press F.E. again, but on Wednesday morning I found it was too late as S.B. had already given the Attorney Generalship to Inskip[13] and made Merriman[14] Solicitor. Poor Douglas was very unhappy for he had realised that when it came to the point he wanted to continue his political career and of course the tragedy is that he is now barred from the chance of becoming P.M. when S.B. retires. To my mind this is a great misfortune for I believe he would have had a very good chance and I am sure he is the best man we have for such a position. You speak as though he would no longer be a member of the Cabinet. Of course that is not so. He will still be there but naturally as Lord Chancellor he will tend to drift out of party politics and to consider himself as at the top of his career.

He and I have been very close together on nearly every point that has arisen and I have a very high opinion of his character & judgement. I would gladly

---

[12] Frederick Edwin Smith (1872–1930). Conservative MP for Liverpool Walton 1906–18 and Liverpool West Derby 1918–19. Solicitor-General 1915; Attorney-General 1915–19; Lord Chancellor 1919–22; Secretary for India 1924–28. Knighted 1915. Created Bart 1918, Baron Birkenhead 1919, Viscount 1921 and Earl of Birkenhead 1922.

[13] Thomas Walker Hobart Inskip (1876–1947). Conservative MP for Bristol Central 1918–29, Fareham 1931–39. Solicitor-General 1922–24, 1924–28, 1931–32; Attorney-General 1928–29, 1932–36; Minister for Coordination of Defence 1936–39; Dominion Secretary 1939, 1940; Lord Chancellor 1939–40; Lord Chief Justice 1940–46. Knighted 1922. Created Viscount Caldecote 1939.

[14] Frank Boyd Merriman (1880–1962). Conservative MP for Manchester Rusholme 1924–33. Member, Lord Chancellor's Committee on Arbitration 1926; Solicitor-General 1928–29 and 1932–33; High Court Judge and President, Probate, Divorce and Admiralty Division of High Court 1933–62. Knighted 1928. Created Baron Merriman 1941.

serve under him as I believe he would under me but I have never regarded him as a rival having no ambition to become P.M. myself and I have on the other hand always looked on him as a man who might well stand between us and a Churchillian domination which would be a very dangerous contingency. I feel very unhappy about it, and all the more because S.B. admitted to me afterwards that F.E. would have gone back to the Woolsack if he had been pressed. But I think he was afraid of possible scandals.

I have had a very harassing time over the scheme, and have even contemplated resignation though the P.M. says the Cabinet would never let me go. But I have been pushed very hard and W.C. has succeeded in winning over all the members of the Committee who were not themselves concerned with Local Government. Fortunately I have succeeded in gaining the adherence of Sir J. Gilmour[15] and we have dug ourselves in and after sustaining a prolonged barrage have presented a minority report which will be considered by the Cabinet on Monday. I am not looking forward to the battles which will ensue but I am determined not to give way and the result must be either that the scheme will be abandoned or more probably that that [sic] a compromise will be found and a modified plan adopted which Gilmour & I can accept. Even then it wont be plain sailing because when the inevitable opposition develops we shall be reproached with having taken out all the drive and there will always be the possibility that the Cabinet will run away and leave us to manage the cart as best we may. It is a trying thing to run in harness with "banditti".[16]

I addressed my future constituents here on Friday, and ever since I have been working at my new Health Insurance Bill the Second Reading of which comes on Tuesday afternoon. It is one of those particularly tedious measures which consists in an endless succession of small amendments without any large general principles and without any novel and striking features. Really it is of great importance for the smoother working of the huge Health Insurance machine with its 7000 Approved Societies & Branches dispensing £30 millions a year in small amounts hardly ever exceeding £1. But it requires prolonged study to master the detail and it is impossible to make it interesting except to those who are actually engaged in its administration. I shall be glad when Thursday night comes and I escape to the solitude of my beloved Dee for I have got a tough week before me. In addition to the Cabinets of which there will be several and which naturally carry some anxiety with them I have got two sittings of the Standing Comee on the Metrop. Common Poor Fund which are highly

---

[15] John Gilmour (1876–1940). Conservative MP for Renfrewshire East 1910–18 and Glasgow Pollock 1918–40. Unionist Whip 1913–15 and 1919; Junior Lord of Treasury 1921–22 and 1923–24; Scottish Whip 1923; Scottish Secretary 1924–29; Minister of Agriculture 1931–32; Home Secretary 1932–35; Minister of Shipping 1939–40. Succeeded as Bart 1920.

[16] Baldwin's name for Churchill and Birkenhead, see Chamberlain to Lord Irwin, Christmas Day 1927, Irwin MSS Eur.c. 152/17/277a.

controversial, a Public Dinner (Metropolitan Water Board) on Monday the Health Insurance Bill on Tuesday a motion on Rural Housing on Wednesday and a debate upon the wickedness of Guardians who employ stone breaking as a task on Thursday!

...

15 April 1928
Westbourne

My dear Hilda,

I too have no epoch making news to give you; only a chat for a few minutes. But there is no need to apologise. Man does not live by news alone and your appreciation of the qualities of my family is very agreeable – none the less so because I have the comfortable feeling that it is *not*! exaggerated even by the partiality of an aunt! Dorothy[17] is all you say of her and in addition her piano playing is good enough now to give real pleasure. As for Frank he is very slow to develop and I feel that one cannot yet speak with certainty of his future. That he will be intelligent truthful sincere and affectionate I am quite certain; what is not yet clear is what initiative, power of taking responsibility and leadership he will acquire. At present his shyness keeps him rather in the background and the fact of his being younger than Dorothy tends to incline him to follow her. But when I look back on my own boyhood I seem to myself to have been an even more timid reserved self conscious boy than Frank. Yet all the time there was a hard core in me that only appeared when circumstances for the time cut away the covering. My experiences in the Bahamas must have exercised a great effect in showing me this core and giving me more self confidence. Probably Frank wont have any such testing time; in fact he has been brought up much "softer" than I was and I wonder sometimes if we aren't spoiling the man in sparing the child. But I think one can only go on watching carefully & keeping a look out for opportunities of making him fend for himself.

...

Having at length finished reading Froude[18] (12 volumes! but intensely interesting) I have started on Grey's[19] "Charm of Birds". If you have not read it I must really lend it you for I am sure you would enjoy it. To me it is especially

---

[17] Dorothy Chamberlain (1911–92). See Appendix I: 'The Chamberlain Household and Family'.

[18] James Anthony Froude (1818–94). English man of letters and historian. Contributed to *Fraser's Magazine* and *Westminster Review* from 1848. Professor of Modern History at Oxford from 1892. Author of many highly impressionistic studies including a twelve-volume *History of England from the Fall of Wolsley to the Spanish Armada*.

[19] Edward Grey (1862–1933). Liberal MP for Berwick-on-Tweed 1885–1916. Under-Secretary, Foreign Affairs 1892–95; Foreign Secretary 1905–16. Succeeded as 3rd Bart 1882. Created Viscount Grey of Falloden 1916. Author, *The Charm of Birds* (1927).

delightful in its description and analysis of the songs of the common birds. Grey remarks truly how few people can distinguish them or pay more than the most general attention to them. He says that until he grew to manhood he only knew two songs, the robin's and "thrushes – and – blackbirds" which he did not distinguish. Stanley Baldwin is just like that. But Grey's descriptions took me back to my youth at Highbury. I suppose when I was 19 or 20 and I began to pay attention to bird songs and got up at 5 o'clock in the morning to identify the singers. I remember making exactly the same discoveries as Grey – learning the difference between the blackcap & garden warbler, being astounded at the disproportion between the size of the wren and the volume and vehemence of its song, puzzling over the two utterly different voices of the woodwren. I have never seen any description which so happily conveys the quality of these songs and the impression they make on the listener. ...

My holiday has not been as successful as on many former occasions partly owing to Miss Robinson's[20] illness (she was in bed upstairs all the time & continually having alarming symptoms) but very largely owing to the weather which was beastly. ... Add to that that I did very badly with the salmon, losing 12 and landing only 3 and you have sufficient explanation of the feeling that oppressed me when I came away that my holiday had not come up to my expectations. I dont go through the agonies that some people do when I lose a salmon. I am very disappointed but I know that I must lose some and I soon put the incident out of my mind. This time however I was obviously doing something wrong. I was fishing with much larger hooks than usual on account of the floods and I believe I did not strike hard enough. But unluckily by the time I had made up my mind what the fault was and how to correct it the cold had come and driven the salmon to the bottom so that I got no opportunity of testing my theory. That's the worst of such a short spell.

...

I have got a horrible session in front of me. Winston will do all the prancing and I shall do all the drudgery. It includes interviews with the Press, broadcasting & phonofilm as well as a dreary rating Bill! And of course I never feel quite sure of getting P.L. Reform through. While I was in Scotland W. started another hare & wrote me a long letter to suggest that there was no reason why I should object. But ... I wrote back to say that I did object & at the same time warned off the P.M. Since I returned I hear that the President of the Bd of Trade also objected and the hare has retired into its form!

---

[20] Miss C.E. Robinson. Chamberlain's secretary for thirteen years until April 1937. Resigned in indignation at his appointment of a second secretary to deal with social arrangements when he became Prime Minister.

21 April 1928
Westbourne

My dear Ida,

...

I had a solitary week in London nearly the whole of which was taken up with Cabinets or long confabs with the P.M. There has been much bitterness of spirit among those who were previously defeated and mass attacks have been made. In one respect I have allowed the plan to be altered although my arguments against the alteration were sufficiently convincing I believe to have enabled me to checkmate it if I had chosen to press my advantage. Time will show whether my objections were well founded or not but in any case I have preserved the conditions which I considered vital and have lost nothing in weight or influence by what I have consented to surrender. But it has been a strenuous time and I am glad that limits of time now make it impossible for our lively colleague to spring any fresh surprises. I believe the Cabinet are committed to P.L. Reform and although I shant feel safe till the Bill is through (and it wont come on till the autumn) the ground is more thoroughly consolidated in the Cabinet where it was most shaky than ever before.

...

29 April 1928
37 Eaton Square, SW1

My dear Hilda,

This has indeed been a tremendous week and the astonishing thing to me is that I feel so fresh after it. I must admit that on Wednesday, harassed by incessant distractions and with the weight of two big speeches on my mind I was irritable & worried and short of sleep. But the moment the incubus is removed I seem to bounce up like a cork and feel no trace of the fatigue. I am assured by some of my friends that I look better than I have for years so I suppose the mental elasticity may be connected with physical health. What that is due to, whether "Bemax" or light rays on innate goodness I dont know – & dont much care.

The Budget has certainly had a remarkably good start and though one expects criticism to grow after the first excitement has passed off the critics show singular difficulty in deciding on what to criticise. The point I remarked on to Winston as likely to be chiefly fastened on was the long delay in giving relief and further observation rather confirms this. W. says he thinks he can give the railway relief this year without disturbing the rates & so he can, but I have warned him off any premature agricultural land relief or grants to necessitous areas and he has promised faithfully to be good. If once he were tempted into making these concessions I should indeed be frightened about P.L. for the country districts & the necessitous areas themselves would say "Why all this bother about Guardians and Local Authorities, upsetting boundaries and attacking vested areas? We have got all we wanted without any disturbance; just go on as you are, and drop the rest". And I fear the demand would be irresistible and my Cabinet would disperse in a rout. But I am sure Winston himself does not want that nor (and this is even more important) do his chief advisers at the Treasury.

The fact that W. is considering a temporary arrangement under which the railways are to be given a subsidy equivalent to their rates in order that they may pass it on to the "basics" illustrates more clearly than ever the point I have consistently made to the Cabinet in considering this matter namely that the proposal is nothing but the thinnest kind of camouflage for a subsidy to coal steel and agriculture as direct as that which we gave to coal in 1925. The permanent plan under which we pay the subsidy to the local authorities in order that they may pass it on to the railways in order that they may pass it on to the selected trades is so utterly illogical, so complicated & so completely contradictory of the opinion universally expressed a little while ago that State subsidies were economically unsound, that I could not imagine that it would not be torn to pieces at once. S.B. on the other hand was always attracted by the scheme and thought the camouflage was sufficient to enable us to get away with it. At the time when he first informed me of this view I told him I felt bound to put my views before the Cabinet but I should not press them beyond a certain point for I had great faith in his instinctive flair for the way in which the man-in-the-streets mind works. The event appears to show that he was quite right. Not a word of criticism has been heard of this most vulnerable proposal. It almost makes one long to be in Opposition to see how hopelessly they have (so far) missed the weak points. Of course it is not my business to point them out and although I still think the railway proposals quite wrong I shall naturally defend them in public since they are part of the common policy. I cant help thinking that Labour feels utterly incompetent to criticise & that Liberals are afraid lest they should incur unpopularity. But the arguments they might have used even if they were unpopular now would have brought them credit & profit in the end perhaps even before the General Election. But there they have to bear the weight of an utterly unprincipled leader. Austen[21] was absent when my criticisms were discussed in Cabinet, but even without him I believe I could have killed the railway project had I not known that S.B. wanted it.

Your account of your conversation with the farmers is illuminating. Dont they deserve to have a Lib-Lab Government and to be put under the harrow themselves!

---

[21] (Joseph) Austen Chamberlain (1863–1937). Liberal Unionist MP for Worcestershire East 1892–1914 (a Conservative from 1906) and Birmingham West 1914–37. Civil Lord of Admiralty 1895–1900; Financial Secretary to Treasury 1902; Postmaster-General 1902–3; Chancellor of Exchequer 1903–5 and 1919–21; Secretary of State for India 1915–17; Minister without Portfolio in War Cabinet 1918–19; Lord Privy Seal and Leader of Conservative Party 1921–22; Foreign Secretary 1924–29; First Lord of Admiralty 1931. Created KG 1925.

I always said they would not be grateful but actually to turn all that we have done for them into a grievance is the limit. I see the D. Mail which is making great efforts to increase its agricultural circulation is making great play with its slogan Relief to the land at once & freedom for the farmer from all taxation on petrol for whatever purpose he may use it as compensation for the murderous assaults made on him by the Minister of Health. Needless to say it lies recklessly and persistently in support of this campaign.

Lloyd George's speech on the Budget was most useful. He really did not understand the proposals & knew he did not. But he hoped to draw corrections as he went along so that he could drop any unsound arguments and concentrate on any weak places. Fortunately I was receiving a deputation and Winston didn't know the answers to Ll.G.'s questions so that he fairly committed himself and gave me a "sitter". It always gives me particular satisfaction to make Ll.G. look ridiculous although this time I took care not to be ill-natured & the Goat laughed away quite merrily himself being relieved to get off so easily. He told K. Wood[22] afterwards that he had misunderstood our proposals but was beginning to get the hang of them now. Which didn't prevent his saying last night at a public meeting that I had been "as obscure & almost as rhetorical" as Winston.

I had a huge meeting at Tynemouth on Friday but it was bad staff work at the C.O. to arrange that Winston should speak in Newcastle the next day. Nevertheless the Tyne district is a good one for our purpose since it has suffered most terribly in its three principal industries coal steel and ship building. Father spoke there in 1903 and I didn't forget to rub in the fulfilment of his prophecies. Even shipbuilders today have at last begun to come round as they feel the draught and old G.B. Hunter,[23] a regular Die Hard, Free Trader & shipbuilder in the old days has written to the P.M. begging him to "safeguard" steel. The trouble is that it is too late, too late at least to do all that might have been done 25 years ago for some markets have gone forever and the internal resources of the trade have been sadly whittled away. But eppur si muove.[24]

The clause in the R. &. V. Bill on which the Times (and today the Sunday Times) has descended so heavily is hated by all the lawyers. It shortcircuits them! The difficulty at present is that these doubtful points *never* get beyond quarter sessions because the amounts involved are so small that people wont incur the risk of loss by appealing to the High Court. But as the decision of one

---

[22] Howard Kingsley Wood (1881–1943). Conservative MP for Woolwich West 1918–43. PPS to Minister of Health 1918–22; Parliamentary Secretary, Ministry of Health 1924–29 and to Education 1931; Postmaster-General 1931–35; Minister of Health 1935–38; Air Secretary 1938–40; Lord Privy Seal 1940; Chancellor of Exchequer 1940–43 and member of War Cabinet 1940–42. Chairman, Executive Committee of NUCUA 1930–32. Knighted 1918.

[23] George Burton Hunter (1845–1937). Principal partner in Swan Hunter, shipbuilders of Wallsend. Knighted 1918.

[24] Translation: it does move all the same. Attributed to Galileo after he recanted his doctrine that the earth moves round the sun.

quarter sessions is not binding on another you get no authoritative ruling and consequently no uniformity of valuation. The clause is not vital to my Bill and if need be it can be dropped. But it would be very useful and if it were in the hands of the Lord Chancellor I am pretty sure I could get it. But I fear F.E. is more than halfhearted & I rather expect he will drop it.

... Yesterday morning Annie & I went to the Leicester Galleries to see an exhibition of pictures by Spencer Gore[25] who died in 1914 but is just beginning to be recognised as a very considerable artist. We were much struck with his pictures over 80 of which have been collected at the Galleries. They show a very remarkable development and a reaching out experimentally in various directions that is most interesting. I am going to see whether one cannot be secured for the Birmingham Art Gallery.

In the afternoon we went to a concert at the Albert Hall where we heard Beethovens Mass in D, Choral Fantasia Pianoforte Concerto and Egmont overture. The last is the only one I had heard before so far as I can remember and I enjoyed the opportunity of enlarging my acquaintance with the great man. I have just been reading a very interesting critical study of him by a man called Sullivan; the best book about Beethoven that I have come across yet. To me he has always been a far more interesting and intriguing figure than Napoleon. After the concert we strolled out into Kensington Gardens & looked at the flowers in the Long Walk ... Altogether it is a good show & yesterday in the hot sun with the young green foliage not too dense and the thrushes & chaffinches in full song it was heavenly. I think we must send you the Grey *now*, while the birds are still at the height of their songs. ...

...

5 May 1928
Westbourne

My dear Ida,

...

I had a new experience last week. I dined with Harry Preston[26] and a Bohemian crowd and then went to see a boxing match at the National Sporting Club ... and as I had long wanted to see a fight I was immensely interested. Neither man was knocked out and neither appeared to suffer much damage though I should not have liked to be the target for some of the blows, especially from the Frenchman who was a ferocious & brutal looking animal. I thought (and so did many others) that he had the best of it but the Referee decided in favour of the Italian. Of course my presence created much interest. Various

---

[25] Spencer Frederick Gore (1874–1914). English painter. Founder member and first President, Camden Town Group 1911.

[26] Harry John Preston (1860–1936). Hotel proprietor and boxing enthusiast. Knighted 1933.

boxers were brought up to be presented, the evening papers had large headlines on the subject and I have since had the offer of a box at Stamford Ring for an international exhibition next month. But I dont propose to make a hobby of it and have refused.

Perhaps you may have observed that in my varied life I also broadcasted during the week – on Milk and public health. It was very short but very tedious. It was however distinctly audible, so I am told, and I understand that that is considered a good thing when broadcasting.

The incident in the House on Wednesday was very ridiculous, and not very creditable either to Leo Amery[27] or A.M. Samuel.[28] But it may truly be said that no other Cabinet Minister would have advised the Under Secretary of another Department to accept an amendment which he had been told to resist, and no other Under Secretary would have taken the advice if it had been given. The Chief Whip's language was sulphurous but the two Oppositions had the merriest night they have enjoyed for a long while.

Of course you are quite right about the R.D.C.'s. There will be nothing left for them to do and they will hardly survive for very long one would suppose. As soon as they tumble to that, they will raise the doose's own delight and I am surprised that they haven't begun already. But probably they are waiting until the tortoise puts its head out, which it proposes to do in about a month's time. I shall then be issuing to L.A.'s a Memorandum setting forth the provisional proposals of the Govt. and after that I expect things will liven up.

I had to give up my Cl.4 of the R&V. Bill after all. The lawyers and the Press were too many for me and the moment anyone says "Bureaucracy is encroaching" no one pays any more attention to argument or even to facts. They just shout "Down with Bureaucracy" and go for it bald headed. I wanted very much to make the equally fair retort that the Bench and the Bar always work together to protect their trade union and what they want is to exploit the public to their hearts content. Fortunately Salisbury[29] said something of the kind and as I told him he relieved my bursting heart. Meanwhile the clause was a most useful

---

[27] Leopold Charles Maurice Stennett Amery (1873–1955). Conservative MP for Birmingham South (later Sparkbrook) 1911–45. Under-Secretary, Colonies 1919–21; Parliamentary and Financial Secretary to Admiralty 1921–22; First Lord of Admiralty 1922–24; Colonial Secretary 1924–29 and Dominion Secretary 1925–29; Secretary of State for India 1940–45.

[28] Arthur Michael Samuel (1872–1942). Conservative MP for Farnham 1918–37. Under-Secretary for Foreign Affairs and Parliamentary Secretary, Board of Trade 1924–27; Financial Secretary, Treasury 1927–29; Chairman, Public Accounts Committee 1929–31. Created Bart 1932 and Baron Mancroft 1937.

[29] James Edward Hubert Gascoyne-Cecil (1861–1947). Conservative MP for Darwen 1885–92, Rochester 1893–1903. Under-Secretary, Foreign Affairs 1900–1903; Lord Privy Seal 1903–5 and 1924–29; President, Board of Trade 1905; Chancellor, Duchy of Lancaster 1922–23; Lord President of Council 1922–24. Conservative leader in Lords 1925–31. Styled Viscount Cranborne 1868–1903, succeeded as 4th Marquess of Salisbury 1903.

lightning conductor and I have safely got through with other clauses which at one time caused me considerable anxiety.

...

Orpen seems to have made a mess of Ll.G. but perhaps that is of good omen.

20 May 1928
Westbourne

My dear Ida,

...

Ouf! I have had a week. Five speeches in addition to long & anxious hours over the new Bill. I should have liked another week or so to work on it for it is surprising how one can overlook obvious defects when one has had one's nose to the grindstone continuously for a long time. But, thanks to the Chancellor's indisposition, we have had an uninterrupted opportunity of improving it and the ninth draft, which is the one we are on now, looks to me fairly weather tight. The opposition are already licking their chops in anticipation of a feast – but we shall see. I expect the Second reading to come on about the 7th June.

Yes, my speech on the Estimates had a great success and almost created something like a sensation. Not only did I hear from many quarters of the delight of our own side, but the Liberal Chief Whip came to say that the Goat was so pleased with it that he had put his papers in his pocket & gone home and the Liberals would not move any reduction. I interpret that to mean that he couldn't find any holes to pick. The Socialists of course did move a reduction but Lawson,[30] a miner from Chester-le-Street came up to me in the lobby to thank me for my deeply interesting speech, which he said had made him see bigger things than ever before. I was really very gratified because he is often very bitter. Of course the journalists, who must always be melodramatic, having for some time represented me as a cold hearted cynic, now declare that the mask was at last lifted & revealed a man "racked with emotion" and "torn with passion". The one picture is just as ridiculous as the other, but perhaps if people will take them together they will get somewhere near the truth.

The ineffable Jix[31] has once again got away with it and has actually increased his reputation by his handling of the Hyde Park case.[32] Stanley told me some time

---

[30] John James Lawson (1881–1965). Labour MP for Chester-le-Street 1919–49. Financial Secretary, War Office 1924; Parliamentary Secretary, Ministry of Labour 1929–31; War Secretary 1945–46. Created Baron Lawson 1950.

[31] William Joynson-Hicks (1865–1932). Conservative MP for Manchester North-West 1908–10, Brentford 1911–18, Twickenham 1918–29. Parliamentary Secretary, Overseas Trade Department 1922–23; Postmaster- and Paymaster-General 1923; Financial Secretary to Treasury (with seat in Cabinet) 1923; Minister of Health 1923–24; Home Secretary 1924–29. Created Bart 1919 and Viscount Brentford 1929.

[32] Although acquitted of indecency in Hyde Park, a Miss Savidge was subsequently interrogated

ago that when he made him H.S. he told him that what he particularly wanted him to do was to change the heads of the police and that he had funked it. I suspect that that is the explanation of a story which at the best is one of incredible bungling and at the worst a scandal of the first magnitude. As usual, in the crisis, Jix was doubtful what to do, but the Cabinet had no doubts and so once again he appears as the strong, if not silent, man (to use the words of the most amusing Times leading article on the correspondence with the Bishop of London). Derby,[33] who sat next me at a dinner on Friday and very frankly gave me his opinions on most of my colleagues, declares that when a photograph recently appeared in the papers of Jix looking at his pigs, à la Baldwin, it showed clearly that they were on the drawing room carpet! You should have heard him say in the House "Of course I *am* the Executive; I mean I represent the Executive"!

Yesterday we came here early as I had to address the Ebenezer Provident Society in the afternoon at the Bot. Gdns. I sweated blood all morning trying to think of something to say, but after all it came out quite well when I got on my feet and I returned feeling thankful that this awful week was behind me.

Annie is very excited at having found an ideal lodging for the holidays in Bamborough Castle, part of which is let off for the summer. ... Ten miles away are moors & hills and the country swarms with the seats of the nobility who may be expected to welcome the Minister of Health's family & possibly even to provide him with fishing!

...

30 May 1928
Westbourne

My dear Hilda,

...

I wonder if you read the P.M.'s speech at Welbeck and noticed again how he mentioned my name. He always does in an important speech and generally mine is the only one. Winston has begun to emerge from his retirement & make himself a nuisance. At present he is endeavouring to make my speech on the 2nd Rdg of the R. & V. bill when he wants me to "unfold" the plan for Local Government. But I say it would be totally irrelevant as well as extremely unwise & I *wont do it*.

---

at length by police leading to Commons criticism of the legality of this arbitrary action. A tribunal recommended greater protection for those interrogated and greater discretion by the police in such cases. Police methods were debated in Cabinet and the Commons on 17 May 1928, CAB 29(28)8, CAB 23/57.

[33] Edward George Villiers Stanley (1865–1948). Conservative MP for South-East Lancashire 1892–1906. Financial Secretary to War Office 1900–1903; Postmaster-General (in Cabinet) 1903–5; Under-Secretary for War 1916; Secretary for War 1916–18 and 1922–24; Ambassador to Paris 1918–20. Succeeded as 17th Earl of Derby in 1908.

3 June 1928
The Manor House, Great Durnford, Salisbury

My dear Ida,

...

Alas! my holiday is drawing swiftly to its close but I have refused to think about work and have returned the "notes on the R & V (Apportionment) Bill" which the office sent me.

Tomorrow I must take it up in earnest.

9 June 1928
Broadlands, Romsey

My dear Hilda,

...

I am very glad to have got that second reading over and I am well satisfied with the debate. It was a very difficult case to put and I had some very late sittings working away at it; but the discussions did not reveal any new point or any concentration of criticism on awkward details. What I was most afraid of was lest our own side should develop cold feet over something but on the contrary they all supported us and some of them made extremely good speeches the best perhaps being that of Geoffrey Ellis.[34] I have made a note of him as a possible successor to Kingsley if he should at any time be reft from me.

Winstons speech on the Finance Bill was one of the least effective I have heard him make. He seemed tired and laboured rather heavily with his statistics. On the other hand he was at his best in replying to Ll.G. on my Bill and scored a notable Parliamentary success. Of course the H of C. enjoys nothing so much as a duel of that kind and it fairly rocked with laughter over the sallies of both. But I doubt if these exhibition bouts, entertaining as they are, really advance the position of the combatants. Ll.G. plainly did not understand either our plan or his own and Winston gets uncomfortable the moment he moves off the broad outlines of the picture.

As I was waiting for a cab after the division, Lunn,[35] one of the Labour Members came up and excusing himself on the ground that we were both Members of the House enquired who had been influencing me the last few weeks! I was floored by this unexpected conundrum and at the moment could only think he meant Winston. However he went on to explain that since I spoke

---

[34] (Robert) Geoffrey Ellis (1874–1956). Barrister, banker and Conservative MP for Holmfirth 1910–12, Wakefield 1922–23 and 1924–29, Winchester 1931–35 and Sheffield Eccleshall 1935–45. Counsel to Crown in Peerage and honours claims 1922–54. Created Bart 1932.

[35] William Lunn (1872–1942). Miner. Labour MP for Rothwell 1918–42. Labour whip 1922; Parliamentary Secretary, Department of Overseas Trade 1924; Under-Secretary, Colonial Office 1929 and Dominion Office 1929–31. Member, PLP Executive 1931–36.

on the distress in the mining areas of South Wales I had been a different man. In my speech on the R & V. Apportionment Bill there was not a trace of that acerbity which I sometimes put in "so beautifully". He & his friends had been discussing it and the conclusion they had arrived at was "That his wife is a gentle lady & she must have influenced him".

Annie is rather pleased at present but I have warned her that she has now a reputation to live up to and there must be no departure from gentleness in future!

...

We dont yet know who we are to have for a Speaker. Hilton Young[36] is ruled out as not being a pucca Conservative. The possibles seem to be Tom Inskip, Sir R. Sanders[37] & Algy Fitzroy.[38] The first would make much the best, but I understand the Labour Party object to him on the ground that he has at times made speeches they didn't like! Aren't they childish. You might just as well say that no advocate should be made a judge. Perhaps a greater difficulty is in finding a successor to be A.G. We are not very strong in law officers with experience. But perhaps Leslie Scott[39] might do for a time & I should like him to have the chance.

Next week the Prayer Book again. I have a feeling that it will get through & I hope it will as I think that it better for us politically than leaving the thing unsettled. But No Popery is still a very powerful cry.

...

17 June 1928
Westbourne

My dear Ida,
...
The excitement of the week has of course been almost confined to the Prayer book. I heard very little of the debate as I was busy elsewhere but my information

---

[36] Edward Hilton Young (1879–1960). Assistant Editor, *Economist* 1908–10; City Editor, *Morning Post* 1910–14. Liberal MP for Norwich 1915–23 and 1924–29 (Conservative from 1926); Conservative MP for Sevenoaks 1929–35. PPS to H.A.L. Fisher 1919; Financial Secretary, Treasury 1921–22; Secretary, Overseas Trade Department 1931; Minister of Health 1931–35. Knighted 1927. Created Baron Kennet 1935.

[37] Robert Arthur Sanders (1867–1940). Conservative MP for Bridgwater 1910–23 and Somerset (Wells) 1924–29. Whip 1911–21; Deputy Conservative Chairman 1918–22. Under-Secretary for War 1921–22; Minister of Agriculture 1922–24. Created Bart 1920 and Baron Bayford 1929.

[38] Edward Algernon Fitzroy (1869–1943). Conservative MP for Northamptonshire South 1900–1906, 1910–18 and Daventry 1918–43. Deputy-Chairman, Ways and Means Committee 1922–23 and 1924–28; Speaker, House of Commons 1928–43. Widow created Viscountess Daventry 1943.

[39] Leslie Frederic Scott (1869–1950). Unionist MP for Liverpool Exchange 1910–29. British delegate, International Conference on Maritime Law 1909–10, 1922–23; Solicitor-General 1922; Lord Justice of Appeal 1935–48; President, National Association of British Councils. Knighted 1922.

confirms the view expressed in the papers that most of those who created a sensation last time were unable to repeat it, that on the whole the Pros had the best of it on this occasion, that the P.M. was ineffective but that by the time he spoke the issue was already decided. What I have not seen brought out except in the Times was that the defeat was really the work of the Opposition. Only 2 Liberals & less than 30 Labour men voted for the book & large numbers of Socialists who abstained last time voted against this week. I fancy political reasons influenced them.

I have no idea what will happen now but the P.M. and our Chief Whip were both very nervous about the results of a defeat. The former must have been disappointed with his own speech for I am pretty sure he thought he was going to make a good one. But the mood of the House was not receptive and he is not a speaker who can at the last moment readily recast his utterances. Winston's behaviour was comic. He was concerned solely with the result of his vote upon Epping and insisted on speaking that he might give his reasons & so conciliate his electors.

I had a very miscellaneous week, beginning with Orpen. He does give one the idea that he concentrates intensely on his work and I found that he has not done himself justice in his self portraits. He is apt to look "common" in them but he doesn't look common in real life. I rather took to him and thought he did to me.

Annie & I came into contact with the Governor of Rome twice on Tuesday – once at the County Hall where he was paying a ceremonial call on the L.C.C. and again at dinner that night as the guest of Sir R. Blades[40] at the H. of Commons. The Governor is a fine looking man tall & well set up with a keen smooth shaven face & marked features. He might have been an Englishman but is of the type that was more common 50 years ago than today. He is certainly a ready and practised speaker. When he arrived at the County Hall he asked me in a whisper what was the form at the ceremony. I told him there would be an address of welcome to which he would be expected to reply. He declared that he had not been warned so I just told him one or two things that I thought might help. A few minutes later with perfect self-possession and in admirable English he made a 20 minutes speech in reply to the address building on what it contained and weaving in the hints I had given him. I was filled with admiration.

…

On Wednesday I went to open St Annes Hill near Chertsey a beautiful bit of wooded hill about 26 acres in extent that has been given to the U.D.C. by Sir William Berry[41] the great newspaper magnate. I went largely to please him as he

---

[40] George Rowland Blades (1868–1953). Alderman of the City 1920–48 and Lord Mayor of London 1926–27. Conservative MP for Epsom 1918–28. Conservative Party Treasurer 1931–33; President, NUCUA 1936. Knighted 1918. Created Bart 1922 and Baron Ebbisham 1928.

[41] William Ewart Berry (1879–1954). Founded *Advertising World* 1901; Editor-in-Chief, *Sunday Times* 1915–36 and of *Daily Telegraph* 1928–54; Chairman, Financial Times Ltd and Associated

is a very good supporter of ours but I was quite glad I went for the gift is a most admirable one and has been admirably treated. ...

On Friday we travelled to Cheltenham where we dined with Agg-Gardner[42] before the meeting in the Town Hall. The hall was packed and many applicants for seats had to be turned away, for I am told that my name is now well enough known to draw an audience. It was a very successful meeting for though the speech was not a fireworky one it held the audience and I could tell by the prolonged applause at the end that they had been pleased ...

24 June 1928
37 Eaton Square, SW1

My dear Hilda,

...

I have had a magnificent week end the weather was perfect and I spent all my time out of doors fishing and watching birds. I have quite made my reputation as a fisherman, for I caught 19 trout while Barlow[43] and a friend of his named Colin Campbell[44] only got 5 between them. I suppose I am learning the game; at any rate I was more successful than I have ever been before and enjoyed myself mightily.

There is very little news to give you. We got through the first two days of Committee on R. & V. very well and this week we shall pass a guillotine resolution much to the delight of the Labour Party who see themselves absolved from the necessity of making a desperate fight over a measure which they suspect is popular in the country. I have been working on the great memorandum which is now ready but we shan't "release" it till after the guillotine resolution is through so as not to give fresh ammunition to the opposition until they are safely shackled. I think it is a very good document and though of course it will be criticised the financial provisions are so favourable that Ll.G. will find the ground cut from under his feet and the L.A.'s ought to be fairly well pacified.

...

Press. Principal Advisor, Ministry of Information 1939. Created Bart 1921, Baron Camrose 1929 and Viscount 1941.

[42] James Tynte Agg-Gardner (1846–1928). Conservative MP for Cheltenham 1874–80, 1885–95, 1900–1906, 1911–28. Chairman, Commons Kitchen Committee 1917–28. Knighted 1916.

[43] (Clement) Anderson Montague-Barlow (1868–1951). Conservative MP for Salford South 1910–23. Parliamentary Secretary, Ministry of Labour 1920–22; Minister of Labour 1922–24. Knighted 1918. Created Bart 1924. Chairman, Royal Commission on Location of Industry, 1937–40. Changed name by deed poll from Barlow to Montague-Barlow in 1946.

[44] Colin Algernon Campbell (1874–1957). Director, Westminster Bank.

1 July 1928
Dawn House, Winchester

My dear Ida,

… I have got to black the boots when I get home this evening, – in other words get up my amdts to the R & V Bill for tomorrow.

…

Annie's party was enormous and highly successful as usual. She has acquired the reputation of having the best parties in London or perhaps I should rather say of being the best hostess in London and people come because they know they will enjoy themselves, and will be made welcome. But it was a tiring day as after the party A. & I had to receive 1700 delegates to the World's Dairy Congress at Lancaster House. I was lucky, for I went home after it was over and thereby missed the all night sitting and 27 divisions!

I have been working hard on the Memorandum and as you will have seen we got it out on the 29th thereby cheating Ll.G. who had prophesied that it would be the last day of the last week before it appeared. It seems on the whole to have had a good reception even the Opposition papers being unable to restrain their admiration of its ingenuity. But of course there will be plenty of opposition and largely on the lines which you state in your letter. Still I don't think it will be quite as destructive of local interest as you seem to think though no doubt that is how it will appear to members of R.D.C.'s. I think that the larger ones will get a good deal of delegation from the C.C.'s and though the latter are in many cases ill equipped for their new duties I hope the effect will be to stimulate them to do better than they have in the past. It was quite clear that it was impossible under the new conditions to keep Poor Law & Roads under the small authorities. Their financial resources will be so much diminished by the derating that they would be unable to stand up to violent fluctuations in their expenditure.

The guillotine went through very amiably the opposition being really very delighted at escaping the drudgery of prolonged sittings and obstruction.

…

I am getting on slowly with Orpen but I haven't been allowed to see the picture yet. He is an amusing little cuss!

…

8 July 1928
Westbourne

My dear Hilda,

…

I had three days on R. & V. last week and once more I was amazed at the futility of the opposition. One would have thought that the guillotine once passed they would have taken a careful survey of the situation, decided which were the most vulnerable points, and concentrated upon them. As a matter of fact there were three extremely difficult questions on which I felt I might have to give something away but only one of them was even discussed because individual Labour & Liberal speakers wasted all the time in discussing and dividing on absolutely ridiculous and childish amendments. Kingsley and I just put our hands in our pockets and lay back while they ran on, playing our game for us. I asked Maclaren,[45] the Socialist member for Stoke why they didn't organise their forces properly. "Oh", he said, "of course you're quite right, but what can you expect. There's no captain of the ship and the whole place is in a state of chaos". And then, with a twinkle, he added "But if you were our leader, can you imagine yourself attempting to keep Wedgewood[46] [sic] and me in bounds?" I replied, also with a twinkle, "Well I would try".

If Labour is ineffective, Liberals are no better. They have a wonderful chance now of showing that small as are their numbers they can be more effective as an opposition than the Socialists. It is true that they haven't got a very brainy lot, but there are quite enough of them, especially if properly advised and organised, to put up a reasoned serious case wherever criticism is possible, – and there is very little in this Bill that can not be criticised. But Lloyd George comes and makes a sort of guttersnipe partisan speech and then goes away and the case is left to Ernest Brown[47] who is full of assurance but otherwise ill-equipped and Harney[48] who is generally more or less fuddled with liquor.

We have issued a sort of Child's Guide to the memo on local Govt, for the use of our members. It is supposed to be by Willie Brass[49] as it exalts the Govt and slates the Opposition, but it was really composed by my late private secretary Douglas Veale,[50] and it is an extraordinarily successful piece of work. A great

---

[45] Andrew MacLaren (1883–1975). Engineer and Labour MP for Stoke Burslem 1922–23, 1924–31 and 1935–45 (Independent Labour from March 1943).

[46] Josiah Clement Wedgwood (1872–1943). Naval architect 1894–1900. Served South African War 1900–1901 and Resident Magistrate, Transvaal 1902–4; Flanders and Gallipoli 1914–15; attached General Smuts' Staff in East Africa 1916; Assistant-Director, Trench Warfare Department 1917. Liberal MP (Labour from May 1919) for Newcastle-under-Lyme 1906–42 when created Baron Wedgwood. Vice-Chairman, PLP 1922–24; Chancellor, Duchy of Lancaster 1924.

[47] (Alfred) Ernest Brown (1881–1962). Liberal MP for Rugby 1923–24 and Leith 1927–45 (a National Liberal from 1931). Chairman, Select Committee on Procedure 1931–32. Parliamentary Secretary, Ministry of Health 1931–32; Secretary of Mines 1932–35; Minister of Labour 1935–40; Scottish Secretary 1940–41; Minister of Health 1941–43; Chancellor, Duchy of Lancaster 1943–45; Minister of Aircraft Production 1945. Leader, Liberal National Group 1940–45.

[48] Edward Augustine Harney (1865–1929). Irish barrister. Member of Australian Senate 1901–3. Liberal MP for South Shields 1922–29.

[49] William Brass (1886–1945). Conservative MP for Clitheroe 1922–45. PPS to Chamberlain 1922–24 and 1924–27, to Amery 1927–28, to Moore-Brabazon 1940–42. Knighted 1929. Created Baron Chattisham 1945.

[50] Douglas Veale (1891–1973). Second Class Clerk, LGB 1914; Private Secretary to Permanent Secretary, Ministry of Health 1920; Private Secretary to Minister of Health 1921–28; Registrar, Oxford University and Fellow of Corpus Christi, Oxford 1930–58. Knighted 1954.

many members have been up to me to tell me how valuable they have found it and how clearly and persuasively it states the case, among them being Philip Snowden[51] who had somehow got a copy and told me he intended to circulate it to *his* friends! I think I must procure one for Ida; I believe she would find it interesting and useful. Meantime I have been reading a very interesting minute by one of my Medical Officers written before he knew that Poor Law Reform was coming in which he elaborates a plan of concentration and cooperation by Boards of Guardians in the use of institutions, taking the Southampton & Bristol areas as examples. Drawing a circle with a 25 mile radius round each of these towns he shows how a vast tract of country (including Odiham) could have the use of the two big hospitals one at each place for maternity cases; how thereby the patients would have the opportunities of specialist treatment & nursing; how at present a vast number of nurses with C.M.B. were employed in the areas who only had about 4 maternity cases a year; how by concentration you could do with far fewer C.B.B. [sic] nurses & give those you kept a far better experience. How, further, by this concentration, you could vastly improve medical teaching and give vastly better opportunities for research. How by similar concentrations you could sort out the tuberculous patients, the mental defectives, the loonies, the M. & C. W. the seniles and the able bodied. How you could deal with each of these classes more effectively and more economically, closing altogether some of the present out-of-date buildings. It is a very interesting and convincing paper and the comment of my officers at the time was "Splendid but you will never get Boards of Guardians to work together like that".

I have got rather a heavy week in front of me. Probably you have not seen that I have been the subject of a torrent of abuse in the Welsh papers because I have declined to replace the chairman of the Welsh Board of Health who has just retired and have decided that there shall be no chairman in future. This is represented as a deliberate insult to Welsh National Sentiment (Syn. Vanity) and a sinister step towards the total abolition of the Board. The real trouble is that the man who would have naturally succeeded to the Chairmanship is a thoroughly disloyal intriguer, a typical Welshman, in fact. I have known him a long time, as Lloyd George planted him on me at the time of National Service. I fancy he has been one of L.G.'s tools for some of his dirty work and I suspect that whenever he has a grievance he makes L.G. take it up lest he should tell some of the things he knows! When I first became Minister in 1923 I found this man, John Rowland,[52] had been quarrelling with the then Chairman whom he was trying to push out in order to take his place. I had to have an enquiry made by Sir Ellis

---

[51] Philip Snowden (1864–1937). Labour MP for Blackburn 1906–18 and Colne Valley 1922–31. Chancellor of Exchequer 1924, 1929–31; Lord Privy Seal 1931–32. Created Viscount 1931.

[52] John Rowland (1877–1941). School master, Cardiff 1902–5; Private Secretary to Lloyd George 1905–12; Chairman, Welsh Board of Health; Administrative Adviser, Corporation of Merthyr Tydfil 1936–37. Knighted 1938.

Griffith[53] (a Liberal ex-M.P.) and his report was discreditable to both but especially to Rowland. I had them both up and gave them a terrible dressing [sic] which the Chairman accepted meekly though Rowland received it with suppressed fury. Ever since he has been trying to make the Chairman acknowledge that he was in the wrong so as to clear his path to the succession. He is at daggers drawn with the most efficient member of the staff and altogether no one who cares about good administration could think of giving him the appointment. I was quite aware that as soon as he knew he was not to have it, he would begin rousing up & exploiting the Welsh National Susceptibilities and of course Ll.G. & the Socialist M.P.'s are anxious to make party capital out of it. So they have had a meeting and I am to receive a deputation. And if they dont get satisfaction – by George, they are going to demand half a day to debate my salary. I suppose it will give me a little trouble but it is all very childish and I dont suppose for a moment that they think they can bully me into submission.

On Tuesday I am to be "on the mat" before the Agriculture Committee to account for my crimes, viz. that I have blocked their Bill for dealing with reconstituted cream which is now cutting out natural cream because of the abolition of preservatives and secondly that I have contumaciously and malignantly returned to the abolition of their friends the Guardians.

I have got some good evidence to show (1) that the dairymen who have complained about the preservatives themselves use sour milk, dirty milk containing bits of paper and dead flies, and vessels imperfectly cleaned (2) that other dairymen say that they have increased their business 30% by the improved methods used since they were no longer allowed to use Borax and that consequently they have been converted & now enthusiastically support the order. As for the Guardians, its for them to say whether they want the rate relief. If so, they must swallow the Guardians, but after all those who care about the *work* & not the position will find ways of still doing it.

A. had as big a crowd as ever on Tuesday and Berry says "We never have anything like that at Downing Street". I think on the whole she is standing the season wonderfully well in spite of all her work. For she is doing a lot. She attended an infant welfare congress one day and was suddenly called on to speak which I need hardly say she did with great success especially as she was able to set the Congress right on a point connected with the Ministry's maternal mortality campaign. On Friday she came down here to open a fête in connection with the Cripples Home which of course meant another speech. And yesterday we both attended our demonstration in the Bot. Gdns. It was a great success. The day was absolutely perfect. At 4 when we went in 6500 had arrived but there was a dense column all the way up the Vicarage Road pouring in and I am certain we

---

[53] Ellis Jones Ellis-Griffith (1860–1926). Barrister and Liberal MP for Anglesey 1895–1918 and Carmarthen 1923–24. Under-Secretary, Home Office 1912–15. Adopted surname Ellis-Griffith in lieu of Griffith 1918. Created Bart 1918.

easily beat all records. Our principal agent hopes to win Kings Norton next time but he evidently thinks we shall probably lose Duddeston & Deritend.

...

15 July 1928
37 Eaton Square, SW1

My dear Ida,

On such a hot night I dont feel equal to answering your criticisms except to say that you cant make omelettes without breaking eggs. But we shall probably make modification which may meet your difficulties to some small extent.

I suppose this has been a light week as they go, for I have had no public speeches since Monday. But it has been very full of Cabinet & departmental work and I was unable to attend A's party. I had two meetings of party committees to address, the Agricultural & the Health & Housing, both on Rating relief & Local Govt reform and (pace you) I was assured after both that I had carried most of the members with me completely.

On Wednesday I had the Welsh Depn. which included the Goat in his most mischievous form. I could see the malice in his eye as soon as he came in. I made a very frank statement and I believe nearly the whole of those present were satisfied to judge by their hear hears & nods of assent. But the Goat seemed beside himself with fury. He fairly shouted lies & twisted or tried to twist what I had said into something quite different. It remains to be seen whether he can do anything; I am not afraid of a debate in the House, but if he could kill me by a thought I should be dead before now. Well, one comfort is that I heartily reciprocate his dislike.

Next week I have 3 speeches, two days on R&V & we are threatened with an "all nighter" on the Tote. I confess I don't think its worth it. I was always against that wretched betting tax and my fears have been fully justified. Its been a bad egg from the beginning.

...

21 July 1928
Westbourne

My dear Hilda,

... I believe that in spite of the hot weather both A. & I are getting through much better than we did last year but of course every now & then one feels rather used up and we are glad to have a little time to ourselves down here to renew our strength. We have just come back from a garden party of one of the Edgbaston branches of the Junior Imps at which we were asked to show ourselves and say a few words. Luckily that does not mean what it once did in the way of worry or I should never have got through this week. Yesterday I was opening the new Sanatorium of the Surrey C.C. at Milford ... On Tuesday I was addressing a luncheon of 350 smart people for Lady Titchfield's Prevention of Tuberculosis campaign and Monday & Tuesday were devoted to the last stages of R.&V. Add to that two dinner parties, Annie's party and two receptions and you will see that we have had a fairly strenuous week. Well, another fortnight will see the end of it.

...

The more I think over Ida's criticisms of L.G. reform the more it seems to me that she has not understood them. I cant understand why she should think that District Nurses should be injured by a concentration of hospital work. Their work would not be affected at all & they will get their maternity fees just the same. But if the scheme of Dr Neilson[54] were carried out women who now are confined in a Poor Law Institution would go to the big hospital at Bristol or Southampton where they would get very much better conditions and would incidentally provide the C.M.B nurses there with more practice than they are now able to obtain.

So far as we have gone at present with Associations of the L.A.'s their attitude is pretty friendly. That of course does not apply to the R.D.C.'s but I have two possible concessions to them in mind which may help. One is that they should have a statutory right to appoint a certain number of their members on the local sub-committees of the C.C.; the other, that these sub-Coms should be named Guardians Committees in the Bill. That would probably mean that the individual members would continue to be known as Guardians. As to roads my solution would be that any D.C. Rural or Urban should be empowered to apply to the C.C. for delegation and should have the right of appeal to the Ministry against the C.C.'s refusal, but I am not sure that I can get Wilfrid[55] to agree. At present my chief worry is to know what to do with the districts where I have appointed guardians. The C.C.'s are already in Socialist hands and the "good" districts will feel it hard to have to pay for Socialist extravagance. I haven't found any satisfactory solution yet.

The Welsh party had a meeting to decide what to do with the Minister of Health but apparently found some difficulty in deciding on any course. First they said they would demand a day. Then someone remarked that the Govt might not give them a day, so they decided to put down my vote on a supply day.

---

[54] Henry John Neilson (1862–1949). Doctor, Nottingham 1888–1915; Major, RAMC 1915–17; Deputy Chief Commissioner of Medical Services, Ministry of National Service 1918–19 and Chief Commissioner, Ministry of Pensions; Divisional Medical Officer, South-West Division of Ministry of Health.

[55] Wilfrid William Ashley (1867–1939). Conservative MP for Blackpool 1906–18, Fylde 1918–22 and New Forest 1922–32. Chairman, Anti-Socialist Union. Unionist Whip 1911–13; Parliamentary Secretary, Ministry of Transport 1922–23; Under-Secretary, War Office 1923–24; Minister of Transport 1924–29. Created Baron Mount Temple 1932.

But neither Libs nor Labs were willing to give up one of their supply days to a subject on which the House was not likely to be very sympathetic. So finally it was left to be raised "some time" on the adjournment or the Appropriation Bill. I expect we shall have a short and futile debate in a thin House on the last day, but that wont carry them any further. They haven't got Jix to deal with!

Orpen is to have one more sitting this month but he tells me he will want several in the autumn. I think he is really interested and determined to make a success of the picture. He has a funny habit of making wry faces at his canvas and whispering to himself. Last Monday he was desperately excited, dashing at his brushes, glaring at me, and then rushing at the picture to put in a stroke or two. "Try to get it; try to get it" I heard him whisper in a wistful tone. At last I said "judging by your expression, you are making the most awful hash of this picture". He laughed & said the more interested he was the more difficult he found it to get what he wanted. And then after a moments silence he suddenly shouted "But there's going to be no hash about this". I like him, and I think he finds something congenial about me.

…

30 July 1928
37 Eaton Square, SW1

My dear Ida,

…

What with A & the children going off tomorrow … and my vote on Wednesday & the big speech on Saturday and Cabinet & committees I am thoroughly rattled! But I suppose it will all come out in the wash.

I see there are great headlines tonight about splits in the Cabinet, but it is grossly exaggerated. Jix made a foolish speech on Saturday & will have to be rapped over the knuckles but I guess he will put up with it.

…

Please excuse scrap; I cannot write any more tonight.

5 August 1928
Lochinch, Castle Kennedy, Wigtownshire

My dear Hilda,

I suppose by now you are on your way to Evian and I hope that before leaving you were able to get satisfactory news of Austen.[56] I only heard on Thursday

---

[56] On 31 July 1928, the day after his disastrous disclosure to Parliament of the Anglo-French compromise on arms limitation, Austen Chamberlain suffered a total collapse from overwork which soon developed into pneumonia. He left for a long cruise and a three-week rest with friends in California before returning to London in mid-November.

afternoon that he had got a touch of pneumonia, which alarmed me a good deal and only on Friday morning could I get through to Ivy. The doctors were with him then but I couldn't stay to hear their verdict as I was just leaving to catch my train so Ivy promised to send me a wire that evening. The wire did not actually arrive till yesterday and said "Doctors satisfied with progress" which is not very enthusiastic but I suppose as much as one could expect. Ivy said he was very weak and I should think that is the worst trouble. Of course Geneva is out of the question and S.B. was making arrangements for Jim Salisbury to sign the Kellogg treaty so I hope Austen will get ample time in which to convalesce. It is really the result of prolonged overwork by a man who hasn't got a great reserve of strength.

I felt myself as if another 3 or 4 days would break me up. The strain during the last week has been unusually heavy. Kingsley was away having gone to Karlsbad, my new P.S. is not as experienced as Veale, my vote was down for Wednesday with one or two awkward points coming up, every section of the Department was remembering that it had some problems which must be solved before the Minister left, in particular important decisions had to be taken on Loc. Govt. Reform, the final Cabinets had portentous agenda with papers of corresponding voluminousness to read, and last but not least this open air meeting was weighing on my mind. I had a headache for two days – I believe from sheer fatigue.

Well anyway its all over now and I feel better already. I expect a few days will restore my equilibrium sufficiently to enable me to enjoy my holidays because though I am tired mentally, physically I am particularly well. Annie declares that she has never felt so well at the beginning of a holiday since we were married, but I am not sure whether this is to be attributed to the car or to Bemax. Anyway it is very satisfactory. ...

I suppose you read all about the Cabinet Split.[57] Jix's performance was of course merely another example of his irresistible passion for notoriety but it was very harmful as it gave rise to all sorts of ridiculous rumours and accentuated the feeling of bitterness already existing between Winston and Leo. We had a little allocation on Wednesday from S.B. on the folly of pinning the protectionism flag to iron & steel, the desirability of letting the safeguarding leaven work with as little advertisement as possible and the necessity of mastering the Rating scheme & expounding it to the people. I thought it was well done and S.B. further showed his tact in his answers to the opposition next day when the portentousness of the question was dissolved in laughter.

---

[57] On 28 July 1928 a Joynson-Hicks speech at Romsey calling for bolder action on tariffs revealed the depth of Cabinet division. On 1–2 August the Cabinet agreed not to change policy on food taxes or a general tariff and Baldwin prepared a letter for publication to set out the agreed policy.

The most interesting incident however was the Cabinet on Thursday called to consider what S.B. should say in a statement on safeguarding to be made public today. At Leo's request I walked down with him beforehand. I am supposed to be the only member of the Cabinet who has any influence with him and I use it to keep him in the shafts instead of prancing about outside. Whether it was due to me or not, on this occasion he behaved admirably and whilst not concealing his own convictions he declared himself prepared to accept the view that we could not at the Gen. Election propose either new food taxes or a general tariff. On the other hand Winston, though himself against the safeguarding of iron & steel, did not see how you could refuse an enquiry into the conditions, which of course implied a duty if the verdict is favourable. I put in some tactful remarks, others followed on similar lines and we dispersed in the utmost good humour, astonished at finding that we had nothing to quarrel about. Stanley was tremendously pleased. He had also received some good news which seemed to foreshadow at last those amalgamations & concentrations in the cotton & steel trades for which we have waited so long and so impatiently. They require the cooperation of many people, very suspicious of one another and very concerned lest the result should exclude them from their positions. They also necessitate the agreement by the Banks who have advanced a lot of money and who have to consent to write off their losses and stand out of their money. But in the end it is the only way of salvation, and if, after carrying out schemes of this kind, steel was still unable to meet the foreign competition, then its case for safeguarding would be unanswerable. Altogether we dispersed in a calm after the storm. Yesterday I said in my speech that the "Cabinet had never been more completely united than it was today" and wondered whether any opposition paper would scent the double entendre.

As a last chance I had lunch on Wednesday with Douglas Hogg to talk to him about Empire Farms before he goes to Canada. There was no doubt in my mind that he was much interested in the idea; he kept saying that it was a most interesting scheme, a great idea, and he will not forget it during his travels. The trouble is that he will be travelling so fast & speaking so often that he will have little time or opportunity to discuss such ideas with people who could forward them. The immigration minister is unfortunately Egan an Irishman who seems to put every possible obstacle in our way and at the last moment has hitched up the plan for harvesters so that in any case it will now be too late to get off more than 7000. But I told Hogg that I only wanted to put the idea into his mind so that he could discuss it if any suitable person and opportunity presented themselves.

...

13 August 1928
Bamburgh Castle, Northumberland

My dear Ida,

...

I was very much afraid you might have to delay your journey on account of Austen. I got exactly the same impression from my brief talk with Ivy as you viz. that his danger lay not so much in the pneumonia as in the deadly weakness. Since then I have had a letter from her in which she gives an account of their proposed trip beginning at the end of this month & ending on the 7th Nov. That ought to do him a lot of good though I have warned Ivy to be careful of Canada where they have no mercy at all on eminent statesmen. But this is a warning and causes me to wonder whether if we come back next year Austen would be able to stand another five years of office.

S.B.'s letter to the Chief Whip which appeared on Sunday seems to have attracted little attention.[58] If he had consulted me about the wording, as he told me he intended to do but didn't, I should have advised him not to use the word Protection lest it should give rise to misunderstandings. As it was, I got a furious letter from Leo who said he had written to the P.M. to say that he regarded it as a breach of the understanding arrived at in Cabinet & that he should hold himself free to take any step he liked in the autumn. I shall write him a soothing letter presently, but he has resigned or threatened to resign so often that I dont think S.B will take him very seriously especially as he doesn't really intend to make any departure from the agreement. The really important sentence in the letter was the one which said No manufacture will be excluded from the enquiry.

Meanwhile S.B. must have been solaced by the delicious communiqué from our incomparable Home Secretary. In case you should have missed it, I repeat it. "Sir W. Joynson Hicks from his 'seat' in the country has authorised the announcement that he fully concurs in the terms of the P.M.'s letter to the Chief Whip". The ineffable conceit & complacency of it. The patronage of the P.M. The underlying assumption that the country could not take the P.M.'s announcement seriously until it knew that he had asked and obtained the Home Secretary's leave to publish it. No one but our one and only Jix could have produced such an incredible gaffe.

...

On the Monday we trained (with four changes) to Peebles where we were met & drove to the Elibanks[59] at Dorn Hall. This was a long promised & long delayed visit, as we dont really care very much for either of them. ...

...

---

[58] Baldwin's letter to Eyres-Monsell on 3 August (published 6 August) 1928 reaffirmed the policy emphasis on derating and downplayed 'the Protectionist red herring' but the ambiguous pledge 'not to introduce Protection' (when he meant a general tariff) prolonged a crisis which the letter was intended to dispel.

[59] (Charles) Gideon Murray (1877–1951). Colonial Civil Service 1898–1917; Food Commissioner

22 August 1928
Loubcroy Lodge, Oykell, By Lairg

My dear Hilda,

...

The weather is lovely. It is too soon to say how sport will turn out but present indications are bad. Grouse appears scarce salmon scarcer and trout very stiff.

I am very well and find I can walk without knee stiffness ...

3 September 1928
Bamburgh

My dear Ida,

...

I hope when you come you will be able to bring the latest authentic story about Austen. The account of his journey to Liverpool & his embarkation there as given in the Times was most disturbing and still more alarming were the photos published in various newspapers which made him look as if he had had a stroke. I presume it is really no more than his excessive physical weakness and mental depression finding expression in neuritic pains, but I should like to hear more. ...

The latter part of my stay at Loubcroy was as you can imagine more cheerful than the first and I feel it did me a lot of good ... Estimating the sport by the actual bag I should say it was the worst season I remember except possibly 1918 when the "vermin" had got very abundant during the war. ...

...

16 September 1928
Craigengillan, Dalmellington, Ayrshire

My dear Hilda,

...

It has been, I should say, an unusually pleasant September this year. ... Our holiday is now very nearly at an end and I confess I am quite ready to go home, but I think I have enjoyed my stay away as much as ever in spite of anxieties & some disappointments. I wish Annie were more able to enjoy her holiday. This strained heel does not seem to get right and she constantly complains of rheumatic pains in different parts of her body. ...

The sport is not very great here. We had two days driving without much result and a day in the snipe bog which was very amusing. But the fishing is disappointing. ...

for West of Scotland 1917–18. Unionist MP for Glasgow, St Rollox 1918–22. Member, Speaker's Conference on Federal Devolution 1919–20. Succeeded as 2nd Viscount Elibank 1927.

...

I am longing to see the garden & the orchids at Westbourne, but not so keenly anticipating the pleasure of Yarmouth & negotiations with L.A.'s. By the last pouch from the Ministry I had six invitations to open buildings attend public dinners &c &c.

...

[P.S.] I see the Scottish Burghs & the Scottish Parish Councils have both met & unanimously condemned the Govts proposals for Loc. Govt. Reform in Scotland.

> 22 September 1928
> Westbourne

My dear Hilda,

...

I have got a very strenuous time before me, as in addition to my negotiations with L.A.'s I have four speeches in my (new) constituency and a number of public dinners and functions. Next week A. & I are attending the Yarmouth [Conservative Annual] Conference where I shall have to speak and then we go to Paris with Dorothy for the week end. Our first Cabinet is on Monday and I shall take the opportunity of a private chat with S.B. when no doubt I shall hear the latest developments in connection with my colleagues.

...

> 28 September 1928
> 37 Eaton Square, SW1

My dear Ida,

...

It is certainly startling to hear that so late as Bermuda Austen was only able to walk round the deck by himself, but I hope he has made more rapid progress since. Kylsant[60] told Annie that his people on board had given him rather a bad account of his condition but probably that was at the beginning of the voyage.

We came back from Yarmouth this morning having had a very pleasant excursion ...

The party meeting was a great success – everyone in great spirits and showing an admirable unity despite the vehement statements of the opposition press to the contrary. I dont know what accounts you may have seen of the Conference

---

[60] Owen Cosby Philipps (1863–1937). Shipowner; Vice-Chairman, Port of London Authority 1909–13. Liberal MP for Haverfordwest 1906–10 and Unionist MP for Chester 1916–22. Served on numerous government committees and enquiries. Convicted of publishing false commercial information 1928 and sentenced to a year's imprisonment. Created Baron Kylsant 1923.

but I had the success of my life there though I am still a little puzzled to know why. The party organisers had rather cold feet about Local Govt Reform and the Chairman tried to prevent my speaking on it, on the ground that it was a difficult subject to treat on a public platform. I set myself to try and put the case in such a way that it could be understanded [sic] of the people and that they could see the broad purposes of the scheme. So far as the words were concerned the speech was mostly impromptu and I lightened it up with such humorous interpolations as occurred to me. The result was astonishing. I had a great reception when I rose but when I sat down there was a perfect hurricane of cheers which went on for several minutes till I had to rise & bow like a singer. And then the whole audience got up and sang "For he's a jolly good fellow". Old hands said they had never seen anything like it before and I was overwhelmed with congratulations. Of course a personal triumph like that is always gratifying but one knows better than to attach too much importance to it. What gives me much more satisfaction is the conviction that the members of Parliament who were there, the correspondents of the Press, and the party officials had their conception of the scheme as an election winner completely altered. I was told that the pressmen were amazed at the enthusiasm and the chief agent himself said to me that the fears of the agents had been completely removed. I am sure that the incident will be most important in its influence over subsequent proceedings and as the Central Office got a verbatim report they will have new material which will enable them to deal with a subject which they have been hitherto inclined to shirk.

S.B.'s speech in the evening was one of the best I have heard from him both in matter & manner. He spoke with weight & confidence, like a leader addressing his followers, and his audience was wildly enthusiastic. The enthusiasm over safeguarding was tremendous and though no doubt the audience would have liked a much stronger pronouncement especially on iron & steel I am sure we are wise in keeping our policy always a little behind what the party is ready for. Even Leo is satisfied to wait though he chafes under Winston's laggardness.

...

6 October 1928
Westbourne

My dear Ida,

...

My week has been divided between work on the Bill and speeches in Birmingham. I think it is now pretty clear that we shant have a great deal of trouble from the Guardians who realise that the game is up, but that the real fight will be over finance. Kingsley had an extremely useful conference with the L.A.'s (including Guardians) in Gloucestershire. After the conclusion of the public proceedings the Guardians asked to see him privately and saying that they realised that abolition was inevitable asked if they might not make suggestions to mitigate the sacrifice. Their suggestions were not very helpful but it shows what the feeling is underneath. I think a good deal of comfort will come to them when they find it provided in the Bill (1) That the local sub-committees of the C.C. Public Assistance Committee are to be called "Guardians Committees" and (2) that they are to be composed of C.C. representing the area representatives of the Districts comprised in the area & coopted persons who may not be more than ⅓ of the whole.

I always knew we should have trouble over finance but that I dont really mind as it is not a question of principle. But Lord! there *are* a lot of controversial points in the Bill; we should never get it through without a guillotine.

...

I came down here on Tuesday for a first meeting in my constituency and had a wretched attendance – only about 250 in a hall that holds three times the number. ... However those who were there had a good speech so perhaps more will come next time I go to Market Hall. I had to go back to London on Wednesday but returned on Thursday to open a School of Pharmacy, where I had a riotous reception from the students ... In the evening I had a meeting for the Edgbaston ward in the Vestry hall and this time the room was packed and my people were more cheerful accordingly.

...

A. asks me to thank Hilda very much for her letter which she enjoyed reading. I agree with her that it is ten to one against my ever being P.M. But as I have not any wish for that very wearing post that does not trouble me a bit.

13 October 1928
Westbourne

My dear Hilda,

...

I see plenty of photographs of Austen in summery clothes and always with the broadest of grins so that I hope he is feeling well and happy. It will certainly be very cold in Ottawa in the middle of November and I should think the Atlantic will be wholly vile. But perhaps that will be preferable to replying to criticism of the Anglo-French "Pact" on the address. Mackenzie King[61] is coming to lunch with us on Wednesday so I shall tell him not to let A. be worried by Canada Clubs and United Loyalists. I get a great many affectionate enquiries about him from all sorts of people; it is evident that he is now established in the popular regard.

...

---

[61] William Lyon Mackenzie King (1874–1950). Canadian economist and politician. Liberal MP 1908–11, 1921–49. Deputy Minister of Labour, 1900–1908; Minister of Labour 1909–11; Liberal Leader 1919–48; Prime Minister 1921–30, 1935–48.

I was in town up to Thursday afternoon working away at the Bill mostly. The heathen are beginning to rage furiously together against it but I am not yet able to gauge the extent or the force of the opposition. I meet the L.C.C. on Monday but their concern is of course with London only. I should like to know whether Ida has any criticism or suggestion to make in connection with the following arrangement which we have evolved for counties. Each county must prepare a scheme for the approval of the Minister dividing up the area into a number of sub areas comprising one or more county districts. It must form a public assistance committee (which may be an existing comee. to which all the transferred functions must be referred but it may assign some of these functions to other committees, education to the Education Comee hospitals & M.&C.W. to health Comee &c. In each area it must form a local committee called the Guardians Committee for the area to deal with out relief subject to such conditions as the Public Assistance Committee may lay down (financial control) and it may at the request of that Comee visit & report on any P.L. Institutions but it may not manage them nor appoint nor dismiss any official. When any business affecting the area is discussed by the P.A.C. the Chairman or other representative of the G.C. has the right to attend & take part in the proceedings but not to vote. The G.C. is to be composed of ⅔ members of the District Councils in the area nominated by them and members of the C.C. representing electoral districts in the area and one third persons including women but not members of the C.C. nominated by the C.C.

...

I had two meetings on Thursday one at Harborne in the baths – a large hall about half full – the other at Quinton where we had for them a very good audience. It will be interesting to see whether I shall get better attendances when they get used to a Cabinet Minister as their member. Meanwhile I think I have done useful work with four meetings and a flower show. ... Tavistock[62] was not too good but fortunately on the right side and not encouraging for the Liberal Conference. I don't think Ll.G.'s speech will do him much good. It is likely to embitter the Socialists and yet it wont win him the trust of those who fear Socialism.

...

Hall was here this morning and gave a more cheerful account of Hoskins. I haven't got the final accounts yet but it looks as if last year would show a small profit & the prospects this year are much better so that we might perhaps hope to get something in the way of a dividend in 12 months time.

...

---

[62] Tavistock by-election, 11 October 1928. A Conservative majority of 1272 in 1924 was reduced to 173 when Labour intervened for the first time.

20 October 1928
The Hall, Six Mile Bottom

My dear Ida,

I am glad to have your news of Austen although I agree that it is rather disappointing. He must be a perfect skeleton to weigh only 9 st and I find it difficult to believe that by the end of November he will be fit to take on the strain of the F.O. again. And then there is the General Election to look forward to towards the end of May which seems most likely to be the fatal date. But I believe that wont worry him as much as it does me. He sleeps in the afternoons when he has speeches to make in the evening!

I am beginning my conferences with the Local Authorities. I had one on Monday with the L.C.C. which I thought on the whole pretty satisfactory and one on Thursday with the C.C. Assn which was not so satisfactory. But I have had a private note since from Lord Strachie,[63] who was one of the deputation saying that he was much impressed by what I said and offering to come and see me in order to discuss how he can help. From a Liberal that is rather encouraging.

I agree that the management of the institutions is very difficult & I am not sure that we have got the best or the final solution. One trouble is that they will probably be divided up among the Committees Hospitals going to the Health Committee M.D. & lunatics to the committees dealing with these subjects already & so on. I think what my people are most afraid of is a demand on the part of Guardians Committees to have institutions of their own and if one were to say that they might manage subject to conditions &c imposed by the C.C. would not that exactly reduce them to the position of school managers? No doubt the arrangement will be subject to criticism and we may happen on some more satisfactory solution than we have at present.

Owing to my engagements I was not able to get here until Thursday night so I missed one day's shooting. But the two I have had I have enjoyed and it has been an interesting experience to be shooting on what is perhaps the crack partridge estate of the country where birds come over in hundreds and one really gets an opportunity of correcting one's faults. ...

The party too has been rather a new experience being a mixture of young smart people and much older ones. The young ladies of today paint themselves up to an incredible and I think disgusting extent but I must say they are not as bad as they look. ...

The fashionable ways are interesting. The ladies breakfast upstairs, the gentlemen downstairs at 8.45. They drive off in a kind of bus to the shoot at 9.45 & the actual shooting begins about 10. There are 15 keepers permanently employed on the estate and on shooting days two or sometimes three squads of

---

[63] Edward Strachey (1858–1936). Liberal MP for Somersetshire South 1892–1911. Parliamentary Secretary, Board of Agriculture 1909–11; Paymaster-General 1912–15. Succeeded as 4th Bart 1901; created Baron Strachie 1911.

beaters each 30 to 40 strong are marshalled & drilled so as to avoid any waiting between the drives. If there are more than a few hundred yards to walk between the drives you get into the bus again.

The ladies come out & join the guns at luncheon which is in a farmhouse & is quite simple though there is a very ample supply of everything. In about an hour a start is made and so well prepared are the arrangements that the last drive ends just after sunset and before the bus has reached the front door again it is dark. On arrival, there is a more or less perfunctory change followed by the tea and then there is a dispersal, the ladies retiring to their rooms & the gentlemen to the smoke room. Dinner is supposed to be at 8.15 when the gong sounds but no one comes down till 8.30 and then we all go downstairs to a sort of basement in which is a gramophone, a ping-pong table a bar and a cinema! Here the party converses or plays ping-pong for a quarter of an hour or so while the younger members consume cocktails and at last we saunter up to dinner about 8.45. I wonder the cook doesn't give notice.

After dinner you may look at the amateur movies taken on a trip round the world by the Reids[64] (rather boring these amateur shows) or play bridge or vingt et un till soon after midnight, but in these "smart" households you dont get away from the ladies again: in other words I get no chance of a pipe till its too late. Well its an amusing experience though I must say a little of it goes a long way with me because the majority of these people seem to have no intellectual interest whatever, and I soon tire of personal gossip.

26 October 1928
Westbourne

My dear Hilda,

Thank you for letting me know about Joe's birthday. It is dreadful how I have got out of touch with Austen's family, because at one time I was quite intimate with them. But since he has had Twitt's Ghyll and Morpeth Mansions all intercourse has ceased and now I only see them at rare intervals and for a moment at a time. ...

...

It has been a busy week with conferences and discussions on the Bill & I have had to sit up rather late once or twice but on the whole I am well satisfied with the progress made. The U.D.C's had prepared a pretty critical report but, as usual with them, they were extremely amiable when they came to see me and after a friendly and reassuring discussion they left declaring that there never had been any Minister in whom they had so much confidence as myself.

---

[64] Alec Stratford Cunningham-Reid (1895–1977). Conservative MP for Warrington 1922–23 and 1924–29, St Marylebone 1932–45 (whip withdrawn May 1942 and defeated as Independent Conservative 1945). PPS to First Commissioner of Works 1922 and to Minister of Transport 1924–29.

I was much more anxious about the Municipal Corporations. They had invited the assistance of my old friend Arthur Collins,[65] formerly Borough Treasurer here and my Director of Establishment at National Service, and he together with a firm of Actuaries has prepared a report which condemns the scheme pretty thoroughly from the financial point of view. Rather foolishly they made counter suggestions as to the construction of the formula which lend themselves readily to counter criticisms, but the A.M.C. warily declined to father any constructive proposal and confined themselves to the statement that the formula required re-adjustment in consultation with themselves. The most unfortunate thing was that the A.M.C. declared it to be "fundamental" that the loss of rates should be separated from the block grant and made up specifically to each authority. On this the Daily Herald came out with huge headlines "Staggering blow for Neville Chamberlain" and a sensational article expressing the view that the only thing for me to do was to "scrap" the Bill & start afresh. The next day however the headlines had shrunk to the width of a column and the day after I retired to a back page with the remark that I seemed disposed to stick to my guns but it was believed [?] I should make some concessions. I call that thoroughly bad journalism. They should never have started such a conspicuous hare as that if they were not going to follow it up. As a matter of fact the A.M.C made a mess of things at their deputation. I knocked the opening speaker off his perch by asking him an innocent question in the middle of his speech, a trick I have often tried before & seldom found to fail. He got in a panic at once, gave the first answer that came into his head & was immediately contradicted by the bulk of the deputation, some 60 in number. But as soon as I had fixed them down to their answer they themselves got frightened & the next speaker begged me not to take either answer as they had not thought it out.

I had a splendid opportunity of rolling them in the mud but a victory in the room might have cost me the victory outside so I was magnanimous and omitted to dot the i's. But their confidence had gone and when I asked the question "Is it really fundamental"? only a few timid voices answered Yes and there was silent acquiescence while I demonstrated that it was nothing of the kind. I was well pleased with the interview and Kingsley and all my people are delighted. I am satisfied that the only real "kick" is over the money and if I can screw a little more out of Winston I dont believe I shall have any very formidable opposition. I am told that a good many of our members are now quite strong on the local government side and feel that it too is a winner for an election. ...

　　...

---

[65] Arthur Collins. Seconded from Birmingham Council to become Secretary and Accounting Officer, National Service Department 1917; Birmingham City Treasurer, 1918–22.

4 November 1928
37 Eaton Square, SW1

My dear Ida,

... I am very glad to hear what you say about the R.W. Housing Act. I can't make out that it is being taken up much more actively in the country generally, but I suppose it will only really begin to move when it is due to expire.

I am sorry I forgot about the Yarmouth speech. ... I don't think I ever said or thought that the Rating &c scheme was an election winner. In fact I think I remember writing that it was too technical and too involved ever to make much appeal to the man in the street. But if we can get it passed we shall have done something that will be remembered to our credit hereafter and we must just hope that we may win the election on more general grounds. I see Garvin[66] in the Observer is busy administering "rude shocks to Conservative complacency" and practically prophesying the triumph of the Socialists. The Sunday Times is lugubrious and Rothermere is I understand going to come out against us so things dont look too cheerful, & the Municipal Elections are not encouraging. However if we go out, we go out & then the other side will have their turn of disfavour. You will be interested to hear that I have redrafted my Bill so as to permit Guardians Committees on the request of the public Assistance Committee to visit & report on or manage a Poor Law Institution subject to such conditions as the C.C. may lay down. My people dont much like it but I think its right.

...

I have had a busy week but managed to get a glimpse of the orchid show in the new [Horticultural] hall. ... I picked up a couple of nice things.

...

16 November 1928
37 Eaton Square, SW1

My dear Ida,

...

I have been worked pretty hard during the last fortnight and begin to feel the effects a little. That wretched speech on Literature & the Press at the Printers Pension Corporation dinner which I undertook at the request of Gomer Berry because he is valuable to the Party weighed like lead upon me. I sat up late night after night working away at it and although finally I got it to my satisfaction and delivered it without forgetting any of it, it has left its mark on me. All the big bugs including F.E. and Winston have attended these dinners in the last few years, and I didn't want to fall below the level. As a matter of fact I think my

---

[66] James Louis Garvin (1864–1947). Editor, *Observer* 1908–42 and *Pall Mall Gazette* 1912–15. Official biographer of Joseph Chamberlain.

effort was quite equal to theirs and old Riddell[67] at any rate expressed unbounded satisfaction with it. ...

It is always when one is busiest that outside engagements pile up and I have had 3 other speeches to make this week. The first was for Lady Londonderry[68] in connection with a new Fund which is to be raised to help maternity services. The next was to the National Farmers Union on the Bill. As you know the N.F.U. have carried on a sort of vendetta against the Ministry mainly on account of the Preservatives Regulations, Synthetic Cream and the Milk & Dairies Order and the Agr. Correspt of the Times never loses the opportunity of having a tilt at the Minister no doubt because he thinks it will be popular with the farmers. In such circumstances I always like to meet my critics, having found that one can usually bring them to a better frame of mind and so it proved in this case. ... They were I daresay flattered at having a Minister come down specially to talk to them. At any rate I found the atmosphere more friendly than I expected and in a few sentences I had them in roars of laughter. After that it was plain sailing. I was bombarded with questions but I had an answer for everything and generally a joke besides. My own impression that I had left them in a thoroughly good humour was confirmed afterwards by various M.P.'s who had seen some of their farmer friends and who all assured me that the meeting had done an immense amount of good and that the farmers were more than satisfied. In face of that it is of no use for Prebendary Propert[69] to demand my resignation!

Meanwhile negotiations with the Assocns continue to proceed according to plan. The C.C. have got out of the cul de sac in which they had landed themselves and are joining the A.M.C. in a joint committee which is empowered to go on negotiating with the Minister. And this joint committee has announced that, while adhering to its views about the separation of derating losses from the block grant (and thus saving its face) *if* the Minister is obdurate, it will then *insist* on – the very concession that the Minister privately whispered into the ear of his old friend, Ald Williams[70] of the A.M.C.! They are to see me next Thursday when we are to debate this new "demand" and after a decent show of

---

[67] George Riddell (1865–1934). Chairman, *News of the World* 1903–34. Created Baron Riddell 1920.

[68] Edith Helen Vane-Tempest-Stewart (1879–1959). Married Viscount Castlereagh 1899 who succeeded as 7th Marquess of Londonderry 1915. Founder and President, Women's Legion 1914–18. President, Conservative Women's Advisory Committee, Northern Counties Area 1930–46. Known as Circe to intimates.

[69] Reverend Prebendary P.S.G. Propert (1861–1940). Vicar in Fulham and Prebendary, St Paul's Cathedral. Vice-Chairman, Fulham Poor Law Union 1896; Chairman, Fulham Board of Guardians for twenty-five years; President, Association of Poor Law Unions 1920 and Central Poor Law Conference 1926. Author of several works on the Poor Law.

[70] Probably Richard John Williams (1853–1941). Mayor of Bangor 1913–20; Alderman, Carnarvonshire County Council and Bangor City Council; Chairman, North-West Wales Pensions Committee. Governor, Council of University College of North Wales. Knighted 1921.

resistance I propose to accept it on the understanding that it forms part of a general agreement. If I can go to the House for second reading with a settlement with the C.C.A & the A.M.C. in my pocket it will be a triumph especially as, according to the Sunday Times "persuasion is not my forte!"

I suppose I shall have to spend all next week working at that (2nd reading) speech. I haven't begun it yet – not had time – but it must evidently be a long and I fear tedious affair.

...

We are having a very pleasant party here [Chevening], and yesterday we were lucky enough to get an absolutely perfect day. Of course we are on very familiar terms with the Stanhopes[71] now and there are no formalities between us any longer. Among the guests are ... Taffy Gwynne[72] (Morning Post) ... Gwynne is very enthusiastic about a scheme for buying a huge estate on the Peace River for colonisation purposes – in fact the very scheme that I was so keen about last July but which the Colonial Office & Treasury succeeded in drowning. I have given him plenty of encouragement but I personally believe (though I didn't tell him) that only a Prime Minister, not merely convinced but prepared to take all the responsibility on his own shoulders could carry through such a plan. It is too spectacular for S.B.

... W. Bridgeman[73] told me he had met an old opponent, a farmer, a Liberal, and the kind who is always vocal in objections, and that he had said that he thought their criticisms had been most fairly met and there was now nothing to complain of in the scheme.

...

8 December 1928
Westbourne

My dear Hilda,
    ... It has been as always a busy week for me but there is not much to tell for my work has been almost entirely administrative except for Cabinet Councils.

---

[71] James Richard Stanhope (1880–1967). Parliamentary Secretary, War Office 1918–19; Civil Lord of Admiralty 1924–29; Under-Secretary, War Office 1931–34 and Foreign Office 1934–36; First Commissioner of Works 1936–37; President, Board of Education 1937–38; First Lord of Admiralty 1938–39; Leader of Lords 1938–40; Lord President of Council 1939–40. Succeeded as 7th Earl of Stanhope 1905.

[72] Howell Arthur Gwynne (1865–1950). Journalist. Reuters' correspondent in Roumania, Sudan, Greece and South Africa; Foreign Director, Reuters Agency 1904; Editor, *Standard* 1904–11 and *Morning Post* 1911–37.

[73] William Clive Bridgeman (1864–1935). Conservative MP for Oswestry 1906–29. Unionist Whip 1911; Junior Lord of Treasury 1915–16; Parliamentary Secretary, Ministry of Labour 1916–19 and to Board of Trade 1919; Secretary for Mines 1920–22; Home Secretary 1922–24; First Lord of Admiralty 1924–29. Created Viscount Bridgeman 1929.

But next week and the week after I shall have to be in the House nearly every day on one thing or another. On Tuesday is the guillotine motion on which I suppose there will be loud and angry protests from the Labour Party although their whips have agreed the time table with ours. I rather fancy that S.B. moves it but I shall probably have to stand by and speak later. Then on Wednesday we take the housing subsidy resolution.[74] The opposition expected something much more drastic and were rather taken aback but of course they will exploit it all they can for party purposes. On Thursday we enter upon our 13 day committee stage.

...

16 December 1928
37 Eaton Square, SW1

My dear Ida,
...
I haven't much to say, but as you opine the subsidy debate when off very well and the guillotine & subsequent committee have gone along smoothly. I have been much occupied with distressed mining areas in addition to everything else but it is finished now. Tomorrow I shall slip out of the House in the course of the afternoon for the critical discussion with the C.C.A. A.M.C. & U.D.C.A. Unfortunately they are quarrelling among themselves & that may make it very difficult to come to terms with them.

...

31 December 1928
Westbourne

My dear Ida,
...
I am glad you were able to see something of Austen. S.B. did ask me whether if the Dominions & Colonial offices were split I should like the Colonies and I said Yes but I did not suppose he was seriously thinking of it as there would be some difficulties about the staffs. But as he mentioned it to Austen there must be something definite in his mind. Perhaps he thought he might get over his difficulty about Leo by leaving him with the Dominions.

...

I had a telephone message from S.B. this afternoon asking us to go and lunch with him on Wednesday and incidentally his Secretary observed that this

---

[74] This abolished the 1923 subsidy on new houses altogether and reduced the subsidy under Wheatley's 1924 Housing Act by £25.

morning's news of the King was rather disquieting. I must say that any but good news now is disquieting for I cant see how he can last out much longer unless he takes a definite turn for the better. Its a terrible fight and I feel very sorry for the Queen.

    ...

3

1929

'There is no Certainty in Politics': Legislative Triumph and Electoral Defeat

6 January 1929
Westbourne

My dear Hilda,

...

You need not regret anything in your letter for you amplified what Ida had said and I was glad to have your own personal impressions of Austen. I think it is particularly satisfactory that he should be cutting down his smoke & his drink. I have long thought that he indulged far too much in both and that sooner or later he would have to pay for it. But I did not think he would take kindly to any expression of such views from me and I did not therefore say anything to him. That he should be doing the right thing now even though rather late is very gratifying.

I expect what S.B. said to Austen about my going to Agriculture arose from my remark to him just before Christmas that it was an extraordinarily interesting office with a wide scope and that at one time I should have liked to try my hand at it. He asked if I would take it now and I said No. It would be a great sacrifice to take it now. The salary is only £2000, the status is that of a minor minister and the difficulties in the way of success are enormous. The other day S.B. asked me if I thought Winston would take it. I again said No, for I thought he would feel the force of the same reasons as influence me. But W. is an extra difficult man to find any office for outside the one he occupies now. No doubt A. will speak to S.B. some time again about all the offices.

We went over to Astley Court on Wednesday to lunch with him [Baldwin]. There was only the family there and after lunch I went to his room and we discussed persons and things at large. I wanted in particular to tell him of my conversations at Swinton with P. Cunliffe-Lister[1] who had asked my advice as to

---

[1] Philip Cunliffe-Lister (1884–1972). Changed his surname from Lloyd-Greame in 1924. Conservative MP for Hendon 1918–35. Parliamentary Secretary, Board of Trade 1920–21; Secretary, Overseas Trade Dept 1921–22; President, Board of Trade 1922–24, 1924–29 and 1931; Colonial Secretary 1931–35; Air Secretary 1935–38; Minister Resident, West Africa 1942–44; Minister of Civil Aviation 1944–45; Chancellor, Duchy of Lancaster and Minister of Materials 1951–52; Commonwealth Secretary 1952–55. Knighted 1920. Created Viscount Swinton 1935 and Earl of Swinton 1955.

whether he should continue in politics. He does not like the H. of C. of which he has not got the ear; he has the usual distaste for his constituency & his wife hates & loathes politics. Nevertheless I advised him to go on, feeling certain that he would always be hankering after the old life if he did leave it, and feeling also that in view of the weakness of our second eleven and his own comparative youth he would be a great loss to the party. Philip was obviously touched and gratified by what I said and before I left he told me that he had had a talk with Molly and decided to take my advice. If we come back therefore, he will still be with us though he would like a change of office.

S.B. was I think genuinely glad to hear that P. was going on though those two are not very sympathetic and never will be. We discussed other members of the Cabinet but he said nothing to me this time about myself and I said nothing more to him on that subject. Of course there was nothing new to say.

Evidently he was not too hopeful about the King. His own country doctor was frankly pessimistic; "it might be sooner or it might be later, but he had never known a man of his age recover when the poison had once got into his system". If H.M. should unhappily die the General Election would inevitably have to be postponed until the autumn. If he should live I imagine he will be more or less of an invalid. But I wish we could get our Honours List out!

...

12 January 1929
Westbourne

My dear Ida,

...

I have had a very busy week as there has been a great deal of office work and I had to go up to town on Friday & spend the day at the Ministry to decide various matters that could not well be dealt with by correspondence. We have also had a number of social and public engagements. On Tuesday I spent two hours in the Art Gallery with Kaines Smith and enjoyed my morning very much. ...

On Wednesday we had Grant Robertson[2] to lunch and I had a long talk with him about the University and the new Hospital on which I am glad to say his ideas are sound. He wants not only to take the Medical School out to Edgbaston but also to make it an integral part of the Hospital which would be staffed to a considerable extent by the Professors of the University. Thus the Professors would be chosen for their fitness as teachers as well as doctors instead of being drawn only from the local men who are senior physicians or surgeons as now.

---

[2] Charles Grant Robertson (1869–1948). Historian and academic adminstrator. Fellow, All Souls 1893–98 and domestic bursar 1897–1920; Tutor in Modern History, Exeter College, Oxford 1895–99 and Magdalen 1905–20. Principal, Birmingham University 1920–27 and Vice-Chancellor 1927–38. Knighted 1928.

Moreover you would get proper team work between the clinical & the non clinical men, the bacteriologists, anatomists, biologists chemists and physicists.

...

Last night we finished up with a visit to an Edgbaston Constituency Ball – a sort of mild forecast of the election. I am to have three opponents I hear. I see the New Statesman opines that of all the wicked members of this Government Austen is the worst. So like the high brow Liberal view.

...

19 January 1929
Westbourne

My dear Hilda,

We had a fall of snow here the night before last but happily it was followed by a thaw so that your fears were not realised and we had quite a comfortable journey up to Liverpool. Edward Stanley[3] came to the station to meet us and we drove out to Knowsley as soon as the photographers (after several failures) had succeeded in firing off their flashlights. ...

I felt beforehand that the relay would add new terrors to the ordeal of speaking but it was not so. I was informed beforehand that there would be several microphones in front of the platform and that I need not cramp myself. As a matter of fact I thought no more about them when I got on my feet except when messages were passed along to say "All halls full" and "relaying excellent".

My own meeting was all I could wish. The hall, the largest in Liverpool, holds 5000 and it was packed from top to bottom. I did not go in for fireworks, having a serious purpose to fulfil, but I just put in enough lighter passages to keep the attention of the audience and they maintained their interest, so far as I could judge, to the end. I spoke for an hour and ten minutes and as usual evoked much amazement by not having any notes. The local paper took up rather a carping attitude this morning but I gathered it was a Liberal organ so it was not to be expected that it would be friendly. I should like to hear from a more impartial source what really was the impression created, but if one may accept the views of M.P.'s and others on the platform they were highly delighted and thought it would do a lot of good. I had rather a difficult point to deal with in the local position at Liverpool as the council profess to have a grievance on which I cannot meet them, but the particular member who had been pressing

---

[3] Edward Montagu Cavendish Stanley (1894–1938). Conservative MP for Liverpool Abercromby 1917–18 and Fylde 1922–38. PPS to his father, the Earl of Derby 1922–23; Conservative Whip 1924–27; Parliamentary and Financial Secretary, Admiralty 1931–35 and 1935–37; Under-Secretary for Dominions 1935 and for India 1937–38; Dominion Secretary 1938. Chairman, Junior Imperial League 1928–33 and President 1933–38; Deputy Chairman, Conservative Party 1927–29. Styled Lord Stanley from 1908.

me about it was impressed by the adroitness with which he considered I had turned it and declared that I had completely taken the wind out of the sails of the critics.

After we got back we had supper & then made a hurried survey of some of the treasures of Knowsley. It is a gigantic place and a regular museum of beautiful & valuable things. ... Altogether it was a very interesting visit & I like Edward Stanley and incline to think I like his wife too, though I should be surer if she did not make a mask of her face by the use of powder & lipstick. Stanley told A. that "we" (meaning I suspect the Whips office) often made Cabinets from which I fear the majority of the present Government are excluded. But it appears that Austen and I are spared. I am destined for the Exchequer from which Winston is expelled and relegated to the Dominions. They like him personally but do not consider that he could be trusted as a leader.

Frank went off very cheerfully on the whole. He enjoyed his last week with his parents very much and there is no doubt that he is developing now at a great pace. ... I wish I knew exactly what he was to do when he is ready to earn his living but whatever it is I feel pretty sure that he is of the kind that will do well. As for Dorothy she writes to her friend Aylott that she hasn't got a "trace of home sickness", though she doesn't choose to give her parents that information. ...

...

... I am having a most interesting correspondence with Bledisloe.[4] I wrote to ask what he had in his mind when he suggested in the Times that there should be a 3-party conference on agriculture. I told him it was no good; no one would trust Ll.G. and Ramsay wouldn't or couldn't play because a successful result must be to our advantage. I said I couldn't understand why he should be depreciating safeguarding which if things went on as they were doing would be practical politics for certain agricultural products within five years, and I expressed my opinion of the folly of farmers in opposing the safeguarding of iron & steel or any other old thing, since every addition to the list strengthened their case. And so on. B. replied at length and gave me his ideas which as I say are very interesting. They involve interference with the middleman and with rents which sounds formidable. But I have told him that I don't shut my mind to either and we are to have a talk as soon as I am through with my Bill. I should feel better satisfied if we could evolve something in the nature of an agricultural policy.

...

---

[4] Charles Bathurst (1867–1958). Active spokesman for agriculture and Conservative MP for Wiltshire Wilton 1910–18. Parliamentary Secretary, Ministry of Food 1916–17 and Agriculture 1924–28; Governor-General, New Zealand 1930–35; Chairman, Royal Commission on closer union of Rhodesia and Nyasaland 1938. Knighted 1917. Created Baron Bledisloe 1918 and Viscount Bledisloe 1935.

Edward Stanley said that of all the speeches he had heard the one he wd most like to have made was mine at Yarmouth. And one of the Liverpool members said the Serjeant-at-Arms told him that my speech on 2nd R. was the best he had heard in the (I think) 47 years he had known the House. So Naow!

26 January 1929
Westbourne

My dear Ida,

I can now answer your question about the relaying as I have seen either someone who was present or someone who has seen someone who was present at each of the three halls. They had simply a chairman who started a speech and broke off when I was turned on and in each case I am told the affair was an unqualified success. The audiences were not very large; they were estimated at 1000, 500 and 300 but it may be that the halls would not hold more. Anyway the voice came through without any difficulty and the people were sufficiently interested to stop and listen right to the end of the speech. At Widnes I was told the audience was mostly working men, many of them belonging to the Labour Party and some came up afterwards to express their satisfaction and to say how very interesting they had found the speech. It is curious that it should be so, but we shall see whether the interest lasts after the novelty has worn off. E. Stanley told me that they only proposed to use the system on special occasions. I understand it costs about £50 to hire the P.O. lines.

I have got through my first week in Committee without undue fatigue and with very marked success. The two difficult points were the Conservative amdt to leave out breweries and distilleries and the Astor[5] amdt to take M.&C.W. out of the block grant. Fortunately the movers of the first gave me an opening as they all adduced different reasons for their proposals. So I fell upon them and knocked their heads together and their colleagues thoroughly enjoyed their discomfiture. They deserved to be laughed at because theirs was a demonstration of mere cowardice but I dont think they expected to get so little support in the lobby. Mr Briggs,[6] who moved, was unmercifully ragged afterwards in the smoking room where he observed that he had never been so knocked about in his life before and he thought he had made a mistake in going in for politics.

The other amdt required much more careful handling. Nancy had been working up the Y.M.C.A. for some time and there was a distinctly nervous feeling in the party. However I sent for Nancy the day before the amdt came on and talked to

[5] Nancy Witcher Astor (1879–1964). Conservative MP for Plymouth Sutton 1919–45. First woman MP to take her seat. Wife of Waldorf Astor.

[6] William James Harold Briggs (1870–1945). Conservative MP for Manchester Blackley 1918–23 and 1924–29. Member, Surrey County Council from 1930.

her like a father after which she announced that she should make her speech before me & say that *if* she were not convinced she should have to reserve her rights &c. So I got together some ideas and in a very full House made a reasoned statement on the whole situation which completely satisfied the nervous ones. In fact one of the whips who was standing at the Bar told me that the men round him were "simply delighted" and said it was the best speech I had ever made. That old familiar phrase!

The last two days have been very dull as so many amdts were out of order that the opposition were at their wits end to fill up the time and rambled about in generalities, false points, misunderstandings & misstatements. I felt very bored yesterday but scored a point with "Cheer up, Cully", a quotation which was obligingly supplied to me by someone in my neighbourhood. But the Press didn't report another incident. Ellen Wilkinson[7] was speaking and making a serious [sic] of offensive insinuations about the Tory party of the most "catty" description. Then she observed that she didn't want to make any "Captious criticism". "*What* criticism?" said I with my feet on the table. "*Captious* criticism". "Oh, I thought you said "Cats criticism". This interjection fairly doubled up the Labour Party with laughter and Red Ellen, not being able to think of the reply, had to join in herself.

Someone told me the other day that a friend of his had been lunching with Lord Thomson[8] and found him supremely confident that his party was coming back to office after the election. In fact they are already dividing out the places and he proposes to take the Foreign Office! Kingsley tells me that Snowden said to him that he was sure they were coming in. But to do that and get a working majority they would have to win about 160 seats and I cannot see where they are going to get them. They may be right, but my impression is that it is pure guesswork. I fancy we shall lose Midlothian but we ought to keep Battersea. Thomson said that both Right & Left wing were united in one thing – their dislike of Mosley![9]

...

---

[7] Ellen Cecily Wilkinson (1891–1947). Labour MP for Middlesbrough East 1924–31 and Jarrow 1935–47. PPS to Susan Lawrence 1929–31; Parliamentary Secretary, Ministry of Pensions 1940 and for Home Security 1940–45; Minister of Education 1945–47. Chair, Labour Party NEC 1944–45.

[8] Christopher Birdwood Thomson (1875–1930). Entered Royal Engineers 1894; Brigadier-General 1918; Supreme War Council 1918. Joined Labour Party 1919. Secretary for Air 1924 and 1929–30 when killed in the crash of airship R.101 at Beauvais. Created Baron Thomson 1924.

[9] Oswald Ernald Mosley (1896–1980). MP for Harrow 1918–24 as Conservative until 1920 and then Independent until joining Labour in May 1924. Labour MP for Smethwick 1926–31 (New Party February to October 1931). Chancellor, Duchy of Lancaster 1929–30. Founder and leader, New Party 1931–32; of British Union of Fascists 1932–40 until interned 1940–44; of Union Movement 1948–66. Succeeded as 6th Bart 1928.

9 February 1929
Westbourne

My dear Ida,

...

Battersea[10] was a bad blow though it would be easy to exaggerate its significance. The main cause of the defeat was apathy, the minor ones the disgruntlement of the bookies & the intervention of the Liberal. But I am pleased to see that of the Liberal revival there is no sign anywhere. In my opinion the sooner they disappear the better, for they dont seem to me to serve any useful purpose and their presence on the whole only aids the Socialists. Also the bye-elections do not indicate any landslide against us so I am not disposed to be pessimistic.

...

16 February 1929
37 Eaton Square, SW1

My dear Hilda,

This weather is too vile for anything ... I got a chill in my room at the H. of C. on Wednesday and though I survived Thursday all right it attacked my liver and I spent yesterday in bed where I am now writing this. It is a great nuisance, but I hope to be all right by Monday ...

The opposition had the greatest difficulty in keeping the debates going on report stage and man after man rose with the obvious intention of spinning out as much time as possible. The coolest thing on McD.'s part is I think to come in at all on Third Reading after having been absent during the whole of the preceding stages.

I see the Times returns to the charge about bureaucracy this morning. The curious thing is that they admit, as did Sir A. Hopkinson,[11] the need for a clause to remove difficulties. Hopkinson said I had proved that up to the hilt. Privately he admitted to me that you could not remove difficulties without "modifying the provisions of the Act". But he didn't want to put those words in the clause "because they might make a precedent". Can you imagine that a sensible person would be so illogical. The Times is just the same & it only shows that prejudice has now been created to such an extent on this matter that the voice of reason is

---

[10] Battersea South by-election, 7 February 1929. A Liberal intervention captured 2858 votes and enabled Labour to overturn a Conservative majority of 5217 in 1924 to win the seat by 576 votes. As predicted, West Midlothian was lost to Labour on 29 January.

[11] Alfred Hopkinson (1851–1939). Barrister and Professor of Law, Owens College Manchester 1875–89 and Principal 1898–1904; Vice-Chancellor, Victoria University, Manchester 1900–1913. Unsuccessful Liberal and Liberal Unionist candidate before becoming Unionist MP for Cricklade 1895–98 and Combined Universities 1926–29. Chairman of many departmental commissions. Knighted 1910.

no longer listened to. The Times complains that my amdts have not altered the substance of the clause. That is true. But there is no way of altering the substance which would satisfy them but to delete it altogether & that they admit would not do. I foresee that this will be the clause which the Lords will fasten their teeth into and I should not be surprised if they threw it out altogether. If so I should let it go for I fancy we shall have to have the inconveniences of such a course demonstrated before we get any sympathy for the clause.

…

I am distressed about the birds at home for I fear no one will feed them and we shall lose many thrushes & chaffinches. Tits generally seem to survive the hard winters, but I always remember how songless the garden was for several years after the last great cold. …

…

I got an hour one day at Burlington House & hope to go again. I didn't think Hals came up to expectation and I was a little surprised at some of the Rembrandts but the Rabbi is magnificent. The Cuyps were satisfying and I must have a much better look at the Vermeers.

…

24 February 1929
37 Eaton Square, SW1

My dear Ida,

…

My trouble was certainly not "flu" and I have felt no effects since beyond a certain depression of spirits. But it was a nasty turn and if I had not taken it seriously and gone to bed until it was over it might have developed into something worse. As it was, my voice about which I was rather nervous on Sunday, was particularly good on Monday and my speech gave great satisfaction to our people. I enclose a cutting from the always carping critic of the Sunday Times; although I was not sympathetic to his complaint that the H. of C. found so little to alter in the Bill that it might as well have stopped at home, he cannot pretend that he represents anybody but "one" i.e. himself.

The House had an object lesson immediately afterwards in what may happen where it is not ridden on so light a rein as I employed. Neither Leo nor Winston distinguished themselves in the debate on the Irish loyalists; the latter in particular had not prepared himself for the debate and was tactless and unsympathetic in manner. Thus he delivered himself into the hands of Linky[12] who hates him and hates the Irish Treaty. Linky is I think the most skilful dialectician in the House

---

[12] Hugh Richard Heathcote Gascoyne-Cecil (1869–1956). Conservative MP for Greenwich 1895–1906 and Oxford University 1910–37. Provost of Eton 1937–44. Styled Lord Hugh Cecil from 1869. Created Baron Quickswood 1941. Member of Mesopotamia Commission 1916.

and on this occasion he used his rapier again and again with deadly effect. I was really sorry for Winston; he is like a child on such an occasion. All the next day he went about with a gloomy brow and a pouting lip. S.B. told me he spent hours in his room marching up and down and revolving 50 different ways of evading a climb down. S.B. was tender with him and at last he arrived at the only possible solution himself and himself wrote out the statement S.B. made. But as Stanley says if he had been leader he would have acted on the first impulse that came into his head, forced a division and split the party from top to toe.

Now that my Bill is through the Commons it is evident that there is a fuller consciousness than usual of the nature of the achievement. I have never received so many compliments on the handling of any measure as during the last week and indeed I have begun to feel that unless the boom stops quickly the usual reaction is inevitable and imminent. On Thursday I was the guest of the Lobby Journalists at luncheon, a function to which I had long been looking forward with unusual alarm. I had been to one or two of those luncheons; there is never any report but the chairman generally delivers a very carefully prepared speech full of elaborate allusions and witticisms polished to the last degree and then the guest is supposed to make a light and airy reply showing how easily he can do the same thing without preparation. On this occasion the chairman was quite up to tradition. He described me as the man of the hour, prophesied that I should be Prime Minister and then spent ¼ hour ragging me as the future dictator "rationalising" the Cabinet and ruling alone or sharing the purple with Austen like the old Roman Emperors of the West & East, "Nevillius and Austinian" taking Home & Foreign Affairs respectively. It was certainly a very good speech and a difficult one to follow, but luckily I had had a brain wave. I related an imaginary conversation with an old and candid friend who had explained to me why I should never be any use to the journalist and had described me as a catalogue of negatives. Then followed a list of the various distinctions or peculiarities of which I could not boast, and as each one was clearly recognisable as a dig at one of my colleagues, this idea had a great succés. The chairman in his speech had observed that the mask was falling and behind the granite face was appearing the warm and human heart!! I heard afterwards that the journalists had been wondering whether N.C. had it in him to be amusing. When they went away they were satisfied that he had!

It was rather a thick week again for on Friday I went to Swindon & addressed a mass meeting of about 3000 in a swimming bath, the speech being relayed to Chippenham Abingdon & Trowbridge. This week I only have a reception on Friday night and a speech next morning in Birmingham, but in March I have already got six biggish speeches and I shall be very glad when Easter comes and I can get away to the Dee.

You, or rather Hilda, have been corresponding with Annie so you know how she is going on. It is not a very easy time for her, but I hope she may manage to keep down her engagements whenever she does not feel equal to them …

…

... I set out a little while ago to raise £10000 for an election fund in Birm. So far I have got £5630 single handed!

2 March 1929
Westbourne

My dear Hilda,

I am very grateful to you and Ida for taking in Annie and making her happy and comfortable this week end. I think she is wonderfully well considering, but as you know she has a trying time to go through and the number of worrying things that keep cropping up with servants and family and what not is surprising. So it will be very good for her to have a little change and it is very comforting to me to know that she likes to go to the Bury House and feels her sisters in law to be a help in steadying her mind.

Alas my garden is like yours; it shows sad devastation ... The ground is like iron an inch below the surface and though I heard a thrush singing this morning I fear there must have been a good deal of mortality among the birds. I read a letter from Jack Hills[13] in the Times recording with great joy the presence of redwings in Mount Street, but I see them every day in St James' Park.

...

Annie will, I daresay, have told you about Calthorpe.[14] I really feel very vexed with S.B. for letting me down, though from what Vansittart[15] told me I suspect it was merely another case of his dismissing a disagreeable topic from his mind. But I dont mean to let it go, for although of course I never made any promise not being in any position to do so, I did allow it to be seen that I was confident of the honour and indeed I had every reason to be. It gives me a nasty feeling in the stomach every time I think of it.

...

I have had a wonderfully quiet week and have quite recovered my spirits. Indeed I have more than once found myself with ½ hour in which there seemed to be nothing particular to do. But that is partly due to the fact that Robinson[16]

---

[13] John Waller Hills (1867–1938). Conservative MP for Durham 1906–22, Ripon 1925–38. Financial Secretary to Treasury 1922 to March 1923 when defeated at Edge Hill by-election.

[14] The Calthorpe Estate owned much of Edgbaston, including Westbourne.

[15] Robert Gilbert Vansittart (1881–1957). Entered Diplomatic Service 1902; Assistant Secretary, Foreign Office 1914; First Secretary 1918; Counsellor 1920; Secretary to Lord Curzon 1920–24; Principal Private Secretary to Ramsay MacDonald 1928–30; Permanent Under-Secretary for Foreign Affairs 1930–38; Chief Diplomatic Adviser to Foreign Secretary 1938–41. Knighted 1929. Created Baron Vansittart 1941.

[16] (William) Arthur Robinson (1874–1950). Entered Colonial Office 1897; Assistant Secretary, Office of Works 1912–18; Permanent Secretary, Air Ministry 1917–20 and Ministry of Health 1920–35; Chairman, Supply Board of Committee of Imperial Defence 1935–39; Permanent Secretary, Ministry of Supply 1939–40. Knighted 1917.

(and several other of the chief officers at the Ministry) is laid up with flu and so there is a block in the stream of traffic that flows up to the Minister.

I met Robbins[17] of the Times one day & he burst out with "What a delightful speech you made at the luncheon" and went on to say that they had been regretting that etiquette had prevented their taking a shorthand note of it for their own pleasure. But I am satisfied that it was much better they should not. In cold print they would have wondered why they thought so much of it whereas now they will talk about it to those who weren't there until it will seem to have been much better than it was. I also had very flattering accounts of the impression produced by my speech at Swindon but already I am beginning to feel oppressed by the thought of Bradford next Saturday. It is I think the C[ounty] B[orough] which comes out worst under the scheme as it has low unemployment, low children high rateable value and being very "progressive" extremely high percentage grants. I imagine the Central Office didn't realise that when they asked me to go there. Including Bradford I have six more speeches to make this month ... but still the cry comes for more and I suppose there will be no peace until the General Election is behind us.

(Sunday morning) L.G.'s speech seems to me to be merely ridiculous. Probably you didn't see the fuller report of the earlier part of it which I found in the Birmingham Post. He was amazingly rude about Austen, who, he said, had made the most boastful speech he had ever read except the one made by his brother on the 3rd Reading of the L.G. Bill. I only hope A. has seen it; it might help to dispel illusions! I noticed that on this occasion Winston was let alone. A little while ago he dined with the Goat and came away in deep depression, having been filled up with confident prophecies of our complete discomfiture at the election. I suppose the cunning animal is trying to make a soft place in the Conservative party for him to sit down on if he should want a seat and the Labour party's furniture is too hard. But it is possible to be too clever and the Goat's reputation is so bad that his guarantee carries no conviction.

I have got another £1350 for my fund which brings my total up to very nearly £7000. I am hoping that presently some one else will do something.

...

I enclose a cutting from T.P.'s article in todays Sunday Times which shows that the legend of the granite face & the warm heart is still being industriously propagated!

---

[17] Alan Pitt Robbins (1888–1967). Reporter, *Yorkshire Post* 1904–8; editorial staff of *The Times* from 1909; Parliamentary Correspondent for *The Times* 1923–38 and News Editor 1938–53.

9 March 1929
37 Eaton Square, SW1

My dear Ida,

Many thanks for your two letters. The first gave useful particulars about the advisory Committee of Doctors and if you carry out the proposal you will be doing exactly what we at the Ministry would like to see. But to attempt compulsion would only be to invite disaster as I have told Dawson[18] and though he keeps trying to get his B.M.A. given some statutory position I think I can count on their Lordships to hold firm. I have spent a good deal of time in the Lords this week. It is a dreary place and I cant think how it is possible to deliver a speech with any spirit there. There are no rules of order. Anyone gets up when he likes and talks about what he likes and no one seems to pay any attention to what is being said. The Lords were rather sticky for some time and distinctly naughty on Thursday night when they defeated us over agricultural cottages & showed their teeth over Supervision of Midwives. But yesterday they were anxious to get through and galloped over some 60 clauses & 12 Schedules without stopping. We even got the Henry VIII clause by offering the amendment which I had had in reserve ever since the trouble in the Commons and as even Douglas had gloomily prophesied that we should never get away with the clause the "bureaucrats" were distinctly elated.

...

I made myself very unpleasant about the failure to get the honour I wanted and have got a definite promise for it next time so I hope it wont fail again.

Newman, the Calthorpe agent, came to see me one day at my request and I explained to him how things were. He then remarked that my lease would soon be coming to an end and enquired what I wanted to do. I said I wanted an annual lease on which he observed that he thought the Calthorpes would desire to meet my wishes. But we did not discuss terms.

I dined alone with the P.M. one day and we had a long talk about Cabinet changes. I know he would like also to meet my wishes but I must of course take into account his difficulties and I am bound to say that at the moment my destination if we should come back, looks much more like Treasury Chambers than the C.O. Apparently the party (in the House) would like to see me there instead of the present occupant but as he has not expressed any views it is obvious that the matter must continue in abeyance.

...

---

[18] Bernard Dawson (1864–1945). Physician and diagnostician. Physician-in-ordinary to King Edward VII 1906–10; to King George V 1910–36; to Prince of Wales 1929–36. Chairman, Consultative Council on Medical and Allied Services 1919; Member, Medical Research Council 1931–35, Army Medical Advisory Board 1936–45. Knighted 1911. Created Baron Dawson of Penn 1920 and Viscount 1936.

On the way up [to Bradford] I met Park Goff[19] M.P. for Darlington. He appears to have been studying the constituencies rather carefully and informed me with great confidence where we should lose seats and to whom. For what it is worth his view was that the Liberals would increase their numbers from 37 to 70 or 80 but that we should have a majority over both the other parties of something between 35 & 55. It appears that at present our M.P.'s are suffering from a bad attack of defeatism, but so far as I can see there is nothing substantial to warrant it, and it is probably due to the attacks of the Daily Mail & Daily Express on various individual Ministers, particularly Jix. I hear that the latter is for once perturbed at the storm he has so gratuitously provoked and complains piteously that his own constituents are turning against him. But his vanity is not likely to be submerged for long and he simply cannot exist without constant publicity.

I see the unfortunate Austen has again been the victim of one of those dirty American journalists, and the Herald (alone among the papers I have seen) publishes a violent tirade against him by Senator Borah,[20] who did not wait to hear whether the story was true but swallowed it whole and greedily. The path of peace with the U.S.A. is hard indeed with such constant sabotage on their side and such unscrupulous partisanship on ours.

...

16 March 1929
Westbourne

My dear Hilda,

...

Many thanks for your birthday wishes. I wonder whether a sense of delicacy has prevented your alluding to the fact or whether you have not realised that I shall be SIXTY on Monday. Certainly I dont feel like that picture in the Dutch Exhibition described as an old man with a thoughtful expression probably aged about sixty. He had a shiny bald head with a fringe of white hair and a lined and ragged face. One would not put him at less than 70 these days. But sixty is a landmark, isn't it.

I must warn you that you and Ida probably wont like the portrait unless Orpen alters it. When I saw it I thought Well he looks a sardonic customer. I told Orpen

---

[19] Park Goff (1871–1939). Conservative MP for Cleveland 1918–23, 1924–29 and Chatham 1931–35. PPS to First Lord of Admiralty 1919; member, British Council of Olympic Games 1920–24 and Chairman 1923–24: member of Select Committees on London Traffic 1919 and Police and Traffic 1921 and of various Inter-Parliament Conferences. Knighted 1918. Created Bart 1936.

[20] William Edgar Borah (1865–1940). American politician. Republican Senator for Idaho 1907–40; Chairman, Senate Foreign Relations Committee 1925–33. Convinced isolationist and instrumental in blocking US entry to League of Nations.

that it seemed to me top heavy and he seemed inclined to think the criticism just. But I must have another look on Monday.

...

I also had a women's meeting to address on Wednesday. I tried to make an encouraging speech as there is so much defeatism about and it was gratifying to read a letter from Mrs Moore Brabazon to Annie that it had been "like a breath of fresh air". I felt myself that it was a successful effort and one can't always have that feeling when one has to make so many speeches.

That night I dined with the Salisburys and had a very pleasant evening. I always like Lady Salisbury and the other guests, the Iveaghs[21] and the Hailshams were also congenial. I had just been introduced to Lady Hailsham[22] once before but this time I had a good talk and liked her very much. I am very glad that Douglas is so happily matched. He made an admirable speech in the Lords on an amendment about voluntary hospitals and thanks to him we got away with it and defeated that bundle of peevish vanity, my Lord Dawson of Penn! I think we are fairly well through our troubles in the Lords and shall come out without any serious damage.

I came down yesterday afternoon in order to address the Central Council last night and go to a social this evening. I have got another £1000 for our local fund so we have accumulated £8000 now and our principal agent wears a happy face.

...

Dr Lyster must be very green to think that on entering the House for the first time he would have a chance of being Minister of Health. If the socialists were to take office Arthur Greenwood[23] would certainly have that place. The ex-Cabinet Ministers left the opposition to the L.G. Bill entirely to him.

24 March 1929
37 Eaton Square, SW1

My dear Ida,

We have just got back from Brighton to find your letter and your most generous but totally unexpected cheque. You and Hilda are the most devoted of sisters and I cant tell you how much I appreciate the help you have given me on

---

[21] Rupert Edward Cecil Lee Guinness (1874–1967). Conservative MP for Shoreditch Haggerston 1908–10, South-East Essex 1912–18 and Southend 1918–27. Chairman, Arthur Guinness & Company 1927–62. Styled Viscount Elveden 1919–27; succeeded as Earl of Iveagh 1927.

[22] Mildred Dew. Widow of Hon. Clive Lawrence, she became Hailsham's second wife in 1929 after the death of his first wife in May 1925.

[23] Arthur Greenwood (1880–1954). Labour MP for Nelson and Colne 1922–31 and Wakefield 1932–54. Parliamentary Secretary, Ministry of Health 1924; Minister of Health 1929–31; Minister without Portfolio responsible for economic affairs 1940–42; Lord Privy Seal 1945–47; Paymaster-General 1946–47; Minister without Portfolio 1947.

so many occasions. But I really dont know whether I can accept it this time; certainly not without telling you that although I am still considerably overspending my income I am no longer anxious about my financial position because I have done so well out of the sale of Elliotts to the I.C.I. that my capital is now larger than it has been for some time in spite of the deficits of recent years. If, as I suspect, the wise virgins have been depriving themselves of a certain amount of light in order to help their brothers I feel that I should be abusing your unselfishness if I were to take your cheque. Accordingly I am returning it, but I am just as grateful to you both as if I had kept it.

All the papers and most of our party seem to have made up their minds that we are in for a débâcle at the election, but I still see no reason to suppose that we shall not come back the strongest party. These bye-elections have certainly shown a great slump in our vote but it seems to me that that is just what one would expect a few weeks before the real struggle and though we are in the trough just now there is still time for the following wave before the end of May.

I am sure it would be a mistake to try and outbid the Goat. Our policy when we declare it after Easter will not contain anything sensational, the strongest cards probably being slums & safeguarding, but we ought to be able to put up a fairly good Budget and if S.B. can make up his mind to reconstruct the Cabinet, which he is seriously considering, that should freshen up our rank and file and give them a fresh talking point. I had another conversation with S.B. a little while ago when he said that if we came back he thought he would like to send me to the Colonies. He thought the native question was so important that we wanted the best man we could get to tackle it. But of course he may change his mind again as I expect the party might indicate its wishes that I should go elsewhere. Anyway this is only pure speculation.

I got through the Lords Amendments in 3 hours on Friday which wasn't bad seeing that there were 220 of them but it added a good deal to the effort that I had this Brighton meeting on my chest. However we had a great gathering and the speech went off very well but I felt fairly done after it and have only recovered today ...

...

Look in the Times tomorrow or Tuesday for a letter from me on seeing a Wheatear in St James' Park!

...

31 March 1929
Cairnton, Banchory, N.B

My dear Ida,

...

The fishing is very bad at present and I dont remember so few salmon being caught since I have been coming here. On Friday nobody caught anything not even Arthur Wood.[24] Yesterday Jack Hills got 2 and I got 1 and lost another. ...

Well the portrait is finished and Annie & Dorothy who came on Thursday to see it had no criticism to make. I think Orpen has greatly improved it since you saw it. ... It is to go into this years Academy and my impression is that Orpen likes it the best of the ones he is exhibiting. I was delighted & rather relieved that you and Hilda were pleased with it before; now I am sure you will be satisfied that your gift to Annie has been well expended.

I had lunch with S.B. on Thursday and a talk afterwards about the programme. I think it should fill out all right & except that it does nothing special for Agriculture it should please our people. I have circulated my ideas on slums to the Cabinet but dont yet know how they have taken them. At any rate they go a little deeper than Ll.G. does; his notions of slums are simply comic.

12 April 1929
Westbourne

My dear Hilda,

...

I began my holiday with 2 glorious days. Not a cloud in the sky obscured the sunshine and it was a joy to be out of doors fishing without a coat. The river was very low and fish scarce and dour but one lived in expectation and a few kelts with an occasional salmon kept us interested. By Monday however there was a complete change. The wind went into the N.E. and brought showers of snow from the Arctic, the water was icy and I dont know that I have ever known it so cold by the Dee. Of course the fish wisely kept to the bottom and altogether I had 4 blank days out of seven two of them without even a touch to enliven the proceedings. However I caught three salmon including one 18 pounder the largest landed while I was there and while I cannot call it a good sporting season I returned much refreshed and very fit.

I came here on Saturday to find A. & the children at Westbourne ... Dorothy ... has made great progress with her technique ... Frank seems very well ... His report is not quite so enthusiastic as some which preceded it but the criticism

---

[24] Arthur H.E. Wood (?–1935). Director, BSA 1907–35. Sole tenant of a water on the River Dee at Cairnton from 1920. Chamberlain fished there every Easter for thirteen years from 1922 until Wood's death in May 1935 and became a disciple of Wood's method of greased line and 12-foot rod.

appears to be directed chiefly at his "quietness" and remembering my own characteristics at that age I don't feel that that need prevent his development into more forceful ways later on.

Annie & I went to London on Sunday night as the P.M. wanted to see me on Monday morning. We had a conference with Winston at Downing St and lunched with him and Mrs W. very pleasantly at No 11. after which I went to the Ministry and did some chores there before returning to dress for the Primrose League Banquet at which I was the principal guest. I don't think I ever addressed a "stickier" audience. They were the most depressing collection of old frumps and I had to work hard to stir them at all. However they appeared to be pleased and S.B. was much delighted with my comparison of Ll.G. to the "Christian General".

Next day we returned here to find it still bitterly cold and the garden very blank and dismal with the wind & frost & drought. On Wednesday I had to go back again. We had a Cabinet in the morning, the P.M. kept me to lunch with him and Mrs B.[25] and then we met again in the afternoon. I had expected to return next morning but I had to attend a Cabinet Committee at 10 and another Cabinet at 12 so that I had only just time to finish my business at the M/H & catch the 4.10.

I dined on Wednesday with the Editor of the Sunday Times & a very interesting & distinguished company including the Ld Chief Justice … Hewart[26] told me that Bonar[27] had twice offered him the Lord Chancellorship after he became P.M. in 1922 which is an interesting piece of inner history.

Our talks in Cabinet were largely connected with the Budget about which I cannot tell you anything yet but I had some private conversations with S.B. about reconstruction of the Cabinet. He has not yet finally made up his mind but I rather think he will postpone it till after the election. On one thing however I think he has decided namely to give me the office I desired or rather the two offices [Colonial and Dominion], but what he will do with the present holder I dont know & nor does he.

Tonight I have been at a dinner to celebrate the attainment of £10M deposits in the Municipal Bank. It is a remarkable figure in less than 10 years and the Corporation is very proud of its unique distinction.

---

[25] Lucy Baldwin (1869–1945). Married Stanley Baldwin 1892.

[26] Gordon Hewart (1870–1943). Liberal MP for Leicester 1913–22. Solicitor-General 1916–19; Attorney-General 1919–22; Lord Chief Justice 1922–40. Knighted 1916. Created Baron Hewart 1922 and Viscount 1940.

[27] Andrew Bonar Law (1858–1923). Conservative MP for Glasgow Blackfriars 1900–1906, Camberwell 1906–10, Bootle 1911–18, Glasgow Central 1918–23. Parliamentary Secretary, Board of Trade 1902–5; Colonial Secretary 1915–16; Chancellor of Exchequer 1916–19; member of War Cabinet 1916–19; Lord Privy Seal 1919–21; Prime Minister 1922–23. Leader of Conservative Party 1911–21 and 1922–23.

27 April 1929
Westbourne

My dear Hilda,

...

I wonder where I left off my last letter to you. I think it must have been about the 14ᵗʰ just before the Budget and I remember you specially asked me to tell you about it as you would not see an English paper. I expect after all you have seen some accounts but in case you should really have missed them I will give you a brief summary. There were a number of minor reforms which took a good deal of time to tell about but were not of much importance in themselves and did not eat up much of the £11 million surplus with which the Chancellor found himself after making the necessary provision for derating. The Betting tax is repealed and replaced by a tax of £40 per telephone installed in the bookie's office. The publican's licenses are reduced and the off licence holders with justice's licenses are allowed to sell ½ bots of spirits. The manufacturers licenses paid by brewers, distillers and tobacco mfrs are increased so as to take from them the rating relief (this is of course pure electioneering, but deprives the Opposition of one of their silliest and most telling criticisms). Railways are let off the passenger duty and have agreed to spend 80% of the capitalised value on modernising their plant & equipment. Rural telephones are to be fixed in 5000 villages & 1300 country railway stations where neither telephone nor telegraph now exists (this is much appreciated by farmers). The increase in the grants for maintenance of classified Roads already announced (50%–60% for Cl. I. & 33⅓% to 50% for Cl.II) is to be extended to grants for improvement & new construction. The public had expected some reduction in tea or sugar but the surprise was great when it was announced that the tea tax would be repealed entirely at a cost of about £7 millions and there were long faces on the Socialist benches and much foolish talk about bribery. There was however another surprise even more complete when Winston was able to say that the derating of Agriculture would be anticipated and brought into operation during the current half year (from April 1). The cost of this operation (a little over £2 millions) comes not out of the surplus but out of the funds accumulated for Rate Relief which have exceeded the estimate. We could not anticipate industrial relief (to *my* great relief) as the apportionment had not proceeded far enough and this has been so generally recognised as reasonable that there has been no criticism of the distinction.

Winstons speech which took 2½ hours was one of the best he has made and kept the House fascinated & enthralled by its wit, audacity, adroitness & power. I think the general public were a little disposed to complain that it was a humdrum Budget; if so, it was because W. has taught them to expect something startling each year, and their anticipations had been aroused accordingly. But frankly it is constructed with both eyes on the Election and from that point of view there is no doubt that it is a very serviceable affair. Indeed it has contributed materially to the marked reaction from the depression in our ranks which was so apparent a few weeks ago but has now largely disappeared.

The press, the clubs & the lobbies have been full of gossip about reconstruction of the Cabinet. I think it is generally accepted that there will be none before the election but it seems almost as universally believed that W. will not return to the Exchequer but will be succeeded by the present Minister of Health. There is where the merlassis [sic] jug is likely to get broken. W. himself keeps silence even to the P.M. but I suspect that he would be glad to leave the Treasury if he could find a new sphere sufficiently in the light. It is certain that India must be very much in the foreground during the next Parliament.

During the Budget week I myself made an Election Gramophone Record and gave a half hours broadcast from 2LO. It is a very curious sensation, sitting alone in a room and talking to the microphone, knowing that you are being heard by listeners who may number millions but unable to obtain the faintest indication of the impression you are making. It was a great relief when it was over to find the B.B.C. people quite enthusiastic. They said every syllable was clear and distinct, pace & tone excellent matter & manner the best they had had yet. Since then I have had many most gratifying testimonials. The London correspt of the Post who is a Liberal said he had heard from 10 other Liberals in different parts of the country and they were without exception "fascinated" being equally impressed by the force of my argument and the moderation of my tone. Sir C. Hyde[28] wrote to Austen that he had listened in to all the political broadcasts (including L.G. & S.B.) and he thought mine "supreme". I am very pleased for I did take a good deal of trouble both in preparation and delivery to appear reasonable & fair and at the same time convincing on the merits of our case.

During the same week I laid the foundation stone of a new housing scheme in Bethnal Green, dined with the Editor of the Mng Post, wrote an article on slums for a Birmingham publication (it hasnt appeared yet but I am rather pleased with it) and moved the 2nd Rdg of my new Agricultural Rates Bill in the Commons. I confess I nearly fainted at the idea of *another* rating Bill, but I guessed the opposition would hardly incur the unpopularity of resisting such a boon to the farmers and this proved to be the case. We had a tedious & dreary debate but there was no division and last Monday in my absence the Bill passed through all the remaining stages in a few minutes.

On the Thursday we (A. & I) attended a great meeting at Drury Lane to hear the P.M. announce the party programme. As usual on such occasions he gave the audience hardly any opportunity of letting loose its enthusiasm and the opening was rather cold but towards the end things warmed up and the general verdict

---

[28] Charles Hyde. Philanthropist and sole proprietor of *Birmingham Post, Birmingham Mail, Birmingham Weekly Post* from 1913. Chairman, War Graves Commission, Hon. Treasurer, Birmingham Lord Mayor's Unemployment Fund 1920–21, 1923–24. Created Bart 1922.

afterwards was quite satisfactory though it was felt that various items would have to be elaborated further if they were to be made intelligible & attractive to the electorate. Once again when in the course of the speech S.B. mentioned my name it was received with such loud & prolonged applause as to show clearly the delegates appreciation of my work and that & other things has caused the Herald to come out with a leader entitled "Neville as the Big Noise" in which it says that evidently my achievements are to be made the feature of our election campaign & then goes on to explain what a callous mean brutal & contemptible bureaucrat I am.

...

Last Sunday I left Westbourne in the morning for London & that night travelled to Aberdeen in order to address a great meeting there on Monday evening. On arrival I went on to Banchory to stay with Wood but to my great annoyance & disappointment found it even colder than at Easter. ... Of course the fish wouldn't take & it was only in the last hour that they began to show signs of life. ... I had to drive 20 miles to the meeting in a car with a hood (and a draught) and felt my throat getting husky as I went. However it was all right for the meeting which was packed while many were excluded. I spoke for 65 minutes to a most attentive & enthusiastic audience and the speech was relayed to 9 other towns. I am told the cost was between £500 and £600 and I can only hope that the expenditure was justified by the novelty of the idea and the réclame it created. After the meeting I had to drive back and by the time I got to Cairnton my voice was good & husky. Next morning I awoke to a heavy snow shower which was repeated soon after I entered the water. It was bitter cold for the first hour and a half but it got a little better then and I was fortunate enough to land 3 salmon before lunch. The afternoon was unproductive but I left a happy man for my night journey back to London.

Unluckily my throat got rather worse than better and it was not improved by a long speech to the Central Ass. for Mental Welfare on Thursday morning. ... The result is that I have had to spend today ... in bed, but I am better & hope to be right by Monday. That evening 104 back benchers ... are giving a dinner to Kingsley & me to congratulate us on our success with the L.G. Bill – a very gratifying tribute which I must not miss.

Polling day is fixed for May 30, the dissolution being on May 10. It is getting horribly close!

5 May 1929
Westbourne

My dear Hilda,
...
... If you have seen Austen since your return you will have got the latest election views so far as he knows them. There is no doubt that the Socialists

have got their tails very much down at present. Some Liberals allow themselves to indulge in quite fantastic ideas of what they might again [sic] but no seriously minded student of politics seems prepared to give them more than 60–70 seats and a good many are doubtful whether they will even increase their present total of 46. On the other hand the average opinion in our party seems to range round a majority of 40 to 50 over the other two. If that proved somewhere near correct we should have a very different time in the H. of C. from what we have had in this parliament. But I have a feeling that we may come out better than that. This is a woman's election and I think the Baldwin legend appeals pretty strongly to women.

When I think that in less than four weeks from now it will be all over I feel inclined to gasp. Its so sudden! I can hardly realise that whatever happens I shall very soon be saying goodbye to the Ministry of Health. It will be a wrench to go, for I have been very happy there and I should like very much to carry through the slums and the new maternity Benefit and the P.G. School and the Lunacy Reform, and see the Voluntary Hospitals established on a proper basis and nurse the Local Authorities over the early stages of their new duties and in short see out the thousand and one things that I have started. But of course in the process a thousand and one *new* things would get started, one never would get to the end and one might well get oneself and the office into a groove.

The office itself is very unhappy in its uncertainty over its future. To have a Socialist Minister steadily undoing all that I have done to restore the administration to sound principles is a possibility which cannot be ignored but which would really break their hearts if they had to endure it. But I cant believe they will though of course I dont know who on our side might succeed me.

I think its pretty well settled in S.B.'s mind now that I shall go to the C.O. [Colonial Office] & retain the D.O. He spoke to Winston about it & he expressed great pleasure at the idea; perhaps he didn't want me at No11! It was rather curious that in a Committee engaged in drawing up the P.M.'s election address on [sic] manifesto (*not* the one appearing today which is dreadful poor stuff) I was asked to draft the paragraph on Colonial Development. It is true that Leo was not present at the moment, but the request came quite naturally & arose out of some remark I made on the subject.

I have had a very busy time this week and so has Annie who has spent part of it here attending Edgbaston Division functions. Neither of us gets a chance to do any chores of our own.

It was a very charming & gratifying function at the House on Monday night when I was "dined" together with Kingsley Wood by 104 back benchers – as many as could be got into the Strangers Room. I believe there is no precedent for such a compliment. Many more would have come if there had been room. Ministers were excluded but S.B. came in after dinner to listen to the speeches and made an informal but most effective one himself. Four back benchers

Geoffrey Ellis, Cyril Cobb,[29] Ruggles-Brise[30] and Lady Iveagh[31] representing Industry, London, Agriculture and Women, sang our praises and those of the Act and they were all exceedingly well done. I gathered afterwards from Whips & P.S.'s that the company dispersed in high good humour and satisfaction with its evening.

On Tuesday I was to have dined with the Middle Temple but as my Estimates were suddenly put down for Wednesday I had to cry off to prepare for them. However as it turned out I wasn't even able to do that as I had to stop at the House to answer Pethick Lawrence[32] who had notified me of a matter he wished to raise on the adjournment. The result was that it was 11.30 before I could begin work on the speech and though I sat up late I literally had not time to work it up as I should have liked. Naturally it was, when delivered, inferior to its predecessors, but all the same it has had a remarkably good press, even opposition papers finding it a "fascinating" review, and several M.P.'s on our side were enthusiastic in their appreciation of its value in providing electoral ammunition.

On Thursday we lunched with the Salisburys and then while Annie came down here I addressed the Health & Housing Comee on slums and finished up by attending the performance of Ruddigore by the Min. of Health Amateur Operatic Society – a painful ordeal!

...

11 May 1929
Westbourne

My dear Hilda,

...

This last week has been a record one almost for me. I had no speech to make – though attending the Court is very nearly as bad, and I had a good number of deputations to see before finishing up. We have worked hard at the declaration of policy comprised in the P.M.'s address (published this evening) and I think it

---

[29] Cyril Stephen Cobb (1861–1938). Barrister and Member, LCC 1905–34; Vice-Chairman 1910–11 and Chairman 1913–14. Conservative MP for West Fulham 1918–29 and 1930–38. Knighted 1918.

[30] Edward Archibald Ruggles-Brise (1882–1942). Landowner and Conservative MP for Maldon 1922–23 and 1924–42. Created Bart 1935.

[31] Gwendolen Florence Mary Guinness (1861–1966). Eldest daughter of 4th Earl of Onslow; married Rupert Guinness 1903 who succeeded as 2nd Earl of Iveagh 1927. Conservative MP for Southend 1927–35. Chair, National Union Women's Advisory Committee 1927–33; Chair, National Union 1930; appointed Conservative Deputy Chair March 1930 but did not take up the post.

[32] Frederick William Pethick-Lawrence (1871–1961). Treasurer, Union of Democratic Control 1916 and Peace candidate Aberdeen South 1917. Labour MP for Leicester West 1923–31 and Edinburgh East 1935–45. Financial Secretary, Treasury 1929–31; Secretary for India and Burma 1945–47. Member, Political Honours Committee 1949–61. Created Baron Pethick-Lawrence 1945.

makes a pretty impressive document. S.B. is in very good spirits and starts his campaign in a confident mood. As he says there is no steam in the Socialists and the prospect of possibly laying out L.G. Rothermere and Beaverbrook[33] all at one go causes him to lick his chops lovingly. There is no doubt that our stock is rising and I hear a good many people (including my Lord Melchett)[34] saying with a sagacious wag of the head "I shouldn't be surprised if we did a lot better than some people think".

Nineteen days! It is not very long, but its like the Channel crossing; one thinks a lot about it before hand and the thoughts are not pleasant. I have nothing like what some will have. Meetings in the rowdier part of Birmingham are not much fun and S.B.'s programme makes my blood run cold. My adoption meeting is on Tuesday and I have seven more at the constituency and two in other parts of Birmingham. Next Thursday I speak at Pontypool Aberavon and Swansea with an overflow at the last place. Whitmonday is nomination day but otherwise a holiday. Tuesday the 21st I speak at Southampton and on the 23rd I go to Rugby instead of Sunderland. I expect I shall be pretty weary by the 30th.

The nearer I get to the end of my term at the Ministry the more sad I feel about it. I shall hate leaving it and I know the office has the same regrets. "We shall have to start in an entirely new atmosphere" Robinson said to me. "We have all got so used to a situation in which the Minister does things better than we do, but it will be very different when we get a new man here". All the same he has no doubt whatever that I am right to go. I should surely have an anti-climax if I stopped, and apart from that it is not well to stop too long in one place – one's mind gets frozen. But I sometimes wonder whether I shall be able to grapple with an office of which I know so little – except that it has a very poor staff! I had a farewell talk with S.B. on Friday. He has got most of the principal offices filled in his mind and I am glad to say that he has accepted my nominee as my successor.[35] After a careful sifting of the available material I picked him out as the best, and Robinson would be very well satisfied to have him.

I have written two articles which A. & I think are rather good. One is on the L.G. Act & will appear in the Sunday Times tomorrow. The other is on slums & has been done at the request of the Telegraph. It may run into two parts but I don't know when it will appear. We shall be curious to see whether I get paid for

---

[33] (William) Maxwell Aitken (1879–1964). Conservative MP for Ashton-under-Lyne 1910–16. Chancellor, Duchy of Lancaster and Minister of Propaganda/Information 1918–19; Minister of Aircraft Production 1940–41; Minister of State 1941; Minister of Supply 1941–42; Minister of War Production 1942; Lord Privy Seal 1943–45. Knighted 1911. Created Bart 1916 and Baron Beaverbrook 1917. Acquired *Daily Express* 1918 and later *Evening Standard*.

[34] Alfred Moritz Mond (1868–1930). Liberal MP for Chester 1906–10, Swansea 1910–23 and Carmarthen 1924–28 (Conservative from 1926). First Commissioner of Works 1916–21; Minister of Health 1921–22. Created Bart 1910 and Baron Melchett 1928.

[35] In March 1929, Chamberlain had proposed Sam Hoare as his successor at the Ministry of Health.

these articles. Winston says I ought not to allow them to go for less than £100 each, but I wrote them for the sake of the party and nothing at all has been said about payment.

...

18 May 1929
Westbourne

My dear Ida,

After all I am able to scribble off a letter for – tell it not in Goth – I have not got another speech till Tuesday and I have just (12.15 am) completed my article for the Daily Mail! I should like to have spurned their request, but in the interests of the party I felt that was impossible, especially as Jix and Winston had written already. So I will begin by wishing both you and Hilda many happy returns of your respective birthdays to carry on your invaluable work and to be the comfort & support of your brothers. ...

Sunday morning. Well anyway I am through the first week. I had my adoption meeting on Tuesday, very well attended & enthusiastic. Thursday was a nightmare. I trained to Pontypool where I lunched with the local people and then addressed a great meeting for nearly an hour in a cinema. Then accompanied by the agent for the next division I motored for two hours during which he talked incessantly, till we got to Briton Ferry about half past five. There, there was a large crowd including a biggish lot of Socialist miners, in a hall and I addressed them for ¼ hour. They gave me a good hearing though there was a good deal of booing at the end and as I drove off. I got to my Swansea hosts house at 6.20 and at once retired to think over my evening speech before dinner at 6.45; I had hoped for more time but there was a lot of traffic on the road which had delayed us. The Swansea meeting included the Gower Division as well as the two borough divisions & it was held in an enormous drill hall, said to hold 5000 or 6000. It was packed full and atrociously hot, and I thought that though they had to stand the great crowd outside which listened to a loud speaker had the best of it. I spoke for just an hour here and was listened to with close attention. I saw little of Socialists but there were a good number of Liberals at the back who contented themselves however with cheering Lloyd George's name and gave me an opportunity of making fun of them. After the meeting I was hustled off to an overflow at another hall some distance away but this was a poor affair. There were only a few hundreds present and a large proportion of them not very lively Socialists. When I got away I felt sorrier than ever for Stanley who has day after day like that.

...

I found everyone in very good spirits in South Wales, rather expecting that Labour might gain some seats at the expense of the Liberals but hoping to win some ourselves. I didn't myself think this optimism justified. There is a bare chance for Pontypool but I doubt our getting any success in Swansea or Gower.

On Friday I had two meetings here in the poorest part of Edgbaston viz Market Hall ward. At the first which was quite full I should think 7 out of 10 were Socialists. They came to make trouble but I handled them tactfully and we got through very comfortably. Our people told me it was a far better meeting than Lowe[36] had last time when they chivvied him until he took refuge in a sulky silence.

My Telegraph article comes out on Thursday. I don't know when the D.M. will publish but I am rather pleased with what I have written. It seems to me "brighter" than either Winston Jix or Snowden.

25 May 1929
Westbourne

My dear Hilda,

We are still alive and moreover we are still quite fresh, for this election has not been anything like so wearing as the last. It is a great comfort to have Edgbaston instead of Ladywood to deal with and we find everyone so friendly and anxious to help that we might have been the member and his wife for ten years. Indeed we see no sign of that apathy which one always associated with this division; the women, in particular, all seem anxious to vote and so far as our canvass is concerned the reports seem generally to agree that it is more favourable than it was last time. I had an opportunity the other day of talking to Edwards[37] our principal agent, and he seemed pretty hopeful of all the divisions except Yardley where we hardly expect to save the situation.

I did get paid for my D.T. article for which they sent me fifty guineas. The Mail & Sunday Times however did not pay nor do I expect to get anything from the News of the World for which I have done an article on housing to be published tomorrow. ...

We are rather surprised to hear of Lady Mosley's[38] remarks as she is a Conservative and does not approve of her son's doings. I suppose she was only repeating what her daughter-in-law[39] had told her. She is even more outrageous than her husband and believes the lies she tells, which is of course more dangerous

---

[36] Francis William Lowe (1852–1929). Conservative MP for Edgbaston 1898–1929. President, Birmingham Conservative Association 1892–1918 when became Joint President of Birmingham Unionist Association; Chairman of Midland Union and the National Union; member, Council of National Unionist Association. Knighted 1905. Created Bart 1918.

[37] R.H. Edwards (1891–?). Central Office agent in Lancashire and Cheshire; Chief Agent for Bristol 1924–26; Chief Agent for Birmingham from 1926.

[38] Katherine Maud Edwards Heathcote (1874–1950). Married Sir Oswald Mosley 1895; mother of Oswald Ernald Mosley. Leader, British Union of Fascists Women's Section from 1933.

[39] Cynthia Blanche Mosley (1898–1933). Daughter of Marquess of Curzon; married Sir Oswald Mosley 1920. Labour MP for Stoke 1929–31 (sitting as New Party MP from February 1931). Member, British Union of Fascists from formation in 1932.

from our point of view. But I hear that in Ladywood the reconditioning policy is very popular.

I had a wonderful meeting in Southampton on Tuesday. There was a rather noisy band of Socialists in one corner of the big hall but they only served to warm up the atmosphere. My speech was the best I have made in this campaign and Apsley[40] who was in the chair said he had never seen the people so roused up. Unfortunately both our candidates are new and one of them is very weak. I think we should certainly hold one of the two seats but I am rather dubious about the other. I got back on Wednesday afternoon and had an excellent meeting in Edgbaston that night. Clara said that at that particular place they usually got a very poor attendance but on Wednesday it was packed and rather to my surprise there was no visible opposition at all though I was told afterwards that there were some Liberals & Socialists present.

On Thursday I spoke at Rugby where we had a very rough house and I have had profuse apologies since from the Chairman & candidate. The real trouble lay in the arrangements. The hall was oblong with the platform at one end. Seats were placed for about half the length & filled by supporters but beyond that was a solid standing crowd tightly wedged together and consisting almost entirely of opponents. A loud speaker was fixed but it was fixed *outside* for the benefit of a crowd of some 800 who stood in a yard and the result was that I had to shout steadily for 55 minutes against a perfect pandemonium. I got my speech through to the sitting audience but a continuous row like that rather cramps one style and I can only hope that the indignation created by the unmannerly behaviour of our opponents will bring D. Margesson[41] as much support as my arguments would have done if I had had a better chance of developing them.

Yesterday I had a womens meeting in the Botanical Gardens which was quite successful in spite of the presence of a number of anti-vaccination and anti-vivisection fanatics who made themselves ridiculous and got well hooted by the audience. Today I have been going round Committee Rooms & talking to the old people in a Home run by the Little Sisters of the Poor. Next week I have five speeches but they are all in Birmingham so I have broken the back of my work.

Annie says she finds the election a rest but she spends a great deal of time in the Committee rooms and is making hosts of new friends who will soon be as devoted to her as those in Ladywood. I suppose in the past the organisation has

---

[40] Allen Algernon Bathurst Apsley (1895–1942). Conservative MP for Southampton 1922–29 when retired and Bristol Central 1931–42. PPS to Albert Buckley 1922, to Moore-Brabazon 1925–28 and to Inskip 1936–39. Killed on active service, 1942. Director of *Morning Post* until resigned in 1935 after disagreement with Editor. Son of 7th Earl of Bathurst and styled Lord Apsley.

[41] (Henry) David Reginald Margesson (1890–1965). Conservative MP for West Ham Upton 1922–23 and Rugby 1924–42. PPS to Minister of Labour 1922–23; Assistant Whip 1924; Junior Lord of Treasury 1926–29 and 1931; Parliamentary Secretary, Treasury and Chief Government Whip 1931–40; Secretary for War 1940–42. Created Viscount Margesson 1942.

been on the slack side in Edgbaston and if all goes well now it will be interesting to work it up. Our agent seems to be doing very well and it is a comfort to deal with him instead of Arthur Walker. I believe the P.M. is coming here on Tuesday and I hope to get an opportunity of a quiet talk with him at luncheon.

One thing has been a great comfort during this election and that is the weather. The garden has been a joy and a relief and I dont know how many years it has been since we spent so long at Westbourne at this time of year. Fortunately too the tulips have been quite marvellous. … and the border in front of the peach house has been such a picture of beauty that I have been obliged to go & stand looking at it several times a day. …

The Buna Fugen has been more wonderful than ever, the lilacs are particularly good and the hawthorns which are only now beginning to open look as if they would be exceptionally well flowered. Irises promise extremely well and I have never seen so many fat buds on the French paeonies. They really are as good as yours!

…

… Well this time next week we shall know all about it!

2 June [mis-dated May] 1929
Westbourne

My dear Ida,

…

After such a week I hardly know where to begin. We (Annie & I) have felt pretty miserable since it became evident how things were going and though we are getting over the shock of the disappointment future prospects do not encourage us to take a cheerful view. Perhaps it is even now too soon to express opinions upon causes and effects but it may be interesting to you if I set out my own unaided meditations and impressions. But I abstain from criticism of our own party. For those who are always pessimists it is easy to say when disaster comes I told you so. Equally it is easy for those who put forward alternative policies to say "If you had taken my advice this would not have happened". It does not follow that their plan or any plan would have produced a different result. And although every man, including our P.M. has the defects of his qualities, we cannot usefully dwell on the defects at a time like this. Therefore I pass to the situation.

The great advance of Labour is in the industrial districts. This is merely a continuation of a process which has been going on for years. We have seen it for instance in Birmingham where the Socialist vote has increased at every election since 1918.

This advance has been assisted materially by the fact that other parties have been in office all the time except for the brief interlude in 1924. The politicians & agitators, working on the most ignorant & credulous section of the people, have had an easy task in attributing the troubles & difficulties of the post war period to the Govt which they have always represented as a class Govt with a bias against working people. Nothing that we have done has helped us to get over this. For example we have probably lost votes by our Pensions Scheme & our housing successes. No one has voted for us on account of these things who would not otherwise have done so but thousands have voted against us because they or their relations or even some one they knew had not got a pension or a house. I see no way of stopping this Labour advance except such a dose of Labour Government as will in turn disappoint and antagonise its supporters.

In the meantime it looks as if the Conservative Party might become predominantly the Agrarian Party, the Socialists representing the industrial towns. Such a demarcation if defined only a little more sharply, might profoundly affect our attitude towards the Protection of Agrarian products!

Now as to the present position. Socialists evidently expect to come in. They plan to carry on for 2 years in such a way as to establish their ability to govern and to govern in some respects better than Conservatives. Then they would frame an attractive Budget & appeal to the country to give them a majority. To their supporters they would say, We have made good so far as efficiency is concerned. But we cannot carry out a proper Socialist programme (including Nationalisation) without a clear majority. Let us have it and you may expect the millennium. I think this plan might well succeed and we should have 7 years of Socialist Government.

On the other hand to resign now would I think put S.B. in the wrong with the country. There is an anti Socialist majority apparently in the House and until the contrary is proved he ought to carry on. But my view is that he should ride for a fall. I regard the suggestion made in some papers today that it would be possible for him to introduce a series of Social Reforms in a form so non controversial that all parties would agree to them as simply fantastic. The Socialists would never accept such a position. They would say (and rightly) if a Government is to be carried on by assent, we are entitled as the strongest party to form that Government. Moreover I think if we by compromising with Liberals kept the Socialists out, we should be represented to the country in the light of capitalists once more combining to cheat Labour of the reward it had won by its own right arm. That would mean a Socialist majority for certain and probably in much less than 2 years. Better put them in at once: it is quite possible that they overrate their powers and though they will endeavour not to repeat the mistakes of 1924 & though they have undoubtedly at the moment got the extremists under, they have not got a strong intellectual outfit and they are always rent by internal jealousies the moment there is any office or place to be handed out.

Therefore my plan would be to ride for a fall. I would not even reconstruct the Cabinet. I would announce that I should challenge the verdict of the House as soon as it met and that only if it was favourable would I fill vacancies and rearrange my Government. And I would put something aggressive in the King's Speech about Safeguarding.

The Liberals would be in a great difficulty and would be very angry. They would say You are forcing us into an impossible situation. We cannot vote for Safeguarding and we will not actively put in the Socialists so we shall abstain. If you are beaten & they come in it is entirely your fault. We should reply. It is you who have created the impossible situation by your folly in running candidates in impossible places. We are not going to be responsible for a Govt which cannot carry out the only policy we believe likely to conquer unemployment. And after mutual recriminations we should go out & the Socialists would come in and once more the Liberals would be in trouble.

We are going up tomorrow to town & no doubt there will be many discussion there on what should be done. I have a feeling that Winston will be against the views I have put down that he will say – at all costs keep the Socialists out even if you have to make terms with L.G. We shall see.

You will observe that I am not giving much consideration to my personal position. My pleasure is in administration rather than in the game of politics. I was astonished when Austen and Ivy lunched here on Friday to find him apparently contemplating the loss of office with equanimity – though he had not intended to remain in Parliament after the next 5 years. To me it makes all the difference to be in office. If I were told that I could never hold office again I should prefer to go out now. And the position as I see it is not very far from that. If I have to wait 7 years how far shall I have travelled down the hill. On the most favourable supposition I cannot expect to have either the energy or the physical strength I have now. Now was my chance when I still retain plenty of physical vigour and when my mental powers are at their zenith. And now the opportunity has been snatched from me in the twinkling of an eye. It is hard to bear & it will take time to recover spirits. But there is no certainty in politics and that is why one does not go out in despair. The most unexpected things may happen and we may return to office sooner than seems possible now. Gladstone & Disraeli were both Prime Ministers in their old age – But they didn't altogether make a success of it!

Austen tells me he (or rather she) has sold Twitts Ghyll to Lord Waring.[42] (I do wish his friends did not all have such disagreeable financial reputations). I thought he was to have another house in the country but he says he cant afford it and that he will confine himself to his flat. We are all going to be poorer now by the bye!

It is a tragedy that he should be so reduced. But Hoskins *may* be able to pay something & when he has retired from politics I imagine him once more pottering round a rock garden in that semi-rural zone which he likes. Ah! me! Oh! dear!

---

[42] Samuel James Waring (1860–1940). Enthusiast of decorative art who promoted New English Renaissance through firm of Waring & Gillow. Member, Tariff Reform Commission and Executive Council of Municipal Reform Society. Created Bart 1919 and Baron Waring 1922.

...

Monday 3rd ...

I am very glad to see from your letter that you had independently come to very much the same conclusion as I upon the course we ought to pursue. I wrote to S.B. to give him my views in case anyone else should be trying to rush him into another course. It is curious that all the papers seem to assume the necessity for reconstruction before meeting the House. That seems to me farcical and it would look as though we really did mean to try and "cling to office".

...

9 June 1929
37 Eaton Square, SW1

My dear Hilda,

...

It is very annoying though not surprising to get the gout again. It is really a very light attack so far as the foot is concerned for I have no pain in it except when I walk. But I cant ever remember any previous attack when I have felt so low and irritable. I think it must be boxed up inside me instead of exhausting itself in local inflammation.

I have had some very nice letters from M.P.'s to whom I had written to condole on their defeat. Nearly all ascribe their misfortunes in the first place to Liberal intervention, but I fear they assume that in the absence of a Liberal candidate, Liberal votes would have been given to them, which seems to me very doubtful.

I think we must be prepared for a long period of Opposition. Labour is making a good start; it has an excellent press; the City has decided that it cant bite and it succeeds to an inheritance of lucky coincidences. We reckoned that on our plans, unemployment would be reduced at least to 600000 during our next term of office. They will take the credit for that. Hoover[43] is apparently disposed to come far nearer to our point of view over disarmament & the freedom of the Seas than Coolidge.[44] They will take the credit for that. Winston told me of a conversation some friend of his had had with Ammon[45] at a public

---

[43] Herbert Clark Hoover (1874–1964). Engineer and US politician. Worked on relief of famine and distress in Europe during Great War; Secretary of Commerce 1921–28; President of USA 1929–33; Chairman, US Commission on European Economic Relief after 1945.

[44] Calvin Coolidge (1872–1933). Lawyer and US politician. Governor of Massachusetts 1919–20; Vice-President of the United States 1921–23; President, 1923–29.

[45] Charles George Ammon (1873–1960). Secretary, Union of Post Office Workers; member, LCC for North Camberwell 1919–25 and 1934–46. Labour MP for North Camberwell 1922–31 and 1935–44. Labour Whip 1922; Parliamentary Secretary, Admiralty 1924 and 1929–31; member, West African Commission 1938–39; Chairman, National Dock Labour Corporation 1944–50; Chief Labour Whip in Lords 1945–49. Created Baron Ammon 1944.

dinner when Ammon said words to this effect. We will keep quiet for 2 years & establish confidence and then by G— we'll give them H—l.

But I am coming definitely to the conclusion that the present situation is better for the country than that we should have taken office again. The lesson can be learned more slowly perhaps but at less cost. Only by the time it has been learned there will be a new generation.

I have already had an offer of the Chairmanship of a new company at a salary far exceeding that of a Minister of Health. I am going to look into the papers but the size of the loot frightens me. I fear that so big a bribe portends a risky transaction and I cant afford to sell my reputation.

...

15 June 1929
37 Eaton Square, SW1

My dear Ida,

...

Generally speaking we are both much refreshed by our visit to Yorkshire. I rather believe Annie is right in thinking that my depression was the result of taking Atophan, a gout remedy which was recommended by Morris but which Hackney afterwards told me had unpleasant effects on some people. At any rate I began to feel better when I ceased taking it.

We were alone with the Cunliffe Listers and the country there was looking very lovely. A. went a tremendous drive of over 180 miles round the Lakes but I spent most of my time fishing. I had very little success but enjoyed the solitude.

Last night I had my dinner to which Annie came. Everything went off admirably and everyone seemed very happy to be there. Robinson made a little speech which was very gratifying because he praised the things which were true and I responded while Kingsley finished up. I gathered that the new Ministers had had a talk with the officials and had learned a good many things about the business which has not been present to their minds when they made their promises. They had had something to sleep on was the verdict.

...

23 June 1929
Charminster House, Dorchester

My dear Hilda,

...

My gout has disappeared at last but I feel still an immense distaste for politics and a disinclination to work of any sort that is positively alarming. I dont think I shall take the Steel chairmanship. Colin Campbell who is a banker & knows all about it says there is no swindle in it but I am afraid it is a more responsible post than I want. I would prefer a plain directorship which would leave me free to do as much political work as I wanted. I see the Times is demanding that the party organisation & its educational propaganda should be put under an ex-Minister. If that idea should materialise I have a horrid feeling that there will be a unanimous desire that the ex-Minister of Health should be the Minister in question.

...

29 June 1929
37 Eaton Square, SW1

My dear Ida,

...

We have had a rather rackety week with social engagements which are pouring in upon us with giddy rapidity and have kept us out of bed till a late hour every night. On Monday we went to Lady Cory's to hear Kreisler[46] but were rather disappointed this time as he gave us a poor programme and seemed very tired. The next day I went to see S.B. and had a talk with him; he seemed rather tired and down, having had a trying time wrestling with dissolution honours. The results dont seem to have been very satisfactory ...

...

Sunday We would have supposed that we should hardly know what to do with ourselves, yet we seem to have very little leisure ...

I have definitely refused the chairmanship of the British Steel Industries after full consideration on the ground that the responsibility involved was too great. So far nothing else has been offered to me but I shall not go round begging. I think something must turn up that will be suitable and in the meanwhile I am not sorry to be free for a while. All sorts of things might happen. As I wrote last week, no sooner did this suggestion of an ex-Minister to take charge of the party organisation appear than everyone said I was the man, and various papers actually declared that I had accepted such a position. As a matter of fact I dont believe S.B. is considering any change and he has given me no indication that he has any new job in mind for me. But if he did ask me it would require very careful consideration before I accepted a position which would deprive me alike of my H. of C. work & of any opportunity of adding to my income. I hear Worthy[47] has secured a job at £10000 a year – through F.E. I fancy Austen has a firm offer of one directorship & a possibility of another which between them, if

---

[46] Fritz Kreisler (1875–1962). Austrian-born American violinist.

[47] Laming Worthington-Evans (1868–1931). Conservative MP for Colchester 1910–29, Westminster St George's 1929–31. Minister of Blockade 1918–19; Minister of Pensions 1919–20; Minister without Portfolio 1920–21; Secretary for War 1921–22, 1924–29; Postmaster-General 1923–24. Created Bart 1916.

they materialise, should make him at least as well off as when in office. Philip Cunliffe-Lister is rejoining his old companies. But I am hoping to get another fifty guineas for an article in the Sunday Times!

I said to Austen that at our age people were not likely to be very anxious to secure our services on the condition that they should be withdrawn whenever office was available in a new Govt. He replied that that was true and if a good offer were made to him on condition that it should not be given up for office he would accept. But I haven't reached that point yet.

I hear privately that L.G. is in a great fright lest his followers should be seduced from him by a non-Socialistic but advanced Liberal series of measures by the present Govt. Accordingly he would like to throw them out in November & would be prepared to do a deal with us now on these lines. There are people who would be foolish enough to entertain such a proposition but S.B. is not among them. Nor is

Your affect. brother

...

13 July 1929
Westbourne

My dear Ida,

We had rather a terrible party at the Peels[48] after we left you. Lady P.[49] herself is not only as ugly as isn't possible but she is a bad hostess and doesn't know how to make the best of her guests. And the guests with two exceptions were very boring. We had the Bristols;[50] he was in the Navy at one time now he is a landowner and Ch. of his C.C. in West Suffolk. He said We have set our faces against giving any assistance under the R.W. Housing Act to people who could quite well afford to do without it, so we decided at once to confine ourselves to loans. I asked him if the owners *were* doing up their cottages without assistance and he said No. I observed that it was no wonder the Act was a dead letter in his county but it seemed rather hard on the labourers. He got very uncomfortable & tried to rattle off a number of other reasons for

---

[48] William Robert Wellesley Peel (1867–1937). Conservative MP for Manchester South 1900–1906 and Taunton 1909–12. Joint-Parliamentary Secretary, Ministry of National Service 1918; Under-Secretary for War and Air 1919–21; Chancellor, Duchy of Lancaster 1921–22; Minister of Transport 1921–22; Secretary for India 1922–24 and 1928–29; First Commissioner of Works 1924–28; Lord Privy Seal 1931. Succeeded as 2nd Viscount Peel in 1912 and created Earl Peel 1929.

[49] Ella Williamson. Eldest daughter of 1st Baron Ashton. Married William Robert Wellesley Peel 1899.

[50] Frederick William Fane Hervey (1863–1951). Entered Navy 1877; retired as Rear-Admiral 1911. Unionist MP for Bury St Edmunds 1906–7; Chairman, West Suffolk County Council 1915–34. Succeeded as 4th Marquess of Bristol 1907.

doing nothing but I changed the subject. ... The exceptions were Sir Francis & Lady Humphrys[51] from Afghanistan. They were both delightful and he was not only very interesting on his subject but also had many amusing tales to tell. He doesn't want to go back but is hoping for a Legation.

We dined at home on Monday but have dined out every night since, thrice been out to lunch, and had one lunch party of our own. Life is very strenuous now one is out of office!

Dont believe Annie's tales of Dorothy's wit brilliance and beauty or you will be disappointed when you see her ...

What I can truthfully say about her is that she has earned the enthusiastic praise of her music master and the affection of many schoolfellows as well as of the Ozannes ... And I will add, that she has improved in looks. ...

We had an uncomfortable week in the House as Leo took the opportunity when speaking on Safeguarding to express publicly his opinion of Winston and to state that he entirely disagreed with him.[52] This exposure of differences shocked the party so badly that a number of young men abstained from voting in the division, a somewhat illogical method of showing their displeasure. I was pretty vexed because the Opposition at once represented that he and I were both advocating full blooded Protection with taxes on food and Winston went about like a bear with a sore head. By persistent prodding S.B. was finally induced to have a meeting to discuss policy and every one present except myself & Leo declared their determination to have nothing whatever to do with food taxes. They refused to consider making any new statement about policy lest the Liberals should take fright but on the whole they were not averse from the idea that we should make Empire the starting point when we did come to consider the future. Of course Leo came to me afterwards as I expected, to say that he was so disgusted that he should retire to a back bench and carry on a crusade freed from all restrictions and though I think I have stopped his doing what I think would be equivalent to self murder I sometimes wish he would carry out his threat for with the best intentions he ruins any cause in which he is interested.

In the meantime I continue to hear from many quarters of the immense interest & hope created by my speech[53] and I shall take every opportunity I can

---

[51] Francis Henry Humphrys (1879–1971). Various political posts on North-West Frontier of India 1904–19. Deputy Foreign Secretary, Government of India 1921; Minister, Afghanistan 1922–29; High Commissioner and C-in-C, Iraq 1929–32; Ambassador, Iraq 1932–35. Chairman, British Sugar Corporation 1939–45 and Iraq Petroleum Company 1941–50. Knighted 1924.

[52] On 9 July 1929, in the debate on the King's Speech, Amery launched a long-suppressed tirade against Churchill's free trade obstructionism and appealed for a comprehensive system of tariffs and Imperial preferences.

[53] On 4 July 1929 Chamberlain's speech to the Empire Industries Association called for tariffs and a more empire-orientated economic policy along with the need for a free hand releasing the Conservatives from the limiting pledges imposed upon themselves before the election.

get of trying to work out my ideas more fully. But Thomas[54] is making great play with Colonial Development and if it were not for Snowdens imprudent declaration of his intention to abolish Imperial Preference if he gets the chance our clothes would all have been stolen from us.

The dissatisfaction on the Govt back benches was so openly and vehemently shown last week that I am getting very nervous about the future. I understand there is to be a party meeting for the purpose of getting the dissentients in hand again and I hope to goodness it will be successful or we shall have the Government riding for a fall and I don't know what would happen if they threw up the sponge early next year.

We came down here this morning after an absence of nearly a month. I do hate being away from the garden for such long periods as of course we have missed a great deal of the beauty. I am confirmed in my previous impression that it is a great gardening year. ...

...

I have got rather a heavy week in front on me with Housing Subsidy Bill, speeches and dinners but I am going down to fish with Monty Barlow again at the end of it and after that I don't think I shall have much more work before the holiday ...

21 July 1929
Charminster House, Dorchester

My dear Hilda,
... Like you I feel in want of a change and I shall be very glad when next week is over and we can all get away.

Down here it is marvellously peaceful and for two days I have forgotten all about politics and given myself up to the joys of trout fishing. I came down on Friday evening with Barlow and had a good beginning that night getting 3 fish on the evening rise one of which was the biggest caught here this season 1lb 3oz. Yesterday morning I got 5 but then the weather changed and last night was a blank and this morning I only got one. But I love the fishing even when I dont get much out and this morning I lost several good ones among the weeds.

...

Later ...

Politics are disgusting. Winston is shoving very hard, with an eye to the leadership it is said, and S.B. remains obstinately in the background. The former wants us to do a deal with Ll.G. over electoral reform and I am afraid Austen is also disposed in the same direction. I cant see what we have to get out of it and if

---

[54] James Henry Thomas (1874–1949). President, NUR 1910 and General Secretary, 1918–24, 1925–31. Labour MP for Derby 1910–36 (from 1931 as National Labour). Colonial Secretary, 1924, 1935–36; Lord Privy Seal 1929–30; Dominion Secretary 1930–35.

as I understand Ll.G. wants to put the Socialists out before they can bring in another budget I believe that is the worst thing we could do. But it looks to me as if things might get rather critical about Christmas time which would of course make it difficult to get away. I believe A. has made up her mind that she would like to go to E. Africa but its rather a shock to find that it costs more than twice as much as the trip to Jamaica.

My successor seems very friendly now he is in office and takes every opportunity of telling me what he is going to do. I fancy he is a bit nervous.

Well I dont seem to have much inclination to write this week end so I will stop ...

28 July 1929
Westbourne

My dear Ida,

...

I did not speak on Monday but got in my West Ham speech on Tuesday.[55] I dont think the Times reported it but I laid a trap for the Socialists into which they marched with both feet. I extracted a quotation from the Webbs latest work on Poor Law to the effect that experience has shown how impossible it is for elected bodies to administer out relief with propriety to their own constituents. I worked up the Socialists first with some provocative statements & then observed that I supposed they would at least admit the sentence above. Of course they shouted jeers & derision and to my great joy Montague[56] the Under Secretary for Air joined in. You should have seen their faces when I expressed my sorrow at having inadvertently revealed another division in their ranks & told them whose words I had been quoting. I dont know whether that put them in a specially bad temper but they called me every name they could think of Murderer, Cad, the most callous & brutal Minister who had ever sat on the front bench and so forth. One of "my people" i.e. the staff told me he thought they had been thoroughly uncomfortable all through the debate.

We finished up with a debate which resulted in much discomfiture for Winston, and I must say he deserved it.[57] All through this short session he has been trying to take the lead away from S.B. and he thought he saw his way to make a real

---

[55] On 23 July 1929 Chamberlain led a fierce attack on the Labour government's proposal to revoke the Order under the 1926 Board of Guardians (Default) Act which suspended three Poor Law Unions and transferred their powers to the county councils.

[56] Frederick Montague (1876–1966). Labour MP for Islington West 1923–31 and 1935–47. Under-Secretary for Air 1929–31; Parliamentary Secretary, Transport 1940–41 and Aircraft Production 1941–42. Resigned Labour whip in Lords 1955. Created Baron Amwell 1947.

[57] On 26 July 1929 Churchill's Commons attack on the dismissal of Lord Lloyd as High Commissioner in Egypt aroused much Conservative disapproval and his well-prepared speech fell flat before a hostile audience.

splash on the adjournment and leave the House the hero of the day. He had warnings of the most definite character as to the case which the Govt could put up but he insisted on rushing on his fate and the result was that while S.B.'s speech was generally applauded as equally dignified and proper Winston was made to look exceedingly foolish. I suppose generally speaking the session is regarded as having gone well for the Govt. All the better, since we dont want to get them out yet. And I am very glad to say that we are entering on this electoral reform enquiry with our hands absolutely untied and without any arrangement whatever with the Goat.

Before leaving London I had interviews with Mackinder[58] & McDougall[59] about Imperial policy. The latter is an Australian attached to the High Commissioners office who is specially interested in trade & seems to be a good deal in Bruce's[60] confidence. Both of them were entirely in sympathy and agreement with the line I have been taking on Imperial Trade Policy and I feel satisfied that it is the right line for our party to take though it wants working out a good deal more in detail. I had a talk with S.B. about it too and tried to get some expression of his views but he would only say that it sounded worth exploring. I do wish he would apply his own mind a little more to these problems instead of leaving things so entirely to others.

I had a long talk with Edward Wood[61] on Friday when we walked into Hyde Park together and discussed Indian & home affairs for a couple of hours. In spite of the immense difficulties of the problem he is not without hope that a plan may be found which will satisfy the more reasonable Indian and at the same time secure the vital services for the ruling power.

When seeing S.B. I sounded him on the possibility of my getting away in December for a couple of months or so and found him quite agreeable to the

---

[58] Halford John Mackinder (1861–1947). Reader in Geography, Oxford University 1887–1905. Principal, University College Reading 1892–1903; Director, LSE 1903–8; Reader in Geography, University of London 1900–1923 and Professor 1923–25. British High Commissioner to South Russia 1919. Unionist MP for Glasgow Camlachie 1910–22. Chairman, Imperial Economic Conference 1926 and Imperial Shipping Committee 1920–45. Knighted 1920.

[59] Frank Lidgett McDougall (1884–1958). Economic Adviser to Australian Government in London from 1923; Australian representative and chairman, Imperial Economic Committee 1935–37; Member, Economic Committee of League of Nations.

[60] Stanley Melbourne Bruce (1884–1967). Australian politician and diplomat. Australian Treasurer 1921–23; Prime Minister 1923–29; Minister Resident in London 1932–33; Australian High Commissioner in London 1933–45. Retired in England. Created Viscount Bruce of Melbourne 1947.

[61] Edward Frederick Lindley Wood (1881–1959). Conservative MP for Ripon 1910–25. Under-Secretary, Colonies 1921–22; President, Board of Education 1922–24 and 1932–35; Minister of Agriculture 1924–25; Viceroy of India 1926–31; Secretary for War 1935; Lord Privy Seal 1935–37; Lord President 1937–38; Foreign Secretary 1938–40; Ambassador to Washington 1941–46. Created Baron Irwin 1925; succeeded as 3rd Viscount Halifax 1934. Created Earl of Halifax 1944.

idea. He said he would be very sorry not to have me here but he did think it would be extremely useful for me to have some first hand knowledge of the colonies in which the most vital & important issues might presently have to be decided. ...

...

5 August 1929
Bamburgh Castle, Northumberland

My dear Hilda,

...

... In a little more than a fortnight I have now had just 20 requests to speak at various functions in October or November alone. I suppose this is a tribute to my growing reputation in the country but I could wish that it took a less embarrassing form. A. & I drove over to lunch with the Runcimans[62] ... R. has a large lake in which he has invited me to fish whenever I feel disposed ... Both he and she made themselves very agreeable and they are to pay us a return visit on Thursday.

...

11 August 1929
Bamburgh Castle

My dear Ida,

...

I had a letter from Austen yesterday. ... I had asked him to give me his views of the Egyptian Treaty and he writes fully on that subject. He thinks Henderson[63] blundered badly over Lloyd's[64] dismissal but I am afraid I reluctantly disagree with him there. Harsh he certainly was, but he made a good case & presented it very skilfully and in the end he got away with it successfully. I found that Runciman, who lunched here one day this week,

---

[62] Walter Runciman (1870–1949). Liberal MP for Oldham 1899–1900, Dewsbury 1902–18, Swansea West 1924–29, St Ives 1929–37 (Liberal National from 1931). Parliamentary Secretary, LGB 1905–7; Financial Secretary, Treasury 1907–8; President, Board of Education 1908–11, Board of Agriculture 1911–14, Board of Trade 1914–16 and 1931–37. Lord President of Council 1938–39. Special Envoy to Czechoslovakia 1938. Created Viscount Runciman of Doxford 1937.

[63] Arthur Henderson (1863–1935). Labour MP for Barnard Castle 1903–18, Widnes 1919–22, Newcastle East 1923, Burnley 1924–31, Clay Cross 1933–35. Labour Party Treasurer, 1904–12, Chairman 1908–10, 1914–17. President, Board of Education 1915–16; Paymaster-General 1916; Member of War Cabinet 1916–17; Home Secretary 1924; Foreign Secretary 1929–31. Labour leader 1931–32. Chaired World Disarmament Conference 1932–35. Nobel Peace Prize 1934.

[64] George Ambrose Lloyd (1879–1941). Conservative MP for Staffordshire West 1910–18 and 1924–25. Governor of Bombay 1918–23; High Commissioner for Egypt and Sudan 1925–29; Colonial Secretary and Leader of the Lords 1940–41. Knighted 1918. Created Baron Lloyd 1925.

quite shared this view. As to the Treaty R. did not like the provisions about the Soudan but thought the rest inevitable though disagreeable. There again I find myself in agreement with him though Austen says he is concerned both with the position of foreigners and with the removal of the troops from the neighbourhood of Cairo. I think it quite possible that foreigners will suffer by the change – I think Egyptians will suffer still more. But I rather doubt if we can help ourselves.

Meanwhile I see Snowden is maintaining a very firm stand at the Hague.[65] There he has the full sympathy of myself & I suppose most other people. But I do wonder what is his way out or whether he has any. City circles thought that a break up of the Conference and a return to the Dawes plan would be the most disastrous thing of all. But surely that must have occurred to other nations too, and I cant help thinking that if Snowden remains firm they will have to drop their bluff. If he returns successful he will be drowned in the butter the Mail and Express will pour over him. Both of them are hard at work writing up the present Government at the expense of the last.

I suppose you followed the Twickenham election.[66] But unless you read the Daily Express you would utterly fail to realise the cynical audacity of modern journalism. Day after day it has been proclaiming that the whole world was watching this election in feverish suspense. Day after day it announced some sensational new adherence to the doctrine of Free Trade within the Empire, although if one read beyond the headlines the alleged credo generally turned out to be nothing more than a vague and generalised hope for progress towards an ideal. But on the day when the result was announced not only did the "Empire Crusade" disappear from its pages but we searched its columns in vain for any mention of the election at all. And yesterday there was a similar blank! What does it take its readers for? And is it not after all correct in supposing that they are like a slate and that you can equally well write anything you choose upon it & wash it all out next day!

...

Monday ... I thought I had written my impressions of the Egyptian Treaty to you but it must have been to someone else. My feeling is that Milner[67] sold the pass and to get it back was almost impossible. We have been trying what is quite impossible viz. to steer a middle course. I hate the idea of all our good work

---

[65] The First Hague Conference, 6–28 August 1929 finally reduced German Reparation payments in accordance with the Young Plan of June 1929.

[66] Twickenham by-election, 8 August 1929. Beaverbrook launched his 'Crusade' for 'Empire Free Trade' in the *Sunday Express* on 30 June 1929 and the Conservative candidate was officially disowned after espousing Empire Free Trade. The Conservative majority of 5966 in the general election earlier in the month was cut to 503.

[67] Alfred Milner (1854–1925). High Commissioner for South Africa 1897–1905; member, War Cabinet 1916–18; Secretary for War 1918–19; Colonial Secretary 1919–21. Created KCB 1895, Baron 1901, Viscount 1902, KG 1921.

going to the devil as it surely will. I would hold on to the Soudan like grim death but I rather despair of Egypt itself.

...

20 August 1929
Loubcroy Lodge, Oykell, By Lairg

My dear Hilda,

... I suppose it *was Sir* Herbert Samuel[68] who confided in you (you call him *Mr* Samuel) but no! on looking at your letter again I see you speak of him as the member for Farnham. Of course that is Arthur Michael Samuel not Herbert – a very different person. A.M.S. was Financial Secretary to the Treasury in the last Government. He was selected by Winston against the advice of his friends, proved a failure and very soon W. refused to speak to him at all. Hence these tears. Of course he is a Jew and looks it, but he really is a very warmhearted rather childlike person whom I always like. He is very generous & always giving things away. He gave me a print of the Bull Ring in Birmingham which must have cost him £15 or £20. He has a fund of knowledge which includes such diverse subjects as Piranesi and The Herring on both of which he has written books & he has also published a very readable volume called the Mancroft Essays. I considered him for Fin. Sec. when I was at the Exchequer but concluded that though clever he was not quite balanced enough for such a responsible position & ought to be tried out first in a less important post.

...

We had some jolly walks and drives at Bamburgh before Frank & I left last Friday. That night we slept at Inverness and came on here on the Saturday. It was pouring with rain & the river was in flood to my great joy. On Sunday I fished ... without success ... Yesterday I flogged the Oykell from 10 a.m. to 7 p.m. had a joyful day. I lost 3 salmon pulled 2 more & rose a sixth out of 8 fish that I saw. I also got 2 fine sea trout so that it was a lively time & I dont mind losing fish like some people do. The thrill is in hooking them. I am off again now for another try.

Frank is having the time of his life. He caught 3 trout on Sunday & yesterday went out with Gerald & shot his first brace of grouse. Today he is to come with me.

---

[68] Herbert Louis Samuel (1870–1963). Liberal MP for Cleveland 1902–18 and Darwen 1929–35. Under-Secretary, Home Office 1905–9; Chancellor, Duchy of Lancaster 1909–10 and 1915–16; Postmaster-General 1910–14 and 1915–16; President, LGB 1914–15; Home Secretary 1916 and 1931–32; High Commissioner for Palestine 1920–25. Knighted 1920. Created Viscount Samuel 1937.

22 September 1929
Tillypronie, Tarland, Aberdeenshire

My dear Ida,

…

I am having a very pleasant visit here. I like my host[69] very much; he was a short time in the House with me but I have never known him before. But besides being a very good fellow who is generally popular he is a man in a good many affairs; Chairman of the Cunard, director of the L.M.S. and the Midland Bank and probably many less well known concerns. He must be very well off and everything here is done in great style or rather I should say with great attention to comfort …

I was hoping to get some fishing here but the weather has been so dry that there is no water in the Don and, it is reported … no fish either. But there is plenty of shooting so that the time passes very pleasantly and I am gratified to find that I can hold my own with any of the guns here young or old though I am considerably the oldest member of the party.

The only guest who would be known by name to you is Sir Francis Humphreys. He has been offered Iraq and has been asking my advice as to whether he should take it. He has just had a very advantageous offer from the City which would make him financially comfortable for life; he doesn't know Arabic nor has he any personal acquaintance with the personages concerned. Moreover he cant stand heat though he doesn't mind cold. I have refused to give advice as only he can balance up the relative weight to be attached to the various factors of material advantage, duty to his family, duty to his country and satisfaction in taking a hand in the making of history. But I have made clear to him what I desire & my view that there is a big job to be done which he can probably do better than anyone else and I have very little doubt that he will accept the offer. But I have strongly advised him to lay down his conditions including what I believe the administrators get in most other hot countries namely a prolonged period of leave in the summer.

…

28 September 1929
37 Eaton Square, SW1

My dear Hilda,

…

I got to Westbourne in time for lunch and was immediately rung up by a local hon sec of a "Business Club" for an address which I promptly refused. This

---

[69] Thomas Royden (1871–1950). Shipowner. Chairman, Liverpool Steamship Owner's Association; President, Chamber of Shipping. Coalition Unionist MP for Bootle 1918–22. Chairman, Cunard Steamship Company. Succeeded as Bart 1917. Created Baron Royden 1944.

makes the 46th request since July! We had a very large attendance at our Annual Demonstration in the Botanics, but I was the only ex-Cabinet Minister present. … D. Davis[70] took me aside to say that he found much dissatisfaction among members of the party with the leader & *Now was my chance*. My answer was that I was not looking for "chances" which do not present any attraction. But I fear he is right about the grousing.

…

13 October 1929
Swinton, Masham, Yorkshire

My dear Hilda,
…
If Austens visit materialises and he does tell you his plans you might report them on to me as I shall not be seeing him for some time. I hope his City business is going to be both congenial and remunerative for the belief grows upon me that he is unlikely to hold office again. I have been unpleasantly surprised to find how quickly his popularity in the party has been dissipated. Nothing seems to have annoyed the rank and file more than his public statement that S.B. had promised him the F.O. again if we came in. Even Bridgeman was vexed and seemed to think A. was one of the "old gang" who ought to make way for younger blood. I had thought that his position and reputation on the Continent were recognised to have a special value which must be preserved, but I can see, although people wont say much to me about him, that a steady stream of propaganda has had its effect and that even in his own party there is a feeling that he is too Continental to be a good representative of England.

In these (Swinton) quarters I meet with severe criticism on S.B. a criticism which I got also when I dined with Sam Hoare last Monday. I sincerely hope that this is only a passing phase and that S.B. will show some energy and drive when we reassemble. But I confess to some nervousness on the subject especially if, as I anticipate, this Government goes on for some time longer, because S.B. does not shine in Opposition. He knows it, and moreover it is so distasteful to him that he might conceivably withdraw from the leadership. In that case the succession would come either to Winston or myself & I dont know which I should dislike most! When I think of the possibilities I feel inclined to retire myself while there is yet time to avoid them!

…

We have had wonderful weather here and though the wind has been rather heavy for shooting the sunshine has been quite delightful. I miss Annie's company

---

[70] David Davis (1859–1938). Member, Birmingham City Council from 1901; Alderman 1913; Lord Mayor 1921–23; Life Governor, University of Birmingham; Deputy Chairman, Birmingham Unionist Association. Knighted 1923.

but being out of doors all day keeps me busy and occupied. Our party includes Lord and Lady Melchett (née Mond) who would be delightful company if they weren't so repulsive! He is quite learned about pictures and furniture & works of art generally and of course full of information on high finance and the most modern forms of industry. But he is almost impossible to understand because he mumbles so and punctuates every sentence with his sharp "What"? He has expressed the desire to have a talk on Empire with Philip & me some time today but I dont know what he is up to unless he is really going to declare for Empire Free Trade. Meanwhile I have heard from Northumberland[71] who wants me to advise the Editor of the Morning Post about Empire policy. I suspect that he is after Peace River Settlement, but as Gwynne is now in Canada he will probably have been able to form some idea of how far such a project would have any chance of acceptance there.

Just before leaving home I got an invitation to go to Liverpool and address 5000 people on Municipal Elections. I have expressed willingness to accept though its a tremendous bore and fag, for I think it might help to rouse the party to some effort and also show that the leaders were not wrap [sic] in slumber as all the papers make out.

...

19 October 1929
37 Eaton Square, SW1

My dear Ida,

I have returned tonight from Six Mile Bottom and am very glad I did as a most appalling amount of correspondence has accumulated during the two days I have been away and I have got two speeches on my mind. I find your letter here, but as the housemaid has gone to bed with my inkstand I must use a fountain pen to write my reply and I never can write properly with those instruments of torture.

I must confess that I was rather disappointed and depressed at not finding Annie better. She looks lamentably pale and weak and though she declares she is better she shows very little sign of vitality & buoyancy and evidently is very "nervy" still. I believe she is better but it looks to me as if recovery was going to be very slow and I had no hesitation in advising her not to go to Hatfield next week.

I dined with Austen on Monday. He had said in his telegram that he wanted a long talk and I had assumed he had something particular to say but if that had been in his mind he must have changed it. He certainly did say that he

---

[71] Alan Ian Percy (1880–1930). Succeeded as 8th Duke of Northumberland 1918. Leading figure in Diehard revolt 1921–22; Chairman, *Morning Post* 1924–30.

thought Baldwin ought to have some meetings to discuss the situation before Parliament assembled but he said nothing about any unauthorised programme and I should have thought that in any case before considering anything of the kind it was necessary to see how far Baldwin was prepared to go. We did not discuss his seat or the personal position of either of us but I agree that there is no necessity for him to make any decision yet. Nor did we talk about his financial affairs or I might have given him some comfort by telling him that though the final figures are not yet complete I am hoping to get something out of Hoskins this year.

...

I had a meeting with my co-directors of the proposed new Trust Company of which I am to be Chairman this week and I think it is going to materialise. Hilton Young is going to join the Board which is satisfactory as I like him and moreover he understands finance.

I am very worried over an accident which has befallen me. On Friday the man next me about 20 yds off discharged his gun in my direction. ... and since then I have been stone deaf in that ear and cant hear my watch when it is held close to it. ... The immediate effect is to fill me with an intense dislike of politics "which is very strange".

22 October 1929
37 Eaton Square, SW1

My dear Ida,

...

I have just met W. Peel who says he hears that just before Ramsay went to U.S.A. he got S.B. to agree to a statement by Irwin that Dominion Status would be granted to India (*ultimately*, I presume) and that S.B gave his consent without consulting any of his colleagues. I trust this is not true. W.P. says Simon[72] is threatening to resign [as Chairman of Indian Statutory Commission]!

Everywhere & from all sides I hear of depression distrust & despair in our party. Politics are not a cheerful occupation just now and I am glad we are going away!

...

---

[72] John Allsebrook Simon (1873–1954). Liberal MP for Walthamstow 1906–18 and Spen Valley 1922–40 (Liberal National from 1931). Solicitor-General 1910–13; Attorney-General 1913–15; Home Secretary 1915–16 and 1935–37; Foreign Secretary 1931–35; Chancellor of Exchequer 1937–40; Lord Chancellor 1940–45. Knighted 1910. Created Viscount Simon 1940.

26 October 1929
37 Eaton Square, SW1

My dear Hilda,

...

We had our party meeting on Wednesday when S.B. had to confirm the India rumour. There was a sort of gasp and as far as I could see no one in the party approved of what he had done. I know quite well how it happened. He saw Edward who told him that there was nothing new in the statement but that it was necessary in order to prevent serious trouble in India in December (two statements which to me appear incompatible with each other). Then he went to Aix and a representative of the India Office came out with a draft & said Ramsay wants to know that you agree to this; Edward is strongly in favour of it. And S.B. reflected I know nothing about this but if Edward backs it it must be all right. I think it was most improper and unfair to ask him to assent to such a statement & of course his assent was personal only, but obviously if his party does not back him, and I certainly dont think they will, he is in a very embarrassing position. We discussed Foreign Affairs at some length but Home Affairs & in particular the position of our own party not at all nor do I know when we are to meet again nor what measures are to be taken to decide on policy. Since then I had an opportunity of about 20 minutes private talk with S.B. when I told him of the criticisms that were reaching me from all quarters about his want of leadership and told him that he must give a lead and be a bit more aggressive if the party was to be held together. He said he was quite aware of the criticism & was conscious that opposition was not his strong suit, but of course leadership is wanted for a Govt as well as for an Opposition.

It is all very depressing and particularly embarrassing for me because every one I meet tells me of S.B.'s failings and many suggest that I should do better in his place. Heaven knows I dont want the job. It is a thankless one at any time & never more so than now when the party is all to pieces. Moreover, S.B. is my friend as well as my leader and I would not on any account play L.G. to his Asquith.[73] If only he would make the effort and regain his place I should be quite happy but at present he doesn't show much signs of doing so and once again I am thankful that for a time I am going to leave the country.

In my conversation he expressed the view that the new policy would have to take the form of an advance in Safeguarding but he didn't say in what the advance should consist. The situation is enormously complicated by Beaverbrooks campaign which you are probably unaware of as you dont see the Express. He is pushing it very hard and very cleverly so as to catch thoughtless & disgruntled Conservatives and every one who knows him tells me his dominating motive is

---

[73] Henry Herbert Asquith (1852–1928). Liberal MP for Fife East 1886–1918 and Paisley 1920–24. Home Secretary 1892–95; Chancellor of Exchequer 1905–8; Prime Minister 1908–16; Secretary for War 1914. Leader of Liberal Party 1908–26. Created KG and Earl of Oxford and Asquith 1925.

detestation of S.B. It is difficult to see how we can have any accommodation with him if that be so.

...

17 November 1929
Westbourne

My dear Ida,

... I was dog tired with late sittings in the House of Commons. Seeing how completely the press has refused to take any notice of the Pensions Bill[74] debates one wonders whether it was worth while to put up any opposition at all. Suppose we had just let it all go through without amendment, would any soul have been the wiser? You yourself say nothing on the subject and I wonder if you realised that we sat from 3.30 on Tuesday afternoon till 8.30 on Wednesday morning and again had a very late sitting on Thursday. I confess I found it very hard to discover anything in the Times that even indicated that an all night sitting had taken place. The Herald, it is true, had a picture of "the Premier leaving the House about 8.45 after the all night sitting" but this was only to pretend that he had been there whereas he slept comfortably in his bed and only turned up at 8.30. I met him then in the Lobby & he said "I was absolutely amazed when I woke up this morning and found you were still on Clause I. Your people put up a magnificent fight".

Your account of the developments in connection with the Local Government Act are interesting as showing how its possibilities are beginning to be realised. I guess it will prove to have been my magnum opus when my obituary notice is written.

On Monday evening S.B. told me that the Beaver had written in a Rothermere Sunday paper an appeal to him to take up Empire Free Trade, saying that if this were done he would be quite ready to retire. S.B. thought the best thing would be to see him but he wanted me to be present. Accordingly on Tuesday morning I went to S.B.'s house where I found him & the Beaver in the library and we three sat & talked for some 2½ hours. The Beaver developed his policy at length, admitting that it was neither new nor properly described as *Free* Trade. But Empire Free Trade was a far better slogan that [sic] "freeer" trade or any other designation which might be more accurate and anyway the term was quite as justifiable as the so-called Free Trade which was only Free Imports. He declared that he had got a great deal of support from the Dominions as well as from Conservatives at home and gave us many figures to show that Canadians were really frightened about the Argentine competition in wheat and their own

---

[74] This extended widows' pensions to the wives of insured men who had either died or were over seventy before Chamberlain's scheme came into operation.

growing dependence on the U.S.A. We afterwards discussed at some length the political consequences of our adoption of such a policy. The B. agreed with S. B. that Winston would be dead against it but thought he had no following and nowhere to go if he left us. Finally S.B. said of course he was not in a position to commit himself but he gave the impression that on the merits he was convinced and he was merely considering political possibilities & expediencies. I believe this impression was a true reflection of his mind; at any rate he said nothing after the Beaver had gone to contradict it. We discussed what he could say next Thursday and I expounded my ideas of a speech beginning with an attack on the Government for their handling of unemployment and then going on to an exposition of world economic conditions leading to the conclusion that in the idea of Imperial unity alone could salvation come. After that he was to say that he was convinced that this must be the central feature of Conservative policy in the future and that we were going to examine every aspect of it in consultation with reprs. of overseas, finishing with a suggestion that it might well be a question for consideration how far it was possible to go without untying our hands & freeing ourselves from hampering pledges.

At the time S.B. was very pleased with this but I am afraid he forgot it very soon because he said some days later that he wished he had written it down there and then. But probably it went a little further than would be wise at this stage and it might be better simply to say that we would approach the whole enquiry "with a completely open mind". I can see though that S.B. has been very considerably damped by talks with cold footers like Worthy and I know from experience that in such a talk he puts up no fight at all and does nothing to counter any arguments that may be brought up. So I don't know what he will say on Thursday, but it is one of those occasions when there is a great opportunity if only he will take it.

Last Thursday I went to the Garvin lunch and there saw the Beaver again. He immediately asked me to join him after the lunch as he wanted to see me and I drove with him to the House. I found he was afraid that S.B. was going the whole hog on Thursday & he wanted to say that he didn't think that would be wise. But he also suggested that S.B. should, through me, show him beforehand what he was going to say that he might give it the fullest support. It is evident that an accommodation is very near but it must be admitted also that it might easily go wrong at any moment.

As I came out from the lunch I ran into the Goat who had been speaking at it and he poured out a whole string of compliments about one of my speeches on Widows Pensions. He had never heard a better presentation of a case, it had absolutely shattered the Ministers arguments. I wondered what he was up to. It *was* a good speech but he must have had some motive for saying so.

...

P.S. ... Austen was to see the Beaver today.

24 November 1929
37 Eaton Square, SW1

My dear Hilda,

...

I have had a very heavy week and I wasn't surprised to find this morning that my weight had gone back from 10st. 1lb which I reached after the holidays to 9st 11. which is usually about my lowest level. But I too feel I am through the worst and my mind is at ease again ...

Yes I am very pleased with Baldwin's speech which went extremely well I am told and has had favourable repercussions in the party, among members of the House, in the Beaver's mind, and in Canada. Sam Hoare who has been most helpful to me all through has just left me, and we agreed that we had every reason to be satisfied with our efforts without which I am certain neither would the breach with the Beaver have healed nor the Albert Hall speech delivered. We have had to picket our leader – peacefully but very closely – all the week as Salisbury, Worthy, and Winston have all been pulling the other way but in the end we have triumphed and I fancy it will be difficult to stop the ball we have set rolling. Just to illustrate the difficulties I see the Sunday Times is today rather critical – cries "Ware Protection" [sic], and wishes that S.B. had said more about economy. This means that Camrose (né Sir William Berry) is jealous of the compliments to the Beaver! and if we are not careful we shall lose our one supporter in the Press in our effort to recapture the other. But what we have got to do now is to stimulate S.B. to get going with the enquiry. He is like a top. You must keep whipping him or he falls over! So Sam & I are going to tackle him again, always separately, and get our other myrmidons to work in the same direction. If I were he I would get into touch at once with some leading agriculturists, industrialists, economists & financiers and talk with them till I could get my own mind clear as to the lines to be followed and then I would set Philip and Sam to work out details with them. But I doubt if he will do it that way for I have never yet been able to persuade him to take any subject under his own wing.

The Committee you allude to is Research. They want me to be Chairman of it but I have refused to commit myself till I come back and see what the conditions are then. It looks to me as if Unemployment Insurance & Coal were going to prove two very awkward and embarrassing snags and the Govt may be in serious trouble before long.

I was thankful to get through the Pensions Bill which afforded very little scope owing to the timorousness of our people who would not vote against 2nd R. I think they would have done themselves no harm if they had but it was very difficult in a safe seat to press them beyond a certain point and anyway I did make them, though very reluctantly, vote against Clause I.

I had to go to Oxford on Thursday to take part for the first time in a Union Debate. It was rather bad having to do it just before [Dorothy's appendix] operation but I got through it – I trust without discredit if not with very conspicuous success. They had the largest attendance they have recorded for years – over 700 voted – and we were defeated by about 40 votes, which I was told was not bad. There were a good number of Indians present and they voted in a solid block with the Govt.

Last night I had another speech – to the London Federation of the Junior Imperial League, and it was a great success. The platform were most enthusiastic saying that the Imps had all been thrilled and that I had given them exactly what they wanted. Needless to say, I gave them the new Empire policy and I feel sure that that is the one subject which will appeal to the need for an ideal which is natural and instinctive among young people. I am glad that my last political speech before I go away should have been on that subject and should have evoked such a warm response.

Yesterday morning we had a meeting of the future directors of the Australian Trust. We have now got Sir Malcolm Hogg,[75] brother of Lord Hailsham, to join us and I am very pleased with him. I hadn't met him before, but he strikes me as a man of first rate quality and as he is a Director of the Westminster Bank he can bring a good deal of useful knowledge to bear. But we aren't over the rapids yet as we have not yet solved the problem of raising sufficient cash to make a start and until we do that it is not certain that we shall ever come into existence. Meanwhile it is pleasant to hear that the composition of the Board is highly approved of in the City and its only doubt arises from its fear that two members, Hilton Young and myself, might at any moment be called off to join another Government. But I dont think there is much chance of that!

...

Hoskins has come in very handy for all of us. My overdraft was rather larger than I cared about leaving behind me, but I think I need not worry about it now.

10 December 1929
37 Eaton Square, SW1

My dear Ida,

I can hardly believe that this is the last night before we start on the great adventure but I suppose by this time tomorrow we shall be on our way to Marseilles. I shall be glad for Annie multiplies work with every hour & no efforts on my part will induce her to get to bed before 12. I am agreeably surprised however at her ability to stand so prolonged a strain. As for Dorothy she is full of life and spirits and there is no doubt that she will extract the fullest amount of enjoyment from her first experience of travel.

---

[75] Malcolm Nicholson Hogg (1883–1948). Joined Forbes, Forbes & Campbell 1904 and its Bombay office 1905; Deputy Chairman, Bombay Chamber of Commerce 1915–17 and Chairman 1917–19; member, Legislative Council of Governor of Bombay 1915–17; member, Legislative Council of Viceroy of India 1917–19; and India Council 1920–25. Knighted 1920.

I have taken no part in H. of C. work for some little time and have only watched the Govt getting into trouble. But I have been working behind the scenes and feel satisfied that things are in train for the working out of a practical Imperial programme to which I hope to come back with renewed vigour & fresh ideas.

I hope you and Hilda will continue to write your weekly letter only altering the date so that they may leave London on Thursday when the post goes. ...

...

18 December 1929
M.V. "Llangibby Castle"

My dear Ida,

It is a week today since we started but already it seems more like a month and home affairs have receded into a vague and misty distance ...

Well, so far, we have been quite extraordinarily fortunate in our weather ...

...

Tomorrow we reach Port Said. I hope I shant find a telegram there to say the Government is out and I am wanted in London immediately!

...

Xmas Eve 1929
M.V. "Llangibby Castle"
In the Red Sea near the straits of Bab-El-Mandib. Temp. 82°

My dear Hilda,

... How glad I am that I am here in this sunshine & warmth instead of shivering in the cold & dark of your December. So far our good fortune has not deserted us; we have had smooth seas with little wind and though it has been warm the heat has never been oppressive ...

...

I am doing a good deal of reading especially about Central Africa and begin to get the atmosphere. We have brief accounts of doings at home by wireless from which we see that the Govt got the second reading of the coal bill by only 2 votes. But it all seems very far away.

...

4

1930
'No Confidence is Felt in S.B.':
Baldwin, Beaverbrook and the Empire Crusade

Chamberlain left London on 11 December 1929 for a three-month tour of East Africa intended both as a holiday and a preparation for a possible future term as Colonial Secretary. Accompanied by his wife and daughter, Chamberlain crossed by land to Marseilles where they boarded the ship which carried them via Genoa, Port Said and Aden to Mombasa by 30 December. Travelling first to Nairobi, Chamberlain inspected schools, hospitals and research laboratories, met governors, coffee planters and local chiefs and fished for rainbow trout in Nyeri. From there he moved on to the Rift Valley to meet the pioneering Lord Delamere where he thrilled at the abundant wildlife and marvelled at the spectacle of vast flocks of flamingos on Lake Naivasha 'like a snow storm of pink snowflakes'. From Kenya the family travelled to Uganda to visit the source of the Nile, the Victoria Falls and on from Lake Albert to the Murchison Falls, although floods prevented the continuation of the tour through Tanganyika. Embarking at Zanzibar on 16 February, Chamberlain arrived back in England on 8 March 1930.[1]

17 January 1930
Kapsilial, P.O. Sergoil, Kenya

My dear Hilda,

I must apologise for the length of time that has elapsed since I wrote last but literally every minute of our time has been filled up and only by taking very firm measures with … our hosts, have we got a few minutes this morning to write letters.

… I am glad to say that we too are all in the best of health and enjoying every minute of our trip except for the packing which is a veritable nightmare and does necessarily recur rather frequently. I think I can only give you general impressions as obviously I cannot squeeze a consecutive narrative of a tremendously busy fortnight into one letter. … Delamere[2] is the outstanding

---

[1] For Chamberlain's detailed travel diary of this tour see NC2/14–15.

[2] Hugh Cholmondeley (1870–1931). Pioneer of colonisation in British East Africa owning 7000 acres near Nairobi. Succeeded as 3rd Baron Delamere 1887.

personality on the Colony. At first sight he is not impressive but on further acquaintance I have begun to see how broad his views are and to appreciate the vision & courage with which he has pioneered enterprise after enterprise often at great loss to himself but with ultimate gain to the Colony. I was therefore anxious to get on as intimate terms as possible with him and to make myself acquainted with his views, so that I welcomed very warmly the opportunity of spending a couple of days with him. We talked incessantly the whole time (so our wives declared) and I have reason to believe that the liking & respect I felt for him was reciprocated. His house – quite a primitive sort of log hut was in the most typically Central African scenery we have come across. ...

I have quite lost my heart to the country. To begin with there is the most marvellous variety of scenery & climate & one is always coming on something totally unlike what one has seen before. ... The sun was hot in the middle of the day, but never oppressive and the birds butterflies & caterpillars were a constant joy.

...

I feel I am beginning to know something about the problems of the country. It would take too long to write about them here but it was rather gratifying to be told by Lord Francis Scott[3] yesterday that I had won the complete confidence of the country and the settlers would do anything for me! This is not derived from speech making as I haven't done any but just from talking with individuals.

All our Tanganyika plans have been washed out by the rains which have washed out the railway and we have had to give up our voyage down the Lake

...

...

26 January 1930
Government House, Entebbe, Uganda

My dear Ida,

We got back here last night from Lake Albert & found A's mail ... I had letters from Philip Cunliffe-Lister & Sam Hoare giving me the political news so altogether it was quite a feast. Sam H. thinks things are blowing up for a crisis in the near future and that I may have to be telegraphed for. I sincerely trust he is wrong for I dont at all want to fly back and leave my family behind, but I confess it appears to me very improbable that the Govt wd go to the country before introducing a Budget though I quite realise that they got a bad shake up over the Coal Bill.

---

[3] Francis George Montagu-Douglas-Scott (1879–1952). ADC to Viceroy of India 1905–10; member, Executive and Legislative Council, Kenya Colony. Son of Duke of Buccleuch; styled Lord Francis Scott.

If I dont comment on your letters it is because I must save space & time & also because they were written a month ago. But dont imagine that we dont look forward to them & enjoy them just as much as if they had been sent off the day before.

...

14 February 1930
Mombasa

My dear Hilda,
...

I am complete ignorant of home affairs, but as I expected we have got through without a General Election. Grigg[4] has just shown me a telegram saying unemployment is up to 1500000 & trade returns most unsatisfactory. They wont want to dissolve on that!

I gathered ... that S.B. had tied himself up again on food and that Amery had claimed his freedom. I am very sorry; I wanted that free hand but must see what exactly S.B. did say before I decide on my action.

24 February 1930
British India Steam Navigation Company

My dear Ida,
...

There is of course no news to give you; we have had a very quiet peaceful voyage so far, pleasantly hot but not too oppressive. The ship is comfortable, the Captain most obliging and I have allotted to me a writing room on the boat deck to which I retreat in the afternoon. ...

...

I see Beaverbrook and Rothermere have launched their new party. The Daily Mail bulletins which we receive on board by wireless give lurid accounts of the enthusiasm which it has excited and of the numbers and quality of its adherents. But reading between the lines I get the impression that it has not really produced the effect intended and may even have consolidated S.B.'s position.

...

---

[4] Edward William Macleay Grigg (1879–1955). Secretary to Editor, *The Times* 1903; Assistant Editor, *Outlook* 1905–6; Head, Colonial Department, *The Times* 1908–13; Joint Editor, *Round Table* 1913–14; Military Secretary to Prince of Wales 1919–20; Private Secretary to Lloyd George 1921–22; Liberal MP for Oldham 1922–25; Governor and C-in-C, Kenya Colony 1925–30; Chairman, Milk Commission 1932; National Conservative MP for Altrincham 1933–45; PPS, Ministry of Information 1939–40; Financial Secretary, War Office 1940; Joint Under-Secretary for War 1940–42; Minister Resident in Middle East 1944–45. Knighted 1920. Created Baron Altrincham 1945.

22 March 1930
Westbourne

My dear Ida,

... Everyone says I am looking so much better that I begin to think I must be, though I cant say that I have been conscious either of the deterioration or the improvement. But it is a fact that having returned with a strong distaste for politics I have now begun to find them interesting again and I have been tackling my new jobs with so much energy that perhaps I have renewed some of my strength in East Africa.

...

I am writing an article for the D.T. on the end of the old Poor Law system. Your account of the way the Surrey C.C. are behaving is disheartening but I believe they are rather the exception than the rule and I agree with you that they will probably see the error of their ways in time, though that is no consolation to those who are made to suffer now. I wonder if you saw the attack upon me in the Daily Mail. They declared that I had made a mistake of £15 millions in my estimates and the Treasury would have to find that amount more than they had expected. I made a smashing reply, a small portion of which they inserted in a back column. Thus does our popular press mislead the public in order to feed Rothermere's vendetta against Baldwin. But I have got a letter tonight from the chairman of the Ipswich Finance Committee showing that in his Borough the estimates have been almost exactly fulfilled and remarking that though a Liberal he is not going to refrain from doing justice to a great statesman even though he be a Conservative.

This has been a busy and eventful week and though I have not been in the public eye I have done a good deal of work for the party behind the scenes. I have now definitely taken over the Research Department which will next month be housed at 24 Old Queen Street with the principal rooms overlooking Bird Cage Walk. The leader and his staff will share the building with us and I expect there will be a lot of colloguing there between us. I found things in rather a mess, for Eustace,[5] who always said he was not the man for the job, had started a number of hares without any clear idea of where he was going, and the office was evidently dispirited and uneasy. But there is a different atmosphere now and they are all rather excited and feeling that they are going to be an important body. I am getting very much interested myself and it seems to me that through my new department I shall have my finger on the springs of policy. With immense difficulty we have got S.B. to set up a sort of inner Shadow Cabinet called the Committee of Business which is to meet regularly and I am arranging

---

[5] Eustace Sutherland Campbell Percy (1887–1958). Conservative MP for Hastings 1921–37. Parliamentary Secretary, Education 1923 and Health 1923–24; President, Board of Education 1924–29; member, Joint Select Committee on India 1933–34; Minister without Portfolio 1935–36. Known as Lord Eustace Percy from 1899. Created Baron Percy of Newcastle 1953.

to take my instructions from and report to them. I am insisting that every committee I set up shall have proper terms of reference, that it shall be strictly limited in number so as to sharpen the individual sense of responsibility in each member, though they are allowed to bring in any one they like to help them, and I am providing that committees shall be composed mostly of young men including back benchers. We shall be at once an Information Bureau providing data and briefs for leaders, and a long range Research body and the results of our work will be supplied not to the public but to the Committee of Business the Central Office and Ashridge College. As a start I am setting up a Research into Unemployment Insurance and Outrelief to work out the proper principles on which an Insurance Scheme should be operated and a proper method of dealing with able bodied unemployed who are not really insurable and weigh down the Fund but at present are excluded from outrelief. I shall have another committee on overproduction which is the new world phenomenon another on social & industrial problems including thrift and co-partnership & finally another on agriculture. I am particularly pleased with the latter, because hitherto all our investigations have simply endeavoured to find some vote-catching device with the result that we bring forward a series of disconnected proposals which have no relation either to one another or to any coherent scheme. I have persuaded my friends that what we want is a survey of the whole position which shall establish the proper proportions of the different kinds of farming – arable, dairy, stock &c. in the light of our soil climate and economic conditions and then a consideration of the measures necessary to establish each kind in its proportion. On this plan we shall be able to rule out many of the really childish suggestions which our agricultural committees have been wasting their time over, and such measures as we propose will fall into their proper place as necessary for the purpose at which we are aiming. It will take time but if it is done in the way I want it should give us for the first time a solid groundwork of principles and a story which we can make intelligible in the towns as well as in the country.

At the same time I have been searching round for a new Chairman of the Party and I believe I have now found him if he will undertake the job. I have not spoken to S.B. because I want first to see my man and sound him discreetly, but if I find him willing I know I can get backing for him and as he seems to me to have just the qualities required I dont despair of making a change.

In addition to all this I have had two rather important interviews. I got Douglas Hailsham to dine with me one night. He has just returned from a six months absence in Japan and India and was in a very disgruntled condition because before he left he had not been summoned to the Shadow Cabinets and he was exceedingly hurt & vexed at having been cut out of the Party Council. Fortunately I had already spoken to S.B. about him and got him to promise that he should be on the Committee of Business and after a long talk in which I put him wise about what had been happening and he told me about India he went away in a thoroughly good temper having as he said greatly enjoyed himself and feeling that he now understands the situation. He is far too valuable a man to offend by neglecting his very reasonable wish to be brought in to our discussions.

My other interview was with the Beaver whom I now call "Max". Once more he was disappointed and suspicious, finding fault with everyone's speeches and declaring that it must be food taxes or nothing. After most absurd difficulties in screwing Stanley up to act, for he does not like what he calls running after the Press, he was at last induced to ask me to see if the Beaver could be got to attend some meetings at which we might discuss the best way of pushing the great policy. It seemed almost doubtful if he ("Max") would not throw any such invitation back in our teeth but I am glad to say that I had a most satisfactory interview and got all I wanted. He has become extraordinarily forthcoming and confidential now and tells me all sorts of secrets about his relations with Rothermere and his opinion of my colleagues! I confess I am getting to like the creature and as I dont hesitate to tell him when I dont agree with him he trusts me and nothing could be more frank and straightforward than his conversations with me. I foresee some stormy interviews with some of my colleagues but I hope all the same that we may manage to run together for there is no doubt that he can be equally a very valuable friend and a very formidable enemy.

The reported "deal" between Libs. and Labs. sent Winston into a fresh panic. He is obsessed with a fear (studiously fostered in his mind by Ll.G.) that there will be a Lib-Lab "Bloc" in the next Parliament against the Conservatives who will thereby be excluded from office indefinitely. I have no doubt that Ll.G. would make a deal with Labour if he could. He would offer to support them in abolishing the plural vote and the University representation in return for the alternative vote, or he would make a compact about seats at the election and either plan would give his party, so he thinks, substantially larger numbers. But I do not believe he had made or can make any such deal because the Socialists simply cant afford the discredit of an alliance with him. On the other hand I think he would equally be prepared to do a deal with us if we could afford it and were willing. But he could not deliver the goods because his own people would not agree to any such bargain with us whom they hate. So the Goat is in a dilemma again and I cant help contrasting him with A.J.B.[6] Both had the chance of becoming the National Statesman, beyond and above Party. A.J.B. took it and did his best work in his last years. Ll.G. was incapable of such heights and today with all his gifts no leading politician exercises less influence on public opinion. I wonder if you read S.B.'s panegyric on A.J.B.; it was one of his best and "the

---

[6] Arthur James Balfour (1848–1930). Conservative MP for Hertford 1874–85, Manchester East 1885–1906 and City of London 1906–22. President, LGB 1885–86; Scottish Secretary 1886–87; Chief Secretary, Ireland 1887–91; First Lord of Treasury 1891–92, 1895–1905; Prime Minister 1902–5; First Lord of Admiralty 1915–16; Foreign Secretary 1916–19; Lord President 1919–22, 1925–29. Conservative Leader in Commons 1891–1902; Conservative Leader 1902–11. Knighted 1922. Created Earl of Balfour later in same year.

last of the Athenians" was an inspiration. To me A.J.B. remained always aloof. I never got on terms with him. I admire his intellectual gifts immensely and realised his charm, but he always seemed to me to have a heart like a stone. I cannot forget his extraordinary coolness when we heard the shocking news of Henry Wilsons[7] assassination at tea in the Botanical Gardens here[8] and it was of a piece with his behaviour to Father.

...

29 March 1930
37 Eaton Square, SW1

My dear Hilda,

...

I have been going to my Research Committee every day & have got my Agricultural Comee going and various other activities including West India sugar on which the Committee of Business suddenly discovered we had no policy. I think they felt it a comfort to have some definite body to refer to.

But my time has been chiefly occupied in trying to bully the C.O. into taking up the new policy. It is proposing a three weeks "campaign" in May for the purpose of stirring up the party and Davidson[9] asked me to go with him to see Max and get his advice about the literature to be issued. As our visit happened on the day after Salisbury's letter[10] the atmosphere was not propitious & you can judge of my consternation when I found that no allusion was made to the new policy in the documents which David produced. Needless to say all cooperation on those lines was refused and the suspicions of our bona fides were only intensified. It is proposed that people should be invited to sign a pledge to support the policy outlined by Mr Baldwin but as it was not stated what the policy was the pledge was not very valuable. I tried to get S.B. to give instructions but finding this useless I suggested that I would draw up the leaflet with David

---

[7] Field-Marshal Sir Henry Hughes Wilson (1864–1922). Deputy, later Assistant, Adjutant-General, Army HQ 1903–6; Director of Military Operations 1910–14. Assistant Chief of General Staff 1914; British Military Representative at Supreme War Council 1917. Chief of Imperial General Staff 1918–22. Unionist MP for North Down February 1922 until assassinated on the steps of his London home on 22 June 1922.

[8] See Robert Self (ed.), *The Neville Chamberlain Diary Letters, Volume II, The Reform Years, 1921–27* (Aldershot, 2000), p. 116.

[9] John Colin Campbell Davidson (1889–1970). Private Secretary to Lord Crewe 1910, to Harcourt 1910–15, to Bonar Law 1915–16, to Chancellor of Exchequer 1916–20. Conservative MP for Hemel Hempstead 1920–23 and 1924–37. PPS to Bonar Law 1920–21, 1922–23 and to Baldwin 1921–22; Chancellor, Duchy of Lancaster 1923–24 and 1931–37; Parliamentary and Financial Secretary, Admiralty 1924–26; Chairman, Conservative Party Organisation 1926–30. Controller of Production, Ministry of Information 1940–41. Created Viscount Davidson 1937.

[10] Lord Salisbury's letter published in *The Times* on 25 March 1930 was dismissive of Beaverbrook's policy and reasserted its author's free trade inclinations.

who should submit it for S.B.'s approval. This was accepted, so I went to the C.O. drew up the pledge myself, making it applicable to the new policy of Empire Economic Unity (including food taxes subject to the Ref[erendu]m.) and Safeguarding alone, and stating the policy in unmistakable words. This was accepted by Davidson & approved by Topping[11] and I left them to get the Leader's sanction. Next day I received a note from D. saying Here is the latest version of the pledge which S.B. has approved and found he had taken out the policy again and mixed it up with other things such as Economy. I found David & asked why it had been altered and he said at first that it was because as drafted it seemed too long. Afterwards he remarked that he had come across Winston fulminating to his followers in the Smoke room & saying there ought not to be a pledge at all. Also, he said Max was trying to force us into supporting food taxes at the Election. I said that if that were so we could have no better safeguard than a pledge which specifically stated our position. David said he thought so too and would try again. The next day he sent word that he would be glad to see me about the pledge. I went to the C.O. where I found him with Patrick Gower[12] and they had actually altered it again and once more taken out the description of the policy. I was quite obstinate in refusing to agree so they said they would try and get it all in. There it stands for the moment but I shant be sure that they will come up to scratch till the document is issued. Meanwhile I have taken the precaution of insuring Sam's & Philip's support. The rest of the business committee knows nothing about it – officially at any rate.

We had a meeting of the Committee on Wednesday and I found it was going through without a word being said about Salisbury's letter. I would not allow that & expressed my feelings though very temperately. Salisbury neither explained nor defended himself. Apparently he consulted no one and I dont suppose he realises the nature of his crime. I lunched at Arlington St on Friday and he was quite friendly and affable as usual. But he has made things very difficult for me who have to try and keep Max from going off the deep end.

I had a long talk with Bruce this week. He looks very well and has been working away at the possibilities of a commercial treaty with Australia which, he tells me, he does not think would require a tax on wheat or meat though they might be very glad of protection for dairy produce. He is also going into the rationalisation as between Australia & ourselves of two typical industries and

---

[11] (Hugh) Robert Topping (1877–1952). Conservative Agent, Dublin 1904–11; Glamorgan South 1911–18; Cardiff, Llandaff and Barry 1918–23; Northwich 1923–24; Central Office Agent, North-West Area 1924–28; Conservative Principal Agent 1928–30; General Director, Central Office 1930–45. Knighted 1934.

[12] (Robert) Patrick Malcolm Gower (1887–1964). Entered Inland Revenue 1910 and Treasury 1919; Assistant Private Secretary to Bonar Law 1917–18; Private Secretary to Austen Chamberlain 1919–22; Private Secretary to successive Prime Ministers 1922–28; Chief Publicity Officer, Conservative Central Office 1929–39. Knighted 1924.

there seems a good possibility of an arrangement which would materially help our people.

Winston is of course crazy about the Lib-Lab. combination. I do not believe they have got anything fixed as yet but no doubt Ll.G. is working for it. There are however so many difficulties in the way that I very much doubt its coming off and it is at least doubtful whether internal dissensions will not break up the Govt before any arrangement could come into operation.

...

P.S. I was forgetting to tell you that I had an interesting conversation on Friday with Sir Percy Loraine[13] whom I met at dinner with the Rayleighs. He told me that Nahas[14] had impressed him as an "upright" man; to me a very unexpected appreciation. To fortify this opinion he said that Nahas had never made any improper use of anything he (Loraine) had told him; on the other hand Nahas had confided to him secrets which if they were disclosed would be sufficient to hang him. (I understood this to mean damage him irreparably with his party, not that he had committed any crime punishable by death!) Loraine said that Fuad,[15] much to his surprise, was very anxious to have the Treaty. It might have been supposed that the withdrawal of British troops would have left him at the mercy of his faithful people, but apparently he has confidence in his ability to hold his own. The Wafd, according to Loraine, have in the last 4 months very considerably modified their attitude. They have been looking round at the conditions in Algeria Morocco Tripoli &c and concluded that British domination is much to be preferred to French or Italian. They have told him that if they get a settlement now they will want a lot of European help, particularly with the police – a matter of great importance if they are to be responsible for the safety of foreigners. Also they realise that economically i.e. in finance and in technical conduct of industry and public works they cannot stand by themselves and they say that if the Treaty is signed they intend to come to us every time both for European staff in police & other services and for help in developing their industries.

I asked him about the Sudan which I regarded as one of the most serious if not actually the gravest risk Henderson was taking. He admitted at once that the Sudan *was* the snag, but thought if we could get a final settlement we might

---

[13] Percy Lyham Loraine (1880–1961). Diplomat. Attaché to Constantinople 1904; First Secretary, Warsaw 1919; Minister to Persia 1921–26 and Athens 1926–29. High Commissioner for Egypt and Sudan 1929–33; Ambassador to Turkey 1933–39 and to Italy 1939–40. Succeeded as 12th Bart 1917.

[14] Mustafa Nahas Pasha (1876–1965). Egyptian lawyer and politician. Succeeded Zaghlul as leader of Wafd 1927. Many times Prime Minister of Egypt. Negotiated treaty of perpetual alliance with Britain 1936; dismissed by King Farouk December 1936 but recalled at British insistence 1942–44. Recalled to power 1950 but displaced by Neguib 1952.

[15] Ahmed Fuad (1868–1936). Youngest son of Ismail Pasha; succeeded as Khedive of Egypt 1917; assumed title of King Fuad I when British protectorate ended in 1922.

agree to an Egyptian battalion. I said Is it possible to get a final settlement now. He said that was really the difficulty; the time was not ripe. But, he added, it would take at least four years before the British troops could be moved out of Cairo. By that time we should know whether the Egyptians meant to play fair or not and we could make our final decision about the Sudan in the light of our experience.

You will see that his views were hopeful and encouraging. He did not say so but I fancied he implied that the removal of George Lloyd had eased the situation in Cairo considerably. Any how I should find no difficulty in believing that to be the case.

4 April 1930
37 Eaton Square, SW1

My dear Ida,

...

The Canadian budget is very encouraging and shows that the U.S. tariff has made them sit up and take notice at last. If they are prepared to go so far without any corresponding preference from us I imagine they would do a good deal more for a bargain. We shall see now what happens in Fulham. My information is that we shall probably win but that it will be a close thing. It is hard to get a reliable account of the feeling there. The Empire Free Traders report unbounded enthusiasm. On the other hand Kingsley says that the canvas [sic] of the back streets shows that the new policy has not caught on. But then he is very lukewarm himself and I rather discount his information on that account.

We saw [Dr] Thomas on Wednesday and his verdict [on Annie] is Nervous Exhaustion due primarily to overwork and secondarily to the climacteric. I am not sure that I agree with his priority but in any case the remedy is the same namely rest, and he is confident that if carried out it will be effective. The question therefore is where to go and he is making enquiries as to the most suitable place. Annie herself is attracted by the Lake of Geneva and I think we shall probably fix on that neighbourhood. If so our idea is that she should go there about the middle of July ...

...

We began our Committee on the Housing Bill on Thursday. The papers of course give a very abbreviated report but the Govt got very tied up and Jowett[16] admitted to me afterwards that clause 1 was very obscure and had been made obscurer by the Ministerial explanations. I am leading the opposition at present but dont feel very much interested in it.

---

[16] Frederick William Jowett (1864–1944). Member, Bradford Town Council 1892–1907 and Labour MP for West Bradford 1906–18 and East Bradford 1922–24, 1929–31. Defeated as ILP candidate by official Labour 1935. First Commissioner of Works 1924.

A. & I went down to Birmingham on Friday morning as I had the Annual Meeting of the Midland Union in the afternoon. The principal feature of the meeting was of course my speech and I think it went off very well. The next day I had Newman, the Calthorpe Agent, to lunch at Westbourne in order that I might show him the house and if possible arrange terms as to the new lease when mine expires in March 1932.

He is treating me very generously and we have arranged terms which are very satisfactory to me. I am to have a 21 years lease with an option to me (but not to the estate) to terminate it any time by giving 12 months notice. ... I have power to pull down the Great Room whenever I choose and I am to pay 25% less rent than I do now.

I rather doubt if I shall interfere with the Great Room. By getting rid of it I could make such alterations as would give me a good room for myself. But on the other hand as long as I am in politics I shall not spend a good deal of time at Westbourne and when I give up my political career there will be nothing to keep me in Birmingham from which nearly all of my friends & relations will have disappeared. But the power to pull down relieves me of the liability to keep up which is worth a good deal.

...

6 April 1930
Westbourne

My dear Ida,
...
You heard from Annie of her wonderful reception from the Birmingham women. The more one hears of it the more remarkable it seems. All of them had to pay 6d. for admission and I suppose many must also have paid for their transport as there were quantities of charabancs and busses from the more distant parts of the town. They would never have come to an ordinary meeting or to hear an ordinary speaker like that; it was just a demonstration of the intense devotion she has inspired in them, which burst out when it had the opportunity of showing itself.

...

I began my week with a good deal of East Africa; the Hilton Young's came to lunch on Monday. Then that evening I addressed a large Committee of our party in the House of Commons on the subject; later on I dined with Sir Samuel Wilson[17] of the Colonial Office and last of all I finished an article on the Future

---

[17] Samuel Herbert Wilson (1873–1950). Soldier and Civil Servant. Assistant Secretary, Committee of Imperial Defence and Secretary, Overseas Defence Committee 1911–14; Home Ports Defence Committee and Imperial Communications Committee 1918–21; Governor and C-in-C, Trinidad and Tobago 1921–24; Captain General and Governor in Chief, Jamaica 1924–25; Permanent Under-Secretary, Colonial Office 1925–33. Knighted 1921.

of East Africa for the Sunday Times. I had to dine with the Wilsons by myself as Annie did not feel like coming, but I had a good talk with S.W. and I think we pretty well agreed. He wants me to see Passfield[18] but I said I wasn't going to ask for an interview. If Passfield wanted my views I should be happy to give them but the request must come from him. Jimmie Thomas, whom I met one day, expressed great desire for a talk on the subject but I think he has too many other irons in the fire to be able to attend to East Africa.

My article in the Telegraph appeared on Monday also. I dont know whether you … saw it. Anyway it seems to have been well received and I was pleased to find that Arthur Robinson who was lunching with me on Wednesday, had read it with strong interest & approval. He tells me that his Minister has made *no* contribution to the New Housing Bill except the Default Powers clauses which are of course pure eye-wash. I have searched through it without finding a single new idea except the per capita grant which strikes me as a clumsy expedient designed really in order to sidetrack the family allowance people. I shall have to spend this afternoon in further study of it as I am speaking on it tomorrow.

Austen has gone off to Cap Martin for which I am sorry as he is useful at our meetings. When Winston gets too intolerable I become speechless lest I should say too much and A. then very often intervenes with those calm and measured utterances which bring the discussion back to earth and common sense. And Winston has been very tiresome lately. He is obsessed by his desire for some sort of coalition or alliance with Ll.G. and continually preaches to his colleagues, to the H of C smoke room, and to his constituents that the Conservative Party is finished and done for. By its attitude on food taxes it has alienated the Liberals and driven them into an anti-Conservative Bloc. Thus at the next Election 8 million Conservatives will be drowned and suffocated under 13 million Lib-Labs. But perhaps even now it is not too late to pull back the machine from the edge of the precipice. And so on, ad lib. It is all very silly and very mischievous – and I might add very foolish. For with all his brilliance Winston does not improve his position in the country and ever contrives to inspire doubt and anxiety instead of confidence.

I did not see the proof of the "pledge"[19] till Thursday when it was brought to me with an intimation that the office thought it too long. So I just took my pen and divided it into two. First paragraph headed "The Policy" second headed

---

[18] Sidney James Webb (1859–1947). Civil servant, barrister, author, Professor of Public Administration and member of various Royal Commissions. Member, LCC 1892–1910. Labour MP for Seaham 1922–29. President, Board of Trade 1924; Dominion and Colonial Secretary 1929–30; Colonial Secretary 1930–31. Created Baron Passfield 1929.

[19] The Conservative Home and Empire campaign was intended to galvanise the party with a restatement of policy on tariffs, agriculture and empire reaffirming the commitment to the Referendum. Besides Baldwin's speech tour in May–June, Circular 3153 enabled party members to sign a 'pledge … to do everything in [their] power to further the policy … for Home and Empire'.

"The Pledge" the latter being merely to support the above policy. David was delighted with this and it has gone off once more for a proof. But I fear it may since have been driven out of his head. On Wednesday I saw the man I have in mind as his successor. I am not sure that you would know his name. Geoffrey Ellis. He was in the last Parlt but lost his seat at the election. He is a banker & business man progressive in politics but with a cool & critical mind. He has taken a great interest in C.O. Reform and is really the author of the new proposals for Provincial decentralisation and the reduction of the National Conference. He is very popular in the office and was well liked and respected in the House where he was head of a small group. I am told the only people who dont like him are the agents because he is the only man who exercises any control over them. He has worked up his own Provincial division in Yorkshire to a very high state of efficiency. From this brief account I think you will agree that he is the very man for the job and I will only add that his ideas about the C.O. & politics generally accord very closely with my own so that I naturally feel confidence in his judgement.

I had been told that he would not take on the chairmanship for two reasons – health, which is not very strong and finance. I therefore saw him and though of course I was not in a position to make him any offer I ascertained that neither of the suggested grounds would prove an insuperable obstacle.

Having thus secured the ground I invited the unhappy David to lunch with me the next day and – in effect – told him he had better go before he was fired out. It was not a nice task and I was very sorry for poor David whom I like personally, but the more I see of his work the more I am convinced that in his present position he is a danger to the party. I fear what I said was a shock to him; he asked me to see S.B. about it, which I haven't had a chance to do yet but shall try for on Monday or Tuesday. David himself said he thought he *had* better go; the difficulty was to find a successor. But to that I merely replied that that was S.B.'s job. In the end he thanked me profusely for having been so frank with him but I expect later on he probably had a bit of a reaction and I must keep up the drive if the change is to be accomplished.

Max has been chasing heretics busily all the week and on Thursday Elibank gave a private dinner at the Savoy to meet him to which Hailsham, Sam Hoare, R. Horne,[20] P. Cunliffe Lister. L.S. Amery & I were invited. I sat next to Max and slated him roundly and openly for his stupidity & unfounded suspicions. He was in a mischievous & puckish mood but when he saw I was really vexed he fell on my neck and took back all he had said. Yesterday he had quite a good article on S.B.'s speech, very different from the way he talked! I put it down to the dinner.

---

[20] Robert Stevenson Horne (1871–1940). Conservative MP for Glasgow Hillhead 1918–37. Minister of Labour 1919–20; President, Board of Trade 1920–21; Chancellor of Exchequer 1921–22. Knighted 1918. Created Viscount Horne of Slamannan 1937.

12 April 1930
Westbourne

My dear Hilda,

...

As you say, some history has been made this week. I saw S.B. on Tuesday and found that my previous talk with David had made everything easy as David had told him he was ready to go and all that remained was to arrange the order of his going. S.B. wants to be able to announce that the duties of the Chairman will in future be altered on David's suggestion so that it may appear that he has either finished or put in train all that he went to the C.O. to do. This would be all right if I were sure that he would recommend the best alterations but I think he will require some assistance if we are to make certain of this. The funny thing is that only 5 people in the world know who is to succeed him, three in London, viz. Geoffrey Ellis Annie & I, and two out of London viz. you two! The fact is the succession must be worked with great tact and delicacy in order to avoid any suspicion that D. is being pushed out for the purpose of putting someone else in. But I have had a further long talk with Ellis who knows all the ins and outs of the C.O. thoroughly and I am more than ever convinced that he is the only man for the job.

I am glad to say that the pledge has now been finally got into proper form and though there are a good many doubters who are fearful about it, I think myself that it is a good thing because it will teach our party that this is a new policy and the principal feature in our programme, at the same time defining in unmistakeable [sic] terms what the policy is. I hear that the Snowdens have agreed with Ll.G. on a great counter campaign for Free Trade but I observed with amusement that the Herald had a very lukewarm balancing leader on the subject and I rather fancy Ll.G. may get let down. At the same time I like to see Libs and Labs getting tied up with Free Trade which is undoubtedly a dying cause.

I read the Beaver's speech at Nottingham with relief even though he did attack Eustace Percy and Billy Gore.[21] I had written him earlier in the week in very plain terms because I knew he was contemplating going down and announcing that he would run a candidate in opposition to O'Connor.[22] O'Connor made a very foolish speech but he has now declared that he stands four square for S.B.'s policy so that war upon him would have been war on us. The Beaver would not at the time withdraw his threat but I see he has not carried it out. He came to the

---

[21] William Ormsby-Gore (1885–1964). Conservative MP for Stafford 1918–1938. Assistant Secretary, War Cabinet 1917–18 and with Military Intelligence Department in Egypt 1918; Under-Secretary, Colonies 1922–24 and 1924–29; Postmaster-General 1931; First Commissioner of Works 1931–36; Colonial Secretary 1936–38; High Commissioner to South Africa 1941–44. Succeeded as Baron Harlech 1938.

[22] Terence James O'Connor (1891–1940). Barrister and Conservative MP for Luton 1924–29 and Nottingham Central 1930–1940. Solicitor-General 1936–40. Knighted 1936.

complimentary dinner given to me on Monday in the House and declared that I reminded him of Bonar Law and that he could not say what "joy and pleasure" he had derived from our short acquaintance!

...

We came down here on Thursday as I had undertaken to speak (with A. Greenwood) at a send off meeting for our New Hospital Centre. This is really one of my schemes though I did not do much more than put forward the idea at an opportune moment. The site (on Fallow's Farm) is 125 acres and 25 acres is allotted to the new General Hospital and Medical School. The hospital has been designed for 740 beds plus 100 more in a paying patient block and the estimated cost of construction and equipment is £1¼ millions. Sixty beds are to be gynacological [sic] and 60 special and there will be 7 operating theatres and extensive laboratories. It is a big sum to find but it is a big idea and will put Birmingham right in the front among teaching hospitals. I suppose I shall have to stump up a goodly sum.

Last night we had our Unionist Assocn Annual Meeting at which I presided as usual. I thought it seemed a little flat, partly because Leo Amery made such an interminable boring speech but no doubt it is rather difficult to whip up enthusiasm at this moment. Generally speaking my reports show that Socialists are sulky and discontented but there is no tide of Unionism yet.

...

20 April 1930
Cairnton, Banchory, N.B.

My dear Ida,

Really the weather since this Government has been in office has been too poisonous. We have had nothing but north east wind since we have been here accompanied by frequent drenching showers of rain varied with sleet or hail. Each day has been worse than the day before culminating yesterday in a gale so fierce that for the first time in my life I was actually driven off the river and spent the afternoon reading a detective story in the hut! It does make one furious when one has only a few precious days to fish; and on Thursday night my toe suddenly flared up so that I had to spend the whole of Friday in bed. Luckily the Aberdeen doctor who attends Arthur Wood is very clever & gave me a new drug and a lotion which between them cleared off the gout by the evening and it seems not to have revived today in spite of fishing part of yesterday. So I suppose it might be worse. Frank was fortunate enough to catch a fish his first day. After that he missed a couple of days but yesterday he caught the biggest that has been landed while we have been here, namely 19½ lbs and was immensely excited and delighted over it. Arthur is most awfully good to him. He wont allow him to go with me but takes him on his beat and gives him lessons which will be invaluable to him, in the arts of casting, hooking and playing.

Jack Hills is the only other guest. He is a very keen, but as you would expect, a slow fisherman.

You can imagine how sick I was to see the Beaver letter in the Times. I saw David on Monday evening. He had been to see the Beaver about a suggested meeting in the Crystal Palace at which S.B. was to speak and the constituencies concerned thought they would like the Beaver in the chair. We thought that most undesirable, if not impossible, and David was sent to explain as nicely as possible. When I met him about 10.30 p.m. he was quite happy. The Beaver had been very nice and had said the last thing he wanted was to embarrass S.B. or the Cons. party and he would explain that he had an engagement which he could not possibly get out of. But David added that Max was frightfully anxious to see me and "would chase me any where" for an interview. Could I see him that night. I said certainly not, but I would ring him up next morning which I did & was told he was very sorry but he was going riding in the country & would not be back till evening. The next thing was the letter which appeared on the following day.

I suspect the trouble to have been David himself. He *always* thinks he has made a wonderful impression and speaks of Max as a "very great friend of mine", little suspecting what Max says about him. He himself told me that he had described the Campaign to Max as intended to *ascertain what the feeling in the party was* about the new policy, and a day or two after, the Daily Mail had an article headed "the Conservative Runaways" in which it said that a strong section *led by the Conservative Central Office* were trying to back out of the policy. Of course the idea of David's *leading* anyone is grotesque, and in any case he is going now (which Max does not know.) But to Max's suspicious mind there are always powerful forces working against him secretly and he is so busy trying to hit them on the head that he has no time to attend to the avowed and open enemies. I wrote a strong letter of protest to him from here, but I fear it will be of no use. He can certainly do a good deal to destroy our party but if he succeeds he will at the same time shatter the only party which can possibly carry the policy he wants. So far my experience of him is very disappointing and confirms what I was so often told, that he wont "stay put".

The Budget is very bad and mischievous and just what I expected. I think it will do us good. The dropping of the Safeguarding duties will absolutely infuriate the people in the industries concerned & will serve further to dismay and weaken the Labour Party many of whom have no sympathy with Snowden's ideas. The 6d. on the income tax was what was wanted to goad those in our own party who had got into the habit of grousing in the club & railway carriages that they didn't see what was the difference between Baldwin's Government & a Socialist Government. They will see better now! The worst feature is the concentration of all the taxation on the few for the benefit of the many. This is calculated to weaken the sense of responsibility down to vanishing point and to carry the West Ham principles through the whole country.

…

10 May 1930
Longford Castle, Salisbury

My dear Hilda,

...

Fulham[23] was I consider satisfactory from our point of view. I should have been very sick if we had lost the seat; on the other hand if Cobb had romped in with an enormous majority the Beaver would have been very difficult to hold. As it is, in spite of the pœans [sic] of triumph in the Daily Express, he seems to be very chastened and has made peace with O'Connor. I have not myself had any further communication with him. Meantime S.B. is very worried over his campaign of speeches having begun to realise how difficult it will be to say any thing new when there are so many of them. From another source I heard that the C.O. (not David) was of opinion that he was getting very rattled and that it wouldn't take much to make him throw in his hand. As a matter of fact he did say something of the kind to me one day but I dont think he meant it seriously. But he was depressed by the constant grousing and inclined to "let them all go to blazes". Finding him in that sort of mood I abstained from making any suggestions about David's successor but I am gradually widening the circle of those who know about G. Ellis and I haven't entirely given up hope that I may get David himself to make the suggestion, though I believe he doesn't like Ellis. I had a talk with him on Monday when he told me the only names he could think of were Kingsley Wood, Douglas King[24] and Plymouth.[25] But I confined myself to finding insuperable objections to all of them.

I spoke at Gravesend on Wednesday and here last night, – a mixture of crabbing the Govt or the Liberals and Home & Empire. ... Today some of the people who were there came to lunch and I had most gratifying accounts of the effect of the speech. ... The audience were not very demonstrative as is usually the case in the country but one could see from their intent looks and open mouths that they were deeply interested.

...

---

[23] West Fulham by-election, 6 May 1930. After being defeated by a 2211 Labour majority in 1929, Cobb (Conservative) won the seat by 240 votes at the by-election in which the Liberals withdrew.

[24] Henry Douglas King (1877–1930). Conservative MP for North Norfolk 1918–22 and South Paddington 1922–30. PPS to Leslie Wilson 1919 and Hamer Greenwood 1920; Unionist Assistant Whip 1921 and Whip 1922–24; Financial Secretary, War Office 1924–28; Secretary for Mines 1928–29.

[25] Ivor Miles Windsor-Clive (1889–1943). Conservative MP for Ludlow 1922–23. Chief Whip in Lords 1925–29; Under-Secretary, Dominions 1929; Parliamentary Secretary, Transport 1931–32; Under-Secretary to Colonies 1932–36 and to Foreign Office 1936–39. Styled Viscount Windsor 1908–23. Succeeded as 2nd Earl of Plymouth 1923.

17 May 1930
Westbourne

My dear Ida,

...

I am feeling "kinder low" myself. Politics are very unpleasant just now and our party is in a very disgruntled and disheartened condition. S.B.'s speeches so far have been very disappointing. I knew he had not really got enough material for them but I hoped he would have given them an air of greater importance & have emphasised their constructive side instead of dwelling so much on what he would not ask people to vote for. I am afraid that he listens too much to David and that the advice he gets is too much like cold water. I hear that Max is thoroughly dissatisfied and rebellious and of course Rothermere and Lloyd George are artfully adding fuel to the flames. I fear I shall have to see him again soon but I dont look forward to the interview because the fact is that there is a considerable amount of justification for his contention that the party is not all out for the policy. I am getting continual rumours of dissatisfaction with the leadership and if David does not make his announcement soon I foresee an explosion. It is not a nice time to be making speeches and I am oppressed with the number in front of me. ... And committees on the Housing Bill are interspersed every other morning and when I go away I have complaints of the conduct of the business by those I leave behind. It is a weary time and I long for Whitsuntide when I can get away to a trout stream again.

...

Saturday. I see the Times has an article on the differences in the Conservative Party over the Naval Treaty. I strongly suspect that the action of the back benchers goes further than the discretion of the Times reveals. In fact they are thoroughly dissatisfied with what they consider to be the want of leadership by the leader and I take rather a serious view of their action which looks to me like the first beginnings of a revolt. In the mood in which S.B. was a little while ago it wouldn't have taken as much as that to make him throw in his hand and I begin to wonder how much longer he can go on. If he should give up a most unpleasant situation for me is certain to arise. I know a great many would like to see me in his place but many others would not. I myself would hate it; it would be the end of all peace and probably of any chance of the C.O. but I should not refuse it if the party wanted it. Lately however it has occurred to me that they might well take Horne as leader. I could work with him all right.

25 May 1930
37 Eaton Square, SW1

My dear Hilda,

I did not think for a moment that you would get Annie to stop over tonight. You cant press her beyond a certain point or you defeat your own object. I had to have some strenuous battles to get her away from her own family everyone of whom I wish at the bottom of the sea. With one accord they all want to come & work up their unhappiness with Annie and the Irish in her rises up to meet them every now & then. It was a job to get her away from Sharon that afternoon; if she had stopped the night, I dont know when she would have got over it. Apparently Herbert hadn't the decency to keep away from the funeral and Horace who bullied & neglected & robbed his mother during her lifetime turned up here one evening in remorse & floods of tears and had to be kept to dinner and pushed out of the door afterwards. Can you wonder that Annie looks pulled down!

Dr Thomas has at length written to say he would be back today. I expect he will see her but I dont see what good he can do. The fact is there is nothing to be done but to try & keep the family at arm's length until we can get A. away altogether. She has written to Evian which seems to attract her and I rather expect we shall decide on it, instead of waiting on for Thomas' suggestions which probably wont help when they come. Until this unhappy shock she was showing distinct signs of improvement, but it has given her a bad knock.

Yes, I was depressed when I wrote and am now, though not for the failure of a single speech. I have made four since then – Albert Hall, H. of. C. Preston & Ipswich and had sufficient compliments about each to have exhilarated me if I had been capable of exhilaration. But at present I dont seem to have any home life and all pleasure has gone out of politics. Next week end I am going down to Briantspuddle and perhaps on the banks of that delightful stream, in solitude, I may find some relief and repose of mind.

My Preston meeting on Tuesday was really a remarkable one. The hall there is the 3rd largest in the country and I should think it holds between 4 & 5000. Although this is a bad time of year for indoor meetings, the people began to cue [sic] up about 6 o'clock and when I arrived the hall was jam full. Over 800 pledges were signed as people went in & the enthusiasm was tremendous. When I mentioned Father's name the cheering was so loud & long that I had to stop for some time and on all sides I heard that the most extraordinary change had come about lately on the subject of safeguarding. I had not intended to give a great deal of time to safeguarding proper feeling that it was less easy to see its application to an export trade like cotton than to trades where the Home Market is predominant. But after what I had heard I decided to make it a feature and the response of the audience was very striking & encouraging. It prolonged the speech to 70 minutes & I felt dog tired after it; all the same I had to sit up "chatting" till 11 and returned by a 7.30 train next day with a headache.

Before leaving for Preston I had had an interview with David. I had learned that after a talk with the Bridgemans he had begun to declare that there was no hurry for any announcement, and even, when a crisis was supposed to have arisen in the fortunes of the Govt, that it might be necessary for him after all to remain at the helm.

If this was a correct account, he did not reveal it to me though it required a direct question – when are you going to announce your resignation – before he would broach the subject. I need not repeat the conversation; I did not mince words and he promised that the announcement should be made before the end of the week. On Friday I heard that he was havering again and on my return from Ipswich yesterday afternoon I had a note saying that S.B. wanted it postponed till next week in order that he might discuss with me the whole question of the succession which might involve the Whips.

Of course I am not deceived. It is David himself who has told S.B. that he has given deep thought to the succession and now come (for the fiftieth time) to a final & definite conclusion. Whatever this conclusion may be it certainly is designed to exclude Geoffrey Ellis and to leave Topping in actual command. S.B., as usual, has offered no suggestion of his own & has been completely swayed by David. I am convinced that it is David who is responsible for the negative tone of these speeches, which read so flatly. I cant imagine anyone being enthused by those of which I have seen reports, and I can understand & sympathise with Max's disgust. I went to see him on Thursday after the Express had published a leading article on my allusions to him at Preston (where I said I wished he would give a little more time to attacking his enemies and a little less to sniping at his friends). I found, as I expected, that he was not in the least disposed to complain. On the contrary, he admitted that he was difficult to work with – though, he said, I believe I am less difficult to you than to any of your colleagues. I told him that Baldwins emphasis on no food taxes was the inevitable reaction of his own attempt to get rid of the Refer[endu]m & reminded him that I had long ago warned him not to be in a hurry to put that forward until our party was consolidated. But I could see I made little impression on him. He harked back again and again to his desire to get in Rothermere. Why couldn't S.B. say a kind word. Rothermere had said nothing worse than many other people had said of political opponents with whom they had afterwards made friends. I told him that B. was further away from Rothermere now than when I returned from Africa. There was only one possible channel of reconciliation and that was himself. If I could re-establish confidence between him and S.B. I would not despair one day of seeing S.B. & Rothermere at the same table.

But he was evidently not prepared now to do business on those lines. He has lost *his* confidence in S.B. and he viciously remarked that in a very short time if he did not alter his ways his leadership would not be worth a curse. Feeling was rising dangerously against him. I believe he is right there; but I feel more and more disinclination to succeed him, and perhaps my want of ambition makes it more difficult for the rank & file to decide to throw the leadership into the melting pot.

...

25 May 1930
37 Eaton Square, SW1

My dear Hilda,

...

I was lunching with Sam Hoare today and he suggested what I have been rather feeling myself, that Ellis hardly carries guns enough to stand the fire that will be aimed at him if he stands alone. He wants me to take him in under my wing i.e. that I should agree to take the Chairmanship for a limited time with Ellis as understudy. I am inclined to give serious consideration to this idea if it is pressed. There is a good deal to be said for it and I think it would buck the party up though it might ultimately break me! But there would be some guarantee that the job would be done.

Sam is going to see S.B. tomorrow & see what he says. Probably S.B. will ask me to see him but whether he will take to the idea remains to be seen. I wonder what you think.

Annie is safely back and is not too low. But she looks desperately tired ...

1 June 1930
37 Eaton Square, SW1

My dear Ida,

...

Lady Bridgeman[26] asked to see me on Thursday and said she was being consulted by the Davidsons about the C.O. & wished to know what advice she should give. It is rather funny that David should go to her and that she should come to me again. I advised that the announcement should be made at once and she then showed me the drafts of the letters which D. had prepared. I thought his own was very bad. He had said not a word about criticism but the bulk of the letter was taken up with a long rigmarole about the difficulties of the work. I told Lady B. how I thought the letters should have been worded and next day it appeared as I had drafted it. I have seen no criticism of it so I think the drafting was all right. The leader's reply I only modified in the last sentence but all the stuff about the changes is David's and therefore means nothing but that he wanted to make his departure look less like an admission of failure. But S.B. has asked me to go and see him tomorrow, when no doubt he wants me to discuss the position with him. As far as I know he is still on the line of a Board or Committee, so I may not be asked to take the Chairmanship. But S. Hoare tells me he broached the idea to Bobby Monsell[27] who said it sounded too good to be

---

[26] Caroline Beatrix Bridgeman (1872–1961). Married William Bridgeman 1895. Prominent figure in Conservative women's organisation. Chair, National Union Women's Advisory Committee 1924–27; first woman chair of National Union Executive 1926. Created Dame 1924.

[27] Bolton Meredith Eyres-Monsell (1881–1969). Royal Navy 1895–1906 and 1915–16.

true. I mentioned to G. Ellis & asked if he would be willing to be deputy chairman or whatever it might be called under me. He said Yes but not under any one else as I was the only person who understood the position. Annie doesn't much like the idea as she thinks it would be likely to prejudice my future career but she agrees that for the sake of the policy it might be worth while.

I made a speech to the United Club on Thursday which quite carried that staid body off its feet. They all got up & sang "for he's a jolly good fellow" at the end & Austen reported afterwards that the smoke room at the House was "buzzing" with it. I was glad it was a success as I was getting rather fed up with speeches.

The Government had a bad day on Wednesday but Mosley had a personal triumph.[28] I thought the matter of his speech showed a fantastic ignorance of realities but the manner could hardly have been improved on. But I was not impressed, as some apparently were, with his sincerity. On the contrary I thought he was clearly acting, though I must say he acted very well.

...

8 June 1930
Swinton, Masham, Yorkshire

My dear Hilda,

... The weather is all that you anticipated and we are enjoying immensely the opportunity of spending these wonderful summer days in the country when every thing out of doors looks its best. Annie finds this place restful and I get away to the river and forget politics for a time.

...

I saw S.B. on Monday and it was evident to me that he did not want me to go to the C.O. The reasons he gave were hardly adequate and I suspect he was prompted by David who in his turn was prompted by Topping. The C.O. must have got wind of what had been going on and realised that if I went there with Ellis there would have been a good deal of disturbance. So they got busy and very soon succeeded in alarming M.P.'s who as Bobby Monsell reported to me told him that if Ellis went there there would be trouble. They said he was a Free Trader & was tactless in dealing with the agents which I think shows the source of their information. Anyhow I have decided not to press my views any more at present. S.B. wants W. Bridgeman to go there and I have declared myself in

---

Conservative MP for Evesham 1910–35. Unionist Whip 1911–21; Treasurer of the Household 1919–21; Civil Lord of Admiralty 1921–22; Parliamentary and Financial Secretary, Admiralty 1922–23; Parliamentary Secretary, Treasury 1923–24, 1924–29, 1931; Chief Whip 1923–31; First Lord of Admiralty 1931–36. Knighted 1929. Created Viscount Monsell 1935.

[28] After a brief formal resignation statement on 21 May 1930, Mosley used the debate on unemployment on 28 May to justify his actions and to outline the proposals contained in his famous memorandum.

favour of that solution. I dont think he will do anything to reform the office but at least he is a white man and his name will be acceptable and he will keep out the Leslie Wilsons[29] & George Lloyds. I shall bide my time but I shant forget the C.O. and some day Mr Topping will have to go and the stable be swept out. Austen knew all about the possibility of my going and did not object provided that the conditions were clearly laid down, but we may take it that that is now off.

Meanwhile the party is in a very disgruntled condition and even David's departure has not satisfied the malcontents. Taffy Gwynne (of the Morning Post) came to see me the other day to unbosom his soul to me. He said he adored S.B. but was convinced he was not the man to lead the party and he wanted to know whether if S.B. gave up I would accept the leadership if it were offered me. I told him that I should hate it, & that I was sure I should be very unhappy if I had it, but that if the party wanted me to take it I could not refuse. I believe, though he didn't actually say so, that he means to go to S.B. & tell him that he ought to give up. I dont think S.B. will pay much attention to him but I know he does sometimes wonder whether he ought to go on & if the Gen. Election should be long delayed I very much doubt if he will stay the course. However I dont intend to think about it; it would be a nightmare and I hope it will never materialise but I should not feel justified in saying No if I were asked though I would much prefer the Colonial Office under some one else.

By the way I hear that Topping who was at the United Club meeting went to S.B. afterwards to complain that my speech was not in accord with the official policy and to ask for instructions! No doubt this was to put difficulties in the way of my going to Palace Chambers.

    ...

16 June 1930
37 Eaton Square, SW1

My dear Ida,

    ...

I hear from Philip that he has seen Bridgeman who doesn't want to take on the Chairmanship so we are back again where we were. The agricultural speeches of S.B. seem to have been pretty well received though I dont think he made them sound like a policy. But that was not exactly his fault as he had not got the material which wont be available until my Committee has finished its work – some time in the autumn I should think. M. Barlow had the usual story to tell of

---

[29] Leslie Orme Wilson (1876–1955). Conservative MP for Reading 1913–22, Portsmouth South 1922–23. Assistant Secretary to War Cabinet 1918; Parliamentary Secretary to Minister of Shipping 1919–21; Parliamentary Secretary to Treasury and Chief Conservative Whip 1921–23; Governor of Bombay 1923–28 and of Queensland 1932–46.

dissatisfaction with the leadership but I agree with you that nothing is likely to happen unless the election should be long delayed in which case I should be nervous about S.B.'s capacity to hold the party. But its no use to worry about it; in politics the expected is the one thing that never happens.

...

21 June 1930
Westbourne

My dear Hilda,

Things have moved on so rapidly since I saw you on Thursday that I hardly know where to begin. I felt so unhappy at the uncertainty and indecision about the party meeting and the Beaver was becoming every moment so much more aggressive and offensive that after leaving you I went & sought out Austen on the Front Bench & took him down to the terrace for a talk. I represented that the time had come for action and no action was being taken. If a party meeting was to be held it ought to be held at once. Then there was the reply to Macdonald's [sic] letter of invitation to the all party conference on unemployment. The Times had announced that we were going to refuse, yet no refusal had been sent & when Sam had asked S.B. what he was doing about it he had answered rather testily that he must have time to think. Finally there was the Chairmanship; a petition was being circulated in favour of Leslie Wilson & another in favour of George Lloyd and both carried with them a condemnation of the long delay. Austen agreed & offered to speak to S.B. that afternoon but said, as I had mentioned G. Ellis' belief that only my appointment could save the leadership, that he should tell S.B. that he would advise me strongly to have nothing to do with it should he think of asking me. He explained that he feared lest I might be involved in S.B.'s own ruin and he saw no reason why I should involve myself in such a risk.

...

Later in the afternoon he and I after a meeting found ourselves alone with S.B. and Austen at once asked him what he was doing about the party meeting. Fixed for Tuesday week, said S.B. Oh that wont do, said Austen. You ought to have it as early as possible and not later than next Tuesday. Oh, you think it ought to be earlier, said S.B. Well I have got two speeches to make this week end but I suppose I must manage it. We'll have it next Tuesday. So that was *one*. Next A. enquired about the letter. Nothing had been done but S.B. promised to ask Hailsham who was coming to another meeting very shortly to draft the reply and later on I myself saw him do this. Finally A. began about the chairmanship, but at this moment I was called away and only heard afterwards from Austen what had occurred. S.B. said he had asked Bridgeman but did not think he would take it. He mentioned my name as another possible, but said no more about it when Austen expressed his strong objection observing that on the whole he thought Kingsley Wood would be the best man. Austen suggested as two more names Eyres-Monsell and W. Elliott[30] [sic] and they then parted.

Later that evening S.B. saw me & said he wanted a long talk with me about many matters next day. I said I would meet him in the House after I had been to my office. In the meantime he gave me a letter he had received from W. Bridgeman which when I read it proved to be a refusal on his own part and a recommendation of Kingsley Wood.

Yesterday morning I went to my office and had a long talk with Ball[31] from whom I learned that although Bridgeman was personally popular his appointment would not be approved because he and his wife are known to be close friends of the Davidsons. While I was still discussing these matters a message came through from S.B. asking me to go up to the House at once. I went and found him in conclave with Davidson and Eyres Monsell. They said they wanted my advice about the procedure at the party meeting. What they proposed was that S.B. should make a strong attack on the growing disposition of irresponsible press lords to dictate to the elected representatives of the people. He should then repeat and emphasise his own policy and conclude by saying, Now I want to know whether you are for me or not. Those in favour please stand up. Above all there must be no discussion. I said at once that I totally disagreed. I thought he might indeed get a majority though only a majority to support him, but that the meeting would go away thoroughly dissatisfied saying that it had been muzzled, and that the essential thing was to let the grousers blow off steam and then answer them. To my mind the crucial point was the referendum and I sketched out what seemed to me the line to take. Who proposed the Refm? Beaverbrook himself. Why did I accept it? Was it because it was an essential & pivotal part of my policy? Not at all. I accepted it as an expedient to preserve the unity of my party. Today B. who hailed my acceptance with gratitude and delight has reversed his opinion and now denounces me because I do not change my opinion as quickly as he does. I cannot tolerate dictation of that kind from anyone. The only thing that would make me change my policy on the referendum would be the conviction, brought about by the representations of my own party that so far from uniting the party the Refm was now a stumbling block to its unity. Today I have no evidence before me that such is the case and until it is forthcoming I stand where I did.

---

[30] Walter Elliot Elliot (1888–1958). Conservative MP for Lanark 1918–23, Glasgow Kelvingrove 1924–45, 1950–58, Scottish Universities 1946–50. Parliamentary Secretary of Health for Scotland 1923–24, 1924–26; Under-Secretary for Scotland 1926–29; Financial Secretary to Treasury 1931–32; Minister of Agriculture 1932–36; Scottish Secretary 1936–38; Minister of Health 1938–40.

[31] (George) Joseph Ball (1885–1961). Career with MI5 1919–27; Director of Publicity, Central Office 1927–30; Director, Conservative Research Department 1930–39; Deputy Chairman, National Publicity Bureau 1934–39; Deputy Chairman, Security Executive 1940–42; Acting Chairman, Conservative Research Department 1943–45; Chairman, Hampshire River Board 1947–53. Knighted 1936.

To this S.B. observed that he could accept that; in fact it seemed to him to differ very little from what he had been suggesting. (but oh! the difference to me!) The trio agreed also to adopt the procedure I had outlined and so far as the meeting goes, if they will only stick to the book, all ought to be well. For you will observe that my suggestion loosens S.B.'s position on the Refm very considerably and transfers the final decision from the Beaver to the party.

The subsequent history of the letter to Macdonald [sic] is rather comic. Hailsham produced his draft rather apologetically saying he was no writer. I at once made 3 criticisms on it which he accepted as good, but as he had to go off to a case S.B. asked me to draft the necessary alterations. I retired to the smoke room and in ten minutes returned with them to S.B. who accepted them saying they were very good. An hour later I met Geoffrey Lloyd[32] S.B.'s secretary who said he was taking the revised draft to show Austen who was at Rutland Gate. Two hours after he came to Eaton Square saying that Austen did not like my draft & had made another, which he had brought for me to see. I did not like his as I thought he had described Macdonald's [sic] proposals in terms which M. would not accept as accurate so that he could say our objection was based on a misunderstanding. I refused however to make a further redraft telling G. Lloyd that really his chief must decide seeing that after all it was supposed to be his letter. This morning I read that "at a late hour last night Mr Baldwin's reply had not reached the Prime Minister".

To return to the chairmanship, and my meeting yesterday morning. They discussed Kingsley & Elliott [sic] and Bobby himself and turned them all down and finally Bobby said "Of course there is only one man who could really completely restore confidence and pull the whole thing together", and here they all looked at me. I said, Well, Stanley, you know you have never asked me yet, and I should want a lot of pressing to consider what is an extremely unattractive task. S.B. said he hadn't liked to ask me; it seemed so much to ask. "But of course if you did take it it would be a wonderful thing for the party. If I could announce *that* on Tuesday, it would make things go".

I had to take this as a definite expression of his desire that I should consider it. He himself with his eternal dislike of a decision, said "Well we mustn't badger him any more now", but I went off and had a private talk with B. Monsell who said "Everybody" was coming to him to say how much they wished I were at the C.O.

Later I had a long talk, at his own request, with Sir R. Horne who wanted to tell me about a dinner at which he and Amery and Beaverbrook had been

---

[32] Geoffrey William Lloyd (1902–1984). Conservative MP for Birmingham Ladywood 1931–45, King's Norton 1950–55 and Sutton Coldfield 1955–74. Private Secretary to Baldwin, 1929–31 and his PPS 1931–35; Under-Secretary, Home Office 1935–39; Parliamentary Secretary for Mines 1939–40, for Petroleum 1940–42, and Fuel and Power 1942–45; Minister of Information 1945; Minister of Fuel and Power 1951–55; Minister of Education 1957–59. President, Birmingham Conservative Association 1946–75. Created Baron Geoffrey-Lloyd 1974.

present. They had had a very stormy discussion but finally someone had suggested a last meeting between Beaverbrook & S.B. and as I was thought to be the only man capable of persuading S.B. to go to such a rencontre he wanted to know whether I would essay the task. I told him of the party meeting which he had not heard of, and suggested that we had better wait till that was over in which he quite concurred. I also told him of the procedure I had suggested which he also approved very heartily being particularly taken with what he called the cleverness of the proposed line on the Refm. I was convinced from the whole tone of this conversation that although he might very likely have said that, if he were asked to lead the party in the event of a vacancy, he would be willing to do so, he had not been engaged in any intrigue to bring that about, so finally I told him of the request I had received to take the Chairmanship and Austens advice and asked his opinion. He said it was not new to him. He had been told that I might be pressed and had said that I ought not to be asked to make such a sacrifice. But if I did take it, and he hoped in that case that I should accept only for a limited term he thought it would be the most splendid thing for the party that could happen.

Well there it is. Sam & Philip both want me to do it and now you come down on the same side. As a matter of fact I made up my mind days ago that I would take it if S.B. asked me and I only put it completely out of my thoughts because he did not seem to want it. I don't believe any one can say with certainty what effect it may have on my chances of the leadership but, as you know, I have no ambitions that way and should not therefore allow any consideration of that kind to weigh with me. My reason for accepting is that I think I see an opportunity of rendering the party a service that probably no one else can do at this juncture, and if things went really well, as they probably wont, it might make just the difference to our chance of winning the next election and carrying the great policy into operation.

There remains the "when" and "how". I should like to get the announcement made in time for Tuesday mornings papers but to do that I must settle before Monday afternoon the terms of letters between Stanley & myself and I must devote some part of tomorrow to working out the conditions I must lay down. I shall want G. Ellis, but probably it would be better not to mention his name yet. I want also to keep the Research Dept.

Annie, after some doubts on personal grounds, agrees with my decision. She quite realises the risks of failure, through no fault of mine, but is prepared to take them for the sake of the possible gains. I suppose it means goodbye to the House of Commons for a time but I dont think I mind that if I can keep in touch with members on our side.

What a screed I have written! But I expect you will like to have the full story of this momentous affair.

...

5 July 1930
Charminster House, Dorchester

My dear Hilda,

... I am so glad to get away to my fishing again & have been looking forward to it ever since I was here before. Our unfortunate host had to go to Germany on some urgent business ... but J. Hills and I came down yesterday for the evening rise and fished again this morning. So far he has caught six to my three, but mine weigh nearly as much as his as I have got big ones. The weather is just perfect and there is enough doing to make it interesting all the time. I can hardly bear to leave off for meals and indeed its only the necessity of having some consideration for my companion that prevents my killing myself with sheer fatigue.

I am still working off old engagements though I refuse to take on any new ones. On Wednesday I presided at the morning session of the National Conference on Maternity & Child Welfare which occupied the whole morning and necessitated a speech. So far as I could see the papers made no mention of the Conference at all and it wasn't really worth doing. ...

As for the Unionist Conference[33] I was very pleased with it. Beginning in rather a bad temper it got quite jolly before the end and though I am against the Agents vote on principle I am glad they passed it as it removes a grievance which might otherwise have been a great embarrassment to me. The D. Herald had a malicious headline about a "rebuff" to me but as a matter of fact the striking feature of the proceedings was the way the delegates ate out of my hand. I only intervened four times and each time my suggestion was accepted at once and without question.

I did not take over till Thursday as David wanted a day to clear up and as I was unable to give the afternoon to the office owing to meetings at the House you can imagine that I haven't got very far yet. But I wrote a letter for the leader to send to Mr Cook[34] on Monday which I hope gets him out of an awkward situation without discredit and I also wrote a short account of Conservative policy on Food Taxes for John Bull which enables me to put it as I think it should be put to 1½ million readers. Snowden and Beaverbrook are also writing on the same subject. Hortley, the local Chairman, will be astounded if we dont win North Norfolk – our agent says we shall lose it. I hope we do lose it – it will make it easier to deal with the Beaver.

I agree with Austen's fears about the Socialists stealing our clothes while we are in the water. We are meditating a vote of censure worded in such a way as to make them all vote against Safeguarding and Imperial Preference.

---

[33] Chamberlain was President of the National Union of Conservative and Unionist Association Annual Conference, London, 1 July 1930.

[34] Thomas Russell Albert Mason Cook (1902–1970). Director of Thomas Cook travel agency. Unsuccessfully contested North Norfolk in 1924, 1929 and 1930; Conservative MP for North Norfolk 1931–45. Proprietor, *Norfolk Chronicle* 1935–55. Knighted 1937.

I daresay Austen told you that we are having a very anxious time about India. Both the Indian Govt and the S. of S. seem to have got badly rattled and there is really no saying what they may do. We are trying our best by alternate threats and cajolery to stiffen their backs.

Imagine my fury when I discovered on Wednesday that there was no meeting of the Business Committee. I had a lot of things I wanted discussed, & Sam came back specially from Wimbledon, missing the match he most wanted to see. None of us had any notice of the change. I made myself excessively disagreeable first to the Secretary & then, as he pleaded that he had several times tried to get instructions & failed, to S.B., who was rather cross but said it should not happen again. I have a private letter from an old member not now in the House but in touch with it. He says there is much dissatisfaction with S.B. as a Parliamentary leader & suggests that Austen should be Deputy Leader & do all the work. If we could have a Deputy Extra-Parliamentary leader too we might get on!

12 July 1930
Westbourne

My dear Ida,
...

I wonder if Austen told you of our interview with Garvin on Monday. It was rather a painful affair. He began to discuss the book at his own desire during lunch while the men were still coming in and out. I had supposed that he would enter upon regrets apologies and excuses. Instead of that he poured out for 20 minutes such a spate of extravagant & complacent eulogy of himself as I have never heard from any man before. What he had performed was a miracle, carried through at the imminent risk of his life, and all previous biographers were put to shame. Simultaneously he had 400000 (or occasionally 500000 in his more excited moments) auditors hanging on his lips to know what the oracle had to impart to them. "I am a mind-changer" he repeated once or twice impressively. "I am a man of my word", he said more than once. At last I rapped out "Haven't you a contract?" He saw the indignation but shouted that that was wiped out long since, and turning to the silent Austen he began his song of self praise again. As soon as I saw an opening I said "You have done irreparable injury to my father's memory". It stung him like a whiplash and he fairly foamed at the mouth, saying he would not tolerate such insults from any man. He would send all the papers back tomorrow. He was as firm as I was but I could think only of my own "confounded point of view". Once more he told of his holidays sacrificed, his health in peril, his half million souls hungry for his word. I said "All this marvellous work does not help me for we have got nothing". Out he burst again. "Dont talk to me in your Parliamentary phrases, I wont bear it. I'll pack up all the papers tomorrow". After this I thought it best to let Austen try and soothe him down but it was quite impossible to bring him to reason. He would revise nothing till the whole was complete. He would not hand over what he had done to be finished by anyone else. He would not promise to complete by any date for was not the world waiting to hear him on India or any other old topic. At last he began to cool down though still making frequent references to my outrageous remarks and every now and then working himself up into another fury. But my shots had told and finally we extracted from him a definite promise that if by the end of January he had not completed the life down to 1903 he would revise the first two volumes for publication. Austen was going to write and confirm this arrangement but on Thursday when I spoke to him about it he had not done so and small though the result is I am convinced we should not have obtained it if I had not deliberately said the most wounding thing I could think of. He is a truly *awful* man to have to deal with. What the life will be like I dread to think of – how much will be J.C. and how much J.L.G.?

I daresay you will have recognised the hand in the vote of censure. I drafted it in the train on the way up from Dorset and it was received with general approval by the party. The object of course is to force the Govt to declare themselves against safeguarding and food taxes, but while thinking what their reply would probably be a horrid thought occurred to me. Why should not the Govt hang on till the Imperial Conference, and then say to the Dominions, "We cannot put taxes on food but short of that we are prepared to go to any lengths by Import Boards, Bulk purchase, quotas, subsidies, &c &c to give you the market you want here. Now what will you give us for that?" I see no reason why the Dominions should not give substantial advantages. And when the Govt goes to the country asking that the bargain may be confirmed. "Surely" they might say "You are not going to slap the Empire in the face by rejecting the bargain they have approved. Surely you dont think if you did that they would come all the way back again for the sake of the Tory food taxes from which you have escaped, thanks to us. All that the Tories promised we have got for you without putting a penny on your bread or your meat and, while they have been talking, we have got the goods and found the true means of curing unemployment at last".

Every one to whom I have disclosed this thought agrees that it is a trump card which even this Govt can hardly be stupid enough not to play but no one has at present found the counter stroke to it. It would spike the Beaver's guns completely and it would spoil half our batteries and perhaps more if they embarked on some sort of safeguarding too. Perhaps some idea may occur to me presently but meanwhile I have told the C.O. to prepare for an election in November.

North Norfolk[35] was perhaps as good as was possible. If we had won the seat the Beaver would have claimed all the credit. As it is he blames us for the result,

---

[35] North Norfolk by-election, 9 July 1930. Lady Noel-Buxton retained her husband's former seat for Labour after he was created a peer, having held the seat himself since 1922.

while our people say we should have had a sitter if he hadn't barged in. I think myself the result was very difficult to explain. It was much better than our canvas showed and the C.O. agent certainly thought that food taxes would do us much more damage than they did. If we knew how the Liberals voted we could form a much clearer & more reliable opinion. I fear that another bye election is likely to recur soon which will I suppose give me more trouble, but the C.O. wont wobble about next time as it did over N. Norfolk. I have written to ask the Beaver to dine with me next Thursday and if he comes I shall endeavour at least to settle whether we are to be at peace or war. We cant carry on both at once and survive as a party.

I have done nothing startling at the C.O. yet as I am still trying to get my bearings. I have to keep running up and down between Old Queen Street and Palace Chambers but it is important to keep a hold on both.[36]

B. Monsell's strategy gave the Govt a narrow shave on Wednesday. In a preliminary division he held back about fifty of our men in St Stephens Club and the Govt had a big majority. Ll.G. was completely taken in and thought he could safely use the stick and only the rebellion of his followers saved the situation. It has shaken him badly but we shant get another chance like that for many a long day.

...

19 July 1930
37 Eaton Square, SW1

My dear Hilda,

...

Well the atmosphere certainly did not seem favourable for our talk with the Beaver for the Express & the Evening Standard had been more than usually offensive to S.B. and I was not very hopeful therefore of a favourable result. However Max turned up first & was in a very friendly mood which was never once ruffled all the evening in spite of plenty of frank talk. I had Sam & Philip with me and they both played up splendidly chipping in with a fresh attack from another angle whenever things seemed a little awkward. We skirmished about all dinner till the servants were out of the room when I led off on politics and after some preliminary fencing we got down to business when I asked him directly whether my succession to the chairmanship had not changed the situation & how were our relations to stand in the future. He began to talk of what might happen in Bromley where there will soon be a vacancy as our member is dying. I said we could not have different plans in different constituencies; we must have common plans for all or nothing. He then asked what I would propose & I

---

[36] The locations respectively of the Conservative Research Department and Central Office.

produced my terms. He must call off all attacks on S.B. & the party, & cease to invite subscriptions to run candidates against official Conservatives. We on our side would allow anyone to express his adherence to "Empire Free Trade" provided he loyally accepted the official policy. He might try and persuade the local association to adopt his views and if they did they could put what pressure they liked on the candidate. But if he failed to convert them he must be content to leave them alone. It took a little time to get all this clear; then he said. A little time ago I would have jumped at these terms. If I were alone I would jump at them now but I cant separate myself from Rothermere. Finally when he rose to go and I asked what he meant to do he said he was going to see Rothermere at once and then would let me know the result. The impression left on all our minds was that he was very anxious to make the deal and intended to do his very best to persuade Rothermere to come in.

In the course of the conversation I asked him whether he thought the Dominions would do a deal with the present Govt on the basis of Import Boards. I dont think he saw what I was leading up to; at any rate, he replied that the Dominions wanted a market & wouldn't in the least mind how we set about to give it them. He thought therefore that though Thomas was a terrible muddler he had an excellent chance to make a bargain which in the case of Canada alone would give us the Canadian market in four articles of first importance viz. Structural steel, steel sheets, steel plates and anthracite coal. This would at once give employment to 50000 Welsh miners while Mackenzie King, if he could go back to Canada & say he had sold the British Govt 100 million bushels of wheat for a number of years would be hailed as the greatest Prime Minister Canada had ever had. I then asked him what would happen if, having made such a deal, the Government went to the country. We would be obliged to support the deal and the Empire question having been thus settled we could not put forward an Empire bargain on other lines as immediately practical politics. That did not necessarily mean defeat for us. On the contrary we should be left with Safeguarding, our own Agricultural policy and the Government's record – all three winners. But Empire Free Trade, Food taxes and the Referendum would all be pushed into the back ground. They could not be a live issue.

Of course no journalist ever admits that anyone else has had an idea which hadn't occurred to him already. And Max wasn't going to admit that he hadn't thought of all these contingencies. Nevertheless I am convinced that the idea was new to him and that he was profoundly impressed – and *de*pressed – by it. I pressed him repeatedly to say what was the counter to it. If he had thought about it before he would have had an answer of some kind, but he had none. And we then urged that the only counter was to get the Govt out before the Conference, or if that were no longer possible, to weaken them by constant attack till they dare not put forward import boards at all.

Really this was my trump card and I think it brought home to Max the absolute folly of quarrelling with our party and the necessity of finding some way of destroying the Labour Party before they destroy his policy. For if it is not carried soon it is difficult to see how it could survive in the face of a fait accompli in the shape of a trade agreement concluded without food taxes.

Sunday. I saw S.B. yesterday morning at his own request to tell him of my talk with the Beaver. I suspect he was half disappointed for he was quite looking forward to saying in public what he thought of him and his colleague. But on the other hand he could not resist my conclusion that if I could pull this deal off things would look fairly rosy for our Party. This view was also that at the C.O. where Topping described my communication to him as the "first gleam of light after many months of gloom". It might also be described as the first fruits of my Chairmanship and if it does come off I cannot help thinking that the prospects are very bright. If the Labour Party goes to the country after the Conference (assuming they make the deal) as would I think be best for them, we should deprive them of credit by accepting their bargain and declaring we could have made a much better one. Meanwhile the food tax bogey would have gone West and we should be free to lam them for all we were worth on unemployment safeguarding and agriculture. The B-R claws would have been cut and they would have to support us. When we got in we should not be expected to do much Imperially all at once but with the permanent secretariat which I assume this Govt would have set up we could get to work on accumulating the material which is really necessary to enable a proper deal to be done. At present to speak honestly that material is not there and though you could do a deal on broad lines such as Max suggested with Canada you want a lot of hard long detailed tedious work before you could frame a proper inter Imperial scheme to cover even a single industry.

Suppose on the other hand the Govt held on say for the Indian Conference which they now talk of postponing till the spring. In that case they would be gambling on an improvement in the Trade position which might very possibly come. But I do not believe it would save them. There is a lot of discontent in their party both in the H of C & the country and it goes deeper than ours. The Liberals would get tired of holding their hands. The electoral reform conference has finally broken down (it has been worked with great skill by Sam Hoare) and Liberals have little hope now of a deal with Labour on the lines of P.R. or the alternative vote. I think in this case of holding on our victory would be postponed longer but would be much more decisive. I hope I am not too complacent in suspecting that, in the inside of a fortnight after taking over, the situation has completely changed – and in our favour.

. . .

26 July 1930
Westbourne

My dear Ida,

...

After a very hectic week I am plunged in gloom and my week end is properly
spoiled. That wretched Bromley vacancy came just at the wrong moment & has
complicated things terribly. I heard nothing from the Beaver till Wednesday but I
heard of him for all the would-be candidates went rushing to him for support and
then rushing back to me for advice which was very difficult to give. I thought it
was hardly playing the game while I was keeping a truce to go on pressing our
candidates to declare themselves Free Traders and I was getting more and more
uneasy. In fact I had made up my mind to ring him up when he rang me up and
said he wanted very badly to see me. I saw him and he said he had seen Rothermere
on Sunday and he (R.) had, after many protests, authorised him to negotiate. I
didn't know what he meant as all he had to do was to say Yes or No but at the
moment I let that pass. (I think I know now what he meant). On Monday however
a certain Col. Combs had announced himself as a United Empire candidate. Now
the so-called United Empire Party is financed by Rothermere and includes odd
things like No surrender in India in its programme as well as Empire Free Trade.
Max had protested that this was very embarrassing to him and had induced R. to
damp down publicity, which in fact he did. But Max explained that he was still
nervous about R. and wanted to find some way of bringing him in and after a lot of
beating about the bush he brought out the suggestion that we should all agree on
Esmond Harmsworth[37] for Bromley. I turned this down at once pointing out that if
I agreed I should split my party, for all the loyal supporters of S.B. would think I
had sold the pass. Moreover he must settle relations before and not after Bromley
for I could support an Empire Free Trader if he was fighting us. He saw the point
and I then told him what I knew he would learn very soon that I was going to meet
R. myself. That morning S. Hoare had come to tell me of a long talk he had had
with Max Pemberton[38] who is a great friend of Rothermere's. Sam had impressed
on him the folly of strengthening the Socialists by weakening the Conservatives &
he had agreed that it was silly and had ended by asking if S. & I would meet R. at
lunch or dinner. I agreed without hesitation and as other dates were inconvenient
to the others I postponed my journey here in order to attend the lunch today. When
I told Max this he was immensely delighted; it seemed to take a load off his mind
and he said he should now wait to see what happened today. As a matter of fact
both Express & Mail have kept quiet till today but this morning the Express had a

---

[37] Esmond Cecil Harmsworth (1898–1978). Son of Lord Rothermere. Conservative MP for Isle
of Thanet 1919–29. Chairman, Associated Newspapers 1932–71 and Newspapers Proprietors
Association 1934–61. Succeeded as 2nd Viscount Rothermere 1940.
[38] Max Pemberton (1863–1950). Author, novelist and Director, Northcliffe Newspapers. Knighted
1928.

most offensive article on the events at Barnes where B. has been trying to force Fremantle[39] to say he is an Empire Free Trader (whatever that may mean) under threat of having another candidate against him. I dictated a warm letter to Max but kept it back till after the lunch and then decided not to send it as the lunch was a failure. The party consisted of Pemberton Sam Hoare Rothermere Esmond & myself, and the two Harmsworths produced the worst impression on us. They treated the negotiations with Max purely from the personal and journalistic view. A row among the Conservatives would be good business for the papers, therefore they did not want it to stop. If Max accepted the terms he would lose the dominating position he held and eventually be smothered in the Conservative ranks. In vain we pointed out that if he split the party he would lose his policy; they cared nothing for the policy but only for the "fun". And at last after long talk the root of the matter came out. R. said that he had asked Max whether there was anyone whom he could trust in the Conservative party and he replied Yes there was one. Was it Horne? No Horne was insincere and a social climber. It was N.C and, said R. "If you make that transformation you get him and you get me 100 per cent". Of course, after that there was no use pursuing the subject and we broke up.

Now you see why I am gloomy. Frankly I dont see what to do. I shall see Max again but I dont believe I can get him without Rothermere & R. wont move unless he can shift Baldwin. The commonest loyalty makes it impossible to listen to such a suggestion and yet the tragedy is that – most reluctantly – I have come to the conclusion that if S.B. would go the whole party would heave a sigh of relief. Everywhere I hear that there is no confidence in his leadership or belief in his determination to carry any policy through. Yet it looks as if I might have to go down fighting for S.B. when my own desire is, as it always has been, to go for the free hand. I addressed the 1900 Club on Wednesday and made a very frank speech as there were no reporters. But at the least shade of criticism of B's slogans I was interrupted with loud shouts of No No and one man kept calling out "We want another leader". I was furious and have written to the Chairman to say I will never address the Club again. I wish I thought it was singular.

Ouf! Lets think of something else.

I dined at the Palace on Tuesday and found the King in tremendous spirits. After dinner he beckoned me up and then we went & sat down together and had quite a long conversation. He was exceedingly indiscreet about his present Ministers but evidently delighted that Jimmy Thomas had got safely back into the Dominions office again …

…

---

[39] Francis Edward Fremantle (1872–1943). Medical Officer of Health, Hertfordshire 1902–16 (later Consulting MOH); member, LCC 1919–22. Conservative MP for St Albans 1919–43. Chairman, Commons Health and Housing Committees; member, Industrial Health Research Board 1929–34 and various other medical committees. Knighted 1932.

4 August 1930
Westbourne

My dear Hilda,

...

First, as to Garvin. I dont suppose Austen wrote all I suggested to him but he did write both to him and to Wargrave.[40] The first produced a reply which began with another squeal "Neville said a word which made me cold and does not assist at all". Ass! but he was touché for he went on to reaffirm his original promise – to Sept 1903 by Jan 31 and if not to revise the 1st two volumes "strength permitting". The second resulted in an appointment with Wargrave ... who was sympathetic and anxious to help. He does not believe G. will ever finish the book but he will remind him of his undertaking from time to time and when Jan 31 comes and he hasn't fulfilled it I think we shall find Wargrave useful as an intermediary. I am afraid if I met G. again I should do him some violence.

An awful lot has happened since I wrote to you last in very gloomy spirits after the interview with Rothermere. Max maintained silence on Monday and on Tuesday I felt I must not delay longer for on Thursday the Bromley people were to select their candidate and I was determined to have an answer before then. Meantime the News Chronicle had learnt of my interview with Rothermere and divulged it with an air of disclosing a portentous secret. On Monday evening I had arranged to meet the 1922 Committee who wanted to ask me questions about the C.O. and of course they were burning with curiosity. I made no secret of it, said I considered it part of my duty to find out what the Press Lords were thinking & doing, explained that I could not reveal a private conversation but hinted that they need not expect too much. The 1922 Comee were quite satisfied and approved what I had done. Next morning Esmond Harmsworth rang me up and said his father had drawn the conclusion from reports of my remarks the night before that I was not altogether satisfied with the interview and evidently he was surprised at this. I said that was not an unfair description of what I had told the Comee. E. then said that now it had got out his father thought we might as well have a further talk. Would I come and lunch with them. I said Yes, but I couldn't come before Friday as I already had luncheon engagements on the other days. So it was settled for Friday at Esmond's house, and he then added that he wished me to know that he didn't want to stand for Bromley but it was Max who was pressing it. I said I supposed Max had told him what I had said about that. He replied no Max had only told him that he had mentioned his name to me in that connection. I said, That is too bad of him he ought to have told you that I could not agree to it and I repeated my reasons.

---

[40] Edward Alfred Goulding (1862–1936). Barrister and member of LCC 1895–1901. Conservative MP for Devizes 1895–1906 and Worcester 1908–22. PPS to Henry Chaplin 1895–98; Chairman, Tariff Reform League Organisation Department 1904–12. Created Bart 1915 and Baron Wargrave 1922.

That evening I went to Max's house at 7 o'clock. He was extra cordial saying he was *delighted* to see me and asked how I got on with R. I said I had been very disappointed with the interview and told him what had happened. He roared with laughter, said that was just like R. but that he didn't mean it, it being R's insistence on the personal injury to Max if he accepted my terms. He went on to say that he had seen R. who had been very much impressed with me and said I "measured right up to the standard he had led him to expect". I went on to say that what had really troubled me much more was that it did not seem to me that he (Max) and I were getting any nearer. He had now kept me waiting eleven days, Bromley would have to be settled on Thursday and I still did not know his mind. To my surprise he at once reverted to Esmond. If I would accept him all would be well. I said I told you before I could not accept him and it is of no use for you to try again. I won't have him now though if we agree I will have him later on. He then said that he had consulted McKenna[41] about my proposals & his own difficulties with R. McKenna had said your course is plain. You can't make an agreement but you can operate its terms. I didnt understand what this meant but he explained that in such a case he would act as if the agreement were in force but de die in diem so that he could break it off when he chose. I had never expected him to sign any formal agreement but as he appeared to be putting his arrangement forward as an alternative to mine I replied very solemnly that it would be an act of faith on both sides but that for my part I was ready to try it and if he told me definitely that he would work on those lines I thought I could find a candidate acceptable to myself who would nevertheless call himself an Empire Free Trader. Once more he began to press for Esmond on which I got a little annoyed and said Will you please take it from me as final that I will not accept Esmond for Bromley and if you want to conciliate R. you must do it some other way. He took this quite calmly and appeared to accept the position, only he said he must still consult R. before giving me a final answer. I said All right but I must have it in good time to decide about Bromley and he promised that he would not fail to comply with that request.

I went away from this interview in high spirits and told my friends including S.B. that I felt more confident of success than at any time during the negotiations. Max's manner and the general line of his talk led me to the conclusion that though he would have been glad if I had taken Esmond he was convinced that the terms he had got were so favourable that he was anxious to clinch them.

The next day, Wednesday, was a busy one. I had many interviews to get through at the Research Dept. and the C.O. and I did not go to the H. of C. till 6 o'clock when I had a meeting of the business Committee to which I wanted to

---

[41] Reginald McKenna (1863–1943). Liberal MP for Monmouthshire North 1895–1918. Financial Secretary to Treasury 1905–7; President, Board of Education 1907–8; First Lord of Admiralty 1908–11; Home Secretary 1911–15; Chancellor of Exchequer 1915–16; declined the Exchequer in 1922 and 1923; Chairman, Midland Bank 1919–43.

submit some Research matters. I had hardly sat down to this when the Secretary came in & said Mr Hannon[42] (who sees a lot of Max nowadays) wanted to see me urgently. I went out & found him in some agitation, saying he was the bearer of a disagreeable message. He then handed me a short letter from Max saying that he had consulted R. & Esmond, that it had been decided to run the latter for Bromley, that his name would be put before the Conservative Exec. Com. and the Association, that he realised that this meant the renewal of hostilities, that it was with the deepest regret that he contemplated our separation, but that the difficulties on both sides were too great.

This was a staggering blow and it hit me in a tender spot. For I saw at once that Max had been playing a double game and I suspected, what I soon found to be a fact, that while he was keeping me quiet with soft words he had been working away at the capture of the most important points in the Bromley position. I had given my trust and it had been abused and I was bitterly humiliated and outraged. However it was a time for action rather than lamentation. I went straight back to my colleagues & told them it was war and I wanted their assent to whatever might be necessary to carry it on. They gave it at once & I had the principal agent over & gave him the news and his instructions. As a result I had an interview next morning with the Chairman of the Bromley Association, another with Campbell[43] one of the candidates who promised to stand firm, and in the afternoon I met the whole executive committee. I told them the story of the negotiations & how they had broken down and I made it quite clear that Esmond, under whatever flag he fought, would receive no support from the C.O., M.P.'s would not speak for him and if returned he would not get the party whip. They retired and shortly afterwards they unanimously agreed to recommend Campbell to the Association that evening. The first round had been won and I went over to the House where my colleagues were summoned to hear the latest news from the front. I need hardly say that they were immensely delighted and relieved, especially Winston, who is nervous about Epping & was very warm in his praise of my "firm handling" of the situation. However we were not out of the wood. I had a further interview with the candidate to make sure he was not weakening and another with the Chairman with whom I discussed every possible contingency at the meeting and agreed with him the best way of countering it. I was pleased with him that afternoon. I had given him confidence and he went off

---

[42] Patrick Joseph Henry Hannon (1874–1963). Conservative MP for Birmingham Moseley 1921–50. Vice-President, Tariff Reform League 1910–14; General Secretary, Navy League 1911–18; Director, British Commonwealth Union 1918–28; Secretary, Empire Industries Association 1925–50; President, Industrial Transport Association 1927–37. Knighted 1936.

[43] Edward Taswell Campbell (1879–1945). East India merchant and Vice-Consul, Java 1914–20; member, LCC 1922–25. Conservative MP for North-West Camberwell 1924–29 and Bromley 1930–45. PPS to Kingsley Wood 1931–43 and to H.U. Willink 1943. Knighted 1933. Created Bart 1939.

in a determined mood. Late that evening the agent telephoned me to my house that all had gone well, the chairman had promptly sat upon any Beaverites who looked like making trouble and Campbell had been unanimously adopted. Round two!

There it stands for the present. Seeing that he had been forestalled Max has kept mum about Esmond and only the Times has let out that attempts had been made behind the scenes to get him adopted. The funny thing is that he still expected me to lunch. I wrote to him on Thursday morning saying that after Max's communication to me of the evening before he would realise that it was no use my lunching with him. Apparently he was away till Friday and then didn't open his letters. So he & his Father waited for me ½ hour & then rang up when Miss Thompson gave them the news that I wasn't coming. I should like to have heard what they said! I fancy R. has some confused idea that politics being entirely a game you can play fast & loose with a man politically and yet keep on terms with him privately. I believe he intended to make further trial of me, alone this time, to see whether I was at all to be attracted by the idea of superseding S.B. and assuming that I must have ambitions that way he would not understand that I could jeopardise them by treating Esmond so roughly. I predict that I haven't seen the last of him – or Max. But Max has made one of his biggest blunders. He has destroyed my confidence in him and when that has happened I dont readily give it again vide L.G.

I went up to Edinburgh on Friday night keeping the gout angry and sullen but not daring to fight down with Navatophan. The exciting events of the last few days had somewhat interfered with my sleep but that night I slept in the train like a baby and woke refreshed. We had a rotten day pouring all morning and showery in the afternoon so that the audience was not what had been hoped for. But the press was hungry that day & I had a good report of what two people have written to me was a "delightfully outspoken" or "straight spoken" speech. If I were leader (which there is no prospect of *whatever*) I should declare at once for the free hand. It would frighten some supporters but enthuse the rest.

August 5 London 6.30 p.m. ...

... I had Hubbard[44] to lunch with me yesterday and was amused to read an Olympian leader in the Post today explaining to an ignorant public the true issues and all the inferences which only a penetrating journalist would have known how to draw from the bare facts.

I was sorry to leave Westbourne where I enjoyed my two lazy days messing about in my garden. The inside of the house has been redecorated & is much improved. Now the outside is being repainted ... I should have liked to rebuild the rose house but I jibbed at the money. However I have at last had the right

---

[44] George William Hubbard (1870–1939). Journalist and Editor, *Birmingham Daily Mail* 1903–6 and *Birmingham Daily Post* 1906–33.

idea as to how to house my seedling Cymbidiums ... without touching the potting shed. ... Of course I cant afford it at present with everything so low that my capital is shrinking away every day. But when we get back to office, if ever, and the trade revival comes, I shall know what to do.

...

10 August 1930
Hotel Astoria, Bruxelles

My dear Ida,

... I had been rather wondering whether events at Bromley might not detain me in England, but up to the time of my departure there was no sign of battle there and I hope I shall be able to work out my full holiday in which case I shall only get back on the eve of the poll. Some of my friends seem to think that we may yet see Max making overtures to me again. That may or may not be. At present I am not taking any chances & indeed if he did make advances I should receive them only with the utmost caution. Meanwhile I can see plenty to occupy me in the C.O. where revelations continue to accumulate, and to show how little of business method has entered into its administration. But I am not going to talk any more politics.

...

16 August 1930
Hotel Astoria, Bruxelles

My dear Hilda,

...

I must say I agree very much with you about the Flemish painters. These early people R. van der Weyden, Memling, Van der Goes, the Van Eycks are very interesting and indeed fascinating in the brilliance of their colour and the accuracy of their reproduction of what they saw. But of course they are very early and one has to judge them always relatively. ... When you come to the later people – well I have always heard from Austen that I did not appreciate Rubens because I had not seen him in Belgium but after seeing him here I am still of the same opinion that, although a fine colourist, his figures are coarse compared with the Italians and that in composition he cannot hold a candle to them. ... But are not F. Hals and Cornelis Dutch rather than Flemish?

... [W]e did ourselves very well in Brussels and saw most of what I wanted. One night we went to the opera & heard Madame Butterfly. It was the first time I had seen it but it confirmed my previous impression that with a few exceptions I dont really care about opera.

...

22 August 1930
Schwarzwald Hotel, Titisee

My dear Ida,

...

When did I write last? Was it from Baden-Baden? If so, I think it must have been before we had had time to examine the neighbourhood or crystallise our impressions. Since then we have been nearly a week in Baden or Würtemburg [sic] and I can say confidently that though there are places in this country which are charming ... and individuals who are likeable (as for instance our chauffeur) on the whole I loathe Germans and detest all their habits & customs. To begin with they are a revoltingly ugly race. I have only seen one woman who was not positively repulsive and I think she ... must have been a Swiss. As for the men with their great shining bald skulls, their little rolls of fat at the back of the neck, and their huge paunches, they are fit mates for their womenkind. I *have* seen one or two children who were quite adorable but either they must have been foreigners or else they were destined early to lose their beauty. German beds infuriate me. They are provided with an enormous puffy eider down stuffed I suppose with feathers. It is short so as to reach up to the top of your stomach. It is insufferably hot and I always throw it away at once, but underneath I am apt to find a *second* eiderdown of the ordinary variety but buttoned on to the sheet. Without it one would catch cold, with it one passes the night wrestling with nightmares. Then the pillows. They too are so soft that the moment you put your head on them it sinks down and all the corners come forward & smother your face. Last night as I struggled to find a slightly less uncomfortable position (my bed is always too short) the corner of the pillow next the wall flung itself across my face with such vigour that it struck a glass of water standing by the bedside & knocked it over sending a cataract into my bedroom slippers. And the food! No wonder Germans always seem to suffer from indigestion. The one who occupied the room next to me at Frendenstadt had to have a siesta after lunch during which, to judge from his groans, he must have suffered horribly. They give you an enormous meal in the middle of the day and a very short but extremely indigestible one in the evening. The domestic calf continues to provide the staple of all meals but it is bravely backed up by the pig, preferably raw, and the sausage in its many but almost invariably sanguinary forms. Their pumpernickel and their Zweiback, their acid wines & mineral waters tasting like "warm flat irons" are equally disagreeable. Only one thing is good here & that is their milk and butter. ...

...

I am not thinking much about politics but in response to an urgent request from the C.O. I sent off a letter to Campbell our candidate for Bromley this morning. I was afraid they would be calling for me to come back early and speak for him so that I was relieved to find that only a letter was wanted. I dont regard Mr Redwood very seriously. I dont think any one believes in the United

Empire Party which does not excite the same enthusiasm as Max's "Crusade" and Max seems to be trying to keep out of it himself. But I am rather troubled over a cutting from the Times which A. sent me and which indicates that C.O. have sent out a revised version of an old leaflet about the Refm. The new version omits mention of the Refm but repeats the pledge to put food taxes before the people from which the Times concludes that the Refm has now been dropped in favour of a second election. I believe this is stupidity – not malice on the part of the C.O. but I have sent a letter to the Director of Publicity which will give him a mauvais quart d'heure and have instructed him not to send out anything else of any kind whatever without my personal approval. Unfortunately S.B.'s own speeches have not been at all clear and I may have to make some definite pronouncement myself either publicly or privately when I get back. For I will be no party to a second election which would in my opinion be fatal to success. The Refm is the furthest I am prepared to go and I shall tell S.B. so.

Another "bye" is to come for I had a telegram yesterday telling me that Douglas King had been drowned in a yachting accident. I am very distressed about it. King was not a flier but one of these men who can always be relied on for loyalty and hard work. He was a very straight plucky honourable little chap and we shall miss him in our party.

...

7 September 1930
37 Eaton Square, SW1

My dear Hilda,

I am very glad to be able to confirm the cheerful account of Annie which I gave you last night. ...

...

I did not ask the Dr Laxing, who came in place of Thomas ... to make any examination, but I gave him an account of her troubles & he rather added to my confidence that all would be well as he evidently considered that all the symptoms were accountable for by the change of life. He struck me as having a head on his shoulders – not the sort of man who doesn't bother to go below the surface.

Provided that there is nothing unexpected and not found by Laturille I think Annie should go on well now. She wont worry with Martin at hand in Birmingham and she will follow any instructions he gives her without rebelling against them. She doesnt yet feel prepared to make that complete break with political duties which I think is necessary but one cant force her too hard all at once and there is nothing actually arranged for, while I have told my agent that he must make no engagements for her.

Your visit to Chateau D'Oex was an immense relief and joy to her and I cant be sufficiently grateful to you & Ida for so promptly coming to her aid in spite of my warnings. I did feel that it was asking too much of you, seeing that there was nothing to be done for her except the mental strengthening ... But A's morale crumbled even more completely than I had expected as soon as we had gone, and she says she wept tears of joy on hearing that you were coming. You have been good Samaritans indeed ...

I have been able to get a good deal of work done since I returned, but the political atmosphere is not very invigorating. A confidential report on Bromley indicates that Redwoods unexpectedly large poll[45] chiefly reflects a general dissatisfaction with the leadership and this is only the echo of a refrain that reaches me from every quarter with a dreary monotony. I understand that S.B. will be back about the 20th and I must then have an earnest talk with him but the confidential view of the C.O. is that the party wont have the Referendum and that S.B. cant give it up. Oh dear!

I hear Austen has refused to take part in the Indian Conference & so has Hailsham. I fear this may be because they do not feel that their views are shared by their leader.

...

21 September 1930
Holwood, Keston, Kent

My dear [Hilda?],[46]

...

You ask about Ruggles Brise & the Quota. The plan is one which has been worked out by one of my Research Comees under Wolmer[47] and the article was written as a sort of kite to draw criticisms. I didn't want Wolmer to put his name to it lest it should be too official but as a matter of fact I think the scheme is watertight as far as wheat is concerned. But I saw in the Times that while I was away Addison[48] had been taking it up and I therefore decided in my speech

---

[45] Bromley by-election, 2 September 1930. The Conservative majority of 7037 over the Liberals in 1929 was reduced to 1606 through the intervention of V.C. Redwood who polled 9483 votes (24.1 per cent) on a substantially reduced turnout.

[46] Confusion arises in the bound volumes about the sequence and location of letters for September 1930, probably due to family efforts to conceal Chamberlain's candid observations about his wife's mental and physical problems during her menopause. This version brings together NC18/1/710A and NC18/1/742 (incorrectly located in June 1931). This represents the correct page sequence.

[47] Roundell Cecil Palmer (1887–1971). Conservative MP for Newton 1910–18 and Aldershot 1918–40. Parliamentary Secretary, Board of Trade 1922–24; Assistant Postmaster-General 1924–29; Minister of Economic Warfare 1942–45. Styled Viscount Wolmer 1895–1941 when became Baron Selborne. Succeeded as 3rd Earl of Selborne 1942.

[48] Christopher Addison (1869–1951). Liberal MP for Shoreditch 1910–22 and Labour MP for Swindon 1929–31 and 1934–35. Parliamentary Secretary, Board of Education 1914–15 and Ministry of Munitions 1915–16; Minister of Munitions, 1916–17; Minister of Reconstruction 1917–19; President, LGB 1919; Minister of Health 1919–21; Minister without Portfolio 1921; Parliamentary Secretary, Ministry of Agriculture 1929–30; Minister of Agriculture 1930–31; Dominion Secretary

yesterday to claim it at once as *our* policy. Thinking things over it has occurred to me that if S.B. were to say that having adopted the quota system he saw no necessity for a tax on either wheat or meat, he might be induced to claim the free hand for everything else and that even in the North where they are so terrified of food taxes they might feel that the exclusion of the two great staple foods would at any rate mitigate their difficulties. Bruce told me some time ago that he did not care about a tax on meat; he would much prefer protection for dairy produce since Australia even with a preference could not put her frozen beef into competition with Argentine chilled beef. Moreover it is possible that the quota system might be applied to beef & mutton though it would certainly be more difficult than with wheat. Since I have thought of this I have felt a little more cheerful and should the idea be found acceptable S.B. might even now save his bacon at any rate for the time.

Apart from some such new development I see little hope for him. Lord Stanley (with whom I am staying here) tells me he has been horrified to find how dissatisfaction with the leadership has grown during the last two months and Topping says frankly that he sees no way of avoiding a change. The question is how far S.B. is aware of what is going on. On that I have heard from Willie Bridgeman (on whose judgement S.B. relies more than anyone else's) that S.B. is going to his place in Shropshire the day after his return to London and wants to see him *alone*. And W.B. says he wants a talk with me first, and is coming to spend Wednesday night at Eaton Square. I may be wrong but I suspect that all this has some relationship to S.B.'s personal position – and mine. Topping says nobody suspects me of wanting to oust S.B. but that I am regarded as his natural successor and the Daily News had an article & a leader a little while ago, stating that S.B. was going to bow to the inevitable & that homage was already being paid to me as the heir-apparent. It was not entirely complimentary but said I was much the best of an undistinguished bunch and that I was possessed of far greater character & determination than S.B. All this is rather the crackling of thorns under the feet but the air is becoming perceptibly hotter & I shall feel easier if my little plan which I shall impart to W.B. comes off.

Meanwhile you may have observed my "unauthorised programme"[49] of an emergency tariff. Although I believe the Cabinet has not accepted the 10% import duty they are so obviously smelling round it that I thought it well to come out with a pronouncement on one side which would take the wind out of their sails. Edward Stanley was very delighted with it & the audience at once took it up with enthusiasm. I believe it will be heartily welcomed in the party.

1945–47; Commonwealth Secretary 1947; Lord Privy Seal 1947–51; Paymaster-General 1948–49; Lord President of Council 1951. Created Baron Addison 1937 and Viscount 1945.

[49] At Crystal Palace on 20 September 1930, Chamberlain outlined an 'unauthorised programme' of drastic economy, reduction in direct taxation, unemployment insurance reform, emergency tariffs for industry, a wheat quota and a 'free hand' for other tariff demands to negotiate imperial preferences.

Another unauthorised observation I made though I'm not sure if it was reported was that we should desire at the earliest possible moment to reduce *direct* taxation. This would of course be hailed by Socialists with joy as an admission that we were out to help our friends. On the other hand our friends would be equally delighted for different reasons and it is our friends whose enthusiasm & loyalty we particularly want to stimulate just now.

From various sources I hear that Max is in very low spirits and anxious for an excuse for reconciliation. Lidiard,[50] our candidate for S. Paddington, who came to see me declared that Max had directly urged him to do so and Lidiard tried hard to be allowed to arrange a meeting saying that Max had said If only I could have 10 minutes with Mr Chamberlain I am sure we could settle everything. But I replied Gammon. Max knows me well enough to ring me up any time of day or night and ask for an interview if he wants one. But he is just manœuvring for position & hopes to get *me* to ask for an interview with him. I shall let him stew in his own juice, for until he has cut free from Rothermere I am sure he cant come to terms with me.

28 September 1930
The Manor House, Great Durnford, Salisbury

My dear Ida,

After all I am here without Annie. She could not bear to take my advice and stick to one doctor whose opinion was backed by that eminent medical authority, her husband, but rushed off to see Victor Bonney [?] (the seventh doctor since this trouble began). I need hardly say that his advice was directly contrary to that of Thomas. ... As a matter of fact A. did what she always does viz. picked out those parts of his advice which she wished to follow & ignored the rest so she decided that she would not be happy if she came here – and as soon as she had done that the whole thing cleared up completely & she was perfectly well. I am sorry as I am convinced that what she wants is to get her mind off herself & the change of surroundings would have given her something fresh to think of. But I know by experience that you cant press her beyond a point or she only goes back on you. She doesn't want to be curetted and as two doctors are in favour & two against she has decided against. On the other hand all the doctors are against radium which she wants because Ivy (whom she insisted on consulting & who told her that none of "these doctors", meaning G.P.'s understand anything about womens troubles) gave her an enthusiastic account of her own recovery by radium. I dont blame Ivy: she could only say what she thought, but it makes it more difficult for me to keep Annie off the radium.

---

[50] Herbert Lidiard (1864–1941). Several times Mayor of Paddington; LCC member for Paddington; Chairman, South Paddington Conservative Association; unsuccessful candidate South Paddington by-election 1930. Knighted 1923.

...

As to the political situation I have not heard a word from S.B. but things are nevertheless much clearer to me than they were. To begin with I have ascertained that he himself has no idea how matters have developed and that he is coming home [from Aix] very pleased with himself, in bouncing spirits and declaring that he is now going to take the gloves off (against R. & B bien entendu, not against R.M.) Bridgeman has heard no more and doesn't know when to expect him & I have had no answer to the letter I wrote asking him to lunch.

You will agree therefore that as there is no question of his voluntarily renouncing the leadership there is no question of my urging him to retain it. I told Bridgeman exactly how feeling about S.B. had developed. He did not seem to me to take it very seriously; said the people who talked like that were just those whose opinion was not worth having and that the sound Conservatives could soon be got back into the fold. All the same he recognised that some move had got to be made and was impressed by what he called my ingenious plan. I cant remember whether I have told you what the plan is. ... In short, S.B. is to announce that he is going to restate Conservative policy and for that purpose to summon a suitably representative meeting. He would start off with a general attack on the Govt leading up to a stiff declaration in favour of economy specially going for unemployment insurance. He would naturally follow on with safeguarding and declare for the emergency tariff (which has caught on like hot cakes). Then he would come to Imperial Development & in the course of his remarks would arrive at the quota system which he would adopt for wheat, pointing out that this makes a tax on wheat unnecessary. Then going on to meat he would show how a tariff could not help the Australasian meat producers though they could be helped in other ways. Thus he would arrive at the conclusion that so far as the two great staples are concerned a tax does not form part of his programme. Thus the object which the Referendum was designed for can be achieved by other means & the Referendum having become obsolete is dropped. Finally, for the rest he would claim a free hand to use any and every means that seems feasible & useful to protect home markets and enable us to make advantageous arrangements with the Dominions. But he would point out that as the Imperial Conference is sitting important conclusions may very soon be reached to which we shall not be parties and we must reserve all rights to criticise or to urge amendments or to insert in our programme any new features which may arise out of these conclusions.

I had the Editor of the Yorkshire Post, the proprietor of the Glasgow Herald & a man from Lancashire to lunch with me last week and put this suggestion before them. They all approved and said it would be very helpful and even the C.O. thought it would be a good move though evidently they feared that S.B. would never get it across. However it seems to me the right thing and I must hope for the best.

...

11 October 1930
Westbourne

My dear Ida,

This has been a most anxious week but it has ended in a real "scoop" for us and as Annie observes it has fairly justified my decision to take the Chairmanship of the Party for I cannot imagine that David would have been equal to the occasion. As soon as I saw the papers on Thursday morning I realised the opportunity that had been given us and collecting Topping from the C.O. I drove off to Upper Brook St to see S.B. who gazed at us expectantly but had no suggestions to make. However he was quite ready to accept mine and driving back to the C.O. I set to work on the draft. By lunch time I had got it ready and read it to Bobby Monsell who had turned up unexpectedly in London & who received it with enthusiasm. However I still wasn't satisfied with it and all afternoon was occupied with further amendments till by 5 o'clock it had taken its final form. I then had the correspondents of the friendly papers up to my room and explained to them the important things to emphasise while Gower hurried off to show it to S.B. & get his final approval. S.B. took it whole & soon after six it was handed to the Press.

It is too soon to say what its whole effect will be but at any rate it bowled out Melchett Morris[51] and Max in one. Melchett looks particularly foolish because the Express printed his offensive letter in large type on the front page with headlines about Too feeble to seize the chance and underneath was the statement showing that the chance had been seized. Meanwhile Empire Free Trade has had a punch in the wind and the Referendum & 2nd General Election have been buried without loss of credit. Now I am at work on the letter which S.B. is to write me next week and if we can get that out with an equal air of decision we may save S.B.'s bacon long enough to enable him to go later without a triumph for R. & B. That he can remain permanently I cannot believe. He has at last I think come to understand how low his stock has fallen but the effect seems rather to cow & stupify [sic] him than to inspire him with any sort of determination or capacity to take a decision. I feel very sorry for him for I am afraid he is very unhappy but though one may temporarily prop him up in the eyes of the country one cannot make him show up as a leader to the House of Commons and when the House meets at the end of the month I fear there may be trouble among our people who will say the policy is all right but we do not believe S.B. will carry it out. Yet perhaps he might, if he is properly supported. I feel that it is of no use to worry about it: one must just await events.

South Paddington is fixed up. Sir H. Lidiard has been quietly transferred to my court and I have seen & approved his election address which ends by

---

[51] William Richard Morris (1877–1963). English motor manufacturer and philanthropist endowing Nuffield College, Oxford (1937) and the Nuffield Foundation for medical, scientific and social research (1943). Created Bart 1929 and Viscount Nuffield 1934.

promising to support the Conservative Party loyally in the House. Max did mean to bring out an Empire Crusader against him but whether he will persist after the events of the last few days remains to be seen. Meanwhile a letter in the Times gave me an opportunity of replying this morning indirectly to the Times own very stupid & unfair comments on the C.O. The C.O. itself is immensely pleased at being publicly justified.

... I had to come here to address a League of Nations Union meeting last night. I know mighty little about the subject but with the help of the Research Dept I produced a lot of stuff that was new to the audience and I think politically it was a very useful meeting. The supporters of the League are always very enthusiastic and they are very apt to believe that we are luke warm because we are not willing to disarm before anyone else. But last night they appeared to be more than satisfied with what I said & a clergyman on the platform declared that his test of how he should vote was the candidates attitude towards the League (!) and after my speech he intended to vote for me.

...

18 October 1930
Westbourne

My dear Hilda,

I am so glad to hear that "Mr Baldwins letter" made such a good impression on you and Ida. It has been a very interesting week and once again it shows that as we thought the chairmanship of the party does enable one to direct the policy though nominally he has nothing to do with it. As a matter of fact S.B. *never saw* the letter till a few minutes before the Business Committee when he read it out as the "result of our meditations". Except for a few minor alterations, therefore, made at the Committee, it was drafted by me from beginning to end! Naturally I was very anxious about its reception in the North but thanks to my luncheon party a few weeks ago the Yorkshire Post & the Glasgow Herald swallowed it like lambs. So here we are with the free hand having got rid of the Referendum without loss of face & so far as I know without a word of protest from any single Unionist organ. I have only seen 3 M.P.'s since, Sir H. Betterton[52] (Nottingham) Sir George Bowyer[53] (Bucks) and Geoffrey Ellis (Yorks) and all three expressed

---

[52] Henry Bucknall Betterton (1872–1949). Conservative MP for Rushcliffe 1918–34. Parliamentary Secretary, Ministry of Labour 1923–24 and 1924–29; Minister of Labour 1931–34; Chairman, Unemployment Assistance Board 1934–41. Created Bart 1929 and Baron Rushcliffe 1935.

[53] George Edward Bowyer (1886–1948). Conservative MP for Buckingham 1918–37. PPS to President of Board of Trade 1921–24; Conservative Whip 1925–35; Junior Lord of Treasury 1927–29; Comptroller of Household 1935; Parliamentary Secretary, Agriculture 1939–1940; Conservative Whip in Lords 1945–47. President, Urban District Councils Association 1923–25 and from 1929. Vice-Chairman, Conservative Party Organisation 1930–35. Knighted 1929. Created Bart 1933 and Baron Denham 1937.

themselves as thoroughly delighted & satisfied. In fact all the information that comes to me indicates that the whole party has been heartened up and feels that it has a policy once more while S.B.'s personal position has been greatly strengthened. Whether he can hold it must now depend on himself, but at any rate I have given him another chance. It is curiously characteristic of him that he hasn't said a word of thanks to me or even shown any sense that he realises what has happened. In fact I doubt whether he does. It certainly saves me trouble when he takes everything I give him without question but I am a little disturbed by the thought of what might happen if some one else were Chairman. But then of course some one else might be leader and have a mind of his own.

It was satisfactory to find that Salisbury showed no sign of distress over the free hand and though he doesn't like the wheat subsidy he is all out for Empire trade for which he is quite ready if necessary to accept a tax on foreign wheat. On the other hand Winston at an early stage began to show signs of emotion. He kept asking questions which to me indicated clearly that he was looking for something to object to. He couldn't postpone the statement because I had inserted in the earlier one the announcement that S.B. would unbosom himself in the following week. At last he discovered that I had so far altered my original suggestions as no longer to exclude meat from the possibility of taxation and after a little while he announced that it was not possible for him to accept the new policy and that he should have to state his disagreement publicly. It was quite evident that his alleged reasons were not the real ones and that he had come determined to find some pretext for running out. He thanked us all for our consideration to him during our 5 years of association, expressed his regrets at parting and declared his intention of acting as the benevolent (and no doubt candid) friend. Clearly it had been thought out beforehand. There was an awkward pause. I wrote on a piece of paper which I showed to Bobby Monsell who sat next me "Vex not his ghost. Oh! let him pass". But Austen came to the rescue and said all the things which I suppose the rest of us ought to have said. He begged and implored him not to do so great an injury to the cause and not hastily to take so grave and irrevocable a step. Winston was moved and (according to Austen) dashed away a tear. He began to say something and broke off. And then we all broke up. Nothing has happened since so I suppose Winston has thought better of it. It seemed to me too good to be true. Some days later I asked S.B. if he had written to Winston as he had promised Austen to do, Austen saying "appeal to his heart; thats the only way to touch him". S.B. said he had and then he added I said something to him, a point which had occurred to me. I dont know whether it will appeal to him. I told him he mustn't feel that if he wanted to go, he would have in any way let me down!! I have laughed till I cried over this. Have you ever heard or read of anything like S.B.'s simplicity in this or any world. What a thing to say to a man who feels that he is at a crisis in his life & that if his highest ideals and noblest sentiments were appealed to he might be capable of the last sacrifice. Ah me! Oh dear!

I enclose the B.P. verbatim report of my speech as the Press Association started, when they had got to a certain hour, to transcribe, and so missed the really important passages about food taxes. You will see that I was very outspoken. I had read a leader in the Daily Herald in the morning saying that clearly the tactics must be to "run Mr Baldwin on to the defensive". So I decided that I would shirk nothing and I must see whether the C.O. should not reprint the salient passages in some leaflet. Our principal agent here was delighted and said it would do an immense amount of good in clearing away doubts and encouraging candidates and if only S.B. would talk like that – ! I saw Derby on Friday. He is going to make a speech on Wednesday and wanted to know what line he should take. I gave him the line and today he has sent me the speech to vet. It is admirable and in Lancashire it will be most helpful. Thus can the Chairman work on public opinion.

I am working away hard at C.O. reorganisation and begin to see light. But the legacies (Ashridge and Ladies Carlton) are heavy burdens to start under. They have played the d—l with our finances.

...

26 October 1930
37 Eaton Square, SW1

My dear Ida,

... I dont think S.B. will believe himself to be a heaven-born leader. He knows, and often says, that he is not a good leader in opposition but it is hardly to be expected that he should be willing to retire just at the nadir of his fortunes and be pointed at all the rest of his life as the man who failed. He therefore wishes to hold on until his star rises when he fancies himself handing over the reins to someone else and departing with the regretful affection & respect of his party. Whether things will work out that way remains to be seen – probably not. But I expect I should dream the same sort of dream if I were in his place.

The Gretton[54] request for a meeting merely said "to discuss the situation" but undoubtedly was directed at the leadership and I thought in the circumstances the right thing for S.B. to do was to challenge a decision at once and for that purpose to call a meeting not merely of M.P.'s but of the body competent to elect or depose leaders viz. M.P.'s & Peers. That is why I left out the candidates so that it should not be said afterwards This meeting had no power to decide the question. I have drafted a resolution dealing with policy only but anticipate that an amendment may be moved on leadership in which case the Chairman is to rule it out of order as an amendment but offer to take it

---

[54] John Gretton (1867–1947). Brewer and Chairman of Bass, Ratcliffe & Gretton. Conservative MP for South Derbyshire 1895–1906, Rutland 1907–18 and Burton 1918–43. Created Baron Gretton 1944. Leader of the Diehards in the Commons.

as a substantive motion after policy has been discussed. In this way I anticipate we may get a solid vote on policy and then strengthened by the approval of the policy I reckon S.B. should get an overwhelming vote of confidence. I have a good deal of evidence that the last letter which showed so remarkable a resemblance to my speech has gratified a great many of our party both in the House & out of it and the Beaver's subsequent behaviour has disillusioned some of his most ardent supporters. The Express keeps up a continuous shout of triumph over Admiral Taylor's[55] alleged miraculous progress, but unless the canvas is hopelessly misleading he hasn't really made a very deep impression. If our worm does come out well on top it will be a smashing blow for the Beaver. If Taylor wins it will be very bad for us but not fatal, whilst if the Socialist should get in it will infuriate our whole party and perhaps be the best of all in the long run. I agree with you in being glad that the Beaver has not taken what seems to me obviously the wise course from his own point of view. By standing out he has demonstrated the personal ingredient in his motive and I believe cut his own throat.

I entertained the Lobby journalists to lunch last Tuesday and we had a very satisfactory discussion at which they ventilated grievances. I have promised to interview them (i.e. the reps of the *friendly* press) regularly every week and have appointed W. Brass as a liaison officer. They were very pleased at that and also warmly expressed their appreciation of the way in which I had talked to them on the two previous occasion when I met them.

   ...

2 November 1930
37 Eaton Square, SW1

My dear Hilda,

I fear S. Paddington must have been a severe disappointment to you after you had sent off your letter. I confess it was to me as we had rather expected that Taylor's and Lidiard's figures would be reversed.[56] At the same time I have never attached undue importance to the result more especially as it has been obvious that S.B.'s letter had cut the ground from under the Beaver's feet and that his stock in the country has been going down ever since. Shipley is really more significant & though we dont expect to win I shall be disappointed if we dont bring down the majority by a substantial amount.

---

[55] Ernest Augustus Taylor (1876–1971). Royal Navy career. Captain 1913; Rear-Admiral retired 1924; Vice-Admiral 1929. Empire Crusader MP for South Paddington 1930–31, adopted as Conservative MP for the same seat 1931–50. Knighted 1952.

[56] South Paddington by-election, 30 October 1930. After unopposed Conservative returns in 1924 and 1929, the official Conservative (Lidiard) lost by 941 votes to Taylor representing the Empire Crusade.

Meanwhile the result of the municipal elections[57] is very striking and it will spread depression still further through the Socialist ranks. But it will tend to postpone the Gen. Election. I heard recently that Henderson was privately expressing confidence that if his party went to the country now they would come back with undiminished strength. He can hardly think so now and I imagine this demonstration of Socialist demoralisation will cause the Govt to cling to office as long as they can hold together.

I was well satisfied with our meeting [at Caxton Hall on 30 October] though at first I was surprised at the size of the minority for the reception accorded S.B. on his arrival was remarkable, the audience all rising & cheering. I had been against a ballot but when I saw the tone of the meeting I changed my mind and I am glad we gave it and made it impossible to doubt that the rebels had polled their last man. They put their case very badly and Hailsham had no difficulty in demolishing them. As for the Beaver he was received with boos and hisses, and perhaps because he was unprepared he said just what I should have wished him to say viz I dont care who is the leader so long as he accepts my policy. This gave all the point that was needed to Douglas['] observation that anyone who succeeded S.B. would have to take his orders from the Daily Express if he were to avoid the same hostility as S.B. had incurred. I think we are now safe for a while at any rate from further intrigues in the party and if S.B. will only play up and follow good advice our position ought steadily to improve.

I am having a strenuous time still for I had to address the Ladies Carlton on Friday & though there were no reporters I had of course to prepare the speech. I had planned to go to Birmingham for the week end but when on Austen's suggestion I undertook to move the official amendment to the Address I felt it necessary to stay here and I have spent most of today and yesterday in slaving away at my speech. I have got it laid out to my satisfaction now but I shall have to do a good deal more polishing and memorising if I am to deliver it effectively. I have another address to make to a political club on Wednesday, also not reported and an incredible number of dinners luncheons deputations and interviews this week. Its as bad as being in office.

...

8 November 1930
37 Eaton Square, SW1

My dear Ida,

... I have not had the "flue" ... I have been working for two months at high pressure and had become conscious that my reserves were getting low. This

---

[57] For the first time in eight years, Labour's municipal advance was halted with a net loss of sixty-five seats. Chamberlain declared it proof of 'Labour's complete failure to cope with the distress under which the country is now suffering'.

week ... was the climax, but I thought I should get through it all right. And so I should have done if I had not picked up a cold on Monday and aggravated it by dining out three nights in succession. ... So when S.B. & Bobby Monsell ... urged me to cut the division on the Education Bill and go to bed I was very glad to follow their advice. ... But ... today I am much better. Tomorrow I shall get up and on Monday I shall enjoy my usual robustious health.

This morning we enacted the last moments of Wolfe. Annie rushed into my room crying They run! (or words to that effect). Rousing himself from his lethargy the dying hero faintly asked Who run? "The Daily Express"! ["]Then I die happy" and unfolding my paper I attacked a breakfast which would have killed anyone whose constitution had been less seriously undermined by prolonged abstinence from food than mine.

To you who dont read the Express this is hardly intelligible so I must explain that its leading article begins by congratulating *Mr Baldwin the Central Office* and the Conservative party upon the Shipley election.[58] And after a handsome admission that the contest was fought on safeguarding with food taxes in the background it concludes by declaring that the victors of South Paddington embrace the victors of Shipley in one general osculatory triumph! To those who have been reading the Express and the Evening Standard daily this article must have come as a bewildering surprise: to the ardent Crusader it must have produced the sensation of a douche of ice cold water. I imagine the disciples asking themselves in doubt & fear "What has come to the Son of Kish? Is Saul also among the prophets"?

To initiate you into the mystery I must go back to S.B.'s famous letter to the Beaver. I think I told you then or soon afterwards that in my opinion he was beaten for the differences in policy had been whittled away till there was too little ground left for him to fight upon. And though he had won S. Paddington I felt that he could get no satisfaction out of a victory which was useless in itself and was unlikely to be repeated. I felt therefore that presently I should find some overture being put forward, and I was not surprised when Sir Abe Bailey[59] telephoned to me on Tuesday asking whether I would dine at his house next day to meet the Beaver and saying that he was sure everything could be settled.

You will wonder what Abe Bailey had to do with it. I have only met him occasionally at big dinners and hardly knew him till a week or so ago when he asked me to lunch with him alone. He was very confidential & rather complimentary but I was not quite sure why he had asked me. He said he had supported all parties in turn according to what he considered to be the national

---

[58] Shipley by-election, 6 November 1930. The Conservatives overturned a Labour majority of 4961 on a 7.6 per cent swing to win a seat held by Labour in 1923, 1924 and 1929. Labour regained it in 1935.

[59] Abe Bailey (1863–1940). A major Transvaal mine-owner. Member of Cape (1902–5), Transvaal (1907–10) and Union of South Africa (1915–24) Assemblies. Knighted 1911. Created Bart 1919.

interest. I think he gave the Labour Party a handsome donation at the last election, but he declared his intention of helping us next time, and he pressed upon me his desire to assist us in other than financial ways at any time. Since then he had sent me brief notes containing extremely confidential (and not always correct) information about the movements and intentions both of the R.-B. combination and the Government. I have heard him described as a born intriguer. He doesnt seem to me to deserve quite such a disagreeable description but he is one of those people who love to feel that they are pulling the wires and making the puppets dance and I believe that his aims are quite genuinely to promote national & Imperial interests. He is immensely rich and keeps in pretty close touch with a great many influential people. It was probably because he had come to the conclusion that the chairman of the Conservative Party was becoming an influential person that he decided to improve his acquaintance and I was included in a vast company of between 30 and 40 men whom he invited to dine at his house to meet Herzog[60] and Havenga[61] on Tuesday.

This was the man who put himself forward as the go-between. I received the advance stiffly. I was speaking at St Stephens Club at a dinner; would not some other day do just as well. Abe replied that he was off to S. Africa on Friday & it was imperative that the settlement should take place before he left. Finally I said I would go after my meeting at 10.30.

I didnt actually succeed in reaching his house till 10.45; I didn't leave it till 12.30 a.m. I hadnt seen Max since just before the Bromley election and this was a New Max whom I had never seen before. All his volubility and assurance had gone. He was slow, hesitating, speaking in a subdued voice, embarrassed and at times almost humble in manner. I on my side was just as sticky as I could be for the first hour. I would hardly open my mouth and made not the slightest effort to break the long & awkward pauses in the conversation. When Abe offered to leave us to ourselves I begged him to stay. At last the Bromley election was mentioned & then I opened up and told Max what I thought of his double faced behaviour. He protested and tried to evade the issue but in the end he could only assert feebly that he *thought* he had told me everything. But I said bitterly that I had had the shock of my life and I wasn't having any more like that.

At last as it was getting late and I wanted to get to bed I asked what he had to propose. He made a long rambling story in which Rothermere & a seat for Esmond came in again. But I said I stood where I did on that. Reconciliation must come first & must begin with R. & B. Esmond might come after. I would

---

[60] Dr General James Barry Munnik Hertzog (1866–1942). South African soldier and politician. Cabinet Minister 1910–12 when resigned to establish National Party. Prime Minister 1924–39; Minister of Native Affairs 1924–29; Minister of External Affairs 1929–39.

[61] Nicolaas Christian Havenga (1882–1957). South African attorney and Nationalist, later Afrikaner politician. Member, South African Assembly from 1915. Minister of Finance 1924–39 and 1948–53; Leader of Afrikaner Party 1939–48 before rejoining Nationalists.

pledge myself to nothing save that if reconciliation were effected I would endeavour to find a seat for Esmond but I must be sole judge of place and time. Max did not protest but said he would go and see the Rothermere brood, that he was prepared to make great sacrifices, that he wanted nothing for himself not even the saving of his face provided only that the policy he cared for was achieved. All which may be considered to represent accurately the mood *of the moment.*

Next morning the busy Abe was round to see me and to assure me that Max meant business. I told him that the danger point was Rothermere and the real question was what would Max do if R. refused to play. Since then he has bombarded me with notes and telegrams even from the steamer assuring me that Max will not let any man stand in his way this time. The article in the Express appears to bear out his assurances.

I dont understand either why the Times crabbed my speech on Monday, but I am sure it did not represent the feeling in the House where I learned that a number of the younger men said it was the best I had ever made. It was I think open to the reverse criticism that for a vote of censure it devoted too much space to an examination of our own policy. But I did this on purpose in order to give our people material for speeches in the country and from the comments made to me afterwards it was evident that they much appreciated it from that point of view. Ramsay's winding up speech was one of the worst I have heard him make; he was much interrupted, though not any more than we used to be, and was so much upset by it that he called out "Swine" to us – a little undignified for a Prime Minister!

...

15 November 1930
Chevening, Sevenoaks, Kent

My dear Hilda,

It was really very good of you to write in the circumstances, but your weekly letter is such an institution that I miss it very much if it doesn't come and I like always to keep in touch with your doings.

Your account of Lady Clinton's[62] activities simply takes one's breath away. How indeed can any human being survive such a tale of responsibilities let alone the physical strain. And the mere recital of them emphasises the tragedy that such people will not recur in the new generations. Our mad system of taxation is rapidly destroying the great landed possessions and the great country houses with the whole semi-feudal system that revolves round them. No doubt the

---

[62] Lady Jane Grey McDonnell (?–1953). Daughter of Earl of Antrim. Married 21st Baron Clinton 1886.

social services will replace the Lady Bountifuls and on the average will produce something much more efficient, but it cant replace the personal relations.

...

... On Thursday I had arranged to pick up S.B. in my car and take him to a theatre where we were to see a "talkie" in which the actor George Arliss[63] made up as Disraeli delivers a series of extracts from his speeches. The idea was that S.B should do an introductory speech and then say also a few words at the end and in this condition the film would go round with our touring vans and also be exhibited at picture houses. However when I got to Brook St. instead of S.B. coming out I was asked to go in and found him sitting in a chair with a stick by his side awaiting the doctor having apparently strained a ligament in his foot during his sleep. Any ordinary mortal would have telephoned to save my going round to his house but the poetic temperament does not work that way and after a short talk I went on to see the film by myself, S.B. has not of course done his part yet but the Disraeli is really quite extraordinarily good and must be most popular. ...

Later on I attended a luncheon given by Camrose but arranged by the Research Dept. to put Scullin[64] in touch with representatives of the party. He had expressed a strong desire to meet Baldwin or myself. S.B. had undertaken to go; I had another luncheon engagement but threw it over as I felt no confidence that S.B. would ever get on to business subjects. I was very glad (and so was Camrose) that I went. S.B. would only make jokes about his leg and couldn't be got into general conversation. But I sat between Scullin and ... his Minister of Trade & Commerce and I had a good talk with them both about what they wanted and what they were prepared to give us. I thought the conversation quite satisfactory. They understand our difficulties – the quota suits them very well for wheat – they wont be too difficult about meat – they want help for butter & fruits – and they are fully prepared to take industry by industry and consider how the Australian market shall be shared between the local manufacturer & the British manufacturer to the exclusion of the foreigner. I have no doubt that we could soon fix up a treaty with them. During the same afternoon I went to Bennetts[65] farewell reception and had a few words with him. He wasnt able to get the other Dominions to join him in the statement he wanted to make condemning the Macdonald [sic] Government root and branch but before joining in the general

---

[63] George Arliss (1868–1946). English actor famous for his portrayal of historical characters. Made his reputation in USA 1901–23 in plays like *Disraeli* (1911); won an Academy Award for *Disraeli* (1929).

[64] James Henry Scullin (1876–1953). Australian politician. Labour member, House of Representatives 1910–13 and 1922–35. Leader of Federal Labour Party 1928–35; Prime Minister 1929–31.

[65] Richard Bedford Bennett (1870–1947). Canadian barrister, businessman and Conservative politician. Member, Federal Parliament 1911–17, 1925–38. Minister of Justice 1921 and 1926; Leader, Conservative Party 1927–38; Prime Minister 1930–35. Created Viscount Bennett 1941.

statement which has since been published he wished to be assured that he would not by doing so in any way embarrass us (the Conservative Party.) Altogether I think we have made good use of our opportunities of making contact with the Dominions and I hope to get the results embodied in a report which will remain on record among our files. It is an immense comfort to my orderly mind to have the Research Department in existence. I wish I knew a rich man who would give it a whacking big sum to endow it.

On Friday I sat with S.B. to receive the N.F.U. in fulfilment of a promise I extracted from him last July. Unfortunately he is in a curiously nervous state just now which causes him to talk incessantly and at terrific speed. Instead of drawing the N.F.U. therefore as I had wanted to do he insisted on talking to them. Even when I seized any chance to ask them questions he took the answer out of their mouths and though he was thoroughly pleased with the interview and believed he had firmly established himself in their affections I venture to say that he never found out what was in their minds. However though I was very disappointed it was better than nothing and I must leave it at that. Fortunately the N.F.U. are very cross with Addison.

...

I dont know how Annie struck you but I have no doubt that she is very much better than she was last summer. Her nerves are ever so much quieter and many of the symptoms of mental disturbance which were so distressing have disappeared. Moreover although occasionally she exclaims at the cramping of her life by this inability to go out with me, she is on the whole worrying very little even about family matters which might be expected to worry her a great deal. Which reminds me that Enid has now definitely separated from her husband and says she wont go back to him. ... So far as I can make out neither of them is prepared to make any sacrifice to meet the other. Each wants to live their own selfish life and prefers to live it alone. ... It all seems to me very deplorable and an illustration of the modern idea which calls itself "freedom to live its own life" but which I call "utter selfishness". ...

...

22 November 1930
Croxton Park, St Neots

My dear Ida,

...

I have had a busy and on the whole a satisfactory week. On Monday I dined with W. Brass to meet half a dozen young M.P.'s whom I did not know. This is about the 5th dinner of the kind and though it was less agreeable than the others chiefly owing to the bad manners of one Irishman, I still think it was very useful. It is surprising how much this young members [sic] think of any attention from a front bench man and how much, conversely, they resent the lack of it. There is no doubt that S.B. has done himself no end of harm by his aloofness. I wrote a note to Edward Stanley to congratulate him on a speech he had made in the House. Last Tuesday we lunched with him to meet the Nawab of Bhopal[66] and Lady Stanley repeated all I had written to Annie and told me that Edward would stand on his head for me. I was so impressed with the effect that I wrote to Eddie Winterton[67] to congratulate him on his West African articles and I had a reply just overflowing with gratitude & satisfaction. What people never realise is that many of us dont ever think of ourselves as "great men" & cannot imagine that any one else does. I lunched with "Max" on Friday of which more anon – and he told me that when I accepted the P.M.G.-ship in 1922, Bonar Law considered it a tremendous coup to have secured me but was surprised that I had not asked for a more important post. And I, at the time when Leo brought me the message, thought that to be head of a department as so much beyond my measure that I begged to be given an Under Secretaryship instead!

...

On Wednesday I made my speech in the City of which no doubt you saw a report in the press. It went off extremely well. The meeting was crowded – they had to turn many away – and when I sat down the applause went on for about a couple of minutes. McKenna came up to shake hands and congratulate me on a most interesting speech and Felix Schuster[68] to say how warmly he agreed with me and to recall how Father had told him to "think Imperially". Several people were particularly impressed with my answer to the Beaverbrook questioner. They could not think what I should say but they felt that my reply had neatly turned him over and yet had left the door open to a friendly gesture.

...

On Thursday I lunched with Camrose who is beginning to think of starting an evening paper in London a proceeding which I did my best to encourage as being likely to keep my volatile friend in order. That evening Sir E. Grigg came to dinner and gave me a very interesting account of a conversation he had had with Ll.G. I confess I discount it a little because I suspect that wily Welshman of having said some things to him *avec intention*. However the gist of his remarks

---

[66] Hamidullah Khan, Nawab of Bhopal (1894–1960). President, Board of Municipality of Bhopal 1915–16; Chief Secretary to his mother's government 1916–22; member of her law and finance departments 1922–26. Succeeded mother as Nawab 1926. Chancellor, Chamber of Indian Princes 1931–32 and 1944–47.

[67] Edward Turnour Winterton (1883–1962). Conservative MP for Horsham 1904–51. PPS to Financial Secretary, Admiralty 1903–5; Under-Secretary, India 1922–24 and 1924–29; Chancellor, Duchy of Lancaster 1937–39 (member of Cabinet from March 1938); Paymaster-General 1939; Father of the House 1945–51. Styled Viscount Winterton until succeeded father to Irish peerage as 6th Earl of Winterton 1907; created Baron Turnour 1952.

[68] Felix Schuster (1854–1936). Banker. Member, Council of India 1906–16; Deputy Chairman, Committee of London Clearing Bankers 1904–13 and 1924; Chairman 1913–15 and 1925. Created Bart 1906.

was that he was not going to lead his little army to destruction i.e. to a General Election, but that he was profoundly anxious about the destinies of the country and the Empire under the present Government. His own inclination would be to join with Conservatives if only they would consent. And his terms were really very moderate. Provided that a tax on wheat were avoided ⅘ of the Liberal Party could be steered (under wise & careful leadership) into the acceptance of a moderate protective tariff including food taxes. R.M. if he resigned would probably not dissolve but pass the buck to S.B. who would immediately be embarrassed by the need of forming a Cabinet with the Old Gang. Really S.B. had not got the men to pull the country through 10 years of resolute government. He himself no longer wanted office – he was old and tired – but he *would* like to see one or two of his friends, *particularly Simon*, (this must have been meant for me) taking a share in administration. And then of course there must be a clear understanding that before going to the country a little measure of electoral reform, say p.r. in the big towns, would be put through Parliament.

The whole argument rests on the assumption that the continued existence of the Liberal Party is a national interest and that a coalition between Libs. & Cons. would be able to hold the fort for at least ten years. I doubt if either of these assumptions could be sustained, but the talk interested me and if S.B. has no objection I am rather inclined to get hold of Simon & find how the situation appears to him. I am not disposed to give electoral reform but if you said "a deal on seats" I might see something in it.

On Monday I saw Horne in the Lobby and he asked if I had heard anything from Max. He then said that Max had not been well and moreover that he was getting restless. He thought it would be a very good thing if I would go and see him. I didn't feel inclined to do that, but I wrote a brief note saying I was sorry to hear that he was ill and no doubt this was why he hadn't written to me. The result was an invitation to lunch which I accepted and I had 1½ hr tête-a-tête with him on Friday. He was extremely forthcoming and told me a lot of interesting incidents in connection with Bonar; I have told you one already. Another was that when Bonar had decided to go he was worrying very much about his successor and said to Max that "if N.C. had had a little more Parliamentary experience he would be the man, for he had the stuff in him". Apparently he never thought of the possibility of S.B. until he heard that the King had sent for him on A.J.B.'s advice.

More than an hour passed before Max got anywhere near business. Indeed like his prototype he appeared "unaccountably shy" & it was really only in the last five minutes that I got anything clinched. Put briefly it amounts to this. Max is still very anxious to get Rothermere in and thinks it may be managed. But he has given up all hope of working through Esmond who is not sufficiently interested in politics to play the part his father wished to give him. Nor is it any use to bring S.B. & Rothermere together. It has all got to be worked through me, but if R. really did refuse to participate in a reasonable plan Max will feel that he is released from all obligations towards him. All he wants now is to find some means of healing the breach without too great loss of face, so as to bring in as many Empire Crusaders as possible and then work for an early election, but it was made pretty clear that all was dependent on faith in my determination to carry the policy through. No confidence is felt in S.B. except insofar as it is felt that I can get him to do what I want. In the end we arranged that I shall draft a new letter from S.B. to Max in which S.B. will repeat what he said in his last & make a fresh appeal for cooperation. Max will draft a reply in which he will nobly accept the olive branch and call upon the Crusaders to remember that policy, not leaders, is what they care for. When these drafts are mutually agreed on R. Max and I are to lunch together and they are to be disclosed to R. If we can get him to say he approves they will immediately be published. If not I suppose Max and I will have to consider what he is to do. You will observe that S.B.'s assent is assumed, but as he is not asked to change anything this time all he really gives is the initiative in writing to Max. No doubt he will be criticised by some for this but as his letter wont be published unless we are sure of its acceptance I dont see that he can be hurt.

It looks as though I had brought off the great achievement "with honour". But people's memories are short. Most of them wont know that I did it and those who do know will forget. Still I shall have my own quiet satisfaction in my consciousness that I have justified my decision to take that Chairmanship.

...

5 December 1930
Westbourne

My dear Ida,

... I had a long talk with Simon on Monday & another with Reading[69] on Tuesday. The conclusions I drew were (1) that Simon wouldn't worry about tariffs if he could get the Government out (2) that he would join a Conservative Administration if asked, should R.M. not dissolve but advise the King to send for S.B. (3) that neither he nor Reading knew what L.G. was up to (4) that both of them would feel things easier if we were able to promise P.R. in the big towns, but failing that they were ready to talk about seats (5) that Simon was not going to try and oust L.G. from the leadership, but that he was confident that a large number of Liberals in the country were in agreement with his views.

The announcement about the Electoral Reform Bill on Thursday, evidently by arrangement with Herbert Samuel, was a surprise and every one is wondering

[69] Rufus Daniel Isaacs (1860–1935). Liberal MP for Reading 1903–13. Solicitor-General 1910; Attorney-General 1910–13; Lord Chief Justice 1913–21; Ambassador to Washington 1918–19; Viceroy of India 1921–26; Foreign Secretary 1931. Knighted 1910. Created Baron Reading 1914, Viscount 1916, Earl 1917 and Marquess of Reading 1926.

what it means. W. Graham[70] told a friend of mine that they had done a deal but he evidently did not know what it was. Max says he is sure they have made an arrangement to which Samuel and L.G. are parties, he admits that the Lib. party have not been consulted but believes that L.G. can control them sufficiently to make them accept his directions. I myself belief that the deal is of the sketchiest description. I know Samuel and Henderson have been working for it very earnestly but it was definitely turned down a little while ago by the Liberal Parliamentary Party. I suspect that thereupon Samuel, who is believed by some of his colleagues to be working either for the Viceroyalty or for a place in the next Labour Government, went to Henderson and said Produce the best thing you can in electoral reform and that will show you mean business. Dont make your Trade Disputes Bill too drastic and L.G. & I will work like beavers to keep you in. Henderson, who keeps hoping that if he can only hang on, trade must revive, would jump at any chance of winning Liberal support. The Goat on the other hand had a more difficult game to play. I suspect that he is humbugging the Govt and is only kidding them on in the hope of putting pressure on us to give him better terms still, which is his real object. To keep his mixed team sweet he had to assert his independence and say rude things to everybody, but he left the impression of a deal (for our benefit) and yet kept the door open by his statement that some things might even make him overrule his fear & hatred of Protection. You would think that even he would blush to tell such egregious lies but he really does not know what truth is. I said to Reading (basing myself on what Grigg had told me) that I did not anticipate that L.G. would make any trouble about tariffs if we agreed to come to an arrangement on expelling the Govt. He laughed & said that he thought L.G. would go further in that direction than anyone in his party!

I had an interesting talk with Max yesterday. The reason he gave for not accepting my letter was that it would not be the same thing as one from S.B. but behind that I think was the feeling that if he had accepted it he would himself soon sink into insignificance and Empire Free Trade would be seen to have failed. Accordingly he propounded a new idea. He wraps up his ideas in such a way that it needs a lot of cross-examination to dig them out and generally I dont seize the full significance of them until I have thought them over afterwards. Consequently I must put his new plan in my words not in his, and indicate the curiously mixed motives which have induced him to put it forward.

"Empire Free Trade" has always been an elastic phrase and Max has used it to cover anything that he thought might be useful. Thus in S. Paddington it merely meant Hands across the seas; blood is thicker than water; Empire Free Trade means prosperity for the country. In Norfolk however it meant taxation of

---

[70] William Graham (1887–1932). Journalist 1905–18. Labour MP for Edinburgh Central 1918–31. Financial Secretary, Treasury 1924; Chairman, Public Accounts Committee 1924–29; President, Board of Trade 1929–31.

foreign agricultural products under cover of reciprocal trade relations with the Empire. When it was pointed out that a tariff on wheat would not save the farmer from Russian dumping or even from Canadian competition it appeared that Empire Free Trade meant a guaranteed price for wheat. And a little later it was extended to mean protection for all agricultural products irrespective of the Empire.

This interpretation is only used in agricultural areas but it is so loudly applauded there that Max has convinced himself that it would go down anywhere and his proposal to me was, Let Baldwin announce casually that when he asks for the free hand that means not only freedom to negotiate with the Dominions but freedom to do whatever seems best to restore our greatest industry to prosperity. Then let him write to me calling upon me to support his party loyally and devotedly and I will answer with corresponding enthusiasm. Incidentally, I believe I can secure the invaluable support of the Daily Mail. Finally, turn over to me the Liberal agricultural seats and I will raise such hell there that I shall detach them from L.G. and either bring them in to our support or beat them out of the field.

If this little plan were to come off Max would still maintain the heroic rôle. Instead of sinking into the background he would be represented by the Express as having pulled the Conservative Party after his policy & he would appear as the Prince Rupert of our army galloping over the enemy on our flanks.

If I took the personal view only I should resent this device for exalting himself. But mixed up with it is a genuine conviction that the policy is right and a genuine desire to see it carried out. *And I share the conviction and the desire*. In fact, I have always chafed at the idea that you might tax a mans boots and clothes, put up his rent, increase the cost of his fuel, but that never never must you tax agricultural imports lest his food should cost him more. I believe that the greatest market for industry is to be found in agriculture and I dont believe you can help agriculture effectively unless you control imports. Therefore I told Max that I would try and get him what he wanted, but it will take a bit of doing. If I were even to suggest it to S.B. he would go off the deep end at once & so would the C.O. Yet I believe that if it were boldly agreed with conviction we might well get away with it in the present state of the country. I had a confidential talk with Edwards this morning. He believes that if we had an election now we could sweep the decks in Birmingham and he tells me that protection for agriculture so far from hurting us would be very popular here. Of course Birmingham is ahead of the North there; still I hardly expected Edwards to say so much.

...

14 December 1930
37 Eaton Square, SW1

My dear Hilda,

I am delighted to find from your letter that it was you who sent me Orwin's[71] book ... As a matter of fact I did read it a fortnight ago while in Birmingham and found it extraordinarily interesting. After going through it I read the Liberal pamphlet on How to tackle unemployment and then the Government Bill on Land Settlement & the Debate on the Second Reading. It was clear enough that the Govt had taken Orwin's ideals holus bolus and that the Liberals had also got much from them though as the large scale specialisation and mechanisation plans would rather increase unemployment than the reverse they practically dropped that part out. I fancy our people are all against demonstration farms and largely against the small holdings extension. I am myself in favour of the latter but I do not like naming 100000 or any number as I expect the process would be slow if it were to be carried out carefully.

With regard to your two observations I think it would be very difficult to pay travelling exes. The area Comees are very large – I think the W. Midlands is about 120 and the exes would be heavy. And I am unwilling to saddle the C.O. with any further expenditure as it is very short of funds and the Nat. Union is really a separate body though we pay the Secretary.

As to the speeches of the agent & candidate I dont see what we can do. We circulate literature which gives the policy but we cannot edit the speeches of individuals. I don't think the cases you give are really typical, but I have no doubt that the general woolliness about policy which prevailed until September has made people less inclined to talk about it.

Max has started a new campaign for Empire Free Trade which is now explained to mean Protection for Agriculture. He has not yet shown his hand but if he is going to begin the old game of directing his attack against *Conservative* candidates threatening to run an "Empire Crusader" unless they toe the line I shall give him up in despair. If he confines himself to Liberal candidates it will be a different matter.

Apparently L.G. did get away with it but I see Simon is taking his own line – and I fancy we shall presently see him forming an independent group which will work with us.

...

---

[71] Charles Stewart Orwin (1876–1955). Lecturer, South East Agricultural College 1903–6; Agent for Turnor Estates 1906–13; Director, Agricultural Economics Research Institute, Oxford 1913–45; member of various agricultural and food committees and author of many related works including *The Future of Farming* (1930).

23 December 1930
Westbourne

My dear Ida,

...

Politics got very nauseating again before the House rose and I was thoroughly fed up with my Party who do nothing but grouse all the time. I heard no more from Simon or Reading and it is very difficult to judge from Lloyd George's last speech what he really means to do. I fancy he will watch how public opinion reacts to the T.U. bill and be guided by that; but I suspect he will discover sufficient reasons for advising his people to vote for the Second Reading and pretend to be very anxious to amend it in Committee. It still looks to me as if we should have an election next year and not very late either, but it is difficult to say how it is going to come. I am plotting to bully Liberal M.P.'s over the T.U. Bill as I believe that is the vulnerable point. They arent called "the Portuguese" for nothing.

...

5

1931
'Well, Well, it's a Funny World':
Financial Crisis and the National Government

3 January 1931
Westbourne

My dear Hilda,

...

Annie succeeded, though with some doubts & anxieties in getting to Swinton but had to spend most of her time in bed. Still she always enjoys her visits there and did not regret the journey. There was a rather unexciting party but good shooting ... I find I shall have to curtail my visit to the Bridgemans and go to London on Tuesday returning next day for functions here. It is Indian affairs that are taking me up but I shant be sorry to have a few hours at the office as there is a "bye" in East Bristol and other urgent matters to attend to.

... I must lend you Winston's book[1] if you haven't read it already. I dont know how reliable it is for facts but it is certainly vastly entertaining – the best he has done yet I think.

...

Politics are not exhilarating, but more than ever it looks doubtful if the government can survive long. If they do go out & we come in our troubles will begin. They will have left us a damnosa hereditas and I dont look forward to any share I may have in clearing up the mess. Austen writes in some alarm about my letter to the Times but he seems to have thought I had pledged myself to reduce taxation instead of expenditure – two very different things.

...

17 January 1931
Westbourne

My dear Hilda,

...

S.B. came on Wednesday and made a very good speech to the Engineering Employers dinner to which I accompanied him. ... I had had a useful luncheon

---

[1] Churchill's volume of *My Early Life* covering his first twenty-six years to 1901 was published on 20 October 1930.

with the Midland Union the same day at which I delivered a speech and after a sort of general discussion replied to the criticisms and suggestions. When you are dealing with chairmen of constituency associations and other workers that is always a valuable method and enables me to clear up many difficulties.

...

25 January 1931
Westbourne

My dear Ida,

...

I think every one would agree that the Govt have had a bad week. The defeat on the Education Bill was unexpected up to the last moment and though the P.M. had evidently considered his action it if should occur and decided to ignore it, no Government likes being humiliated by its own supporters and none could stand many repetitions of such an occurrence. The attitude of the Liberals over the T.U. Bill is therefore the more disappointing to the Government because it follows immediately after the defeat and because it shows what some of us have always maintained that Ll.G. can make bargains but cannot deliver the goods. I still think they will scrape through their second reading but for all practical purposes their bill is dead & before very long the corpse will begin to stink.

I am to wind up for the opposition on Wednesday. My speech must to a large extent depend on the course of the debate and in particular on Simon's speech but the line I am thinking of is to assert what seems to me the essential thing namely that the Bill is a Bill to legalise the General Strike. I believe that is what the country will be chiefly interested in and the evasions of the Government speakers indicate that in their view it is the vulnerable spot.

I thought the Attorney General's speech a very clever piece of advocacy and it greatly pleased the Socialists who cheered him for a long time when he sat down. I whispered to S.B. that they were astonished to find what a plausible case could be made for so bad a bill, whereupon he got up and said that their cheers showed only too clearly that his supporters felt he had made out a very plausible case!

On the legalising of the General Strike the A.G.'s argument appeared to me to be that in his opinion it was legal before we made it illegal and that his clause would make it legal again. But that did not matter because the right way of dealing with General Strikes was not to make them illegal but to wait until they occurred and then get emergency powers to control them. If no one else does it first I shall put this interpretation on his speech & argue that the essential thing is to prevent such strikes not to cure them, and that on such a vital question abstention from recording any opinion is a shirking of responsibility which will not easily be forgiven by the country. Evidently Liberals hope to catch Simon by adopting his alternative definition of an illegal strike, moved by him as an amendment to our 1927 Bill. But I imagine he will say It was one thing to substitute that amendment for a new proposal, it is quite another to tear up the existing law and so introduce fresh uncertainties into the industrial situation. I don't suppose I shall be reported as I shall speak late, but it will be an exciting evening. In the meantime I suppose I shall have to spend many weary hours on the bench listening to a debate most of which will be terribly dull. It is amusing that the speakers from our front bench having been chosen by a committee and not including Winston, he has nevertheless insisted on speaking. He was not going to let a debate of that importance go by without coming into the picture.

When it is all over I am having a meeting of my office committee and that will be probably its last meeting except for the approval of the report. I have got the structure settled in my mind during the recess and have since seen all the members but one individually so that I think the ground is prepared for a unanimous decision. But if a General Election is coming very soon I shall have to wait till it is over before I carry out the alterations and as it is essential that I should not leave them to someone else I am providing for an office of Deputy Chairman to be filled on the recommendation of the Chairman when required and for a definite term only. This would allow me to remain Chairman and exercise a general supervision even though in office.

...

31 January 1931
Westbourne

My dear Hilda,

... I wrote to Hartington[2] to say that in the present precarious condition of politics it was impossible for me to think of going away and he sadly recognised the justice of my views. But since then the corrupt bargain between Liberals and Socialists has been drawn closer and it is evident that an election is no longer imminent. ...

Of course my speech would not in any case have been commented on in the press but Winstons brilliant performance was bound to fill the stage. As an entertainment it was superb, and perhaps as good as anything that even he has yet done in that line. I cannot help suspecting that it was deliberately prepared as a preliminary to his break with S.B. and his entry upon his India campaign. If so, it was skilfully conceived and carried out with admirable verve and dash. It set every one talking about him and raised his prestige to a higher level than

---

[2] Edward William Spencer Cavendish (1895–1950). Conservative MP for West Derbyshire 1923–38. Member, British delegation to Paris Peace Conference 1919; Under-Secretary for Dominions 1936–40, for India and Burma 1940–43 and for Colonies 1943–45. Styled Marquess of Hartington 1908–38; succeeded as 10th Duke of Devonshire 1938.

ever. But considered as an attack on the Bill, I do not think it was specially helpful to us or damaging to the Socialists. Though restive at his description of the privileges of Trade Unions the Government supporters soon forgot their irritation in their enjoyment of his banter and I am sure their feeling at the end was not that they had suffered any injury but that they had had one of the best laughs they had enjoyed for a long time. I felt that my task was not rendered any easier but nevertheless I was on the whole well satisfied with my speech and though I always discount the compliments one receives because the House is so amazingly generous on these occasions I believe our people were very pleased and did feel that I had got home. The debate over the three days was really a very interesting one. It was clear to me from the first that the weak point was the legalising of the General Strike. The persistent evasions on this question showed where we had to keep on hammering and I was like every one else amazed when at the eleventh hour the Solr General[3] answered the question in the opposite sense to what I believed was the view of the Attorney-General. I therefore demanded that Thomas should tell us whether or not the Solr General's view expressed the intentions of the Cabinet, but with his usual adroitness he managed to speak for nearly forty minutes without getting near the Bill and by damning lawyers all round he threw doubt on his Solr without actually contradicting him or disowning him in particular. In private conversation with me the next day he gave me an amusing if rather lurid account of the affair. "It was d—d awkward you see", he said. "You kep' on askin' those b— questions and I kep' lookin' at the b— clock. Mac says you aint goin' to answer Jim, and I says, not a b— answer". I enquired whether Cripps had consulted his colleagues before making his statement. "Not a b— one" says Jimmie. "They come runnin' in to my room and says Look 'ere what Cripps 'as said. So I says Oh 'ell! I shall just 'ave to play b— 'ell with the lawyers"! Today I see that Ramsay, no doubt anxious to reassure the T.U.C., has said right out that the General Strike was not a political strike and therefore ought not to be made illegal. But then what becomes of Herbert Samuel, who said at Darwen that no momentous question of principle was involved, because all parties were agreed that the General Strike must be made illegal and that that was the effect of the Bill.

I am considering whether I wont start a poster campaign in Liberal constituencies calling attention to the fact that Liberals are selling the country for party purposes. I cant help thinking that a direct attack of that kind, especially in seats like Darwen where the Liberal hold is precarious would make the member very uncomfortable about voting with the Government.

---

[3] (Richard) Stafford Cripps (1889–1952). Labour MP for Bristol East 1931–50 and Bristol South-East 1950. Solicitor-General 1930–31; British Ambassador, Moscow 1940–42; Lord Privy Seal 1942; Minister of Aircraft Production 1942–45; President, Board of Trade 1945–47; Minister of Economic Affairs 1947; Chancellor of Exchequer 1947–50. Knighted 1930.

I agree with your criticisms on the Baldwin Churchill correspondence[4] but I believe the explanation is that B. never thought it would be published. Winston certainly said nothing about publication and S.B. did not show his reply to anyone. I had no idea that it was going any further till the Press began to ask me about it and then I learned that it was Winston who had asked for its publication, no doubt again with a view to his Manchester speech. Whether he intended it or not I can see quite well that the effect of his action is going to be very damaging to S.B.'s position. Sam Hoare dined with S.B. on the night of Winston's India speech in the House in order to coach him in his reply. Afterwards he told me that S.B. had conducted himself so clumsily that he had stirred up all our die-hards who had been satisfied with his own account of our official position but felt that S.B. had departed from it as much on one side as Winston had on the other. I am afraid the explanation is that S.B. has never taken the trouble to master the situation and that in his anxiety to dissociate himself from reaction he laid all the emphasis on the advance he would like to make and slurred over the safeguards without which no advance ought to be made. Yesterday I had all our area agents up in conference to consider the line to be taken over a General Election and one of the most intelligent of the women told Gower afterwards that the feeling against S.B. in Lancashire was terrible. I am certain it will be much worse after Winston's speech and of course the 2 Press Lords have seen their opportunity and are going to make the most of it. The longer an election is delayed the more difficult it is going to be to keep the party behind the leader. But all the same I am profoundly thankful that we are rid of Winston, for obviously he could not now be included in another Conservative Cabinet if one were formed.

I have at last completed my scheme for the organisation of the C.O. It has not come out in the form I had originally contemplated, but I am pretty well satisfied that I have devised a practical scheme which will add greatly to the efficiency of the machine and will lead to great economy also. By seeing each member of the Committee separately I have got a unanimous concurrence and a report is now being drawn up which will place our conclusions on record. If no Election comes I shall proceed to carry it out at once but in the contrary event it would have to be postponed for a time. In any case however it is clear that I must myself see it started and in working order and accordingly I am creating a new office of Deputy Chairman to be filled if I enter a Government. This would allow me to delegate most of the work I am doing now but would keep me available to control developments until I can be sure that the thing will run of itself. In the meantime I am the target for the Beaver and his friends but they wont find it as easy to dislodge me as David! though they may to some extent undermine my popularity. Ça m'est bien égal.

---

[4] On 27 January 1931 Churchill formalised the rift over India by resigning from the Business Committee. Baldwin's reply next day agreed the decision was 'correct in the circumstances'. Churchill spoke to the Indian Empire Society at Manchester's Free Trade Hall on 30 January.

... A. is spending the day in bed and Dorothy is with Hazel Wiltshire whom we don't much like but whose company is we think better for her just now than that of Mr Lloyd![5]

...

8 February 1931
Westbourne

My dear Ida,

...

[Annie's] meeting was a small one of the Edgbaston women but she came back from it very happy and excited, saying that she had got back her voice and her power over her audience and making plans for further exercise of both. It is very satisfactory that she has passed this first test of the beginnings of recovery, but I shall endeavour to restrain her ardour as I fear she might easily get a set back if she presumed too much upon her strength. But she is really better. ...

I expect you have seen my correspondence with the P.M. over the Trades Disputes Bill. His letters have been very rude but I do not think he has scored as he has shown up his own dishonesty in trying to conceal the real meaning of his Bill. At any rate I have achieved my purpose for I see today that Herbert Samuel has declared at Darwen that Liberals would amend the Bill in Committee so as to make it clear that the General Strike is illegal. A little while ago in the same place he was maintaining that the Government had disclaimed any intention to make it otherwise so he has learned something.

Simon came to dine alone with me on Wednesday and was very friendly & forthcoming. But it is clear that he has not got sufficient hold even over his meagre following to unite them into a body of dissentient Liberals. He had intended to speak & vote against the Electoral Reform Bill but found that Lambert[6] meant to vote for it. So he compromised on an agreement that they should all abstain. He is however going to do a lot of speaking in the country against the Government & against the Lloyd Georgian policy of expenditure and I think he will draw a great number of Liberals to him. So I shouldn't wonder if the political situation undergoes a further change pretty soon. When the confidence of the country has gone it does not take much to upset the administration & if only we could make public the information we have got about the enormous pressure the P.M. and others have put on the railway companies to suppress the charges against Socialist M.P.'s of abusing their railway vouchers there would be

---

[5] Stephen Lloyd (1906–92). See Appendix I: 'The Chamberlain Household and Family'.

[6] George Lambert (1866–1958). Farmer and Liberal MP for South Molton 1891–1924 and 1929–45 (Liberal National from 1931). Civil Lord of Admiralty 1905–15. Chairman, Liberal Party 1919–21. Created Viscount Lambert 1945.

a pretty storm. They have withdrawn Mardy Jones[7] from the House just in time but I am told there is a much worse case which has not yet been disclosed and if we can prevent them hushing it up we shall. In any case they have got this Unemployment Insurance Commission on their backs and they have deserved it. It's not easy to see how they will escape from that dilemma.

Meanwhile I am wondering whether it would not be worth while for the Lords to pass the Electoral Reform Bill and so force an Election. It would be a bit of a gamble of course but what a sell for R.M!

The Islington story is amusing, is it not. We got Critchley's[8] election address when he stood in 1929 and found him relating how Mr Baldwin had laboured for the country for $4\frac{1}{2}$ years and you shouldn't swap horses in the middle of the stream. One can hardly believe that even London electors will vote for a man whose Master says he is out to smash the Conservative Party, and I shall be very disappointed if he does not cut a ridiculous figure. If, all the same, we lose the seat because of his intervention it may not be a bad thing, as it will certainly unite our people against the Beaver who has come out very badly on this occasion. In spite of the trumpeting and crowing of his papers I am told he is very depressed and unhappy.

Winston is busy making all the mischief he can over India, but Sam Hoare had a very good article in the Morning Post and I am going to publish it as the official statement of policy so as to try and prevent our people from being stampeded.

I have got a magnificent group of Cymbidiums in the Conservatory. They give me immense pleasure and my only regret is that there are so few people to show them to. But eventually I shall cut them and carry them up to London to exhibit when we give our swell luncheon to the Willingdons.[9]

    ...

---

[7] Thomas Isaac Mardy Jones (1879–1970). Parliamentary Agent, South Wales Miners' Federation. Labour MP for Pontypridd 1922 to February 1931; resigned when charged with illegally allowing his wife to use his MP's rail voucher. Unsuccessfully stood as Independent Labour in 1931. Staff Officer, Ministry of Supply 1942–44; Education and Welfare Officer with British forces in Middle East 1945–46.

[8] Alfred Cecil Critchley (1890–1963). Brigadier-General, Canadian Army. Unsuccessfully contested Manchester Gorton 1929 and Islington East February 1931 (the latter as an Empire Crusader). Conservative MP for Twickenham 1934–35. Director-General, BOAC 1943–46; Chairman, Skyways Ltd 1946–54.

[9] Freeman Freeman-Thomas (1866–1941). Liberal MP for Hastings 1900–1905 and Bodmin 1906–10. Lord-in-Waiting 1911–13; Governor of Bombay 1913–18 and of Madras 1919–24; Governor-General of Canada 1926–31; Viceroy of India 1931–36; Lord Warden of Cinque Ports 1936–41. Created Baron Willingdon 1910, Viscount 1924, Earl 1931, Marquess 1936.

14 February 1931
Westbourne

My dear Hilda,

...

You cant think how magnificent the Cymbidiums are. I dont believe I have ever had so much pleasure out of them as this year when I have been lucky enough to have a good many week ends at home ...

Politics are a fair mix up. I hear the Government are saying now that they have got another two years. Undoubtedly Ll.G. has very much tightened his hold on the Socialists and I am told that A. Henderson is playing up very hard for the leadership again. I believe he is one of those who are rather in favour of a closer alliance with the Libs. whereas Jimmy Thomas is against it. Herbert Samuel again wants alliance – Simon told me he considered him "a lost soul" – and he and Ll.G. seem to work together though I am told they dont love one another. All the same I still remain of the same opinion that the Govt cannot maintain themselves in office for many more months. The policy of spending will have its effect in the money market and public opinion will make itself felt in condemnation somehow or another. Mosley & Ll.G. would make an unholy combination and a dangerous one but the danger largely arises out of the weakness of our leadership and the consequent loss of confidence in our party. Every week I get more and more evidence of the spread of distrust and unless we do get an election soon it seems to me that we shall be unable to prevent an explosion.

Sunday morning. Last night A. & I attended a dance of the Harborne "Imps" and even there I had to listen to criticism of our leader's want of firmness and decision. Last Tuesday I addressed the candidates association at the Constitutional Club. It was a very good meeting and after I had spoken for $\frac{3}{4}$ hr I allowed the candidates to ask questions. One of the questions was "Why cant Mr Baldwin come out with a plain statement about India like Mr C. has made here this afternoon. That would clear away all misunderstandings". Yet I had not said anything more than we had all agreed upon, or than S.B. himself could have said. But he *will* not put any punch into his speeches and his stock is rapidly falling again.

I heard rather unpleasant accounts of Islington a little while ago, but now they seem to be better again. Luckily Critchley is hopeless on the platform and the hecklers give him a poor time though you would never suspect it from the accounts in the Express & Evening Standard. Asked what he thought of Dizz's views on Empire he observed that Disraeli was a Liberal statesman but he was afraid he did not know what his views on Empire were! He is said to be going back & the Beaver also is exciting less interest. He has got nothing new to say and cant keep it up.

Dorothy & I went to Queens Hall to hear the Lener Quartette one night this week and enjoyed ourselves very much. They played three quartettes Brahms, Beethoven & Mozart in that order. As usual the Beethoven rather overshadowed the other two but they were all very good. ...

...

I have not given incredible pleasure to five gentlemen of the C.O. who on Friday afternoon received 3 months notice to quit. I hear there is a considerable "flutter" in Palace Chambers & I suppose the trouble will begin next week. These are the tallest poppies but they are not all that will be felled by the mowing machine!

21 February 1931
Westbourne

My dear Ida,

...

I have had a pretty hot week but on the whole a useful one. On Monday I addressed the 1922 Committee in the House and afterwards answered about 20 questions on various points of policy. I heard from several of those present that members were very pleased and appreciated very much the straight & definite answers they got. On Tuesday I dined alone with Lord Camrose. The purpose of the dinner was to discuss the starting of an evening paper about which he had begun to have doubts as to whether it would be a success because of the want of faith in the party in their present leader. He said he himself had a great regard and respect for S.B. but was coming definitely to the opinion that he could never bring his party to victory. He said that if I were leader he thought confidence would come back and he as good as suggested that I should leave the C.O. which he evidently thought was standing in my way. I said that I was not yet ready to leave the C.O. unless I did so with the deliberate intention of taking S.B.'s place and that I would not entertain. He seemed disappointed but said he didn't believe S.B. could go on much longer anyhow. We got along extremely well together and before leaving I asked whether if I could get him £250000 he would go on with the paper. He said he probably would, so next day I sent for David and asked if he could help. David said he thought he knew where to find the quarter million and has gone off (very pleased at being asked) to try for it. I believe David to have real gifts for raising money – his trouble is that he doesn't know how to spend it.

On Wednesday we had a very successful lunch party to meet the Willingdons. I cant think that she will be very popular in India, she is such a terrible egoist and talks continuously about herself in a high pitched voice. He, on the other hand, has all the charm that she lacks and his talk about his job sounded wise and sensible. But his friends tell me that he lacks firmness. We shall see.

On Thursday morning I had a visit from Sir H. Frank[10] who came to tell me that though no politician his work brought him into contact with all sorts &

---

[10] Howard Frank (1871–1932). Estate agent; head of Knight, Frank & Rutley. President, Estate Agents Institute 1910–12; Governor, Royal Agricultural Society representing London Division on Council 1907–22. Knighted 1914. Created Bart 1920.

conditions of men in all parts of the country and he thought he ought to tell me that everywhere he found profound dissatisfaction with S.B.'s leadership and anxiety for a change. I asked who they wanted and he said "Mostly you". I replied that I got similar representations from others but his answer showed how impossible it was for me to make any move. He said he recognised that and thought he would write to Derby about it, to which I said Well anyhow dont show me the letter or tell me anything about it. He added that he thought both R. & B. would accept my leadership, but with their hostility to S.B. he did not see how he could lead the party to victory.

When he had gone I was told that Linlithgow[11] was waiting to see me. He took a little time before he came to the object of his visit, but finally it appeared that he thought he ought to tell me that the people he came across were all losing faith in S.B. Even in Scotland where he had stood very high, his name was going down and the question was what was to be done about it. I was one of those whose name was mentioned as his successor but more and more he found people turning to the idea that after all Hailsham might be the best man in spite of not being in the Commons. He felt that my position was prejudiced by my having taken the C.O. but he realised that I had acted deliberately, and took off his hat to me for it. I said that the difficulty about a Peer as leader was more in opposition than in office. The duties of P.M. were becoming so onerous that it was increasingly difficult for him to attend to the H. of C. and if he was to have a deputy there was a good deal to be said for his not being a member himself. Linlithgow said this was a new point to him and he thought there was a good deal in it. He left offering to help in any way he could and I promptly booked him for my Research Committee on H. of L. reform. As he is Chairman of the Independent Peers an unofficial body which has sometimes been tiresome in the past this was a useful move.

That night I dined with the Nat. Fed. of Iron & Steel Mfrs and made a very clear and explicit statement to them on the Emergency Tariff, coupling it with warnings against raising prices or delaying rationalisation. As two of them told me afterwards it was the best speech they had ever had, I felt that the evening had not been wasted. Some of these manufacturers are very suspicious and it is very desirable that they should be convinced that we really mean business.

...

Today London seems to be buzzing with sensational accounts in the Herald & the Evening News of violent turmoil over Mr Chamberlain's dismissals of staff at head-quarters. The Herald declares the office is "seething with discontent" but

---

[11] Alexander John Hope (1887–1952). Civil Lord of Admiralty 1922–24; Deputy Chairman, Conservative Party Organisation 1924–26; Chairman, Royal Commission on Indian Agriculture 1926–28 and Joint Select Committee on Indian Constitutional Reform 1933–34; Chairman, Medical Research Council 1934–36; Viceroy of India 1936–43. Styled Earl of Hopetoun 1887–1908; succeeded as 2nd Marquess of Linlithgow 1908.

my impression is that the public will only say "I thought he'd be getting at them soon. And high time too!" I have I fancy rather queered their pitch by telling the 1922 Committee about the reorganisation and reductions on Monday.

1 March 1931
37 Eaton Square, SW1

My dear Hilda,

Your letter arrived plumb in the middle of the crisis and as you suggested Topping has been the deus ex machina. He asked me last week whether he might send me a memorandum on the feeling in the Party about the Leadership, intimating that he considered it his duty to give me formal warning of the dangerous situation we were getting into. I said I should receive his memo with reluctance but I could not refuse to receive it. Accordingly he brought it to me on Thursday. It stated that things were much worse than at the time of the Caxton Hall meeting, that there was a general feeling that the Party could not win the election with S.B. as leader, and that there was a serious danger lest Churchill should seize the leadership himself if something were not done quickly.

I asked Topping to alter a couple of phrases which I thought too wounding for S.B. to read & decided to let him have it over the week end with a short covering letter. Before doing so however I determined to interview various colleagues to make sure that they agreed and that, if S.B. were to consult them, they would know the facts. So I had a talk, separately, with Sam Hoare, Philip Cunliffe-Lister, Austen, Bobby Monsell, Hailsham and last night I saw Willie Bridgeman. Everyone without exception agreed that I was in duty bound to show the document to S.B. Every one confirmed the view expressed by Topping of the rapid decline in S.B.'s position. Every one I think, except Willie Bridgeman, was of the opinion that S.B. would have to resign.

I had mentioned to Hailsham that S.B. had a big speech to make on Friday next – the only one he has been booked for, and he urged me not to present the memo till this speech was over. I did not like the delay – I was afraid of missing the bus – but my position is singularly delicate and I did not want anyone saying that I had been hustling S.B. off the throne. So I consented to the postponement and at the Speakers party I told Austen and others. However yesterday Austen rang me up to say he was not happy about the delay and that the fact of the speech being imminent was a reason for letting S.B. know the real position, not one against it. I really agreed with this view, but any remaining doubts were settled by the announcement in the Evening Standard last night that Moore Brabazon[12] had

---

[12] John Theodore Cuthbert Moore-Brabazon (1884–1964). Pioneer motorist and aviator. Conservative MP for Chatham 1918–29 and Wallasey 1931–42. Parliamentary Secretary, Ministry of Transport 1923–24 and 1924–27; Minister of Transport 1940–41; Minister of Aircraft Production 1941–42. Created Baron Brabazon of Tara 1942.

withdrawn his candidature in St Georges rather than champion S.B. After that it was clear that S.B. must know at once and this morning I have sent the memo to him by hand.

But what effect will St Georges have on him & on the party? I have very little doubt that Petter[13] is standing at the instigation of R. & B. We cannot possibly sit down under that or allow S.B. to resign at their bidding. Therefore just at the moment when the train was laid and the match actually lighted Max has once more blundered in and upset the apple cart. I dont think that even so Baldwin can survive. But it is going to make for delay, for difficulty & humiliation for him, and, incidentally, it is going to involve me more deeply with him while Winston who has left the Sinking Ship, amid the cheers of the disgruntled for his "courage", will remain unaffected except in so far as he rallies to himself those who wish to express their disgust with the failure of S.B. to lead. This is the irony of politics. But somehow I don't believe that Winston will win, even though I lose.

As far as I can learn the procedure is for the H. of C. to choose its Leader in the Commons. But the matter cant be left there. The party must have a Leader to fight the Election and for that purpose I think both Houses must be brought in. I expect the Lords would like Hailsham. The Commons I am told are more inclined than for some time to listen to the idea of a leader in the other House although there is some slight misgiving about the soundness of Hailsham's judgement, there is great admiration for his vigour and determination. If therefore S.B. does disappear there is a strongish possibility that the two Houses would unite in choosing Hailsham as Leader.

In that case he might make it a condition that I should lead the Commons as I know he has a profound distrust of Winston and I dont think he has a high opinion of Horne. In our conversation on Friday he told me that he did not *want* to be Leader he could not imagine anyone desiring to take on such a load. But if the Party insisted on it he would not shirk the call. On the other hand if the leader was to be a H. of C. man he wanted me and would gladly serve under me. I told him that my position was exactly parallel to his. I said that in discussing the situation with Austen he had said that he believed that a system with the Leader in the Lords & his deputy in the Commons was unworkable. Salisbury had told him that only his relationship with Balfour had made their position tolerable. But, I said to Hailsham, I didn't take that opinion as final. It depended on the relations between the two men. In our case any difficulties would be more his than mine, because he knew that in the H. of C. decisions had often to be taken on the spot, without consultation with anyone.

Austen's view was that in any case Winston would put up a strong fight and that there might then be a suggestion that he & I might both retire in favour of

---

[13] Ernest Willoughby Petter (1873–1954). Mechanical engineer and designer of one of the first British cars. Unsuccessful Conservative candidate for Bristol North 1918 and 1923 and as Independent Conservative at Westminster St George's 1931. Knighted 1925.

a third man viz Horne. This would be a repetition of the Bonar Law episode but though I dont rule out Horne I think Austen overrates Winstons influence. Once you take away the Anti-Baldwin irritant his followers would shrink to a handful.

Well you see that the crisis is right here and that important developments must arise very shortly. As you say the general position has confirmed my instincts and there can be no doubt of the extreme tenuity of the thread by which the Govt hold on to office. The fury of the Labour Party with the Liberals is comic; the latter are half frightened and half proud of their importance. On Wednesday we shall vote on the Alternative Vote and there will in all probability be a number of Labour abstentions so that if *our* people come up to scratch we might even defeat the Govt.

In any case the alliance about which they were all so cock-a-hoop a couple of weeks ago has vanished; Garvin no longer screams that by our folly we have established the Socialists for 2 years; the National Party idea has faded out again; the "New" Party[14] looks somewhat ridiculous. Our position ought to be one for rejoicing and exhilaration, instead of bitterness, anxiety and distrust.

I have been closely in touch with Grigg who is anxious to come out as a Liberal Unionist. He tells me that Simon who is to speak at Manchester on Tuesday is going to declare for a tariff. Grigg was going to write a letter to S.B. asking for his approval of the idea of a L.U. wing acting in alliance. But now I dont know what will happen.

You will perhaps have seen the announcement of further change in my office. So far from seething with discontent it is settling in to work and the only unhappy ones are those who to their astonishment and dismay are being asked to do something to earn their salaries. I was rather pleased the other day at what Topping said to me when I was talking to him about his memorandum. I said I supposed he realised that if any thing happened to S.B. I might have to leave the office, and he replied that there was not one of them in the office who would not be very sorry indeed if I left because they all realised how much I had done for them in the few months I had been there. For the first time they had been given a strong lead. He himself had had a rotten time during the 3 years he had been there. But he was happy now and I had laid down the foundations so securely that he felt that they could go along safely and confidently even if I had to leave them. And if I went to be Leader they would know there was someone in that position whom they could trust & come to in times of difficulty.

I thought that that was rather a nice tribute especially as it was entirely spontaneous and impromptu. I dont know what the Research Dept feel but I think there too I could safely hand over now for the lines are settled and the staff

---

[14] The New Party was established by Mosley in February 1931 to support his radical economic policy supported by three Labour MPs – his wife, John Strachey and Robert Forgan – and an Ulster Unionist.

know their job. As to Mr Ball he says his ambition is to be my Principal Private Secretary at 10 Downing St!

On Wednesday I had an Exhibition to Candidates, M.P.s & Peers, of a selection of the films we are showing in our cinema vans. Everybody was delighted with them and we are rapidly getting filled up with bookings. It is very remarkable how they can get publicity when meetings fail. During the L.C.C. Elections on two nights when large halls had been booked & good speakers brought down only about 50 people turned up. On the same two nights speakers going round with the van reckoned they addressed audiences amounting in aggregate to over 3000 each night.

...

P.S. 4.30 p.m. *Very Secret.* S.B. has decided to go at once.

7 March [mis-dated February] 1931
Westbourne

My dear Ida,

I dont wonder you were upset when you saw my letter to Hilda after what I had written on Sunday. Up to 10 oclock that night S.B. and Mrs B. were quite decided on going, but apparently Willie B. rolled up then pooh-poohed the idea of resignation and urged that S.B. should come out and fight himself in St George's. Mrs B. jumped at the idea, all the personal secretaries backed it up with enthusiasm and by the time I got to Upper Brook Street the decision had almost gone the other way for Mrs B. was urging her husband to consult no one but to act. Fortunately he was not prepared to do that, but he refused to consult Austen or Sam or Topping as he knew what they would say. Luckily Geoffrey Dawson[15] happened to call upon him during the afternoon and he took the same view as I did. I believe that really settled it, but in any case I think he would have had to give it up as Camrose said he would not support him.

It comes back to my original idea when I first heard that Petter was going to stand as an Anti Baldwinite and Brab had run out. I thought then that that would make things too difficult for S.B. to go and I did not anticipate that he would make up his mind to do so when he read the memorandum. He sent for me on Sunday afternoon and when I saw him and Mrs B. at 3 o'clock they had been discussing where they would live and what they should do with their secretaries. Later on he saw Sam who was astounded at the length to which he had gone and so when we heard of the reversal next morning it was a bombshell for both of us.

Now none of us know where we are. My guess is that S.B. has said to himself that he will postpone his decision until after the election is over and then see

---

[15] (George) Geoffrey Dawson (1874–1944). Private Secretary to Milner in South Africa 1901–5. Editor, *Johannesburg Star* 1905–10; Editor, *The Times* 1912–19, 1923–41. Known as Robinson until 1917.

how things are, though he told Kingsley on Thursday that he did not intend to go till he was kicked out! But the memorandum remains and on Thursday I gave him two letters from candidates reporting that in their constituencies people were saying that we should do no good unless there was a change. Personally I do not believe anything but a very early General Election can save him and evidently other people think so too as my friends tell me that there is any amount of lobbying going on for Winston and Horne as successors.

So far as I am concerned I am doing nothing except that I dined with Hailsham privately on Thursday night and discussed the whole situation with him. He had not heard anything of what took place over the week end until then but he agreed with me that in the circumstances we ought to consider what might happen if there were a change. He does not want Winston at any price and considers Horne unfitted to be leader though if he were chosen I dont think either Hailsham or I would refuse to serve under him. But we were in complete agreement that either of us would serve under the other and that either of us would accept the party's decision as to who should lead. Geoffrey Ellis who came to see me says that the Hailsham N.C. combination is what the City would like and that if it were known that we would act together no other alternative would have a chance. So that's how things stand at present. Just now the general feeling is that in spite of the quarrel over the T.D. Bill the alliance is unbroken and that the prospect of a general election has once more receded into the dim distance. I dont agree. I think the Govts position is still very precarious and a bust up might happen at any moment. I am told that what Snowden is suffering from is not "flu" but some kidney trouble and that it is quite on the cards that he may not be fit to introduce the Budget. I don't think that would help us but it brings in a new factor of uncertainty.

The Indian agreement[16] has for the moment strengthened S.B.'s position for in spite of George Lloyd and Winston it is generally welcomed and the India Committee which had been stirred up by Winston's henchman Bracken[17] to demand that S.B. should make a public protest against the Gandhi[18] conversations are now thankful that he refused to accept their advice. But I don't think the

---

[16] On 4 March 1931 the Viceroy and Gandhi signed an agreement in which the latter accepted the constitutional principles laid down by the Round Table Conference and agreed to attend when sessions resumed. Civil disobedience was also abandoned.

[17] Brendan Rendall Bracken (1901–58). Conservative MP for Paddington North 1929–45, Bournemouth 1945–50 and Bournemouth East 1950–51. PPS to Churchill 1940–41; Minister of Information 1941–45; First Lord of Admiralty 1945. Chairman, *Financial News* 1926–45 and *Financial Times* 1945–58. Created Viscount Bracken 1952.

[18] Mohandâs Karamchand Gandhi (1869–1948). Indian nationalist leader. Called to Bar, London 1889; practised in South Africa 1889–1908; leader of passive resistance campaign against discrimination towards Indians in South Africa 1908–14. From 1914 increasingly dominant force in Indian Home Rule movement and Indian National Congress; assassinated in Delhi by a Hindu extremist.

Newton Abbot speech was a great success as it reads very dull and uninspiring. The 4 point programme was a suggestion which I made to him and I think it was a good one but somehow he didn't make it sound like a trumpet call.

Meanwhile I am pursuing my various ends and making progress. On Tuesday I went up to Leicester to lunch with the Executive Committee of the newly formed East Midlands Provincial area. It was a very successful function. About 130 sat down to lunch and afterwards I addressed them for about 50 minutes and then answered questions. I believe they were very pleased & found the answers I gave satisfactory and helpful.

Next day I had a private meeting with Sir R. Hutchinson[19] & G. Lambert two Simonian Liberals. Eyres Monsell was present and we had a satisfactory discussion after which they agreed to draft a statement of their position and get it signed by as many as possible for publication. We are to see the draft and provided we are satisfied with it I shall try and get Conservative opposition withdrawn in the constituencies of the signatories. If this succeeds I believe it might have a considerable effect on Liberal opinion both in and out of the House. The Libs. are the Portuguese and this is the weak point in the allied line against which I propose to direct my offensive. Last night I addressed my Assocn down here and made a definite appeal for Liberal support. I don't see any report in the London papers but something may have appeared in the later editions.

Negotiations for the new Evening Paper are proceeding and Camrose is now getting out a definite scheme, so something may presently occur there which will not be pleasant for B. & R. They are very sick at our having got Duff Cooper[20] for St George's and though my office is very pessimistic I myself think he ought to scrape in. I hope so for it will make things easier for S.B. who might retire then with relatively good credit, though there is always the possibility that he might consider that he was sufficiently rehabilitated to go on.

...

I am very pleased to hear what you say about the Rural Workers Housing Act. If the C.C.A. could really be moved to make a representation for the extension of the Act it would be very satisfactory whatever was the result. I dont believe the Govt would do anything because they have committed themselves so often

---

[19] Robert Hutchinson (1873–1950). Liberal MP for Kirkcaldy Burghs 1922–23 and Montrose Burghs 1924–32 (Liberal National from 1931). Chief Liberal Whip 1926–30; Chairman, Liberal National Organisation 1936 and Treasurer 1940. Paymaster-General 1935–38. Knighted 1919. Created Baron Hutchinson of Montrose 1932.

[20] (Alfred) Duff Cooper (1890–1954). Conservative MP for Oldham 1924–29 and Westminster St George's 1931–45. Financial Secretary, War Office 1928–29 and 1931–34; Financial Secretary, Treasury 1934–35; War Secretary 1935–37; First Lord of Admiralty 1937–38; Minister of Information 1940–41; Chancellor, Duchy of Lancaster 1941–43; British representative with Free French 1943–44; Ambassador in Paris 1944–47. Created Viscount Norwich 1952.

246   THE NEVILLE CHAMBERLAIN DIARY LETTERS

to a complete condemnation of it but of course it would be quite easy to include it in the Expiring Laws Continuance Act.

...

The usual weekly letter for 14 March to Hilda was almost certainly never written. From his 'Sporting Diary' it is clear that Chamberlain abandoned his plans for a fishing trip to Ireland, but a pencil note in his pocket diary referring to the '6.15 Winchfield' (the nearest station to Odiham) suggests that he visited his sisters to unburden himself at a time when his patience towards Baldwin had reached breaking point. On 11 March, news of Baldwin's anger towards some colleagues for 'plotting against him' and soreness towards Chamberlain 'for not having supported him more stoutly' was something which Chamberlain 'found ... difficult to stomach without resentment'. At the Business Committee the same evening, Austen bluntly asked Baldwin to release his half-brother from the party chairmanship in terms which made it 'pretty plain what he had in mind'. By this stage, Chamberlain had also concluded that he could not continue at Central Office with any satisfaction. Before despatching his letter of resignation, a cold and at times irritable meeting with Baldwin on 13 March only intensified Chamberlain's feeling of wounded resentment. 'To me it seemed astonishing that he should have expressed no single word of surprise, regret or satisfaction at my decision to leave the Central Office and no single word of appreciation of my work there', he noted bitterly in his diary. 'Surely no "leader" ever accepted more or gave less to his followers than S.B.' Chamberlain then curtly completed his letter of resignation, suspecting that Baldwin would seek to continue in office: a situation which, he believed, would not save his leadership but would 'probably render impossible the full restoration of our original relations'.[21]

18 March 1931
37 Eaton Square, SW1

My dear Ida,
...

S.B. has appointed 10.30 tomorrow morning to see me. From his manner this week and from secret information I gather that he has been a good deal disturbed at the idea of any rift and is anxious to make it up. The trouble is that it is I who am feeling sore now and it remains to be seen whether he will give me an opportunity of getting my grievances off my chest.

We ought to be in a splendid position with both the other parties at sixes & sevens. But we aren't.

---

[21] Neville Chamberlain Diary, 11 and 14 March 1931, NC2/22.

What do you say to Johnnie Stonehaven[22] as my successor?

My office is very confident of a triumph tomorrow [at the St George's by-election].

21 March 1931
Westbourne

My dear Ida,

...

I went and saw S.B. on Thursday but got no satisfaction. He did indeed begin by telling me that he could not say how much he was obliged to me, but he conveyed the impression that he said it because he had been told by David or someone that I was annoyed because he had not said it before. He made no reference to our personal relations nor to the memorandum nor to his own intentions and indeed it was evident that he had put these and all other disagreeable thoughts out of his mind. So we went on to discuss my successor. Bridgeman had suggested Stonehaven and the suggestion had already reached me via David and Ball. I am a good deal inclined to accept it. Johnnie is perhaps not very clever but he is absolutely straight, he has been an M.P. he has sufficient position to impress the local chairmen and, last but not least, I think he would listen to any advice I might give him. Accordingly I gave my blessing but I was left without any clear indication of what my leader means to do except that he suggested Easter as a suitable time for me to go. Apparently however he considers that I *have* gone, for I read this morning that he intends to take a leading part in a new campaign of which he has omitted to give me any previous notice.

I was disappointed that Duff Cooper did not do better.[23] Five thousand off our last poll is pretty serious especially as he probably got a considerable number of Socialist votes. But if it be true that Winston's Albert Hall meeting[24] did him harm, it did more harm to Winston about whom some pretty hard things were being said afterwards.

The Liberals meantime are in a pretty mess. Pontypridd[25] has once more rapped at their door and shown them the result of too close association with a

---

[22] John Lawrence Baird (1874–1941). Diplomatic service 1896–1908. Conservative MP for Rugby 1910–22 and Ayr Burghs 1922–25. PPS to Bonar Law 1911–16; Under-Secretary for Air 1916–19 and Home Office 1919–22; Minister of Transport and First Commissioner of Works 1922–24. Governor-General, Australia 1925–30; Chairman, Conservative Party 1931–36. Succeeded as Bart 1920. Created Baron Stonehaven 1925 and Viscount Stonehaven 1938.

[23] St George's by-election, 19 March 1931. Duff Cooper won the seat with 17,242 votes and 59.9 per cent of the vote to Petter's 11,532 votes and 40.1 per cent.

[24] At the Albert Hall meeting of the Indian Empire Society on the day before the St George's by-election Churchill accused Conservative leaders of collusion with socialists to betray India and suppress opposition to a policy he denounced as 'a crazy dream with a terrible awakening'.

[25] Pontypridd by-election, 19 March 1931. The Liberal vote fell from 36.8 to 24.2 per cent.

Socialist Government. The Goat is busily engaged in his usual intrigues, but it seems very unlikely that his rank & file will submit to anything in the nature of a close alliance while the Labour back benchers are equally distrustful of the value of Liberal support. I expect the result of Ll.G.'s manœuvres will be to drive the dissentients together. Lambert came to see me the other day to find out what sort of help he and his friends could expect from me in the constituencies and I told him I would do all I could if they would join up into some coherent body but not otherwise.

...

Eaton Sq. Many thanks for your letter wh. I found here. I also found a note from S.B. saying that he had sounded Stonehaven who was diffident but liked being asked and that he had recommended him to go & talk it over with W. Bridgeman! Why not with me? I expect Johnnie will come to me he will be a great fool if he does not.

I have been a long walk with Sam Hoare this afternoon. He is very depressed as I expect all our people are who know. He does not think anything particular will happen on Tuesday and I agree. I dont see quite what Ll.G. can propose that will offer the Libs any security which is what they are after. Lady Ampthill[26] who came in while I was having tea with the Hoares had been talking to Willie (Beauchamp[27] I suppose) & said he was all against an alliance but that H. Samuel was dying to join the Govt. The trouble was the Labour Party did not want any more Liberal M.P.'s they wanted Peers.

28 March 1931
Westbourne

My dear Hilda,

...

This has been a harassing exciting exhausting week and I dont yet know whether it has ended in disappointment or triumph. There have been two chapters, The Struggle with Baldwin and the Struggle with Beaverbrook. The incidents of the two overlapped in time but to make them clear I must tell them separately and I will begin with the first as that is finished while I am still waiting for the last words of the second.

I am not surprised at your strong language about S.B. But I believe that in trying to analyse his motives you have not made sufficient allowance for his literally incredible stupidity, stupidity in the sense of total inability to see how

---

[26] Lady Margaret Ampthill (1874–1957). Lady-in-Waiting to Queen Mary. Married 2nd Baron Ampthill 1894.

[27] William Lygon (1872–1938). Lord President of Council 1910 and 1914–15; First Commissioner of Works 1910–14. Liberal leader in the Lords 1924–31. Styled Viscount Elmley until he succeeded as 7th Earl of Beauchamp 1891.

things will appear to other people. This reaches such a point that I confess to having had doubts myself whether there was not at times a departure from that loyalty and candour which I have always hitherto believed in. However I proceed with my story. On Monday I saw little of him but I was still feeling very resentful at the publication of the intention to start on a campaign without informing me. Also I had a note from S.B. saying that he had sounded Stonehaven who was diffident but liked being asked and that he had advised him to talk to *Bridgeman* about it. He expected he would make up his mind in a few days.

I thought this an extraordinary proceeding. Why had he not advised Stonehaven to talk to the man who alone knew the present position in the office. I wondered whether he had advised Stonehaven to consult anyone else whom he had not mentioned in his letter & in a talk which I had with S. on Friday he innocently replied to a question from me that he had in accordance with a suggestion from S.B. consulted Davidson! You can imagine that this note did not calm my mind but when on Tuesday morning I read in the Times that the plans for Mr B's campaign were being mapped out and that he intended to pay special attention to the north I could no longer contain my indignation. Having ascertained by telephone that the office had heard nothing I wrote a fierce note to S.B. saying that if this withholding of his confidence was intentional I would publish my resignation that afternoon, if not, I considered his behaviour inexcusable. Having sent this to Upper Brook St. I went to the Kings Levée; when I returned I found a messenger on my doorstep with S.B.'s reply. It was apologetic, full of excuses, but while it vehemently protested his unabated affection and confidence it offered no adequate explanation. However it asked me to see him and as I had already agreed to meet Stonehaven in S.B.'s room at 5 o'clock I appointed 4.30 for a personal interview first.

I lunched that day at Philip Sassoons[28] and walked away with Sam Hoare to whom I related what I had done and who shared to the full my resentment and indignation. He had had a long talk with Geoffrey Lloyd who is one of S.B.'s secretaries but used to be Sam's P.S. and now poured out his heart to him. He told Sam that S.B. was very bitter against his colleagues for what he considered their disloyalty to him, that I was apparently excepted from the general charge though the soreness extended to me, that he was particularly annoyed with Austen for his intervention about my position at the C.O. and finally that he was filled with the most intense dislike and mistrust of Topping. At this moment I felt totally incapable of doing a stroke of work for the Party, but I saw clearly that there would have to be some frank not to say brutal talk.

Well the interview took place. It was long and painful, though S.B. made no attempt to hit back. I let him see – for the first time – what had been in my mind

---

[28] Philip Albert Gustave David Sassoon (1888–1939). Conservative MP for Hythe 1912–39. Private Secretary to Haig 1915–18; PPS to Lloyd George 1920–22; Under-Secretary for Air 1924–29 and 1931–37; First Commissioner of Works 1937–39. Succeeded as Bart 1912.

about his conduct and he had nothing to plead in excuse but his own shyness and inability to say the things he felt most. But the conversation revealed one thing to me and that was that S.B. has already constructed a view of his action on the famous Sunday which is quite contrary to my recollection and to the notes which I wrote down at the time. And though I have now twice corrected him he holds to his tale and I have no doubt entirely believes it. His account is that on receiving the memorandum he sent for me and asked me whether his colleagues wished him to go I replied that they did and to a question whether I concurred in that view I nodded my head. Thereupon he decided at once to go since he could not carry on in opposition to the views of those most closely associated with him.

My account, which I fancy I wrote or told you at or about the time, is that when I got to his house he said that his & Mrs B's first reactions were identical and they were to go. Mrs B. then left the room & S.B. talked of their future life which he said he & Mrs B. had been discussing. How he should live in a smaller house which his son-in-law would lend him, how he would sell his superfluous furniture & belongings. He asked if Annie would take over Mrs B.'s P. Secretary & discussed what Geoffrey Fry[29] would do. At one time he said I shan't consult my colleagues I shall merely tell them of my decision. I therefore supposed & I think reasonably supposed that I was in the presence of a chose jugár [?] & the question which he asked me later on was according to my recollection whether his colleagues would agree with the course he was taking. To that I said Yes I thought they would & I should give the same answer again, adding my own concurrence. But clearly that is quite different from saying that they wished him to go. On that I should have expressed no opinion not having been authorised to do so. The fact is S.B. & Mrs B. had quite made up their minds to go before I arrived & it was only afterwards that he based his decision on the supposed wishes of his colleagues.

After I had had my grievances out I told S.B. that the state of feeling among his colleagues was extremely serious. He had bottled up his resentment & said nothing to them but they were getting reports of what he had said about them to others & they were extremely cross about it. (I didn't tell him that the worst things had been said by Mrs B. & in company too!) I said the only way to clear them up was to call his colleagues together and have a frank & open talk. He was very reluctant to do this but finally consented & we had the talk on Wednesday. It was a painful ordeal for him and Austen in particular showed him little mercy but it had the desired effect and I think everyone felt better after it (except S.B.) The result appeared next day when to Ramsay's amazement he made a sudden & viscous [sic] attack on him in the House!

---

[29] Geoffrey Storrs Fry (1888–1960). Called to Bar 1913. Served Home Office 1915–17 and Treasury 1917–19. Private Secretary to Bonar Law 1919–21, 1922–23 and to Baldwin 1923–39. Created Bart 1929.

To finish up this chapter I found that Johnnie S. had accepted the chairmanship without seeing me and without having been told one single word of the circumstances in which I had given up the office. I thought this was very unfair to him, so I gave him 2 hours on Friday and told him the whole story. I think he will do all right. He knows very little about politics as they are at present but he seems anxious to have my help and as I am anxious to give it we ought to be able to work together. I found S.B. had said nothing to him about coming to the Business Committee so I advised him to write at once & say he considered it essential and he said he certainly would. I expect the announcements will be made about Wednesday or Thursday next.

Now to turn to my second chapter. Last Sunday I went for a walk with Sam and he strongly urged me to see Max again before I handed over. At first I was reluctant to do so but on thinking it over I concluded that it might be worth while to explore the ground as Max was likely to be a good bit chastened after St George's. So I sent a note asking if he would care to have a talk. A very cordial reply came back & I went & spent an hour & a half with him on Tuesday and came away with a peace protocol in my pocket. I needn't repeat the whole lengthy conversation but in the course of it he expressed a strong desire to come to terms. I asked what he wanted and his reply seemed to me to mark such an advance that I suggested he should write it down & let me see how it looked on paper. Now in dealing with Master Max you have to be very smart because he is as tricky as a monkey and I wasn't at all surprised when the written words came out quite different from the spoken. However when I said "that wont do" he replied "Well, we'll try again". The second draft was better but still unsatisfactory, but I then made suggestions and in the end he gave me the draft of a letter in his own hand which was to be written to me and the terms of which appeared to be entirely satisfactory inasmuch as they entailed no departure from our present policy. Max told me that if my people would accept them he thought he could get Rothermere to come in and also the so-called Agricultural Party in Norfolk.[30] The next day we had the frank talk I have spoken of and then I produced Max's draft. Much to my astonishment it was promptly and unanimously approved. S.B. of course obviously didn't like it but he made no objection and so on Thursday I saw Max again and took him a draft reply which he at once approved. He had already seen R. & was confident he would come in and he had sent for his farmers who were coming the next day Friday. So far so good. But yesterday Max telephoned & said the drafts appeared to him a little dry & lacking in the spirit of going out to conquer. He had accordingly altered his by inserting a few little ornaments which didn't affect the substance & would send them round after he had seen his farmers. I said I had to leave by the 4.10 to preside at the

---

[30] Formed by the Parliamentary and Policy Committee of the Norfolk branch of the NFU in January 1931 to contest all seats where the candidate did not accept their food tax programme.

annual meeting of the B.U.A. last night so he must let me see everything in the final form if it was to be released for the press the same evening. About 3 o'clock a messenger arrived with the new draft and a letter calling attention to several alterations. I felt that I must be careful and on comparing the two drafts I at once perceived an alteration not mentioned in the note namely the insertion of the word "now" so that it read "I understand that Conservative Agricultural policy *now* proposes" etc. Of course the effect of this was to make it appear that we had changed our policy in order to secure the agreement, and I at once wrote to say that "now" must come out. In about 20 minutes another note came back signed by all the farmers saying that they insisted on the "now" and if I did not agree they asked that I would receive a deputation. So I wired to Birmingham to say that I could not catch my train and went off to Stornaway House where I found 14 or 15 farmers. The Beaver lay doggo in another room while I wrestled with them. I had to be very firm but eventually suggested words which I said I would accept and which I thought would meet them. They said they must consult Max, so I went out and had a few words with him first. We settled that we would not publish anything before Sunday and he undertook to try and get my words accepted. Then I went off to catch the next train and got to the meeting in time to deliver my speech. This morning Gower rang me up, evidently with the Beaver in the room, & said the farmers wanted to publish a letter saying that they approved the correspondence in which the Conservative party proposed to *accept* the policy for which they were fighting. I at once replied that I would not agree to that & that if they insisted on it the deal was off. Thereupon he at once read an alternative draft which was quite innocuous and he has since telephoned again to say that Max has telephoned this draft & the farmers are meeting today to decide if they will accept it. If they do the whole thing will appear on Monday morning. If they dont I dont know what will happen but Max is evidently anxious for a settlement and he wants it before I leave the Chairmanship.

There, now I have told my long story & you will realise why I said that it had been an exciting and exhausting week. If I have brought off this coup it is a good wind-up for my chairmanship and I believe a sigh of relief will go up from the party & a groan of consternation from the Lib-Labs. Of course incidentally it will once again strengthen S.B.'s personal position, but I dont suppose he will appreciate what I have done for him.

     ...

5 April 1931
Cairnton, Banchory, N.B.

My dear Ida,

Thanks for your congratulations. The uncertainty continued almost to the last minute for when I got to town on Sunday I found Gower on my doorstep saying that those tiresome farmers had turned down the alternative draft letter. I had to go to Stornaway House again myself and see Max explaining to him that since the Observer had given away the secret it was absolutely necessary to give the press the details that night. Max said that Garvin had got the news from him earlier in the week and that he had had a most painful surprise when he read the Observer. But I am not disposed to quarrel with Garvin for his dirty work as it forced Max's hand and made him take the responsibility of drafting and authorising me to publish the farmers commentary in a form which I could approve.

I have been overwhelmed with congratulations which have come from all quarters (except S.B. who cant bear the thought of making it up with the Press Lords and doesnt see how it has helped his own position) There are of course a great many who say I wonder how long it will last and this feeling of doubt has been encouraged by comments & cartoons in the Beaverbrook & Rothermere Press which somewhat depart from the spirit if not the letter of the agreement. But then Max is very like Gandhi. He is posing for his idolaters very often and everything he says has to be discounted. I think he will give us endless trouble but if S.B. can be induced to say the right things I believe we can have Max's support in the Gen. Election. And that may just make all the difference!

Reflection has brought me very definitely to the conclusion that painful as it really is to me to leave the C.O. I was right to go. And of course I have been unbelievably lucky in pulling off my coup actually after I had made up my mind to leave & written my letter of resignation. Everything has seemed to work in as though preordained. Winstons behaviour which had made it impossible to keep him as our champion made it seem so natural that I should give up Palace Chambers to take his place that no breath of any want of harmony seems to have been heard or listened to. From Winston's letter I see that S.B. never wrote to him. Yet on Wednesday he asked me whether I thought he ought to send him a line and I said "certainly". I suppose he forgot. I know he forgot to answer my letter of resignation and I should never have received it if on the morning of the day when the correspondence was to be handed to the Press I had not sent for his secretary Sir Geoffrey Fry and told him that I must have the letter by 4. that day. So I got it at 4.40! having to hand it to the Press at 5.

I had a long talk with Simon on Monday and another with Grigg next day. It is extraordinary how difficult it is to get these Liberals to do anything. Grigg indeed is anxious to go forward and form an organisation but Simon wont move. I got him so far as to say that he would certainly join a Committee of Liberals (if they would call themselves Independents and not Unionists) to vote against the Govt. but he did not seem to think he could count on more than *four* to join. On the other hand he was very anxious to have an assurance that all opposition in constituencies should be withdrawn in the case of any Liberals who support our vote of censure. But one cannot found an appeal to local Conservatives to sacrifice their organisation for a single vote and an ineffective one at that.

I am not quite sure what will happen to negotiations of this kind when I am no longer Chairman. But I daresay I shall still be wanted to take part in them just as I dont expect to part entirely from the office. The staff who seem most genuinely grieved and upset over my departure are anxious to maintain contact after I go and my retention of the Research Dept will make it easier to ensure this.

...

18 April 1931
Westbourne

My dear Ida,

This has been a pretty busy week for me as you can imagine and I am not sorry to have a quiet Saturday down here. ...

I did not take part in the debate on the M/H estimates on Monday as I rather wanted to separate myself from the Ministry, but I listened to Greenwood and thought I had never heard a more paltry or dreary effort. When I did my estimates I used to make them the occasion for a survey of the health of the country but he had evidently not taken any trouble to survey anything and he had a pretty bad day in consequence. On the following afternoon he had a go at his Town & Country Planning Bill but it was evident again that he knew little about it and was chiefly reading from a brief supplied him by the Department. I made a considerable speech on the subject but it is not one that lends itself readily to popular treatment and so with the exception of the Telegraph which was very complimentary the Press did not pay much attention to it.

I handed over to Stonehaven the same day introducing him to the principal officers. ... I think the whole office is very much cheered by the knowledge that I am going to attend their office Conferences. They feel that continuity is now assured and that there will be a definite time when they can be sure of seeing me if there is anything they want to bring up.

I asked Johnnie if he had written to S.B. about the Business Committee. He said No, but he had spoken about it & said that it really was a sort of condition of his taking the office. I said What did he say? "Oh he said that would be all right". I said You will see, he wont do anything. To Johnnie's astonishment no summons came for the Wednesday meeting. I went to Geoffrey Fry and told him that the Chairman had not had his invitation. He asked if he should telephone him at once. I said Well I think you had better mention it to S.B. first. At the meeting, no Johnnie. I said nothing then but next morning I asked Geoffrey why he had not been there. "S.B. wouldn't have him". But I spoke to S.B. myself & he said it would be all right & I know Stonehaven did the same. "Well I dont know about that, but S.B. wouldn't have him last night". Did you ever know such a man to move? In the meanwhile I put it in the papers that he was coming and I shall just go on nagging till he does. On Friday I introduced Johnnie to the Press representatives and then we sat down and had a talk as we have done every week they all asking questions and I answering. I thought it a good object lesson for Johnnie & as soon as they had gone he exclaimed that he should now write & tell S.B. he couldn't carry out his duties unless he was admitted to the Business Committee.

S.B. did very well I thought on Thursday[31] but I find that there was a certain amount of criticism on the ground that he treated the subject too jocularly. Johnstone's[32] [sic] performance was simply lamentable and must have been very disappointing to his own people for there was nothing in the manner to make up for the total want of inspiration in the matter. Ll.G. however had every reason to be pleased with his tactics. He had effectually frightened the Government & Ramsay's intervention, which proved to be quite unnecessary, was I am sure arranged to enable him to make his heavy threats about a General Election at once if he was beaten. After Ll.G. had spoken Ramsay would have done better to have kept silent but I expect he was afraid that the Libs. might run out at the last moment. Ll.G.'s own speech was a masterpiece of artistry. There was of course nothing in it but false history and irrelevancies but it sufficed for his purpose and was received with delighted laughter by the Socialists as well as by his own people. I did not expect much comment in the press on my winding up speech but *our* own people were immensely pleased with it and I had more congratulations on it than I think I have ever had for a speech in the House. I enclose a note George Bowyer sent me which shows that it was appreciated by the other side too and I was very glad it was a success as I am to take so much more part in the proceedings to the House in future.

…

Mr Wright[33] is a cad who cannot be trusted to carry out an honourable understanding but neither the Express nor the Mail gave him any special prominence. I am lunching with Max on Monday to see where he stands now but I am not much afraid of his attempting any serious break though no doubt he will continue to give us plenty of trouble.

Ramsay told a lie last night in what he said about the Libs who voted with us on Thursday. But I am in negotiation with some of them & they tell me they think they can get 12 to join a new Independent group at once and might get another 10 if we could help them in the constituencies. Twenty two would be worth talking about and I do not share the pessimistic view of some of our

---

[31] On 16 April 1931 the new Lord Privy Seal, Thomas Johnston, defended the government's employment policy against a Conservative censure motion.

[32] Thomas Johnston (1882–1965). Founder of *Forward* 1906, and Editor 1919–46. Labour MP for Stirlingshire West 1922–24, 1929–31, 1935–45 and Dundee 1924–29. Under-Secretary for Scotland 1929–31; Lord Privy Seal 1931; Scottish Regional Commissioner, Civil Defence 1939–41; Scottish Secretary 1941–45; Chairman, Scottish Forestry Commission 1945–48; Chairman, North of Scotland Hydro-Electric Board 1946–59; Governor of BBC 1955–56.

[33] J.F. Wright. Leader of the Norfolk Farmer's Party.

people that the Government are now safe for another year. They have some nasty snags in front of them and I rubbed in the humiliation of the I.L.P. who in spite of "utter despair" at the Governments proposals announced their intention of voting with them and were consequently treated with the contempt they deserved.

...

27 April 1931
37 Eaton Square, SW1

My dear Hilda,

...

The political situation is very discouraging and our people are properly in the dumps. Labour believes it is in "for the duration" and that it can count on sufficient Liberal support to ensure its survival whatever it does. So far I think they are right but I refuse to take the pessimistic view because I do not believe in the staunchness of the Libs. I lunched with Max on Monday and suggested he should start attacking them in their constituencies. He was just off to Berlin and seemed to like the idea and promised to go through a list with me on his return. If he can be kept to it, there will be the additional advantage that he will be occupied in useful service instead of harrying our candidates. But if S.B. should say anything foolish at Liverpool on Tuesday, M. would probably go off the deep end. I have seen G. Lloyd & very carefully instructed him and as he has written out the salient passages it shd be all right.

...

2 May 1931
Westbourne

My dear Hilda,

...

Ashton was a great victory.[34] The C.O. refused to prophesy beforehand but I always declared that Mosley would make very little impression on the Labour Machine. I dont want to see a New Party in the field and so I am delighted that he has had such a blow. Moreover I believe that if one could discover how the 6600 Liberals who voted at the General Election distributed their votes this time we should find that about ⅓ came to us, ⅓ to the Socialists and ⅓ abstained. If I am right the Socialist drop was about 4000 (their usual figures in these days) and the anti Lloyd George faction was much stronger than their representation in

---

[34] Ashton-under-Lyne by-election, 30 April 1931. A Labour majority of 3407 in the 1929 general election was turned into a Conservative majority of 1415 largely due to the collapse in the Liberal vote. Mosley's New Party polled 4472 (16 per cent of an 80 per cent turnout) but probably took votes from the Conservatives.

the House would indicate. I shall anxiously await the result of Scarborough which is quite as important as Ashton.

Many thanks for your congratulations. I did have a good week in the House. The little speech on Monday was very well received all round and I had compliments on it from all parties. One Socialist whose name I can't remember came up to me to say It was the nicest thing ever done in the House. Clynes[35] too said "it was so 'uman' and Snowden was so pleased" & Ramsay tossed across a characteristic note "May I say how delightful you were". The Tuesday speech cost me much labour. Annie who is a good critic thought it was not as good in delivery as the one on the vote of Censure & I think she was right but our people were very pleased and it seems to have been well received in the country. One of the Whips told me that it was just what they wanted, that every sentence told & that it provided the hard hitting that they missed in Winstons more brilliant efforts. Winston himself was a little nervous lest I should poke fun at him but he told me that he had no complaint to make at all and in fact I took pains to say nothing offensive to him. I dont want to play into the hands of the enemy by widening the breach but I fancy it will go on widening of itself and I dont much mind if it does.

Last night I had a great meeting at Blackburn – about 3000 people including many Liberals. I spent a good deal of time over the Emergency Tariff with special reference to the cotton industry and our people there agreed that the speech would be most useful to them. They said they had never heard the case put like that before – in fact they did not know how to put it but now they had had a lead and they would take care to follow it up. The conditions there are awful. Eighty out of 130 mills in Blackburn are closed and they are at their wits end to know what to do. They told me that the whole district was fed up with the Government and they were confident that they could win both seats. In fact one man who was formerly in the House said we should sweep Lancashire and Yorkshire at the next election.

I agree with you, by the way, that we should have won Ashton without Mosley. I do not for a moment believe that his 4000 votes were all taken from Labour.

...

---

[35] John Robert Clynes (1869–1949). President, National Union of General and Municipal Workers. Labour MP for North-East Manchester 1906–18, Manchester Platting 1918–31 and 1935–45. Vice-Chairman, PLP 1910–11, 1918–21 and Chairman 1921–22; Deputy Leader 1923–31. Parliamentary Secretary, Ministry of Food 1917–18; Food Controller 1918–19; Lord Privy Seal 1924; Home Secretary 1929–31.

9 May 1931
37 Eaton Square, SW1

My dear Ida,

...

Austen was very dissatisfied with his speech on Monday after Snowden's statement but the circumstances were extraordinarily difficult and he really did much better than he thought. The speech contained a good deal of very pertinent criticism and had a good press. It was in the delivery that he was not quite up to his form and he got put off his train of thought by an interruption.

I had to dine in the House three nights running and on Thursday the Socialists were rude so we made them sit up till their last train had gone. I got to bed at two but I expect some of them had very little sleep. I hope so. I didn't do a lot of speaking but I intervened late on Thursday and apparently pleased my team. They in turn pleased me very much for they worked hard and were always ready to carry on the debate even when the material had run rather dry. So far I am told they are very well satisfied and I consider that we had the best of the argument all through. Snowden who looks very ill took no part in the debate and it is confidently asserted in the Lobby that he will very soon retire, perhaps to the Lords, and be succeeded by Graham, Alexander[36] or Thomas. I rather expect it will be Alexander – Graham is not wearing well.

I have had some information this week, which I believe to be reliable, about the interim Report which the R[oyal] C[ommission] on Unemployment Insurance is going to present at the end of this month. According to my informant they mean to carry on transitional benefit for 6 months administering it through the Ministry of Labour on a means test & according to a scale. But no enquiries are to be made the applicants word being taken for the family earnings &c. If this is right, not only will it involve overlapping, but as the scale will be more liberal than the practice of the best P.A. Comees there will at once be a concerted effort to level up the P[ublic] A[ssistance] Comees to the R.C. scale. The Govt will of course accept the recommendations the Liberals will support them and we shall have to come out into the open and define our attitude. If the party is left to itself it will certainly take the line that although this is not what we would have done still as the R.C. has recommended it we cannot oppose it. That would be more than I could stand and I am therefore anxious that a lead in the other direction should be given. So I have got a special Business Committee called for Monday to which I have got permission to bring anyone I like and I am taking Hilton Young & Betterton who can be relied on to stand firm and Walter Elliott [sic] &

---

[36] Albert Victor Alexander (1885–1965). Cooperative MP for Sheffield Hillsborough 1922–31 and 1935–50. Parliamentary Secretary, Board of Trade 1924; First Lord of Admiralty 1929–31, 1940–45 and 1945–46; Minister without Portfolio 1946; Minister of Defence 1946–50; Chancellor, Duchy of Lancaster 1950–51. Created Viscount Alexander 1950 and Earl Alexander of Hillsborough 1963.

Kingsley who cant. I would rather run the risk of losing the election than give way on what seems to me a really vital matter.

...

[P.S.] Scarborough was excellent & St Rollox, though not a win, is very good.

16 May 1931
Westbourne

My dear Ida,

... I quite understand that your speech will take you some time because, like me, you like to have clearly in your mind beforehand what you are going to say. I dont believe I could "ramble on indefinitely" about anything though at need I can do a certain amount of improvisation. But even a trifling affair like the proposing of a toast ... costs me quite a lot of labour beforehand and an anxiety altogether out of proportion to its importance.

The more I think over the two reports about the R.C. on Unempt Insurance the more I see that they are not so inconsistent as they seemed at first sight. It all depends on the way the thing is presented. The Report has not yet been actually drafted and I gather that the attitude of some of the members is still subject to alterations from day to day. But if Robinson is right the argument would be something like this. The problem is so difficult that it is not possible to come to any conclusion without further consideration. All questions of principle are therefore reserved for our final report. But in the meantime something must be done to ease the strain on the Exchequer. Taking covenanted benefit first, if borrowing is to be reduced you must either increase contributions or reduce benefits and we leave it to the Govt to decide which if either of these courses they will take. As regards uncovenanted benefit we propose that for the next six months the M/Labour carries on as at present except that they should revert during that time to the means tests adopted by the Rota Committees during the Conservative administration of / 25 and /26. These tests were very similar to the tests used by Guardians except that relief was either given in full or withheld altogether.

If the case were put in this way it would be difficult for us to oppose it and on the other hand, should the Govt adopt it they will surely get into hot water with the T.U.C. If Robinson is correct in saying that all members of the R.C. are impressed with the danger of setting up a third body to deal with the able bodied unemployed that bodes well for the final Report. But I am going on with my preparations for I am told that the Govt are confident that they see their way through their difficulties and that sounds ominous. Moreover it is pretty clear that our leader does not relish the prospect of a fight.

Graham asked Austen and me to see him on Thursday to propose an arrangement about the Finance Bill. I expect Austen has told you that after consultation with the Whips we refused it. Graham was very disappointed though as amiable as ever and I have no doubt they will guillotine us, though I dont know yet whether they will let us run for a couple of days before introducing the instrument. For my own comfort I hope not as in the absence of a guillotine I think we shall have to blood our hounds by giving them an all night sitting or two. Meanwhile I have undertaken to move the rejection of the Bill on Second Reading on Tuesday and as I have to unveil a Milner Memorial on Monday and broadcast on Tariffs on Wednesday I shall be glad when the end of the week comes.

...

25 May 1931
The Manor House, Great Durnford, Salisbury

My dear Hilda,

...

I was pretty weary by the time the House rose, but well satisfied with my week. ... The speech on the Finance Bill did I believe shake up the Labour M.P.'s a bit and our people said there was a tremendous lot of ammunition in it for the platform which is what they like. The broadcast too appears to have been successful if I may judge from the enthusiastic letters I have received. It was a piece of luck getting the last turn. On Thursday I saw Max and succeeded in getting an arrangement with him over S. Paddington which in effect leaves the decision in the hands of the local Exec. who will be free to keep Williams[37] if they like. This is no better than I expected and everyone is delighted except the man who ought to be most pleased of all namely Herbert Williams. I have just had a telegram to say that he "strongly objects" but he doesn't say why and anyhow I dont see what he is going to do about it.

Generally the political situation looks worse than for some time owing to the consolidation of the Lib.Lab forces. I should not be surprised to see a Lib. like H. Samuel in the Government on the next vacancy. The Libs have in fact ceased to be an Opposition and the Govt has become a majority Government.

One thing has pleased me this session in connection with Austen. I have, I believe, recovered the Second position in the party, Winston having separated himself from his colleagues while Hailsham has, perhaps unjustly, somewhat lost credit for his handling of the Lords and Horne has receded into the background. For this reason perhaps I have noted a new attitude on Austen's part. He has never before quite abandoned the elder-brother manner. But now he treats me as an equal and as a result I feel much more sympathetic than at any time since we have been in the House together.

---

[37] Herbert Geraint Williams (1884–1954). Engineer. Secretary, Machine Tools Department, Ministry of Munitions 1917–18. Conservative MP for Reading 1924–29; South Croydon 1932–45 and East Croydon 1950–54. Parliamentary Secretary, Board of Trade 1928–29. Member, Select Committee on Expenditure 1939–44. Chairman, London Conservative Union 1939–48 and NUCUA 1948. Knighted 1939. Created Bart 1953.

31 May 1931
Westbourne

My dear Ida,

...

I met at Charminster the Chairman of one of the big banks who is also connected with many other City institutions. I never heard such an appalling account as he gave of the state of things there. Whoever is Chancellor next year is I believe going to be faced with an unprecedented deficit.

P.S. ... Annie asks me to write about the car that you and Ida have offered to give the children. I cant say how grateful and how touched we are by your generosity. ... But I think we must give it further consideration before we accept. I dont know how much longer I can go on before taking the plunge and getting into a smaller house. I have been postponing it thinking that things might get better and that I might be in office again. But the prospect grows more remote. Last year my expenditure was more than double my income and I had to sell out capital at a heavy loss. This year it will be worse. Dividends have come down all round and capital depreciation seems to find no bottom. In such circumstances to incur extra expense seems almost mad, and I can't see how the extra car could be run on less than £100 a year ...

...

6 June 1931
Westbourne

My dear Hilda,[38]

...

['Page two destroyed. Health details of his wife.']

South Paddington. It is a very difficult position not made easier by Herbert Williams, the candidate's temperament and I am by no means out of the wood yet. But so far I have succeeded in keeping Max in good humour and he was more amiable and friendly at my last interview on Thursday than I have seen him for a long time.

On Tuesday night we had some people to dinner who had been kind to us in Uganda ... Next day we had Sir Malcolm & Lady Robertson[39] to lunch. He

---

[38] After the usual discussion of domestic and garden details, at the top of sheet 3 there is a note (possibly in Annie's handwriting) stating 'Page two destroyed. Health details of his wife' with the last line of the omitted sheet on South Paddington also added. As in September 1930, this almost certainly related to Annie's gynaecological problems.

[39] Malcolm Arnold Robertson (1877–1951). Entered Foreign Office 1898; First Secretary, Washington 1915–18; the Hague 1918–19; Deputy British High Commissioner, Rhineland 1919 and High Commissioner 1920–21; Consul-General, Tangier 1921–25; Minister, Buenos Aires 1925–27 and Ambassador 1927–29. Chairman, Spillers Limited 1930–47. Conservative MP for Mitcham 1940–45. Chairman British Council 1941–45. Knighted 1924.

was our Minister in Buenos Ayres [sic] and is now Chairman of the great milling firm of Spillers. He had been making speeches against the quota and I wanted to see what the trouble was. Fortunately I found it to rest on a misapprehension of our proposals and Robertson went away saying that he was profoundly relieved and completely satisfied. But I could never have achieved this result if it had not been for the work of the Research Department. On Thursday I lunched with Sir P. Sassoon ... and on Friday I had Lord Francis Scott and 2 other members of the deputation from Kenya to lunch for discussion of East African affairs. When I add that Annie had a number of social engagements of her own you will agree that our pleasures are very hard work.

We had a good day (very badly reported) on the guillotine resolution. I narrowly missed making a fool of myself but fortunately had the idea of looking up my speech on the guillotine on the Local Government Act. A perusal of this showed that I must be careful not to object to the principle and this was made easier by the fact that (to my great joy) officious Liberals kept pointing out that I was reserving myself for a guillotine on a Tariff Finance Bill and that I should then be able to claim the authority of the P.M. Also I went into the Library while questions were going on and there got an admirable quotation from L.G. who said of A.J.B. that he was always blundering into difficulties & calling them Parliamentary emergencies to which he wanted to apply measures calculated to destroy freedom and liberty of debate. The P.M. played into my hands by saying that the guillotine was necessitated by a Parliamentary emergency namely the obligation to pass legislation on coal and Unemployment Insurance before the end of the session; so my quotation exactly fitted him.

Snowden, as you may have seen, himself turned up and, looking surprisingly well, made a short speech. In the Lobby he took occasion to thank me very warmly for my "most graceful speech" (on the Budget opening day), which he described as a "perfect little gem". I was glad he spoke about it as up to then he seemed to be the only one of the major members of the Cabinet who hadn't made some allusion to it.

Later in the evening we got a concession from him on the allocation of time in the Report Stage. Later still we had a glorious bluff on an amendment to make closing time midnight instead of 10.30 on each of the guillotine nights. This put Ministers in a most awkward position. Graham tried to turn it off with a joke and I rebuked him for his frivolity in my best heavy father style. Our people got in a panic that the Govt were going to accept it and in fact both Graham and the Attorney General told the P.M. he ought to do so. But he knew that acceptance would mean a revolt among his back benchers and remained firm as I had counted he must. There was a sigh of relief on our benches when it was seen that all the Ministers had gone away and left the unhappy Pethick (or "pathetic" as he is called) Lawrence to bear the brunt with instructions to stand firm at all costs. But it will make a good platform point. Rather than sit up an hour and a half extra before midnight this Govt, as lazy as it is incompetent, insists on driving through its proposals undiscussed!

I have brought down the Royal Com. report on Unempl Insurance to read carefully as we are going to discuss it in a special meeting of the Business Comee on Monday. I think it obvious that the Govt. will not accept the recommendations. They daren't, and the Liberals wont take the odium of backing what they know to be right. But I expect the Govt will decide to accept the reform of the abuses and will then fix on some item in the recommendations or perhaps put up some substitute to reduce the drain on the Exchequer. That is their real dilemma. As I have pointed out all along unless they can straighten out Unt. Ince the whole Budget crumples up and its falsity is exposed.

Now they have got a new trouble in the Liberal Land Tax amdt to allow Sch. A to be deducted. My information is that out of the £3 millions of revenue Snowden reckons on from his 1d in the £ this amendment will destroy £2,700,000. Naturally Snowden kicks. But the Liberals dont care two hoots about the tax. What they want is the valuation and then they would hand the whole business over to the Local authorities and say Those Tories deprived you of ⅔ your rateable value. Here is a whole new field for you to dig in and from which you can extract enough to enable you to embark on any schemes you have a mind to. Not an unpopular plan probably among the L.A.'s. But this will loosen the bond between Libs & Labs and if the Lords will only do what I want them to viz pass the Electoral Reform Bill *with the alternative vote in it* the Libs will have no reason left to want to keep the Labs in any longer.

...

14 June 1931
37 Eaton Square, SW1

My dear Ida,

I must write you a short letter tonight as I have a terrible lot to do. ...

The fact is that I am being worked harder than ever & shall be I suppose till the [Finance] Bill is out of the way. ...

...

I went to Newcastle on Friday night and spoke there yesterday afternoon to a good audience. I thought it was one of the best speeches I have made recently although I was tired after a hectic week in the House. After it was over I drove with my host & hostess some 35 miles up the Tyne and had a couple of hours fishing but though I rose a salmon I did not succeed in hooking one. But it was a lovely spot and I felt refreshed in spite of the late hours involved.

I feel sure that L.G. will find some way of compromise but it will be interesting to see what form it takes. Our Whips have laid a deep plot for a snap division tomorrow & I have devised an amendment which sounds harmless on paper but which if carried would make their Bill look uncommonly foolish.

…

20 June 1931
Charminster House, Dorchester

My dear Hilda,

…

I got down here yesterday afternoon after many alarms as to whether I could manage it. When it was known that Unemployment Insurance was to be taken on Monday there was a demand that I should speak for the party as it was thought that we should have to say something about our policy and people were afraid the wrong thing would be said. However in the end it was considered that S.B. ought to do it and he has undertaken the task. Of course he has been coached but as he never seem to take in what is said to him I dont know that that is much good. We had a number of discussions on policy last week and I got my way in the end so that it is agreed (1) that we do not pledge ourselves not to reduce benefits (2) that we do say, whenever we consider the proper time to say it has arrived, that those who are not within the insurance scheme *must* be subject to a means test. I have been putting forward a new idea however namely, that instead of a flat rate you should have a series of classes or categories each with its different rate of contribution and corresponding benefit, and the workman should be allowed to choose what category he would enter with power to shift his class on giving the prescribed notice and fulfilling the required conditions. The advantages would be considerable. A man's benefit could bear some reasonable relation to his ordinary standard of living whereas now it is too high for the agricultural labourer and too low for the first class mechanic. It would enable us to bring in the agricultural worker (who is now in danger of unemployment with the increased use of machinery and the fixation of wages without fixation of prices) and yet not upset the scheme and particularly it would give the insured a choice instead of forcing them all into the same Procrustean bed. They have a system of classes in Germany but, as you would expect, there is no choice the class being determined automatically by the wage rate.

What I want to do from the political point of view is to shift the issue from "The Tories will cut your dole" to a constructive scheme of a more attractive kind, but I also think it would be a much better plan from the social point of view.

The "snap" came off beautifully. The Socialists were quite unconscious until they were actually in the lobby and it was as good as a play to see the change of expression go all the way down the bench when the Whips brought in the news. The party has had the horrors ever since. They are always convinced that we have got some new trap for them and the rank & file are being made to cling to the House like limpets.

As for the Land Tax it has got them into a fair tangle. The Chairman of the Board of Inland Revenue, who was my P.S. when I was at the Treasury told me that he thought the Revenue had been halved and was now not worth collecting. And now the Lord Advocate being hunted rather hard has promised an appeal on questions of fact as well as questions of law which has pretty well killed the valuation. Benn[40] told S. Hoare that they would have had an election when L.G. pressed them so hard only they had no money. I fancy they must still be expecting one soon or surely they would have done something more in Unemployment insurance.

I had a hard week but am thoroughly enjoying my fishing. I had a successful evening last night with 7 fish. This morning I only got a brace but it was delightful by the river. I really cant consent to die until they arrange some fishing in the next world.

...

n.d. [28 June 1931]
[37 Eaton Square, SW1]

[My dear Ida][41]

...

S.B. has suggested to me that I should take a brief holiday when I am through with the Finance Bill and as I am getting pretty tired I am disposed to take him at his word. ...

Snowden ground the faces of the Liberals in revenge for having had to give them a concession & they are filled with bitterness. L.G.'s attack on me was spiteful in the extreme & not provoked by what I said which was not anything very hard but I will find an opportunity of giving him one back. On the whole we have done well over the Bill & it has made a lot of friction in the Socialist & Liberal Parties. It is quite on the cards that they may give up one of these days but Uncle Arthur doesn't want to lose his Chairmanship of the Disarmament Committee & advises against an election.

S.B. was more exasperating than ever on Monday and ran out at the last moment. He had agreed to lay down our principles but jibbed when it came to the point and now Winston has done it instead.

---

[40] William Wedgwood Benn (1877–1960). Liberal MP for Tower Hamlets 1906–18 and Leith 1918–27; Labour MP for Aberdeen North 1928–31; Manchester Gorton 1937–42. Junior Lord of Treasury and Liberal Whip 1910–15; Secretary for India 1929–31. Vice-President, Allied Control Commission for Italy 1943–44; Air Secretary 1945–46. Created Viscount Stansgate 1942.

[41] The first page of this letter has also been removed but references to the Bristol Honorary Degree confirm the date. Again, the motive for this censorship was a desire to conceal details of Annie's gynaecological problems. In the preceding week she had a preliminary examination and Chamberlain anticipated and wanted 'a more complete one under an anaesthetic'.

I am to meet a number of M.P.'s and candidates on Wednesday to sound them on Unempt Insurance but I feel rather spiritless about it. It is such a Sisyphean task rolling S.B. up the hill and watching him roll back again.

...

4 July 1931
Westbourne

My dear Hilda,

...

At last I have got through the Finance Bill ...

I suppose you will have seen a report of the speeches in the House yesterday. I took the opportunity of making a dignified reply to Ll.G. and he responded by disclaiming any charge against my "honourable career". Then he went on to attack Simon and kept up his attack for half an hour with astonishing venom and bitterness. The Socialists rocked & rolled about with laughter and applause but some of them admitted afterwards that the thing was overdone. I said to Mike Thompson[42] [sic] "A music hall turn with 2½ millions of unemployed" and I see the Times said the same thing this morning. I thought it a sorry performance & I wondered what the Socialists would have said if they had known that at the very moment when they were applauding him L.G. was secretly negotiating with us! This is very secret and is in fact only known to one or two, not including S.B.! I rather doubt if anything will come of it, but last Monday I was told by a member of a conversation with L.G. in which he intimated that if we would let him have the alternative vote he would turn out the Government. He was nervous about it because, as he said, once before he had entered upon similar conversations with Winston, Winston had told S.B. and S.B. had told Ramsay! Very embarrassing no doubt and others who carried on negotiations simultaneously with Jacobites and Hanovarians suffered similar embarrassments at times. However, as I am not much concerned about the results of the alternative vote and do want to get the Govt out I encouraged my informant to have further conversations, which he has done. Meanwhile before I knew this I had suggested to Midleton[43] the amendment since passed by the Lords to limit the A.V to a certain number of boroughs. This

---

[42] William Lawson Mitchell-Thomson (1877–1938). Conservative MP for North-West Lanarkshire 1906–10, North Down 1910–18, Glasgow Maryhill 1918–22, South Croydon 1923–32. Director, Restriction of Enemy Supplies Committee 1916–19; Parliamentary Secretary, Ministry of Food 1920–21 and to Board of Trade 1921–22; Postmaster-General and Chief Civil Commissioner 1924–29. Chairman, Television Advisory Committee 1934–38. Succeeded as Bart 1918; created Baron Selsdon 1932.

[43] (William) St John (Fremantle) Brodrick (1856–1942). Conservative MP for Surrey West 1880–85 and Guildford 1895–1906. Financial Secretary, War Office 1886–92; Under-Secretary of War 1895–98; Under-Secretary, Foreign Affairs 1898–1900; War Secretary 1900–1903; Secretary for India 1903–5. Succeeded as 9th Viscount Midleton 1907; created Earl of Midleton 1920.

of course would not suit the Govt. But there are two possible alternatives. The Government may decide to withdraw their Bill and put it through again under the Parlt Act in which case it will probably never become law. Or they may decide to fight now and disagree with the Lords Amdts. In this case L.G. says he would give us the plural vote (very important for us) minus the vote for wives of business men (which has always seemed to me indefensible) and in return for the A.V. he would undertake to get the Govt. out by April. I think we should want him to promise an earlier date and of course he might not be able to deliver the goods. But anyway we should be no worse off than we are and we should have our plural vote back which means a considerable number of seats. L.G. says he believes that in default of an "arrangement" with us he can keep the Govt in for two years which I very much doubt. But what a man!

I had an interesting morning with the M.P.'s and candidates and I think a useful one. It was obvious that they were all very nervous and that it was highly necessary to let them know what we had in mind lest they should pledge themselves to the contrary. One man said he was continually asked what his attitude was towards the R.C. [on Unemployment Insurance] and added with simplicity that he always "evaded the question" by saying that in no case would he increase contributions or reduce benefits! The one new feature to my mind was the general conviction that it would be fatal to suggest that the people on Transitional Benefit would be thrust on to the Poor Law. But I dont think it is necessary to say that in so many words and when I reported the result of the meeting to the Business Committee. S.B. asked me to prepare a formula for him to use at Hull where he is to speak in about a fortnight. I ask for nothing better.

Well, we have got our holiday fixed up with Ernest[44] and go to Moor Lane House on Tuesday afternoon till the following Monday. I am eagerly looking forward to it for this last week has been the hardest of all and I am in that condition when I need a rest if I am to do justice to my work. Meanwhile I wish we could have had another day here for I have never seen this garden lovelier & yet there are heaps of things just about to come out. ...

...

11 July 1931
Moor Lane House, Briantspuddle, Dorset

My dear Ida,

...

Of course I entirely agree with what you say about the Housing Bill, but I think its mostly eyewash. I had a talk with Arthur Robinson about it and he

---

[44] Ernest Ridley Debenham (1865–1952). Married to Cecily (died 1950), daughter of William Kenrick of Birmingham. Created Bart 1931.

made no secret of the fact that it was brought in only as a sop to the Liberals. But he added that the Ministry had taken all the sting out of it and that he didnt expect that more than about 4000 houses would be built under it. If that turns out to be the case it will at any rate do little harm.

I dont think I have told you of another piece of information that came to me after I had heard of the conversations with the Goat. A mutual friend of the P.M. and of Stonehaven came to the latter with Ramsay's knowledge and said that he was desperately anxious about the country. So serious was it that he doubted if any Party could be strong enough to put it right. A National Government was required and he himself would be quite ready to hand over the Premiership to S.B. and serve as his Foreign Secretary. He hated the idea of being tied up to L.G. and he did not want to be forced to oppose the two things necessary viz a tariff and reform of Unemployment Insurance. Snowden Thomas and Greenwood thought as he did and would be prepared to join the coalition but not "Uncle Arthur" Henderson who was believed to be anxious for the succession to the Premiership.

Stonehaven said he must tell all this to me & Hailsham as well as to S.B. but that he was sure it would split both the Labour Party & the Conservatives from top to bottom. (N.B. Austen has not been told.)

This shows that Stonehaven is getting the hang of things. It is a curious story. One wonders how far it was seriously meant & how far it was only an expression of weariness with an anxious and trying position. If there was any seriousness in it R.M. must have got a long way off realities for such a combination is clearly impossible.

...

18 July 1931
Westbourne

My dear Hilda,

...

I cant say that I felt really rested after my holiday but it was as you put it a let up and we have not long to go now before the end of the session. ...

The political situation becomes more and more obscure. The P.M. seems either carelessly or perhaps deliberately to have communicated his hints to leaky vessels, and I keep getting fresh evidence of it. Elibank who is always trying to act the honest broker sent me a pressing invitation to have a talk with him. I didn't know what he wanted to discuss but I lunched alone with him and soon perceived that he was working laboriously round to a National Government. At last he informed me that he had it from a friend of Ramsay's that the P.M. would not be averse from considering such a plan. I asked whether Henderson was prepared to come in and at first Elibank said "Oh. Yes." but on being pressed he admitted that Henderson's name had not been mentioned and he undertook to go back and get more information. At the time I was under the impression that R.M. contemplated only an alliance with Conservatives leaving Liberals out, in which case I understood he would want the Foreign Office, and I could hardly suppose that that idea would smile to Henderson. However since then I have further news. Lloyd George asked Kingsley to go and see him again to discuss the Electoral Reform Bill and spoke as follows. "I think it only fair to tell you that since we last talked my ideas have changed. At that time I thought I could carry the Government comfortably for another two years. But I have come to the conclusion that matters are working up to a crisis, and that by the autumn the situation of the country may be so serious that only a National Government will be able to deal with it."

So he has got wind of it! And if he knows then Henderson knows too, because all the Lib-Lab negotiations have been conducted by Henderson. I fancy that L.G. will work for this solution for all he is worth. Obviously it opens up a new and most enthralling prospect for him. For if Conservatives refuse to join R.M. then L.G. will say, "For my part, I am before all a patriot, and I cannot refuse the call to serve my country. Therefore I am ready to join up and take a subordinate place with, of course, some colleagues in the Government", and once in, the cuckoo wont be long in hoisting the nestlings on to its shoulders and out of the nest.

As things are now, it is certain that we could not accept an invitation from Ramsay. But I can conceive that if things did get very serious in the autumn, with perhaps a crisis in the city, unemployment soaring up to three millions and the prospect of a £100 million deficit on the Budget you might get a very powerful movement backed by the Daily Mail and possibly the Express for a National Government, which would change the aspect very materially. Even then you certainly would not get unanimity. The diehards in our party and the I.L.P. with a considerable contingent of the more extreme Socialists would be hostile and the combination would find it hard to reconcile their fundamental differences. I myself hate the idea and hope it wont come to pass. But on the other hand the prospect of a Lib-Lab coalition is not very alluring and it would certainly be a good deal stronger than the present lot are alone.

Anyway nothing will happen this month and during the recess when members get into contact with their constituencies their views are sure to undergo some change.

...

25 July 1931
Westbourne

My dear Ida,

According to your letter "Politics get more and more satisfactory". But I hardly think this is what you meant to say for I expect you would agree with me that they are like the weather – couldnt be worse, and wont be better till we get another Government. ...

...

This has been quite a busy week in one way or another. On Monday I had Edward Irwin to dinner and we had a long and very interesting talk on both home and Indian politics. He doesn't seem at all changed to me and in spite of all criticisms I retain my belief in him. Did you see his damaging quotation from a speech of Winston's in 1921 (after the Dyer incident) in which he twice proclaimed that India must be given "Dominion Status"?

On Tuesday I went and did a "talkie", not directly political but to please British Movietone News (Ye Gods! What a name) who have helped the C.O. a good deal in cinema work. They are opening a News Reel Picture House in Birmingham and my performance is an introduction and a welcome. I consented to do it partly because I thought it would be good practice and I was gratified to find that it came much more easily than on either of the two previous occasions.

On Wednesday Lord Grey came to lunch. We invited the Hilton Youngs too as he is very keen about birds & she can talk about anything and we had a very pleasant party, Grey chatting about fishing and birds and Lloyd George of whom he remarked "He is a very difficult man to follow"! Curious, but yesterday morning in the course of a conversation between S.B. Ramsay and myself R.M. observed (of Ll.G.) "Oh! that man! The way his mind works – is a positive danger to the country".

Which leads me to a humorous incident. Kingsley has been following up his talks with Ll.G. about a deal over the Electoral Reform Bill but has reported that he thinks his mind is now set upon a reconstruction of the Government which would enable him to slip in. The little man however has been keeping K.W. on the string always saying he would see him again so that it was with some surprise that we heard that the Liberals had concerted a plot to get the Bill through the Commons on Monday. This piece of news was let slip by Addison in the course of a conversation with Hailsham about land utilisation and Hailsham came hot foot to tell us to look out. The idea was that the Liberals whose turn it is to choose a subject for supply on Monday would put down Coal Mines but would close off the discussion quite quickly when the Electoral Reform Bill would come on. So a question was asked on Thursday as to what business would be taken after supply was finished on Monday & Snowden answered Any of the Bills mentioned on the 9th July (when he had gone through a list including the E.R. Bill) but in no case would the House be asked to sit late. The game was now clear and a team of Conservatives has been got together to talk about Coal Mines till it is too late to take anything else. You will observe that

1. Ll.G. began by humbugging the Government to whom he did not disclose that he was talking with us and

2. He is now trying to humbug us by keeping from us his plan to get the Bill through without any deal

3. Addison humbugged Ll.G. by disclosing the plot to Hailsham

4. Snowden humbugged us by not explaining that he contemplated taking the E.R. Bill on Monday and

5. He humbugged Ll.G. by intimating to us that we could stop the Bill by merely talking it out. Finally

6. We have humbugged Ll.G. by not telling him that we know all about his little game and have devised a plan to stop it.
Truly, as Adam Smith said, the politician is a cunning and crafty animal.

...

I understand that the Conference was not very successful and that another "crisis" was expected in about a month. But Ramsay said yesterday that things were looking more cheerful and that he hoped to get the French in with us and the Americans in tiding the Bosch over the worst. I gave Austen an account of the situation yesterday. I dont think he had realised at all the sort of position we may find ourselves in when the autumn comes and he had rather a shock. I am told that the Economy Committee have signed their Report, that they anticipate a deficit of £130M in the Budget & that they say the Unempt. Insurance Comee didn't go nearly far enough in their recommendations. It looks as though we should presently find ourselves in the same condition as Australia and have to take the same sort of measures. But I have seen this coming for some time now.

It is possible that I may speak in the House on Thursday but otherwise I have finished until the autumn. The Research Department continues to pour out large Reports of unequal value but some of great importance. I believe my House of Lords Committee has nearly finished its work and has rather unexpectedly found itself unanimous with the possible exception of Duff Cooper who apparently thinks it ought to be left exactly where it is. That seems to me impossible.

...

2 August 1931
Dalchosnie, Kinloch Rannoch, Perthshire

My dear Hilda,

...

I am almost afraid to give you our first impressions of this place lest they should seem extravagant but we all agree that it is the nearest to perfection we have yet experienced. ...

This morning the children and I went a grand walk up the moor. ... The heath was out though not the heather and we found the two sorts of staghorn moss and various other flowers including the wild yellow saxifrage. It was good to be on the moors again & smell the bog plants and the birches.

There are any amount of rabbits to shoot, and Sir John has left word that he would like us to kill three brace of grouse on the 12th. The keeper tells me that there are ptarmigan on the tops and a few snipe. Also there are trout in the burn to be obtained with a worm, and the fishing in Loch Rannoch is better than usual this year. Moreover he declares that he has seen 2 salmon ... in our pools so I expect we shall have a go at them some time. Today has been delightfully warm & sunny and altogether things could hardly have begun better.

There was so much talk going on about a National Government last week that I thought it was desirable to have a talk before we separated so I got Austen, Hailsham, Philip C-L. & Sam to dine with me on Wednesday night and we had a long and useful discussion. None of us want a coalition and I am inclined to think we may manage to avoid it but we agreed that it might be unavoidable though only on condition that tariffs were accepted. The usual talk is of our joining a Labour Govt. but I think that if it came at all it would be much more probable that R.M. would resign and that a certain number of the present Government would come into an administration under S.B. But all my guests declared that the greatest difficulty in such an event would be S.B. himself as his defects are just those which would be most undesirable in a Coalition leader.

You will have seen what happened on Thursday. I had intended to make a strong attack on the Government, but I found the City was so nervous that that sort of line followed by a provocative speech by Snowden might have precipitated a flight from the £. So I went to see Snowden and told him that if he would give an assurance that he would use the recess to study ways & means of economy I would tone down my speech, say nothing offensive, express confidence in the soundness of the position and end with an appeal instead of an attack. Snowden at once jumped at the offer. He warmly agreed that sooner or later the country had got to face up to the realities and expressed great concern at the seriousness of the position. I think he does realise the situation though probably he is the only member of the Govt who does. On Thursday I sent for Peacock[45] one of the directors of the Bank of England who has a great reputation for wisdom & sanity and told him the line I proposed to take which he warmly approved. It was amusing to watch the Socialists during the debate. They didn't understand my speech at all and kept making the usual party interruptions but when they heard Snowden expressing his gratitude for my self restraint, confessing that my criticisms of his Budget were justified & promising to adopt my suggestion about economy they simply didn't know where to look. Snowden played up extremely well and generally the debate was very successful. Our people seemed very pleased, the Deputy Governor of the Bank[46] sent me a message to express his great satisfaction, the City plucked up spirit again and I see today that even the Observer (Garvin apparently being away) declares that I made a masterly

---

[45] Edward Robert Peacock (1871–1962). Canadian-born British merchant banker. Director, Bank of England 1921–24 and 1928–46. Director, Baring Brothers 1924–54; Director, Canadian Pacific Railways. Knighted 1934.

[46] Ernest Musgrave Harvey (1867–1955). Entered Bank of England 1885. Comptroller, Bank of England 1925–28; Deputy Governor 1929–36. Knighted 1920. Created Bart 1933.

speech! The Goat must be vexed to be out of action when the waters are so troubled but we shall not see him again for some time as I am told he will have to go for a sea voyage when he is convalescent.[47]

...

9 August 1931
Dalchosnie

My dear Ida,

...

Well, this place seems to be all that we could wish for and the more we see of it the more in love with it we are. ... I am going to try a dry fly in the Inverhadden burn and the keeper who has evidently not had a fisherman here for a long time is quite excited at the prospect. ...

... One afternoon I took the two boys with the keeper up to our highest point 3300 ft where we shall go later on for ptarmigan. We had wonderful views from the summit and I found there Loiseleuria Procumbens [alpine azalea] which I have only met before on Ben Eoina at Loubcroy. I have also found 2 Saxifrages. The commonest is the yellow aizoides which is very abundant and grows in great patches in all the wet places. Hypnoides is more local and Stellaris I come on very occasionally.

...

We get our papers here regularly and I have got the Economy Committee's report to read. I see that the talk of a National Government is being damped down pretty vigorously by the friendly press and the Sunday Times even declares that the alternative of a financial dictatorship is being talked of in high circles. I dont think this need be taken seriously but there is no doubt that the City is still very nervous and there seems a general consensus of opinion that this Government at any rate will never have the guts to do anything effective in the way of economy. I think one can best leave things to go on simmering for the present.

...

16 August 1931
Dalchosnie

My dear Hilda,

...

... Since the 1st week we have hardly seen the sun and yet we have had practically no rain so that the burns & river have persistently fallen & become

---

[47] Lloyd George had a prostate operation on 29 July 1931 which kept him out of active politics throughout the political crisis.

less & less fishable while a continuous northeast wind has kept the temperature low. This sounds truly vile but the place is so delightful that we have enjoyed it in spite of the weather ... I took the three boys ... to collect the 3 brace of grouse which I had been allowed. ... Unluckily Frank did not succeed in dropping a bird himself though he had several chances, but he thoroughly enjoys going about with a gun. ...

...

I wonder how much you will have heard or seen about political developments here. Things suddenly boiled up in the city and as a result the whole situation has undergone a complete change the outcome of which no one can at present foresee. I was getting daily letters from the indefatigable Smithers[48] but was paying no attention to them when I received a communication from the Deputy Governor of the Bank saying in effect that the position was desperate & begging me to come to London at once. So I had to take the night train on the 12th and the next morning met S.B. who had also been summoned from France. We saw the P.M. and Snowden that afternoon. They said they had decided that the Budget must be balanced & that economies must be made to the extent though not necessarily in the precise ways suggested by the Economy Committee. They felt however that the occasion demanded sacrifices all round and they were considering in what way these could be obtained. They would be ready by next Tuesday afternoon to give us a general outline of their proposals and while they would take full & sole responsibility for them they would gladly consider any suggestions we might have to make. If they could be assured of our general support they proposed to summon Parlt in the 1st fortnight in September to pass a supplementary Budget and an Economy Bill.

Here is an astonishing change. Some people, including Austen, thought I was rash in saying many months ago that I would not join a Govt which was not pledged to reduce national expenditure in its first year. Yet so perilous has the state of the national finances grown to be that a Socialist Govt. is actually contemplating a cut of £100 millions a year!

To secure such a measure of relief and to do it though a Socialist Govt seems to me so important in the national interest that we *must* give it our support provided the proposals for "equal sacrifice" do not imperil British credit or too brazenly affront ordinary rules of justice & fair play. And I dont think they will do either. Ramsay & Snowden had not by any means got their ideas worked out on Thursday but the talk I had later with the Bank of England directors coupled with the hints of ministers indicated a tax on all fixed interest whether from War Loan, Corporation or Colonial Stocks, Railways or Industrial Debentures. I dont think Preference stocks would come in as they are not really "fixed".

---

[48] Waldron Smithers (1880–1954). Conservative MP for Chiselhurst 1924–45 and Orpington 1945–54. Knighted 1934.

Anyway the decisions are left to me as S.B. is not coming back. I think he would agree that crises of this kind are not his forte. He had apparently given no thought to the situation, asked no intelligent questions, made no helpful suggestion and indeed was chiefly anxious to be gone before he was "drawn into something". He left a final message for me that he was most grateful to me for sparing him the necessity of returning and he would "back me to the end"! So I go back tomorrow night. I have asked Sam Hoare to come & attend the conference with me and very possibly I may summon Austen, Douglas & Philip to discuss my proposed action on Thursday. But that will be rather to help in concocting a letter to the P.M. which shall most advantageously represent our position than because I want any assistance in coming to a decision. I know now pretty well what are the limits within which I can promise support and I desire to support if possible.

Et après? There might be a new alignment of parties, as some think. Or there might be an appeal to the country in conditions offering us the utmost advantage, seeing that we could no longer be saddled with the unpopularity of economy, but could concentrate on tariffs & Imp. Preference as the restorers of prosperity. Thank Heaven Ll.G. is not here to plague us. It looks as if *his* plan of reckless expenditure was finally bust.

By request of the Press I saw them on Thursday in conference just as I used to do when I was Chairman. The result was a remarkable unanimity among our London & Provincial papers on the lines I wanted. I am going to see them again next week.

Alas for my holiday! And my pocket. For these little trips which serve to interest & amuse the public will cost me a pretty penny. And the result will be further to curtail my income in order that *my* sacrifices shall not be less than those of others! Well, well, its a funny world.

23 August 1931
37 Eaton Square, SW1

My dear Ida,

…

I expect you will have seen some further home news which has given you a better idea of our crisis. Anyhow my last letter told you of its origin. After all the Chancellor was not ready on Tuesday and it was not until Thursday morning that Sam & I with Samuel & Maclean[49] met him again with the P.M. at Downing St.

After hearing his proposals I said at once that they were inadequate. Really the two Ministers agreed but they asked us to give them further consideration

---

[49] Donald Maclean (1864–1932). Liberal MP for Bath 1906–10, Selkirk and Peebles 1910–18, Peebles and Midlothian South 1918–22, Cornwall North 1929–32. Chairman, Parliamentary Liberal Party 1919–22 and Acting Leader in Commons 1919–20. President, Board of Education 1931–32. Knighted 1917.

and see them again after they themselves had discussed them with the Cabinet. We saw them accordingly next day, but instead of better their figures were much worse, and as they said that was final it appeared that nothing could stay the financial catastrophe. However we & the Liberals consulted together & went again that night to Downing St. to see the P.M. when we told him that if that were the last word we would combine to kick him out as soon as Parlt met. If however he could reconstruct his Govt so as to be able to put forward adequate proposals we would do all we could to support him. Nothing was said about a Nat. Govt. but it was obviously not excluded. He said he intended to make his own proposals to the Cabinet & those that didn't like them would have to take their own course.

Next day (Saturday) we were assembled once more & R.M. said if we would agree to an intermediate figure he thought he might possibly get his Cabinet up to it. I thereupon cross examined him on the meaning of "agree" and he defined it as meaning that we would allow him to put his proposals before the House and express our views by means of amendments. Now the only way in which the economy figures could be raised was by cutting the dole and if once we could fasten that on the Labour Party they would be irrevocably split. R.M.'s proposal therefore suited me down to the ground the only question was whether it wd become practicable or whether the other Ministers would not rather refuse to accept it in wh. case there would be nothing left but resignation. R.M. was to have another Cabinet yesterday afternoon & after it was over it was announced that there would be a final one this evening. We are now waiting for this final decision but since I began this letter H.M. has seen S.B. & told him that the P.M. has reported that he cant carry his colleagues nor his party. So unless they change their minds in the next few hours this Govt will come to an end and S.B. will be sent for tomorrow. I have just wired to Austen to come back.

Well, I have had a strenuous time these last few days but have nothing to regret & no reason to be dissatisfied with the part I have played. It looks however as if a much more strenuous time was ahead, but I shant mind that if we are *doing* something.

...

Well as you see I am in a state of complete uncertainty still, but you will I daresay know much more before this reaches you.

P.S. Of course S.B. could do nothing without the Libs. & if sent for he would have to see them at once. I have strongly advised him to make every effort first to get Macdonald [sic] & one or two other Labour men in with him. In that case I have little doubt the Libs would play & we could carry the Economy Bill and – then dissolve.

27 August 1931
37 Eaton Square, SW1

My dear Hilda,

It will be no surprise to you now to find that I am here in the Government again. The story is too long for me to tell now but I write for two purposes.

First, I am anxious that Annie should stay at Dalchosnie as long as possible in order that she may build up her strength for the strenuous times ahead. I have put this to her and explained how little she would see of me here and she has consented to delay her return. I suggested to her that she might at least await your arrival ... I dont really quite know how her mind is now but I am sure you will do all you can to steady her and prevent any rash decisions.

The second thing is to warn you against any congratulations to Austen. He is in a terrible state of mind and there was a painful scene at Deans Yard this evening when he rather lost control of himself.

I suppose he had hoped that he would get the F.O. again and most unhappily there was a misunderstanding about a code telegram which he sent to Ivy & which she interpreted as meaning that he had got it. Now he feels utterly humiliated and declares that he has made a fool of himself and has allowed himself to be treated as a back number. He is very very bitter about it. I feel very sore for him and hardly know how to help him though I feel sure he has made no mistake and will presently realise that he was right to take the Admiralty since he could not have what he would have liked. But he wants very tender handling just now and congratulations are dust & ashes to him.

...

We have a terrible job in front of us. I hope we shall come through with it.

12 September 1931
37 Eaton Square, SW1

My dear Hilda,

...

Things have gone well for us in the House. Snowden was quite excellent on Thursday. His voice was clearer & louder than on either of the two previous Budget occasions and it made a deep impression on the House. Members had a shock over the deficits and the Socialists were evidently dismayed at the way in which the direct tax payers were hit whilst our people took the news with admirable cheerfulness and readiness. Of course I wasn't in the House yesterday but evidently Thomas' revelations were extremely damaging and must have taken the heart out of the opposition. I notice that they have selected all the intransigents to put their case and kept in the background those who were prepared to go further a fact which I think I must comment upon when I speak on Monday. Even now people dont seem to realise that Henderson and some of his colleagues did accept a cut in benefits which though it took the form of a levy and a deduction was a cut just as much as if the benefits themselves had been lowered.

Things are moving very rapidly in the direction of a tariff. R.M. has asked me to serve on a Committee with Snowden & Reading to consider the adverse trade balance & what should be done about it & we are to meet on Monday and report to the Cabinet on Wednesday. I feel pretty sure that the P.M. himself is ready to go the whole hog, but I cant believe that either Snowden or Samuel would accept it. Snowden doesn't matter so much; probably he would be ready to retire but if Samuel went the question is how many Liberals would he take with him and what would be the effect on our majority. The Stunt [?] press is now shouting for action by *this* Govt. I wonder what our people would say if their policy were carried out under Macdonald [sic] instead of Baldwin. It is very obscure and difficult to see how things are going to work out but it is evident that there will be rapid developments in the course of the next week.

You will have seen that my proposal for Transitional payments has appeared and in the general melee it does not seem to have attracted a great deal of attention though I expect we shall hear more of it presently. But the fact that the late Govt were in favour of a needs test is awkward for the opposition even though they did not propose the intervention of the P.A. committees.

This is a short letter, but I am feeling a bit tired & I think bed is called for. I am glad to say that the gout did not materialise and I have felt no more of it.

19 September 1931
Westbourne

My dear Ida,
...

This has been a terrible week though the public does not in the least realise it, and I hardly like to write a detailed account of it. But between mutiny in the Fleet, the imminent danger of a crash in the £, a first class financial crisis in India, and the refusal of the Liberals either to face a tariff or to find any other way of redressing the trade balance, the atmosphere has been as depressing as it is possible to imagine. The Prime Minister is worn out and seems unable to make up his mind to decisions, S.B. is useless and everything seems to fall on me. On top of that one's own personal affairs are not calculated to raise one's spirits. I believe Annie wrote to Hilda about Eaton Square. I suppose we shall have to wait until we know about the election before we can take any definite decisions but I must make economies here too and I am afraid it means dismissing our second man. I must certainly get rid of my store and intermediate house but I have not yet come to any conclusion about the cool orchids though if I keep them a little longer I expect they will have to go later.

All of us in the Cabinet except Samuel and Reading want an election as soon as possible and indeed I think it is inevitable. We cant stop in and do nothing while our popularity crumbles and the Libs. wont face the tariff. In fact Ll.G. wants to choose this moment for a Free Trade Campaign. I think it would be a good thing if he did drag his people into it for that would be the end of them.

But if we do go to the country how are we to go? Our idiotic party thinks it has the game in its hands and wants us to fight on party lines. I believe the only way to secure the sort of majority which would give the world confidence is to go as a National Government, perhaps even as a National Party carrying Macdonald [sic] and his colleagues with us together with as many Liberals as we could get. It is very interesting to find that Topping wants this too, though you could hardly find a stronger party man. He is coming to see me about it on Tuesday and I must see what I can do though it is difficult because in addition to my other duties the P.M. wants me to take charge of the Economy Bill which means constant attendance in the House every day next week except Tuesday.

...

10.30 p.m. They have telephoned for me to go back tomorrow morning for a Cabinet. More trouble no doubt. I will take this with me.

Eaton Square 7.30 p.m. *Sunday* I guessed as much! The £ has gone & we must suspend the Gold Standard Act tomorrow. If only it had been possible to peg it while we got our Economy Bill through, but of course we shall have a very embarrassing series of debates now with prices going up. I hope it wont go very far. Herbert Samuel of course jumps at the idea that this has made a tariff unnecessary as it must check imports and help exports. Ergo, a General Election must be unnecessary too. That remains to be seen, but doesn't everything go wrong perversely, just before you can get it right. Dont write any more about "restful week-ends". They are not for the likes of me. It *was* a lovely morning, but I have had a *beastly* week end.

Thanks for your letter. I am for moderation in cutting down as in everything else. But some folks are always in extremes & one extreme provokes another.

26 September 1931
Westbourne

My dear Hilda,

The offer which you and Ida make in your postscript is just one more piece of your illimitable generosity and we do, both of us, appreciate it most warmly and thank you for it from the bottom of our hearts. But I cant accept it. I have got to reduce my expenditure permanently, so far as I can see and to postpone it for a year would only make people think that there was no real need to economise at all. ... I hope by getting rid of the store & green house plants and by not replacing the Woods we may make a substantial reduction here and if we can find a tenant or purchaser for Eaton Square and I continue to draw my (reduced) salary I shall fill some of the deficit in my Budget. But even so, unless trade improves and my shares appreciate very markedly I shall still be living beyond my means and I dont disguise from myself that further economies may presently be necessary. However I believe that the worst part is in making the change and as the majority of people in this country contrive to be happy on a much smaller income than I shall have left I don't take too tragical a view of my situation.

It has been a very anxious week, with crisis after crisis coming upon us. No sooner had we taken the necessary measures to go off the gold standard than the situation arose which necessitated the reduction of the cut in the Navy & other defence forces, police and teachers. It was maddening to have to give way about the teachers after their behaviour and as I expected it has quite upset my panel doctors who, up to then, were quite pleased with their sacrifice. I must say those Admirals have shown up badly; they must be completely out of touch with the men and I hope Austen wont let the matter rest where it is, though I haven't had any opportunity of talking to him about it. We have all been humiliated and our whole scheme of economy jeopardised. The fall in the value of the £ has of course been a heaven-sent opportunity for the Opposition who keep rubbing it in that Macdonald [sic] justified the cut in unemployment benefit by the fall in the cost of living.

No sooner had we dealt with the second crisis than a third equally formidable descended upon us from India. Of course nothing of this has appeared in public but we have had a battle royal with the Viceroy & his Council & it was touch and go whether they did not resign in a body. In the end they gave way but I fear the trouble may reappear at any moment. My information is that Gandhi is now seeking a pretext to break up the Round Table Conference and go back to India and make trouble there.

Meanwhile we are rapidly approaching the moment when we must take our decision about the election and our programme. I was vexed at first when I heard the P.M. was going away but I came to the conclusion that he was probably wise. He was so tired that he could not make up his mind and could only wander round and round his problem. Meanwhile public opinion has definitely hardened in the right direction. I have been seeing the press pretty constantly and thanks to my experience with them at the C.O. I am now on extremely easy terms with them personally. They send word to me when they want to see me and then a dozen or so representing all the principal Conservative journals in London & the provinces come to my room where I talk to them for ½ hour and answer questions. The result is a remarkable unanimity in favour of a prompt election and a national appeal which has I think had a great effect. There was a remarkable meeting of the Business Committee on Thursday (though it took some trouble to get it called) at which all present without exception declared themselves in favour of an appeal with Macdonald [sic] as P.M. & in the event of victory the formation of a National Government *under him*. How astonished the Labour Party would have been if they could have been present! In fact no other party is so ready to subordinate party consideration to national interests, though perhaps one should add that such a situation could hardly have arisen if S.B. had not been our leader. Of course we are all risking our personal futures for what they are worth but there has not been a sign that anyone has allowed that to influence him.

Although you may think that my share in all this is not recognised that is not quite the case. The D.M. the other day said that "Mr Chamberlain is more and more over-shadowing Mr Baldwin as the real leader of the Conservative party" and I notice that the Herald when purporting to give the attitude of different people towards an election puts my views first and represents S.B. as being pulled along after. Topping too says that I am the one man on whom the party relies and though I think he is prejudiced in my favour I have other evidence to the same effect in the way people come to see me when they want things done. The latest is Oswald Mosley! I have had a message that he would like to play with us at the election and I have said I would see him next week.

It is evident to me that Herbert Samuel is very uncomfortable about his future and he is working like a beaver to gain time and find some bridge. But I am determined that he shall swallow the whole programme or go out and though Ll.G. fulminates from his sick room and threatens to flood the country with Free Trade candidates I believe we may safely call his bluff.

The present indications point to an early dissolution and an election near the end of next month. The £ has up to the present followed the course predicted by the bankers. It may go lower yet but will probably settle down to something between 12/- & 16/-. I am told the cotton orders are the consequence of the rise in the price of silver which has increased the purchasing power of China & India. We shall probably keep prices of commodities in the shops fairly steady till stocks are exhausted but then of course they are bound to go up which is another reason for an early election.

...

Sunday Samuel has circulated to the Cabinet a very well reasoned paper against an election. He makes out a formidable case with rising prices discontented unemployed etc. and I think I must spend a little time in concocting a reply. But this will only be to clear my own mind as we shall be discussing the subject in Cabinet tomorrow afternoon.

I am a good deal disturbed in my mind about Dorothy. She is a very difficult child to deal with as she has a strong will and considerable independence. But with this she combines an inconsequence and lack of purpose that confounds and distresses me. Just now her C.C.H.F. work is at an end, and she has made no effort to find anything to take its place. She hates social functions and makes her music a constant excuse for refusing other engagements. Yet she is no longer seriously pursuing her music and her practice is neglected. Day after day & night after night she goes to the "pictures" or the theatre or the opera or concert room but all without method. I have been suggesting to her a course of domestic economy at which she grasps eagerly showing that the right spirit is there if one can give it a suitable opportunity. Can you help me with any suggestions and do you happen to know of a good school?

4 October 1931
37 Eaton Square, SW1

My dear Ida,

You are right in thinking that this has been a most anxious & harassing week, though I am glad to say it has come out right in the end.

When I wrote last, I thought we were rapidly approaching the crisis but although Macdonald [sic] had not actually defined his intentions I believed from what Thomas told me that he was prepared to carry on whatever the Liberals might do. You can imagine my consternation when on Monday he circulated a memo which meant if it meant anything that he was not prepared for a dissolution unless H. Samuel and Reading remained in the Government and agreed the policy. On receipt of this memo I went to see Samuel to find out how far he was prepared to go, but though he was very forthcoming and evidently anxious for an agreement he was extremely reticent & non committal on policy and talked chiefly about the necessity for avoiding an election. The Cabinet that afternoon was very unsatisfactory the P.M. showing every sign of going back on us and I proposed that I should have a further interview with Samuel, hoping that in the meantime I might see the P.M. myself. I did in fact get an appointment with him for 9.30 but before then he sent word that he had gone to bed with a bad headache. This sounded ominous but I saw his P.P.S. and made another appointment for 10.30 on Tuesday morning. That night I determined to compose a sort of draft memorandum for a National Government programme so worded as to secure the P.M.'s assent. I thought if he accepted it and then H.S. objected he might get annoyed and perhaps be ready to go on without him. Instead of insisting on a tariff I based the crucial passage on the necessity for checking imports, leaving the method of control open (i.e. either prohibition tariffs or any other means). Next morning early I showed my draft to S.B. who approved it and then took it to Ramsay who read it attentively and then said "I agree with every word of this and I shall work upon it". Everything went according to plan. Ramsay produced my draft (the now famous formula) at the Cabinet, Samuel immediately objected to it and the P.M. got very cross indeed with him. He declared that I had made a very substantial contribution to a solution of our difficulties & said plainly that a speedy election was inevitable. Next day we met again and Samuel & Reading asked for more time to allow them to see L.G. Samuel went that afternoon to Churt where he got a proper dressing down from L.G. who objected vehemently to an election and wanted the Liberal members of the Govt to resign. Next day Thursday Reading went on a similar pilgrimage with the same result and when we met at 6.30 we expected the break would come. To our astonishment Samuel said he could not surrender his judgement to L.G. and he thought that with some small alterations to the formula, an agreement might be possible. The P.M. then suggested a committee of three to examine the formula and S.B. at once asked me to represent him. So the P.M. Herbert Samuel and I met after dinner to see what we could do. I was searching for a breaking point, but it was no good. Samuel was determined to come in and after some small alterations which gave nothing away I was obliged to give my assent. There was one more chance. Samuel said he must consult the Lib. Ministers to get their confirmation and once more we adjourned for half an hour to give him time for this. We were in a nice stew, not believing that the Libs were converted and seeing every kind of difficulty in the constituencies but not being able to find any good reason for refusing to cooperate with them if they accepted our formula. However when we met again at 10.30 Samuel said Ministers would not accept. Once more we hoped that the P.M. would clinch & say in that case we must go on without them. But he could not make up his mind and as the Liberals declared that they wanted more time and that it was not fair to rush them we agreed to give them till 2.30 on Friday. The P.M. was going to Seaham that day which seemed a misfortune but after all it turned out to be providential. When we met on Friday the Liberals proposed an alteration the effect of which was to say that we would only control imports if it were found necessary. Here at last was my opportunity and I jumped upon it. I said that the words in the original document did imply a commitment to deal with imports that they were always intended to commit us and that we could not give way on that point. The unlucky Samuel found himself caught. He had been told not to commit himself to anything but an open mind (which meant a free hand to resist a tariff) and he dared not give way. So at last in Ramsay's absence we came to the breaking point and separated. Luckily that afternoon there were Liberal party meetings which passed stiff Free Trade resolutions so I dont think Samuel can go back. We still have to carry the P.M. to the next step but I think even he cannot now refuse to go on.

It has been a wearing business but I have nothing to reproach myself with and I think I have played my cards successfully and got what I wanted.

You ask about dates & I think you can take it that nomination day will be Oct 19 & polling day the 27th. I saw Max on Thursday and he will support us "all out". He believes we shall get a sweeping majority.

…

10 October 1931
Westbourne

My dear Hilda,

…

Things went all wrong again after I wrote to you last. The P.M. had a letter from L.G. asking to see him and went to Churt on Monday morning. You can imagine how artfully the little man went to work, playing on his feelings, showing him how we and the Liberals would be at loggerheads at once, and how he was being made a tool of by those wicked Tories. L.G. declared that I "lived" at Stornaway House and had made a sinister pact with Max at Ramsay's expense and drew an awful picture of the fool he would look when we demanded food taxes as soon as the election was over. The result of all this was that Ramsay's nerve went all to pieces and when S.B. & I went to see him at 4 o'clock that afternoon he produced a draft manifesto that would have simply horrified our people. We told him that it was out of the question, that he must go back to my manifesto in which I offered to make a slight alteration which I thought might make it a little more acceptable to Liberals and that finally he must come to some decision that evening. He agreed then to summon the Cabinet for half past ten and we went to it resolved to resign if he tried to postpone a settlement any longer. To our consternation he announced that as he had failed to achieve agreement he saw nothing for it but to go on as we were without an election. Samuel & Reading of course purred their satisfaction – the rest of us declared that we could not accept such a course. Thereupon Ramsay said in that case the election was decided and it only (!) remained to consider how we should appeal. Snowden[50] then produced the suggestion that the P.M. should issue his own manifesto asking for a free hand and the two Party Leaders should each issue their own programmes and to our astonishment this was at once accepted by the Liberals. Ramsay afterwards told me privately that he had only made his suggestion of no election in order to convince Samuel that it was impossible, but I dont altogether believe him. I know he told someone definitely that day that he had decided against an election and I believe he tried it on in the hope that we would accept it.

Anyway, here we are now committed to this extraordinary proceeding under which we go to the country as a united Government, one section of which is to advocate tariffs while the other declares it has an open mind but is unalterably convinced of the virtues of Free Trade. And Ramsay Muir's[51] secret letter to Liberal candidates now revealed shows how he proposes to interpret the situation. Denounce the election, denounce the Free Hand and oppose protectionists even if they support the National Government. I never fought an election under such a difficulty.

I wonder what you thought of S.B.'s manifesto. Austen was delighted with it but it never occurred to him that I had spent most of Thursday morning in re-writing the dreadful wishy-washy document which S.B. presented for my criticism. I hope we may win the victory which we anticipate but if we do I foresee a peck of troubles as soon as the election is over, first in the formation of the Government and then in the formulation of policy.

---

[50] This is an error. Samuel suddenly and unexpectedly produced a typed statement with the proposal. See Chamberlain Diary, 5 October 1931.

[51] (John) Ramsay Bryce Muir (1872–1941). Professor of Modern History, Liverpool and Manchester Universities, 1906–21. Liberal MP for Rochdale 1923–24; unsuccessfully stood elsewhere 1926, 1929, 1931 and 1935. Chairman, Organising Committee of Liberal Party 1930–31; Chairman, National Liberal Federation 1931–35 and President 1933–36.

Well, its no use to meet trouble half way and for the next two weeks I suppose each minute will be worse than the last. I am to have a Socialist opponent but as he is only being adopted at the last moment I am not going to have more than 3 meetings in the constituency spending the rest of my time speaking about the country. I believe I am to broadcast on Thursday.

We had a great meeting here last night and S.B. was quite at his best. Enormous numbers of people were turned away from the doors and the crowds in the street were like those on polling day. We ought to do well here though I was rather astounded to hear today that Ramsay had demanded that we should hand over the Erdington seat to a National Socialist. You can imagine the fury of our people.

Dont be surprised if I fail to write next week. I shall probably be dead!

18 October 1931
Westbourne

My dear Ida,

I am not dead by any means so I think I might spare time to send you a line as usual.

...

I was so wrong about the last election that I dont like to prophesy about this one. But I do know that the Socialists themselves expected to lose many seats and wherever I have been I have found our people very confident. There is much more interest than there was last time and everyone of my meetings has been packed out and quantities of people turned away. ... As for "savaging" I have seen nothing of it so far. There were a good many Socialists at Wakefield but they were as tame as white mice.

Austen told me last week that he didn't think he would accept office but that he hadn't told you yet. Of course if he were offered the F.O. he would certainly take it but he realises that is very unlikely. I do sympathise with him very deeply. It is perfectly beastly for him to feel that his work at the F.O. was not appreciated by his party and the only other place that would I think be acceptable to him is the one now occupied by S.B. But I confess I don't quite see what S.B. could have done unless he had asked that he should be in the Cabinet instead of one of the others and he felt that if we were only to have four inside it would be very difficult to ask for two Chamberlains. If he went on at the Admiralty I think there is no doubt that he would be in the Cabinet but he doesn't seem much inclined to accept that position.

Dont count too confidently on my going to the Exchequer. It is my belief that we shall have much more trouble with the P.M. than with Samuel and I have a feeling that he would very much prefer Runciman to me in the key position. He is terrified of being made the servant of the Conservative Party and I feel sure he will struggle to get the largest possible number of Liberals and Socialists into his Government.

Well, I have got 5 speeches done and there are five more this week but so far I am not as tired as I expected. …

… I met my opponent at the nomination – a pleasant but quite ineffective person I thought.

Annie is going round & seeing people but finds it tires her a good deal and interferes with her sleep. She will have to go slow again or she will knock herself up.

It is pleasant to think it will be nearly over this day week.

24 October 1931
Westbourne

My dear Hilda,

After all at the end of the second week I find myself still quite fresh though I am very glad not to have do [sic] a third. Of course I dont suffer like I used to do when I began speech making but even now I am so uncomfortable beforehand that sometimes I feel before a meeting that I really cannot face it. I have to take myself sternly in hand and consider that in a couple of hours it will be over and that I have always got through it before. And when finally I am on my feet I lose my nervousness and feel that I can dominate my audience.

I have never before had such crowds to address nor so little interruption. People seem to want to hear every word that may enlighten them and even the Socialists remain quiet and subdued. At Bolton the huge drill hall, the largest in the country was packed to the doors and a large riding school opening out of it was also crammed. The speech was relayed into it so that all could hear without difficulty and the local people estimated that there were from 8000 to 10000 present. It was interesting, as showing the want of enthusiasm among the opposition, that Henderson who had a meeting only a few days before in the same place had an audience of about 2000 … The canvas appears to show a much more favourable result than last time and every canvasser has stories of Socialists declaring themselves "fed up" with their own people and determined to vote "National". I hope that we may presently develop into a National Party and get rid of that odious title of Conservative which has kept so many from joining us in the past.

…

I see the Herald gives Austen's seat as one that the Socialists are to win but I dont think the local members of the Party have any such expectation. They have some hopes of winning back Kings Norton and expect to retain Deritend, Duddeston and Yardley but the indications are that they wont come off with more than 2 seats in Birmingham. I am hoping that Austen will get a really substantial victory for his last fight.

S.B. has written to say he wants a good talk with me after the election and in the meantime he asks me to think over the "horrible problem" of who should be in & who should be out of the new Government. I fancy it will be easier to do that after we see the results, but it is a good sign that he wishes to discuss it with me. On the whole I think Macdonald [sic] has behaved well during the election and as far as I can see he has said nothing to make things more difficult for us afterwards. As for Snowden I quite agree with your view. If I had let what he said pass we should have been accused of a breach of faith if we had brought in a tariff. As it is Snowden has accepted my view, but I was struck myself by his use of the word "we" to which the Times called attention and I have been wondering whether that means that he is still to be a member of the Government, though no longer at the Treasury. If so that takes away another office from our party but I dont see that we could raise any objection, especially as he has done so much to win us the election.

Whatever happens to me I dont think I could be asked to remain at the Ministry of Health.

...

...

Well, when I write next the die will have been cast and I suppose a new crop of troubles will have sprung up. It looks as if the Round Table Conference was going fut and I see the D.H. is trying to put the blame on the National Government as you would expect.

...

7 November 1931
Moor Lane House

My dear Hilda,

... Except for a half hour when the Evening News telephoned me that Simon was going to the Treasury I never thought that R.M. could put anyone there who was not a member of our party, and in that case it must lie between S.B. and me. At any rate there is this consolation now that any doubts which existed were not directed against my capacity but against the views I was known to hold on Protection. Of course I was disappointed at not having Philip to work with and I should have preferred Simon to Runciman who has the reputation of being a difficult colleague. But Simon refused the Bd of Trade on the ground that it would give him a status inferior to Samuel! And so what are called the key positions are given to two men who as it is supposed will cancel one another out. Its a comic idea, but fortunately I like Runciman personally and I fancy he likes me so that at least we ought to start fair. I think I shall ask him to come and have a talk at once so that I may see where he stands.

I rather doubt by the way, whether you are right in supposing that my family connections have stood in my way on this occasion. In fact I always feel that in my political life I have to a large extent escaped the handicap which certainly afflicted Austen in being his father's son. The fact that they were for a long time actually in the House together made comparison inevitable. On the other hand to the majority my contemporaries in the House Father is a name only and they judge me on my own record. But, as I wrote to Austen the other day, he has now succeeded in establishing his own personality apart from Father's, and his latest action has greatly strengthened the "legend" that was already growing up of the "great gentleman" and model of chivalry. I fancy you dont take the Morning Post and so did not see the leader which declared that he had relinquished his claims because he felt himself to be "old and worn out" in the public service. A. was naturally much annoyed and I was so furious when it was brought to my attention that I wrote a "snorter" to Gwynne. I expect apologies are awaiting me at Eaton Sq. meanwhile, I was interested to see that he had tried to make amends yesterday in a long tribute.

Although I did want Philip at the Board of Trade I think that from his point of view he has got a more interesting and useful post. I have already had a few words with him and he says he is anxious to discuss any ideas I may have when I go to Swinton after Xmas.

S.B. tried hard to get something for Amery, but without success though R.M. says he thinks there must be a certain amount of reconstruction before long and if so there might be another chance. But I confess I am not very hopeful, partly because, although Amery's knowledge and brains are generally recognised, no one has any belief in his judgement, and partly because I have no belief in the likelihood of Liberals leaving the Govt. We may very likely get rid of Maclean but I believe Archie Sinclair[52] and "our Herb" will stick to their offices like leeches.

...

15 November 1931
Croxton Park, St Neots

My dear Ida,
... [T]here is a possibility of a European Economic Conference in December dealing with Reparations War Debts & frozen credits. ... I am afraid there can be no certainty about this Conference for some time yet ...

I had supposed that I should not be wanted to attend the Ottawa Conference in July, but there is some doubt about that too now. So there is the cheerful possibility of my getting no summer holiday in 1932 as well as in 1931 & no winter holiday either. Fortunately I remain well ...

---

[52] Archibald Henry Macdonald Sinclair (1890–1970). Personal Secretary to Churchill 1919–22. Liberal MP for Caithness and Sutherland 1922–45. Temporary Chairman of Committees in Commons 1925–30; Chief Liberal Whip 1930–31; Scottish Secretary 1931–32; Air Secretary 1940–45. Leader, Liberal Parliamentary Party 1935–45. Succeeded as Bart 1912. Created Viscount Thurso 1952.

The P.M. settled with Thomas and made his public announcement without giving his colleagues any opportunity of expressing an opinion on the subject. My Treasury people tell me that he and Snowden rode roughshod over the last Cabinet and I expect that has got him into bad ways. But if he continues to act as though he were Dictator & not P.M. I shall watch for a suitable opportunity & then show my teeth. I think he realises that at any time I choose he will have to deal with me and not S.B. and I dont at present observe any desire to get "across" me.

Indeed so far, no thanks either to him or S.B., we have had a success in the Cabinet which has fairly dumbfounded some of our friends like Bobby Monsell & Harry Betterton who are fresh to Cabinet work.

You would hardly believe it but at our second meeting when the sole item on the Agenda was the debate on the Address the P.M. gave a sort of outline of our programme which made no mention of dumping at all! It looked as if we might break up without any allusion to the possibility that the subject might be raised by our people. However I asked permission to give the Cabinet a warning against rash talk on the stabilisation of the £. From that I passed to the adverse balance of trade on which I had had the latest figures prepared and that easily led to the movements of imports, which as I informed the Cabinet showed signs of marked increase in November. "Our Erb" took alarm at once but he could not refuse the P.M.'s proposal to refer it to the Ch. of Exch. & the Pres. of the B/T. to investigate facts & report.

Runciman accordingly saw me that afternoon & himself proposed an enabling Bill to give him power to impose a 10% duty on excessive imports. I told him he must not tie his own hands more than necessary. He should therefore name not an invariable but a maximum rate with power to vary downwards at his discretion & for this 10% was not enough. I didn't mention any figure but he sent me a draft memo in which the 10% was increased to 20%. I didn't like his draft so I re-wrote it and left the figure blank, explaining that there was a danger lest the Cabinet shd spend all its time in arguing the rate instead of the principle. Let them accept the outline of the Bill, I said, and then we will settle the rate. Runciman accepted my draft and my suggestion and in Cabinet after the usual protests and feeble attempts at sabotage by Samuel & Maclean we came to the rate. I at once asked Snowden what he would suggest and, as I had hoped, he said What about 100%? Runciman at once agreed, Samuel couldn't think of any objection – so there it is. Comic, isn't it, to think of the Free Traders giving power to two Ministers to put a 100% duty on any mortal manufactured article they like!

I tried on Friday to get food drink & tobacco included. It was skilfully done & I believe we might have got it if Runciman Snowden & Sinclair had not been absent. R. told me he was going to see his old mother; the Treasury tell me he had a shooting engagement. Anyway his absence gave the P.M. a good excuse for shirking Food Taxes & I thought it unwise to press the issue when no notice had been given that it would be raised. But logically we are right to leave Agriculture out as our Bill is to prevent forestalling and you can't forestall perishable things like black currants. We shant satisfy the agriculturists but I think we may get away with it by explaining that this is only a temporary measure & we are working out the agricultural policy which will be ready before the powers given by the Bill expire.

I am very glad to hear what you say about Austen. On the whole I think his action *has* been appreciated & has added a good deal to his prestige. I spoke to him about another directorship on Friday which I think I may be able to turn his way & which might give him another £1000 or even £1500. Possibly it might enable him to hang on to Rutland Gate. Next week I am going to Birm. to attend a meeting of Trustees & I hope I may get time enough to go into *my* financial affairs & settle finally what we are going to do. It seems impossible to sell my orchids and I am thinking of letting G.H.K. take anything he wants and handing the rest over to the Botanical Gardens.

...

21 November 1931
Westbourne

My dear Hilda,

...

... I am evidently in for that Government Conference on War Debts &c. I expect it wont meet till the new year but they say it will last for weeks when it once begins and that will be very awkward if the Cabinet is discussing policy meanwhile.

...

So far the Abnormal Imports Bill has gone extremely well and Runciman has made quite a reputation by his handling of it. But the agricultural people are very stirred up as I expected by the omission of their products and the P.M. has been made to realise that they cant be neglected. Gilmour has now put in a memo asking to be allowed to promise a wheat quota and I believe he is also going to put in a plea for a pronouncement on luxury fruits & vegetables. That will raise a new question in the Cabinet and I think a good deal will depend on Runciman's attitude. But I dont myself see how he can oppose it as he himself wanted to curtail luxury imports and if he approves I think Samuel will have to give way.

The next point will arise on Thomas' instructions. Is he to be allowed to negotiate for preferences on Empire food products? He himself seems very nervous about it but obviously the success of the [Ottawa] Conference is bound up with it and again I don't see how the Free Traders can oppose it. If they do they will I think have to go and it is certain that nothing would please our people so much, for which reason I doubt their going. I had a brush with Thomas himself in Cab. Comee. He proposed that any preferences given by us should apply to the whole Empire & that we should trust to them to give us an equivalent. I, on the other hand, declared for Treaties with each Dominion, to be afterwards ratified by the Empire as a whole and I supported my case with such good arguments that J.H.T. immediately turned round & said that was what he meant. I fancy this horrified his staff for when it came to recording the conclusions he tried very hard to whittle them away & bring them back nearer to his original proposal. He didn't succeed but we are to have another meeting next week with Simon & Runciman who were absent before and then I shall fight it out again. To my mind the point is fundamental and the only way to tie Thomas down to his instructions. On Monday I am dining with Bennett & Bruce at Hailshams, and I shall raise the question then & see what their attitude is. At present I have Philip & Jack Gilmour with me.

Meanwhile we have a series of first class problems in India & the international financial situation to deal with which require firm handling. Luckily I think both Hoare & Simon are very sound and though our P.M. constantly threatens to go off the rails we have hitherto always succeeded in bringing him back again. I am to dine with Simon on the 29th to meet Flandin[53] the French Finance Minister & shall be very glad of the opportunity as I think he will be one of my principal stumbling blocks.

I hope next week to be in a position to deal in Cabinet with Land Taxes on which (without asking the Cabinet) I have promised the House to make a statement before it rises.

...

This morning I attended a meeting of the Highbury Trustees. The Ministry of Pensions is giving it up at the end of the year and its future use has to be decided on in consultation with the Corpn who have the right to ask that it shall now be transferred to them. I thought it was an opportunity to return to my old idea so after the meeting I got hold of the Lord Mayor and Sir James Curtis[54] & suggested that they should consider the possibility of keeping the hall and the rooms on the ground floor as a memorial to Father. Unfortunately Austen allowed most of the furniture books &c to be sold so that it is not possible to restore it as it was, but I believe if the idea was accepted a surprising lot of objects connected with Father would come to light and form a collection which in days to come

---

[53] Pierre Etienne Flandin (1889–1958). Chef de Cabinet to French Prime Minister 1913–14. Entered Chamber of Deputies 1914. Director, Allied Aeronautical Service 1917; Under-Secretary, Air 1920; Minister of Commerce 1924, 1929 and 1930; Minister of Finance 1931 and 1932; Prime Minister 1934–35; Foreign Minister 1936. Tried and acquitted of collaboration 1946.

[54] James Curtis (1868–1942). Fifty years' service in local government. Midland Food Controller 1917–21 and 1936–41; Vice-Chairman, Central Valuation Committee of Ministry of Health 1928–38 and member, Railway Assessment Authority; advisor on Divisional Organisation to Ministry of Food 1941–45; member, Departmental Committee on Unemployment Insurance and Local Government Reconstruction. Knighted 1919.

would prove singularly interesting. It outrages my feelings that there should be no memorial to Father in Birmingham except the fountain put up to commemorate his municipal service. Indeed as Austen & I have both now made a certain reputation our association with the house might add something to its interest and if the right person were found to look after it, the collection might include a good deal of other things connected with other members of the family – B[eatrice] for instance. The Ld. Mayor & Curtis seemed rather taken with my idea and promised to examine it carefully.

29 November 1931
Chevening, Sevenoaks, Kent

My dear Ida,
Many congratulations on being an Alderman ... As to the "luck" in getting it I agree that there is a certain amount of chance in the attainment of all such things including Chairmanships of Committees and Councils, membership of Cabinets, Mayoralties, Premierships & so on. Sometimes people who scheme for them succeed in achieving the office and then, because they weren't really quite good enough, make nothing of it & leave no name behind. I always say that to be Prime Minister is very largely a matter of luck. To be recognised as capable of being Prime Minister is quite another matter. That at least puts you in a class on merits – and I think you can say the same about an Alderman!
...
Our National Government goes ahead at a giddy pace. As I expected we got Runciman with us over agriculture; Snowden growled but almost inaudibly, & the Samuelites offered no objection. Do you remember Hilda Mary dragging one our dogs about on a lead and when we protested that he was half choked & utterly miserable, declaring, "No, he *likes* it"! Samuel "likes it". But as for me I laff & laff twall I kin laff no mo'. The declaration has been taken extremely well. It is true there is still some grumbling about sugar beet, and barley and the neglect of Scotland. But the great majority see that we have done all that could be expected of us and are duly grateful. If you look back only to last July what would have been said then if it had been proposed to give the Ministers for Trade & Agriculture such powers as these. We have witnessed a political revolution in 3 months and though bloodless it is none the less effective. Particularly is this last advance valuable because it it [sic] is a breach in the defences of the anti-food taxers which will reveal the intrinsic weakness of their position, and immensely simplify our next task.
Our next task is to attack the Empire problem. I am myself very anxious that we should make some statement on the subject before the House rises and I hope, as soon as we get this accursed Indian problem out of the immediate foreground, to tackle the P.M. seriously about it. We had a very interesting and valuable talk at Hailshams last Monday. He and Bennett & Bruce, P. Cunliffe Lister & Amery,

Howard Ferguson[55] the Canadian High Commissioner and I. We established inter alia (1) that the Canadians are extremely anxious that J.H.T. should not visit the Dominions where they say he would degrade the whole Dominion conception of a British Statesman and the representative of a British National Government. (2) They are anxious for a speedy decision and announcement of a Dominion Wheat Quota. This would be very valuable to Bennett personally even though we announced that we should want something in return. Incidentally, the Dominions dont ask for a guaranteed price like the Home farmer. (3) The Canadians anticipate that if a Democrat should be returned at the next Presidential Election (by no means impossible) he would at once make an offer of Reciprocity so attractive that no Canadian Government could afford to refuse it. There is therefore no time to lose.

In the Cabinet however Samuel & McLean [sic] may & probably will make all the difficulties they can and they will be backed by Snowden who hates the quota. But he hates the Home quota more than the Empire Quota, and as the former is already decided he may not think it worth while to hold out very firmly against the latter. Runciman will be all right so long as we dont tax wheat & meat. His attitude appears to me utterly illogical but fortunately it doesn't matter as we dont require *at present* to tax either of these things, & by the time we do the cost of living may not be a matter of so much importance as now. So I am not on the whole without hope that I may get my way here too.

There are however two private difficulties which cause me some concern. The first is the Land Valuation scheme. Snowden while remaining very pleasant to me personally has taken my proposal to drop the valuation very badly. In effect he says this is using the Tory majority brutally & ruthlessly to force Tory medicine down his throat & that this Government has no mandate to drown his lively little kitten. He even threatened withdrawal if it were persisted in. This is all very well, but I cannot see how I can defend the retention of the kitten in my nursery and *I* may have to threaten withdrawal if it is *not* drowned. Of course I can defeat Snowden if I stand firm but I should be sorry indeed if he went and I can imagine that Samuel might seize the chance to go too on a pretext which he might think would give him more favourable ground than food taxes.

The other matter concerns the P.M. himself. I have discovered that he is holding meetings of economists & bankers including people like Keynes,[56]

---

[55] (George) Howard Ferguson (1870–1946). Canadian barrister and politician. Conservative MP for Ontario 1905–30; Premier of Ontario 1923–30. Resigned to become Canadian High Commissioner in London 1930–35.

[56] John Maynard Keynes (1883–1946). Economist. Fellow, King's College, Cambridge. Civil Servant from 1906; Treasury 1915–19. Principal Treasury Representative, Paris Peace Conference. Member, Macmillan Committee on Finance and Industry, 1929–31. Economic Adviser to government during and immediately after the Second World War.

McKenna Arthur Salter,[57] Stamp[58] & a number of others at which he discusses with them Government policy on currency, banking, international debts commercial & political, & Reparations. He does this while I am discussing the same things with the Governor of the Bank but there is this difference. The Governor and I are the responsible people who have eventually to take action; the others have no responsibility but a good many of them are financially interested in the results of the policy to be adopted.

I was invited to the last of these meetings & sent a message that I was already engaged. S.B. however went and gave me an account of what took place which made my hair stand on end & sent the Governor into hysterics.

I have got to go to the P.M. therefore & tell him that I must decline to attend his meetings, that I hope he will have no more of them but that if he does he will leave Govt policy out of the discussions (of course impossible) and finally that I am proposing to set up a Committee of my own, which will make his unnecessary. You will perceive that this conversation is likely to be of a somewhat delicate character and though the P.M. has seemed to me to be definitely making advances in my direction lately I am wondering whether I have any velvet glove thick enough to overcome the disagreeable impression of the metallic substance inside.

And yet how could any Chancellor carry on his work, in times like these when secrecy is one of the first essentials, in such circumstances? I doubt if there has ever been a time when so many grave dangers to the financial situation were present. The responsibility on the Chancellor is overwhelming and if he is to bear it, he must not be tripped up because it amuses the P.M. to tie strings across the grass.

I had a very heavy and harassing week which rather culminated on Thursday when I had two speeches to make one at the Advertisers luncheon the other at a dinner to the Beaver in the House. I felt rather below form with a good deal of headache & a bit of catarrh & a touch of gout but I suppose the necessity was the mother of effort and I came through not only successfully but with flying

---

[57] James Arthur Salter (1881–1975). Admiralty Transport Department 1904; Director of Ship Requisition 1917; Secretary-General, Reparations Commission 1920–22; Gladstone Professor of Political Theory and Institutions, Oxford 1933–44. Independent MP for Oxford University 1937–50; Conservative MP for Ormskirk 1951–53. Parliamentary Secretary to Ministry of Shipping 1939–41 and Ministry of War Transport 1941; head, British Merchant Shipping Mission to Washington 1941–43; Chancellor, Duchy of Lancaster 1945; Minister of Economic Affairs 1951–52; Minister of Materials 1952–53. Knighted 1922. Created Baron Salter 1953.

[58] Josiah Charles Stamp (1880–1941). Economist and statistician. Entered Inland Revenue 1896 and Board of Trade 1898; resigned from Civil Service 1919. Secretary and Director, Nobel Industries 1919–26; British Representative on Reparations Committees of 1924 (Dawes) and 1929 (Young). Member, Samuel Commission on coal industry 1925; Director, ICI 1927–28. Joint Secretary, Royal Statistical Society 1920–30 and President 1930–32. Knighted 1920. Created Baron Stamp 1930.

colours. The Advertisers I went to in order to please Lord Luke[59] (of Bovril!) who has been very good (financially) to the Research Department and from whom I am hoping to get further help. Incidentally it is through him that I heard of the Crosse & Blackwell Chairmanship for A.C. The dinner to the Beaver turned out to be a personal triumph for – me. Max was by no means equal to the occasion. After dinner speaking is not in his line and he was heavy in hand & packed his speech with too many statistics. But I have heard from many quarters that I had made the speech of my life "never been so like your father" "inspired us all" &c, and I was genuinely gratified because some of the "New Boys" were there and I have had no opportunity of making myself heard in the House except at question time.

...

We drive home this afternoon in order that I may dine with the great Flandin tonight. Isn't it amusing to see how the foreigners are all flocking to our doorstep to ask whether it wouldn't be good time [sic] for a talk about tariffs? France, Germany, Holland, Belgium & Denmark *already*. Of course we always said they would.

...

                                                      6 December 1931
                                                      37 Eaton Square, SW1
My dear Hilda,

...

I do see very little of Austen now and am so busy in the afternoons that I am generally not in the House & so dont even hear his speeches. I hear of them however and gather that, as you say, they produce a great effect and give him perhaps a greater weight in this House than if he were a Minister. I did meet him at lunch on Thursday and we had a few words but not on personal matters. I believe however that the Directorship (Crosse & Blackwell) *will* be offered him that it will carry a good salary and that the "catch" is that it is in a pretty bad way and will require at least some years of hard & well directed work to put it back into a paying condition. In his position I should certainly take it.

As to houses ... [i]t appears impossible at present to let or sell this place so Annie has given notice to all the servants & is going to try and manage with a different kind of staff. I am rather afraid it wont be anything like enough and though I dont want to do anything hastily I find it growing upon me that we shall

---

[59] George Lawson Johnston (1873–1943). Businessman and philanthropist. Father founded Bovril; joined Board 1896; Vice-Chairman 1900; Chairman 1916; Managing Director 1931. Close association with King Edward's Hospital Fund from 1901–43 and Royal Northern Hospital 1909–23. Introduced Voluntary Hospital (Paying Patients) Act 1936. Chairman, *Truth* and Business Committee of National Publicity Bureau. Knighted 1920. Created Baron Luke 1929.

have presently to give up Westbourne. Hoskins has made a loss this year as I fully expected. I think Hall has done well to get through with a trading deficiency of £4000.

Now to continue my story and answer some of your questions, the position of the £ does give me a good deal of anxiety. So long as it doesn't go below where it is now and there is no panic we can manage. What I fear is a wholesale withdrawal of foreign holdings of sterling which still amount to a very large sum. The drop which has already taken place has of course depreciated very seriously the value of these holdings and if they are realised the holders will suffer severe losses. If therefore they think that the £ is likely to recover they will hold on and that is why the French are so anxious to see us return to the gold standard. On the other hand if they anticipated a further serious fall in the value of the £ they might think it necessary to cut their losses. With what seems to me an extraordinary failure of that logic which is supposed to be their special characteristic they insist on Reparations before commercial credits from Germany, thus "freezing up" British financial resources and threatening the stability of the £ which they are so anxious to restore. The absurdest part of their conduct is that while they keep the whole of Europe in a state of nervous anxiety and are thereby precipitating the advent of Hitler[60] to power, they are making it impossible for Germany to pay any Reparations. The only chance of her ever doing so is to be put in a position to trade so as eventually to provide the surplus from which alone Reparations can come. Altogether France is behaving pretty badly just now and if she thinks she can bully us into supporting her on Reparations by putting 15% on our coal she is very much mistaken. But I should not be surprised if she attempted to squeeze us by operating on her sterling balances next week and I expect to see the £ drop again.

The fact is that France and America are both thinking of their forthcoming elections. Any Reparations settlement or adjustment must be accompanied by a corresponding settlement or adjustment of war debts. Hoover knows it but daren't say so. Unless he says so France darent move and so we are all locked in a suicidal embrace which will probably drown the lot of us!

Reflect on this (1) We remitted nearly £400 millions of France's debt to us. (2) If the U.S.A. had agreed to fund our debt on the same terms as she gave to France we should have so overpaid that to put it right we should pay *nothing* for another 9 years! Did ever a country exploit her misfortunes more successfully than France? But on Sunday Flandin began the conversation by enquiring whether "you are going to ruin my poor country!" He was a hard nut and we got nothing out of him. On the other hand I don't think he got much out of us.

---

[60] Adolf Hitler (1889–1945). Born Austria-Hungary. Corporal, German Army 1914–18. Became leader of National Socialist Workers Party 1921; staged unsuccessful Munich *putsch* November 1923 for which imprisoned 1924; published *Mein Kampf* 1925. Chancellor of German Reich 30 January 1933–45; Chief of State August 1934. Committed suicide, Berlin April 1945.

I saw Snowden again on Tuesday and found him quite immovable. If I pressed the suspension of valuation it would be an abuse of the Tory majority & he would resign. If I postponed the decision till February he would still resign but his resignation would not matter so much. I was of opinion that a resignation now, accompanied as it would be certainly by McLean [sic] & possibly by Samuel, would be too dangerous & might precipitate a financial crisis and so I told the P.M. when I saw him on Wednesday morning. I therefore said that I was willing to face my own party though I thought I was being very unfairly treated. The P.M. however said that Snowden was an "awfully difficult colleague" and he would see him. Apparently however he was unable to get Snowden to see him so he wrote, and received an uncompromising reply in which the little man persisted in regarding any attack on his darling as a "dirty Tory trick", and the P.M. wrote to me asking me to postpone my decision till February. But in the meantime I found the Treasury did not take such an alarmist view of the effect of Cabinet changes as I had done and moreover several of my colleagues say they would rather have the break now & be freed from the difficulties which Snowden would surely make about tariffs. In the end I have got a Cabinet called for tomorrow afternoon & I have circulated a memo in which I strongly recommend suspension. So we shall join battle at once but I think the issue depends on the P.M. I dont mean to make it a resigning matter now, but I will not consent to postpone a decision longer than February & I shall say so.

On Wednesday we got the Dominion Quota through the Cabinet pretty easily, but postponed discussion on food taxes. I feel sure that D. McLean [sic] will make their inclusion as a possibility in Imperial trade agreements an excuse for leaving the Govt in which he is getting more and more uncomfortable. The P.M. said something the other day, which I confess frightened me, to the effect that the people of this country would never stand to [sic] food taxes. To go into the Conference saying we rule out food taxes would be to kill it before it had started and I will never consent to that. I think therefore this coming week will be the most critical in the history of the Govt. It will be obliged at last to face the realities. I wish I thought we should get some help from S.B.

I had a plain talk with the P.M. over this "Advisory Comee" which I have refused to attend and I must say he was very nice about it & took it extremely well. Not only did he assure me that he had no wish to poach on my ground or to interfere with my conduct of finances but, as I heard afterwards from Runciman, when the Committee met he began by reminding them that they were there merely to enlighten him on questions with which he was not very familiar and that any question of Government policy was entirely outside their sphere! He is beginning to expand more to me and if we dont quarrel this week we may yet get a good deal more mutual confidence though his temperament is too different from mine for us ever fully to understand one another.

As I came out from the P.M.'s room on Wednesday I found Mr Gandhi quiled [sic] up on a sofa waiting to say farewell. So I introduced myself and had a couple of words with him. He is a revolting looking creature, without any redeeming feature in his face that I could see. Not that it was wicked or sly looking – there was just no charm whatever. I think the [Round Table] Conference has ended very satisfactorily when one considers how many unfortunate ways there were in which it might have come to a conclusion. It looks to me as if presently we should have one or more provinces asking for autonomy without waiting for the centre, and in that case we shall try & give it them. That is what I have always wanted & what I said to Edward when he went to India. Let them make their experiments in self government so that they and we may see what they make of it. If they are successful, well & good. That will give us confidence in going further. If on the other hand (as I think more likely) they fall down directly a really nasty situation arises, then there will be still a strong central Govt to step in and clear up the mess.

...

12 December 1931
Westbourne

My dear Ida,

I understand that my last letter *did* reach you untouched but Southon's trop de zele gave me some uncomfortable moments as the contents were not meant for publication. However the P.O. took the trouble to send a man round to assure me that the letter had been found & sealed and so I hope none of the P.O. Bolshies read it.

I think I said last week that I thought the next few days might be critical for the Government. Perhaps I should say the same again today, but I have a feeling that the crisis has passed. The struggle over the land taxes was the worst fence we have encountered but thanks to some preliminary propaganda Snowden found himself in a minority of one and decided that the moment was not opportune for resignation. Arthur Robinson whom I saw in the gallery a few days after was chuckling over the memorandum I had circulated to the Cabinet which he considered to be a masterpiece.

We are now at last getting down to what "our Jim" politely calls "the guts", i.e. our fiscal policy. The P.M. circulated some impossible proposals, examination by "experts", then a policy Committee of 4 viz N.C. Snowden Runciman and Hilton Young & finally a political Comee to consider any difficulties that might arise consisting of himself, Simon, Samuel & S.B. That is one Labour two Libs and a Conservative who could be depended on not to make trouble. I was horrified and got to work at once with the result that the experts and the political Committee have gone West and the policy committee has been enlarged by the addition of Simon, Philip C. Lister, Thomas, Gilmour and Samuel. This means that the fight will come in Committee. I shall be Chairman and we hold our first meeting next week. I am aiming at a decision for a tariff before we break up for

Xmas and I think it must be an Emergency Tariff to be introduced as soon as we return or otherwise the country will be swamped with imports. I am glad to say the P.M. is coming along very sweetly. He is getting much less stand offish to me and even called me by my Christian name the other day! It is true a member came to me and told me last week that he had reliable information that the P.M. had had 2 meetings with Socialists one with those in the House & the other with those out of it at which he had sought to know whether if he rejoined them he would find the leadership still open to him. One of the meetings my informant said had replied in the affirmative. He did not know which, but would find out and let me know. There may have been such meetings but I cant think that any idea of the course suggested can seriously have been in the P.M.'s mind.

On the whole I am well pleased with the way things have gone. I suppose it is partly due to my being Chancellor but in fact I find myself in a different position in this Cabinet from any other that I have sat in. It seems to me that I carry more weight. I certainly speak more; the P.M. shows much deference to what I say and as S.B. mostly remains silent our people look to me for the lead and I see that they get it.

My speech in the House went very well and was received with great satisfaction in the City. I am not entirely happy about the revenue which I shant be sure of for another month at least but my people are fairly confident & in fact I watered down what they had suggested I should say on the subject. ...

What struck me about this House both when I was speaking and when listening to others was its silence. In the last House one was always subjected to a good deal of barracking but the opposition are too cowed to say much and our own people want to listen. They are a good deal influenced by speeches but so far have behaved extremely well.

I see that Amery has begun to show his resentment at being left out by increasingly sharp attacks. I think he is foolish from his own point of view but perhaps he thinks he has no chance of office now. I was speaking here last night and replied really to his criticisms but I avoided any mention of his name as I dont want to be the first to begin personalities.

...

6

1932

'A Very Momentous Year':
The Tariff, Lausanne and Ottawa

3 January 1932
Westbourne

My dear Hilda,

...

I had a nice letter from Austen who felt I think a little conscience stricken at having so vigorously douched his brother with cold water just at Christmas time. As he has withdrawn all opposition to the Highbury scheme I regret nothing that I have done and have had a further communication with the Lord Mayor who replies obediently that he will see that all my suggestions are faithfully carried out. Meanwhile I have written a *very* nice letter to Austen to explain that I still want his help in political matters. I shall write to Mary today and tell her a little of why I want the Highbury memorial.

...

... The Reparations preliminary talks have got into rather a trough and I dont seem to be quite in agreement with Simon, but I hope a talk may put matters right. I assume all the time that I go to Lausanne,[1] but have heard no word from the P.M. His famous letter to Laval[2] was sent without a word to either Simon or me, but I have since had a copy & I am glad to say it seems quite harmless. But the allusions to it in the press caused Snowden to send me a confidential letter of warning in which he complained in the bitterest terms of the way the P.M. had "butted in" on previous occasions. How these Labour men did love one another!

I feel that this is going to be a very momentous year for me. Probably it will be the turning point or perhaps I should rather say the critical point in my political career. If I dont make a success of it I shall slowly drop back. There's some luck about it, but most depends on myself, and I am not down hearted.

---

[1] An international conference on Reparations was scheduled to meet at Lausanne in January 1932 but was cancelled until 16 June because of impending French and German elections.

[2] Pierre Laval (1883–1945). French politician. Socialist Deputy 1914–19, 1924–27; Senator 1927–44. Minister of Public Works 1925; of Justice 1926; of Labour 1930 and 1932; Prime Minister and Foreign Minister 1931–32; Colonial Minister 1934; Foreign Minister 1934–35, 1940 and 1941–43; Prime Minister 1935–36; Deputy Prime Minister and Minister of Information 1940; Minister of Interior 1942; Deputy Head of State 1942–44. Executed for treason 1945.

17 January 1932
37 Eaton Square, SW1

My dear Hilda,

...

You were quite right in your deduction from what you saw in the Times. I did interview first our own press & then the Press Agencies on Thursday and yesterday as usual I saw the Sunday Times man. The position does not at the moment look as well as it did on trade policy but my experience teaches me not to be disheartened. In every really difficult negotiations there are times when things look black, but with patience & concentrated effort one can usually find some way out. ... When the [Balance of Trade] Committee met to examine my memo Snowden went back on his promise to Runciman and declared that he was opposed to the whole thing. We had to listen to an old time Free Trade disquisition and it was only by very tactful handling that I got him back to the discussion of the memo paragraph by paragraph. Then Samuel took up the wondrous tale & put up objection after objection, nor could I get any response to hints that I might be willing to meet him by widening the area of exclusion from the 10% tariff. Finally, seeing that we could get no further that day I proposed that Runciman shd get some more information & that we should meet on Monday to discuss it. I then asked Samuel to come to my room and told him that we must come to a final decision on Tuesday. He agreed but wanted us to confine ourselves to reporting that if the Cabinet took a certain decision such & such things would follow. I said this would not do; we must make definite recommendations as to what the Cabinet should decide. The question was what should be the nature of the decisions. After further discussion, Samuel said he would support wholeheartedly a proposal for powers to impose selective duties but he could not support or vote for any proposal for a flat rate tariff at any level or subject to any exclusions. I said I was sorry as I considered that essential and he thanked me warmly for so frankly discussing the situation and went away. I then saw Runciman who was very indignant over Samuel's intransigence and declared that he would resign if we didn't have a 10% tariff! After that I saw the P.M. He approved of the lines on which we were proceeding, rather thought Samuel would not carry things to an extremity but was concerned about Snowden's attitude. He had already heard about it from a third party and told me very confidentially that he had ascertained that Lady Snowden[3] was responsible for her husband's change of view. So on Friday I wrote a long confidential letter to Snowden using the arguments I thought most likely to weigh with him & begging him not to run out if we arrived at conclusions on Monday with which he did not agree. There is how things stand at present and I suppose tomorrow I

---

[3] Ethel Annakin (1881–1951). Married Philip Snowden, 1905. Campaigner for women's suffrage and temperance. Member, Labour Commission of Enquiry to Russia 1920 and Royal Commission on Food Prices 1925. Member, first Board of BBC 1927–33.

shall know my fate. Meanwhile I have drafted the committee's report in outline so that we may lose no time in getting it before the Cabinet. By the way I told the P.M. that I contemplated a Bill to be introduced the same week as his announcement of our policy and he raised no objection.

In foreign affairs, it is very curious to see how things seem to be working round to the course I suggested while I was at Beyn [?] namely that as we could not get a permanent settlement now we should work for a short extension of the moratorium coupled with a postponement of the Conference until we could assemble it with some prospect of a final settlement. I also urged that we should make no public statement which would link up Reparations & War Debts but deal with Repns first & then go to U.S.A. and ask them to make their contributions. At first I had every one against me the F.O. the Treasury the Bank and the Germans & French. By degrees each of them has come round and though we are by no means agreed yet and the French are being as difficult as they can it looks to me as if there were now a good chance at least of our coming to terms on something like these lines. We may not be able to avoid the conference altogether but if Ministers have to go I hope it may only be to ratify an arrangement which the "experts" will have worked out already. I saw the Italians this week and I am glad to say they are in complete accord while the Governor now says he agrees entirely with my proposals.

… I lunched with Esmond Harmsworth and the Editor of the Mail on Wednesday and instructed them on the true gospel with I hope useful results.

To turn to my domestic affairs which are sufficiently complicated. To begin with, I had hardly left the house on Friday to go and shoot with Weir in Suffolk when Annie went & took the flu. …

Next this miserable curate who has been making love to Dorothy for some weeks brought things to the test last night. I am glad to say that she rejected him, but she does like him very much (she is I fear rather too susceptible) and this has been a day of utter misery for the poor child. A. & I are now thankful to Stephen Lloyd for saving us from worse things, but the trouble is that D. isn't quite certain where she stands with Stephen. If only some "Tertius"[4] would step in with all the qualities (and possessions) we could desire! But it is ticklish work balancing on this tight rope and very difficult to know how to give advice that will be at once sound and satisfactory to Dorothy.

…

I am waiting (7.20) for a summons to Downing St to discuss the latest message from France. I spent an hour there this morning, but our P.M. has an insatiable appetite for tasks which would be better left to the men whose job it is to do them.

I walked to and from Downing St this morning. This afternoon D[orothy] & F[rank] & I picked up S.B. and took him to the zoo! After an hour's walking

---

[4] Translation: a third party expecting to profit from two others' quarrel.

there I walked all the way home. Pretty good for me, n'est ce pas? And yesterday I shot more pheasants than anyone else.

Here is the summons. When shall I get my dinner?

23 January 1932
Westbourne

My dear Ida,

As Lausanne is off for the present A. & I decided to come down here for the week end. ... We had ... to dine in the train instead of here but we ran into Willie Bridgeman at the station and so dined together.

Naturally he was much interested, as doubtless you have been, in the latest development of constitutional practice and now I must go back to the beginning of the week. Snowden replied very cordially to my letter. He was not moved by argument but was obviously touched by my appeal to his loyalty and though he did not say what he would do he promised to weigh up very carefully what I had said.

We had our last Committee meeting on Monday. All agreed to my proposal except Samuel and Snowden but the latter's attitude was quite different from what it had been. Instead of continually raising difficulties he remained silent until Samuel proposed further investigations when he said we ought to come to a conclusion at once. I said Samuel had better put his views on paper and, to save time, circulate them direct to the Cabinet. He objected to the 10% general tariff but was prepared to accept the other part[.] Snowden asked if I minded his also circulating his views and I said no. I got the report finished that night and next day the three papers were circulated. I reported to the P.M. what had happened saying I did not think Samuel would go but suggesting that when the right moment came the P.M. might tell Snowden that he would be at liberty to express his dissent in public & still remain in the Cabinet. Accordingly we met on Thursday morning and adjourned at lunch time for a further meeting the same afternoon. I still thought things would go all right, but as I afterwards heard the four dissentients lunched together and determined on resignation. When we reassembled Samuel who had left off in the middle of his case resumed in a perceptibly harder tone though he still said nothing about resignation. Finally the P.M. expressed his own views coming down in favour of the proposals and then Samuel sprang his mine declaring that he could not support them. McLean [sic] immediately followed on the same lines and Snowden and Sinclair announced their agreement. On that the P.M. said he would take no decision that night and we broke up. When we met again on Friday the P.M. who had gone through another agony of indecision drew attention to the disastrous effect abroad of a break-up & then dwelt on his own embarrassment forced as he would be to fill all the vacancies with Tories! However he had made up his mind to stay but only on condition that he was requested to do so. Samuel then took up the wondrous tale, claiming that he and his friends were free to act as they thought right, expressing his regret at the necessity of parting, re-affirming the impossibility of accepting the proposals but expressing his willingness to sit down again and see if we could find any other plan on which we could agree.

I thought it necessary to intervene at once. I said I had no reproaches to make. Samuel & Co were free to do what they chose, and must take the responsibility for their action. It was of no use to sit down again; we had gone thoroughly into the question and if it had been possible to find alternatives I was sure the ingenuity of the Home Secretary would have produced them. As for the P.M. if we had to go on without our colleagues it would make no difference to our attitude towards him we should still consider ourselves a National Government and we should withdraw nothing of our confidence in him. This observation drew warm assent from all our men and the P.M. was obviously gratified. At this moment however Hailsham intervened with the proposal that all the dissentients should be allowed to express their objections & to disclaim responsibility for the proposals while remaining members of the Government and he justified this departure on the ground that we were a National & not a Party Government. I confess I had not thought it possible for members of the House of Commons to take such a course though I had contemplated that Snowden might do it. However to my astonishment McLean [sic] at once said that such a proposal merited careful consideration. After a little more discussion the 4 dissentients withdrew to consult and after about ¼ hr they came back and said they would accept. All that remained to do was to draft a communiqué to the Press & accordingly Simon Samuel & I proceeded to work out the statement that you have seen.

Of course this novel plan will be very hotly criticised by the opposition but it has had a pretty good press and I think the general verdict will be as put by the Daily Mail that this is a sensible arrangement which will be approved by all practical men. It is the dissentients who will suffer embarrassment. I am well satisfied, for not only have I got my way but the dissent of the Free Traders cuts the ground from under the feet of the critics in our own party. They cannot say I have sold the pass. I may have some further trouble with Samuel but I think I may fairly claim that he is not entitled to use his position in the Cabinet to obstruct or hamper the proposals approved by the majority. There will be difficulties at bye-elections, and I suppose Samuel & Co will vote against the 2nd Reading of my Bill. But he cant go on voting against us all through Committee or take part in a Free Trade Campaign.

Lausanne gets no easier, and I have had endless meetings with Simon & the P.M. with the object of trying to find a way out. I think we shall soon have to make a public statement of our views but we have withheld it up to now lest we should bring about a definite breach with France. What I am anxious to get is a sufficient moratorium to allow us to discuss the possibility of a final settlement *after* the French & German elections and in spite of all the difficulties I haven't yet given up hope of doing so.

Dorothy has got over her troubles pro tem as the curate refuses to take his disappointment tragically and says he will get over it like measles. ... We hope indeed that the experience may be useful in showing Dorothy how far it is possible for her to care about different men and also how much pain & trouble she can make for herself by doing so. Certainly she is much more doubtful about the wisdom of marrying Stephen than she was a year ago and that I think justifies us in the way we have treated the affair.

...

6 February 1932
37 Eaton Square, SW1

My dear Ida,

I was so delighted that Hilda was in the gallery on the great day of my life.[5] I wish indeed that both my sisters had been present to see Father's triumph for it was really his.

If I had obeyed my own instincts I should have kept my emotions entirely to myself. But when I saw how the Press was talking of the historic fitness of the occasion I knew that if I said nothing it would not be understood and people would have felt that there was something missing. It wasn't easy to say it, for though I didn't fear that I should break down I did fear that I might not be able to control my voice. However by going slow I did manage it and I have no doubt now that it was right to do it and that the House was moved as it is not often.

One thing I was anxious about & that was that Austen should not be left out. You are the only person who has mentioned it – the press didn't understand but I think Austen did.

Looking back it still gives me cold shivers to think how near we were to a colossal blunder. I dont think I have told you the story, but if I am repeating myself you must forgive me, for it is an interesting bit of inside history.

In my original plan I intended to give the Dominions the $\frac{1}{3}$ preference which has been accorded to them on all the safeguarding duties, leaving the remaining $\frac{2}{3}$ to be discussed at Ottawa. This $\frac{1}{3}$ appeared in all the memoranda which I prepared for my committee but just before our last meeting Thomas came to me and begged me to leave it out as he wanted all he could get to bargain with. It seemed rather difficult for me as Chancellor to urge a project involving a loss of revenue against the Minister responsible for the Department which was to benefit and I supposed that he knew his business well enough to be sure that no mischief would be done. I was however relieved when Max Beaverbrook told me that in

---

[5] Chamberlain introduced the Import Duties Bill on 4 February 1932 concluding with a moving personal tribute to his father's frustrated vision and the consolation that 'the direct and legitimate descendants of his own conception, would be laid before the House of Commons ... in the presence of one and by the lips of the other of the two immediate successors to his name and blood'.

his opinion the Dominions would mind nothing except the duty on flour which he thought the Canadians would dislike. He knew (I dont know how) that I had wanted to give the ⅓ but said he was glad I had not done so. That was on Thursday 28ᵗʰ Jan. Judge of my astonishment when on the following Monday the Express came out with a violent article declaring that we were about to commit a capital blunder in taxing the Dominions. I was sure that Max had not intended this when I saw him and it suddenly occurred to me that he must have learned something from Canada. Thomas had meanwhile gone to Geneva and feeling that something must be done I sent for Howard Ferguson the Canadian High Commissioner who is in close touch with Bennett and asked him if he had heard anything.

What he said confirmed my worst fears. He said he had warned Thomas 3 weeks ago and had tried to see him on Saturday but Thomas had refused saying he was just off to Geneva and it would be "all right at Ottawa". Bennett was in a state of great agitation saying that if we were going to put the 10% on Dominion products there would be no use in having a Conference at all and he would be forced at once to raise the Canadian tariff against the Home Country. Ferguson begged me to put off the operation of the duties till after Ottawa. Bennett was holding a meeting of his Cabinet that day and was going to cable the result and if I liked he would give me a confidential copy of the telegram. There was a party at Londonderry House that afternoon where I saw Baldwin & told him what I had done. I found he was in nominal charge of the Dominions office, which I did not know before, but he entirely approved my action. After the party I went straight to the P.M. and told him the story. He was very much concerned and at once communicated with the Dominions office who told him that they attached great importance to giving nothing away and that Thomas felt very strongly about it.

Next day Ferguson brought me the cable from Bennett, repeating that the course proposed by Thomas would be disastrous & that if it were persisted in he believed the Conference would never meet.

That day there was much telephoning with Geneva and it was reported that Mr Thomas was greatly upset & was talking of resigning. However on Wednesday I read Bennetts cable to the Cabinet and urged that we could not afford to jeopardise the Conference and should at once make up our minds to say that the duties would not come into operation for the Dominions until it was over. On Macdonald's [sic] suggestion I was asked to telephone to Geneva and tell Thomas that the Cabinet wished to adopt my suggestion and hoped he would agree. So I went out there & then and telephoned in the next room. Thomas said it was a conspiracy between Max[,] Bennett and Ferguson to do him in and he strongly resented it but presently he said he would call together the Dominion representatives at Geneva and talk to them and he would telephone again in the evening whether he would "drop it or chuck it". I guessed that to mean that he would drop it but asked if in the meantime I might go on drafting my statement on the assumption that my plan was adopted. To that he said yes and in the evening he rang me up here to make his report. His account was obscure but I gathered that with one accord the Dominions had shouted that if we put the duties on the game would be up and he concluded "You know 'ow 'ellishly I feel Nevil but I agree" and I read him the passage I had drafted. That was why I had to read it in the House but when I mentioned his name there were such derisive cheers that I was afraid someone had "blown the gaff". However I am assured that these jeers only meant that the opposition considered Thomas would agree to anything and they therefore thought it necessary to scoff at my observation that the proposal "had his full concurrence".

If he had not been away I should never have seen Ferguson and as he and Ferguson do not love one another he would probably never have guessed the reactions. There would have been a howl of indignation all round the Dominions and either we should have had to humiliate ourselves by a retreat or the Conference would have bust. Whew! It still makes me sweat to think of our narrow escape!

Samuel made a fearful bloomer and I hear the lobbies were like a hornet's nest after his speech [on the Import Duties Bill]. I sent for D. MacLean [sic] & told him the only way to clear up the mess was for him to speak in the debate on Monday and pull the thing back into its proper perspective. Poor Donald, who *is* a gentleman, was quite conscious of the mess his colleague had made and is going to do his best but I don't envy him his job. But I guess Samuel has really spiked the guns of his own side for if that sort of speech were ever repeated his position would be untenable.

I have had an enormous lot of letters and telegrams ranging from the King to my tailor. I will show you some of them some day for they are very pleasant reading and some of them very affecting. ...

Well, I suppose we shall gradually realise that the great change has come and is not a dream but it is hard to believe it yet. ...

...

13 February 1932
Westbourne

My dear Hilda,

...

I entirely share your disgust with the N.F.U. They really are intolerable. The more you do for them the more they curse you for not doing something else. But they will do nothing for themselves, except hold indignation meetings.

Every one else seems pleased on the whole though of course we shall be bombarded with requests for further admission to the free list. It is rather curious that Runciman who began by wanting to tax even cotton & wool, is now finding himself compelled to put in quite a long list. I myself have given way very reluctantly because once any article gets on to the free list you can't take it off again although if it is not included it can be added afterwards. But it was difficult to justify taxation of articles not produced here or in the Empire except on grounds of revenue and I cannot at this stage declare my Budget hand.

I only put in the provision enabling the Committee to recommend additions to the free list after 6 months at the last moment. But it was clear to me that there ought to be such a power because as soon as the general tax was proposed we began to get representations about the vital importance of all sorts of articles of which we had never heard. The whole Bill is drafted so as to give the greatest amount of flexibility and I think it is a good Bill. But its success will depend a great deal on the [Advisory] Committee.

We tried to get Sir Ralph Wedgwood[6] as chairman but he has declined on the ground that he is too much of a free trader, on which Runciman promptly turned him down. I am thinking now of a man whose name is not so well known but who has a very good reputation in the City.

I understand that Sinclair is going to speak on the second reading of the Bill. He makes a bad impression on us in Cabinet where he talks much too much and fails to carry conviction. If he makes a speech like Samuel our people will be so angry that it will be almost impossible for Liberals of the Samuel breed to remain in the Government. But I should think he would be more careful, and in that case the situation will clear itself. After all in a fortnight the Bill will be on the Statute Book and in operation. The issue therefore will be decided and it seems to me that the Free Trade Liberals if they support the Government will have to accept that and say no more about it.

...

We have at last succeeded in getting a formula accepted by the French and if the Germans will also agree we shall have moved forward a very, very little way. It amounts to this that we agree to a Conference in June at which we are to try and find a lasting settlement of Reparations and then go on to consider other things which are not specified but include War Debts currency distribution of gold and tariffs. Nothing is said about a further moratorium because the French wont agree (before their election) to any total suspension of payment and the Germans wont agree (before their election) to anything which suggests a payment at all. And we cant mention War Debts because the Americans wont agree (before their election) to consider any relaxation. As for the standstill agreement that comes to an end on the 29th but the bankers have agreed to renew it provided that the French dont refuse to renew a credit they have granted to the Reichsbank. They have (the French) have [sic] been very tiresome about it but I hope now

---

6 Ralph Lewis Wedgwood (1874–1956). Deputy General Manager, North Eastern Railway 1919–21 and General Manager 1922; Chief General Manager, London & North Eastern Railway 1923–39; Chairman, Railway Executive Committee 1939–41; Member, Central Electricity Board 1931–46. Created Bart 1942.

they will be more reasonable and meanwhile on seeing our retaliation clauses they have promised to withdraw the surtax on coal at once.[7]

As for disarmament I dont think anyone takes the French proposal seriously except her satellites, the Poles & the Little Entente. Whether we shall get anything we care about such as abolition of submarines or heavy bombers or reduction in size of battle ships seems very doubtful. It is difficult to go on talking about disarmament with Japan in her present condition. Our ambassador in Tokyo says he feels as if he were in a lunatic asylum.

...

20 February 1932
Westbourne

My dear Ida,

I am very much interested to hear of your remarkable rate reduction and particularly that it is to come mostly out of roads. I have just pruned the M/ Transport estimates rather drastically and justified it on the ground that big reductions by L.A.'s were probable. Of course Pybus[8] was not willing to admit this but what you say confirms my view. Here in Birmingham they are reducing 6d, which is not bad especially as roads dont count for much in a County Borough.

It has not been a very hard week really though I have had to be on the bench pretty continuously. My winding up speech on 2 R went very well – in fact I think it was the most successful thing I have done in that line, but the papers never report much of the debate after dinner. What particularly pleased our people was my allusion to Samuel "a marvellous backhander" Southby[9] (one of our Whips) called it. I was so pleased with it myself that I must tell you how it was done without giving Samuel any cause for complaint. Sinclair had spoken in the afternoon and I described his speech as eloquent and in places impassioned. Moreover I went on, it appeared to me to be unexceptionable [sic] in tone and taste. At this there were sympathetic cheers from all parts of the House, some applauding because they had heard the speech but more because they like the word "taste" which seemed to them to mark a contrast. However I proceeded "It differed in many respects from the speech of the Home Secretary" – but here

---

[7] In response to the French imposition of 15 per cent surtax on British coal on 12 November 1931, the Cabinet retaliated with a draft anti-discrimination Bill. The French withdrew the duty on 10 December.

[8] Percy John Pybus (1880–1935). Engineer and Liberal MP for Harwich 1929–35 (Liberal National from 1931). Minister of Transport 1931–33. Created Bart 1934.

[9] Archibald Richard James Southby (1886–1969). Entered Navy 1901; retired as Commander 1920. Conservative MP for Epsom 1928–47. Assistant Government Whip 1931; Junior Lord of Treasury 1935–37. Created Bart 1937.

there was such a roar of applause that I had to wait a full minute before I could continue without altering my expression "and in particular I could not discover in it any support for the Home Secretary's protectionist proposals." Some of the papers reported the incident but spoiled the neatness of it which consisted in the juxtaposition of two phrases in such a way as to make their proximity appear accidental.

As for the Committee stage, it is the softest job I ever had put upon me. After such things as the Contrib. Pensions Bill, the L.G. Bill and above all the R. & V. Bill this is childs-play. One has only to smile and the opposition withdraw their amendments. You may have seen that hitherto I have declined to give any information about the [Import Duties] Advisory Committee. I saw that about a week ago Wolmer had suggested that Austen was the sort of person who ought to be selected as chairman. I thought no more of it but to my intense astonishment and dismay Austen himself took an opportunity of telling me that he did not want to be excluded because it was thought that he would never accept such a place. That while he would never ask for it, nevertheless if it were offered he would accept it and give up his seat in Parliament. Fortunately I was able to say that I had already offered the chairmanship to some one else and was expecting his answer next day. But does it not strike you as very extraordinary that Austen of all people should not see the gross impropriety of such an appointment. Leaving aside all question of his competence, how could I appoint anyone who had taken an active political part in advocating Protection for years, and above all how could I give this well paid post to my own brother and the son of J.C.? It makes my blood run cold to think of the cynical comments which would burst out everywhere.

Entirely for your own private ears the man I had asked was Sir George May[10] (Chairman of the Economy Committee) and he has now accepted. He seems to me eminently the right man, with plenty of drive, very practical and competent, with a wide experience of business but not associated with industrial concerns and with no known hostilities. I reckon myself very lucky to have got him.

...

I wonder what has been happening in Shanghai since eleven o'clock last night.[11] I suppose we shall hear something tomorrow but it seems almost

---

[10] George Ernest May (1871–1946). Entered Prudential Assurance Company 1887, becoming Secretary 1915–31. Manager, American Dollar Securities Committee 1916–18; Director, British Overseas Bank to 1931; Chairman, Economy Committee 1931; Chairman, Import Duties Advisory Committee 1932–39. Knighted 1918. Created Bart 1931 and Baron 1935.

[11] After invading Manchuria in September 1931, on 28 January a Japanese force from the international settlement at Shanghai marched into the Chinese suburb of Chapei. After a month of fighting, Anglo-American efforts secured a truce on 5 May and the Japanese withdrew from Shanghai.

impossible for the settlement to escape without serious damage to property and perhaps loss of life. And we are not in a position to do much to help while if we got into a real quarrel with Japan she could blow our ships out of the water one by one as they tried to get out of the Whangpoo. The Irish election is another unpleasant change. I am told that a stale mate is the best we can hope for now.[12] I dont much mind about the French Government's fall. Whatever new one is formed seems likely to be better not worse than Laval's. But nothing can be settled till they have had their election.

Meanwhile there are some good features at home. The astonishing gold mine we have discovered in India's hoards has put us in clover. The French can take their balances away without our flinching. We can accumulate credits for the repayment of our £80M loan and we can safely lower the Bank rate. So there is great rejoicing in the City and sterling remains steady while stocks are beginning to mount again.

...

27 February 1932
37 Eaton Square, SW1

My dear Hilda,

...

Annie has gone off to Down House for the week end. She has been very "nervy" all the week and the various social engagements which she had undertaken have been a sore trial for her. When she gets these fits she suffers from what we call nowadays an "inferiority complex" and according to her account does everything wrong. I suspect that others don't notice it, but if she feels like that it is just as bad as if it actually happened. I think a few days by herself is the best thing for her and hope I shall find her nerve restored when I join her in Birmingham on Monday. She has a women's meeting and I a Chamber of Commerce dinner that evening.

... I am very happy that the Bill has gone through so well. I was at the Speakers Levée last night and talked with all and sundry (I did not know the names of a good many) and it was very gratifying to hear such unanimous satisfaction with my conduct of the measure. You ask about the maize. I was of course anxious to have the revenue and also to give some help to Kenya as we had put hemp on the free list but I felt all along that the economic arguments were the other way. So when I saw Pollock[13] the Finance Minister for Northern

---

[12] In the Irish Free State the moderate Cosgrove government was replaced by one led by De Valera who immediately began to sever links with Britain.

[13] Hugh McDowell Pollock (1852–1936). Harbour Commissioner 1900–1921; President, Belfast Chamber of Commerce 1917–18. Ulster Unionist member of Stormont Assembly 1921–36. Minister of Finance 1921–35.

Ireland and heard his story I resolved to make that the decisive reason. I knew that if I put it on that ground Ulster would be eternally grateful and I should moreover cut away the principal argument of those who wanted to tax meat. If we had done that we should have lost Runciman & moreover a 10% duty would not have been enough to give the farmers protection. I could have carried the maize tax and still defeated the meat taxers but it would have left a very sore feeling & probably an agitation would have sprung up which might have forced us to give way later. I therefore made up my mind to throw over maize, and try to get hemp out instead. I had to make my peace with Runciman and Philip C.L. but sisal is more important than maize to East Africa and Runciman though nervous about the rope makers finally gave way with a good grace.

I carefully abstained from coupling the two things together as the rope makers would have said I had sold them to placate East Africa for losing maize. So I announced the maize concession first and then allowed myself to be converted on sisal. The result was that I got a flaming letter of gratitude from Craigavon[14] and pæans of joy from the sisal men, both of them being much more grateful than if they had had the concession at first!

I had another succés in winding up on 3rd R. after a very tactless speech from Foot[15] who goaded our people to the last pitch of exasperation. I myself thought I did better on 2 R. but apparently our men considered the last the best so I did not contradict them.

I had a disappointment during the week as the man I wanted as Deputy Chairman of the Advisory Committee declined the honour on the grounds of health. But I am glad to say that I have secured the 3rd member in Sir Allan Powell[16] who was Clerk to the Metropol. Asylums Board and is now principal officer to the Public Assistance Committee of the L.C.C. – a very good man and a hard worker who can be relied upon to get off the starting point promptly. Accordingly on Tuesday – the day the Act comes into force I shall be in a position to announce the names of the Committee & the Secretary & to say that they have held their first meeting in their new office that morning. I think the

---

[14] James Craig (1871–1940). Unionist MP for East Down 1906–18 and Mid-Down 1918–21. Treasurer of the Household 1916–18; Parliamentary Secretary, Ministry of Pensions 1919–20; Parliamentary and Financial Secretary, Admiralty 1920–21. Sat in Northern Ireland Parliament for Co. Down 1921–29 and North Down 1929–40. Prime Minister of Northern Ireland 1921–40. Created Bart 1918 and Viscount Craigavon 1927.

[15] Isaac Foot (1880–1960). Liberal MP for Bodmin 1922–24 and 1929–35. Member, Round Table Conferences on India and Burma 1931; Secretary for Mines 1931–32. Lord Mayor of Plymouth 1945–46.

[16] (George) Allan Powell (?–1948). Clerk, Metropolitan Asylums Board 1922–30; organised new Public Assistance Department of LCC, 1930–32; member, Import Duties Advisory Committee 1932–39; Chairman, BBC 1939–46; Vice-Chairman, Food Council 1925–29 and Chairman 1929–32. Knighted 1927.

House will be rather pleased at that. I have seen May again and am very favourably impressed by him. He asked what was my idea of the way to get to work and I said Take a rapid survey and recommend a scale of additional duties to cover the field for a year. Then you can go to work at leisure to build up a scientific tariff. He did not say if he would do that but he nodded and I think he probably will (our emergency tariff!).

You ask about the Indian gold. The answer is simple. The rupee is linked to sterling, therefore just as here people get 27/6 for a gold sovereign so there they get the equivalent in rupees and it is so profitable that as the news goes round the poor Indian brings out his hoards and turns them into rupees or silver. We are getting about £2M a week and we shall be able to pay off about £30M of our foreign credits next week after which we shall safely abolish the restrictions on the export of capital & reduce the bankrate. The City is buzzing with activity, the Govt stocks are booming the foreigners are buying sterling and we are sitting with all our weight on its head lest it should soar up to undesirable heights. Hopkins[17] tells me he feels happier than he has done since 1927 and it is indeed wonderful that the National Government should have so quickly restored confidence when we seemed about to plunge into disaster only a few months ago.

Ottawa is still wrap [sic] in mystery so far as the delegates are concerned but Thomas who can never keep his mouth shut has been bragging to a journalist that he was going to head the delegation and that he would "take" Runciman Philip and Hailsham with him. On the other hand the Dominions people are determined not to have him at the head if they can help it, but I have no doubt he knows that and I have an idea that he is trying to keep me out lest I should displace him in the leadership. I dont care tuppence about the leadership but I do care about the success of the Conference and so on hearing what J.H.T. had said to the journalist, I went to S.B. and suggested that he should take the leadership himself & "take" me with him. It seems very possible that we may finish our business and get the House up by the end of June so that it would then be possible for any Ministers to get away & undoubtedly if S.B. went at the head of such a team as I have mentioned it would give the Conference an altogether exceptional prestige. S.B. went to Canada a year or two ago when he was P.M. and left a very good impression there and although he would not contribute much to the practical part of the business it would be extremely useful to have him there to make dignified speeches and do things which we might not have time for. I enlarged on this theme to S.B. and although the idea came as a surprise to him I could see he was much tickled by it and it seems to me the solution of the difficulty.

---

[17] Richard Valentine Nind Hopkins (1880–1955). Member, Board of Inland Revenue 1916 and Chairman 1922–27; Controller, Finance and Supply Service of Treasury 1927–32; Second Secretary, Treasury 1932–42; Permanent Secretary 1942–45. Knighted 1920.

Annie & I have been invited by de Fleuriau[18] to meet the Caillaux[19] at lunch and we are going. It will be the first time that I have shaken hands with a murderess – she shot dead Calmette, the Editor of the Figaro but was acquitted – I suppose for extenuating circumstances. These foreigners are tumbling over one another to make themselves agreeable to us, "cette noble nation". I hear 1500 Danes have come over to buy at the Industries Fair – organised I fancy by the Danish Government. The Argentines too are all in a dither, just as we always said they would be.

5 March 1932
37 Eaton Square, SW1

My dear Ida,

...

I am sorry to say that Annie's visit to Down House didn't do her any good and she felt so like a nervous breakdown that she went off on Wednesday to Lilian's.[20] I have heard from her since but she doesn't seem any better and I am rather in despair to know what to do with her. She returns tomorrow and I shall have to see then what she feels like but she is rather a difficult patient. The physical and mental are so mixed up in her that one doesn't know which is really the cause of the trouble.

I have had nothing to do in the House this week but have been dining and lunching out a great deal. On Tuesday we lunched at the French Embassy to meet the Caillaux. I sat next the murderess who was of the fair fat & forty type and afterwards had a talk with Caillaux who was very vigorous and voluble – a clever man but I should say not to be trusted. Yesterday I lunched with Vansittart to meet Chastenet the editor of the Temps a very pleasant and intelligent young man. He was very emphatic that the future of the world depended on the re-establishment of the Entente and was anxious that we should lose no time in beginning conversations. We are being very much courted at present. At the Birmingham Chamber of Commerce dinner where I was speaking on Monday they told me that they had never had so many foreign buyers at the B.T. Fair and I think one may safely put that down to their anxiety about our tariff. I quoted Horatio on how "the sheeted dead did squeak and gibber in the Roman Streets" when Julius Cæsar fell, and suggested that we had heard similar sounds in the H. of C. on the passing of Free Trade.

---

[18] Aimé Joseph de Fleuriau (1870–1938). Entered French Diplomatic Service 1892; Counsellor, London Embassy 1913–20; Minister to Peking 1921–24; Ambassador to London 1924–33.

[19] Joseph Caillaux (1863–1944). Socialist Radical Deputy 1898–1919 when convicted of treason; amnesty 1924; Senator 1925–44. Minister of Finance 1899–1902, 1906–9, 1911, 1913–14, 1925, 1926, 1935; Prime Minister 1911–12; Chairman, Commission of Finances 1937–40.

[20] Lilian Cole. See Appendix I: 'The Chamberlain Household and Family'.

We are not likely to go out of our way again to keep the Samuelites in the Cabinet, but I doubt very much if they mean to go. On the other hand I have been very much annoyed by the antics of the Press, suggesting that I should be able to reduce taxation all round next year so when I saw the Lobby correspondents on Thursday I damped them down and the last two days they have been writing in the opposite sense. As a matter of fact the indications are not too good for next year's revenue & it is certainly too soon to begin dividing up the skin of the bear.

I heard on Tuesday night from Camrose that J.H. Thomas had a regular set to with Ferguson the Canadian High Commissioner at a private dinner a few nights ago. Austen was there and ticked them both off very effectively but it shows how dangerous it would be if J.H.T. were to go to Ottawa in command and I have been to S.B. and made him promise to write to the P.M. at once to get his consent to S.B. going himself. As an extra precaution I have also myself written to the P.M. who had sent me his congratulations on the repayment of the £43M.

I hear that Ll.G. tires very easily and there are many rumours to the effect that he is "finished" so far as politics are concerned. They may be exaggerated but I cannot conceive that the old Ll.G. could have remained quiet so long.

The Budget, by the way, is fixed for the 19th April but this is not yet public property.

...

12 March 1932
Westbourne

My dear Hilda,

...

This has been an easy week for me as I have not had to attend in the House except for questions till yesterday when I had rather unexpectedly to make a speech on currency. I hadn't prepared it but it seems to have been well received in the City. The speculators have been busy operating on sterling and as we couldn't stop them we had to let it go but it hasn't gone up as much as I feared and presently we may be able to give it a bump downwards again. I don't want to see it soaring just now though some of our foolish press can't help exulting over the rise without understanding what has brought it about.

My little plan for the Ottawa delegation seems to be coming off, though the Times has been very tiresome about it. I was much annoyed by a paragraph in one of its supplements in which it was stated that I was hoping to make substantial reductions in indirect taxation as well as taking 6d off the income tax. I wrote to Dawson to protest and received a full apology & an explanation that he hadn't read it. Then the same day as I had this apology the Times published its leader saying that S.B. ought to head the Ottawa delegation and giving the names of the ministers who should go but leaving me out. I sent for Robbins to ask what this meant and after seeing Dawson he came back to say that it was pure inadvertence.

Dawson was very sorry but he hadn't read the article and thought it would be disastrous if I didn't go! Two apologies in one day! It appears he had independently come to the conclusion that S.B. should be leader & was very relieved to hear that I wanted it too. On Friday S.B. told me that he had had a talk with J.H. Thomas who had been very worried over his position. He didn't mind S.B. & would (in order to save his dignity) propose it himself, but he didn't want me for fear I should overshadow him. S.B. told him that I had said I didn't care tuppence about the leadership but that I wanted to be there to complete father's work and he suggested that in any printed lists J.H.T.'s name should appear second to his. This apparently entirely relieved the situation and J.H.T. is now quite content that I should go. I fear he will find that his precedence doesn't really depend on his place in a list but I am glad he is satisfied.

We have had a lot of social engagements this week including the Buckingham Palace party at which the Monarch again engaged me in a long conversation. He is very pleased with the way things are going.

19 March 1932
Westbourne

My dear Ida,

...

... I am now in a position to know that this will not be an interesting Budget but I hope I may have opportunities of improving on it in later years. Meanwhile I thought it wise to damp down the expectations of the press so I broke through my rule for once and gave them in advance the passages in my speech of last night which related to the Budget and Master de Valera.[21]

With regard to the latter it seemed to me that he ought not to be allowed to go on airily talking of breaking his engagements without a word from us so I went to the P.M. yesterday morning and suggested that I should give him a warning. The P.M. appeared to think so too but suggested that we should consult our Jim. So Jim was sent for and at once observed "I beg you will not say a word but let him 'ang himself with his own rope". We asked how long he was to be allowed and whether people would not think we were afraid. Thereupon Jim began to hedge and suggested I should refer to an answer he had given to a question in the House. But when the answer was turned up it was so diplomatic that you couldn't tell what it meant & finally Jim had to agree to my proposal with a few verbal alterations. I shall be much interested to see the result.

---

[21] Eamon de Valera (1882–1975). Sinn Fein MP for Clare East 1917–21; member of Dáil for Co. Clare 1921–59; President of Dáil 1919–22; President, Sinn Fein 1917–26; President, Fianna Fail 1926–59. Minister for External Affairs 1932–48; Taoiseach 1937–48, 1951–54, 1957–59; President of the Republic 1959–73.

We had a full and most enthusiastic meeting last night and Bishopp ... said he was there and "he hadn't heard a speech like that since he listened to Mr Chamberlain in Bingley Hall"!

On Tuesday night Austen & I were the guests of the Unionist Club ... at a "banquet". ... The fact is that the Chamberlain stock stands very high at this moment; we will hope it will not presently have a catastrophic fall!

...

27 March 1932
Cairnton, Glassel, Aberdeenshire

My dear Hilda,

...

I got here on Friday morning with Montague Barlow and found things better than they had been since there was plenty of water in the river but not what they should be as the fish would not take ...

In these circumstances a large bag is not to be looked for and I have been lucky in landing the only fish caught here these last two days. ... But it is a joy to be by the river and moreover till today we have had beautiful bright sunshine so that for moments one has felt a delicious warmth on one's back.

There are oyster catchers & dippers and gray and pied wagtails busily at work along the banks & calling and twittering as they fly over one's head. And on the opposite bank the birches and larches make a purple mist with old gold patches in it which always excites my wonder every time I come back to it. I've never seen the effect anywhere else.

I have forgotten all about politics while I have been fishing but others have been trying to keep them alive. I had not been on the water a quarter of an hour before the first camera man arrived. You can imagine his delight when I promptly got into a fish and he was able to return to Aberdeen half an hour afterwards with a bag full of plates showing what was afterwards described as the Chancellors "holiday budget".

...

I had a good talk with the P.M. on Wednesday. It is evident that he is much happier about his own position & that of the Govt than he was and if we can survive my Budget he will be satisfied that we are not to break up for a long time.

I have plenty of troubles ahead of me but I am not going to think of them for another week.

9 April 1932
Westbourne

My dear Hilda,

It was very pleasant to have such an appreciative account of our family from you. You and Ida have done so much for them that it would be strange if they did not show some recognition but they might of course do that and yet not want to go to Odiham. So we too rejoice that they feel themselves so much at home there and enjoy spending part of their holidays with you. They are, I think, an attractive pair because of their honesty and genuine interest in life and moreover they are very sound all through so that I feel confident that they will make good whether they follow in the family footsteps or not.

...

... I do not know how much truth there is in the French belief that the Germans & Italians blocked agreement from purely political motives.[22] The Italians certainly made a bad impression; they knew very little about the case and appeared to be merely acting on instructions. The Germans on the other hand argued with moderation but very persuasively and I was convinced that a great deal of what they said required close study & might well involve some modification of the original plan. Unfortunately Tardieu[23] had committed himself to Benesh[24] [sic] beforehand not to consider a meeting of the 9 Powers and with Geneva on top of us we could not get any further.

I am satisfied that the real reason for the breakdown was want of preparation. This was I think unavoidable but if we had known beforehand as much of the German view as we did of the French we might have got an agreement. As it was I saw what I thought was a hopeful opening on Thursday and following it up privately with Flandin on one side & Buelow[25] [sic] on the other I feel pretty sure that I was on right lines, but Macdonald [sic] was rather slow in understanding it and there really was not time enough to carry the idea through. I am however still pressing it. Runciman sees its importance and I am not without some hope that even now it may be found possible to use it as a starting point for fresh negotiations.

---

[22] Four Power Danubian Conference, 6–8 April 1932. Called to consider a possible Federation of Danubian States. A French scheme for economic collaboration designed to enhance French influence in Central Europe came to nothing given opposition from Germany and Italy.

[23] André Pierre Gabriel Amédée Tardieu (1876–1945). Journalist and French politician. Founder and leader, Republican Centre party almost continually in office 1926–32. Prime Minister, 1929, 1930, 1932.

[24] Eduard Beneš (1884–1948). Czech statesman. Leading member of Czechoslovak National Council, Paris 1917–18; Czech Foreign Minister 1918–35; Prime Minister 1921–22; President, Czechoslovak Republic 1935–38 and 1945–48; President, Czech National Committee in exile in London 1939–45.

[25] Bernhard Wilhelm von Bülow (1885–1936). German diplomat. Secretary of State for Foreign Affairs 1929–36. Author of several books defending pre-1914 German diplomacy and attacking Versailles Treaty.

I am not enamoured of International Conferences after this first experience. They entail many hours of concentrated attention and a terrible lot of meals of an official or unofficial character. In fact I had only one meal (dinner on Monday) at home all last week and I feel a bit weary in consequence. I suppose I ought at this moment to be "immersed" in my Budget speech. Winston used to make his six months beforehand, a very awkward plan as my office explains, because it was always being revised. But I haven't begun mine and am ready to take any pretext for putting it off. Anyhow I lunched with the P.M. yesterday and squared him. I have squared Snowden already and now have only to see Samuel. I shant tell the Cabinet anything till Monday week. J.H.T. is too expansive to be given a secret to keep for a whole week.

Lausanne is provisionally fixed for June 16 which is nearing pretty close. We are beginning to wonder whether we might not postpone Ottawa a little longer especially as Bennett is said to be very much behind with his preparations.

17 April 1932
37 Eaton Square, SW1

My dear Ida,

One cant work at Budget all day long. Moreover I have sent my notes up to the Treasury to have amendments retyped and they wont be back till after tea. ...

This ridiculous Press keeps on ringing up and sending round callers to ask for another photograph or to know what I am doing now. Lambert says they have been told to make a "story" and darent go home without one. I sent word to the last comer that I was taking all my meals as usual and reading a book. I wonder what he will make of that.

They didn't find out that we all went to see "Helen" on Friday. I confess that the modern stage rather takes my breath away though in this instance the decencies [?] are saved by the ridiculous George Robey.[26] I wonder what the play would have done without him. It must be over a year I think since I went to the theatre (oh no, I forgot The Derby Day at the Hammersmith Lyric) and I conclude that I personally get more pleasure out of the concert room.

Austen came to dine last night. He preferred not to know the contents of the budget so we confined our political talk to the Danubian question. He is very anxious to help and offered several times to put himself at Simon's disposal if he would care to consult him. But although I did not say so to him I could not help feeling that Europe had already changed since he was F.S. and that his advice though most loyally offered could not really be of much help except after a fresh term of service in touch with what is going on. He told us about his projected American tour next autumn. He is contemplating 20 lectures before Christmas

---

[26] George Robey (1869–1954). Music hall performer and actor.

& 20 after at the rate of 4 or perhaps 5 a week. It sounds terrific, though he would do it more easily than I; and if he can get through without a breakdown he will have earned a substantial sum in a short time.

...

23 April 1932
37 Eaton Square, SW1

My dear Hilda,

I have had a pretty measly time since the Budget as the lumbago came on as soon as I sat down on Tuesday ... I saw Sir Robert Woods[27] on Wednesday morning and had some treatment but of course as he said I ought really to have been in bed. That was impossible and I had to stick it out till I had replied to the debate but I promised Sir Robert that I would spend the week end in bed ... The trouble is that while the lumbago is certainly better I woke up early this morning with a sharpish attack of gout. I dont like that, not only because it is very painful but also because I cannot avoid the conclusion that it is a sign of overwork on the machine. I know I have been running it pretty hard lately but I have been so well that I thought I could carry it off, but this is an unpleasant warning that there are limits.

Macdonald's [sic] eye trouble ... has a bearing on this. If he should declare himself unable to return to the House this summer Baldwin might be unable to go Ottawa [sic] and in that case I suppose my share of the work would be proportionately greater. That is another reason for hoping that J.R.M. will carry on. If I understand the position rightly what is feared is not recurrence of the glaucoma in the eye already operated on but its appearance in the other one & the necessity for a similar operation on that. I should be afraid in that case of the effect on J.R.M's nerves, for he found the last one exceedingly trying and to have to go through it again would I am sure upset him very much.

I agree with you that I have got off very cheaply with such an unpopular Budget. I had quite a lot of support from the speeches of back benchers and though there was a very strong feeling about the beer duty I am told that it was a good deal better after I had made my explanation and that we shall be able successfully to resist an amendment.

I get a certain number of abusive letters – mostly from beer drinkers, but on the other hand from people who count, including a good number in the City ... I have had some very gratifying comments showing that the wisdom as well as the courage of refusing to make concessions yet is widely recognised. The Governor writes that it is almost the first honest Budget since the War. Trenchard[28] told my

---

[27] Robert Stanton Woods (1877–1954). Consulting Physician, London Hospital; Consultant Adviser to Emergency Medical Service during the war. Knighted 1929.

[28] Hugh Montague Trenchard (1873–1956). Entered British Army 1893. Commanded Royal

P.S. that having read the speech very carefully it had quite restored his faith in politicians, for he had never believed that any one of them would have had the courage to make so realistic a statement[.] I have even got a series of verses, better perhaps in intention than in execution, on the "Budget of Prudence". Only the Times has been consistently disagreeable – I dont know why. Dawson always disclaims any such intention but perhaps his leader writer has some grouse.

The broadcast seems to have gone very well and I have heard from many quarters, including Snowden who is I think a good judge, that it was just what was wanted. I am very glad as I attach much importance to it and it was constructed at short notice & in great pain. I did a draft first & then Fergusson[29] & Gunston[30] criticised. I accepted all their criticisms and suggestions, cut out a lot of what I had prepared & rewrote it on somewhat different lines so they were entitled to a good share of the credit. ...

The mistake the other night was due to my P.P.S. who told me just before I rose that the business was exempted. About 10.55 a note was passed to me to say it was *not* exempted but I, thinking it was a repetition of what I had been told already, brushed it aside without reading it, and it was only on the stroke of eleven that several behind me giving me warning, I realised that I must stop at once. I dont think it mattered; I had already dealt with the points members cared most about and there will be other opportunities (if I can get rid of the gout) to say what I had to leave out.

...

30 April 1932
Chevening

My dear Ida,

I am afraid my letter this week must be a very poor one since I have nothing to tell except my ailments. This is a real bad go, the worst I have had for many years. I got over the violent pain by Wednesday but it started again the moment I tried a gout boot and I haven't been able to put my foot to the ground since. Annie has now got me a pair of crutches which are a great comfort and they are very good to me here even carrying me up & down stairs in a chair which they fortunately possess for that very purpose.

Flying Corps in the First World War and a founder of RAF in 1918. First Chief of Air Staff 1918–29. Commissioner, Metropolitan Police 1931–35. Created Viscount Trenchard of Wolfeton 1930.

[29] (John) Donald Balfour Fergusson (1891–1963). Entered Treasury 1919; Private Secretary to Chancellor of Exchequer 1920–36; Permanent Secretary, Ministry of Agriculture 1936–45 and Ministry of Fuel and Power 1945–52. Knighted 1937.

[30] Derrick Wellesley Gunston (1891–1985). Conservative MP for Thornbury 1924–45. PPS to Kingsley Wood 1926–29; to Neville Chamberlain 1931–36; to Edward Grigg 1940–42. Created Bart 1938.

... The worst of it is that it (or the medicines they give you) do depress one so & make one's inside such a burden that life seems insupportable at times. I am wondering whether I shall really be well enough to return to work on Monday or walk in a procession on Friday, but there's no use in worrying over that at present though Fridays speech weighs very heavily on my mind.

...

The beer drinkers & the brewers continue to rage furiously together and I get a fair lot of abusive letters but I think a firm attitude will bring the H. of C. into line and I am sure that to give way wd only raise a fresh crop of troubles.

... I had an excellent letter from the defeated candidate at Wakefield saying that the Budget had lost the election but that all the same it was right & he wished me all success in carrying it through. He must have good stuff in him.

...

15 May 1932
37 Eaton Square, SW1

My dear Hilda,

...

I am very glad you approved my speeches last week for they cost me more work & worry than they ought to have done. It was really a pretty stiff finish. On Monday I had to wind up on the Finance Bill, which of course meant pretty close attention all day. On Tuesday I had a Cabinet Committee all morning and in the afternoon after answering my questions & listening to some of the debate I finished preparing my speech for the bankers that evening. It went extremely well so that I felt encouraged and strengthened after it, but as soon as it was over I had to go back to the House & move the resolution on the new silk duty. That also went well and I got home at 1 o'clock tired but well satisfied. There however I found a box full of urgent & important papers and I had to sit up another hour to do them.

Next morning I had to be up good and early so as to have a little time in the office before the Cabinet which occupied the rest of the morning. In the afternoon I had a long Cabinet Committee on Reparations & Debts (I am Chairman of this & also of the Tuesday Committee) and when that was through I went home to dine and go to the Court. I always find that very tiring as the stiff uniform & the long standing combined take it out of one. When I got home about 11.30 I went & changed into easier clothes & then sat up trying to compose a humorous & witty speech for the Newspaper Press Fund dinner! Thursday morning was spent in a series of interviews prolonged into this afternoon and then Annie & I had to go and "receive" at a little before 7. Strange to say, I did grind out quite a good after dinner speech which I was told pleased the journalists very much but it nearly killed me.

...

I came down here (Dorchester) with M. Barlow on Friday arriving about 4 and we went out that evening for the late rise. ... I secured a brace and went to bed early with a great sense of relief. Yesterday I woke feeling an awful worm with heavy cold sore throat headache and foot bruised & painful as though it had been thoroughly beaten with a mallet! But on getting out on to the river I soon felt wonderfully better. The flowers were delicious, cowslips, bluebells purple orchis [sic] & primrose & the sedge warblers were singing lustily. ... I was hoping for better things today but alas I woke in the small hours with gout in the *other* foot and I am writing this with a toe which, though not now actually painful, is very uncomfortably hot & tingly. Of course fishing is out of the question and I wonder whether I shall get better tomorrow or whether my holiday is bust. Anyway I cant do anything but wait so I shant worry my head about it. ...

Except for the breakdown in my health I have every reason to be satisfied with the way things have gone. As I had all along planned for, the anxiety about silk had been growing until at the psychological moment I not only announced the concession but carried it through with dramatic swiftness. So overjoyed were the critics that they almost forgot about the beer duty and in any case they bear me no grudge for it any more. I am the more pleased about this as that beast Banman had written in the Evening Standard that though I was the most obstinate member of an obstinate family I should be beaten over the Beer duty.

On economy I determined to give the grumblers a run for their money and make them face up to realities. I have been very cautious and guarded in my language & have not committed myself to any thing specific. But I have intimated that if anything big was to be done it will be very disagreeable and they are wondering now what I have in mind. It will be best to keep them guessing for the present because in the process they talk & the atmosphere is gradually created in which the disagreeable things become possible. I dont think Winston cuts any ice by his criticisms, but it was really the limit when he scoffed at the idea of any "hard thinking" being necessary and declared that I had only to tell the Treasury how much I wanted 10, 20, 50, million & they would produce a scheme for it. I remember that he, without doing any thinking at all, said in the first year of his Chancellorship that he was going to aim at a cumulative saving of £10M. per annum and he wd begin by abolishing the Ministries of Mines Transport & Overseas Trade. Then somebody else had to do a little hard thinking and the result was that not a single one of his proposals was ever carried into effect. The party never recovered from the discredit he brought upon them. Up to the formation of the Nat. Govt our people always said "You had promised economy, you had an unprecedented majority, and you never did a thing". I remember I had to write a very strong letter to the Times when I was Chairman to say I would not join or remain in a Govt that did not actually reduce national expenditure in its first year.

My information is that a Govt of the Left in France is likely to be much more amenable than Tardieu & Co. But I believe Brüning[31] does not take that view. On the contrary he thinks that being already suspect on the point they would be extra cautious. In any case the key of the situation lies in U.S.A. not France, and Uncle Sam's view is that the scheme of Total Cancellation is a cynical plan for putting the whole burden on his shoulders. If you asked him *what* burden, I think he would find it difficult to give an intelligible reply. The fact is the real burden is that brought about by his own insistence on payment of debts while refusing to allow them to be paid for in goods & services.

Fortunately it is difficult to put a limit to human powers of endurance. Which leads me to the conclusion that perhaps we shall all last out long enough to enable even the Americans to learn a little sense.

...

21 May 1932
The Manor House, Great Durnford, Salisbury

My dear Ida,

...

I could not go through this second bout [of gout] without realising that it would be foolish to go back to work as soon as that became physically possible and hope that the trouble would not recur. After the first go I hoped that a little rest & change would set me up. When that notion broke down so completely I had to recognise that something more dramatic was necessary, though I did not myself form any idea of what I ought to do.

However at this stage Annie developed very definite ideas of her own namely that I should go as soon as I could get away next week to Harrogate & put myself again under Dr Morris who seemed before to understand my complaint. This plan at once seemed to me practical and likely to produce the desired effect in the shortest possible time. It involved the practical abdication of my control over the remaining stages of the Finance Bill but after all, the main outlines are already settled and what is left does not compare in importance with Lausanne & Ottawa. If I were unable to attend them I should have to begin to consider my position in the Government; in fact this last week I have had to face the possibility of my retirement from politics. I dont want that just yet, even when I am feeling most depressed and I am ready therefore to make a considerable effort to avoid it.

...

---

[31] Heinrich Brüning (1885–1970). Served in Prussian Ministry of Health 1919–21; adviser to German Christian Trade Union movement 1922–29; Centre Party member of Reichstag 1924–33; Chancellor of Reich 1930–32. Emigrated to USA 1934; Research Fellow, Queen's College Oxford 1937–39; Professor of Government, Harvard 1939–52 and Cologne University 1951–55.

29 May 1932
7 Valley Drive, Harrogate

My dear Hilda,

...

Apart from weather our stay here has so far been most satisfactory ... As a result my foot has improved every day and though I cant remember when it has taken so long to return to normal, I suppose that only means ... that this has been an exceptionally severe attack. ...

...

It is evident that I have chosen an excellent moment to be away. The accounts I get show that Walter Elliot has done extremely well and has developed a restraint & caution which he has not always shown in the past. This shows how responsibility tests a man. If he is really below his reputation he crumbles at once; on the other hand, if he has the right stuff in him the responsibility brings it out. The most astonishing part of the beer duty incident was given very little attention in the papers, but all my correspondents (M.P.'s) wrote at length about it, and evidently they had been greatly impressed.

Winston apparently intended to make a striking speech on the subject and when he came down to the House & found that the clause had never been moved he was very much annoyed. Not having been much in the House he was not in touch with it, and thinking that other people were as much vexed as he was he moved to report progress on the ground that in the interests of the country the subject must be fully debated. But the House had only been amused at what had happened; it saw that Winston only really wanted to have an opportunity of letting off his own speech; it jeered and laughed at him and when Lansbury,[32] in a flood of indignation, denounced his impudence & effrontery in demanding time for himself and commented bitterly on people who came in without hearing the debate, delivered a speech & then walked out "as though God Almighty had spoken" and there was nothing more to be said, the House recognised the truth of the picture & cheered vociferously. And then a little later when Page Croft[33] got up and tried to continue the argument the House actually howled him down. My people were all in tremendous spirits over it.

I see that Ormsby Gore & Tom Inskip taking my speech to the bankers as a text, but embroidering upon it according to their own ideas, have created a

---

[32] George Lansbury (1859–1940). Member, Poplar Council 1903–40 and Mayor 1919–20 and 1936–37. Labour MP for Bow and Bromley 1910–12 and 1922–40. Editor, *Daily Herald* 1913–22; Chairman, National Executive of Labour Party 1925–26; Leader of Labour Party and Opposition 1931–35.

[33] Henry Page Croft (1881–1947). Conservative MP for Christchurch 1910–18 and Bournemouth 1918–40. Under-Secretary, War Office 1940–45. Prominent protectionist: Chairman, Organising Committee, Tariff Reform League 1913–17; Chairman, Empire Industries Association Executive 1928–45. Leading Diehard and Principal Organiser, National Party 1917–22. Created Bart 1924; Baron Croft 1940.

regular slump on the Stock Exchange and some violent protests against defeatism.

I am not disposed to criticise them myself, I believe we have got to make further great economies, and I am not sorry that this impression should get about and that the public should begin to think and consider more exactly than it has yet done where the economies are to be made. There is a very useful article in todays Sunday Times by Scrutator (Sidebottom)[34] probably the most intelligent journalist we have and it points the way. I have taken the first step myself by giving a preliminary warning to certain Ministers that I shall want to see them when I get back and they had better be thinking in the meanwhile what they can do.

...

5 June 1932
Harrogate

My dear Ida,
    ...
My foot has progressed steadily all the week and though still a little tender, I dont think I need fear any recrudescence. I have done so much work here that I dont think there should be a very great accumulation though my Secretary is rather concerned over the heavy programme I have for this week. The Conferences look worse than ever now that Bruning has gone & been succeeded by the egregious Von Papen.[35] In Paris they think that the new German Govt will be aggressive & truculent and if so that will of course make the French as difficult as can be. As for those "idiotic Yankees" they are quite cynical and advise us "as a friend" what we should & should not do with sole regard to their own party politics. They simply infuriate me and unluckily the P.M. still thinks he has special influence with Stimson[36] with whom he insists on exchanging telephonic negotiations while the unhappy Simon tries at the same time to carry on through the usual channels.

---

[34] Herbert Sidebottom (1872–1940). Editorial staff, *Manchester Guardian* 1895–1918; military correspondent, *The Times* 1918–21; political adviser, *Daily Chronicle* 1922–23. Contributor to *Daily Despatch, Sunday Times* (as 'Scrutator') and *Daily Sketch* (as 'Canditus').

[35] Franz von Papen (1879–1969). German statesman. Military Attaché, Washington 1914–16; expelled on charges of sabotage. Chancellor of Reich 1932; member of Hitler's Cabinet 1933–34; German Ambassador, Vienna 1934–38. Acquitted by Nuremberg War Trials 1946.

[36] Henry Lewis Stimson (1867–1950). American politician. Joined New York bar 1891; US Attorney for New York Southern District 1906. Unsuccessful Republican candidate for New York Governor 1910; Secretary of War 1911–13; Governor-General, Philippines, 1922–27; Secretary of State 1929–33; Secretary of War 1940–45. Author of the 'Stimson Doctrine' opposed to Japanese aggression in Manchuria.

11 June 1932
Westbourne

My dear Hilda,

I certainly have had rather a heavy week to start off with but fortunately I have got off another speech on Monday. The Opposition had asked for a debate on Lausanne and it appeared that as the P.M. was going to Paris today I was the only minister who could take it. However I pointed out how very difficult it would be to make a statement without a serious risk of saying something which might be misunderstood or resented in one of the foreign capitals & Ramsay promised to see Lansbury and ask him to withdraw his request. It appears that ever since Lansbury was cheered by our side for his attack on Winston he has been so pleased with himself that he eats out of our hands & accordingly he made no difficulty. I am very delighted as I have a free mind for my week end instead of another speech weighing over me.

As a matter of fact I have got through very well. All my people were very anxious to spare me as much as possible and I got off with one speech on the beer duty & one on the Equal[isatio]n Exchange account on Report. Third Reading gave me an opportunity of doing something to correct the rather pessimistic ideas which have been gathering head lately and I was told yesterday that our people were very pleased and the press gallery "enthusiastic". As a matter of fact there is mighty little that is tangible to make me cheerful. Trade is in fact distinctly worse. But I think one must take a longer view and there are some more hopeful signs. Gilt edged stocks have got so dear that investors are beginning to slop over into public utilities & even industrial preferences. That is a beginning and if nothing untoward occurs to disturb the market we shall presently find that the industrials will be able to borrow freely again. There the I.A.C. [Import Duties Advisory Committee] has got the steel industry well under weigh [sic]; May tells me he is very hopeful about it and if he can persuade them actually to carry through the reorganisation plans which they have in hand it will be a great achievement & may have far reaching effects on other industries like cotton which have hitherto resisted all efforts to set them on their feet. Finally there is Lausanne about which I am beginning to be really hopeful. The awful situation in Central Europe has convinced the French Govt that no half measures are any good and provided they can be sure that we shant run out when it comes to talking with the Americans they will I believe agree to total cancellation. I have been very nervous about our P.M. who believes he has special influence with Stimson and consequently is inclined to pay more attention to his advice than I think wise. But since I came back I have found him much more amenable and as he is very anxious to have the Presidency of the Conference he sees the necessity of a solution to which the Conference will agree. He fears that the American will force us into Repudiation. I dont think they can unless we choose and so far as I am concerned I have made it very plain that I dont choose. We may be forced to postpone payment and of course I dont like that, but postponement is very different from Repudiation which is "Langism"[37] & Bolshevism.

Ottawa is not going too well at present and I expect there will be a good deal of disappointment and abuse over it. But as I think I have said before its real importance lies in starting the Empire on the new path of mutual preference and provided it does that any initial failures are of minor importance. Our own industrials are very frightened lest we should forget our foreign trade which as they point out is more important to us than Empire Trade. What they seem to me to lose sight of is the future possibilities of Empire trade which must be infinitely greater than anything we can hope for from the foreigner.

As I was busy in the House yesterday I didn't see de Valera but the report brought back from Ireland offered no hope of any agreement.[38] Our emissaries found him in a world of his own, quite sincerely convinced of his rectitude but totally incapable of taking in any one else's view. Now that the Senate has wrecked his Bill he must choose between waiting another 18 months or hazarding his fortunes in a new election. If he sends his Ministers to Ottawa we shall treat them with politeness but we shall make no agreement with them and I hope the Dominions will do the same. But I dont trust Havenga.

...

> 19 June 1932
> Lausanne Conference, British Delegation,
> Hôtel Beau-Rivage Palace, Lausanne

My dear Hilda,

Would you believe it? I have got this accursed gout again. It came on quite unexpectedly this morning early; I have been lying on a sofa ever since, but alas, it is getting worse not better and I fear that it is going to cripple me for a few days just as if I hadn't been to Harrogate. Well, as Father used to say, it is of no use to kick against the pricks and I suppose I must put up with it.

At any rate this is a better place to have it in than Harrogate. ...

---

[37] John Thomas Lang (1876–1975). Australian Labour politician. Prime Minister and Treasurer of New South Wales 1925–32. Rather than accept the Federal 'Premier's Plan' involving deflationary measures and a real reduction in the standard of living to address Australia's economic crisis in May 1931, Lang suspended interest payments to overseas bondholders, reduced interest on internal loans and imposed state control over wages, prices and profits. After the collapse of the NSW Savings Bank and acute tension with the conservative Federal government, Lang was dismissed by the State Governor on 13 May 1932.

[38] As part of its campaign to cut links between the Irish Free State and Britain, on 21 April the de Valera government introduced a Bill to abolish the Oath of Allegiance and withhold payment to Britain of land annuities. Thomas and Hailsham visited Dublin on 6–8 June 1932 but obtained no concessions.

We had a very strenuous time when we came sitting up late and wrestling with the Powers over the declaration which we finally got them to sign. The idea & the form of the declaration we owe to Simon and he and I carried on the negotiations. We had a lot of trouble & I thought we were going to miss the bus but I made myself disagreeable to Herriot[39] and after that he came round quickly.

I dont know why the Times suppressed my speech in the Conference which was in their hands in plenty of time. My people are furious about it and it certainly was extremely stupid of them if not worse, for it made a great impression and gave us the lead. I came out very definitely for cancellation all round [of war debts and reparations] and although the French are very sticky at present our people are not discouraged and still think we shall bring them round.

All the Dominions representatives were very pleased with my speech. The N.Z. man said I'm proud to belong to you, and the Australian and Canadian declared it was the only one with any meat on it. As for Von Papen he shook me warmly by the hand & expressed his admiration for its "plainliness". He speaks French better than English and I thought his own speech which was in French was excellent both in matter & manner. I fancy Neurath[40] had a good deal to do with its composition as Von Papen is very new to all this sort of thing and moreover he does not strike one as having much personality though he is very well groomed and has a pleasant manner.

Simon and I had Herriot to dinner on Wednesday & lunched with him on Thursday. I must say he is very attractive, a great talker with a fund of amusing stories & a capital raconteur. But he is very woolly and evidently does not understand the subject we are discussing. Germain Martin, the Finance Minister, understands much more but is also woolly and though he sticks closely to his idea of the way to settle Reparations I don't think he has worked out his plans in detail. He dined alone with me yesterday and I was not looking forward to the occasion as he speaks English with great difficulty. However I have been relieved to find that I understand French better than I expected and though I have to reply in English he did not seem to have much trouble in understanding me. I believe if I have to stop here another two weeks I shall presently be able to talk a little in French myself.

This morning the P.M. came to my room and we had a long and useful talk with our staff. We think the best line is to try for something much wider than an agreement on Reparations only. There is no doubt that the French would like to

---

[39] Edouard Herriot (1872–1957). Mayor of Lyon 1905–47; Senator 1912–19; Deputy 1919–40. Minister of Public Works 1916–19; French Prime Minister 1924–25, 1926, 1932; Foreign Minister 1926–36; President, Chamber of Deputies 1936–40; President National Assembly 1947–54; President, Radical Party 1919–40 and Socialist Radical Party 1945–57.

[40] Baron Constantin von Neurath (1873–1956). German Ambassador to Italy 1921 and to Britain 1930. German Foreign Minister 1932–38; Gauleiter for Bohemia and Moravia 1939. Jailed by Nuremberg War Trials; released 1954.

come to terms with us but they are extremely nervous about their position with the Chamber and if they could get some large arrangement which would cover disarmament, an assurance of some kind about the German Eastern frontiers, the basis of an arrangement about the Danubian countries, & perhaps some mutual engagement with us not to worsen the economic position by further quotas & tariffs they would have talking points sufficient perhaps to enable them to swallow cancellation [of reparations].

I was truly sorry to hear of Donald Maclean's death. He was a thorough gentleman & I had begun to like him very much.

20 June 1932
Lausanne Conference

My dear Ida,

...

I didn't have a bad night and I dont think my foot is worse today though I fear it's no better. ...

...

Ramsay has just been in to tell me of his talks with the Americans yesterday. He didn't get back from Geneva till after 1.30 a.m. but my Secretary tells me he saw him walking in the garden here at 8 this morning. ... I hear G.M. was very pleased with his dinner and told his staff that he had enjoyed himself very much.

... I am much encouraged by the P.M.'s report. G.M. makes a great point that the Americans dont want cancellation which they wd consider was merely transferring the burden from the shoulders of Europe to their own. I know that Stimson has in fact expressed that view both to the French & ourselves. But I told G.M. that he must not take it for granted that what Stimson said today would represent American opinion next November after the election. The important thing was to say nothing to them now but to come to a settlement ourselves. If that settlement commended itself strongly to world opinion I could not believe that America would find it possible to upset it.

It now appears that Norman Davies[41] was saying much the same thing to Ramsay yesterday. If we could so arrange that it was not necessary to call upon the Americans to make any decision now it might be possible to keep Repns & War Debts off the party platforms. Then in Nov. Hoover might say we cant settle this question finally between now & Dec 15 (when the next payments become

---

[41] Norman Davis (1878–1944). American banker and diplomat. Financial adviser to Wilson at Paris Peace Conference 1919; Assistant Secretary to Treasury 1919–20; Under-Secretary of State 1920–21; US delegate to Geneva Economic Conference 1927; to World Disarmament Conference 1932–33; to London Naval Conference 1935; to Nine-Power Brussels Conference 1937. Vansittart considered him 'the most wearisome' of the 'American Amateurs'.

due) but we shall not expect any payment then and we can sit down & talk completely after that.

This is not only gratifying because it is exactly the way I have said things should be handled with America all along, but also because it helps to keep R.M. himself firmly in the path of cancellation which I have sometimes feared he might leave under pressure from the Yanks.

26 June 1932
Lausanne Conference

My dear Hilda,

After a week of perfectly d—ble weather, during which I have been gibbering with cold and plunged in gloom in consequence of the prevailing darkness there is today some rise in temperature and a feeble and watery sun seems to be attempting to show itself. In these circumstances it is possible to sit by the open window again and I can begin my reply to your letter in a somewhat better temper than would otherwise have been possible.

I had two days in bed and three which I spent in my room with my foot up. This is the third day, since that, on which I have been able to go out, but only with a gout boot. Isn't it maddening? Of course its nothing like as bad as it was before, only subacute. I have had burning & tingling and great tenderness, but none of the violent pain. But it is so disappointing to feel that I am still liable to a return & so humiliating to be unable to pull my weight here and so infuriating to be unable to take any exercise or to spend any of my leisure time in climbing the mountains to where the flowers are.

However I mustn't complain too much. Yesterday I took two of my young men out in my Rolls Royce to Les Avants where I gave them lunch and after that going a bit higher up the road we came to a valley the sides of which were just white with Narcissus. By the roadside were also quantities of yellow Trollius & Potentilla, a white branched potentilla with a large flower, blue centaurea & prunellas, purple cranesbill & orchis, and pink knotgrass as well as a few other things familiar in appearance though not by name. ...

...

This has been an education for me in the ways of the foreigner. He simply cant contemplate getting down to business without long preliminary sparring and skirmishing. To disclose at an early stage what you really want & how far you really mean to go is, to his mind, to lay yourself at your opponent's mercy, and it seems inconceivable to him that anyone should be so foolish. When therefore we, in our impatient blundering way, blurt out our intentions without any prologue, the foreigner cant believe that we could be so simple. He says Of course les Anglais must begin like that. But what is his game? What is he concealing and how far is he really prepared to come away from the position he has taken up. And if you dont come away he is inclined to say that you have tricked him. Of course they all have their different methods. The French talk at interminable length on generalities, they protest their loyalty, their frankness, & their disinterestedness. Meanwhile they send out an army of agents (they have a staff of about 50 here) who nose round and try and find out what the other fellow means to do & where is his last ditch. The Italian affects an air of utter boredom & indifference. Apparently he goes to sleep in the corner but in reality he is listening all the time and as soon as the others seem likely to come to some conclusion he jumps up and cries How is it that I have not been consulted. Am I to put up with such an insult. How much will you give me to agree not to make a row.

The Belgian on the other hand works the hardest of all. He knows better than to thrust himself in with the big dogs but nothing can fall to the ground from the table without his seeing it and snapping it up before any of the other little dogs have noticed that it is there. Meanwhile he makes himself useful carrying messages and receiving confidences and when the day of reckoning comes he will put forward the most outrageous claims for personal satisfactions and rewards & somehow get away with them.

We passed this week through the second stage in the accepted routine, the stage when you leave principles and generalities and come to the application. Immediately the difficulties became apparent and it was a case of pull devil pull baker to see which would give way first. It almost came to ordering the special train before we could get a move on and even then we had to propose a change of venue & suggest that a Franco-German exchange should begin. By that time the French were getting alarmed & gladly accepted the proposal; they are now beginning the 1st stage (generalities) with the Germans. The next crisis will probably work up by about Wednesday and we hope that before the end of the week all the bluffs will have been called and we may get to business.

There have been many moments when nothing but a breakdown seemed possible, but I have had a feeling all the time that a game was being played and I am more than ever of that opinion now. My belief at present is that while we may be unable to secure an open and complete cancellation we shall get the substance of what we want and it will be clear to the world that no more payments will in fact be made. Failing that we might still fall back on one final lump sum but it would have to be a very small one and I am not sure that it would help the French.

I am afraid you are right about Hoover. He did not consult any of us, not even our P.M. to whom he had given a promise to do so, and the proposals themselves are made to suit American interests and are put forward for electioneering purposes.[42] That is what makes the high moral tone so infuriating. As a matter of

---

[42] On 22 June 1932 Hoover proposed a specially summoned meeting of the General Commission to consider disarmament through proportional cuts of a third in existing forces.

fact, Samuel who has been sent to Geneva as a sort of permanency has been carrying on conversations with the French *and the Americans* there which were I thought most hopeful & helpful until Hoover butted in. ...

4 July 1932
Lausanne Conference

My dear Ida,

... Annie told me you had guessed that I had come back to announce the Conversion Scheme[43] and I thought you might possibly penetrate the omissions in my letter. But we did accomplish an extraordinary feat in carrying on our preparations for so many weeks without a whisper getting out. The Times lobby correspondent said to me I take off my hat to your people – we hadn't an idea and as an Austrian here remarked to me yesterday There is no other country in which secrecy could have been preserved. Even in the H. of C. I believe half the members thought I was going to make a statement about Lausanne and the other half although they anticipated that some conversion operation was coming never thought of our tackling the whole 2000 millions. It has had a wonderful send-off and I dont think there can be much doubt of its success. The only difficult decision I had to take was whether to proceed with it on the 30th when it was possible that on that day or the day after some bad news would go out from here. But I did not hesitate as I felt the risks of missing the right moment outweighed those of a breakdown here.

I had less than 24 hours in London as I had to come back on an urgent message from the P.M. When I left things seemed to be going unexpectedly well but hitches arose and they were all in a tangle when I got back on Saturday. We were hard at it all that day & straightened out our affairs with the French but when we met the Germans they said our proposal was impossible because their people would not stand it & would throw them out at the forthcoming elections. Counter offers have been made & do not at the moment show any hope of agreement but Herriot who has been to Paris returns tomorrow morning and we shall make fresh efforts. Meanwhile the Italians have raised a fresh difficulty and have made themselves so unpleasant that I had to be disagreeable myself and at this moment they have just gone away in a very bad temper. So it goes on & time is flying. We have sounded the Dominions about postponing the Ottawa Conference for a fortnight if necessary and they are not unsympathetic but I do hope it will not be necessary as I foresee it means another slice out of my holiday.

At any rate I do not feel that I am wasting my time here. The P.M. is I think getting to rely on my help very much. He has a good deal of difficulty in

---

[43] On 30 June 1932 Chamberlain announced the conversion of £2,085 million of 5 per cent War Loan 1929/47 to a $3\frac{1}{2}$ per cent basis.

following the more technical side and he doesn't understand French, so he likes to have me about and in fact he wont now conduct any conversations with the other delegations without having me there too. I get on very well with the French – the Wigrams[44] declare that Herriot "adores" me and also with the Germans though I must say the latter especially von Papen are incredibly stupid. I can quite understand the blunders he made during the war now I see how he behaves here. Von Neurath is more sensible but not very brainy and Count Schwerin[45] though clear headed is very timid & nervous. The Italians I dislike very much but I have not seen anything of Grandi.[46]

Runciman & I went a lovely drive today to the upper country & had lunch at a hotel high above & beyond Lake Neuchatel. … The flowers up there were lovely in the open meadows among the spruce woods. Though I didn't have time to do any walking I have worn a boot today without any ill effects.

Now I must close. I still hope for a settlement though just now the snags look particularly large and formidable.

17 July 1932
R.M.S. Empress of Britain
Mouth of the St Lawrence

My dear Ida,

I doubt if I shall have much time for writing after I get on shore, so I will try and give you some account of my doings …

I dont know whether you saw that I spoke again on Tuesday in the Lausanne debate. The P.M. sent for me on Monday night & I found him in a very nervous condition, saying that his mind would not work & that he could not find a line to satisfy him. He did hate making speeches in the H. of C. he said. I was sorry for him, he was so evidently overstrained & I was also rather concerned as to what sort of a speech he might make. So I told him above all to insist that Lausanne had been a striking success and said that Runciman & I would stand by if Ll.G. required answering. He seemed somewhat relieved, but I am afraid that, except

[44] Ralph Follett Wigram (1890–1936). Temporary Secretary, British Embassy, Washington 1916–19; Third Secretary, Foreign Office 1919; Second Secretary 1920; First Secretary, Paris Embassy 1924–33. Counsellor, Foreign Office and head of Central Department 1934.

[45] Lutz Graf Schwerin von Krosigk (1887–1952). Entered German Civil Service 1910; appointed Regierungsrat 1920; Director of Reich Ministry of Finance 1929–32; Minister of Finance 1932–45 and member of Hitler's first Cabinet; Reich Minister of Foreign Affairs 1945. Sentenced to ten years by Nuremberg Military Tribunal 1949; released 1951.

[46] Dino Grandi (1895–1988). Italian diplomat. Journalist and Fascist organiser in north Italy 1920–21; Member, Fascist Grand Council. Elected to Chamber of Deputies 1921; Deputy President of Chamber 1924; Under-Secretary, Foreign Affairs 1925–29; Foreign Minister 1929–32; Ambassador to London 1932–39; Minister of Justice and President of Fascist Chamber 1939–43. Brought about Mussolini's fall 1943; condemned to death by Verona rump government 1944. Created Count 1937.

for an admirable passage about America, Ishbel's[47] verdict that it was a very bad speech was not far from the mark. Exposition is not his forte, and the woolliness of the phrasing somehow gave the impression that there was something not divulged. Then came Ll.G. to cross the T's & dot the i.'s. Under his skilful handling the whole transaction assumed a sinister aspect and fantastic as his suggestions were they did not seem altogether incredible to the House. Unfortunately for Ll.G. he wanted also to make an Elder Statesman speech about the general situation, a rôle which he really cannot keep up for more than two minutes at a time. He had nothing new to say; it was platitudinous & dull. Then he got interrupted by Black Rod & that knocked him off his perch. He was never able to regain his confidence & finally the House got bored. I knew the Lord had delivered him into my hand and I had a sweet 20 minutes. He was speechless he sat there gazing at me with his mouth open and a comically indignant expression like a ruffled cockatoo and when I put questions he had nothing to answer. That was a grand send-off; to have rolled up Ll.G. & utterly discomfited him. But it was also most gratifying to find that the House was completely satisfied. They laughed at the mare's nest Winston & Ll.G. had found & Winston himself was so chastened that he had to withdraw his previous speech and make some sort of excuse for his mischievous behaviour. Lots of people told me it was the best speech I ever made in the House. There was something familiar about that phrase!

This ship is a marvel, but for my taste she is too luxurious and too big and I look back on the trips I made across the Atlantic in the 90's with a feeling that they were much more enjoyable. ...

I am so thankful that I was able to come with the others on this ship as I have been able to direct things as I wanted them. I make S.B. summon conferences continually and when he says there's nothing to talk about I bring things up. Early in the 1st meeting I got unanimous assent to a proposal that we should draw up a series of general propositions for the approval of the Conference both in order to give the lead to the Dominions and the outside public and to form a test to which every proposition afterwards put forward could be submitted. Later on I went & myself wrote out my propositions which were accepted not only unanimously but with enthusiasm. After that I demanded to know the line of S.B.'s opening speech and after some delay he gave us a series of notes that were received with blank dismay by the whole party. There was nothing to do but to tear them up & let me write a new speech for him which I did and that has also been approved. I have insisted that it shall be typed and read so as to have no possibility of mistake!

---

[47] Ishbel Allan MacDonald (1903–82). Eldest daughter of Ramsay MacDonald, acting as his political hostess and aide, accompanying him on official visits. Member, LCC 1928–34; licensee, Plough Inn, Spen 1936–53. Married Norman Ridley 1938 (died 1950) and James Peterkin 1953 (died 1955).

We have had a very good voyage. I see the sea is described in the log as rough on several days but there has been practically no motion. S.B. had to retire one day from our conference & P. Cunliffe-Lister soon followed him but they must be very bad sailors. ...

You will be glad to hear that I have had no gouty feelings and in fact I think I am in very good form. I hope I shall be able to say the same in a month's time.

...

27 July 1932
Imperial Economic Conference,
United Kingdom Delegation,
Parliament Buildings, Ottawa

My dear Hilda,

... The voyage seems very far away now but I believe I forgot to mention that we finished up with a fire on Sunday night and a collision in the fog on Monday so it was not uneventful.

You will not be surprised to hear that the chief burden of the British side of this Conference is falling on me. Consequently I am being worked so hard that my P.S. is getting seriously alarmed though there is no need for his anxiety. ...

I dont quite know where to begin. We are all housed at the principal hotel here, the Chateau Laurier, in magnificent suites and we also have offices in the Parliament House where I am writing now. The weather has been warm & some of my colleagues would say hot. ... I have had precious little time for air and exercise. Three times, I think, I have been out for an hour or an hour and a half's drive and sometimes I walk the 200 or 300 yds that separate this building from the hotel, but for the rest I have spent my time in interviews and Committees beginning about 9.30 and lasting till dinner and occasionally afterwards. Except when I am dining out, which is fairly often, I dine in my room but I often have someone to dine with me in order to carry on discussion and I have practically never been in bed before 12. In the circumstances I consider it creditable that though my bedroom opens on to a street with a tramline on a hill, up and down which the trams roar thunderously most of the night I pay no attention to them but sleep peacefully through it all. The gout is asleep too ...

It is still too early to pronounce on what will emerge from this Conference but it has not gone badly so far. We are within sight of an agreement with the Indians who have played up splendidly. The South Africans who I feared might be out for mischief have on the contrary been very helpful and I have no doubt we shall do a deal with them. I like Havenga who seems to me a very straightforward fellow and his companions though rather grim looking Dutchmen seem to be quite sympathetic. ...

The Irish are lying very low & carefully abstain from making trouble. They are out to curry favour with the Dominions & recognise that at the least sign of disloyalty they would be ostracised. O'Kelly[48] is trying to get some private talk with Bennett & I cant help thinking that he is looking for some face saving device to escape from the position the Irish have got themselves into. B. is cautious; he doesn't want to get his fingers into the hinges, but I have told him that he must not let any chance of making up a foolish quarrel slip and he is going to hear what O'K has to say.

Bennett himself has been my greatest anxiety. He keeps everything in his own hands; his own Ministers dont know what he means to do and he has hitherto confined himself to very vague generalities. I saw very early that the only chance of progress was for me to get a private talk with him but it was not till two days ago that I got my chance. Luckily he has great confidence and a great regard for me. The Governor General has been telling me today that B. will take from me what he wouldn't take from any one else and I have now succeeded in getting on terms with him as a result of which we met last night, all our delegation on one side and 4 ministers on his, and got down to business. So far he has not made any satisfactory offer but we know pretty well what he wants & he knows what we want.

Of course my absence at Lausanne had put me a bit out of touch but a few days here enabled me to grasp the situation and I have evolved two ideas on which I am working. There is no doubt that the Dominions want preference on meat & wheat & if we had to put against that merely the actual trade we could expect next year from increased preference from them, even if we got all we asked, we could not make a satisfactory picture to our people at home. What I am working for therefore is an agreement over a series of years with progressive decreases in the duties against British goods. Bennett sees the advantage of such an arrangement and though he hasn't yet committed himself he has gone so far as to admit to me that it is an excellent idea, which will make for solidarity & offer a prospect of increasing Imperial Unity. My second idea concerns a number of agricultural products in which more than one Dominion is interested such as meat and butter. The Dominions notion is that we should restrict foreign imports till the price rises to a level which will enable their people to live. But in fact it is the Dominions themselves who have broken the price by increasing their production and my idea is that instead of our restricting their imports they should themselves restrict their production. If this were done on a 5 year plan or a 10 year plan we could secure stability in the industry and at the same time we could progressively increase the Dominion share. It is true that the Dane or the Argentine would have to come into the agreement but he would have his

---

[48] Sean Thomas O'Kelly (1882–1966). A founder of Sinn Féin. Member, Dáil Eireann for Dublin North 1918–45; First Speaker of Dáil 1919–21. Irish envoy to Paris and Rome 1919–22 and to US 1924–26; Vice-President of Executive Council and Minister for Local Government and Public Health 1932–45; Minister of Education 1939; Minister of Finance 1939–45; President of Ireland 1945–59.

compensation in a stable price and the Brit. Govt. could stand over the agreement & guarantee that it would be kept. For we could undertake that if any party to it did not play the game & tried to do more than his share we would put a prohibitive duty against him. The idea is so simple that it seems extraordinary that no one thought of it before. I devised it on the ship and everyone to whom I have suggested it agrees that it would work. Bennett said it was "dead right". Weir[49] was equally pleased, Coates[50] thinks it splendid and though there is lots more to be done on it, I am hopeful of getting it accepted in the end. One of the troubles which has arisen here has been the competition of Russia. The Canadians were terribly afraid we should refuse to do anything but when it came up for discussion I made a speech which apparently delighted them. B. told the G[overnor] G[eneral] that I had made a magnificent statement & since then I have devised a plan which I communicated to Bennett today. He had an idea of his own but he at once said mine was "way ahead of his" and unless any snag appears which I haven't thought of I believe he & Bruce will accept it and in that case it will remove one of our most difficult problems.

...

3 August 1932
Chateau Laurier, Ottawa

My dear Ida,
...
Since I wrote last there has been very little for the press to take hold of and I think they find this a very dull Conference. But in my experience of conferences no news is likely to mean good news and I am more than satisfied with the progress we are making. I think I told you that I had developed two ideas and these are shaping into the twin pillars of the structure we hope to raise. I confess I thought it would be a tough job to get them accepted in the time at our disposal but things are moving so fast that I really begin to believe we shall manage it.

I got my chance to air my views about restriction & regulation of supplies on the Monetary Committee. All the other delegates spoke first & some of them talked as though it were possible to raise prices by monetary manipulation alone. I had a morning in which to prepare my reply, and by employing two

[49] William Douglas Weir (1877–1959). Shipping contractor and pioneer manufacturer of steel houses and motor cars. Scottish Director of Munitions 1915–17; Member of Air Board 1917; Director-General of Aircraft Production 1917–19; Secretary for Air 1918; Air Ministry Advisor 1935–39; Director-General of Explosives 1939; Chairman, Tank Board 1942. Knighted 1917. Created Baron Weir 1918, Viscount 1938.

[50] Joseph Gordon Coates (1878–1943). New Zealand Reform Party politician. Minister in Massey Government 1919–25; Prime Minister 1925–38; Minister of Public Works 1931–35; Finance Minister 1933–35. Represented New Zealand at Ottawa (1932) and London Conferences (1935). Member, New Zealand War Cabinet 1940–42.

stenographers I got it done in time. I thought myself that it was a very original and interesting document and I am told that it created a profound impression on the delegates. Bennett indeed wanted it published to the world at once & I wish it could have been because of its educative value. But Coates (who is excessively stupid though a very good fellow) was alarmed lest some of it should be misunderstood in N.Z and others were afraid lest it should be taken as the final word before they had discussed it. So it was decided not to publish but all the same it has exercised a strong influence over the minds of the delegates and has materially helped in the development of our plans.

We saw the fruits today when we had a long discussion with the Australians. They had decided that they could get no further with unofficial discussions and asked to meet our 7. We were quite ready and it was decided that I should be our spokesman. S.B. was quite certain that Bruce would turn down our proposals at once but on the contrary he accepted them, in principle at any rate, without hesitation. Horace Wilson[51] (our chief adviser) told me that my statement was "really masterly" and the others too seemed very pleased with it and with the way things went. To sum up very briefly, although we did not ask Bruce to give us a final answer he is apparently prepared to accept our proposal for (1) substantially increased preference against the foreigner in goods not produced by Australians (2) a progressive decrease of protective duties against us till only so much remains as will countervail the difference in costs i.e. the British manufacturer is put in the position of a domestic competitor.

August 4 We are terribly pleased about this and think that if we can get Bennett to adopt the same principle (and he has said that he will) we shall have established an Empire policy which will increasingly work to our advantage and at the same time do so by reduction of barriers among ourselves rather than by raising them against other people. On the other side we have agreed to give a number of increased preferences the most important of which has reference to mutton & lamb. But Bruce (and the other Dominions) were not satisfied with a duty alone. They wanted us also to restrict foreign imports, a very difficult matter and one which would probably have necessitated the setting up of Import Boards. We have refused to do this and instead have put up the idea of voluntary restriction. To my great gratification Bruce not only raised no objection but warmly welcomed the scheme and said Australia would gladly cooperate. Meanwhile Lord Weir to whom I communicated the idea on board ship has been working away with Australian producers and he tells me that they have assured him that the necessary machinery to control production could be set up in 14 days!

---

[51] Horace John Wilson (1882–1972). Entered Civil Service 1900. Assistant Secretary, Ministry of Labour 1919–21 and Permanent Secretary 1921–30; Chief Industrial Adviser 1930–39; seconded for special service at 10 Downing Street by Baldwin 1935–37 and Neville Chamberlain 1937–40; Permanent Secretary, Treasury and Head of Civil Service 1939–42. Knighted 1924.

So things look very bright and as I have supplied all the constructive ideas I am very pleased & happy. Of course I shant get the credit which will probably go to S.B. but honestly I dont worry about that so long as the purpose is attained. And even credit sometimes comes where it isn't expected. Last night Herridge,[52] who is R.B. Bennett's brother-in-law & the Canadian Minister in Washington was telling me that the Americans had been very pleased with the success at Lausanne & added "for which they give the credit to you"!

I am keeping as fit as a fiddle and the weather is not oppressively hot. Last week end I stayed at a fishing club on a lake about 80 miles from here. It was a lovely spot ... and all of us caught some. But Canadian fishing is a coarse unscientific affair like deep sea fishing. However it was very enjoyable and I am off to another place tomorrow.

P.S. We have fixed up with the Indians who have accepted the principle of preference (!!) and given us advantage over a wide range of products!

11 August 1932
Chateau Laurier, Ottawa

My dear Hilda,

...

Saturday Aug 13 ... I sent off my last to you on the 4th when if I remember right I was very optimistic and thought all was going well. That mood was a bit shaken on that same day when Bennett brought the Canadian proposals. They were embodied in a huge bundle of papers containing lists of articles in the Tariff schedule and of course it was impossible to get any idea of what they meant. But B's manner was so extremely aggressive and his desire to force us into saying that his offer was most generous and liberal before we knew what it was, was so obvious that I had grave doubts and those doubts were more than

Monday August 15 8.a.m. Well, this letter will give you perhaps some idea of the drive that is going on. I couldn't even get my ten minutes and haven't had another minute to myself till now ... I now go on from where I left off ...

confirmed when our people had examined it carefully. As an example B. said he had given us concessions on steel which would be worth £10 million to us. It turned out that the "concessions" actually put us in a rather worse position than before & meant a loss of trade of about £50,000! As soon as this got to Bennett's ears he sent for his people and cursed them for letting him down while at the same time he loosed off to the Press a denunciation of the British "Whitehall Bureaucrats" especially Sir Horace Wilson who was a Free Trader & out to wreck the Conference.

---

[52] William Duncan Herridge (1888–1961). Canadian Minister to US 1931–35. Unsuccessful parliamentary candidate for universal conscription 1940.

In the meantime this Conference wrecker (Wilson) was urging me to see Bennett as the only chance of saving the Conference and as I got from other quarters an intimation that this course might be acceptable to Bennett I sent him a message that I wanted to see him, and on Tuesday the 9th he came to my room and I had a long talk with him. I pointed out that wrangles about the money value of concessions were not only irritating but useless as even if we agreed on estimates that would not settle the actual results. I said that we were convinced that the Dom. could not give us any concessions which for immediate effect could be compared with those we gave them. We therefore had to look for our reward to the future and what we wanted was a declaration on future policy which would ensure its turning in the right direction. As all this was received with the most cordial agreement I went on to suggest that I should draft out the heads of a treaty and submit them to him. He said he had done some drafting himself & suggested that we should meet again next day I bringing Hailsham and he "someone" to exchange views.

It didn't take me long to draft out what I wanted & apparently it was so much better than his own that his version faded quietly out of the picture. Practically he accepted mine and then last Friday we agreed to give him the other side of the picture. That was where the second and more unhappy hitch came in. He received the communication wh. Hailsham & I made to him with evident signs of annoyance and Herridge his brother-in-law who turned out to be the "someone" did his best to confirm his disappointment. It was not till later that we discovered that what aroused his ire most was that he believed we had deliberately withheld until the last moment the fact that the bacon question was referred to a Royal Commission & could not therefore be decided now. His language (to others) was violent. He said that he had never been so mad in his life; that Americans would not have treated him so, that he had been let down at the last moment & made to look foolish for maintaining to Herridge that Englishmen could be trusted to play straight. Thus we learned that our suspicions of Herridge were justified & that all along he has been a snake in the grass.

But what a man! Fancy his bringing his brother-in-law who is Canadian Minister to Washington into the business at all instead of his Cabinet. And what a childish suspicion. The information had been the subject of many talks between Gilmour & his own Minister of Agriculture. Hailsham & I of course thought he knew all about it but if we had wanted to deceive him we could have found some better way than that.

Since then my relations with Bennett have been extremely unpleasant. He has accepted that after all Hailsham is a good boy as while I was seeing the Press H. got an interview with him and had it out. But he still treats me as though I were a thief. So marked is the difference that today in putting to him a proposal which I had drafted about Russia I handed it over to Hailsham who proposed it as something which he personally had devised while I kept silence. You can imagine how mortifying all this has been and I am feeling as sore as possible. But I cant let personal slights interfere with the attainment of my objects and I am reserving what I shall have to say to Bennett till everything is safely signed & sealed. But then I must tell him what I think of him.

I appreciate the observation of an American that Bennett has the "manners of a Chicago policeman & the temperament of a Hollywood film actor".

The other agreements are rapidly coming to a head & though we havent yet finished with Bruce I believe we shall settle today or tomorrow.

I am well though I have had a very worrying time. I count the days till Saturday when I sail and I never want to see Canada again. I shall sing "Oh, Canada" but in the same sense as "Oh God Oh Montreal"!

…

21 August 1932
R.M.S. Empress of Britain

My dear Ida,

…

Well, here I am on board again, rather gouty, very weary, but with a mind at rest for after all the fogs & reefs & hurricanes we did in the end get safely to port. But I hope I may never have to go through such an experience again. I dont think I ever worked so hard in my life, for the heaviest of the strain fell on me. Hailsham who had the next most strenuous time nearly collapsed on Friday night, and before we left he told me that he had never been so close to a nervous breakdown in all his experience.

As the Duke said … of Waterloo It was a d—d close run thing. So close indeed, that I only initialled the Canadian agreement at 1.30 on Saturday morning after a prolonged and desperate battle with Bennett. I had begun my days work on Friday at 9.a.m. & had been fighting all day with almost every delegation in turn. It was only by the exercise of almost incredible patience, self restraint in face of outrageous provocation, ingenuity in finding new ways round unexpected obstacles and complete confidence in one another that we achieved success. On that very Monday on which I last wrote to Hilda, Bruce and Coates refused to make an agreement unless we gave them the duty on meat. We had a late meeting of the delegation at which J.H. Thomas expressed his admiration of the way Hailsham & I had carried out our work and his indignation at what he called the blackmail which was being attempted. He said he would not embarrass his colleagues but if a duty were given he would just fade quietly out of the picture when we got home. Runciman said the same. He pointed out with truth that he had come a long way but reminded us that both he & the P.M. had pledged themselves at the election against the taxation of wheat & meat. I said that resignations would break up the Government. I hated to put pressure on those who had come so far to come farther but I should regret the failure to come to agreement with Australia as the failure of the Conference and the thought filled me with despair. About midnight we broke up; we had come to no decision but J.H.T. was to telephone the P.M. early next morning and tell him the position. After the others had gone I stopped behind with S.B. I told him that I had felt that it would be unfair as well as distasteful to bandy resignation about with my colleagues, but that I could not retain my position if the Conference failed because we had refused a duty on meat, and I thought the P.M. ought to know that before he gave his answer. S.B. at once sent for Thomas to come back. I dont exactly know what passed but it ended by Thomas saying that he had never had such splendid colleagues, that he thought anything was preferable to a breakdown of the Conference, & that he would sacrifice his own opinions and "lie to Mac" in the morning. Accordingly the next day we had a message from Mac (which was tapped by our friends the Canadians!) saying that he had complete confidence in us and would back us in any decision we came to. In our turn we played the game and keeping a bold and unflinching front we got our agreement without the duty after all.

In spite of the anxieties they caused us I have no complaint to make of the Australians or the New Zealanders. They had to think of their difficulties with their own people who were expecting much more than was reasonable, and, if they drove rather a hard bargain with us they were quite straightforward about it.

Bennett was a different proposition. I gave you an American description of him in my last; here is another given by a Liberal correspondent to the New Chronicle. "As passionate as a spoilt child, as slippery as an eel, as stubborn as a mule, and as hysterical as a woman who has lost her lover". To which I will only add that he lied like a trooper, and that he alternately blustered, bullied, sobbed, prevaricated, delayed and obstructed to the very last moment. Lord Weir, who went to say goodbye to him, finished his conversation with the following concluding shot: "I never knew any man go so near to wrecking a Conference and get through with it after all. *Damn* you!"

Well I am still too fagged to give you a diary of events but I will make a few observations on the results. As you know I was very anxious to get a series of resolutions agreed to which would go some way towards laying down the principles of Imperial trade policy. I was chairman of a committee, containing representatives of all the delegations which was entrusted with the task of drafting a resolution for submitting to the final session and I got out an admirable paper which set forth in general terms what I wanted. If Bennett had been a real President of the Conference he would have given special attention to this matter & might have helped me materially. But he was never anything more than the leader of the Canadian delegation. On my committee he appointed his Secretary of State, Cahan,[53] a man of 73 who must always have been stupid & is certainly

---

[53] Charles Hazlitt Cahan (1861–1944). Canadian barrister and Conservative politician. Member, Nova Scotia Legislative Assembly 1890–94; Federal MP 1925–40. Secretary of State 1930–35.

now incapable of comprehending any broad & statesmanlike policy. When I submitted my paper not a single delegation would accept it and the South Africans made it clear that they did not want anything which suggested that the Empire as such had either principles or policy. In the end I got through a milder resolution which, when read in the light of the individual agreements, does contain much of the heart of the matter. But it would not be clear to the man in the street which is of course what both the S.A. & the Indians wanted.

This was my one disappointment. The agreements themselves are excellent. The Indians … have accepted the principle of Imperial preference. The South Africans have given us considerable concessions and will denounce the German treaty so as not to give them equally to the Hun. The Australians & Canadians have agreed by progressive reductions of duties to put the British manufacturer in the position of a domestic competitor and have said in so many words that they will not use protection to bolster up industries which have no real chance of success on economic lines. Both of them have given us considerable advantages against the foreigner and Australia & N.Z. have come into my meat scheme. It is true that they have only bound themselves for an experimental period, but if the scheme works successfully I have little doubt that they will make a success of it.

I see from Hilda's letter that some features of the scheme have puzzled you. The argument she uses about a young country requiring to expand is precisely that employed by Coates. But what is the use of expanding production unless there is a corresponding expansion of consumption. You must remember that for this surplus meat the U.K. provides the *only* market and that is why over production during the last few years has led to ruinous falls in price. The essence of my scheme is that production shall keep pace with consumption and that leaves two great opportunities for the Dominions. In the first place they can have the benefit of any increase in absorbing capacity that we dont want to reserve for our own farmers. In the second place we announce our policy to be one which will give the Dominions an increasing share of our market at the expense of the foreigner. In other words the foreigner has got to accept a progressive reduction in his exports while the Dominions get a progressive increase in theirs.

…

To go to another subject I know the P.M. has had hankerings after a visit to America in the autumn but I have reason to believe that the Americans dont want him and I hope therefore that we shall hear no more of the project.

…

"Jimmie" tells me that he has been telephoning to London & hears that we have an enthusiastic press except for the Free Traders.

I ought to add after giving such an account of Bennett that it was he who asked that I might sign the Canadian Treaty and that when he said goodbye at Quebec he begged me not to bear malice against him & finished with love to Annie & God bless you.

30 August 1932
Westbourne

My dear Hilda,

... It is a great addition to my satisfaction that Ottawa has given you two so much pleasure and that there are still so many of the family left to rejoice in the fulfilment of Father's policy. The more one thinks of it, the more miraculous it seems that all this should have come about in one short year. And just in time!

... On the whole I think we have no reason to be dissatisfied with the reception of our agreements. It is perhaps just as well that the public should have no idea of Bennett's behaviour. As for my part, I am quite content to let that remain obscure. It amused me to read how Mr Baldwin was closeted with Mr Bennett until the small hours of Saturday when he initialled the agreement & then settled the organisation of the plenary meeting. He was tucked up in his little bed long before that & it was my initials & not his that were appended to the agreement. But whatever the papers say I dont think any one believes that S.B. had a great deal to do with the practical work and anyhow he did admirably what we took him there to do. All his little after dinner speeches & speeches of thanks were models of their kind and his address to the Canada Club which was not reported here was in his best style full of the deeper things which mean so much to him and which produced all the greater impression on his hearers because there is no one in Canada who can think & speak on that lofty level.

...

We had a Cabinet which lasted most of Saturday. Snowden showed no sign of disturbance at what we had done but Samuel asked many carping questions and reserved his position until he had consulted with his friends. I dont think we could have another agreement to differ and if he were to go I should rejoice for he is a most uncomfortable colleague and I believe his departure would draw the rest of us closer together.

I am slowly picking up but still feel pretty tired ... I am besieged by the press here and shall be glad to get away. ...

...

4 September 1932
Tillypronie, Tarland, Aberdeenshire

My dear Hilda,

...

... Last night [Sir Francis Humphrys] was telling me about his interview with the Shah.[54] The Shah does not speak anything but Persian and generally has his

---

[54] Muhammed Reza Khan (1878–1944). Shah of Persia and founder of Pahlavi dynasty. Served Persian Cossack Brigade; helped to engineer coup 1921. Minister of War 1921; Prime Minister

Prime Minister Timurtache[55] [sic] to interpret for him. Humphrys however speaks Persian himself and refused to have an interpreter, with the result that the Shah was so much interested in his conversation that he asked him to stop to lunch. It is the first time that any Englishman has been asked to lunch for 10 years, and I have no doubt that Humphrys impressed the Shah as he does all these wild potentates with a sense that here was a man who could be trusted and whose friendship was worth having. He told Humphrys that the shackles which the Russians imposed on him were intolerable and he was terribly bitten with the notion of freeing himself from them by connecting up Tehran with the new Haifa-Baghdad railway. The railway has of course not been begun yet and I fear that presently I shall be told that a Treasury guarantee is necessary. But I would look favourably on a scheme of that kind, if Govt assistance was really wanted, and should think it a far better investment than a luxury Cunarder or a new "speedway".

...

My host & hostess thought they had never seen anyone look so awful as I did on my arrival (this is a gross exaggeration!) but declare that I already appear a new man. Anyway I can shoot my share of the grouse so there cant be much the matter with me.

...

12 September 1932
Littlewood Park, Alford, Aberdeenshire

My dear Ida,

... According to present plans we return to London on the 23rd and then Frank & I go for a week's fishing to Dorset. ... I am looking forward to the pleasure of instructing Frank in the gentle art, though I dont believe there is much that I can teach him. As you say, he is a pleasing contrast to the Amery boy,[56] but if you had ever set eyes on that little gutter snipe you would feel no surprise at anything he might do.

We had a most successful and enjoyable visit to Tillypronie and Annie made friends with our host & hostess ... She was able to make some return to her hostess who was overwhelmed with stage fright on being commanded to dine at Balmoral ... As a matter of fact the whole things was very informal. I went first alone in ordinary clothes taking my evening clothes with me and the men were allowed swallow tails & trousers instead of kneebreeches.

1923; chosen as Shah 1925. Considered a Nazi sympathiser and abdicated after allied occupation in 1941 before deportation to South Africa.

[55] Mirza Khan Timurtash. Persian Court Minister.

[56] John Amery (1912–45). Leopold Amery's elder son. Known as 'Jack'. Became a Fascist, broadcasting enemy propaganda from Italy during the war. Hanged for treason 1945.

The King was in great form shouting and guffawing away with immense gusto. Although I had ¾ hr's audience he asked practically nothing about Ottawa, but contented himself with retailing some of the more lurid of Jimmy Thomas' stories. They were not new to me as I had witnessed the process of their construction and I was rather disappointed that Majesty did not take a more serious view. I tried to pump him by expressing the hope that he was satisfied, but after first replying Oh Yes he proceeded hastily to qualify by adding "Of course I haven't read all your papers yet". On the other hand though so cautious about Ottawa he was extremely rash in declaring that we must on no account annoy the police, thereby inserting himself into a highly controversial & difficult problem. The May Comee recommended that the police pay shd be cut 12½% in two sniks. When the navy mutinied every one's cut, including the police, was reduced to 10% but the 2 stages were maintained for the police. From the very first Samuel funked this and tried to get out of it. He took a Cabinet minute about economies, to the effect that the Minister might select the place to make them so long as he saved the required amount, as an authorisation to *substitute* administrative economies for pay cuts, though no other minister understood it in that sense; and indeed it is clear that you could not modify the pay cut in one case without raising violent jealousy & dissatisfaction elsewhere. However on the strength of his interpretation Samuel made rather definite statements to the Police Council & the H. of C. which he now claims have committed the Cabinet. Last May the subject was remitted to a Comee of which I was Chairman to make a report on. The evidence as to the effect of any change in the 2nd cut (due 1st Oct) on the services the teachers, the Doctors, civil servants & unemployed was so overwhelming that Samuel (& Sinclair who hunts in couples with him) agreed that the cut was inevitable but asked if they might propose some concessions which would mitigate the blow. This was agreed to, but on the pretext that I was away they have never submitted any proposals. They have waited till we come back from Ottawa & then put up a memo to the Cabinet saying that they & we are committed against the cut that the police would strike if it were enforced and that they cant find any concessions worth offering to them. It fairly makes my blood boil and I have written most seriously about it to the P.M. I dont know what the result will be but I hear that they (the cold foot ministers) are thinking of resigning over Ottawa. I hope they do for I am fed up with them!

...

18 September 1932
Lanfine, Newmilns, Ayrshire

My dear Hilda,

...

I got a telephone message on Monday from the Treasury to say that at the P.M.'s request Warren Fisher[57] was coming up to Scotland & would arrive at Aberdeen next morning ... While I think of it, I may as well add that I am now quite refreshed and feel able to work again, though I think if I can build up a bit of reserve in the remainder of my holiday I shall find it quite useful later on. A certain amount of tenderness remains in the foot joints, perceptible especially when walking over rough ground or wading in heavy brogues. But it does not seem to leave any inflammation and as soon as I get my big boots off I dont feel it any longer.

I thought when I heard of Warren's mission that the P.M. was trying to get me to give way to our 'Erb about the police. But that was not so. The police indeed remains an open point and I am still making myself as disagreeable as possible about it. But the real point of the mission appeared to be this. Snowden, Samuel & Sinclair have intimated their intention of resigning on Ottawa, together with 7 or 8 Under Secretaries. Thereupon R.M. feels very lonely and dispirited. He knows he will be told that he is more than ever the slave of the Tories, that he has sold his soul for office and other pleasantries of that kind. In these unhappy conditions he felt much in need of a comforter and, according to Warren he turned to me. So I sent him back a note, bidding him be of good cheer, assuring him that the defection of our colleagues would only strengthen our own loyalty, & that we looked to him not to be the leader of the Tory Party but as the symbol of our faith that until prosperity returned country must come before party. Finally I told him that the separation was inevitable but that it would in my opinion strengthen the Govt after the first unpleasant reactions had passed. I have only so far had a note to say that a letter from him is coming but Warren reports that he is perceptibly comforted and strengthened.

I believe firmly in what I wrote. Samuel's behaviour over the police is an eye-opener: he is emphatically not a man to go tiger hunting with & with his disappearance & that of his satellite "Archie" we should be far more homogeneous and we should get rid of the friction over bye-elections. In fact we should move towards the fused party under a National name which I regard as certain to come.

This place should make a good finish to our Scotch holiday. Cayzer[58] is as rich as Crœsus and we are therefore in the midst of luxury. He is giving us 2

---

[57] (Norman Fenwick) Warren Fisher (1879–1948). Deputy Chairman, Board of Inland Revenue 1914–18 and Chairman, 1918–19; Permanent Secretary at Treasury and Head of Civil Service 1919–39. Knighted 1919.

[58] Herbert Robin Cayzer (1881–1958). Shipowner. Conservative MP for Portsmouth South 1918–

days shooting and has made interest with friends in the neighbourhood to give
me 2 days fishing in the Don. ...

25 September 1932
Moor Lane House, Briantspuddle, Dorset

My dear Ida,
...

Hilda was right in supposing that a Cabinet had been summoned for Wednesday
when the dissentients will hand in their resignations. ...
...

I had a talk with the P.M. on Friday. He is quite calm now about the resignations
and not in the least inclined to fill up all the places with Simonites as W.
Runciman coolly proposes. We may have more trouble over the reconstitution
than over the resignations, for I still think the latter wont do us any damage. In
fact they have been discounted already.
...

15 October 1932
37 Eaton Square, SW1

My dear Hilda,
...

I was not in the conversation with him [Herriot] but I dined with Simon on
Thursday & found myself next to him so that I found a chance of a good talk.
Tyrrell[59] had written that he was most anxious to see me repeating that
"Chamberlain, c'est du cristal" and he was demonstrative in his evident pleasure
at our meeting again. He was in great form and told many stories with much
humour and spirit. ...

Austen was both gloomy and aggressive demanding to know what the
Government's foreign policy was and expressing his belief that they hadn't got
one. I sympathise with his impatience but think he does Simon somewhat less than
justice. Anyway Herriot was very pleased with his visit and the agreement come to
seemed to me very satisfactory though I see Germany is making fresh trouble.

Well we have finished tonight with De Valera and on a very satisfactory note
so far as our position is concerned. That is to say that though I would have been

---

22 and 1923–39. President, Chamber of Shipping 1941–42. Created Bart 1924 and Baron Rotherwick
1939.

[59] William George Tyrrell (1866–1947). Entered Diplomatic Service 1889; Principal Private
Secretary to Foreign Secretary 1907–15; Assistant Under-Secretary 1918–25; Permanent Under-
Secretary 1925–28; Ambassador in Paris 1928–34; President, Board of Film Censors 1935–47.
Knighted 1913. Created Baron Tyrrell 1929.

only too glad to make a reasonable settlement, De V. was frank enough to make it clear that no such settlement was possible. He declared bluntly that the Irish people would never be satisfied with any arrangement under which they remained liable to pay a single penny to the U.K. & that though he would have kept any arrangement he had made with us he could not guarantee that it would not be challenged by some successor, if under it any liability remained.[60] Moreover he intimated that even if we abandoned all pecuniary claims it was probable that the Irish people would still desire and do their utmost to obtain their complete independence as a Republic. In face of such a declaration accommodation was clearly impossible and no one can criticise us for not giving way.

I have a rather hard time in front of me as in addition to Ottawa on which I kick off on Tuesday I have a number of outside engagements which will be an unwelcome addition to my labour. However I suppose I shall get through somehow. I agree that the publication of the schedules has been well received and though Samuel will give us trouble that will be nothing to the trouble he will have. Did you see Ll.G.'s letter refusing to go to Queen's Hall, with his description of Samuel's "call" muffled with the rags of Whiggery and poltroonery! What a spiteful little man it is.

Meanwhile I have succeeded with much trouble in carrying the police cut through the Cabinet. I expect we shall have an unpleasant time but it would have been worse if we had caved in. Trouble is also working up over the Means Test and it is clear that my original plan of putting the able bodied unemployed on to the local authorities as the permanent solution is hopelessly prejudiced by the delay and the transitional arrangement and above all by the hopeless failure of the Royal Commission [on Unemployment Insurance, 1930–32].

In these circumstances I have conceived a bolder plan which I have imparted to the Minister of Labour and upon which the permanent officials are now working. It is nothing less than taking the whole relief of the able bodied away from local authorities and ministers & putting it outside party politics by entrusting it to a Statutory Commission. It rather takes people's breath away at first and I have not yet communicated it to the P.M. or to S.B. but it is the sort of plan that might properly be introduced by a National Government and I cant help thinking that it might command the support of a good many of the sounder working men. Until it is worked out I cant say what the immediate financial effect would be but I am sure that it would save money in the long run because it would avoid the danger of the relief being put up to auction by the parties. Moreover I conceive that the Commissioners might be entrusted with the duty of providing some interest in life for the large numbers of men who are never likely to get work. I am convinced that no return to prosperity is going to swallow up more

---

[60] At a meeting held at de Valera's instigation to discuss land annuity payments on 13 October, he restated his earlier position in more peremptory terms and demanded compensation for the over-taxation of Ireland since the Act of Union in 1801.

than a proportion of those now unemployed and that we must regard our problem for the rest like that of dealing with the permanently disabled after the war. How is life to be made tolerable for them? They must be given organised recreation physical exercise and where possible a bit of ground and if it were part of the Commissioner's duty to study the question I believe they would with the means at their disposal find ways of enlisting voluntary effort. Their own work would be more interesting & inspiring than if they were only concerned to give the least amount of relief necessary.

Well, there's a new idea for you and I should be interested to hear your comments.

22 October 1932
Westbourne

My dear Ida,

I am glad you approved my line on Ottawa. The Times was no doubt correct in saying that some of our party would have found my speech more amusing if I had violently attacked Samuel, but I was told by many members that our supporters were very pleased and my purpose was to educate them on what Ottawa meant rather than to make an effect which would have quickly been forgotten. They have had their fun with Samuel since.

So far we are well satisfied with our reception. Except for the personal interest of the Simon–Samuel duels, the debate after the first day has been as dead as mutton and the difficulty has been to shake up speakers to carry it on at all. The official opposition has been half hearted & the Liberals are only flogging dead horses so that it has been decided (with the approval of all parties) to wind up the 2R. at 7.30 on Thursday and go on to something else. This means that I shant speak on 2R. at all, but really there is nothing new to say and I shall have plenty of opportunities of intervention on Committee & Report.

With regard to the Hush-Hush scheme this has made much progress since I wrote last. At the P.M.'s request I explained it to the Cabinet and it is now being worked out at the Ministry of Health with the aid of officers from the Treasury & the M/Labour. I haven't seen Robinson, but Sir E. Strohmenger[61] who was at Health with me and has now come over to the Treasury tells me that it has been received there with great enthusiasm & I was very glad to hear this as I have a very high opinion of Robinson's judgement on such matters.

As soon as they get something on paper they will bring it to me and I shall see how it shapes, but I anticipate that the R[elieving] O[fficer]'s will have to be

---

[61] Ernest John Strohmenger (1873–1967). Entered Civil Service 1893. Deputy Comptroller, National Health Insurance 1913; Deputy Accountant General, Ministry of Health 1919–30; Deputy Secretary, Ministry of Health 1930–32; Under-Secretary, Treasury 1932–34; Deputy Chairman, Unemployment Assistance Board 1934–37. Knighted 1927.

taken over by the Commissioners as it would be very undesirable to have 2 machines working side by side. I understand that the M/Health are in some doubt as to whether even medical out door relief should be left to theP[ublic] A[ssistance] Committees or whether they should not be confined to the Institutions. I should like them to keep the whole medical side but the difficulties may be insuperable.

I contemplate that the Comrs would enlist a good deal of voluntary assistance on the constructive side; whether they should be given a chance of availing themselves of the Guardians experience on the relief side I am not sure. One does not want the system to become too bureaucratic but our experience of the voluntary work in the changed conditions of today has not been encouraging.

In any case I am satisfied that the present system could not continue and I believe we should have an increasing number of L.A.'s throwing in their hand. I needn't say that the scheme must be kept absolutely secret for some time yet but it has been so heartily welcomed by the majority of the Cabinet (no one has opposed it) that I feel pretty sure that it will emerge as part of our programme for next Session.

The new Home Secretary & S.S. for Scotland have had their interviews with the police and things went a good deal better than they expected. We shall have trouble in London if anywhere but it is already evident that our late colleagues exaggerated the dangers of a firm stand.

… That [Birmingham Municipal] Bank is really a marvel. The deposits are now over £14 millions and over £4 M has been advanced to house purchasers on mortgage. They have put an inscription on the stone to say that I originally conceived the idea and was principally responsible for its establishment. I came away with a silver trowel and a mallet "suitably inscribed".

Austen told me about the Life which he had read the first vol in proof with intense interest. I have a feeling that I shall be more critical than he but I agree with you that even if one's feelings are sometimes jarred by the style the facts will be there to form a quarry for future historians & biographers.

This has not been a very peaceful week end and I have been recalled to London for a Conference with the pundits about the exchange.[62] It is too bad that we should have a set back there just when things were really beginning to look a little better. What with hunger marchers and relaxation of the means test and doubts about the American Debt there is plenty of material for the scare merchants to work upon.

…

---

[62] After a slump to $3.23 in early December 1931, sterling stabilised at around $3.40 before a further slide saw it fall to a trough of $3.14 in December 1932.

30 October 1932
37 Eaton Square, SW1

My dear Hilda,

...

How long the Hush-Hush scheme will remain a secret I dont know. Sir Allan Powell writes to the Times to advocate it & I have just got an advance copy of the L.A. economy Report in which it is definitely recommended. Whether they had heard something and hastened to scoop in the credit, or whether they thought of it independently I dont know, but there it is and of course their recommendation will help to establish it. I regard it as settled that we shall adopt it now.

Meanwhile I have been pushing the idea of regulation of production which as I think I mentioned in my last is adopted in the Pig Commissioner's report. I descanted on it to the Sunday Times man on Friday and I see he drew attention to it today and I have also been briefing Leith Ross[63] on the same subject for the World Conference. I haven't discussed the brief with the P.M. but I have got it agreed by Runciman so I think it will go all right.

I have also been suggesting a new Disarmament plan to Simon who came to me in despair this week to ask if I could make any suggestion as he was stumped. I sent him a long screed on Friday night but as there hasn't been time to hear from him I don't know whether he will think there is anything in it. It amuses me to find a new policy for each of my colleagues in turn and though I can't imagine that all my ideas are the best that can be found, most of them seem to be adopted faute de mieux!

I heard from someone else of Wickham Steed's[64] wireless on the Unemployment Debate. You are quite right & he was quite wrong. The general verdict was that Samuel had the best of the duel between him & Ll.G. and that the "constructive" part of Ll.G.'s speech was nothing but a rehash of his old story. The coolness of his question Why dont you make plans of your own if you don't like mine was characteristic of him. We *are* making plans & carrying them out too.

The debate on the Ottawa Bill is as dead as mutton and though the Labour Party pretend that they are anxious to discuss matters of real importance it is

---

[63] Frederick William Leith-Ross (1887–1968). Private Secretary to Asquith 1911–13; British representative on Finance Board of Reparations Commission 1920–25; Deputy Controller of Finance, Treasury 1925–32; Chief Economic Adviser to Government 1932–46; Director-General, Ministry of Economic Warfare 1939–42; Chairman, Inter-Allied Post-War Requirements Committee 1941–43; Deputy Director-General, United Nations Relief and Rehabilitation Administration 1944–45; Governor, National Bank of Egypt 1946–51; Deputy Chairman, National Provincial Bank 1951–66. Knighted 1933.

[64] Henry Wickham Steed (1871–1956). Acting Berlin correspondent, *The Times* 1896; correspondent, Rome 1897–1902; Vienna 1902–13; Foreign Editor, *The Times* 1914–19; Editor, *The Times* 1919–22; proprietor and Editor, *Review of the Reviews* 1923–30; broadcaster on world affairs, BBC Overseas Service 1937–47.

evident that that is only an excuse for getting rid of a debate which they dont feel competent to carry on.

So far we have had no sign of trouble in the Police and the H.O. say they are too angry with the Communists to attend to their own cuts. One man who kicked the Inspector on the ground after he had been badly injured by a missile was taken to the police station and searched when he was found to have £30 in his pocket. "Hunger Marcher!"[65]

Very secret De Valera has made further advances and we have been having conversations with an emissary. Our terms are stiff but we are told that since De V. went to Geneva and saw what went on there for himself, and since he heard the Ottawa delegates account of what went on there he has decided that the Free State had better remain in the British Empire!

5 November 1932
Westbourne

My dear Ida,

...

We came down here last night for me to attend a dinner (with speech) and to get a little rest afterwards as I have had a gruelling week. Every single morning I have had a Cabinet or a Cabinet Committee & very often one in the afternoon too in addition to the Ottawa Bill in the House. I had 3 pretty competent Under Secretaries to whom I left a great deal but every now and then it became necessary for me to intervene, notably one evening when a nasty storm boiled up over meat following a not very successful interview which the P.M. and S.B. had had with a deputation of agricultural members. I was only just in time, but after I had spoken the thunder gradually rolled away and though the Beaver is doing his best to stir up more trouble I feel pretty confident that we shall get our team quieted down.

Indeed I am disposed to believe that the emergency which has arisen may in the end be a good thing because it will force the interests concerned to take the idea of voluntary restriction more seriously. It is of course a new idea to most people and they are slow in grasping all its implications. What I want is education and I am doing all I can to educate. I spoke on the same subject on 3R. and if you read your Sunday Times you will find that increasing attention is being given to it in the columns of that paper, the editor of which comes to me every Friday for guidance. But the education even of Cabinet colleagues proceeds slowly. S.B. is beginning now to sit up and take notice and he made an allusion to it in his speech to the United Club the other day. But Walter Elliotts [sic] idea of the way to meet the emergency was to bring in legislation to curtail imports

---

[65] The communist-led National Unemployed Workers' Movement organised eighteen contingents of the 'Great National Hunger March against the Means Test' to meet in London on 27 October 1932 to present a million-signature petition. This ended in much violence from both sides.

from the Dominions & the Argentine and of course Runciman went off the deep end at once as that would have exploded all chance of doing a deal with the latter, while, as I had to point out, we had debarred ourselves from imposing any further restriction on Australian & N.Z. imports till June 1934. However after strenuous argument I got both Elliott [sic] & Runciman to see sense and to agree to meet the Dominions & the Argentine & *ask* them voluntarily to restrict imports. This has been done and a most promising start has been made both parties taking quite a reasonable view. Of course as I expected they wanted to know what the British farmer was going to do to help and here we come up against a difficulty because there is no means at present of controlling production here. But I think Elliott is now convinced that control must come before we can carry out any long term policy and everything points to the development of an agricultural policy on the lines I first suggested when we were in opposition, namely to settle for each branch of agriculture what is the level of production we want to aim at and how long we shall take to get there. Once you have got that laid down you can work out the distribution of the balance between Dominions and foreigners any way you like, and so you lead on to the ultimate regulation of the supplies of all the primary commodities by Inter Imperial and international agreements. This, as it seems to me, is the practical solution of the great problem of how to raise wholesale prices, though I dont deny that there is also a monetary factor to be taken into account. But it is the economic factor which is the governing one and it can be tackled independently. Under consumption is only another aspect of over production. It means a restricted market and if you can deal with under consumption either simultaneously or afterwards you can, if you control supplies, regulate them to suit the state of the market, but regulation is the more important of the two. I have got the Research Department working on the problem of distribution which is so well illustrated in the examples you give. It is not insuperable but it involves an amount of interference with individual action which would encounter very fierce opposition. What a pity I never had the opportunity while I was Lord Mayor of working out that milk scheme. If I had carried it through it would have been an object lesson which might have been of incalculable value.

I have made enquiries about the origin of the L.A.'s recommendations on the relief of the able bodied and find that they came to it independently. But their recommendations will make our task more easy. I think you are right in supposing that it will put an end to the Guardians Committees as it seems difficult to imagine how they could work in with such a scheme.

Simon did not take kindly to my suggestion and the P.M. was disposed to turn it down on the ground that it would never be accepted in Geneva. But in the course of a 5 hours Cabinet discussion on Disarmament my colleagues found on every point that they were blocked unless they came back to it. The 1st Lord and Hailsham both told me that they thought it the only way of making progress and in the end a Committee was appointed of which I was a member to work out a draft proposal which now embodies my plan. It is really very simple and amounts to this; that since the difficulty about disarmament lies in the fears of France & her Allies lest Germany should take advantage of it to re-arm we should all agree that disarmament should take place in successive stages each stage being dependent upon the good behaviour of Germany during the preceding period. The advantages are that confidence would proceed also by stages being based on actual experience rather than promises, that actual reduction would begin at once but not on such a scale as to frighten any one, that arms now in stock would live out their life & then be succeeded by less formidable ones, that armament makers could form their plans according to a known programme i.e. that no one would spend money on developing an arm which would probably be prohibited in five years, and finally that an ultimate objective could be fixed which would satisfy the people who are genuinely anxious to abolish war but who defeat their object by asking for everything at once. When I explained this scheme to S.B. he remarked that it was so simple that he couldn't think why nobody had thought of it before. But I believe that was the comment upon a celebrated solution by the late Christopher Columbus!

India has been another frightful problem during the week. We are getting down to the bone there now and the bone is the question of handing over to an Indian Government the responsibility for finance. We ought never to have promised responsible Government at the centre till we had tried out self government in the Provinces but past prime ministers & particularly R.J.M[acDonald] [sic] have made statements which have committed us and the problem is, as I put it to my colleagues, how to give the Indian child the knife which it is demanding and at the same time to contrive that the knife wont open till the child is old enough to use it without danger to itself and other people. It is one of the worst fences I have come up against and I dont see my way clear yet but I am working towards some sort of solution.

Ireland is off for the present. We shall give them another smack this week and my secret information is that there is a possibility of a Coalition government there soon in which case we may have further approaches. I dont think they can stand our fire long.

All is quiet on the police front. I suppose you have seen the Moscow letter.[66] It is another Zinovieff!

Next week c/o Sir Gomer Berry[67] ... where we go for a shooting party. Flandin is one of the guns.

---

[66] On 4 November 1932 Sydney Elias, chairman of the National Unemployed Workers' Movement, was charged with incitement to disturbance and sedition on the basis of a letter sent from Moscow to the National Unemployed Workers' Movement leaders conveying instructions from the Third International.

[67] James Gomer Berry (1883–1968). Newspaper proprietor and brother of Lord Camrose. Chairman Kemsley Newspapers Ltd and Editor-in-Chief, *Sunday Times* 1937–59. Trustee of Reuters from 1941 and Chairman 1951–59. Created Bart 1928, Baron Kemsley 1936 and Viscount 1945.

13 November 1932
37 Eaton Square, SW1

My dear Hilda,

...

We got back this afternoon earlier than I had intended as I had to return in order to interview the Press on the note to the U.S.A. [on war debts] which is to be published tomorrow. ...

...

I had several long talks with Flandin and got on very confidential terms with him. He asked if I would communicate with him so as to keep him in touch with British policy and I think it would be a good thing to do. But I told him that I should have to have a talk with Simon first as I must be careful not to poach on his preserves. Flandin evidently thinks that Herriot is likely to come to grief before the end of the year on finance and he seems to anticipate a fresh combination between his own party minus the diehards and Herriots Radical-Socialists & Radicals, leaving out Socialists, Dissident Socialists, & Communists. French politics are very confusing!

...

19 November 1932
Yattendon Court, Nr Newbury, Berkshire

My dear Ida,

... [O]ur host was very disappointed with his bag yesterday. ... but I enjoy the small days even and a bag of 200 or 300 pheasants to eight guns gives one plenty of fun. ... I dont think you know the Iliffes.[68] He was in the House for some time but found it impossible to spare the long hours there from his business of journalism. He is with the Berry's in the Daily Telegraph and the Sunday Times and their other papers. I dont exactly know what he does but it is evident that he is most comfortably rich. ... and he seems to have bought up most of the county in the very laudable endeavour to preserve its amenities. They are very nice people and are very good to their servants and tenants; it is a comfort to know that there are still a few left who can afford such luxuries and when I think of the people we have stayed with recently, the Roydens, the Macleans, the Cayzers, the Berrys and the Iliffes I feel that we haven't yet got to the end of our accumulated wealth in this country.

...

I understand that Simon was very pleased with the reception given to his speech, but although he has put in my idea of disarmaments by stages he has

---

[68] Edward Nauger Iliffe (1877–1960). Newspaper publisher and Conservative MP for Tamworth 1923–29. Controller of Machine Tools, Ministry of Munitions 1917–18. Joint proprietor of *Daily Telegraph* 1928–37; proprietor of *Birmingham Post* and *Birmingham Mail* from 1943. Knighted 1922. Created Baron Iliffe 1933.

emphasised it so little that I fear attention will be focussed [sic] on other points and that we may do what we have so often done before, namely get nothing by asking for too much at once. I was rather struck by an observation made to me by Flandin who lunched with me on Thursday and afterwards stopped for a talk. He said, why not tie up German equality of status with an agreement about the eastern frontier, and when I asked how it was possible to get such an agreement he replied that many Germans would welcome it and he would invite Germany & Poland to accept arbitration by Great Britain and France jointly. I have asked Tyrrell whether he has heard this suggestion from any other quarter in France. If there were any chance of arbitration being accepted it would be worth following up. I also had a discussion with Flandin about naval disarmament and agreement with Italy. He said France was not interested in naval power as such, but she was greatly concerned about the safety of her lines of communication with North Africa and if Gt. Britain could guarantee that, she would accept equality with Italy. As however it did not seem to me that he had quite thought out this idea I asked him to consider it further on his return to Paris and let me have a memorandum about it and this he has promised to do. We also discussed the World Economic Conference. Unfortunately on the monetary side the policy of France and ourselves is fundamentally different and it will be very difficult to get any agreement there. However we both thought that if we began on the economic side we might get closer together and I took the opportunity of airing my views on the regulation of production. The idea was evidently new to him but when he had got over the shock he said he was not against it only he thought it ought to be discussed. I told him, what I have not yet told my colleagues, that I thought the only way to make anything of the World Conference was to get agreement beforehand on some major points between France U.S.A. and ourselves, that I myself was trying to frame some sort of programme and that when it was more advanced I thought it might be useful to discuss it with some French representative. He was very much interested in this and asked if he might tell Herriot to which I replied Certainly, provided he understands that these are only my own personal views. Evidently he and Herriot are in close touch.

The same day the new Soviet Ambassador M. Maisky[69] came to see me – a revolting but clever little Jew. I had nearly an hour's talk with him on the subject of the Trade Treaty and Ottawa and I talked very straight to him. The most interesting feature of our conversation was that he asked whether we could not arrange a quota system for timber like that we have made for meat. Ça marche! I said he had better talk that over with Runciman when he came to discuss the

[69] Ivan Mikhailovich Maisky (1884–1975). Russian diplomat. Menshavik was exiled to Siberia before escaping to Germany; lived in London 1912–17. Returned to Russia 1917; became a Bolshevik 1922. Counsellor, Soviet Embassy in London 1925–27; Soviet Ambassador in London 1932–43; Deputy Foreign Minister 1943–45; Soviet member of Reparations Committee 1945–48; imprisoned during a Stalin purge 1949–53. Attached Soviet Academy of Sciences 1957–75.

new Treaty, but I have sent a note to Runciman calling his attention to the importance of the suggestion which if it could be carried out would remove some considerable sources of embarrassment & difficulty. I sent a note of the conversation to Simon, which in his absence came into Vansittart's hands. The result was a telephone message just before I left to ask if I had any objection to the notes being circulated to the Cabinet as the F.O. considered it extremely important.

As to War Debts, I am not surprised that the City is in a state of great nervousness, for the American attitude as expressed by their papers is hopelessly unresponsive. We have had no official indication of any kind as yet but I remain of the opinion that after passing through some mauvais quarts d'heure we shall get our moratorium and then our real troubles will begin. My Treasury people are in a terrible stew about leaving negotiations in the hands of the F.O. as they say they always run away the minute the Yanks say Boh and they are trying to fix up a scheme which will prevent anything being done or said without my approval. I feel pretty confident however that Simon wont do anything without consulting me and that the Treasury fears are unnecessary.

Sunday I am sorry for the Conservative back benchers whose Economy Report[70] has been submerged under the ridicule poured upon them for their apparent anxiety to escape from the responsibility of it. Of course it was a very crude affair and is really better buried. The real article comes out I think on Tuesday but I am afraid it may be some time before we decide how much of it to adopt.

...

26 November 1932
Westbourne

My dear Hilda,

...

I do congratulate you on your success ... No good thing ever seems to come without a lot of trouble and set back and the reason why so many gifted people fail to accomplish much is because they haven't the necessary persistence. Winston is the most conspicuous example; he always loses interest in his schemes after his first impetuous rush and unless someone else does the spadework his schemes come to nothing.

I find it very hard to control my feelings about the Americans. They haven't a scrap of moral courage about any of their prominent men (they have no leaders). Even the P.M. is furious with them at last and all the more because he

---

[70] Backbench pressure for more severe economies led to an Economy Inquiry in 1932 under the auspices of the Conservative 1922 Committee which recommended cuts well beyond those most MPs were prepared to contemplate. In November 1932 the report was dropped and Gervais Rentoul resigned as chairman of the 1922 Committee.

has so long believed that they would behave like gentlemen out of personal regard for himself. I saw with trepidation that he had been speaking yesterday on the subject but when I read the speech I really thought it was very good. As for me there was a dangerous moment in my speech when I saw my audience ready for a smack at Master Hoover and I nearly brought it out. But fortunately my natural prudence restrained me and I refrained. Now, To pay or not to pay, that is the question. I have not even yet abandoned hope that Congress may give way, but I am almost alone in thinking that such a thing is remotely possible and in the next day or so we must decide what we are going to do if they remain obdurate.

It is a most difficult and anxious decision. To refuse is to be accused of repudiation of doing the very thing we have lectured De Valera and the small debtor nations of Europe for doing. On the other hand to pay is to give away our case and to justify the cynics in the U.S.A. who have been saying keep a firm front and we shall get the dollars. Let Europe take care of her own troubles we are only concerned with ours. And I dont know what would be the effect in Europe where every one would be thrown into agitation about their debts to us. Only Germany would remain calm since she is quite determined to pay no more Reparations.

I think it really requires more courage to refuse to pay than to pay; but at present that is the course I am inclined to. I should not repudiate; I should expressly admit the obligation but at the last moment I should inform the Yanks that my conscience would not allow me to take a step which I was convinced would upset the world & throw back all chance of recovery for an indefinite period. I have to go back to town tomorrow and shall be in consultation all afternoon with the Governor & the Treasury and finally with a Cabinet Committee, when perhaps we shall make up our minds.

Whatever we do there will be plenty of people to condemn us on both sides of the Atlantic.

I hope to get some economies out of the official report but I think you can make your mind easy about the Bury, as although we are going to abolish the subsidy under the 1924 [Housing] Act, we shall for a time retain the one for slum clearance and in fact rather suggest to L.A.'s to concentrate on that side of the work. ... I am very gratified to find that the Rural Workers Housing Act has come to the top again. For its purpose it has proved in practice to be the cheapest and most effective method of procedure and it always gives me particular satisfaction because the idea owed nothing to the Dept but was worked out by me with the help of you two.

The Unempt Insurance proposal seems to have escaped notice up to now which shows that our secret has been well kept. I have got a Cabinet Committee appointed with myself as Chairman to work at it but we haven't met yet.

This has been a pretty strenuous week for me. On Wednesday I lunched with the new Company of Newspaper Makers which has been founded by

Blumenfeld,[71] the late editor of the Express. I worked off a little joke on him which completely took him in & a good many others of the Company. Of course there were allusions to the prospect of a reduction of taxation and I began by saying it was a reasonable curiosity on their part but before satisfying it I wanted to interpolate a few observations. I then made my speech & when I had finished said I would now return to the Budget. They would not expect me to enter upon many details but would doubtless be satisfied if I outlined one or two main features which of course they would treat as strictly confidential. The first thing I intended to do was – at this point I pretended that Blum had interrupted and called out "What"? as I turned to him. Blum looked very surprised & whispered that he hadn't said anything. However I bent down and pretended to have a hurried conversation and then turning to the company announced that I had just been saved from committing a frightful blunder. Blum had just told me that the greatest disservice you could do to a journalist was to tell him in confidence what he could find out for himself. I had too much faith in their abilities to doubt that they could easily find out for themselves what was in the next Budget & therefore in deference to the Chairman's maxim I must now hermetically seal my lips. Iliffe who was present, said he had no idea that I was such an actor. He is having a series of shocks, because he told a mutual friend that he had had no idea that the Chancellor could shoot till last week. Apparently the Chancellor is regarded as a sort of Don who is not expected to have any sporting tastes or at any rate any skill. A paper called Everyman that was sent to me had a paragraph saying "I cant imagine Mr C. doing any execution with a shotgun. His temperament is that of a fisherman". But Londonderry[72] who was at Hall Barn the week after we were said the people there declared I never missed anything, an embarrassing exaggeration in the opposite direction.

Macmillans have sent me a copy of the Life and I have just begun it. I must try and keep an open mind but my first impression is that it is far too detailed for modern taste. No doubt later on in the Life the details will have importance but I fear the day has gone by when people are interested in childish years of great men and Garvin seems to me rather to strain the implications of our remote ancestry on Father's youthful mind. His style too jars a little; these constant rushes into the historic present and out again and the journalistic delight in

---

[71] Ralph David Blumenfeld (1864–1948). American journalist. Editor, *Evening Telegraph* (New York) until 1894; journalist, *Chicago Herald* 1884; London Correspondent, *New York Herald* 1887–93; News Editor, *Daily Mail* 1900–1902; Editor, *Daily Express* 1902–32 and Chairman, 1933–48. Founder member, Anti-Socialist Union.

[72] Charles Stewart Henry Vane-Tempest-Stewart (1878–1949). Conservative MP for Maidstone 1906–15. Under-Secretary for Air 1920–21; Leader of the Northern Ireland Senate and Minister of Education 1921–26; First Commissioner of Works 1928–29, 1931; Secretary for Air 1931–35; Lord Privy Seal and Conservative Leader of Lords 1935. Styled Viscount Castlereagh 1884–1915. Succeeded as 7th Marquess of Londonderry 1915.

dramatic contrasts seem artificial and affected. As a record for the family I wouldn't lose a word of it but I am a little nervous about its reception by the public. Still, the tremendous personality of the subject cant fail to excite & retain interest and surely there can never have been any public man whose whole career from start to finish, private as well as public, was so startlingly original and arresting. How exasperating to think that we shall have to wait all that time for the completion.

...

4 December 1932
At Chevening

My dear Ida,
  ...

Annie has certainly been overdoing it, though whether her luncheon parties are most to blame or her Birmingham meetings I am not sure. I suspect the latter because she has been having a tremendous lot and they do take it out of her. It is impossible to deny that they give a great deal of pleasure to the workers, who, as far as I am concerned, have to live on the satisfaction of continually seeing my name in the paper. But I wish they could be spread out a little more so that A. did not have to spend so much time in trying to recover from the effects of her good works.

... An occasional late night does not trouble me and though at the beginning of the week I had some anxiety over Cabinet differences these disappeared, at any rate for the present.

The Note[73] has received such high praise and there have been so many inaccurate accounts of its preparation that you may like to know its true history, for far from its being the composition of the Cabinet, the Cabinet never saw it until it appeared in print. My first idea was to address myself solely to the moratorium so as not to allow the American mind to be prejudiced about that by its unwillingness to think about cancellation. Accordingly I instructed the Treasury to prepare a draft which they did. When I saw it however I found it very thin and unconvincing. It was impossible to state with sufficient conviction that the actual transfer would create disastrous consequences. It was not even certain that Sterling would fall; in fact the Governor declared his opinion that it would do the opposite. Such a meagre case as the Treasury was able to put up was worse than useless and we were driven back rather reluctantly to the idea that the whole case must be fully stated in order to give the background against which alone could be seen the importance of suspending the December payment.

---

[73] After a first Note on 10 November, the full case for suspension of war debt payments was submitted on 1 December 1932.

As a matter of fact it is not possible for me to state publicly the real reason why I so intensely dislike the payment. I have always said that our real task was to educate first French & then American opinion on Repns & War Debts. We managed to succeed with the French: the Americans being more remote require more time. But the longer they go without payment the more easy will it be for them to accept the prospect that there never will be any payment. And, per contra, once they receive an instalment they wont see why they shouldn't have another. You will see something of this in the Sunday Times today. But to return to the note. The new case was written by Sir F. Leith-Ross assisted by a man called Waley,[74] of the Treasury, and sent down to Westbourne on Saturday the 26th. I read it and made a number of alterations in it on my journey to London next day Sunday. By appointment, the Governor came to see me that afternoon and told me that by the intermediary of a third party he had got into communication with Ogden Mills[75] Secretary to the Treasury. Mills was extremely friendly to us; he took the same view of the Debt as we did viz that it was harmful to all the world to pay, including U.S.A. He was anxious to help and had sent us a hint as to which however the utmost secresy [sic] must be maintained. Any leakage would mean that he would have to deny all knowledge but if we chose to put up his proposal as our idea he thought it would go through. The proposal was to divide the procedure as regards principal and interest. Of the $95½ million $30 was repayment of principal and under the Debt Funding agreement we have power to give 90 days notice to suspend that repayment for 2 years. We have not given that notice but the Secretary to the Treasury has power without reference to Congress to waive the notice. Accordingly we should ask for waiver and the Secretary would grant it.

As regards interest, we should divide the $65½ M into three and give bonds for $20M, $20M, & $25½M respectively maturing in one two & three years, to carry interest & be held by the U.S. Government. This proposal would require the assent of Congress.

I asked the Governor two questions. First, could the President get Congress to assent. He thought he could. Second, would the arrangement apply also to France. Certainly not; the Americans were bitterly hostile to France & would give her nothing. I said that seemed to me very serious, for it would involve the default of France and the non ratification of Lausanne.

---

[74] Sigismund David Schloss (1887–1962). Assumed mother's surname Waley in 1914. Entered Treasury 1910; Assistant Secretary, Treasury 1924; Principal Assistant Secretary 1931; Under-Secretary and head of Overseas Finance Division 1939–46; Third Secretary 1946–47; Chairman, Furniture Development Council 1949–57; Chairman, Sadler's Wells Trust 1957–62. Knighted 1943.

[75] Ogden Mills (1884–1937). American lawyer and politician. Republican Member, New York State Senate 1914–17; Member, US House of Representatives 1921–27; Under-Secretary of Treasury 1927; Treasury Secretary 1932–33.

With this information I went to a meeting that evening with Simon Baldwin and the P.M. As you may remember when I wrote to you last I was inclining to the view that we ought not to pay if in the last resort America refused to accept suspension. But almost from that moment I began to veer to the other point of the compass and finally I definitely came to the opinion from which I have not budged since that on this occasion we must pay. (Vide Scrutator in todays Sunday Times). It seemed to me that the consequences of non payment were so serious, that though they might in the end prove inevitable, we ought to avoid them as long as there remained even a remote chance of a happy ending. If we defaulted, whatever name we gave it and whatever justification we found for our own consciences, we should for ever be pointed at by Americans first and then by De Valera & all the small states who have difficulty in meeting their obligations, as the country who sanctioned non payment of debts when it was convenient to the debtor. That would administer a terrific shock to a very large number of the best of our people who would feel that Englands name had been dragged in the mud and would suffer humiliation accordingly. I found that S.B. took this view very strongly and on these very rare occasions when he expresses an opinion of his own he is generally right. As a matter of fact we arrived at no conclusion on this occasion, though we talked it over, but our time was spent in discussing Normans[76] information. I said I was very anxious to accept the proposition provided the French could be got to agree to it, and I proposed that we should at once send Warren Fisher, who could pass without notice, to Paris to tell Herriot exactly the position and ask his views. This was agreed to and Simon & I went up to my room to see Fisher & Vansittart and give them the necessary instructions. Here however difficulties arose. Van said the French would go through the roof at once; Simon suggested various ways of not giving the fact in all its nakedness that the French could not get the same treatment as ourselves, Fisher declared that he was the worst person in the world to carry off a half truth and the situation got so difficult that we adjourned to Van's house for dinner about 10 o'clock and continued to talk there. Finally we concluded that the best plan was to have Tyrrell over at once and he was sent for to arrive on Monday evening.

On Monday morning the P.M. sent for me and said he didnt like the draft note but he hadn't any definite ideas as to alteration except that it should be shorter and cover far less ground. Eventually his notions about this, after I had a shorter draft prepared, faded out.

On Monday afternoon we had a Cabinet at which I definitely announced that I had come to the conclusion that we ought to pay if called on to do so. I said nothing about the Governor's plan, though I declared that I had not given up hope of a postponement. Rather to my surprise three of my colleagues, Cunliffe-

---

[76] Montagu Collet Norman (1871–1950). Governor, Bank of England 1920–44. Created Baron Norman 1944.

Lister, Hailsham and Runciman expressed themselves as against payment. However as they found the majority of the Cabinet with me I judged that they were not going to die in the last ditch.

Tyrrell missed his train on Monday and it was Tuesday morning before he met the P.M. S.B. and myself. By this time the Governor had been interviewed by Fisher & Van who had come to the conclusion that no reliance was to be placed [sic] on his information & that even if it were true we could not possibly accept it in view of the position in which it would place the French. Accordingly we did not tell Tyrrell about this plan, but informed him that the Cabinet was engaged on a new note stating our case afresh that if that produced no effect we should pay in gold and that we should probably say so in our note. Tyrrell said that Herriot wished to pay, but was alone in his Cabinet & perhaps in the Chamber in that view. But Tyrrell thought that if he could say he was acting with us there was just a chance that he might carry through payment. Afterwards he appears to have said to S.B. that Herriot would do *anything* for me & that it would be a good thing if at some time I went over to see him.

Meantime another Cabinet was to meet on Tuesday evening at which the P.M. asked me to give verbally the line of the proposed note. He would then ask the Cabinet to approve the line & leave it to a Comee to polish up.

However that afternoon the Governor turned up again in my room in the H. of C. and brought me a written statement which I took to be the intermediary's view of the position in U.S.A. It repeated the previous proposal and said it was essential that our Ambassador should at once put it forward to Mills before sending any Note. When the actual wording was agreed it should be put into the Note itself. The Governor reiterated his own conviction that this would go through Congress. I said that it wd put France in an impossible position if she were excluded. In such a condition her Chamber would undoubtedly default. That would destroy any chance of an agreed settlement between her & U.S.A. Without such a settlement she could not ratify Lausanne & all our work for the establishment of confidence in Europe would be undone. Moreover if we concocted this plan which we knew was not applicable to her behind her back & then produced it when we knew it would be accepted she would say we had sold her for our own advantage and betrayed the understanding between us that we should consult together. The Governor said if we were going to refuse we ought to let Mills know the ground of our objection. I thought this reasonable & right so I sent at once for Simon who set to work on a suitable despatch to Lindsay.[77]

The Cabinet met at 6 & I considered the time had come to tell them what had been happening. To my consternation I found a strong section who advocated

---

[77] Ronald Charles Lindsay (1877–1945). Entered Diplomatic Service 1898; Assistant Under-Secretary, Foreign Office responsible for Near East 1921–24; Ambassador to Turkey 1925–26 and Berlin 1926–28; Permanent Under-Secretary, Foreign Office 1928–30; Ambassador in Washington 1930–39. Knighted 1925.

that we should accept an offer so advantageous to ourselves and let the French go hang. Cunliffe Lister & Hailsham appeared to be the principals in this view and they got some support in other quarters, but I found Runciman who was at Lausanne was now no longer with them. Things got a bit warm, as I would certainly have resigned rather than accept what I should have considered a betrayal of our Ally and a fatal blow to Lausanne. However the P.M. finally proposed that we should send our note without saying we should pay and at the same time find out whether Mills stuck to his proposal. I said I would agree to this though adding that I wanted Lindsay to urge very strongly that all the European countries should be treated alike as regards moratorium leaving differentiation to the final settlement if the Americans insisted on it. Finally this was agreed to and after I had given my verbal account of the line of the note it was approved & I was left to finish it off.

In the light thrown by the Governor's statement on the attitude of the American Administration I had to do a good deal of alteration. The note at that stage was pretty aggressive and showed no appreciation of any advance towards our position by the U.S. Govt. I finished it about 2 o'clock & went to bed satisfied that it was now pretty good. It was however further modified next day when I read my draft to the P.M. He made several suggestions, mostly good, and I put them into words & sent the note off that night.

Since then Lindsay has seen the State Department but they have introduced an alteration into the proposal as given to the Governor, which makes it quite unacceptable and in the absence of the P.M. Simon & Baldwin I turned it down at once. So at the moment things look pretty bad but I dont yet give up hope.

...

10 December 1932
Buckland, Faringdon, Berks

My dear Hilda,

I cant remember now where exactly I left off in my long account of the note last week but I think I did tell you how the Americans let us down as usual by changing the proposal they had made to us unofficially into a form which was quite unacceptable. That put an end to efforts to find some method of postponement and the only thing that remained was to decide what we should say when we made the payment. It seemed to me that the time had come to be a little more outspoken and accordingly I got a final note drafted which was warmly received by the Cabinet and approved also by the P.M. when I met him next day in Paris. In this I explain that we are not resuming payments under the old agreement but making an advance as it were against the final settlement to be taken into account in the discussions. While the note does not say in so many words that we wont pay any more, which would be repudiation, it warns the Americans pretty plainly that there are limits to our squeezability – and it will I hope carry the process of educating the American public a stage further. Their last note to us is much more friendly in tone than their usual style, but in fact it does not carry us any further and their suggestions about "tangible compensation" appear to contemplate trade concessions which would be quite impossible to give. I can see public opinion over here getting quite disagreeable about the whole business presently.

I dont think the payment we make next week is going to depress the exchange; in fact I think it may even have some effect in the opposite direction when the contents of the note become known on Wednesday. But of course any notion that we were going to continue to make payments would be a very different matter.

My visit to Paris was very brief but I think quite satisfactory. The P.M. was content to leave me to do the talking and Herriot & Germain Martin were very pleased with what I told them. They were very uncertain as to the best course for them to adopt but after hearing what I had to say Herriot seemed convinced that ours was the best course and he said he should try and get his people to do the same. He had to begin with the Select Committees of his two houses and he doesn't seem to have got on too well with them as he has sent an S.O.S. to ask if we cant make a statement of our intentions which he can quote in his statement on Monday afternoon. I am going to see if I can do what he wants by private notice question as although I dislike very much going off at half cock in this way I do think it is very important to keep the French in step with us if possible.

The presentation[78] to me was a great surprise up to the last moment as I had only been told that I was being entertained to dinner. It was very gratifying and very nice things were said by all who spoke. I was very disappointed that Austen could not be there but he wrote a letter which made a great impression and was particularly agreeable to me because he pointed out that Ottawa had only been possible because of what I had done before, in uniting the party on a tariff programme and as a member of the National Government in getting the policy of the Import Duties Act agreed upon. I don't think this is at all realised and perhaps as Austen observes in a letter to me only those who knew the inside history could be aware of it. I suppose you know that what he has been suffering from is paratyphoid. I dont quite know why he persists in calling it lumbago or food poisoning but he seems to think that the less familiar complaint will arouse exaggerated ideas of its seriousness.

I have now nearly finished the Life and on the whole I am very pleased with it. I think rather more space is given to the Gordon affair than was required seeing how little part Father had in it personally. It would seem that Garvin himself feels strongly about it and so had to tell the story again & express his indignation. But apart from this and the earlier part which still seems to me

---

[78] On 5 December 1932 Amery and Hannon organised a dinner of Birmingham's Conservative MPs to present Chamberlain with a large silver salver inscribed with the family crest and the inscription, *Quos pater incepit post bis tria lustra labores Optatum ad finem filius expediit.*

overlaboured I think it is quite excellent and it seems to have been found interesting by the public. Annie met the Garvins at dinner one night and Mrs G. said it had had the best sale of any biography since Morley's Gladstone. I think it brings out well the tremendous power and drive of the subject and the astonishing way in which Father always seemed to dominate whatever Cabinet he was in. It is true he didn't by any means always get his way but he had to be counted with every time. It does strike me that Cabinets were very different in those days. What we call the "team spirit" seems not to have existed. There must have been a dozen occasions during those 5 years when Father either wanted to or did actually offer his resignation and others did so almost as often. And the speeches he permitted himself to make when a Minister of the Crown make one gasp a little even now! It will be difficult to wait patiently for the new volume.

...

I saw Craigavon on Friday in the hope that he would be able to make some suggestion which might be helpful for the Irish trouble. But he had none. "Stick it" was his advice but I fear his mind sees nothing better than to ruin Ireland when she may be glad to remain in the Empire at the cost of the English taxpayer.

17 December 1932
Brocket Hall, Lemsford, Welwyn Garden City

My dear Ida,

Many thanks for your congratulations. I had a greater success than I was aware of at the time, for I did not feel sure that I had got "home". But my P.S. told me next morning that he had been astonished at the number of back benchers who had been to him to express their satisfaction that the British case had been presented with so much dignity & completeness, and Robbins, the Times Lobby correspondent, told Eden[79] who told me that he thought my speech the best I had ever made in Parliament. When I see you I must tell you of my retort to Winston in my second speech which the Times omitted from its report to my great disappointment.

The situation is distinctly puzzling and one must wait for some further elucidation. When Americans praise us & say we shall be rewarded by much better treatment than they give those wicked Frenchmen, I feel all they really mean is that they will *if possible*, treat the French even worse than they treat us. I have no doubt that we shall have a very difficult task when it comes to bargaining,

---

[79] (Robert) Anthony Eden (1897–1977). Conservative MP for Warwick and Leamington 1923–57. Under-Secretary for Foreign Affairs 1931–33; Lord Privy Seal 1933–35; Minister without Portfolio responsible for League of Nations Affairs 1935; Foreign Secretary 1935–38, 1940–45, 1951–55; Dominion Secretary 1939–40; War Secretary 1940; Prime Minister and Conservative leader 1955–57. Knighted 1954. Created Earl of Avon 1961.

but unless the French pay meanwhile I cant see how how [sic] we can be expected to pay any more. On the other hand unless the French pay I cant see how they can ratify Lausanne.

I was very glad that Austen made a plea for reconditioning slums and he certainly made a profound impression on the House. But not necessarily in favour of reconditioning, and it is so difficult to work out a practical scheme and there is so little enthusiasm among the permanent officials at the Ministry of Health that I doubt if there is anyone but myself who could carry it through.

Meanwhile our Minister of Labour has come out in opposition to our Unemployment Relief scheme & has put up a very good case against it. It is only before a Committee at present and I was at first rather disconcerted by his change of mind. But on the whole it is better to get this sort of criticism at the earliest possible moment for it is bound to come some time and the sooner it comes the more time there is for working out the counter arguments. I am glad to say that the M/Health has not changed *his* mind and we are going to have a preliminary engagement on Tuesday.

...

7

1933

'Few Chancellors Have Had a More Difficult Task': The Riddle of War Debts and Unemployment Insurance Reform

4 January 1933
37 Eaton Square, SW1
(From Swinton)

My dear Ida,

...

De Valera has acted rather cleverly in getting in an election before the Opposition have had time to consolidate. I rather fear he may get back.

...

8 January 1933
Highfield Park,
Heckfield, Basingstoke

My dear Hilda,

...

The P.M. informs me (this is very secret) that he has got in touch with Roosevelt[1] who is sending over an emissary to discuss War Debts. The emissary, whose name I dont yet know,[2] will arrive about the 21st & spend a week end at Chequers after which the P.M. asks me to be on hand. Meantime I wrote a long letter to Ramsay giving my ideas as to the way the thing should be tackled & he has replied saying "We are in complete agreement", which is satisfactory. From what I hear Roosevelt has a very long way to travel before he gets to our position, but I think this is the best way of beginning his education. We must try for a moratorium on June 15 to give us time & I should then work for a settlement on the lines of Lausanne. This means (1) a 3 year moratorium (2) a final settlement of all European debts for £150M. to be worked off in bonds to

---

[1] Franklin Delano Roosevelt (1882–1945). Assistant Secretary, US Navy 1913–20; Governor of New York State 1929–33; President of USA 1933–45.

[2] William Christian Bullitt (1891–1967). American diplomat. Entered US State Department as attaché 1917; accompanied American delegation to Paris Peace Conference and negotiated with Lenin 1919; managing editor with US Movie Company in 1920s; Ambassador to Moscow 1933–36 and to Paris 1936–40; Ambassador-at-Large and Assistant Secretary to Navy 1941–44.

be marketed from time to time (3) a cancellation of all bonds not marketed say in 15 years time (4) no conditions concerning disarmament, compensation, or tariffs to be attached. It sounds quite hopeless, but so did Lausanne beforehand.

I am watching Ireland & S. Africa with the greatest interest. Both look a little more hopeful than they did a few days ago.

...

14 January 1933
Westbourne

My dear Ida,

... We had a very pleasant visit to Highfield. ... I looked hopefully about for Crossbills among them for I had been repeatedly told at Elveden that they were common there and though I did not succeed in seeing any I found the cones which they had stripped of their seeds lying on the ground beneath the larger trees. I found similar cones at Highfield but as no one had ever heard of Crossbills there I wonder whether the grey squirrels produce the same results.

One evening Enid showed us the movies she took in Canada ... which included myself in various scenes ... and also one of me signing the Canadian agreement. It is rather weird and not altogether agreeable to see oneself as others see one.

...

Annie is going to stop on here by herself next week to get a little more rest. She does not feel that she has accumulated any reserve to speak of yet, but I hope that being alone will enable her to get a more complete relaxation than is possible when the family is here too.

Meanwhile I reflect with dismay that my holiday is over & that very soon I must begin making speeches again. I could have done with another week very well, but still I have very much enjoyed the break & shall return to work refreshed and re-invigorated. ...

...

29 January 1933
Westbourne

My dear Ida,

...

I enclose a cutting from the Yorkshire Post which may amuse you. It is extraordinary what interest my letter about the Wagtail aroused. Buckmaster[3] wrote that it had given him more pleasure than all the rest of the Times put

---

[3] Stanley Owen Buckmaster (1861–1934). Liberal MP for Cambridge 1906–10 and Keighley 1911–15. Solicitor-General 1913–15; Lord Chancellor 1915–16; member Inter-Allied Commission on Finance and Supplies. Knighted 1913. Created Baron 1915 and Viscount 1933.

together (not surprising perhaps!) Another man spoke of his delight in reading it and declared that it was "like a gleam of warm, bright sunshine coming through the murky gloom of politics". S.B. says that it has firmly established my popularity in the great heart of the nation and then and there (in Cabinet) composed a letter announcing his discovery of a pelican in St James' Park! Gilbert Murray[4] told Austen that this was the sort of thing that completely puzzled Siegfried.[5] He could not understand how grave people could write to grave journals on such trifling incidents. But the fact is that we are an intensely sentimental people, and while *my* interest was prompted by my inborn love of Natural History, the public loves to hear about "dear little birds" and to believe that generally callous statesmen have a "yuman" soft spot about them somewhere.

...

Last night we all three went to the Jewellers dinner which was a great success and had nearly a record attendance. Austen amazed me once more by calmly going down without a note or any attempt at preparation and then making an impromptu speech which was amusing and moving and lofty in tone & phrasing & all so perfectly constructed that it rolled out like an essay and could in fact have been literally transcribed into one. ... Bruce made a most useful speech on Ottawa emphasising that it was not to be measured by the Schedules but by the new spirit it had evoked and he dwelt on the revolutionary charge in the protective policy of Canada & Australia with a conviction which coming from an Australian was well calculated to bring this salient fact home to his audience. I always feel that, when I say it, people may think I am over sanguine, but when Bruce himself declares it they must believe him and I was delighted that his speech was broadcast.

I had some good talk with Austen while he was here. Egged on by him I had an interview with Hilton Young last week and sketched out a possible slum policy to him. He seemed very much attracted by it and, as it were, relieved. For, he said, he was in agreement with all my ideas, many of which had passed through his mind. But he had not been able to put them together and make a picture of them as I had. Since then I have dictated a memorandum on the subject but as owing to repeated summonses by the P.M. I have ... not yet been able to see the typescript & send it on to Hilton. However I repeated my ideas to Austen last night and he is I think delighted with them and if they should be adopted would be well satisfied. ...

While I was about it I thought I would try out my Statury [sic] Relief Commission on my experienced brother and gave him a full account of it. We discussed it in Cabinet for several hours on Wednesday but adjourned without a

---

[4] (George) Gilbert Aimé Murray (1866–1957). Professor of Greek, Glasgow University 1889–99; Regius Professor of Greek, Oxford University 1908–36. Liberal candidate for Oxford University 1918–29; Chairman, Executive Council of League of Nations Union 1923–38; President, United Nations Association 1945–49.

[5] Andre Siegfried (1875–1959). French economist and historian particularly noted for studies of Canada, United States and Latin America. Author of *Post-War Britain: A French Analysis* (1924).

decision. A considerable amount of opposition manifested itself and I am nominally to produce further information but really to see whether I can find any way of mitigating objections. I took the trouble to find out before going to the Cabinet what Betterton would do if the principle was decided against him. I ascertained that he would not resign and so informed the P.M. before we began!

Austen's first observation was that it was very interesting and made him reflect how much closer my mental outlook was to Father's than his own! In reply to my question what he meant by that he said, "Well you are always constructive. You are very bold but your audacity is always founded on a very careful examination of the thickness of the ice on which you are going to venture. In this case the only chance of securing approval of reform is to make it big enough & novel enough to strike the imagination and the very features which frighten some of your colleagues, may well prove to be your salvation".

This is of course entirely my own view. I think I must find some concession but I believe I shall carry the Cabinet all right.

I had rather a success in Leeds where they reported a record attendance & were very gratified by what they felt to be the great importance of my speech. It was true that the Americans now say they are sick of the whole question, but they were not the only people to whom I was speaking and moreover it has had its effect even on them. I noted with pleasure the remark of one paper that Great Britain was hard as a rock and would offer nothing in return for remission. The French are *very* pleased with my remarks which have steadied them on Lausanne and the effect here has been to harden public opinion against payment, which was what I wanted.

One thing I am very pleased about. I got the P.M. to recall Lindsay. This was (though I didn't say so to him) chiefly with a view to making him (Lindsay) the intermediary with Roosevelt and to my great delight the P.M. had the same idea independently. Now I see in today's paper that R. has invited Lindsay to an interview before he goes. That's the best news for a long time and if we can keep the talk in those channels and abstain as long as possible from going to Washington ourselves we may have some chance of progress.

...

4 February 1933
Westbourne

My dear Hilda,

...

I am afraid these American correspondents have played me a dirty trick. They invited me to lunch with them to talk about the Economic Problems & the World Conference. I didn't want to go but consulted the Foreign Office who thought it would be ungracious to refuse. So I went & in my speech said nothing at all about War Debts. After I had finished they asked a number of questions which I answered and these did, some of them, refer to War Debts though mostly they were on other things. The Times, the same evening, read me a summary which they had obtained from some one who was present; and it appeared next day on their front page. At the time I remarked that when thus compressed it sounded to me rather stiffer than what I had actually said but this referred to the manner rather than the matter.

What the correspondents sent to America I have not yet seen though I have asked my people to find out. But judging by the comments that have come back which talk of my refusing to discuss Economic Problems & of my shouting curt challenges across the Atlantic they must have set themselves deliberately to make mischief by distorting my words and positively inventing things I never said at all. It is really wicked when such important issues are at stake and once more one is forced to the conclusion that we have the misfortune to be dealing with a nation of cads.

Last night I made my speech here with a talkie cinema operating on me. I shant do it again. The whole platform was flooded with light so that I could see nothing beyond the first two rows and was half boiled into the bargain. Its really not good enough but the C.O. was so anxious to have it done that I consented to try especially as they said they were not going to have strong lights.

For the first time for I dont know how long Annie & Dorothy & I went to a play this week with the Hilton Youngs. If you havent seen Mother of Pearl I recommend you not to try it. For the most part I was bored. … The whole play revolves round sex and though it is sufficiently farcical to avoid being taken seriously I find that a very little of it goes a long way & became monotonous.

…

12 February 1933
37 Eaton Square, SW1

My dear Ida,
   …

Well, you have no doubt read, and I hope steadfastly disbelieved, the accounts in the papers of our conversations with Lindsay. They are all misleading where they are not untruthful but I can summarise the truth quite shortly.

It soon became apparent that in Lindsay's opinion it was quite impossible to get any satisfactory settlement through Congress at present. This really only confirmed our previous impressions – I had long ago said that a moratorium was the thing to work for. The question then arose, how were we to get this moratorium. Here Lindsay was singularly unhelpful and the P.M. would only repeat that we could not get one unless we sent a Minister. I argued that no President could get Congress to agree to a moratorium on the ground that he had now talked with a British Minister for 2 weeks and as there were only 2 months before the next payment became due it was obvious that the time was insufficient to enable an agreement to be reached! To this neither Lindsay nor the P.M. could find any reply. Simon sat back to see where the P.M. was coming out, Runciman was only concerned to make it clear that he would not be the Minister & S.B. insisted on saying not one single solitary word! So at last I produced a new plan. Lindsay should go back to Roosevelt & begin by showing him that *his* plan was quite impracticable. When this was done which I expected would not be without time & heat, R. would ask what *we* proposed. L. would explain that we wanted Lausanne applied to U.S.A. debt. R. wd reply that this was out of the question as Congress wouldn't look at it. Having established the deadlock & R. being unable to get any further L. would suggest that R. send a message to Congress as follows. That after most friendly and satisfactory (!) talks with John Bull they had come to complete agreement that debts could not be settled before other questions had been discussed (prices, currencies, trade barriers &c). That these were all on the agenda of the World Conference and indeed required the concurrence of other countries to enable effective action to be taken. Therefore we two govts had agreed that the Conference must be pushed on and Debts discussed concurrently but not at the Conference and for this purpose the President must ask for various powers including power to suspend collection of debts during the proceedings of the Conference.

So far I have got agreement after much discussion but the P.M. is at present against the final part of my proposals namely that we should offer our support for the changing of the place of meeting of the World Conference from London to Washington or if that were too hot some other place in U.S.A. I believe this proposal would go a long way to sweeten Congress and Lindsay is very strongly of my opinion that the American Press wd be much easier to control on the other side and that the education of Americans would go on much faster there. Of course I should make it a condition that the P.M. should continue to be Chairman of the Conference. This might make a difficulty though I cant believe it wd be an insuperable one, but I am convinced that it is the doubt that makes the P.M. shy away from the proposal. He has set his heart on the chairmanship, and I think quite rightly as he, if properly backed, would probably have a better chance of making it a success than anyone. But if he could go to U.S. as chairman & not to settle debts, debts could be concurrently discussed and he could exploit his personal popularity there without being saddled with failure, if failure resulted. I dont think he will agree yet, but it may come later.

In the meantime I see no particular objection to sending a Minister over in March, if R. still wants it after hearing Lindsay, provided it is made clear that he goes to discuss the whole situation by way of preliminary not to settle or bargain about debts. But I shouldn't care to go myself, the P.M. certainly wouldn't go, nor S.B. The P.M. has said mysteriously that he has someone in mind but he hasn't said who. I guess Hailsham; and that wouldn't be a bad choice if someone has to go.

Lindsay soon found out how the land lay on the Comee & asked to see me privately. So I saw him alone on Thursday and we had a useful talk. I think he fully understands my mind.

I have made progress this week too with Unempt Insurance Reform. I have made some modifications in the original plan with a view to meeting Cabinet criticisms and after various interviews with malcontents I think I can now feel pretty confident that the general principles will be approved at the next Cabinet on Wednesday. On the whole I have had less trouble there than at one time I expected.

...

I wonder if you saw the correspondence in the Times about S.B.'s use of the phrase "Try Out" condemned by the Public Orator as an Americanism and defended by others as good old English. The joke of it (unknown to them) is that S.B. found himself so completely out of his depth that he asked Rutherford to write his speech for him & "try out" was R's phrase. This S.B. told me himself. But would you not say that to talk of a person being "fired out" was very modern if not American phrasing. Yet I find the following.

"But this shall I ne'er know, but live in doubt
Till my bad angel fire my good one out."
in Shakespeare's Sonnets!
I darent write to the Times again!

18 February 1933
Westbourne

My dear Hilda,
...

You are right in supposing that I have had a strenuous week. I knew anyhow that I had to be the chief speaker at the F.B.I. dinner on Wednesday and at the Conservative Club last night but I hadn't reckoned on speaking for the Govt on the vote of censure [on unemployment], which had been allotted to Runciman. But on Wednesday morning I received an urgent message to go and see the P.M. at 10.30 before the Cabinet and my mind at once jumped to what proved to be the correct conclusion. Runciman had refused on the ground that he didn't see what he could say and the rest all turned to me. ... I must confess that I was a little depressed when after all the work I had put in on it I didn't succeed in carrying the sentiment of the House with me. I did not perceive at the time the coldness which the Times reported but I could see afterwards by the absence of enthusiasm among my friends that it had not gone well.[6]

---

[6] On 16 February 1933 Chamberlain's comprehensive statement of government policy in reply to a Labour censure motion created much despondency by categorically rejecting growing demands for public works and predicting that abnormal unemployment might continue for ten years.

However on further reflection I have recovered my equilibrium. I deliberately said unpleasant things because I thought that it was necessary that people should be told the truth. The House did not respond as I had hoped, but they will presently see that I was right and respect me all the more for saying what others are afraid to say. I repeated it last night to local Conservatives and amplified it and when I sat down they all jumped to their feet and cheered and many said that I had made the finest speech they had ever heard in that room. I shouldn't wonder if I returned to the subject next week at Edinburgh.

I dont think you need worry about my not getting my way over America. Up to the present I have got all I wanted except the holding of the World Conference on the other side and that may yet come. In the way things are now developing, that is if Roosevelt falls in with the plan of sinking War Debts in the World Conference and getting a moratorium for that, I think there is a good deal to be said for a personal visit by the P.M. to Roosevelt. For in that case, it would be publicly stated beforehand that he was not going to settle War Debts or anything else but merely to discuss in a friendly spirit a number of problems of common interest and the result might be considerably to strengthen Roosevelts hand with Congress. I feel pretty confident that the P.M. if he were alone would be very cautious as he is really quite conscious that the examination & decision of specific points is not his forte and though I have told him that I must entirely suspend judgement upon both the personnel and scope of any mission until we get Roosevelt's reaction to Lindsays report of our views, I am quite disposed to think that he may favour a visit from the P.M. and in that case I might be prepared to support it. I must say that considering his own inclinations the P.M. has behaved very well and very loyally all through and I can see that he continues to place increasing reliance on my loyalty to him as well as on the soundness of my judgement.

I am glad to say that after a somewhat difficult passage I have got my Statutory Commission into port and the Cabinet Comee has now been directed to work out the details. We have improved the original plan from the political point of view to meet criticism and the Minister of Labour is not any longer opposing the principle. I haven't yet quite made up my mind whether it is possible and desirable to keep the tramps to the L.A.'s or whether they should go with the Commission. I had Hubbard to lunch here today and as he has a certain flair in these things I described the idea to him and was glad to find it made a favourable impression.

I guess from your letter that you did not see a letter in the Times on "American Prepositions" signed C.E. or that if you did you did not guess that C.E. meant Chancellor of the Exchequer! When I found a passage in Henry V. in which the King speaks of "trying it out" I couldn't resist sending it to the Times along with the lines about "firing out" the good angel, but I thought it prudent to be anonymous this time.

...

25 February 1933
Westbourne

My dear Ida,

...

I am glad to say that my lumbago has pretty well gone. I gave it rather a severe test this week. Eight hours in the train then a big public meeting in Edinburgh. After that a visit to the Unionist Club and another speech followed by a night in the train. Cabinet all morning and Committee and Cabinet from 3 till a quarter to nine. Dinner at the Home Secretarys to discuss certain troublesome affairs with Trenchard about the police and then boxes till 1 a.m. After all that I seemed to be quite fresh when my doctor examined me on Thursday morning so I think I may feel that I haven't much to complain of in the way of health.

The Times is really intolerable. I see it returns again to its pontifical scolding. The Government hasn't economised to speak of and it obstinately refuses to spend the nations money. Anyway taxation must be reduced and the Chancellor shouldn't be afraid to "risk" a deficit. This last phrase is a peculiarly bad example of its low cunning for the ordinary person would read it to mean That I ought to Budget *for* a deficit whereas what it actually says is that I ought to estimate for a balanced Budget optimistically and risk the estimate being out by a million or two. In this way it is safe to be able to say that whatever I do or dont do is wrong. I wonder whether it ever reflects upon the effect of 6d or 1/- off the Income Tax on the mind of the Middle Western Farmer!

I have had a weary time with the Cabinet over the question of what we are to do about arms for China & Japan. My view is that we cant make any distinction for two reasons, one that if we sent arms to China, Japan will seize them on the way, and, two, that since the quarrel with Japan is the League's quarrel not Great Britain's, any differentiation should be by the League & not by G.B. But to send arms to both on the ground that if any profit is made we ought to have our share of it seems to me the negation of all we have been saying in the Peace Pact & the Disarmament Conference. No arms can be exported from this country without a Govt license and we cannot therefore fold our arms like those smug Americans & say we cannot help it if our people *will* sell ammunition & machine guns.

The trouble with the Cabinet is that no one has any fixed ideas. They agree with me and then go back on it & then agree again and then go back again. Only Jimmy Thomas remains faithful. As for S.B. he says nothing except that this is a most difficult question and he sees no way out. We spent hours over this business last week and after it was decided Simon came back to tell me that he thought our decision was wrong.

Lindsay has reported most gloomily on his conversation with R[oosevelt]. But for my part I see no reason as yet for any special gloom. R. agrees that no statement is possible now and apparently he does not object to a moratorium but he sees great difficulty in getting it. So do we all, and so we always have. In the meantime he thinks he was in too much of a hurry and the question of R.M. going over is at present in abeyance. The situation is bad but, as it seems to me, no worse than it was. The Monarch has sent word that he wants to see me but I have no idea whether it is about America or beer duty.

You are right in saying that I have been making a preposterous number of speeches and I haven't got to the end yet. ...

...

4 March 1933
37 Eaton Square, SW1

My dear Hilda,

I must confess to feeling a bit tired today but it is not due to overwork so much as to worry over all the troubles that have suddenly sprung upon us. To have the conflict in the Far East, Germany in hourly danger of an explosion, the Disarmament Conference at the brink of dissolution and the banking crisis in America one on top of another gives even me a pain in the stomach though I generally manage to preserve my equanimity.

If only we could have got a settlement with America immediately after Lausanne I believe half these troubles would never have materialised but that wretched constitution made it impossible to move for months and in the meantime the whole situation has crumbled. The best opinion seems now convinced that the Germans are only looking for an opportunity to declare that the Disarmament Conference has failed in order to re-arm and defy the world. You can imagine that the French are terrified and Poland and the Little Entente have all their bristles up while Italy takes every opportunity of supporting the Germans in the hope of presently annexing some of Yugo-Slavia. We are sending the P.M. out to Geneva to make a last effort to pull something out of the blaze but it is a forlorn hope and we hardly expect anything to come of it.

I got my way about the Embargo – as S.B. said, by knowing my own mind and sticking to it, but I must say I did not expect our decision to be so badly received abroad. I can understand the Chinese being vexed, but that the Japs should be resentful seems to me incomprehensible. The other nations are simply annoyed because they have a bad conscience and resent what they call our assumption of virtue. But of course they make no allowance for the fact that we are in the unique position that no export of arms can take place without a license from the Govt and our Govt therefore must assume a direct responsibility either for export or non-export whereas they can sit back and say they have no control. But our action was not taken to please them but to satisfy our own people and it was received with general approval in the House. Events seem to be confirming my view that the whole thing would be over in a very short time and that no export of arms by us or anybody else would be of the slightest use to China, for I see tonight that the Japs have already swept through Jehol right round to the Great Wall and if they stop there our troubles may soon be over in that quarter.

As for U.S.A. they are going from bad to worse. They are practically off gold now and though they say they will be on it again next week I hae ma doots. We are the one rock which stands fast and if the Times had its way we should soon be adrift too. I must say I thought its leader after the debate on Wednesday was the limit of evasion suggestis falsi and suppressis veri. They never dare face up to the logical consequences of their own implications but they are furious with me for pointing them out. I am told that these leaders are written by Colin Coote[7] and if so that explains much. He entered the House in 1918 and was in till 1922 I think. I remember him as a sort of high brow Coalition Liberal with theories about everything but no practical experience of anything.

I had a very good meeting at Derby, hall packed and people standing up all round and I returned again to the ten years and elaborated it further. It was gratifying to hear last night from the London correspondent of the Post that my repetition of my point had created a great impression. He said he heard from various sources including opposition camps that the critics were coming round and recognising that they had misunderstood my point which was after all a real one and one which had to be met. This confirms my instinctive feeling that the best reply to criticism was to go on repeating the offence and so force people to think about it. Meanwhile I am working away at the idea of spreading the work. The P.M. is greatly interested and warmly approves my efforts and though I cant say that I see much daylight at present I have succeeded in stirring up the Ministry of Labour to a certain activity.

I had a good talk with the P.M. early in the week about this and slum policy. I didn't go into details about the latter – details are not his strong point – but I said enough to convince him that it was possible to construct a plan that would convince people that we knew what we were after & he was immensely pleased and declared that we had had a most helpful talk. I wish I felt more confidence that Hilton Young could "get it across". He seems to appreciate my suggestions but when it comes to passing them on to the public they dont appear to materialise.
…

It was rather hard luck having that Press Gallery dinner on Friday but I didnt see how I could refuse. One of the men there told me that when L.G. came his hands fairly trembled and he admitted an altogether unusual nervousness. I dont quite know why that should be, but I also particularly dislike addressing the Press. Perhaps one feels that they are specially critical. Anyway on this occasion I managed, rather to Annie's surprise, to grind out quite a lot of impromptus and

---

[7] Colin Reith Coote (1893–1979). Coalition Liberal MP for Isle of Ely 1918–22. On the staff of *The Times* 1923–42; joined *Daily Telegraph* 1942: Deputy Editor 1945–50 and Managing Editor 1950–64. Knighted 1962.

though my epigrams were not reported the Pressmen quite enjoyed my chaff ... One man afterwards said there were two Americans at his table who were "tickled to death" with my observations about their country, but I have a feeling that if they had been transmitted across the Atlantic Uncle Sam would have been very angry again!

...

18 March 1933
Westbourne

My dear Hilda,

Thank you and Ida very much for your birthday wishes. I dont know how many more I may have before me but I do hope some of them may be left after I have put off the burden of public affairs. I saw in some paper a statement that Austen had hinted in a recent speech that he might not stand again. ... I suppose it is possible but he has not told me of any such intention.

...

The presentation took place this morning and I haven't got over it yet. When I got up to speak I could hardly get my words out and after the first sentence I had to stop. My mind became a blank and I wondered whether I should ever be able to go on again. There was a much larger audience than anyone had expected and they cheered sympathetically so after a time I collected myself and said what I wanted to say. Its the first time I have really broken down and I felt very much ashamed of my loss of control, but the occasion was too much for me. I hope the Press doesn't report it. Annie received not only the pendant but a brooch as well, both lovely ornaments and she made a charming speech as usual. After the ceremony we were respectively entertained by the Hannons at large luncheon parties, hers at the Queens and mine at the Conservative Club. We had many courses and champagne but I drank water as I didn't want to finish up with a headache.

I had an all day talk with Bonnet[8] yesterday and I am glad to say that we found ourselves d'accord all through. He is a typical Frenchman and has the logical precise mind that I find most congenial. He knew exactly what he wanted to ask and never left any topic till he had got to the bottom of it. After he had finished I had nearly an hour with Keynes. I did not expect or attempt to convert him but did succeed in elucidating his ideas which were even worse than I had supposed. He does definitely want to unbalance the Budget and the trouble is

---

[8] Georges Bonnet (1889–1973). French politician. Socialist-Radical Deputy for Dordogne from 1924. Minister for the Budget 1925, for Pensions 1926, for Commerce 1930; President of Stresa Conference 1932; Minister of Finance 1933 and 1937, of Commerce 1935; Ambassador to Washington 1937; Foreign Minister 1938–39; Minister of Justice 1939–40; Member, National Council 1941 and Council of State 1946. Honorary Knighthood 1938.

that he is so plausible & confident that people like the ordinary back bencher who have not much knowledge are very likely to be attracted especially when he is backed so strenuously by the Times.[9] I foresee plenty of trouble for me over my second Budget.

Ramsay's effort at Geneva[10] has gone off much better than I expected and I hope his visit to Mussolini[11] will be equally fortunate. Roosevelt now wants him to go to U.S.A. to discuss disarmament and when Lindsay observed that it would be impossible to prevent people assuming that he would discuss debts & economic questions too Roosevelt assented & observed that he thought they might settle them both at the same time. What a terrible gulf there is between Europe and America.

With storms blowing up over India, the uncertainty as to what Hitler and Goring[12] [sic] will do next and the Russian outrage the situation is more threatening than I have known it for a long time. The Minister of Labour is making more trouble over the Insurance scheme and the Ministry of Health is getting disheartened. In short life is one damed [sic] thing after another.

...

25 March 1933
Westbourne

My dear Ida,

...

I was vexed when S.B. sent for me on Monday to ask me to take the debate on Wednesday but on reflection I did not really see who else could do it, so I assented. He was a good deal fussed at the alleged unrest among our people who were said to have been very much interested and attracted by the Times and Keynes together. But as a matter of fact when Keynes came out into the open he

---

[9] In four articles in *The Times* between 13 and 16 March 1933 Keynes made a sensational impact by employing the 'multiplier' concept to argue that depressed business expectation required the Chancellor to pump in additional purchasing power, not only by loan-financed public works but also by remitting taxation without reducing current expenditure. This appeal for 'deficit finance' was part of a plan for world reflation. These proposals were expanded and reprinted as *The Means to Prosperity* later in the month.

[10] On 16 March 1933 MacDonald presented specific proposals and figures for military and air disarmament to the Disarmament Conference at Geneva.

[11] Benito Mussolini (1883–1945). Founder of Italian Fascist Party 1919; President, Council of Ministers 1922–26; Prime Minister 1926–43; Foreign Minister 1924–29, 1932–36. Head of German puppet Social Republic in Northern Italy 1943–45. Captured and shot April 1945.

[12] Hermann Goering (1893–1946). Follower of Hitler from 1923. Air adviser to Denmark and Sweden 1924–28; elected to Reichstag 1928 and its President 1932–33; Prime Minister of Prussia 1933; C-in-C German Air Force 1933–45; Commissioner of Four-Year Plan 1936; President, General Council for War Economy 1940. Committed suicide before the Nuremberg Court's death sentence was carried out, October 1946.

shocked the Committee on Monday and from that moment his stock began to fall. Macmillan[13] made rather a halting case on his lines and was demolished by a very clever young man named Horobin[14] whom I have noted before as an exceptionally good & sometimes brilliant speaker. My own speech seems this time to have pleased our people and as Hilton did extremely well in winding up the Govt had rather a good day. The Times is now in full retreat.

We had another good day on Thursday. The P.M. was certainly extremely woolly, as you say, but Winston although he made rather spiteful fun of him overdid his case and never got the House with him at all. But the speech of the day was Eden's. I didn't wait to hear it as I had to prepare one myself but all accounts agree in giving it high praise. That young man is coming along rapidly; not only can he make a good speech but he has a good head and what advice he gives is listened to by the Cabinet.

...

I have been counting up & find that I have made 18 speeches since the beginning of the year. I have no more public ones now before the Budget though I have an informal dinner next Wednesday with a "group" in the House at which I shall have to make a few observations. But I am going to try hard to cut down now & so is Annie ... It is very difficult to refuse when they will ask you so long beforehand.

We have heard nothing from America save what has appeared in the Press. I fancy that Congress has been kicking and the White House has been obliged to issue semi-official denials.

Winston is to make the speech of his life next week on India. He will introduce a number of imaginary dialogues which he has already rehearsed several times to his friends. He *is* a curious creature.

...

1 April 1933
Westbourne

My dear Hilda,

For once I have had a week without a speech, but all the same I was glad to get down here last night for a rest, for it has been rather hard work the last few

---

[13] (Maurice) Harold Macmillan (1894–1986). Conservative MP for Stockton-on-Tees 1924–29, 1931–45 and Bromley 1945–64. Parliamentary Secretary, Ministry of Supply 1940–42; Under-Secretary, Colonies 1942; Minister Resident, North-West Africa 1942–45; Air Secretary 1945; Minister of Housing and Local Government 1951–54; Defence Minister 1954–55; Foreign Secretary 1955; Chancellor of Exchequer 1955–57; Prime Minister 1957–63. Created Earl of Stockton 1984.

[14] Iain Macdonald Horobin (1899–1976). National Conservative MP for Southwark Central 1931–35 and Conservative MP for Oldham East 1957–59. Parliamentary Secretary, Ministry of Power 1958–59. Knighted 1955. Gazetted as Life Peer 1962 but withdrew acceptance.

days. I wonder if there has been so much barracking of the Chancellor before the Budget in any year since the war. Or is it only that as it comes on me I notice it more. But the Times has an article almost every day demanding reduction of taxation and the Mail & Express are adding their shriller notes now. I receive deputations from M.P.'s who urge "imaginative finance", from Brewers & publicans & hopgrowers, from distillers and theatre managers & actors & cinema proprietors and railway and motor lorry users. And every one of them represents that his particular interest is in a moribund condition entirely owing to taxation. I foresee that I shall soon be the most unpopular man in the country while at the same time I receive rather grudging & very belated praise for a "sound" Budget last year and for the Conversion which it made possible. I should think few Chancellors have had a more difficult task than I and I add (between ourselves) my conviction that few men in my position would resist the temptation to bid for popularity.

We had a very good India debate and a triumphant majority at the end. I cant help laughing at Ll.G.'s cunning. No doubt he egged Winston on while he lay doggo himself and now he must be chuckling over Winston's discomfiture. I should be sorry for Winston had he not pursued his campaign so recklessly regardless of the consequences to the country. I have no doubt he has persuaded himself that he is the saviour of our Indian Empire but he has never taken the trouble really to go into the case thoroughly and as I know from past experience he can work himself up into a passion of conviction on anything and on any side of it. On this occasion I had a committee which prevented my hearing him after the first ten minutes but I thought he made a bad start and when Wardlaw Milne[15] interrupted him he seems to have completely lost his control and his nerve. Perhaps he has been cooking this speech too long, but I fancy the explanation is to be found in the incredible quantity of alcohol he is in the habit of taking. I have never heard of his being seen the worse for liquor but he takes enough habitually to knock over less seasoned topers and on this occasion I am told he went to the Smoke room three times before his speech to have a whisky & soda. That must tell on his nerves and his liver and I am afraid he is storing up increasing trouble for himself hereafter.

The American President is renewing his appeal to Ramsay to go over & discuss things with him and I have been urging him to accept the invitation but to try and extract a preliminary promise from Roosevelt that he will recommend a moratorium to Congress. The P.M. of course wants to go and I fancy things

---

[15] John Sydney Wardlaw-Milne (1879–1967). Business career in India. Member, Bombay Municipal Corporation; additional member, Bombay Legislative Council and Viceroy's Council 1915. Conservative MP for Kidderminster 1922–45. Member, Imperial Economic Committee 1927–29 and Joint Committee on Indian Reform 1934–35; Chairman, Select Committee on National Expenditure 1939–45. Chairman, Conservative India Committee 1930–35 and Foreign Affairs Committee 1939–45. Knighted 1932.

will turn out as I am suggesting. As you know I have been aiming at this for a long time.

Unemployment Insurance has been bowling along pretty well lately and I hope to get it through Cabinet on Wednesday and to make an announcement before Easter. The Min. of Labour still kicks but more feebly.

What a business in Russia.[16] It is terribly difficult to hit them without hurting ourselves a great deal more. If they are driven too hard they will probably repudiate all their debts & unfortunately they owe us a great deal. I fear our ambassador has not been a wise guide, but his return here will keep the Russians guessing and no doubt they are very uneasy about their future. The Express is publishing some interesting articles by a man who has lately been there & speaks Russian. If he is to be trusted they look like coming an almighty cropper before long.

...

9 April 1933
37 Eaton Square, SW1

My dear Ida,

...

... I have suddenly become aware that with the constant distractions from which I cannot escape even for a day I have but little leisure to make that Budget speech to which so many people are anxiously looking forward. I dont want either to work at it in Scotland or to curtail my brief holiday to work at it here and so I must try & get it pretty well completed before I go away. But it is hard & tedious work & besides it makes me feel uncomfortable inside ...

I spent most of yesterday & this morning on it & this afternoon we are going to Kew to try & freshen up for this evening. Annie & I went yesterday morning to look at an exhibition of David Muirhead's water colours. There were many delightful drawings among them and though nowadays we cant afford luxuries of that kind Annie allowed me to give her one little bit as a birthday present. It is a perfect little gem – a sea beach with an old Welsh castle on a headland, a clear and delicate bit of colouring which will stand looking at always.

...

The Minister of Health got out his circular [on slums] before I had time to suggest alterations in it. He has made his timetable too short & will presently be reproached with having failed to carry out his promises. But he means well. I think he is waiting for the report of his Comee before saying more about reconditioning.

---

[16] After their arrest on 11 March 1933, six British Metro-Vickers engineers were tried in one of the first Stalinist show trials for organising a sabotage ring with twelve Russians. Despite heavy British diplomatic pressure, two received jail sentences.

We had 3 Cabinets last week in addition to several Cabinet Committees. Unempt Insurance Coops & Russia are all difficult. The former is coming along all right though it is such a big thing that it takes time. Co-ops are a terrible tangle and I dont see my way through. Russia has gone well in the House but it remains to be seen what the Soviet Govt will do. I have a feeling that they are riding for a fall. All our information points to their being near a smash and it may be that they are looking for an excuse to default on their debts. If so that means more trouble for me.

Roosevelt is going ahead well and although he has hitherto maintained silence on debts I have hopes that in the atmosphere of the P.M.'s visit he will be able to get power to grant a moratorium.

...

16 April 1933
Cairnton, Glassel, Aberdeenshire

My dear Hilda,

There! Now I am certain! I thought I heard a curlew this morning while I was dressing but just now the delicious sound was unmistakeable [sic]. You say you have not seen a swallow yet. I saw two yesterday morning – the first that have been seen here but I have heard neither chiffchaff nor willow wren. But a thrush sings divinely on a tree just outside my window every morning.

It is a joy to be here so much later than usual and to see the birches and larches just developing their foliage. Most things are much later than in London but when I am usually here there is no sign of green leaf at all – only catkins. Last year was a particularly cruel Easter with bitter winds & snow showers and the fish were very dour too so that I noted in my diary that I came away "very cold and very cross". Somehow I felt that I had been cheated out of a proper holiday and what with gout & conferences I had very little fishing last year.

This year I hope it will be different. I had to work desperately hard at my Budget speech last week for Cabinets and Cabinet Committees took up all my days and the work had to be done late at night or not at all. Even then there was generally an hour's work on other subjects before I could get to the speech and it required very great efforts of will after all that to put one's mind away and get to sleep. In spite of it though and in spite of the night in the train I arrived pretty fresh and the only sign of overwork has been the early morning headaches with which I have waked. Fortunately they go as soon as I get up and anyway this morning's was not as bad as yesterday's.

I am not working too hard so far … That means I dont actually fish for more than 7½ hours in the day, but if the weather is suitable and I get very strong I might increase it a bit next week.

...

Austen has made the Germans very cross[17] – as was indeed to be expected, but he is the one man whose name is known abroad who can say those things. And they certainly wanted saying, for the Germans choose to shut their eyes to what other people are thinking in their new spirit of complacency and confidence. I must say that so far as Hitler is concerned he has really been the best of the bunch since he has been in office. But whether he can hold Goring [sic] remains to be seen.

I understand that you are both coming up for the Budget speech. I warn you that it is going to be very long and *very* dull. On the strong advice of my experienced Private Secretary I have cut out or refrained from inserting all levities & frivolities. He says he has never known a joke that was not the subject of criticism and the most successful speech he remembers was Horne's in 1922 when he accepted word for word a speech written for him by Niemeyer.[18]

But, as to the substance; well I have done some hard thinking and I feel much better about it than I did. In fact omitting Mr Keynes & the Times I think the public will not be too ill pleased with it.

23 April 1933
Westbourne

My dear Ida,

I dont seem able to get free from my work for very long together and on Friday I had a telegram asking me to return at once [from Cairnton]. ...

I was very unlucky in striking such a bad patch in Scotland. The whole week we had a north east wind and it was bitterly cold. ... The salmon simply sulked and in the last 3 days I only got one. All the same I didn't really do so badly as I landed 9 as well as 4 kelts. My fishing has improved so much that with any luck I generally manage to get in touch with something and if only we had had the sort of weather one might usually expect at the end of April I should have made a really good bag. ...

Although very disappointed at losing a day I was glad I came back as I found three problems of major importance to be settled and it would have been too late to deal with them if I had waited till Monday. I spent most of Saturday at the office and when not there I was able to put in a lot of work in correcting my

---

[17] On 13 April 1933 Austen Chamberlain launched his first uncompromising attack in the Commons on the 'new spirit of German nationalism', warning that it was not a country to which 'we can afford to make concessions'.

[18] Otto Ernst Niemeyer (1883–1971). Entered Treasury 1906; Assistant Secretary, Treasury 1919–22; Controller of Finance 1922–27; Member, Financial Committee, League of Nations 1922–37; Director (later Chairman 1937 and Vice-Chairman 1964), Bank of International Settlements 1931–65; advisor, Bank of England 1927–38 and Executive Director, Bank of England 1938–52. Knighted 1924.

speech and bringing it into better form. I am glad to note that my secrets have been well kept.

The press are fearfully busy and kept Arthur Wood constantly at the telephone to his great joy. Now the photographers keep watch outside the house and today one actually pursued Dorothy & me to the Zoo and followed us round till I went up to him and ordered him off. It is a curious idea that just because the Budget is due in a few days the public should be supposed to want to see the Chancellor looking at the gorillas!

...

29 April 1933
Westbourne

My dear Hilda,

...

The Debate on the Budget was the flattest thing ever known. There was no attack on it really from any side. The unbalancers were so riddled by my opening statement that they never put up a case and my information is that the Socialists were completely flummoxed and unable to find any vulnerable spot. I ought therefore to be well satisfied but I confess I thought my ingenuity deserved a little more commendation than it has received. I did indeed see that young Hall Caine[19] described the Budget as a "work of imagination with a touch of genius", but for the most part it is voted dull and "orthodox". Anyway if it was a poor thing, it was mine own. I settled that I must reduce the beer duty long ago, but the reversion to the half and half Income Tax[20] was a brain wave almost at the last minute and the application of the Depreciation Fund to it was a stroke on which I rather prided myself.

Well, it has had the effect of silencing the grumblers for a bit longer but there will be no praise for the Chancellor till one of my successors is fortunate enough to come in on the upward turn of trade. For myself I must be content to do my duty as I see it and trust to recognition in the future.

But it is a depressing business to be in politics at present and I get very weary of it sometimes, seeing nothing ahead to look forward to, but only long struggles against a gradually more & more disgruntled public opinion. I wonder whether it will seem worth while to go on after the next Election. I cannot tell yet but I have not got Fathers joy in battle and intense conviction that whatever he was pursuing was vitally important. After all most of what I have worked for has

---

[19] Gordon Ralph Hall Caine (1884–1962). Conservative MP for East Dorset 1922–29 and 1931–45.

[20] The reversion to the old system of half-yearly payment of Income Tax instead of three-quarters in January and the balance in July cost the Treasury £12 million but was nearly covered by the Depreciation Fund attached to the 5 per cent War Loan which was no longer required.

been done and now the chief task is to keep the ship steady on the course till she can make port again. Sometimes I thank God that I am where I am and not Winston. Sometimes I think it wouldn't be Winston anyhow and perhaps someone else would be a better pilot than I.

I too am reading the 2nd vol [of the *Life of Joseph Chamberlain*] and have got about as far as you. I find it rather painful reading. What a frightful succession of tragedies it is. Everything blown to pieces over and over again and such long years when the talents were wasted. And never given the real opportunity which comes to so many lesser men. I think the second volume better than the first. Nothing will convince such bitter partisans as Gardiner[21] but if a younger generation ever reads such a colossal work I think it will see more clearly than prejudiced contemporaries. I particularly admire the way Gladstone is treated. There is no direct word of condemnation but the wickedness of the old man his cunning and treachery and his determination to go his own way while he has time are plain to see. I feel my old resentment burn up again as I read. I wonder how Garvin will deal with Ll.G. when he comes to him. S.B. by the way tells me that in his forthcoming book Ll.G. takes it out of H. Samuel and that Keynes having published or re-published some derogatory remarks about him Ll.G. got the M.S. back from the publisher & inserted a last minute dose of pure vitriol! How like Ll.G.

...

I have got a City dinner next week in addition to H. of C. work and I suppose there will be much discussion over Washington. I believe Roosevelt has made up his mind to give us the moratorium but he is not thinking of devaluing the dollar and if he persists it is difficult to see how the World Conference is going to do much good.

I hear the German delegate at Geneva has become most accommodating[.] I suspect Austen's speech has shaken up the German Govt more than they care to confess.

...

7 May 1933
37 Eaton Square, SW1

My dear Ida,

I had no time to reply to your letter while I was at Broadlands as I spent all my spare hours on the river. Nature and man between them were very unkind. The weather was unpropitious with sheets of rain ... and the river was very dirty ... Annie spent most of her time in bed which was just as well as Lady M.T. [Mount Temple] drives her to fury.

---

[21] Alfred George Gardiner (1865–1946). Author and journalist. Editor, *Daily News* 1902–19. President, Institute of Journalists 1915–16.

It is very disappointing & perplexing that she seems more tired than ever physically & mentally. ...

I was not tired by my exertions but one sometimes gets "fed up" when things dont go well and in these times things dont. The situation in Germany is very alarming[22] & in spite of the P.M.'s optimism the Americans do not encourage one to hope that they are going to be helpful.

My Budget resolutions went through without a division; no one can recall a precedent for it and I should think it will drive Punch to distraction. The Equalisation Resolution did the same. And now the Cabinet have agreed to tax the Coops but keep this very secret as I dont want it to get out yet. I must say our Jim has behaved very well and loyally over it & carried the P.M. along with him.

I think the German agreement was not a good one and I fear Runciman doesn't take enough trouble. The Jewellers Association have passed a resolution expressing their "deep regret and astonishment" that as a Birmingham member I did not support Austen.[23] How is one to make such people understand the Cabinet system!
...

14 May 1933
37 Eaton Square, SW1

My dear Hilda,
...
The accounts of the American situation about War Debts published in the papers are most alarming. Luckily Lindsay's reports are not quite so gloomy but he has nothing definite to go upon.

I have a horrible time in front of me with this awful World Conference coming on in June. The P.M. thinks it wont be over by Christmas! And it is difficult to see how anything valuable can come out of it.

It is after midnight so you must forgive my brevity.

26 May 1933
Treasury Chambers, Whitehall

My dear Hilda,
...
I have been "going it" so hard the last two weeks that I marvel at myself to be so well and unstrained. But I think my power of throwing off worries in what

---

[22] On 2 May 1933 the buildings of the Socialist Trade Unions were occupied and all German union leaders were arrested.

[23] The Birmingham Jewellers' & Silversmiths' Association opposed the Anglo-German Trade Agreement and on 1 May 1933 Austen Chamberlain made a very effective attack on it, forcing a division and leading fifty-four other Conservative MPs into voting against the government.

little leisure I get and of sleeping soundly at night save me from getting into the sort of condition that reduces Ramsay at times to a nervous wreck. I was quite sorry for him on the day of the Co-op debate. Sitting next him on the bench I could feel him trembling all over and when he got up his face was quite ghastly.

...

I hadn't time to prepare properly for Ashridge[24] but I had some headings & discoursed for 50 minutes on Finance War Debts Economic Conference & such like, after which questions were called for. ... I must say I was very much impressed with the way in which everybody seemed to be enjoying themselves. I am sure this is largely due to Hoskins'[25] personality, but I feel a lot happier about Ashridge after my visit than I did before.

...

The Times now carries its vendetta so far that it is not content with continually writing nagging carping leaders. It actually gives a false impression of the debates and no one reading it would guess that I had had two very considerable successes in the House this week.

The Coops had endeavoured to rouse a tremendous storm of indignation and expectation over the debate on Monday.[26] I was besieged with Press photographers anxious to take a snapshot over "setting out for the House" etc. When I rose there was a great roar of cheers from our side and an answering roll of counter cheers from the opposition. I set myself to lower the temperature and to give such a moderate and reasonable account as would make the fuss appear ridiculous. In this I succeeded so well that half an hour after I sat down someone remarked to me "This debate is dead". And so it was; nor have all Master Alexander's efforts succeeded in bringing it to life again since.

The other success was over oil. There really was a tremendous drive against the duty and a great number of amendments were put down, nearly all by our party. But I have had a good deal of experience now in piloting difficult measures through the House and my plans worked admirably. I got the Chairman of Committees to accept a plan by which amendments were grouped together according to their general character and a general discussion taken on each group, the individual amendments being divided on at the end if challenged but without further discussion. This plan was acceptable to the House first because they saw it would save time by avoiding repetition, and secondly because it enabled everyone to be sure that his particular view would be put. But from my

---

[24] Bonar Law Memorial College, Ashridge near Berkhampstead. Operated from 1930 as the Conservative Party College until requisitioned during the war.

[25] Major-General (Arthur) Reginald Hoskins (1871–1942). Entered Army 1891; C-in-C, East Africa 1917; retired 1923. Principal, Philip Stott College 1928 and Bonar Law College, Ashridge 1929–38. Knighted 1919.

[26] Co-operative Societies had previously been exempt from taxation on trading profits and investment income. In late January 1933 the Raeburn Committee recommended they should be taxed and Chamberlain persuaded the Cabinet to do so despite MacDonald's strong opposition.

point of view the great advantage I foresaw was that everybody who was not anxious to speak on the group under discussion would go into the Smoke room until they heard the division bell ring when they would return, having heard nothing of the debate, and vote as they were directed by the Whips. Everything went according to plan[.] Speaker after speaker got up and spoke against the duty but I remained calm and when the whips enquired if I was worried I said Not a bit. I sat patiently on the bench till nearly 9 o'clock when I got up. I began with platitudes & jokes till the House filled up and then I delivered a carefully balanced argument on the lines that Bonar Law used to follow so effectively, giving the impression that everything has been weighed up and the final judgement arrived at by an irrestible [sic] process of logic. The audience were convinced except the speakers & we only had 57 all told in the lobby against us.

My concession – on coastwise shipping – I had contrived to reserve till yesterday. Again I kept Belisha[27] out of the way (he is not like my Kingsley) and would not speak till I had heard the whole case against me, when I got up and explained that I had been convinced by the powerful arguments adduced during the afternoon. When it came to the concession I pretended for some time that I was only going to give them half the duty and in the end I flatter myself that I got every ounce out of the concession that was to be had. Indeed there was such general jubilation that those who had been sent empty away appeared to have for the time forgotten their grievances. I should indeed have finished the Bill in Committee last night if Austen had not mischievously intervened on the German agreement and thrown us all out of our programme.

...

I think Geneva is more hopeful and we shall probably escape a complete & open breakdown. But the real question remains unanswered at present; Is there any change of heart in Germany? As for Roosevelt we can get nothing more out of him on Debts but Lindsay still hopes that he is intending to spring a surprise on Congress at the last moment. Provided he doesn't spring the surprise on us!

...

3 June 1933
The Manor House, Great Durnford, Salisbury

My dear Ida,

What a comfort to be in this peaceful place and in such gorgeous weather too. A. & I got here last night about 7.30 and I went out after dinner to cast fly at the earliest possible moment. ...

---

[27] (Isaac) Leslie Hore-Belisha (1893–1957). MP for Devonport as a Liberal 1923–31, Liberal National 1931–42 and National Independent 1942–45. Parliamentary Secretary, Board of Trade 1931–32; Financial Secretary, Treasury 1932–34; Minister of Transport 1934–37; War Minister 1937–40; Minister of National Insurance 1945. Created Baron Hore-Belisha 1954.

Now that I have got away I do begin to feel a little tired but the week has not been as heavy as I anticipated. I thought we should have at least one if not two very late nights but I was never kept at the House after 11.30. This was partly due to a very docile opposition which much dislikes late sittings but still more I flatter myself to a judicious handling of our own side. After all I ought to know how to manage the H. of C. after all my experience at the Ministry of Health and by taking care to adopt a conciliatory manner and giving a concession now and then on something unimportant one gets one's way on the things that really matter. The Exchange Equalisation Account was a good example. My people wanted to stone wall, but I knew how sensitive the House is about control, so I said, show me the best you can do remembering that if the outside is reasonably attractive the inside doesn't matter. So they cooked up an ingenious plan by which the Public Accounts Committee are to be given an elaborately calculated average value of gold & foreign securities in the a/c. As they wont be allowed to know the sterling this cant be any good to them but I had the malcontents into my room and after proving that everything they had asked for was impossible I produced this plan impromptu as it were. They were delighted at having got something to take home and I had no more trouble with them. Of course it drives the Times to fury to see me get away with the Budget like this. This morning's leader once more betrays their disappointment and annoyance but I can afford to laugh at them now. It is something that they recognise Austen's position which is very remarkable and must be very gratifying to him. He has quite eclipsed all the other ex-Cabinet Ministers just by being himself and he is greeted with general cheers whenever he gets up.

...

Dorothy is very excited because Stephen Lloyd who has had malaria followed by a partial paralysis of the legs is probably coming home on sick leave. They dont seem at all doubtful of his recovery but he will probably make quicker progress in a cooler climate. We rather hope he will come as a meeting is likely to be more natural & less embarrassing under those circumstances.

...

10 June 1933
37 Eaton Square, SW1

My dear Hilda,

What a wonderful Whitsun this has been. I don't think I ever remember such an unbroken series of cloudless days. For fishing indeed it was not ideal, but I would always be ready to take my chance of the fish provided I could have such perfect weather.

We had a very pleasant quiet time with the Tryon's. They have got a delightful house with a lawn sloping down to the Avon and great big trees planes, cedars and hickory (!) scattered about. Some nuthatches had built in one of the planes and as I stood by the river the young birds were squeaking away round me as they followed their mother from trunk to trunk.

...

I got up early on Friday in order to discuss the American situation with my people before the Cabinet at 2.30. Roosevelt has made up his mind that Congress has got into such a temper as to make a moratorium impossible. He has accordingly suggested a part payment. In the form in which he made it, his suggestion was not acceptable but it seemed to me that if we could get him to accept a small token payment and to declare that that was not equivalent to a default it was worth while to meet him. Accordingly I made that recommendation to the Cabinet and though I had some trouble in making my colleagues understand what I was proposing they finally accepted it. So I drafted a message for Lindsay yesterday afternoon and I am glad to say that we received this morning a reply which seems to me to be satisfactory. I am not quite sure whether we shall have the President's statement in time to tell the H. of C. on Tuesday but if it comes fairly soon I think I can get away with it all right. It will be a comfort if it works out according to plan for it is not a nice thing to default and yet payment again really was not possible.

...

17 June 1933
Westbourne

My dear Ida,

...

The end of this week has been somewhat of an anti-climax after the earlier excursions and alarums. We kept at cross purposes with R. up to the end but somehow got into step at last, and it is amusing to see that after all there has been practically no protest in the U.S.A. Here of course there has been profound satisfaction and relief and it is pretty evident to me that if I had been unable to get the clean bill from Roosevelt & had just defaulted there would have been some very disagreeable criticisms. As it is I can look back over the whole course of the negotiations without feeling that I should have acted otherwise than I did at any point.

The scene in the House after I had made my announcement was one of the most interesting I remember. Stafford Cripps for once did just the right thing and made no attempt to qualify his satisfaction or his congratulations. Samuel was equally wholehearted but challenged Horne by talking of those "whose speech is always silver". Horne who had not expected the payment in silver felt that he could not say nothing yet did not quite know what to say. In the end he said three things first that to have defaulted would have been bad business because our own debtors would have done the same, second that by paying in silver we should save money and third that we should remember the difficulties of the

Americans. Each of these remarks was true and each was singularly inopportune at the moment. What was so interesting was to see the unerring instinct with which the House instantly perceived the impropriety and conveyed its disapproval. Horne floundered and made desperate efforts to get out of the bog. And then Winston who had been sitting with his head in his hands racking his brains to find a vulnerable point saw his chance to climb into favour over Horne's shoulders and leaped up to say two sentences of approval for the Govt & more approval for Roosevelt with just a suggestion of the labours in which he himself had so long engaged. It was admirably done and he got louder cheers than he has for many a day, though I fancy he might easily draw too big a conclusion from his temporary rehabilitation. But it was just one of those incidents which happen only occasionally but make the House such a fascinating study.

I have had many congratulations both on War Debts and on my speech to the [World Economic] Conference which seems to have impressed the delegates very favourably. But we are only now beginning to approach the real difficulties after much scrapping between the Americans & the French for the empty honours of official positions. I expect next week will develop serious differences but I am well aware that the Conference has got to pass through the regular phases. Unfortunately it is a very trying and worrying process for the Leader of the British Delegation especially when he has got his Finance Bill on in the House and has no great confidence in his Financial Secretary.

...

... [T]oday lunched with the Vansittarts in their beautiful old 1600 house at Denham before going on to the garden party at Windsor. We worked hard on the delegates there so hard that I never spoke to the King, but there are other opportunities for that. ...

...

24 June 1933
Westbourne

My dear Hilda,

...

The week has not been nearly so exhausting as it sounds and I have come through it very comfortably. The whole family went to Oxford [for the Honorary degree ceremony] ... and though the rain prevented our walking in the usual procession it cleared in the afternoon for the garden party. ...

...

The Finance Bill has gone so quietly that I never went into the House on the second day when the Coops amendments were taken. I couldn't get there (on account of the Conference) till 6.30 and by then it was practically over. I am sure Jack Hills is quite wrong. Ned Grigg told me he never had any trouble about Coops though there are a great many in Altrincham. The Labour Party laughed heartily when I told them that some day, when the political propagandists had started a fresh hare, the Coops would be very grateful to me for having given them the charter for their divi. But I seriously believe that to be true. The only real fear they had was that my proposal would be the stepping stone to the taxation of the divi and when I put in a sub-clause to make the divi non taxable they were actually made more secure than they had ever been before. It is fashionable to say that no one likes this Budget. I am certain that too is untrue. Of course it cant be popular in the sense that one reducing taxation all round would be popular. But no one expected that. They expected something off beer and they got more than they had hoped for. They didn't think they would get anything off income tax and they got a lump which will be very welcome next January.

But how long I can go on holding the fort I dont know.

After the success of the week before this one has been dull, but I am not disturbing myself too much about the Americans. If Roosevelt pulls off his policy[28] it will be embarrassing because people will want to know why I haven't done the same. If, as I think more probable, it presently comes to grief, he will throw us all into frightful confusion. But the Conference will have been useful in any case. It is making a lot of people think. And it is showing where the differences lie.

...

Midnight, 10 July 1933
37 Eaton Square, SW1

My dear Hilda,

...

We had a delightful week end [at Briantspuddle] and I was able to forget for a brief space the behaviour of the American President and the French Delegation. In the two days I caught 27 trout ...

Today I had to make my statement to the House & then to wind up. It was a very difficult and delicate task as I wanted to imply something of my feelings & yet to say nothing which would give an excuse for an outburst against us. The debate went extremely well and I can now go to bed with a fairly easy mind. The figures of unemployment came in most opportunely to show that we were holding our end up. But there are always a number of people who will have more faith in a quack than in an qualified practitioner. That sometimes enables the quack to be successful where the qualified man has failed and we must hope

---

[28] During the hundred-day special session of Congress following his Presidential inauguration in March 1933, Roosevelt launched his first New Deal with a flood of economically expansionary legislation. Congress passed the National Recovery Act on 16 June conferring unprecedented powers on the President.

that Roosevelt's experiment will succeed. But it hasn't succeeded yet and in the meantime he has certainly torpedoed the Conference.[29] We must finish it up with all the trumpets we can sound but I find it very difficult to see how we can get much value out of it now.

The latest jibe in Conference circles is that the President's message was a sin against the Moley[30] Ghost!

What will happen now I can't foresee, but I fear the President may have in mind to devalue the dollar at a rate which will wreck the gold countries and start a competitive depreciation. In that case we shall get it "in the neck" as the competition of Germany Belgium & France will be much more serious than U.S.A.

R.M. thinks he will adjourn the Conference about the end of the month. If so I should be able to get away early to Scotland and I hope I shant be required to go to U.S.A. before the end of October.

Last week was trying in the extreme but I hope this one will be more peaceful.

Stephen Lloyd has returned and D. has been visiting him in hospital. Apparently he is still paralysed in both legs and the Drs have not made up their minds what the prospects are. D. is very happy and no doubt both the young people think themselves very much in love. But one cant help wondering if he will ever get right. However it is no use meeting evils half way.

...

15 July 1933
Westbourne

My dear Ida,

Certainly this week – when Monday was over – was not so exacting as the week before but we had so many social engagements that it could not be called restful. On Tuesday we dined with the Readings to meet "Tom" Lamont[31] a partner of Morgans and a well known figure over here. I had a little talk with him during the evening & found him very depressed. He has no faith or confidence in Roosevelt (whom he has known all his life) and he considers that he is

---

[29] On 4 July 1933 Roosevelt's 'bombshell' message effectively torpedoed the World Economic Conference by rejecting the idea of agreement on international currency stabilisation as it would hamper national policies designed to raise domestic US purchasing power.

[30] Raymond Moley (1886–1975). Professor of Public Law and Presidential advisor to Roosevelt on the New Deal; Assistant Secretary of State 1933; Presidential emissary to London on economic and banking policy 1933. His agreement with Britain and France on currency stabilisation on 29 June provoked Roosevelt's 'bombshell' on 4 July 1933 condemning stabilisation and led to Moley's subsequent removal.

[31] Thomas William Lamont (1870–1948). American banker. Chairman, J.P. Morgan. Represented US Treasury on American Commission at Paris Peace Conference 1919; Chairman, International Commission for Adjustment of Mexican Foreign Debt.

making a series of experiments so disastrous that his only hope lies in his belief in the probability of their not being proceeded with. But he was wrong for some of the things that he thought would never happen have happened even since I saw him. After this dinner we went on to India House where the High Commissioner was giving a reception and thence we went to the Beaver's Lodge where he had a party and dance. I hadn't seen the little man for over a year and he was absolutely delighted that we should have looked in. We didn't stop long but he never left us for a moment and actually came down stairs and saw us off himself. The next night we went to a reception at Africa House and on Thursday we dined at the Iraqui Legation to meet Faisal[32] who was very anxious to have a talk with me about his railways. He seemed to think that I had only to say Yes and all he wanted would be done; I had to explain that things weren't put through in that way and that he must talk to the Foreign Office. Fortunately Francis Humphrys was at the dinner & I got to know what was in the wind before I talked to the King.

You will have seen that R.M. proposes to "adjourn" the Conference on the 27th. Not content with the presidential message (described in Conference circles as a sin against the Moley Ghost!) the Americans have been sabotaging every other bit of our work. Apparently Cordell Hull[33] had instructions to keep the Conference going & he voted for my proposals. But when one of the Sub-Committees began to discuss the Cooperation of Central Banks Senator Pittman[34] came down and said that in the opinion of the Federal Reserve Board any such discussion was untimely & the only subject on which it was worthwhile to proceed was – Silver! Since then, just as the Sub had got an agreement about Silver he (Pittman) introduced an amendment to his resolution which would make agreement conditional on our increasing the silver content of our coinage at a cost of some £14M! The only other subject on which the Conference has been able to get agreement so far is sugar but that is now held up as the Americans say they have no instructions!

I should think there has never been a case of a Conference being so completely smashed by one of the participants. It recalls very forcibly to my mind the view I

---

[32] Faisal I (1885–1933). King of Hejaz and prominent in Arab revolt against Turkey 1916–18. Became King of Iraq 1921.

[33] Cordell Hull (1871–1955). American lawyer and politician. Democrat member, Tennessee House of Representatives 1893–97; Judge, Tennessee 1903–7; member, US House of Representatives 1907–21 and 1923–31; Chairman, Democratic National Committee 1921–24; US Senator for Tennessee 1931–33. US Secretary of State, 1933–44; Chairman, US Delegation to World Economic Conference in London 1933. Nobel Peace Prize, 1945.

[34] Key Pittman (1872–1940). US lawyer and politician. US Senator for Nevada 1912–40. Advisor and speech-writer to Roosevelt 1932; President *pro tempore* of Senate from 1932; US delegate to World Economic Conference 1933, secured international silver purchase agreement and played a key role in US Silver Purchase Acts 1934 and 1939; Chairman, Senate Foreign Relations Committee 1933–40 assisting Roosevelt gain flexibility on US neutrality legislation.

expressed some months ago that the only way to get the U.S. to take any interest in the Conference was to hold it in America. I doubt its reassembling except perhaps in some modified form. Whether it will have done any good it is perhaps too early to say. Annie thinks it has and in my buoyant moods I say so too, but if so it is the kind of good which you cant put in the shop window.

... One thing which I had thought I was going to take off your shoulders viz the P[ublic] A[ssistance] C[ommittee] will probably survive. At intervals where I could squeeze it in I have been pegging away at Unemployment Insurance. It has been a terrible job & I should never have got any result if I had not been very determined and persistent. In the end I have saved my Commission for the ablebodied unemployed but the "normal" poor will remain, for the present at any rate, in the hands of the P.A.C.'s. I hope to get it cleared up and the Cabinet decision taken during the next fortnight.

...

23 July 1933
Moor Lane House, Briantspuddle

My dear Hilda,

...

... In spite of all the anxiety which my colleagues had felt about my proposition, the debate on the dollar bonds offer was over in about an hour. I confess that I was very relieved though when I saw the press on the announcement of our intentions I was satisfied that we should have no serious trouble. But if I had been mistaken undoubtedly the Cabinet would have blamed me as I rather pushed them into what a good many of them didn't feel quite happy about. As it turned out I think they will be fortified in their reliance on my judgement. It was interesting to notice that the Times – almost alone – carped at my proposal and said the Govt had missed a fine opportunity of striking a blow for the sanctity of contracts. It was, I thought, very characteristic of them that they emphasised more than once in their account of Friday's debate the dislike felt by the House to the proposal, but they quite omitted to point out that the ground of such dislike as was expressed was exactly the opposite of their view & was to the effect that we were not justified in paying more than we were legally obliged to. As a matter of fact that was only the Labour view; on our side I believe most took the view expressed by the Daily Mail namely that the Treasury was to be congratulated on having found so satisfactory a way out of a very difficult situation.

...

From one remark in your letter I am afraid I misled you in what I said about the Unemployment scheme. The Commission will deal with all able bodied unemployed who come under Health Insurance, which of course includes agricultural workers domestic servants and railwaymen. It will also have those who have been unemployed since they were 16. So the P.A.C. will be left with those over 65 and the sick and the children. I dont think it will be too bad a scheme to begin with and it will perhaps grow in future.

...

I understand that the Opposition desire another debate on the Conference and that I shall have to take part in it again. One thing I cant help chuckling over and that is the awful slump on the N.Y. Stock Exchange. It has absolutely silenced the critics who were asking why our Chancellor could not be brave as well as wise like the American President. No one, least of all Americans, know what he may do next but his experiments look more chancy than ever and I think our people may gradually come to realise that our slower and less sensational methods are more satisfactory in the long run. Meanwhile I am endeavouring to deal with the Dominions. Smuts[35] put out a Memorandum on monetary policy which called for action nominally by everyone but really of course by the U.K. in the direction of depreciation of sterling and a huge programme of public works. He wanted a declaration on this subject by the "sterling bloc". At the moment I merely parried by saying I should welcome a declaration by the British Empire to which other countries could adhere if they chose. But on thinking it over I can see my way to a sort of sequel to Ottawa saying that we have taken the opportunity of reviewing the situation after a year and that we were dead right then and meant to go on etc. etc. This would (1) counteract the failure of the Conference (2) brighten up Ottawa which is getting a little dull & tarnished (3) please the F.B.I. and the Monarch and others who say why doesn't the Empire do something (4) direct the Dominions from subjects they dont understand and on which they can be embarrassing to us. It remains to be seen whether I can shepherd them into the fold but I have seen Smuts who has been acting as bell-wether and he seems favourably impressed. ...

30 July 1933
Westbourne

My dear Ida,

...

I was very pleased to be able to bring off the Dominions declaration. It was no easy job as the sheep kept running out just as I thought I had got them all into the fold. However in the end I not only got them where I wanted but they

---

[35] Jan Christian Smuts (1870–1950). South African advocate, general and politician. Fought against British in South Africa War 1899–1902. Commanded British forces in German East Africa; Minister of Finance and Defence 1910–19; represented South Africa at Imperial War Conference; appointed to War Cabinet 1917–19. Prime Minister of South Africa 1919–24 and 1939–48; Deputy Prime Minister 1932–39.

themselves were thoroughly pleased with the situation and I have left them all (except the Irishman) in high good humour and on the best of terms with us as well as one another. The statement was very well received in the City and has put the £ up just as I was thinking it would have to come down. Altogether it did a good deal to redeem the Conference failure. It was characteristic of J.R.M. that he has never said a word about it to me, in fact if I make any allusion to it he looks vague and after a while says "Oh, that". He takes no interest except in what he is personally concerned with. On the other hand I must say he was very nice when I went to see him about the War Debt on Friday and accepted at once & without question all my suggestions both on procedure and on the lines on which we should negotiate. I heard nothing more of his proposal that I should go to Washington in September.

...

Austen is also very well and very pleased I think with the influential position he has attained. It is perfectly true that he has never had so much influence in the H. of C. & I fancy there is a large measure of truth in his own remark that it would not survive 3 months on the Treasury Bench.

I think the papers in their effort to be bright are making a perfectly ridiculous fuss over L.G.'s speech. I did not think it very good; the end was particularly feeble. To make a sensation out of his conversion to protection with special emphasis on food taxes is absurd. He is as he always has been an opportunist & he thinks the farmers would approve a tax on meat. But they wont trust him.

27 August 1933
Tillypronie, Tarland, Aberdeenshire

My dear Ida,

...

What a wonderful season this is. I think I am having the best holiday that has come to my lot for many years and I shall look back upon it with satisfaction for the rest of my life. ...

We had a splendid day on the Tuesday after you left ... Since then I have been here in a very pleasant party, in the most luxurious conditions and with immense quantities of grouse. Indeed they are beginning already to accumulate in packs and hundreds of birds sometimes pass over two or three guns in a continuous stream from which but a small toll can be taken. On our first day, which was much the biggest, nine guns bagged 227 brace which is a record for that particular beat, and I myself had 33 birds down at one drive. It was very good fun but I really enjoyed even more the next day when we got only 34 brace, but shot over a high ridge which commanded immense views in almost every direction. It was warm without being oppressive and one of those days when clouds pass constantly across the sky throwing blue and purple shadows which chase one another over the slopes and valleys. It was enough to sit & just look at the prospect even if there had been no birds at all, but every now & then one got a real sporting shot that gave one more of a thrill than a dozen low birds.

...

3 September 1933
Cairnton, Glassel, Aberdeenshire

My dear Ida,

...

I am sorry to say that I shall have to go to London tomorrow night. I still cant see what need there is for us to be called together but the F.O. has got the wind up about the European situation.

...

10 September 1933
Dalchosnie, Kinloch Rannoch, Perthshire

My dear Hilda,

...

I stayed on with Arthur Wood till Monday evening. ...

I picked up Jimmy Thomas, coming down from Balmoral, in the train at Glassel and we travelled together to Aberdeen. He told me he had had two long walks with the King one that morning for 2½ hours and the King had poured out to him his family troubles (no doubt about his sons). "By God he is a great yewman creature" said Jimmy and went on to say that when he went to say goodbye to the Queen she burst out "I cant tell you what a lot of good you've done the King & how you have cheered him up". Jimmy did not dwell upon these remarks or try to brag about his intimacy with Royalty, but I thought the incident was very creditable both to him & to H.M. It shows that J.H.T. doesn't merely amuse the King with his "b—y"s & his stories but that H.M. feels he can trust him & respects his judgement on common domestic problems.

After all we need never have had a Cabinet as I suspected all along. I dont mean that there were no troubles about, but there was no need to bring Ministers from Scotland to settle them. The P.M. kind of apologised, saying that after all things had settled down more quietly than the F.O. had expected but of course he could very easily have cancelled the meeting if he hadn't wanted to impress the public.

...

17 September 1933
Westbourne

My dear Ida,

...

We finished up with 191½ brace which is 1½ in excess of what the last tenant got. ... But though we wanted to please Donald and Sir John by beating the record, we ourselves attached no importance to that. It was sufficient that we enjoyed ourselves thoroughly & I must say I got as much fun out of the days when we came home with 6 or 7 brace of grouse after walking over the high ground with those wonderful views as I have often done out of much more impressive drives with 40 or 50 brace. ...

Apart from [a gouty eczema] I have been wonderfully fit all through. I wish I could say the same of Annie, who has been very up and downish with fits of jangled nerves and depression. This change of life business is terribly protracted & though I think she is slowly working through it, she does have a bad time. She has retired to bed now (after lunch) and says she probably wont come down till dinner.

...

24 September 1933
Moor Lane House

My dear Hilda,

... By the way, I found Catt very proud because Sanders man had called while I was away & told him that the big plant of Cymbid. Insigni the photo. of which was published in the Orchid Review was a record for the whole country, and on seeing the plant he declared that they could not get bulbs or foliage like that.

We got off to Norfolk on Tuesday afternoon and spent a very pleasant two days there. ...

Annie was rather dreading the visit & showed some signs of wanting to run out. However I persuaded her to come and as it turned out she quite enjoyed herself and though she would never make an intimate friend of either Sam [Hoare] or Maud she found, as I expected, that she liked them much better in their own home than she had ever done before.

We came back on Friday and I spent the rest of the day working at the instructions for Leith-Ross. I had him & Lindsay to discuss the proposals and I think in the form I have got them we shall not do badly if we can get Roosevelt to accept them. But we are all in the dark as to what is in his mind, if there is anything in his mind. The Governor had half an hour's talk with him and says he spent the whole of it in telling what he had done and explaining that all these complex questions could be reduced to quite a simple form in which they could be decided very easily. R. reminded the Governor of Ll.G. which as I told him was the worst thing I have heard about him yet. He thinks things are going badly over there and says the best opinion (probably meaning the bankers) considers that if America had been content to go slow she would have made more progress and been free from the uncertainty and anxiety which is the inevitable accompaniment of "ballyhoo".

Meanwhile we are making slow but solid progress and my information is that generally speaking people are well satisfied with the National Govt & have no wish to change it. I read with irritation in the Observer today that there was no excuse for the Governments failure to assist the Cunard in building its two monsters & thus assuring Britain the lead in the Atlantic. Their nervous hesitation to throw themselves boldly into the stimulation of industry was their one outstanding fault. That sort of cheap criticism, without any knowledge of the facts could be put up by any fool, and I daresay a good many other fools will accept it. As a matter of fact I am working at it continuously but I am not going to finance the Cunard's venture unless they first come to terms with the White Star and unfortunately they have got a very tiresome and obstinate chairman. I shouldn't be surprised if he had to resign before we get any real progress.

...

Stephen Lloyd is said to be better but we are a good deal concerned about him. The specialist who has I think only seen him twice says he thinks there is something wrong with the spinal chord [sic] & that he will never be any better. The other man who is constantly attending him & who is supposed to be very good does not agree & thinks he will get all right except perhaps for a slight permanent lameness. Stephen himself & Dorothy keep up their spirits and take a cheerful view but evidently all is still uncertain. In any case I should think he could never go back to India.

...

30 September 1933
Westbourne

My dear Ida,

...

I am very sorry my holiday is over but it has been a real good one and everyone remarks on how well I look. I saw S.B. & the P.M. when I got back. The former is very fit and pleased with things in general but the P.M. is in a rather nervy condition, not improved by a bad cold or rather cough. He says he is not sleeping and has been talking again, though not to me, about not being able to go on. But I don't attach any importance to that as I think he only does it to be told that he is indispensable.

I have got a nasty week in front of me – Bankers dinner on Tuesday – speech on India on Friday morning & vote of thanks to S.B. that night. I feel a strong desire to run away and hide!

... Cabinets dont begin till the middle of Oct but I shall have to be in town before then.

7 October 1933
Westbourne

My dear Hilda,

...

A. & I are rejoicing this afternoon to have got through our jobs and to have the house to ourselves. Of course the [Conservative Annual] Conference does not go on long but it is strenuous while it lasts. ... It is quite tiring just to sit from 10.30 to 1 and from 2.30 to 5 even if you have not to take any part but on this occasion the Indian discussion imposed a very serious responsibility on me and I was very thankful when it was over.

I have not seen any good or even accurate account of the debate but as a matter of fact we were delighted with the result. G. Lloyd had staged his Defence debate for the day before to get a good atmosphere and the Conference which was exceedingly jingo and anti-foreign cheered every sentence of a speech which was really a very vicious attack on the Government. He was furious because no Minister was there to reply, but the absence was deliberate and I have no doubt it was good tactics. Winston hovered about wondering whether to speak and seeing that the atmosphere was favourable he decided to take a turn in the sunlight and followed Lloyd with further attacks on us for our neglect of defences. Remembering however that he had been Chancellor he observed that the audience, if they approved these sentiments, must tell the Chancellor that they were prepared to pay for them, whereupon all these very foolish people cheered vociferously. Having thus basked in the popular favour at the expense of the Government the conspirators went to bed very hopeful. They had whipped up all their supporters for a great effort and they had the Morning Post, Daily Mail and Express to support them. The first named had rows of sandwichmen walking round with legends about surrender & betrayal and a pamphlet with wide black borders was handed to the delegates at the doors. The hall was fuller than on the first day and the tension was perceptible.

Wolmer started off with a very well delivered and plausibly argued speech from which it appeared that his resolution was only an expression of the fears which "the Conservative party" felt and which they wished to submit to the Committee (presumably in case the Committee should forget to enquire about Finance defence policy or the welfare of the Indian peoples!) Every body else was giving evidence before the Committee.[36] Why was "the Conservative Party" alone to be denied access to them? These sentiments were received with howls of delight by the audience and the situation looked by no means pleasant. In the end however I concluded that Wolmer's speech was the best vote catcher they had. Hartington was also good particularly on the transparently disingenuous point that he and his friends were the last people to be disloyal to the Govt or the

---

[36] A Joint Select Committee on India met between April 1933 and November 1934 to consider the proposals of the Round Table Conference published on 18 March 1933.

leaders and if they were caused some embarrassment now it would help them in the end. Just as the Heavy Father, as he spanks his young hopeful, says "This hurts me far more than you, my boy. Someday you will be thankful to me for what I am doing now". But George Lloyd was not effective and was thrown out of his stride by a sharp interruption, while Henry Page Croft completely spoiled the effect of a passionate peroration by imploring the audience to "vote for the amendment" instead of for the motion.

If you read the Times you will see that I had little difficulty in carrying the audience with me, and presumably therefore little credit was due to my performance. On the other hand Edwards, our chief agent here, thought it was touch & go and that our 2 to 1 majority was a personal triumph. Geoffrey Lloyd & Derrick Gunston my P.P.S. were of opinion that it was the best speech I had ever delivered (which we have heard before). My own opinion is that as a piece of advocacy it did the trick and that after all was the important thing. I tried to get two things into their minds. First that they were not competent to express an expert opinion on such a difficult subject and second that if they wanted to support the Government they must vote for the amendment. I believe I succeeded in this task and I am confirmed by the rage of the M[orning] P[ost] which sheds crocodile tears over my wounding aspersions on Wolmers innocence. I believe now the critics have shot their bolt and that they wont get as good an opportunity of bolting the party again. On our side I told Topping to treat the vote not as a suspension of opinion but as a definite approval of the general lines of the Government's policy – which in fact it was.

After the division all the "Indians" disappeared and we saw them no more. We had a capital meeting last night and S.B. made an extremely good speech which was very warmly received.

… S.B. says he has got to loathe Americans so much that he hates meeting them and he actually refused an invitation to dine with Ramsay on Monday to meet the James Roosevelts, he being Franklin's son. I myself am going – to look at the creature.

…

18 October 1933
37 Eaton Square, SW1

My dear Ida,

…

And now I am just off to shoot a couple of days with Exeter after which I go to Birmingham where I am opening the 40000th house built by the Corporation on Monday.

…

We dined with our septuagenarian brother last night. He appeared to be in rude health.

21 October 1933
Westbourne

My dear Hilda,

...

I had a very well attended and extremely decorous meeting at Nottingham. ... The real trouble was that I had nothing particular to say and the journalists with their usual lack of perception missed the one new point of interest namely a hint of House of Lords reform. ...

Some of my people at the Treasury listened in to Sir J. Simon and reported a very unfavourable impression of his broadcast which they said was like a smart advocate addressing the jury. I thought myself, judging by his conversation that he was obsessed far too much by the personal side of his controversy with Neurath. I expressed the view that the public would not be interested in what it would feel to be a minor point and that what it would want was a brief & clear account of our proposals and how they had been received by other nations. The White Paper[37] just issued is an attempt to meet this view & on the whole I think it is successful. The B.B.C. man Bartlett[38] was outrageous and I believe the P.M. gave Reith[39] & Whitley[40] a good dressing down.

The situation is obscure and everyone seems to be waiting for someone else to move. Mussolini is playing the usual double game, the Americans are chiefly anxious to convince their people that they are not going to be drawn into doing anything helpful to the rest of the world, the Germans are propagandising with a view to dividing France & England, the French are in trouble over their Budget

---

[37] When the Disarmament Conference resumed on 14 October 1933 Simon proposed a period of international supervision of armaments with no further rearmament before the implementation of disarmament bringing all to an equality with Germany. The White Paper on 20 October included a statement on the conversations conducted since 23 September.

[38] (Charles) Vernon Oldfield Bartlett (1894–1983). Staff of *Daily Mail* 1916; Reuters Agency 1917–19; Special European Correspondent of *The Times* 1919–20; Rome correspondent 1921–22; London Director of League of Nations 1922–32; correspondent of *News Chronicle* 1934–54; political commentator, *Straits Times Singapore* 1954–61; South-East Asia correspondent, *Manchester Guardian* 1954–61. Regular broadcaster on foreign affairs 1928–34 and during the war. Independent Progressive MP for Bridgwater 1938–50.

[39] John Charles Walsham Reith (1889–1971). Engineering career from 1913. Admiralty Engineer-in-Chief Department 1918; responsible for liquidating munitions engineering contracts 1919; First General Manager, BBC 1922; Managing Director 1923 and Director-General of BBC 1927–38; Chairman, BOAC 1939–40. National MP for Southampton 1940. Minister of Information 1939–40; Minister of Transport 1940; Minister of Works 1940–42; Director, Combined Operations, Material Department, Admiralty 1943–45; Member, Commonwealth Telecommunications Board 1946–50. Knighted 1927. Created Baron Reith 1940.

[40] John Henry Whitley (1866–1935). Liberal MP for Halifax 1900–1928. Junior Lord of Treasury and Liberal Whip 1907–10; Deputy Chairman, Ways and Means 1910–11; Deputy Speaker and Chairman, Ways and Means 1911–21; Speaker of House of Commons 1921–28. Chairman of Committee on Relations of Employers and Employed 1917–18; Chairman, Royal Commission on Labour in India 1929–31; Chairman of BBC 1930–35.

and our Foreign Office in the absence of "Van" seems to have no mind of its own. I think we must be very cautious for it would be very easy to make a mistake. But common prudence would seem to indicate some strengthening of our defences and happily we are no longer expecting a deficit at the end of the financial year. News from Washington is pretty bad. So far from being helpful the President is keeping a very stiff countenance on War Debts and it looks as if we shall have to content ourselves with another makeshift till things get more settled on the other side [of] the water.

...

28 October 1933
Westbourne

My dear Ida,

What you say about restoring cuts in municipal salaries shows that the L.A.'s are fairly on the run. They have (taking them as a whole) behaved badly. They were as slow in making cuts as they have been hasty in restoring them and their action is bound to be embarrassing to the Government. In fact the teachers have already begun to stir up an agitation on the ground that we are committing a "breach of faith" in not restoring their salaries when other municipal salaries are being put back to what they were. ...

On sewage and water the M/H will probably be proposing a new scheme next year (with some assistance from me) but of course you must keep this information deathly secret.

Fulham[41] made the P.M. very miserable but I confess I did not lose a minute's sleep over it. The press put it all down to Housing & lies about War. Both no doubt were factors but I heard yesterday from a friend who had been talking to a speaker (street corner) in Fulham what I had all along suspected, that the real attack was on the means test. I hear that the same thing is the one subject in all our local municipal contests. The Socialists have now become quite shameless in offering this form of bribery and they make things so unpleasant that no good men will go on the Public Assistance Committee. This confirms what I have felt all along, that the putting this duty [sic] of investigating needs on to the local authority not only involves a breakdown in one or two bad spots; it is demoralising and disintegrating local government even where its traditions are soundest. The Times in its campaign against bureaucracy has never mentioned this aspect but those who are doing the work now are only too conscious of it. To go back to Fulham I agree that it must

---

[41] East Fulham by-election, 25 October 1933. A Conservative majority of 14,521 in 1931 was turned sensationally into a Labour majority of 4840 on a 29.2 per cent swing against the government. Although the result reflected electoral discontent with housing and domestic issues, Labour's emphasis on disarmament during the campaign was widely interpreted as a vote against rearmament and supposedly had a major impact on Baldwin's policy.

be regarded as highly unsatisfactory whatever be the explanations & excuses. But it is absurd to be down hearted about it. It is no criterion of what would happen in a General Election today, much less two years hence. But I long ago recognised that we *must* lose many bye-elections and that if we got back (as I think we shall) it would be with a greatly diminished majority.

...

I expect you saw that I was opening the 40 thousandth house built by the Corpn on Monday at Wesley Castle estate between Selly Oak and California. The Lord Mayor and his colleagues were "frightfully" nice (as Frank says) to us. They sent a car to take us to the Council House & then the Ld Mayor & Lady Mayoress took us in different cars to see a small scheme in the middle of the town where they have built a number of "maisonnettes" on the site of the old cavalry barracks. ... You can imagine what a change this is from the old filthy back to back den ... We then drove out to Wesley Castle and saw the estate which is delightfully laid out on modern lines and finally we arrived at the site where we found a considerable crowd of councillors residents & friends. ... There the Ld Mayor delivered an address, and invited me to open the house. ... When we came out I was presented with an ivory and silver cigar box decorated with views of the estate and the house in enamel, and having the Corporation & my arms on the top. ... As we drove off there was quite a little crowd outside to see & cheer us[,] a proceeding which astonished me as I never somehow expect to be honoured in Birmingham. Yet they are much kinder to me than they were even to Father – portrait freedom casket cigar box – these things are fairly being rained upon me nowadays.

The P.M. asked me to give the Cabinet an "appreciation" of the Rooseveltian policy as several of them did not understand it. So I made a rather humorous story of it representing the Yanks as a barbarous tribe and Roosevelt as a medicine man whose superiority over other medicine men consisted in the astonishing agility with which when one kind of Mumbo Jumbo failed, he produced another. The N.R.A. [National Recovery Administration] was put forward as a means of raising the prices of commodities. Unfortunately the tiresome things went back whereupon the backwoodsmen from the Middle West beat their tom toms and prepared to march upon the capital. But the medicine man without losing a moment broadcast a new plan even more infallible than the last by which prices would surely be put up just where he wanted them. After which they would stay there for generations. And it was all to be done by buying & selling GOLD which still has a magic significance. I told the cabinet that so long as he confined himself to American mined gold it wouldn't work and that within a few weeks he would be forced into the world market. Then (if he could get the gold) dollar prices *might* rise, or they might stop still & gold prices might fall. No one can tell but you may be sure it wont turn out as Roosevelt thinks or says it will. Now I see he has begun to buy gold and the dollar is *rising* and prices are *falling*.

I hear from America that confidence is crumbling. Some prophesy a crash in the spring. Many say the President is the victim of his malady. It has given him a sort of fictitious self confidence. If things go badly he will relapse into helpless crippledom. I expect these are exaggerated and unfriendly views for they come from banking circles where there is no love for the President. But I look upon him as a dangerous and unreliable horse in any team.

I doubt if we shall get any permanent debt settlement. I have devised a new short term proposal but I had quite a lot of trouble over it in Cabinet. A good many would like just to sit back & refuse any payment, but they haven't got my responsibilities and I am still of opinion that it is worth our while to pay something though not too much to avoid being denounced however unjustly as defaulters.

...

4 November [mis-dated October] 1933
Yattendon Court, Nr. Newbury, Berkshire

My dear Hilda,

I am not disturbed about the Municipal Elections[42] which came out much as I had expected. The poll was very small – only 35% in Birmingham – and I dont think the results are any indication of what would happen at a Parliamentary election. Kilmarnock[43] on the other hand was a disappointment to the Labour party and an immense relief to the P.M. But really bye elections at this distance from the General Election aren't much of a guide. We shall doubtless lose many more and at best we could not expect to repeat 1931 in 1936. But barring unforeseen developments I see no reason to think that we shall not come back with a good working majority.

I am not dissatisfied with my interviews with the L.A.'s. Of course they are bound to say that they ought to be relieved of all liability in respect of able bodied unemployed, and as I said to them I could make an equally good case for putting education on to the Exchequer. But they dont expect anything of the kind and I expect they wont be very dissatisfied in their hearts at the end. ... Anyway none of the Press proprietors whom I have seen privately appeared to be shocked by anything in the proposals and such comments as they made were favourable.

It is not correct that the President has coupled debt settlement with currency stabilisation. Indeed that is what bankers in U.S. want and they are very cross with the President because he still refuses to consider stabilisation even of a temporary kind. But he is getting, as it seems to me, deeper and deeper into the

---

[42] In the municipal elections of November 1933 Labour made 181 gains to only 5 losses and returned 444 of 880 candidates. The Conservatives gained only 6 seats and lost 112.

[43] Kilmarnock by-election, 2 November 1933. National Labour held the seat with a majority of 2653 compared with 7036 in 1931.

mire as his schemes fail to produce the effect he hoped for and this really makes it impossible for him to settle anything about debts. All I can get at present is acceptance of another token payment but (with some grumbling) I have got the Cabinet to authorise my taking this to go on with.

...

11 November 1933
37 Eaton Square, SW1

My dear Ida,

... I have got to see Hilton Young on Monday as he wants to consult me about the Moyne Report.[44] Unfortunately I have not yet had time to read it though I hope to do so tomorrow but the Research Dept tell me it is open to serious criticism and they much prefer the proposals sketched in my memorandum to which indeed they cannot find anything to add.

I rather thought our Unempl etc Bill would have a good reception but it has been better than I thought. My interviews with Press proprietors were supplemented by Betterton who saw the Editors and Lobby correspondents so the ground was well prepared, but the Bill has really won approval on merits. One of the weightiest provincial papers is the Manchester Guardian and they have had excellent notices, pointing out in particular how the Labour members of the Holman Gregory[45] Commission [on Unemployment Insurance] had advocated compulsory training on even more rigorous terms than are provided in the Bill. Even the Express which I reckon as an Opposition paper nowadays is a warm supporter and the Herald has dropped into discreet silence after the discovery that all its anticipatory statements of the contents of the Bill have turned out to be false. Our people in the House are very pleased and the Local Authorities though anxious to get the best possible financial terms are pleased to be relieved of the Means Test.

It was Hilda who said you were "up in arms" about the figures in the D.T. but I hadn't seen the relevant paragraph in the D.T. There will be a good deal of argument about the method of ascertaining the cost (which will be the cost to each individual L.A.) but what they are really most concerned about is lest the Board should push off large numbers on to them on the ground that they refuse to accept training. I have offered to reduce the period of 5 years before review to meet this point.

---

[44] Walter Guinness had been created Baron Moyne in 1932 and became chairman of the Departmental Committee on Housing which reported in 1933.

[45] Holman Gregory (1864–1947). Liberal MP for South Derbyshire 1918–22. Recorder for Bath 1916–24 and Bristol 1924–29; Judge, London Court 1929–32; Common Sergeant of City of London 1932–34; Recorder, City of London 1934–37. Chairman, Departmental Committee on Workmen's Compensation Acts 1918–20 and Royal Commission on Unemployment Insurance 1930–32. Knighted 1935.

Master Roosevelt is shoving the dollar down with a vengeance now and I expect there is a good deal of anxiety in France & Holland, though of course they dont admit it. My Debt arrangement went well. The most encouraging thing to me was the complete apathy with which it was received in U.S.A. It makes me more hopeful about ultimate cancellation.

I have had a busy week with Cabinets, Cabinet Committees, lunches dinners & speeches. ...

...

On Wednesday Flandin came to lunch. I had Sankey[46] Runciman and S.B. to meet him and he stopped on afterwards for a long talk. He thinks they are in for serious financial difficulties & sees no very bright prospects for Sarraut.[47] We are the only big country with a balanced Budget.

I got and read L. Pearsall Smith's[48] book on Shakespeare last May and entirely endorse all you say in its praise. I also noted that All Trivia was his only other original book but I haven't yet got that. I was however instigated by him to get Prof. Stall on Art and Artifice in Shakespeare which is on my table waiting till I can get time to read it.

...

Tomorrow we are going to visit the Zoo where I want particularly to see the humming birds feeding & the Birds of Paradise in their nuptial display.

...

Did you see the P.M.'s tribute to the Chancellor of the Exchequer at the Guildhall? He does not often do such things.

18 November 1933
Croxton Park, St Neots

My dear Hilda,

...

We are quite a large party here. ... Newton[49] is a great agriculturist and has done a lot of pioneer work in various ways. ...

---

[46] John Sankey (1886–1948). Judge, King's Bench Division 1914–28; Lord Justice of Appeal 1928–29; Lord Chancellor 1929–35. Chairman, Royal Commission on Coal Industry 1919. Knighted 1914. Created Baron Sankey 1929 and Viscount 1932.

[47] Albert M. Sarraut (1872–1962). French politician. Radical Deputy for Aude 1902–24; Senator 1926–40. Junior Minister of Interior from 1906; Governor-General of Indo-China 1911–14 and 1916–19; Minister of Colonies 1920–24; Ambassador to Turkey 1924–26; Minister of Interior 1926–28, 1934, 1938–40; Prime Minister 1933 and 1936; Minister of State 1937–38; member, Assembly of French Union and its president 1951.

[48] Logan Pearsall Smith (1865–1946). American-born British writer; essays collected as *All Trivia* (1933) and *Reperusals and Recollections* (1936).

[49] George Douglas Cochrane Newton (1879–1942). Conservative MP for Cambridge Borough 1922–34. Assistant Secretary, Ministry of Reconstruction 1917–19; Chairman, National Agricultural

Newton is producing pigs under contract according to the pig marketing scheme. So far the scheme seems to be going well but I have some fear that we shall get a reaction soon on the ground that the English bacon is inferior to the Danish that it is dearer and that it is not regular. It is an extraordinary thing that no factory has put down a tank cure plant which is a far cheaper process than our dry cure. I am sending Major Ball of the Research Dept to Denmark next week to investigate the industry on the spot and I believe I may be able to get someone to start a tank plant after we know more about it. The Research Dept is helping the Ministry of Agriculture a good deal in various ways and it is now working on coal where I think it may also be very useful.

We have had a terrible time with Simon this week and I feel that somehow or other there will have to be a change at the F.O. before long. He would insist on trying to get the Cabinet to consider an amended Disarmament Convention to be put forward at Geneva so that we might not be blamed for breaking up the Conference. I opposed this plan which seemed to me to have every vice. It was obviously futile with Germany away; it was almost certain to embroil us with our friends and it was moreover extremely distasteful to our own Services. I maintained that we should state one or two broad considerations which not being technical could be understood by every body, that we should recognise the reasonableness of the two main German objections and declare that the Conference must be adjourned while we and Italy explored the possibilities of the situation in Berlin & Paris through diplomatic channels. What I call the chief German objections are those which seem reasonable to many people here and which I would paraphrase thus. You have insisted on our undergoing a 4 years period of penance and humiliation during which we are to remain unarmed while everybody else remains armed. And when it is over the French General Staff will find some excuse for saying that they are released from their obligations and we shall be no nearer disarmament than before.

Simon made every kind of objection but the Cabinet gradually came round to this view and from the telegrams I have seen it looks as if no other course would have had a chance of success. But Simon has no nerve and he seemed unaccountably frightened by Henderson's threats of resignation.

...

On Thursday the House was up early and Annie & I went to the Philharmonic Concert at Queen's Hall. We enjoyed our evening very much: I wish I could go more often to hear music; I know what I am going to get not like the theatre where you pay more and may find yourself landed with some insufferably tedious or vulgar performance.

...

Council 1922–23; official adviser to British delegation, Ottawa Conference 1932 and World Economic Conference 1933. Created Baron Eltisley 1934.

25 November 1933
Cransford Hall, Saxmundham

My dear Ida,

...

The [Edgbaston] Ball [on Thursday] was very successful and we did our duty first dining with a rather pushing lady who has helped the party and remaining to talk with constituents till after midnight. Next morning we had a private view of the [Municipal] Bank Building which is certainly a most creditable performance both inside and out. The modest Mr Hilton whom I engaged in 1916 when he was a clerk in a West Bromwich Bank will now preside in a noble apartment with furniture in Italian walnut and powder blue upholstery and from time to time will emerge on to a marble balcony (copied from the Doge's Palace) to cast an eye over the central hall. The building paid for out of profits will cost £110000 including land and I should say it is very cheap at the price.

Apart from these travels the week has been rather uneventful. ... On Tuesday I saw the L.A.'s again, but I took the precaution of sending for Sir W. Ray[50] in the morning and found out from him how the land lay. In the afternoon I sent for him again and gave him the draft of a new clause to meet the fear that L.A.'s would be landed with so many "discards" by the Board as to eat up their relief. As a result I got agreement with the County Councils & the L.C.C. and though the A.M.C. still pretend to stand out I think the back of their opposition is broken.

On Wednesday ... I lunched in the City with Sir R Roy Wilson[51] at the Bank of South Africa and dined with the Amerys to celebrate his 60th birthday. I wondered what the company would be and was not surprised when the Lloyds appeared. However I keep on friendly terms even with him and I like her[52] so long as we keep off politics, so we spent a pleasant evening next to one another at dinner.

...

---

[50] William Ray (1876–1937). Alderman, Hackney Borough Council 1918–34; member, LCC 1913–34; Leader, Municipal Reform Party 1925–34. Conservative MP for Richmond 1932–37. Knighted 1929.

[51] Roderick Roy Wilson (1876–1942). Conservative MP for Lichfield 1924–29. Manager, Bank of British West Africa to 1924; Director 1929–37 and Vice-Chairman 1937–42. Knighted 1929.

[52] Blanche Isabella Lascelles. Daughter of Commander Frederick Canning Lascelles and cousin to 6th Earl of Harewood. Maid of Honour to Queen Alexandra 1905–11; married George Ambrose Lloyd 1911.

9 December 1933
Westbourne

My dear Hilda,

I wonder how you learned that my speech on Monday was a success[53] – since the Times, as usual, said very little about it. As a matter of fact it was one of the most successful I ever made in the House. My P.P.S. Capt. Gunston said the new members had never seen anything like it before (meaning the debating points) and J.H.T. informed me that I had no idea what a sensation I had created in the Labour Party who, according to him, were delighted to see Mr "Annoyin'" Bevan[54] made to look foolish. It has been rather a hectic week for I had to speak on Newfoundland on Thursday, and down here yesterday, in addition to a number of Cabinets & Cabinet Committees. Our Foreign Secretary proposed to send a telegram to Berlin on Hitler's proposals which I thought certain to send the French into a fit of hysterics while it irritated the Germans. However in the end and after many hours of argument I got it withdrawn and another substituted on lines which I suggested. Simon was very good about it and showed no resentment at having his despatch riddled so I cant complain but it is surprising to me how such a clever man can occasionally fall into such errors of judgement.

...

We had one of our rare dinner parties on Wednesday to meet Mr Stevens[55] the Canadian Minister of Commerce who is over here for a short time. We got the Baldwins the Leith Rosses the Iliffes and Lady Leitrim and I think Stevens had a very interesting evening as well as a pleasant one. We have also started a series of small lunches for M.P.'s and we had our first on Wednesday – three young men and a woman. I think it does a lot of good to meet some of the new M.P.'s occasionally outside the House. I get to know their faces and of course they like to meet the Chancellor socially.

The Local Authorities have been very stupid over the Unemployment Bill. I did think of making a small further concession to the so called distressed areas but instead of asking for that they turned up with the old story that the Exchequer ought to bear the whole cost. Seeing that we do bear over 95% I am rather fed up with this greediness. The fact is that everyone is beginning to ask for money now they see such good returns. ...

...

---

[53] On 4 December 1933 Chamberlain defended the Unemployment Bill from Labour allegations of meanness and 'Treasury pedantry' during the Second Reading debate.

[54] Aneurin Bevan (1897–1960). Miner's Agent and Labour MP for Ebbw Vale 1929–60. Minister of Health 1945–51; Minister of Labour and National Service 1951. Expelled from Labour 1939 and Whip withdrawn 1955. Editor, *Tribune* 1942–45; member, PLP Parliamentary Committee 1952–54 and 1955–60; Deputy Labour leader 1959–60.

[55] Henry Herbert Stevens (1878–1973). Canadian accountant, broker and politician. Conservative (later Reconstruction) MP 1911–40. Minister of Customs and Excise 1926; Minister of Trade and Commerce 1921, 1930–34. Leader of Reconstruction Party 1934–38.

17 December 1933
Chequers, Princes Risborough, Bucks

My dear Ida,

...

I had rather a grim time this week. It began pretty well for the concession I made on Monday gave general satisfaction except to the official opposition who found a promising line suddenly cut off. I was so cross with the Local Authorities that I was disposed to give them nothing, especially since I got the impression that members on our side had also been very disgusted with their behaviour. However I made some careful and discreet enquiries and came to the conclusion that the small concession to the distressed areas would cut away the most formidable part of the opposition, conciliate the County Councils and relieve the minds of the M.P.'s who sit for doubtful seats in the North. I have no doubt that this was the effect and I got the most I could out of my announcement.

I had no idea that we were going to have an all night sitting on Thursday, nor, I fancy, had anyone else except Maxton[56] and his friends who had decided that the Newfoundland Bill provided a splendid opportunity of baiting our Jimmie, and at the same time putting the Labour Party to shame. Jimmie played into their hands by his rather tactless procedure in moving the closure without replying to one of Mander's[57] speeches and the Labour Party found themselves compelled to join in the hunt. In the end Betterton and I who had to take the money resolution on the Unemployment Bill were obliged to wait all through the night not knowing when we should come on and finally found ourselves beginning our work at 8.30 just as we were getting hungry for breakfast. I got mine at about 9.30 and at mid day I had to leave to change & bathe before leaving for Halifax. It was rather rough having an all nighter before a big speech like that ...

...

You will have seen that I was able to announce the successful conclusion of the Cunard affair on Thursday.[58] To the papers this means just the dramatic completion of the big ship. But I have been after much larger game namely the establishment of a single powerful British Shipping Company in the North Atlantic. The Cunarder has merely been the lever by which this result has been obtained but there is no question that without it we should never have brought the Cunard & White Star together. To my mind this is an excellent example of

---

[56] James Maxton (1885–1946). Teacher and Labour MP for Glasgow Bridgeton 1922–46. Chairman of ILP 1931, 1934–39.

[57] Geoffrey Le Mesurier Mander (1882–1962). Liberal MP for Wolverhampton East 1929–45. PPS to Sir Archibald Sinclair as Air Minister 1942–45. Joined Labour Party 1948. Knighted 1945.

[58] In the North Atlantic Shipping Act (1934), the government provided £9.5 million to enable recommencement of construction on hull no. 534 (a Cunarder later named *Queen Mary*) and to assist the merger of Cunard and White Star to keep the latter out of American control.

how National financial resources can & should be used to remove an otherwise insuperable obstacle to the effective working of private enterprise.

Another exceedingly interesting method of employing our credit will perhaps never be known. The Indian Govt have been negotiating with Japan for a limitation of the latter's imports of cotton piece goods into India. In the course of the negotiations, which were started by the Japs with a boycott of Indian cotton, it appeared that the quota of imports proposed by the Japs included a proportion of a certain line which is now supplied by Lancashire. India represented that she could not pretend that Indian interests required this line to be excluded or limited and if she put forward Lancashire interests it would make trouble among her own people. The Japs very skilfully played on their fears by suggesting that the depreciation of the dollar made it advantageous to buy American cotton and the Indian Govt fairly got the wind up. The India Office saw no alternative but to allow the Indian Govt to give way; the Cabinet was frightened of what Lancashire would say and referred it to a Committee with the Chancellor in the chair. I saw that the crux of the situation lay in the fear of the Indian Govt that they would lose the market for their cotton crop. So I boldly announced that I would stand behind the Indian Govt if they wd buy the crop themselves. With this encouragement they told the Japs that their proposals were quite unacceptable and privately let them know that there was no longer any anxiety about the crop. Thereupon, instead of bouncing out of the room, the Japs, finding their bluff called, said they must refer to their Govt & the last I hear is that we shall probably be able to settle with them on our own terms.

Appendix I:
The Chamberlain Household and Family

Although full biographical details accompany the first reference of all characters mentioned in the letters, a number of members of the Chamberlain household and extended family merit further detail.

Bee or B   Beatrice Chamberlain (1862–1918). Eldest child of Joseph Chamberlain. A compelling character who rather dominated Austen as a child but who selflessly took over the running of Highbury after the death of her father's second wife in childbirth. Utterly devoted to her father and of all his children she is generally agreed to have most resembled him in personality, intellectual capacity and fertile imagination. She also possessed a 'beautiful nature' which was 'simple warm ... guileless and incapable of ill-thinking'.[1] Regarded by Neville and his sisters as 'our guide, philosopher and friend'. In later life, she developed many 'funny little ways' which amused the family – not least a complete disregard for dress.[2] Died soon after the Armistice in the influenza epidemic. *The Times* obituary noted she had 'the mind of a great man with the heart of a great woman'.

Byng   (Wilfred) Byng Kenrick (1872–?). Cousin and close friend of Neville and his younger sisters from childhood, accompanying him on his Asian tour in 1904–5. Active member of Birmingham Council from 1914; Chairman, Education Committee 1922–28, 1931–43; Lord Mayor 1928; Alderman 1929; Freeman 1938. Also active in Birmingham Unionist Association and as chairman of the Edgbaston constituency association invited Neville to become their MP in 1926.

Catt   P.G. Catt. Gardener at Westbourne from Chamberlain's arrival

---

[1] Beatrice Webb Diary, 28 May and 30 August 1886, Norman and Jeane Mackenzie (eds), *The Diary of Beatrice Webb* (4 vols, London, 1982–85), I, pp. 170, 175.

[2] 'Recollections of their own father's childhood written for Dorothy and Frank by their Aunt Ida Chamberlain, January 1941', BC5/11/1.

in 1911 until his death in 1940. His slow speech and odd phrases were much imitated. Lived in the lodge at the entrance to the property.

Diane   (Beatrice) Diane Chamberlain (1912–98). Second child and only daughter of Austen and Ivy. Married Terence Maxwell in 1935. Two sons and one daughter.

Dorothy   Neville Chamberlain's first child (1911–92). Left Westbourne to study the piano in Paris in September 1928. Married Stephen Lloyd in July 1935. One son and three daughters.

Frank   Neville Chamberlain's second child (1914–65). After Winchester and Trinity College, Cambridge, travelled in France, Spain and Germany during the late 1930s. Joined 6th Royal Warwickshire Regiment (Territorial Army) in 1937. Active service in the Second World War. After the war he took up farming before joining Hoskins & Company as Sales Director. Active interest in social and welfare work – particularly for the disabled. Vice-President, Birmingham Federation of Boys' Clubs and Chairman, Birmingham Fellowship for the Handicapped. Life Governor, Birmingham University. Married Roma Parrott in 1953. One son and one daughter.

Uncle George or GHK   George Hamilton Kenrick (1850–?). Bachelor living in Edgbaston. Member, Birmingham School Board from 1880 and the Council from 1902. Long-standing Chairman, Education Committee from 1902; Lord Mayor 1908; Alderman 1909. Knighted 1909. Major benefactor to City and to Neville, his favourite nephew whom he resembled in character and appearance and whom he taught to fish and shoot.[3] Visited Loubcroy Lodge in Scotland together every September. Left Neville a substantial legacy on his death.

Hilda   (Caroline) Hilda Chamberlain (1871–1967). Fifth child of Joseph Chamberlain. Cared for her father after his stroke in 1906 at the cost of her own social life and prospect of marriage. Moved with Ida to Odiham in Hampshire in December 1914 after the death of her father and the disposal of Highbury. The more sociable and outgoing of the two sisters with the 'more feminine

---

[3] E. Sandford, 'Neville Chamberlain', *The [Birmingham] Central Library Magazine*, January 1948, p. 286.

side'.[4] Stalwart of the local Women's Institute and National Treasurer, Federation of Women's Institutes. With her sister built and donated seven houses to the Rural District Council in 1923 and established a recreation ground for the village in memory of Beatrice. Governor of Odiham Grammar School, 1923–47.

Ida (Florence) Ida Chamberlain (1870–1943). Fourth child of Joseph. Although the shy and sensitive one of the two sisters, 'she was the man of the partnership in the sense that she did all the things that the man would do'.[5] Active in local government. Member of Hartley Wintney RDC from 1918 and on Hampshire County Council from 1925 until her death. Chairman of Public Health, Housing and School Medical Services Committees. First female Alderman on County Council.

Ivy Ivy Muriel Chamberlain (née Dundas). Married Austen in 1906. Three children.

Joe Joseph Chamberlain, eldest child of Austen and Ivy (born 1907). Married Gina Macdonald. Two sons.

Lawrence Second son and third child of Austen and Ivy (born 1917). Married Anne Eastwood. Three sons.

Leamie Miss Evelyn Leamon (1884–1976). Nanny to Neville Chamberlain's children for nine years until 1928 when Dorothy left to begin her musical training in Paris. Recalled as wise, tactful, affectionate and sensible. Often acting *in loco parentis*, she was liked and respected by Neville although the sparks flew with Annie over their different ideas about child-rearing.[6] Continued to visit Westbourne over Christmas and New Year during the 1930s and remained close to Dorothy, Frank and their own children until her death.[7]

Lilian Lilian Cole (née Williams). Canadian. Mother of Norman and first wife of Herbert Chamberlain, Joseph Chamberlain's brother who died in 1904. Second marriage to Alfred Clayton Cole of

---

[4] Dilks transcript, NC20/1, fol. 30.
[5] Ibid.
[6] Ibid., fol. 23.
[7] Interview with James Lloyd, 19 June 2001.

West Woodhay, Berkshire. Aunt through marriage to Anne Vere Cole and introduced Neville to his future wife. President, Birmingham Women's Liberal Unionist Association.

Mary

Mary Crownishield Endicott (1863–1957). American. Daughter of Secretary for War in Grover Cleveland first administration. Married Joseph Chamberlain 1888. Married Canon Carnegie in August 1916.

Norman

Norman Gwynne Chamberlain (1884–1917). Son of Herbert and Lilian Chamberlain. Member, Birmingham City Council from 1911 and Chairman, Parks Committee. Joined Grenadier Guards 1914; Acting-Captain 1915; killed with all his Company 1 December 1917. Extremely close friend to Neville who deeply respected and admired his pre-war work with Birmingham Boys' Clubs, the Street Children's Union, Children's Courts, Women's Settlements. After Norman's death, Neville took up many of these causes.

Stephen

Stephen Lloyd (1906–92). Studied Greats at Lincoln College, Oxford; Indian Civil Service 1930–35 when invalided out after contracting polio and married Dorothy Chamberlain July 1935. Joined Guest, Keen & Nettlefold as Joint General Manager in 1935, later responsible for overseas development. Member, Birmingham City Council for Sparkbrook and later Edgbaston 1939–74 and Alderman for 19 years. Member, City of Birmingham Symphony Orchestra Management Committee and chairman for eighteen years.

Willie

William Hartley Carnegie (1860–1936). Canon of Birmingham 1905–13 and Westminster from 1913; Chaplain to the Speaker of the House of Commons 1916–36. Archdeacon of Westminster 1918–19. Married Neville's stepmother in August 1916. Generally regarded as something of a bore.

Appendix II:
Primary Sources Consulted for Volume Three

Private papers and diaries

Addison MSS	Papers and diaries of Christopher Addison, 1st Viscount Addison, Bodleian Library, Oxford.
Altrincham MSS	Papers of Sir Edward Grigg, 1st Baron Altrincham, microfilm consulted at the Bodleian Library, Oxford.
Astor MSS	Papers of Nancy Witcher Astor and Waldorf Astor, 2nd Viscount Astor, Reading University Library.
Baldwin MSS	Papers of Stanley Baldwin, 1st Earl Baldwin of Bewdley, Cambridge University Library.
Beaverbrook MSS	Papers of Sir William Maxwell Aitken, 1st Baron Beaverbrook, House of Lords Record Office, Hist. Coll. 184.
Bridgeman MSS	The Political Diaries of William Clive Bridgeman, 1st Viscount Bridgeman, courtesy of Mrs A. Stacey and the Trustees of the Bridgeman family archive, Shropshire Record Office, SRO 4629.
Cecil MSS	Papers of Lord Robert Cecil, Viscount Cecil of Chelwood, British Library, Add. MSS.
Austen Chamberlain MSS	Papers of Sir Joseph Austen Chamberlain, Birmingham University Library.
Beatrice Chamberlain MSS	Papers of Beatrice Chamberlain, Birmingham University Library.
Neville Chamberlain MSS	Papers and diaries of Arthur Neville Chamberlain, Birmingham University Library.
Croft MSS	Papers of Sir Henry Page Croft, 1st Baron Croft, Churchill College, Cambridge.
Dalton MSS	Diaries of Hugh Dalton, 1st Baron Dalton of Forest and Frith, British Library of Political and Economic Science.
Davidson MSS	Papers of Sir John Colin Campbell Davidson, 1st Viscount Davidson, House of Lords Record Office, Hist. Coll. 187.

Derby MSS	Papers and diaries of Edward George Villiers Stanley, 17th Earl of Derby, Liverpool City Central Library.
Gladstone MSS	Papers of Herbert John Gladstone, Viscount Gladstone, British Library, Add. MSS.
Gwynne MSS	Papers of Howell Arthur Gwynne, Bodleian Library, Oxford. Courtesy of Vice-Admiral Sir Ian Hogg.
Hankey MSS	Papers and diaries of Sir Maurice Hankey, 1st Baron Hankey, Churchill College, Cambridge.
Hannon MSS	Papers of Sir Patrick Hannon, House of Lords Record Office, Hist. Coll. 189.
Headlam MSS	Papers and diaries of Sir Cuthbert Headlam, Durham Record Office.
Hewins MSS	Papers and diaries of William Albert Samuel Hewins, Sheffield University Library.
Hopetoun MSS	Papers of the Marquess of Linlithgow, National Register of Archives (Scotland), Edinburgh.
Hopkins MSS	Papers of Sir Richard Hopkins, Public Record Office, T/175.
Irwin MSS	Papers of Edward Frederick Lindley Wood, Baron Irwin (later Earl of Halifax), as Viceroy of India, Oriental and India Office Collections, British Library.
Law MSS	Papers of Andrew Bonar Law, House of Lords Record Office, Hist. Coll. 191.
Leith-Ross MSS	Papers of Sir Frederick Leith-Ross, Public Record Office, T/188.
Lloyd George MSS	Papers of David Lloyd George, 1st Earl Lloyd-George of Dwyfor, House of Lords Record Office, Hist. Coll. 192.
Lothian MSS	Papers of Philip Henry Kerr, 11th Marquess of Lothian, National Archives of Scotland, Edinburgh.
MacDonald MSS	Papers and diaries of James Ramsay MacDonald, including the papers of Miss Rose Rosenberg, Public Record Office, London. The diaries are used in accordance with MacDonald's wish that they were 'meant as notes to guide and revive memory as regards happenings and must on no account be published as they are'.
Magnum Opus MSS	Papers of Sir Maurice Hankey, 'Magnum Opus' files CAB/63, Public Record Office.
Markham MSS	Papers of Violet Markham, British Library of Political and Economic Science.

Milner MSS	Papers and diaries of Sir Alfred Milner, 1st Viscount Milner, Bodleian Library, Oxford.
Newman MSS	Diaries of Sir George Newman, Public Record Office, MH 139/1–5.
Phillips MSS	Papers of Sir Frederick Phillips, Public Record Office, T/177.
Rey MSS	Papers of Sir Charles Rey, Rhodes House Library, Oxford.
Runciman MSS	Papers of Walter Runciman, 1st Viscount Runciman, Newcastle University Library.
Salisbury MSS	Papers of James Edward Hubert Gascoyne-Cecil, 4th Marquess of Salisbury, by courtesy of the 6th Marquess of Salisbury, Hatfield House.
Samuel MSS	Papers of Sir Herbert Louis Samuel, 1st Viscount Samuel, House of Lords Record Office, Hist. Col. 128.
Sanders MSS	Papers and diaries of Sir Robert Sanders, 1st Baron Bayford, first consulted at the Conservative Research Department and now held at the Bodleian Library, Oxford.
Sankey MSS	Papers and diaries of Sir John Sankey, 1st Viscount Sankey, Bodleian Library, Oxford.
Selborne MSS	Papers of William Waldegrave Palmer, 2nd Earl of Selborne, Bodleian Library, Oxford.
Steel-Maitland MSS	Papers of Sir Arthur Steel-Maitland, National Archives of Scotland.
Strachey MSS	Papers of John St Loe Strachey, House of Lords Record Office, Hist. Coll. 196.
Swinton MSS	Papers of Sir Philip Cunliffe-Lister, 1st Earl of Swinton, Churchill College, Cambridge.
Templewood MSS	Papers of Sir Samuel Hoare, 1st Viscount Templewood, Cambridge University Library.
Thomas MSS	Papers of James Henry Thomas, Centre for Kentish Studies, Maidstone.
Veale MSS	Interviews with Sir Douglas Veale by Professor Brian Harrison, British Library, National Sound Archive.
Worthington-Evans MSS	Papers of Sir Laming Worthington-Evans, Bodleian Library, Oxford.

Government Records

CAB 23	Cabinet Conclusions
CAB 24	Cabinet Papers
CAB 27	Cabinet Committees
CAB 32	Ottawa Imperial Economic Conference
CAB 58	Economic Advisory Council and Committee on Economic Information
MH	Ministry of Health
T	Treasury
T 172	Chancellor of Exchequer's Office
T 175	Sir Richard Hopkins papers
T 177	Sir Frederick Phillips papers
T188	Sir Frederick Leith-Ross papers

Conservative Party archives

Birmingham Conservative and Unionist Association, Minute Books, 1914–40, Birmingham Central Library.

Ladywood Division Unionist Association, Minute Books, 1914–40, Birmingham Central Library.

Ladywood Women's Unionist Association, Minute Books, 1919–33, Birmingham Central Library.

Midland Union Executive Committee, Minute Books, 1919–40, Conservative Party Archive, Bodleian Library, Oxford.

Index

Where a note reference is given, this signifies a short biographical or explanatory note on the person or event concerned.

Chamberlain, (Arthur) Neville, career
in Opposition (1929–31)
continued
183, 185, 188, 192, 204, 209,
219, 238–41, 244, 246, 260; on
Labour government, 145, 150,
152, 256; forecasts next election,
197–98, 227, 229, 230, 232, 236,
237, 257, 265; talks with 'Liberal
Unionists', 22–23, 224, 228, 245,
248, 253, 255–56; Trade Union
Bill, 226, 229, 231–33, 235;
India, 232, 234, 236, 237; harries
Labour Government, 197–98,
242, 257–58, 260, 263–64, 266;
cuts in unemployment insurance,
17, 24, 25, 26–29, 258–59, 264,
276; economy and balanced
budgets, 25, 26, 27, 237, 273–76;
financial crisis, 23–24, 269, 271,
273–80; idea of National
Government, 24–25, 27–28,
268–69, 272, 276

career in National Government
(1931–33), 32, 33, 279, 294;
sense of destiny, 33, 300; general
election (1931), 30–31, 278–79,
280, 281–87; appointment as
Chancellor, 285, 287; tariff
policy, 30–31, 33, 34, 35–36,
59–61, 69, 278, 282, 283, 289–90,
292, 301–4, 305, 309–10, 311–13,
327; economies in public
expenditure, 61, 63, 309, 323,
326; attempts to force free trader
resignation, 30, 31, 35, 40–41,
280, 281–84, 347–48, 349;
Balance of Trade Committees,
278, 298–99, 301–3; Lausanne
Conference, 39, 43, 45–46, 47,
48, 50, 54, 288, 290, 300 & n,
304, 324, 327, 328–34, 337, 340,
363, 365–66, 369, 371, 373, 375,
379; Ottawa Conference, 36–41,
288, 290–91, 305–7, 313, 315–16,
320, 324, 328, 333, 335–46, 347,
350–51, 353–54, 367 & n;
monetary policy and 'cheap
money', 41–42, 44, 59, 60, 61,
69, 311, 313, 350, 400; managed
currency and value of sterling, 42,

43, 44–45, 281, 296, 313, 315,
352 & n, 362, 367, 401; War Loan
conversion (1932), 42–43, 59,
333 & n, 384; budgetary policy,
42, 61–72, 216, 315, 319, 320–21,
323, 326, 376–77 & n, 378, 380,
381–83, 388, 396–97, 412;
taxation, 315, 378, 384, 389, 396;
importance of 'confidence', 43,
44, 61–62, 66–67, 313; disdain
for 'imaginative finance' and
public works, 42, 61, 65–72,
381–82, 384, 396–97, 400, 403–4,
409–10; industrial policy, 60–61,
327, 346, 404, 416–17 & n; need
to restrict production, 71, 170,
337–39, 344, 353, 354–55, 358;
criticism of economic policy,
58–59, 61, 63–66, 70, 376–77 &
n, 378, 380, 382, 384, 404;
economic outlook, 311, 313, 327,
352, 388, 408, 415;
unemployment, 350–51, 353, 376,
380, 396; war debts, 45–56, 68,
69, 288, 290, 294, 296, 302, 308,
324, 329, 330–31, 352, 357,
359–60, 362–67, 368–69, 370–71,
373, 376–77, 378–79, 389, 390,
392, 394–95, 397, 401, 403, 406,
408, 410, 412; World Economic
Conference, 52, 353, 358, 375,
377, 389, 390, 395, 369–99,
400–1; NC on international
conferences, 318–19, 331–32,
338, 395; India, 356, 404, 405–6;
housing and slums, 369, 372, 380,
382, 411; radical reform of
unemployment insurance,
350–51, 353, 355, 360, 369,
372–73, 376, 377, 382, 385,
399–400, 411, 415–16; favours a
'National Party', 30, 40–41, 242,
279, 286, 348; workload, 322,
336, 342, 350, 354, 360–61, 378,
379, 383, 386, 390–91, 404; gets
'fed up' with setbacks and
criticism, 376–77, 384, 388, 390,
404; NC's rising dominance,
57–58, 72, 278, 281, 284, 289,
293–94, 297, 299, 300, 353, 378,
399